ADVANCES IN NEUROPSYCHIATRY AND PSYCHOPHARMACOLOGY
VOLUME 1

SCHIZOPHRENIA RESEARCH

ADVANCES IN NEUROPSYCHIATRY AND PSYCHOPHARMACOLOGY

EDITORIAL BOARD

Ross J. Baldessarini *(Boston, Massachusetts)*
Floyd E. Bloom *(La Jolla, California)*
Benjamin S. Bunney *(New Haven, Connecticut)*
William E. Bunney, Jr. *(Irvine, California)*
Graham D. Burrows *(Melbourne, Australia)*
William T. Carpenter, Jr. *(Baltimore, Maryland)*
Roland D. Ciaranello *(Stanford, California)*
C. Robert Cloninger *(St. Louis, Missouri)*
Alec Coppen *(Epsom, UK)*
Joseph T. Coyle *(Baltimore, Maryland)*
Jeffrey L. Cummings *(Los Angeles, California)*
Kenneth L. Davis *(Bronx, New York)*
Daniel X. Freedman *(Los Angeles, California)*
Jes Gerlach *(Roskilde, Denmark)*
Elliot S. Gershon *(Bethesda, Maryland)*
Frederick K. Goodwin *(Bethesda, Maryland)*
Hans Hippius *(Munich, FRG)*
Philip S. Holzman *(Cambridge, Massachusetts)*
Jerome H. Jaffe *(Baltimore, Maryland)*
David S. Jankowsky *(Chapel Hill, North Carolina)*
John M. Kane *(Glen Oaks, New York)*
Kenneth K. Kidd *(New Haven, Connecticut)*
David J. Kupfer *(Pittsburgh, Pennsylvania)*
Bernard Lerer *(Jerusalem, Israel)*
Herbert Y. Meltzer *(Cleveland, Ohio)*
Julian Mendlewicz *(Brussels, Belgium)*
Charles B. Nemeroff *(Durham, North Carolina)*
Steven M. Paul *(Bethesda, Maryland)*
Elaine K. Perry *(Newcastle Upon Tyne, UK)*
Michael E. Phelps *(Los Angeles, California)*
Robert M. Post *(Bethesda, Maryland)*
S. Charles Schulz *(Cleveland, Ohio)*
B. B. Sethi *(Lucknow, India)*
Solomon H. Snyder *(Baltimore, Maryland)*
Carol A. Tamminga *(Baltimore, Maryland)*
Daniel R. Weinberger *(Washington, DC)*
David de Wied *(Utrecht, The Netherlands)*
Itaru Yamashita *(Sapporo, Japan)*

ADVANCES IN NEUROPSYCHIATRY AND PSYCHOPHARMACOLOGY
VOLUME 1

SCHIZOPHRENIA RESEARCH

Editors

Carol A. Tamminga, M.D.

Maryland Psychiatric Research Center
Department of Psychiatry
University of Maryland School of Medicine
Baltimore, Maryland

S. Charles Schulz, M.D.

Department of Psychiatry
Case Western Reserve University
School of Medicine
University Hospitals of Cleveland
Cleveland, Ohio

RAVEN PRESS ◆ NEW YORK

Raven Press, 1185 Avenue of the Americas, New York, New York 10036

© 1991 by Raven Press, Ltd. All rights reserved. This book is protected by copyright. No part of it may be reproduced, stored in a retrieval system, or transmitted, in any form or by any means, electronic, mechanical, photocopying, or recording, or otherwise, without the prior written permission of the publisher.

Made in the United States of America

Library of Congress Cataloging-in-Publication Data

Schizophrenia research / editors, Carol A. Tamminga, S. Charles Schulz.
     p.   cm.—(Advances in neuropsychiatry and psychopharmacology; v. 1)
  Includes bibliographical references.
  Includes index.
  ISBN 0-88167-675-6
  1. Schizophrenia—Research. I. Tamminga, Carol A.
II. Schulz, S. Charles. III. Series.
  [DNLM: 1. Research. 2. Schizophrenia. WM 203 S33798]
RC514.S33635 1991
616.89'82—dc20
DNLM/DLC
for Library of Congress   90-8946
                                                                                        CIP

    The material contained in this volume was submitted as previously unpublished material, except in the instances in which credit has been given to the source from which some of the illustrative material was derived. Great care has been taken to maintain the accuracy of the information contained in the volume. However, neither Raven Press nor the editors can be held responsible for errors or for any consequences arising from the use of information contained herein.
    Authors were themselves responsible for obtaining the necessary permission to reproduce copyright materials from other sources. With respect to the publisher's copyright, materials appearing in this book prepared by individuals as part of their official duties as U.S. Government employees is not covered by the above-mentioned copyright.

9 8 7 6 5 4 3 2 1

Preface

Neuroscience has burgeoned over the last decade. Scientists have worked steadily to reveal complex aspects of neuronal function. The field has generated detailed information about brain structure, neurochemistry, neurophysiology, and integrated neuronal processes. Moreover, the field has fostered the development of new techniques for clinical investigation. Brain imaging, molecular biology, and neurochemistry have produced new techniques currently being applied in mental health research. The knowledge generated has created an unparalleled opportunity and enthusiasm for addressing biologic questions about schizophrenia.

Schizophrenia is an illness whose basic pathophysiology remains unknown. The disease is defined by clinical characteristics but has no verified biologic criteria. A common set of clinical, demographic, and course of illness characteristics exist which define the syndrome. However, such individual variability exists in symptom expression that most investigators consider subgroups likely. Nonetheless, considerable progress has been made in defining clinical phenomenology, neuropsychologic and physiologic characteristics, and their assessment, thus optimizing scientific exploration.

The goal of this volume is to facilitate the application of current neuroscience and psychosocial knowledge and techniques to schizophrenia research. It reflects the current status of scientific information in several areas of the field. Each section was selected as an area of particular interest and new development. Chapters exemplify specific scientific directions in an area. The chapters are not intended to be comprehensive of the area as a whole, rather the best in scientific direction and discoveries in explicating schizophrenia.

This effort has been conducted not only by the two of us, as editors of this volume, but also by our Executive Secretary, Ms. Susan Nusbaum. It is our wish that research in these pages may challenge, model, and perhaps stimulate projects in the future that will ultimately contribute to a full understanding of schizophrenia.

Carol A. Tamminga, M.D.
S. Charles Schulz, M.D.

Contents

Part I: Biochemistry of Schizophrenia

1. Biochemical Characterization of D_1 and D_2 Dopamine Receptors...... 3
   Michael D. Bates, Joy A. Gingrich, Susan E. Senogles, Pierre Falardeau, and Marc G. Caron

2. Mechanisms of Phencyclidine (PCP)-*N*-Methyl-D-aspartate (NMDA) Receptor Interaction: Implications for Schizophrenia.................... 13
   Daniel C. Javitt and Stephen R. Zukin

3. Recent Developments in Genetic Linkage Studies of Schizophrenia .. 21
   James L. Kennedy and Luis A. Giuffra

4. Gene Expression: Implications for the Study of Schizophrenia and Other Neuropsychiatric Disorders... 31
   Edward I. Ginns

5. Molecular Approaches to Neuroleptic Action: Tyrosine Hydroxylase and Cholecystokinin mRNA Levels in the Substantia Nigra and Ventral Tegmental Area.. 39
   Sandra L. Cottingham, Jacqueline N. Crawley, and David Pickar

Part II: Neurobiology and Physiology of Schizophrenia

6. Neuroplasticity of Mesotelencephalic Dopamine Neurons at the Network and Receptor Level: New Aspects of the Role of Dopamine in Schizophrenia and Possible Pharmacological Treatments 51
   Kjell Fuxe, Luigi F. Agnati, Michele Zoli, Emilio Merlo Pich, Roberta Grimaldi, Börje Bjelke, Sergio Tanganelli, Gabriel von Euler, and Anna Marie Janson

7. Neuropeptides and Schizophrenia: A Critical Review.................... 77
   Charles B. Nemeroff

8. Localization and Quantification of μ-Opiate Receptors by [11]Carfentanil and PET: Application in Schizophrenia.................... 91
   J. James Frost

9. The Limbic System in Schizophrenia: Pharmacologic and
    Metabolic Evidence 99
    *Carol A. Tamminga, Hiro Kaneda, Robert Buchanan, Brian Kirkpatrick,
    Gunvant K. Thaker, Mary Beth Yablonski, and Henry H. Holcomb*

10. Autoimmunity and Schizophrenia 111
    *Cathy G. McAllister, Mark Hyman Rapaport, David Pickar, and
    Steven M. Paul*

11. Neuropharmacologic Techniques in the Molecular Biology
    of Schizophrenia 119
    *George R. Uhl, A. Jayaraman, Toshikazu Nishimori, Shoichi Shimada,
    Marcus Rattray, and Bruce O'Hara*

Part III: Behavior and Schizophrenia

12. An Animal Model for Childhood Autism: Memory Loss and
    Socioemotional Disturbances Following Neonatal Damage to the
    Limbic System in Monkeys 129
    Jocelyne Bachevalier

13. Stress and Schizophrenia 141
    Alan Breier, Owen M. Wolkowitz, and David Pickar

14. Neuropsychological Study of Schizophrenia 153
    Ruben C. Gur, Andrew J. Saykin, and Raquel E. Gur

15. Wisconsin Card Sorting Deficits and Diminished Sensorimotor
    Gating in a Discrete Subgroup of Schizophrenic Patients 163
    Robert W. Butler, Melissa A. Jenkins, Mark A. Geyer, and David L. Braff

16. Electrophysiological and Behavioral Signs of Attentional
    Disturbance in Schizophrenics and Their Siblings 169
    *Stuart R. Steinhauer, Joseph Zubin, Ruth Condray, David B. Shaw,
    Jeffrey L. Peters, and Daniel P. van Kammen*

Part IV: Schizophrenia Spectrum

17. The Biology of the Boundaries of Schizophrenia 181
    Larry J. Siever

18. The Schizophrenia Spectrum Concept: The Chestnut Lodge
    Follow-Up Study 193
    Thomas H. McGlashan

19. Pilot Studies of Borderline and Schizotypal Subjects 201
    Gunvant K. Thaker, Marianne Moran, Adrienne Lahti, Helene Adami,
    Carol Tamminga, and S. Charles Schulz

20. Cerebral Structural Abnormalities in Schizophreniform Disorder and
    in Schizophrenia Spectrum Personality Disorders 209
    Carlo L. Cazzullo, Antonio Vita, Gian M. Giobbio, Massimiliano Dieci,
    and Emilio Sacchetti

21. Nonschizophrenic Psychotic Disorders 219
    Peter Berner

22. Ex Multi Uno: A Case for Neurobiological Homogeneity
    in Schizophrenia 227
    David G. Daniel and Daniel R. Weinberger

Part V: Psychosocial Treatments

23. Long-Term Community Care Through an Assertive Continuous
    Treatment Team 239
    Mary Ann Test, William H. Knoedler, Deborah J. Allness,
    Suzanne Senn Burke, Roger L. Brown, and Lynn S. Wallisch

24. A Review of Psychoeducational Family Approaches 247
    Samuel J. Keith, Susan M. Matthews, and Nina R. Schooler

25. Management of Risk of Relapse Through Skills Training of
    Chronic Schizophrenics 255
    William C. Wirshing, Thad Eckman, Robert P. Liberman, and
    Stephen R. Marder

26. A Neuropsychiatric Model of Treatment 269
    Paula T. Trzepacz and Christopher Starratt

Part VI: Pharmacological Treatments

27. Persistence of Antipsychotic Drug Levels and Effects 277
    Bruce M. Cohen, Ross J. Baldessarini, Alexander Campbell,
    Tomohiro Tsuneizumi, and Suzann M. Babb

28. Neuroleptic Noncompliance in Schizophrenia 285
    Peter J. Weiden, Lisa Dixon, Allen Frances, Paul Appelbaum,
    Gretchen Haas, and Bruce Rapkin

29. Pharmacological Approaches to the Development of
    Atypical Antipsychotics 297
    David M. Coward

30. BMY 14802: A Potential Antipsychotic with Selective Affinity for
    σ-Binding Sites 307
    Duncan P. Taylor, Michael S. Eison, Sandra L. Moon, Frank D. Yocca

31. Presynaptic D_2-Receptor Selectivity of Roxindole (EMD 49 980):
    Possible Indirect Effects on Postsynaptic Striatal
    Cholinergic Neurons 317
    Christoph A. Seyfried, Anton F. Haase, and Henning Böttcher

32. Neuroleptic-Induced Anhedonia: Recent Studies 323
    Roy A. Wise

33. Dopaminergic and Serotoninergic Mechanisms in the Action
    of Clozapine 333
    Herbert Y. Meltzer

34. Biochemical Effects of Clozapine in Cerebrospinal Fluid of Patients
    with Schizophrenia 341
    Jeffrey Lieberman, Celeste Johns, Simcha Pollack, Stephen Masiar,
    Peter Bookstein, Thomas Cooper, Michael Iadorola, and John Kane

35. Differential Changes in Dopamine and Serotonin Receptors Induced
    by Clozapine and Haloperidol 351
    Gerald J. LaHoste, Steven J. O'Dell, Clifford B. Widmark,
    Raymond M. Shapiro, Steven G. Potkin, and John F. Marshall

Subject Index 365

Contributors

Helen Adami, M.S.W.
Maryland Psychiatric Research Center
University of Maryland School of Medicine
Baltimore, Maryland 21228

Luigi F. Agnati, M.D.
Institute of Human Physiology
University of Modena
Modena, Italy

Deborah J. Allness, M.S.W.
Wisconsin Office of Mental Health
School of Social Work
University of Wisconsin
Madison, Wisconsin 53706

Paul Appelbaum, M.D.
Department of Psychiatry
University of Massachusetts Medical Center
55 Lake Avenue North
Worcester, Massachusetts 01655

Suzann M. Babb, M.S.
Mailman Research Center
McLean Hospital
Belmont, Massachusetts 02178

Jocelyne Bachevalier, Ph.D.
Laboratory of Neuropsychology
National Institute of Mental Health
Building 9, Room 1N107
Bethesda, Maryland 20892

Ross J. Baldessarini, M.D.
Mailman Research Center
McLean Hospital
Belmont, Massachusetts 02178 and
Departments of Psychiatry and Neuroscience
    Program
Harvard Medical School
Boston, Massachusetts 02115

Michael D. Bates, M.D., Ph.D.
Departments of Cell Biology and Medicine
Howard Hughes Medical Institute
Duke University Medical Center
Durham, North Carolina 27710

Peter Berner, M.D.
Psychiatric University Clinic
Allgemeines Krankenhaus der Stadt Wien
Währinger Gurtel 18–20
1090 Vienna, Austria

Börje Bjelke, M.D.
Department of Histology and Neurobiology
Karolinska Institute
Stockholm, Sweden

Peter Bookstein, M.D.
Hillside Hospital/Long Island Jewish Medical
    Center
Glen Oaks, New York 11004

Henning Böttcher, Ph.D.
Department of CNS Research
E. Merck
Frankfurter Strasse 250
6100 Darmstadt, Federal Republic of Germany

David L. Braff, M.D.
Department of Psychiatry
University of California, San Diego
La Jolla, California 92093

Alan Breier, M.D.
Department of Psychiatry
Maryland Psychiatric Research Center
University of Maryland School of Medicine
Baltimore, Maryland 21228

Roger L. Brown, Ph.D.
Department of Family Medicine
University of Wisconsin
3805 Alumni Hall
Madison, Wisconsin 53715

Robert Buchanan, M.D.
Maryland Psychiatric Research Center
University of Maryland School of Medicine
Baltimore, Maryland 21228

Suzanne Senn Burke, B.A.
Mendota Mental Health Institute
301 Troy Drive
Madison, Wisconsin 53704

Robert W. Butler, Ph.D.
Department of Psychiatry
University of California, San Diego
La Jolla, California 92093

Alexander Campbell, M.Phil.
Mailman Research Center
McLean Hospital
Belmont, Massachusetts 02178

Marc G. Caron, Ph.D.
Department of Cell Biology and Medicine
Howard Hughes Medical Institute
Duke University Medical Center
Durham, North Carolina 27710

Carlo L. Cazzullo, M.D.
Institute of Psychiatry
Milan University School of Medicine
via F. Sforza 35
20122 Milano, Italy

Bruce M. Cohen, M.D., Ph.D.
Mailman Research Center
McLean Hospital
115 Mill Street
Belmont, Massachusetts 02178 and
Departments of Psychiatry and Neuroscience
 Program
Harvard Medical School
Boston, Massachusetts 02115

Ruth Condray, Ph.D.
Biometrics Research
Department of Veterans Affairs Medical Center
Highland Drive
Pittsburgh, Pennsylvania 15206 and
Department of Psychiatry
Western Psychiatric Institute and Clinic
University of Pittsburgh School of Medicine
Pittsburgh, Pennsylvania 15213

Thomas B. Cooper, M.A.
Nathan Kline Institute
Old Orangeburg Road
Orangeburg, New York 10962

Sandra L. Cottingham, M.D., Ph.D.
Clinical Neuroscience Branch
National Institute of Mental Health
Bethesda, Maryland 20892

David M. Coward, M.D.
Sandoz Research Institute Berne Ltd.
CH-3001 Berne, Switzerland

Jacqueline N. Crawley, Ph.D.
Clinical Neuroscience Branch
National Institute of Mental Health
Bethesda, Maryland 20892

David G. Daniel, M.D.
Clinical Brain Disorders Branch
Intramural Research Program
National Institute of Mental Health
Neuroscience Research Center at Saint
 Elizabeth's
Washington, DC 20032

Massimiliano Dieci, M.D.
Institute of Psychiatry
Milan University School of Medicine
via F. Sforza 35
20122 Milano, Italy

Lisa Dixon, M.D.
Maryland Psychiatric Research Center
University of Maryland School of Medicine
Baltimore, Maryland 21228

Thad Eckman, Ph.D.
Clinical Research Center for Schizophrenia and
 Psychiatric Rehabilitation
University of California at Los Angeles School
 of Medicine
Los Angeles, California 90024 and
Department of Psychiatry and Behavioral
 Sciences
West Los Angeles Veterans Administration
 Medical Center (Brentwood Division)
Los Angeles, California 90073 and
Camarillo State Hospital
Camarillo, California 93011-6022

Michael S. Eison, Ph.D.
CNS Biology
Pharmaceutical Research and Development
 Division
Bristol-Myers Squibb Company
5 Research Parkway
Wallingford, Connecticut 06492-7660

Pierre Falardeau, Ph.D.
Departments of Cell Biology and Medicine
Howard Hughes Medical Institute
Duke University Medical Center
Durham, North Carolina 27710

CONTRIBUTORS

Allen Frances, M.D.
Department of Psychiatry
New York Hospital-Cornell Medical Center
525 East 68th Street
New York, New York 10021

J. James Frost, M.D., Ph.D.
Departments of Radiology and Neuroscience
Johns Hopkins University School of Medicine
School of Hygiene and Public Health
Room 2001, 615 North Wolfe St.
Baltimore, Maryland 21205

Kjell Fuxe, M.D., Ph.D.
Departments of Histology and Neurobiology
Karolinska Institute
P.O. Box 60400
S-104 01 Stockholm, Sweden

Mark A. Geyer, Ph.D.
Department of Psychiatry
University of California, San Diego
La Jolla, California 92093

Jay A. Gingrich, Ph.D.
Departments of Cell Biology and Medicine
Howard Hughes Medical Institute
Duke University Medical Center
Durham, North Carolina 27710

Edward I. Ginns, M.D., Ph.D.
Section on Molecular Neurogenetics
Clinical Neuroscience Branch
National Institute of Mental Health
9000 Rockville Pike
Bethesda, Maryland 20892

Gian Marco Giobbio, M.D.
Institute of Psychiatry
Milan University School of Medicine
via F. Sforza 35
20122 Milano, Italy

Luis A. Giuffra, M.D.
Section of Neuroanatomy
Yale University School of Medicine
333 Cedar Street
New Haven, Connecticut 06510

Roberta Grimaldi, M.D.
Institute of Human Physiology
University of Modena
Modena, Italy

Raquel E. Gur, M.D., Ph.D.
Departments of Psychiatry and Neurology
Brain Behavior Laboratory
University of Pennsylvania
10 Gates Building
Philadelphia, Pennsylvania 19104

Ruben C. Gur, M.D., Ph.D.
Departments of Psychiatry and Neurology
Brain Behavior Laboratory
University of Pennsylvania
10 Gates Building
Philadelphia, Pennsylvania 19104

Gretchen Haas, Ph.D.
Department of Neuropharmacology
University of Pittsburgh
Western Psychiatric Institute and Clinic
3811 O'Hara Street
Pittsburgh, Pennsylvania 15213

Anton F. Haase, Ph.D.
Department of CNS Research and Biological
   Research
E. Merck
Frankfurter Strasse 250
6100 Darmstadt, Federal Republic of Germany

Henry H. Holcomb, M.D.
Maryland Psychiatric Research Center
University of Maryland School of Medicine
   and
Nuclear Medicine Department
Johns Hopkins University
Baltimore, Maryland 21205

Michael Iadorola, Ph.D.
National Institute of Dental Research
National Institutes of Health
Bethesda, Maryland 20892

Ann-Marie Janson, M.D.
Department of Histology and Neurobiology
Karolinska Institute
Stockholm, Sweden

Daniel C. Javitt, M.D., Ph.D.
Departments of Psychiatry and Neuroscience
Albert Einstein College of Medicine and
Bronx Psychiatric Center
Bronx, New York 10461

A. Jayaraman, M.D.
Departments of Neurology and Neuroscience
Johns Hopkins School of Medicine
Laboratory of Molecular Neurobiology
 Addiction Research Center, NIDA/NIH
Baltimore, Maryland 21224 and
Department of Neurology
Louisiana State University School of Medicine
New Orleans, Louisiana 70112

Melissa A. Jenkins, B.A.
Department of Psychiatry
University of California, San Diego
La Jolla, California 92093

Celeste Johns, M.D.
Hillside Hospital/Long Island Jewish Medical
 Center
Glen Oaks, New York 11004 and
Department of Psychiatry
Albert Einstein College of Medicine
Bronx, New York 10461

John Kane, M.D.
Hillside Hospital/Long Island Jewish Medical
 Center
Glen Oaks, New York 11004 and
Department of Psychiatry
Albert Einstein College of Medicine
Bronx, New York 10461

Hiro Kaneda, M.D.
Maryland Psychiatric Research Center
University of Maryland School of Medicine
Baltimore, Maryland 21228

Samuel J. Keith, M.D.
Division of Clinical Research
National Institute of Mental Health
5600 Fishers Lane
Rockville, Maryland 20857

James L. Kennedy, M.D.
Departments of Human Genetics and
 Psychiatry
Yale University School of Medicine
333 Cedar Street
New Haven, Connecticut 06510

Brian Kirkpatrick, M.D.
Maryland Psychiatric Research Center
University of Maryland School of Medicine
Baltimore, Maryland 21228

William H. Knoedler, M.D.
Program of Assertive Community Treatment
Mendota Mental Health Institute
108 South Webster
Madison, Wisconsin 53703

Gerald J. LaHoste, Ph.D.
Department of Psychobiology and
Center for Neuroscience and Schizophrenia
University of California at Irvine
Irvine, California 92717

Adrienne Lahti, M.D.
Maryland Psychiatric Research Center
University of Maryland School of Medicine
Baltimore, Maryland 21228

Robert P. Liberman, M.D.
Clinical Research Center for Schizophrenia and
 Psychiatric Rehabilitation
University of California at Los Angeles School
 of Medicine and
Departments of Psychiatry and Behavioral
 Sciences
West Los Angeles Veterans Administration
 Medical Center (Brentwood Division)
11301 Wilshire Boulevard
Los Angeles, California 90073 and
Camarillo State Hospital
1878 Louis Road
Camarillo, California 93011-6022

Jeffrey A. Lieberman, M.D.
Department of Psychiatry
Albert Einstein College of Medicine
Bronx, New York 10461 and
Hillside Hospital/Long Island Jewish Medical
 Center
Glen Oaks, New York 11004

Stephen R. Marder, M.D.
Clinical Research Center for Schizophrenia and
 Psychiatric Rehabilitation
UCLA School of Medicine and
Department of Psychiatry and Behavioral
 Sciences
West Los Angeles Veterans Administration
 Medical Center (Brentwood Division)
Los Angeles, California 90073

John F. Marshall, Ph.D.
Department of Psychobiology and
Center for Neuroscience and Schizophrenia
University of California at Irvine
Irvine, California 92717

Contributors

Steven Masiar, M.D.
Hillside Hospital/Long Island Jewish Medical Center
Glen Oaks, New York 11004

Susan M. Matthews
Division of Clinical Research
National Institute of Mental Health
5600 Fisher's Lane
Rockville, Maryland 20857

Cathy G. McAllister, Ph.D.
Department of Psychiatry and Pathology
University of Pittsburgh
Pittsburgh, Pennsylvania 15213-2582

Thomas H. McGlashan, M.D.
Yale Psychiatric Institute
New Haven, Connecticut 06519; formerly of
Chestnut Lodge Hospital
500 West Montgomery Avenue
Rockville, Maryland 20850

Herbert Y. Meltzer, M.D.
Department of Psychiatry
Case Western Reserve University School of Medicine
2040 Abington Road
Cleveland, Ohio 44106

Sandra L. Moon, Ph.D.
CNS Biology
Pharmaceutical Research and Development Division
Bristol-Myers Company
Wallingford, Connecticut 06492-7660

Marianne Moran
Maryland Psychiatric Research Center
University of Maryland School of Medicine
Baltimore, Maryland 21228

Charles B. Nemeroff, M.D., Ph.D.
Department of Psychiatry and Pharmacology
Duke University Medical Center
P.O. Box 3859
Durham, North Carolina 27710

Toshikazu Nishimori, Ph.D.
Laboratory of Molecular Neurobiology
Addiction Research Center, NIDA/NIH and
Departments of Neurology and Neuroscience
Johns Hopkins School of Medicine
Baltimore, Maryland 21224

Steven J. O'Dell, Ph.D.
Department of Psychobiology and
Center for Neuroscience and Schizophrenia
University of California at Irvine
Irvine, California 92717

Bruce O'Hara, Ph.D.
Laboratory of Molecular Neurobiology
Addiction Research Center, NIDA/NIH and
Departments of Neurology and Neuroscience
Johns Hopkins School of Medicine
Baltimore, Maryland 21224

Steven M. Paul, M.D.
Clinical Neuroscience Branch
National Institute of Mental Health
Bethesda, Maryland 20892

Jeffrey L. Peters, M.D.
Biometrics Research
Department of Veterans Affairs Medical Center
Highland Drive
Pittsburgh, Pennsylvania 15206 and
Department of Psychiatry
Western Psychiatric Institute and Clinic
University of Pittsburgh School of Medicine
Pittsburgh, Pennsylvania 15213

Emilio Merlo Pich, Ph.D.
Institute of Human Physiology
University of Modena
Modena, Italy

David Pickar, M.D.
Clinical Neuroscience Branch
National Institute of Mental Health
Bethesda, Maryland 20892

Simcha Pollack, Ph.D.
Hillside Hospital/Long Island Jewish Medical Center
Glen Oaks, New York 11004 and
Department of Quantitative Analysis
St. John's University
Jamaica, New York 11439

Steven G. Potkin, M.D.
Department of Psychiatry and
Center for Neuroscience and Schizophrenia
University of California at Irvine
Irvine, California 92717

Mark Hyman Rapaport, M.D.
Clinical Neuroscience Branch
National Institute of Mental Health
Bethesda, Maryland 20892

Bruce Rapkin, Ph.D.
Department of Psychology
New York University
6 Washington Place
New York, New York 10003

Marcus Rattray, Ph.D.
Laboratory of Molecular Neurobiology
 Addiction Research Center, NIDA/NIH and
Departments of Neurology and Neuroscience
Johns Hopkins School of Medicine
Baltimore, Maryland 21224

Emilio Sacchetti, M.D.
Institute of Psychiatry
Milan University School of Medicine
via F. Sforza 35
20122 Milano, Italy

Andrew J. Saykin, Psy.D.
Departments of Psychiatry and Neurology
Brain Behavior Laboratory
University of Pennsylvania
10 Gates Building
Philadelphia, Pennsylvania 19104

Nina R. Schooler, Ph.D.
Western Psychiatric Institute and Clinic
University of Pittsburgh
3811 O'Hara Street
Pittsburgh, Pennsylvania 15213

S. Charles Schulz, M.D.
Department of Psychiatry
Case Western Reserve University School of
 Medicine
University Hospitals of Cleveland
Cleveland, Ohio 44106

Susan E. Senogles, Ph.D.
Departments of Cell Biology and Medicine
Howard Hughes Medical Institute
Duke University Medical Center
Durham, North Carolina 27710

Christoph A. Seyfried, M.D.
Departments of CNS Research and Biological
 Research
E. Merck
Frankfurter Strasse 250
6100 Darmstadt, Federal Republic of Germany

Raymond M. Shapiro, M.D.
Department of Psychiatry and
Center for Neuroscience and Schizophrenia
University of California at Irvine
Irvine, California 92717

David B. Shaw, Ph.D.
Biometrics Research
Department of Veterans Affairs Medical Center
Highland Drive
Pittsburgh, Pennsylvania 15206

Shoichi Shimada, Ph.D.
Laboratory of Molecular Neurobiology
 Addiction Research Center, NIDA/NIH and
Departments of Neurology and Neuroscience
Johns Hopkins School of Medicine
Baltimore, Maryland 21224

Larry J. Siever, M.D.
Department of Psychiatry
Mount Sinai School of Medicine and
Bronx Veterans Administration Medical Center
130 W. Kingsbridge Road
Bronx, New York 10468

Christopher Starratt, Ph.D.
Allegheny Neuropsychiatric Institute
Medical College of Pennsylvania
7777 Steubenville Pike
Oakdale, Pennsylvania 15071

Stuart R. Steinhauer, Ph.D.
Biometrics Research
Department of Veterans Affairs Medical Center
Highland Drive
Pittsburgh, Pennsylvania 15206 and
Department of Psychiatry
Western Psychiatric Institute and Clinic
University of Pittsburgh School of Medicine
Pittsburgh, Pennsylvania 15213

Carol A. Tamminga, M.D.
Maryland Psychiatric Research Center
University of Maryland School of Medicine
Department of Psychiatry
Baltimore, Maryland 21228

Sergio Tanganelli, Ph.D.
Department of Pharmacology
University of Ferrara
Ferrara, Italy

Duncan P. Taylor, Ph.D.
CNS Biology
Pharmaceutical Research and Development
  Division
Bristol-Myers Squibb Company
5 Research Parkway
Wallingford, Connecticut 06492-7660

Mary Ann Test, Ph.D.
School of Social Work
University of Wisconsin
425 Henry Mall
Madison, Wisconsin 53706

Gunvant K. Thaker, M.D.
Maryland Psychiatric Research Center
University of Maryland School of Medicine
Spring Grove Hospital Grounds
Baltimore, Maryland 21228

Paula T. Trzepacz, M.D.
Consultation/Liaison Program
Western Psychiatric Institute and Clinic
University of Pittsburgh School of Medicine
3811 O'Hara Street
Pittsburgh, PA 15213

Tomohiro Tsuneizumi, M.D.
Mailman Research Center
McLean Hospital
Belmont, Massachusetts 02178

George R. Uhl, M.D., Ph.D.
Laboratory of Molecular Neurobiology
  Addiction Research Center, NIDA/NIH and
Departments of Neurology and Neuroscience
Johns Hopkins University School of Medicine
Baltimore, Maryland 21224

Daniel P. van Kammen, M.D., Ph.D.
Biometrics Research
Department of Veterans Affairs Medical Center
Highland Drive
Pittsburgh, Pennsylvania 15206 and
Department of Psychiatry
Western Psychiatric Institute and Clinic
University of Pittsburgh School of Medicine
Pittsburgh, Pennsylvania 15213

Antonio Vita, M.D.
Institute of Psychiatry
Milan University School of Medicine
Policlinico, Pad. Guardia II
via F. Sforza 35
20122 Milano, Italy

Gabriel von Euler, Ph.D.
Department of Histology and Neurobiology
Karolinska Institute
Stockholm, Sweden

Lynn S. Wallisch, M.A.
Schizophrenia Research Project
School of Social Work
University of Wisconsin
425 Henry Mall
Madison, Wisconsin 53706

Peter J. Weiden, M.D.
Schizophrenia Service
Hillside Hospital/Long Island Jewish Medical
  Center
Glen Oaks, New York 11004

Daniel R. Weinberger, M.D.
Clinical Brain Disorders Branch
National Institute of Mental Health
Neuroscience Center at St. Elizabeth's
Washington, D.C. 20032

Clifford B. Widmark, M.D.
Department of Psychiatry and
Center for Neuroscience and Schizophrenia
University of California at Irvine
Irvine, California 92717

William C. Wirshing, M.D.
Clinical Research Center for Schizophrenic and
  Psychiatric Rehabilitation
UCLA School of Medicine and
Department of Psychiatry and Behavioral
  Sciences,
West Los Angeles Veterans Medical Center
  (Brentwood Division)
11310 Wilshire Boulevard
Los Angeles, California 90073

Roy A. Wise, Ph.D.
Centre for Studies in Behavioral Neurobiology
Department of Psychology
Concordia University
Room H-1013
1455 de Maisonneuve Boulevard West
Montreal, Quebec, Canada H3G 1M8

Owen M. Wolkowitz, M.D.
Department of Psychiatry
University of California at San Francisco
San Francisco, California 94143

M. B. Yablonski
Maryland Psychiatric Research Center
University of Maryland School of Medicine
Baltimore, Maryland 21228

Frank D. Yocca, Ph.D.
CNS Biology
Pharmaceutical Research and Development
   Division
Bristol-Myers Company
Wallingford, Connecticut 06492

Michele Zoli, M.D.
Institute of Human Physiology
University of Modena
Modena, Italy

Joseph Zubin, Ph.D.
Biometrics Research
Department of Veterans Affairs Medical Center
Highland Drive
Pittsburgh, Pennsylvania 15206 and
Department of Psychiatry
Western Psychiatric Institute and Clinic
University of Pittsburgh School of Medicine
Pittsburgh, Pennsylvania 15213

Stephen R. Zukin, M.D.
Departments of Psychiatry and Neuroscience
Albert Einstein College of Medicine and
Bronx Psychiatric Center
Bronx, New York 10461

PART I
Biochemistry of Schizophrenia

1

Biochemical Characterization of D_1 and D_2 Dopamine Receptors

Michael D. Bates, Jay A. Gingrich, Susan E. Senogles, Pierre Falardeau, and Marc G. Caron[1]

In the human central nervous system, derangements of the dopaminergic pathways have been implicated in a number of pathological conditions, including schizophrenia, tardive dyskinesia, Gilles de la Tourette's syndrome, Parkinson's disease, and Huntington's chorea (for review see ref. 1). In addition, dopamine acts in the periphery to regulate diverse physiological functions such as hormone release and vascular tone. Dopamine exerts its central effects through two major classes of receptors, termed D_1 and D_2 dopamine receptors (2,3). Peripheral receptors designated DA_1 and DA_2 receptors, similar to but distinct from their central counterparts, have also been described (4).

D_2 dopamine receptors have been implicated in the regulation of several signal transduction systems, including the inhibition of adenylyl cyclase, stimulation of K^+ channels, and inhibition of Ca^{2+} channels (for review see ref 5). Such regulation occurs by coupling of the receptor to the effector via a guanine nucleotide-binding protein (G protein). These receptors are found most prominently in the anterior and neurointermediate lobes of the pituitary gland, where they inhibit the secretion of prolactin and α-melanocyte stimulating hormone, respectively; and in the basal ganglia, particularly the corpus striatum, where they inhibit neurotransmitter release and cell firing (for review see ref. 6). In the retina, D_2 receptors are also involved in light adaptation (for review see ref. 7)

D_1 dopamine receptors were originally defined as those dopamine receptors that activate adenylyl cyclase (3); this presumably occurs via the G protein, G_s. D_1 receptors are found throughout the central nervous system, especially in the basal ganglia, where their physiological role has proven difficult to define, and in the retina, where they control gap junction permeability (for review see ref. 7). They are also found peripherally in the parathyroid gland, where they stimulate release of parathyroid hormone (8).

The study of receptor systems using biochemical and molecular approaches has provided much insight into the functioning of these systems. Important structural and functional information regarding the G protein–coupled receptors and recognition of a gene family for these receptors has been obtained using the techniques of molecular biology (for review see ref. 9). This family, which includes adrenergic, muscarinic, serotonin, and peptide hormone receptors as well as the visual opsins, is characterized by the presence of seven hydrophobic, presumably membrane-spanning, domains in the receptor protein. Our approach to the

---

[1]Departments of Cell Biology and Medicine, Howard Hughes Medical Institute, Duke University Medical Center, Durham, NC 27710.

study of the D_1 and D_2 dopamine receptors has been to use subtype-selective antagonists as the basis for the development of specific probes to specifically identify and purify these receptors. This approach has yielded important information about these distinct receptors. It is hoped that these tools will allow the detailed study of receptor structure and function in health and disease.

SPECIFIC IDENTIFICATION OF DOPAMINE RECEPTORS

To study the dopamine receptors at a biochemical level, we first needed to have the ability to specifically identify each receptor in various preparations. Such specificity may be achieved using a high-affinity receptor-selective ligand as the basis for the development of probes that can be radiolabeled to high specific activity and that can be covalently incorporated into the receptor ligand binding subunit. The use of such probes allows the study of receptors in membrane preparations in which they are only minor protein components. For the D_2 receptor, a photoaffinity labeling probe was developed using the D_2-selective antagonist spiperone. For the D_1 receptor, the D_1-selective antagonist SCH 23390 was used as the basis for the development of a ligand that could be used to label the receptor by photocrosslinking.

N-(p-azido-m-[^{125}I]-iodophenethyl) spiperone ([^{125}I]N_3-NAPS), whose structure is shown in Fig. 1A, was developed in our laboratory by derivatization of the D_2 antagonist spiperone as a high-affinity, high-specific-radioactivity (~2200 Ci/mmol) photoaffinity probe for the D_2 receptor (10,11). [^{125}I]N_3-NAPS contains an azido function, which forms a highly reactive nitrene upon light activation, allowing covalent incorporation. For photoaffinity labeling, [^{125}I]N_3-NAPS was incubated in the dark with crude membrane preparations from the tissue of interest. The membranes were washed by centrifugation, resuspended in a small volume, and photolyzed for 1 to 2 minutes using a high-intensity lamp to cause the covalent incorporation of the ligand. Following further washing, the membrane samples were run on sodium dodecyl sulfate–polyacrylamide gel electrophoresis (SDS-PAGE), and the gels were subjected to autoradiography. Figure 1B shows the results from photoaffinity labeling the D_2 receptor of rat anterior pituitary and corpus striatum. In both tissues broad bands of $M_r \approx 80,000-120,000$ are identified. Such bands are labeled in other tissues and other species as well (11). Pharmacological specificity of labeling is demonstrated by incubating [^{125}I]N_3-NAPS with the membranes in the presence of competing ligands. Coincubation with (+)butaclamol demonstrates only a small component of nonspecific labeling. Use of other competing ligands (agonists and antagonists) demonstrates further the pharmacological specificity of labeling, with labeling blocked according to potency of the ligands at D_2 receptors. For example, the (+) isomer of butaclamol was more potent than the (−) isomer, and, among agonists, a rank order of potency, N-propylnorapomorphine > apomorphine > dopamine, is observed. Depending on the tissue source, various nonspecifically labeled bands are also seen; labeling of these peptides is not blocked by D_2 or other receptor ligands.

A radioiodinated bromoacetyl derivative of NAPS was developed in order to specifically label purified preparations of D_2 receptors (Fig. 1A and ref. 12). Such derivatives are highly reactive, and their use is only appropriate for highly purified preparations of receptor. [^{125}I]N_3-NAPS was found to be unsuitable for labeling purified receptor due to its hydrophobic nature and low incorporation rate. In purified preparations of bovine anterior pituitary D_2 dopamine receptors (see below), [^{125}I]bromoacetyl-NAPS labels a peptide of $M_r = 120,000$, as visualized by SDS-PAGE and autoradiography. This labeling is blocked

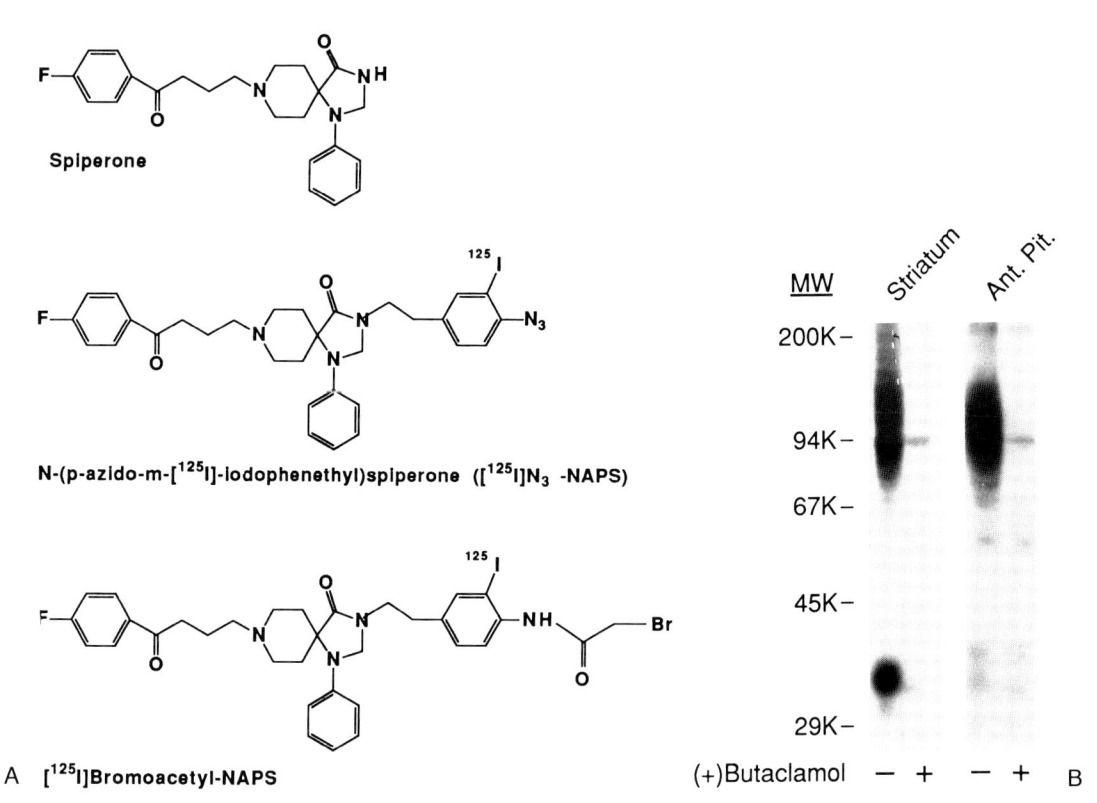

FIG. 1. Photoaffinity labeling of D_2 dopamine receptors. **A:** Structure of the D_2 receptor-selective antagonist spiperone and its derivatives, N-(p-azido-m-[^{125}I]-iodophenethyl)spiperone ([^{125}I]N$_3$-NAPS), a photoaffinity probe for the D_2 receptor, and [^{125}I]bromoacetyl-NAPS, a D_2 alkylating reagent. **B:** Autoradiograph of SDS-PAGE gels from the photoaffinity labeling of D_2 dopamine receptors in rat striatal and anterior pituitary membranes using [^{125}I]N$_3$-NAPS. See text for the method of labeling, which was carried out in the absence ($-$) or presence ($+$) of 1 μM ($+$)butaclamol to define nonspecific labeling. Molecular weight markers are shown.

with appropriate D_2 pharmacology (see below and Fig. 5).

The ligand-binding subunit of the D_1 dopamine receptor was identified by photoaffinity crosslinking. Unlike photoaffinity labeling, the crosslinking technique requires, following ligand binding, the use of a heterobifunctional crosslinking reagent to covalently incorporate the ligand into the receptor ligand-binding subunit. SCH 38548, the 3'-amino derivative of the D_1 selective antagonist SCH 23390, can be radioiodinated to high specific radioactivity (~2200 Ci/mmol; Fig. 2A and ref 13). [^{125}I]SCH 38548 is allowed to bind to D_1 receptors in membrane preparations. The membranes are washed, and the crosslinking agent, N-succinimidyl-6-(4'-azido-2'-nitrophenylamino)hexanoate (SANPAH; Fig. 2A) is incubated with the membranes in the dark to allow the chemical derivatization of the bound ligand. The bound derivatized [^{125}I]SCH 38548 is then crosslinked to the receptor protein by photolysis of the membranes as described above for D_2-receptor photoaffinity labeling. Using this technique, a peptide of $M_r \approx 72,000$ was identified by SDS-PAGE (Fig. 2B). Labeling of this peptide was blocked with appropriate D_1 dopamine pharmacology. For example, labeling was blocked in a stereospecific manner [($+$) greater than ($-$)butaclamol,

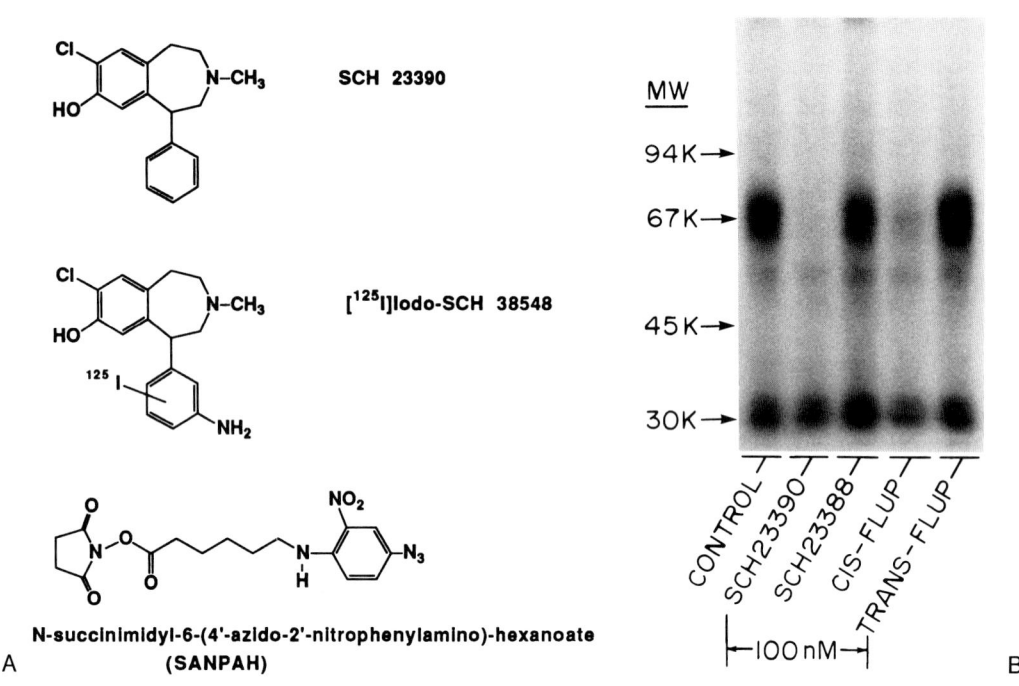

FIG. 2. Photoaffinity crosslinking of D_1 dopamine receptors. **A:** Structure of the D_1 dopamine receptor-selective antagonist SCH 23390 and its iodinated 3' amino derivative, [^{125}I]iodo-SCH 38548, which is bound to D_1 receptors and crosslinked to the receptor using N-succinimidyl-6-(4'-azido-2'-nitrophenylamino)hexanoate (SANPAH). **B:** Autoradiograph of an SDS-PAGE gel from photoaffinity crosslinking of D_1 receptors in rat striatal membranes as described in the text. Nonspecific labeling and stereospecificity of labeling were assessed by carrying out labeling in the presence of 100 nM of SCH 23390 and cis-flupentixol and their inactive enantiomers. Reprinted with permission from ref. 13, © American Society for Pharmacology and Experimental Therapeutics.

and cis- greater than trans-flupentixol] by antagonists and was blocked by agonists with D_1 specificity (SKF 38393 > apomorphine > dopamine), whereas specific ligands for other receptors did not affect labeling. Thus, the ligand-binding subunit of the D_1 dopamine receptor can be identified, allowing further molecular characterization of the receptor in membrane preparations.

PURIFICATION OF DOPAMINE RECEPTORS

More detailed studies of receptor structure and function will require purification of the receptor protein from other receptor and signal-transducing proteins or even purification to homogeneity. The latter is also required to generate amino acid sequence data used for molecular cloning of the complementary DNA (cDNA) or gene for the receptor. To purify a receptor protein, a source of tissue for purification must first be identified. The tissue needs to be relatively abundant in receptor protein and be easily obtainable in large quantities. Because the receptors are membrane-bound proteins, solubilization of the receptor of interest in detergent is necessarily the first step in any purification scheme, and solubilization from the tissue of interest must provide high yields. For both the D_1 and D_2 dopamine receptors, we found that solubilization in the detergent digitonin provided the highest yield of functional receptors (based on ligand binding). Bovine anterior pituitary and rat striatum were used for the purification of D_2 and D_1 dopamine receptors, respectively. Experience with the purification of other guanine nucleotide-binding protein (G protein)–coupled receptors has indicated that affinity chromatography is the most useful method of receptor purification. (Immunoprecipitation has been used to purify other types of receptors; however, antibodies suitable for immunoprecipitation of G protein–coupled receptors have not been available). In affinity chromatography, a receptor-selective ligand is immobilized via a sidearm to an insoluble matrix. The receptor protein adsorbs to the matrix in a biospecific manner, that is, by the immobilized ligand interacting with the receptor's ligand binding site. After washing to remove nonspecifically bound proteins, the adsorbed receptor can then be eluted by passing free ligand through the column. Following affinity chromatography, other chromatographic steps such as lectin, ion-exchange, or gel permeation chromatography may be used in series to obtain purified preparations of receptor protein.

We recently reported the purification of the bovine anterior pituitary D_2 dopamine receptor to apparent homogeneity (12). Purification of the D_2 receptor from this tissue requires an approximately 33,000-fold enrichment of receptor activity. Such an en-

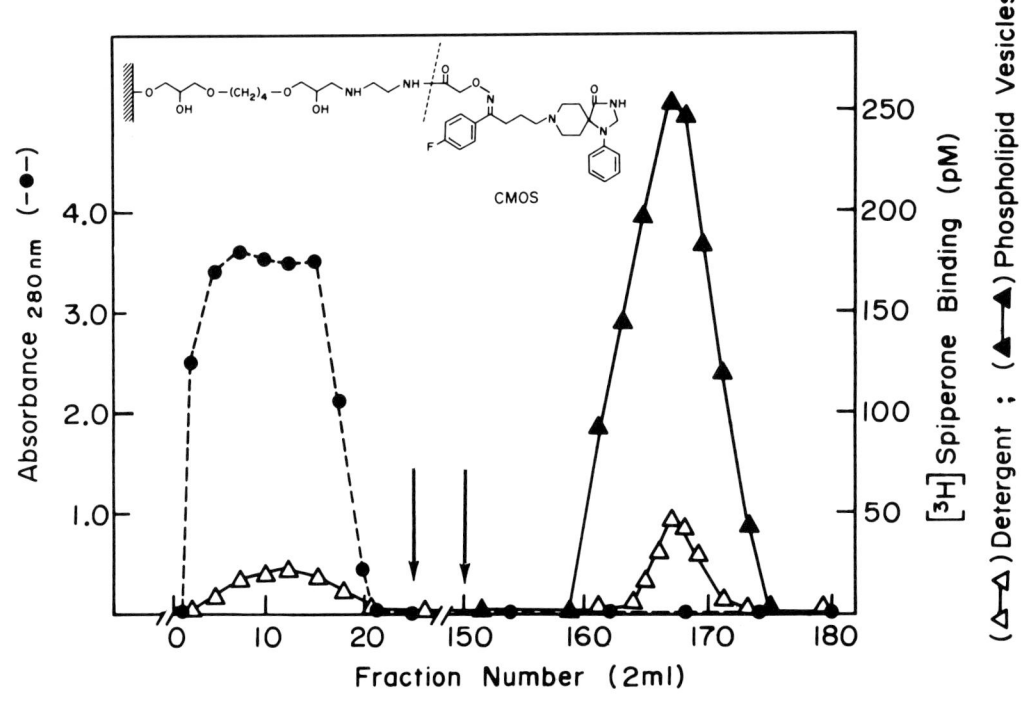

FIG. 3. Affinity chromatography of D_2 dopamine receptors. Digitonin-solubilized bovine anterior pituitary D_2 receptor was incubated with CMOS-Sepharose as described in the text. Most of the protein passes through early (*closed circles*). The *arrow* at fraction 23 indicates the start of washing. The *arrow* at fraction 150 indicates the beginning of elution by the addition of 10 μ*M* of naloperidol. Note that the amount of eluted receptor is greatly underestimated by [^{3}H]spiperone binding in detergent (*open triangles*) compared with the amount present when reconstituted into phospholipid vesicles (*closed triangles*). *Inset:* Presumed structure of the CMOS-Sepharose sidearm. Reprinted by permission from ref. 14, © 1986 American Chemical Society.

richment was achieved by solubilization of membrane-bound receptors in the detergent digitonin followed by successive steps of affinity, lectin, and hydroxylapatite chromatography.

For affinity chromatography, the (carboxymethylene)oximino derivative of spiperone (CMOS) is immobilized to Sepharose 4B via a sidearm (see Fig. 3 *inset*; ref. 14). Solubilized receptor is then allowed to adsorb to the gel in a batchwise fashion overnight. The gel is washed, and the specifically adsorbed receptor is eluted from the gel using the D_2 selective antagonist haloperidol (10 to 50 μM; see Fig. 3). This procedure enriches the receptor approximately 1500-fold. Following this step, reconstitution of the digitonin-solubilized receptor into phospholipid vesicles (a process that is 60% to 70% efficient) is required to observe ligand-binding affinities similar to those observed for membrane preparations. Therefore, [^{3}H]spiperone binding to reconstituted receptors is used to measure D_2 receptor activity following the affinity step. Interestingly, the affinity-purified receptor displays biphasic, guanine nucleotide–sensitive agonist competition curves upon reconstitution (see below). The affinity-purified receptor is then passed over a gel containing immobilized *Datura stramonium* (DSA) lectin, so that the glycoprotein receptor can be purified on the basis of its oligosaccharide structure. A tenfold purification results following elution by N,N'-diacetylchitobiose. The affinity- and lectin-purified receptor is then subjected to hydroxylapatite chromatography to achieve final purification. At this point the purified protein migrates as a single band of M_r = 120,000 on SDS-PAGE as visualized by Coomassie blue stain, silver stain, or by labeling with [^{125}I]Bolton-Hunter reagent (15), as shown in Fig. 4.

Several criteria can be used to characterize the purified protein to demonstrate that it represents the D_2 receptor. First, the specific activity of the purified reconstituted

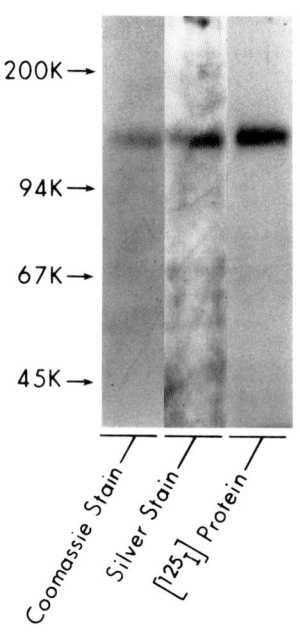

FIG. 4. SDS-PAGE of purified bovine anterior pituitary D_2 dopamine receptors. D_2 receptor was purified through CMOS affinity, DSA lectin, and hydroxylapatite chromatography. Twenty picomoles of purified receptor was run on SDS-PAGE. The gel was stained with Coomassie blue (*left lane*), photographed, and then completely destained and restained with silver (*middle lane*). Right lane shows autoradiography of purified D_2 dopamine receptor iodinated using Bolton-Hunter reagent (15). Molecular weight markers are shown. Reprinted with permission from ref. 12, © American Society for Biochemistry and Molecular Biology.

material (~5.3 nmol/mg protein) is close to the theoretical specific activity based on molecular weight (~8.3 nmol/mg protein). Second, the reconstituted purified protein displays the pharmacological and biochemical properties expected for the D_2 receptor, including antagonist and agonist binding with appropriate rank orders of potency and affinity and G protein coupling. Finally, [^{125}I]bromoacetyl-NAPS specifically labels the purified D_2 dopamine receptors (Fig. 5). Furthermore, protein-stained and affinity-alkylated preparations migrate identically on SDS-PAGE, with M_r = 120,000.

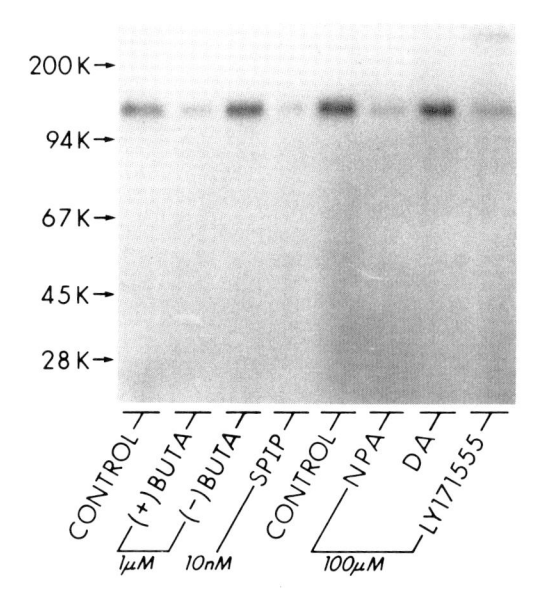

FIG. 5. Affinity labeling of purified bovine anterior pituitary D_2 dopamine receptor. Purified receptor was labeled by incubation with [^{125}I]bromoacetyl-NAPS (structure shown in Fig 1A) in the absence (control) or presence of various D_2 dopaminergic ligands. Molecular weight markers are shown. Reprinted with permission from ref. 12, © American Society for Biochemistry and Molecular Biology.

Large scale purification is required to obtain amino acid sequence information needed for the identification of cDNA or genomic clones for the receptors. Peptides are generated chemically or proteolytically from pure protein and are subjected to microsequencing. The sequences so obtained are then used to design oligonucleotide probes to screen cDNA or genomic libraries. This approach has been used successfully in the isolation of the cDNAs and genes for the β_2-, α_2-, and α_1-adrenergic receptors (16,17,18). To isolate cDNA clones for the bovine anterior pituitary D_2 receptor, purified receptor was cleaved by cyanogen bromide and pepsin. The peptides were separated by reverse-phase high-performance liquid chromatography (HPLC), and individual fractions were subjected to gas-phase microsequencing. Partial amino acid sequences so obtained are currently being used in an attempt to isolate a cDNA clone for the purified protein.

Progress has been made in our laboratory on the purification of D_1 dopamine receptors as well. SCH 39111, the 4′-amino derivative of SCH 23390, retains a high affinity for the D_1 receptor. The amino function allows the immobilization of the ligand onto Sepharose via an extended sidearm (see Fig. 6 *inset*; ref 19). Receptor preparations from rat striatum solubilized using digitonin are adsorbed to the SCH 39111-Sepharose in a batchwise fashion overnight. Adsorption of receptor to the gel is biospecific: it is blocked by the addition of SCH 23390 or (+)butaclamol but not by the less active enantiomers SCH 23388 or (−)butaclamol. The affinity gel adsorbs 75% to 85% of the solubilized receptor. Following extensive washing of the gel, including washes with high NaCl (250 and 500 mM) and low pH (6.0; see Fig. 6), the specifically adsorbed receptor is eluted from the gel using the antagonist (+)butaclamol (100 μM). Other D_1 antagonists and agonists are able to elute the receptor as well; ligands for other receptors are not able. The ligand-binding properties of the D_1 receptor are retained following affinity chromatography, including stereospecificity and rank order of potency. A yield of 35% to 55% of the bound receptor is recovered by elution, with a purification of 200 to 250-fold by affinity chromatography. The specific activity of the eluted material, 300 to 375 pmol/mg protein, is approximately 40-fold short of the theoretical specific activity based on the molecular weight of the protein.

Coupling of the SCH 39111-Sepharose chromatography with several steps of ion exchange and lectin chromatography has yielded a purified preparation of D_1 receptor from rat striatum. Treatment of this preparation with cyanogen bromide and isolation and microsequencing of the peptides obtained has yielded sequence infor-

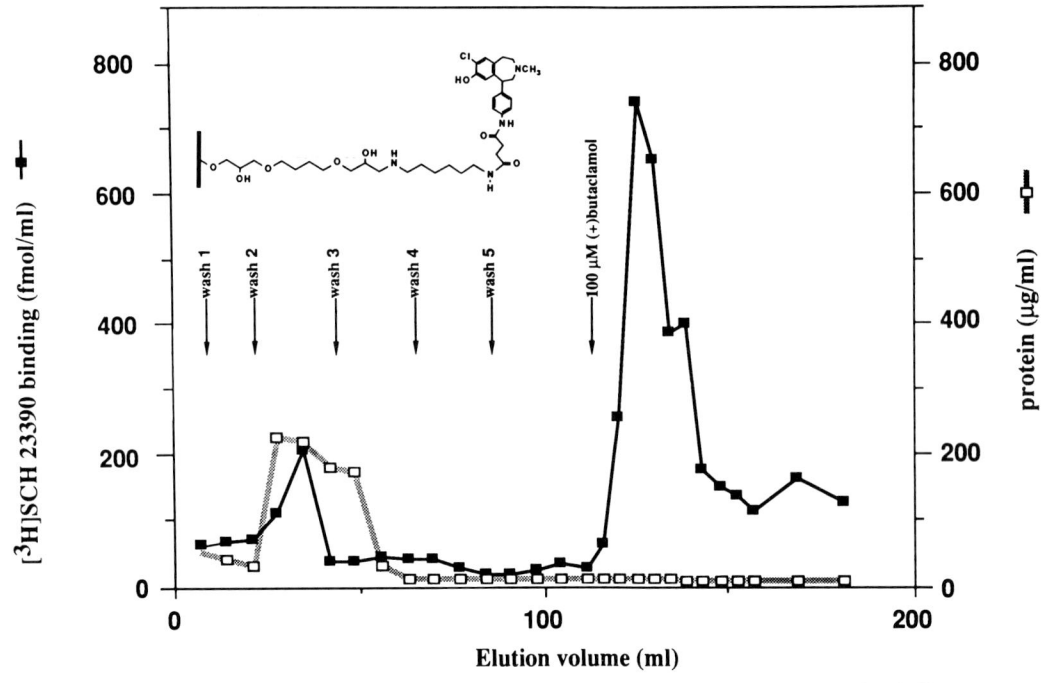

FIG. 6. Affinity chromatography of D_1 dopamine receptors. Digitonin-solubilized rat brain D_1 receptor was incubated with SCH 39111-Sepharose as described in the text. Arrows indicate various wash steps; significant amounts of protein and receptor were eluted at washes 2 and 3, where the concentrations of NaCl were increased to 250 mM and 500 mM, respectively. The final arrow shows elution of the receptor by the addition of 100 µM (+)butaclamol. *Inset:* presumed structure of the SCH 39111-Sepharose sidearm. Reprinted with permission from ref. 19, © 1988 American Chemical Society.

mation that is being used to isolate a cDNA clone for the D_1 receptor.

CHARACTERIZATION OF D_2 DOPAMINE RECEPTOR FUNCTION

As stated above, the affinity-purified bovine anterior pituitary D_2 dopamine receptor displays biphasic, guanine nucleotide–sensitive agonist competition curves upon reconstitution into phospholipid vesicles (14). Such characteristics are not observed if the nonhydrolyzable GTP analog guanylylimidodiphosphate [Gpp(NH)p] is included while washing the affinity gel prior to elution. These observations imply that a G protein is being copurified with the D_2 receptor at the affinity chromatography step. Further work (20) demonstrated the specific association with the receptor of a pertussis toxin substrate of $M_r \approx 40,000$. Peptide maps of this protein were distinct from those of the G proteins G_i, G_o (both from brain) and transducin, known pertussis toxin substrates. In addition, Western blots of affinity-purified preparations demonstrated the presence of material reactive with antibodies raised against and specific for one form of G_i and G_o. These data suggest that the D_2 receptor of bovine anterior pituitary couples to a novel G protein. In recent work using purified D_2 receptor and purified, resolved G proteins reconstituted into phospholipid vesicles, we have shown that the receptor couples preferentially to G_{i2} compared to G_{i1} and G_{i3} and does not couple to G_o (21).

CONCLUSIONS

The use of subtype-selective dopamine receptor antagonists as the basis for the development of subtype-specific probes has allowed the identification and purification of both D_1 and D_2 dopamine receptors. Besides their distinct pharmacology, the ligand-binding subunits of these receptors are distinct at the molecular level. The use of purified receptor preparations and the molecular cloning of the cDNAs and genes for the receptors will allow detailed characterization of dopamine receptor structure and function and their derangement in pathological states.

ACKNOWLEDGMENTS

This work was supported in part by NIH Grant NS 19576. MDB and JAG were supported by NIH Medical Scientist Training Program Grant P32 GM 07171, PF by a fellowship from the Fonds de la Recherche en Santé du Québec, and SES by NIH Fellowship NS-07922.

REFERENCES

1. Seeman P. Dopamine receptors in human brain diseases. In: Creese I, Fraser CM, eds. *Dopamine receptors*. New York: Alan Liss, 1987;233–245.
2. Spano PF, Govani S, Trabucchi M. Studies on the pharmacological properties of dopamine receptors in various areas of the central nervous system. *Adv Biochem Psychopharmacol* 1978; 19:155–165.
3. Kebabian JW, Calne DB. Multiple receptors for dopamine. *Nature* 1979;277:93–96.
4. Kohli JD, Goldberg LI. Dopamine receptors: a classification based on physiological studies. In: Creese I, Fraser CM, eds. *Dopamine receptors*. New York: Alan Liss, 1987;97–114.
5. Vallar L, Meldolesi J. Mechanisms of signal transduction at the dopamine D_2 receptor. *Trends Pharmacol. Sci.* 1989;10:74–77.
6. Stoof JC, Kebabian JW. Two dopamine receptors: biochemistry, physiology, and pharmacology. *Life Sci* 1984;35:2281–2296.
7. Burnside B, Dearry A. Cell motility in the retina. In: Adler R, Farber D, eds. *The retina: a model for cell biology studies*. Orlando: Academic Press, 1986;151–206.
8. Brown EM, Carroll RJ, Aurbach GD. Dopaminergic stimulation of cyclic AMP and parathyroid hormone release from dispersed bovine parathyroid cells. *Proc Nat Acad Sci USA* 1977;74: 4210–4213.
9. Dohlman HG, Caron MG, Lefkowitz RJ. A family of receptors coupled to guanine nucleotide regulatory proteins. *Biochemistry* 1987;26:2657–2664.
10. Amlaiky N, Caron MG. Photoaffinity labeling of the D_2-dopamine receptor using a novel high affinity radioiodinated probe. *J Biol Chem* 1985; 260:1983–1986.
11. Amlaiky N, Caron MG. Identification of the D_2-dopamine receptor binding subunit in several mammalian tissues and species by photoaffinity labeling. *J Neurochem* 1986;47:196–204.
12. Senogles SE, Amlaiky N, Falardeau P, Caron MG. Purification and characterization of the D_2-dopamine receptor from bovine anterior pituitary. *J Biol Chem* 1988;263:18996–19002.
13. Amlaiky N, Berger JG, Chang W, McQuade RJ, Caron MG. Identification of the binding subunit of the D_1-dopamine receptor by photoaffinity crosslinking. *Mol Pharm* 1987;31:129–134.
14. Senogles SE, Amlaiky N, Johnson AL, Caron MG. Affinity chromatography of the anterior pituitary D_2-dopamine receptor. *Biochemistry* 1986;25:749–753.
15. Bolton AE, Hunter WM. A new method for labelling protein hormones with radioiodine for use in the radioimmunoassay. *J Endocrinol* 1972;55:30–31.
16. Dixon RAF, Kobilka BK, Strader DJ, et al. Cloning of the gene and cDNA for mammalian β-adrenergic receptor and homology with rhodopsin. *Nature* 1986;321:75–79.
17. Kobilka BK, Matsui H, Kobilka TS, et al. Cloning, sequencing, and expression of the gene coding for the human platelet α_2-adrenergic receptor. *Science* 1987;238:650–656.
18. Cotecchia S, Schwinn DA, Randall RR, Lefkowitz RJ, Caron MG, Kobilka BK. Cloning and expression of the cDNA for the hamster α_1-adrenergic receptor. *Proc Nat Acad Sci USA* 1988; 85:7159–7163.
19. Gingrich JA, Amlaiky N, Senogles SE, et al. Affinity chromatography of the D_1 dopamine receptor from rat corpus striatum. *Biochemistry* 1988;27:3907–3912.
20. Senogles SE, Benovic JL, Amlaiky N, et al. The D_2-dopamine receptor is functionally associated with a pertussis toxin-sensitive guanine nucleotide binding protein. *J Biol Chem* 1987;262: 4860–4867.
21. Senogles SE, Spiegel AM, Padrell E, Iyengar R, Caron MG. Specificity of receptor-G protein interactions: discrimination of G_i subtypes by the D_2 dopamine receptor in a reconstituted system. *J Biol Chem* 1990;265:4507–4514.

2

Mechanisms of Phencyclidine (PCP)–N-Methyl-D-Aspartate (NMDA) Receptor Interaction:

Implications for Schizophrenia

Daniel C. Javitt and Stephen R. Zukin[1]

Phencyclidine (1,1-phenylcyclohexylpiperidine; PCP or "angel dust"), originally developed as a general anesthetic in the late 1950s, was found to produce loss of consciousness and analgesia sufficient to allow the performance of surgical procedures while not causing significant respiratory or cardiovascular depression (1–3). However, a significant proportion of patients subjected to PCP anesthesia developed psychotic episodes typically lasting 12 to 72 hours but occasionally as long as 7 to 10 days. These episodes were characterized by excitation, unmanageability, paranoia, concreteness of thought (1,2) and "maniacal episodes" (3). Subanesthetic doses (0.1 mg/kg intravenously [IV]) were subsequently found to induce psychotic episodes in normal volunteers and also to rekindle presenting symptomatology in recompensated schizophrenic subjects (4–7). In addition, subanesthetic doses of PCP, but not LSD, amobarbital or amphetamine, could induce abnormalities in tests of abstract reasoning, cognitive processing, attention, motor function and proprioception in normal volunteers that closely resembled those seen in patients with chronic schizophrenia (7,8). These findings led to the proposal that the mechanisms of action of PCP may be relevant to the pathogenesis of schizophrenia (6,9).

PCP binds with high affinity to a specific brain PCP receptor (10–12). Several lines of evidence indicate that the PCP receptor is a site within the ion channel gated by the NMDA-type excitatory amino acid receptor. First, PCP and NMDA receptors are colocalized in the central nervous system (13). Second, PCP receptor ligands have been shown to inhibit NMDA receptor–mediated conductances noncompetitively (14) in a voltage- and use-dependent fashion (15,16). Finally, binding of PCP receptor ligands is enhanced by NMDA receptor agonists, such as L-glutamate or NMDA, and is diminished by competitive NMDA receptor antagonists such as D(−)-2-amino-5-phosphonovaleric acid [D(−)AP5;(17–19)]. Such data suggest a model in which NMDA and PCP receptors represent distinct sites associated with a supramolecular NMDA receptor complex. The identification of noncompetitive inhibition of NMDA receptor function as the mechanism underlying the psychotomimetic effects of PCP sug-

[1] Departments of Psychiatry and Neuroscience, Albert Einstein College of Medicine and Bronx Psychiatric Center, Bronx, NY 10461.

gests that elucidation of the functioning of the NMDA receptor complex may reveal mechanisms relevant to the pathogenesis and treatment of schizophrenia.

MECHANISMS OF PCP-NMDA RECEPTOR INTERACTION

In order to elucidate mechanisms underlying NMDA receptor activation, binding of the selective PCP receptor ligand [^{3}H]MK-801 was determined in the presence and absence of L-glutamate and either glycine or D-serine, agents that had previously been shown to stimulate binding to PCP receptors (12,20). L-glutamate has been shown to mediate its actions as an agonist at the NMDA recognition site, while both glycine and D-serine mediate their actions at a non-strychnine-sensitive glycine recognition site associated with the NMDA receptor complex. For these studies, rat forebrain homogenates were subjected to extensive washing, freezing, and thawing in order to reduce the high endogenous concentrations of L-glutamate and glycine present in crude brain homogenate. Specific binding of [^{3}H]MK-801 was determined at 12 to 16 time points between 5 minutes and 24 hours using a filtration radioreceptor assay in the presence of a 5 mM Tris buffer system adjusted to pH 7.4 and a low (30 μM) concentration of Mg^{2+} (21).

These studies resulted in three novel findings. First, analysis of association curves using a computer-assisted, nonlinear curve-fitting technique revealed the presence of two distinct components of [^{3}H]MK-801 binding: a fast component with a $t_{1/2}$ value of approximately 5 minutes and a slow component with a $t_{1/2}$ value of approximately 3 hours (Fig. 1). This suggests that PCP-like agents do not gain access to their receptor only via open channels, since channel-blocking drugs that interact exclusively with open channels should manifest single exponential association and dissociation (22). A model of PCP-NMDA receptor interaction consistent with bi-exponential association of [^{3}H]MK-801 would be one in which PCP-like agents can gain access to their recognition site via two distinct paths, each corresponding to one of the observed kinetic components of binding. It has been suggested that channel-blocking drugs hav-

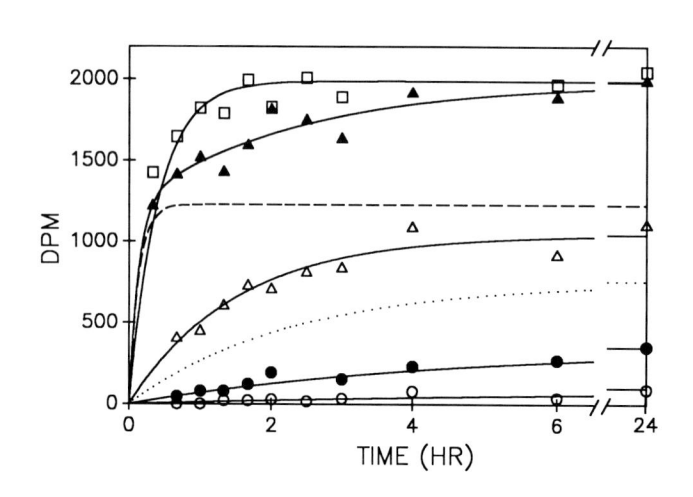

FIG. 1. Association curves of 1 nM of [^{3}H]MK-801 under control conditions (*filled circles*) or in the presence of 10-μM concentrations of D(−)AP5 (*open circles*), glycine (*open triangles*), L-glutamate (*filled triangles*), or L-glutamate plus glycine (*open squares*). Under control conditions or in the presence of D(−)AP5, binding was best fit by single exponentials with apparent $t_{1/2}$ values of 3.2 and 5.8 hours, respectively. In the presence of combined L-glutamate and glycine, binding was best fit by a single exponential with an apparent $t_{1/2}$ of 12 minutes. In the presence of L-glutamate alone, binding was best fit by dual exponentials with apparent $t_{1/2}$ values of 5.5 minutes and 1.6 hours for the fast (*dashed line*) and slow (*dotted line*) components, respectively. (Reprinted from ref 21).

ing pK_a values near physiological pH may associate with their binding sites via both fast hydrophilic and slow hydrophobic paths (22). At pH 7.4 MK-801 (pK_a = 8.2; ref 16) would exist in both deprotonated and protonated forms. The former would be capable of association via both hydrophilic and hydrophobic paths, while the latter would be capable of association only via a hydrophilic path. When channels were maximally activated in the presence of combined L-glutamate and glycine, we found that more than 90% of [^{3}H]MK-801 binding displayed fast kinetics of association, suggesting that the fast path represents binding of [^{3}H]MK-801 to its receptor following diffusion to the binding site via a path corresponding to the open NMDA receptor channel. In the absence of added L-glutamate or in the presence of D(−)AP5, more than 99% of [^{3}H]MK-801 binding displayed slow kinetics of association, suggesting that the slow path represents binding of [^{3}H]MK-801 following diffusion to the binding site via a path associated with closed NMDA receptors channels. The latter path could involve diffusion of deprotonated [^{3}H]MK-801 through the lipid bilayer, through hydrophobic domains of the receptor complex or through the (closed) NMDA receptor gating mechanism. Biexponential kinetics of association of [^{3}H]MK-801 in the presence of L-glutamate alone indicate that association via fast and slow paths can occur simultaneously, supporting the concept that different underlying processes must be involved. The ability of PCP-like agents to reach their binding site within closed NMDA channels over the course of hours may be relevant to the course of PCP intoxication since it suggests that PCP can reach its site of action even in the absence of NMDA receptor activation.

A second finding of these studies (21) was that L-glutamate significantly increased total steady-state [^{3}H]MK-801 binding while D(−)AP5 significantly decreased total steady-state [^{3}H]MK-801 binding (Fig. 2), presumably by displacing endogenous agonists from the NMDA receptor. This

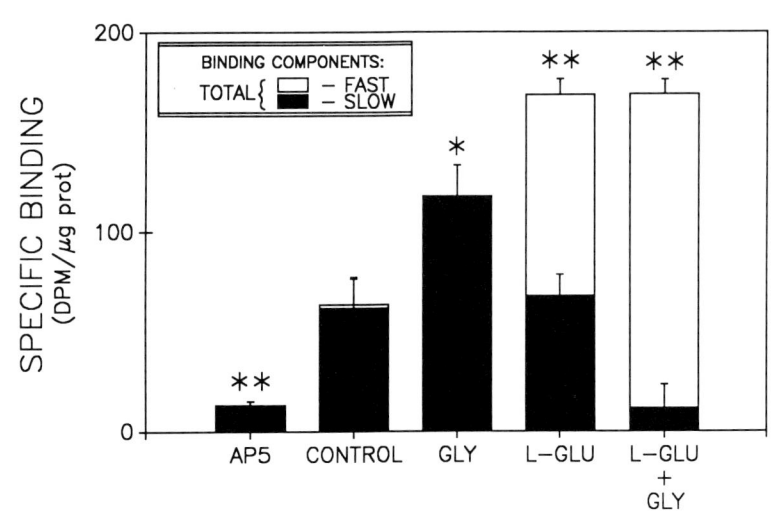

FIG. 2. Specific binding (mean ± SEM) of 1 n*M* [^{3}H]MK-801 to fast (*open bar*) and slow (*filled bar*) components under control conditions or in the presence of 10-μ*M* concentrations of D(−)AP5 (AP5), glycine (GLY), L-glutamate (L-GLU) or L-glutamate plus glycine. Total bar height represents total steady-state binding of [^{3}H]MK-801 under conditions specified. Significant between-groups variation was found for fast ($p < .001$), slow ($p < .01$) and total ($p < .001$) steady-state binding. Values represent mean ± SEM of four to six experiments. *$p < .05$ relative to control. **$p < .01$ relative to control. (Reprinted from ref 21).

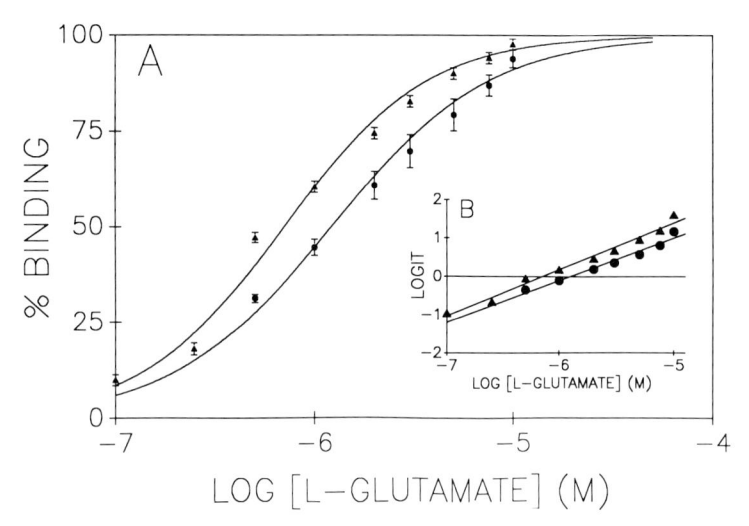

FIG. 3. Stimulation of specific 1 n*M* [³H]MK-801 binding by L-glutamate in the absence (*circles*) or presence (*triangles*) of 10 μ*M* of glycine following 24-hour incubations. Fifty micromoles of D(−)AP5 was added under all conditions to decrease basal binding. *Inset:* Hill plots of specific 1 n*M* [³H]MK-801 binding. Correlation coefficients were $r > .95$ for both plots. In both the absence (*circles*) and presence (*triangles*) of 10 μ*M* of glycine, Hill coefficients were significantly greater than unity. (Reprinted from ref 21).

finding differs from those of previous studies that had reported no change in equilibrium binding following the addition of glutamate and glycine (23,24). A third finding of our studies (21) was that the Hill coefficient for stimulation of [³H]MK-801 binding by L-glutamate was significantly greater than unity (Fig. 3). While glycine shifted the dose-response curve to the left, it did not alter the Hill coefficient significantly. This finding suggests that more than one molecule of agonist is required to induce NMDA channel activation.

A model of NMDA receptor functioning that could account for these findings is one involving the existence of two independent sets of agonist recognition sites within each functional NMDA receptor complex. Occupation of both sets by agonist would be required for channel activation and fast [³H]MK-801 binding. Partial activation would not permit channel opening but would permit slow diffusion of [³H]MK-801 to its binding site via a hydrophobic path. In the total absence of agonist, however, the channel would remain closed and in a conformation to which PCP receptor ligands would not be able to bind. This model is similar to models that have been proposed to account for the functioning of nicotinic acetylcholine (25) and $GABA_A$ (26) receptors. If future studies confirm a functional similarity between NMDA and nicotinic receptors, it may indicate that NMDA receptors are structurally homologous to receptors of the Class I superfamily of ligand-gated channels, which includes nicotinic, $GABA_A$, and strychnine-sensitive glycine receptors as well (27).

ROLE OF NMDA RECEPTORS IN PCP PSYCHOSIS

The ability of PCP-like agents to bind with high potency to a site within the NMDA channel suggests that PCP-induced NMDA channel blockade may be relevant to the clinical effects of PCP. The degree to which PCP receptors mediate the psychotomimetic effects of PCP has been a subject of controversy in the literature. Both haloperidol-sensitive σ (28) and monoamine reuptake (29,30) sites have been proposed as potential alternative sites for mediation of the psychotomimetic effects of PCP. Several lines of evidence, however, support a unique role of the PCP receptor in this regard. First, PCP receptors have been shown to mediate the discriminative stimulus effects of PCP in rodents (31). The rank order of potency with which a large number of drugs from distinct chemical classes can induce the PCP response in animals trained to discriminate PCP from saline corresponds to these drugs' rank order of binding to PCP receptors and inducing NMDA receptor blockade (31). By contrast, agents that selectively bind to the σ and/or dopamine reuptake sites neither induce PCP-like discriminative stimulus effects nor antagonize the discriminative stimulus effects induced by PCP receptor ligands (31). These findings suggest that PCP receptors mediate the introceptive cues induced by PCP and PCP-like agents. Second, psychotomimetic effects similar to those induced by PCP can be induced by ketamine, a related arylcyclohexylamine derivative (32). The psychotomimetic effects of ketamine are induced by doses approximately 10-fold greater than PCP (32), which is consistent with its tenfold lower potency of binding to PCP receptors (10, 11). By contrast, ketamine is essentially inactive at both dopamine reuptake (33) and σ sites (11). Finally, PCP-induced psychosis has been found to be associated with serum concentrations of PCP as low as 20 nM, while serum concentrations greater than 400 nM are associated with gross impairments in consciousness (34). PCP receptors have been shown to bind PCP with an affinity of approximately 30 to 50 nM (12,35,36), suggesting a highly significant degree of receptor occupancy by levels of PCP present during low-dose PCP psychosis. By contrast, σ binding sites and DA reuptake sites have been shown to bind PCP with affinities of approximately 600 (36) and 700 (33) nM, respectively. The affinity of PCP for these sites is thus significantly lower than its affinity for PCP receptors. Furthermore, the affinity of PCP for these sites suggests that they would be affected only to a limited extent by concentrations of PCP that have been demonstrated to cause robust psychotomimetic effects.

In summary, PCP induces psychotomimetic effects that closely resemble those of schizophrenia. Our experimental data from experiments measuring the effects of NMDA receptor activation on binding of [^{3}H]MK-801 to PCP receptors support a model of NMDA receptor functioning in which two molecules of agonist are required for NMDA receptor activation. This model is similar to models that have been proposed for the nicotinic acetylcholine receptor, suggesting the possibility of functional and structural homology between NMDA receptors and members of the Class I superfamily of ligand-gated channels. The psychotomimetic effects of PCP are observed at serum concentrations similar to the concentration at which PCP binds to the NMDA-associated PCP receptor. These findings suggest that endogenous dysfunction or dysregulation of NMDA receptor–mediated neurotransmission may contribute to the pathogenesis of schizophrenia, and that novel agents influencing NMDA receptor functioning could prove of interest as potential treatment for schizophrenia.

ACKNOWLEDGMENTS

This work was supported in part by USPHS grants DA-03383 to SRZ and MH-00631 to DCJ, grants from the Ritter Foundation and the David Berg Family Fund for Research in Manic Depressive Illness to SRZ, and by the generous support of the Department of Psychiatry of the Albert Einstein College of Medicine, Herman M. van Praag, MD, PhD, Chairman.

REFERENCES

1. Greifenstein FE, Yoskitake J, DeVault M, Gajewski JE. A study of 1-aryl cyclohexylamine for anesthesia. *Anesth Anal* 1958;37:283–294.
2. Meyer JS, Greifenstein F, DeVault M. A new drug causing symptoms of sensory deprivation. *J Nerv Ment Dis* 1959;129:54–61.
3. Johnstone M, Evans V, Baigel S. Sernyl (Cl-395) in clinical anesthesia. *Br J Anaesth* 1958;31:433–439.
4. Davies BM, Beech HR. The effect of 1-arylcyclohexylamine (Sernyl) on twelve normal volunteers. *J Ment Sci* 1960;106:912–924.
5. Luby ED, Cohen BD, Rosenbaum F, Gottlieb J, Kelley R. Study of a new schizophrenomimetic drug—Sernyl. *AMA Arch Neurol Psychiatry* 1959;81:363–369.
6. Luby ED, Gottlieb JS, Cohen BD, Rosenbaum G, Domino EF. Model psychosis and schizophrenia. *Am J Psychiatry* 1962;119:61–65.
7. Rosenbaum G, Cohen BD, Luby ED, Gottlieb JS, Yelen D. Comparison of Sernyl with other drugs. *AMA Arch Gen Psychiatry* 1959;1:651–656.
8. Cohen BD, Rosenbaum G, Luby ED, Gottlieb JS. Comparison of phencyclidine hydrochloride (Sernyl) with other drugs. *Arch Gen Psychiatry* 1962;6:79–85.
9. Domino EF, Luby ED. Abnormal mental states induced by phencyclidine as a model of schizophrenia. In: Domino EF, ed., *PCP (Phencyclidine): Historical and Current Perspectives*, Ann Arbor: NPP Books 1981;400–418.
10. Zukin SR, Zukin RS. Specific [^{3}H]phencyclidine binding in rat central nervous system. *Proc Natl Acad Sci USA* 1979;76:5372–5376.
11. Vincent JP, Kartalovski B, Geneste P, et al. Interaction of phencyclidine ("angel dust") with a specific receptor in rat brain membranes. *Proc Natl Acad Sci USA* 1979;76:4678–4682.
12. Reynolds IJ, Murphy SN, Miller RJ. ^{3}H-labeled MK-801 binding to the excitatory amino acid receptor complex from rat brain is enhanced by glycine. *Proc Natl Acad Sci* 1987;84:7744–7748.
13. Maragos WF, Penny JB, Young AB. Anatomic correlation of NMDA and ^{3}H-TCP-labeled receptors in rat brain. *J Neurosci* 1988;8:493–501.
14. Anis NA, Berry SC, Burton NR and Lodge D. The dissociative anesthetics, ketamine and phencyclidine, selectively reduce excitation of central mammalian neurones by N-methyl-aspartate. *Br J Pharmacol* 1983;79:565–575.
15. Honey CR, Miljkovic Z, MacDonald JF. Ketamine and phencyclidine cause a voltage-dependent block of responses to L-aspartic acid. *Neurosci Lett* 1985;61:135–139.
16. Huettner JE, Bean BP. Block of N-methyl-D-aspartate-activated current by the anticonvulsant MK-801: selective binding to open channels. *Proc Natl Acad Sci USA* 1988;85;1307–1311.
17. Javitt DC, Jotkowitz A, Sircar R, Zukin SR. Non-competitive regulation of phencyclidine/σ receptors by the N-methyl-D-aspartate receptor antagonist D(–)2-amino-5-phosphonovaleric acid. *Neurosci Lett* 1987;78;193–198.
18. Fagg GE. Phencyclidine and related drugs bind to the activated N-methyl-D-aspartate receptor-channel complex in rat brain membranes. *Neurosci Lett* 1987;76:221–227.
19. Loo PS, Braunwalder AF, Lehmann J, Williams M, Sills MA. Interaction of L-glutamate and magnesium with phencyclidine recognition sites in rat brain: evidence for multiple affinity states of the phencyclidine/N-methyl-D-aspartate receptor complex. *Mol Pharmacol* 1987;32:820–830.
20. Javitt DC, Zukin SR. Interaction of [^{3}H]MK-801 with multiple states of the N-methyl-D-aspartate receptor complex of rat brain. *Proc Natl Acad Sci USA* 1989;86:740–744.
21. Javitt DC, Zukin SR. Bi-exponential kinetics of [^{3}H]MK-801 binding: evidence for access to closed and open N-methyl-D-aspartate receptor channels. *Mol Pharmacol* in press.
22. Starmer CF, Grant AO. Phasic ion channel blockade: a kinetic model and parameter estimation procedure. *Mol Pharmacol* 1985;28:348–356.
23. Kloog G, Haring R, Sokolvsky M. Kinetic characterization of the phencyclidine-N-methyl-D-aspartate receptor interaction: evidence for a steric blockade of the channel. *Biochem* 1988;27:843–848.
24. Bonhaus DW, McNamara JO: N-methyl-D-aspartate receptor regulation of uncompetitive antagonist binding in rat brain membranes: kinetic analysis. *Mol Pharmacol* 1988;34:250–255.
25. Hess GP, Cash DJ, Aoshima H. Acetylcholine receptor-controlled ion translocation: chemical kinetic investigations of the mechanism. *Ann Rev Biophys Bioeng* 1983;12:443–473.
26. Aoshima A, Anan M, Ishii H, Iio H, Kobayashi S. Minimal model to account for the membrane conductance increase and desensitization of gamma-aminobutyric acid receptors synthesized in *Xenopus* oocytes injected with rat brain mRNA. *Biochem* 1987;26:4811–4816.
27. Barnard EA, Darlison MG, Seeburg P. Molecular biology of the GABA$_A$ receptor: the receptor/channel superfamily. *Trends Neurosci* 1987;10:502–509.
28. Su TP, London ED, Jaffe JH. Steroid binding at sigma receptors suggests a link between endocrine, nervous, and immune systems. *Science* 1988;240:219–221.
29. Smith RC, Meltzer HY, Arora RC, Davis JM. Effect of phencyclidine on [^{3}H]catecholamine and [^{3}H]serotonin uptake in synaptosomal preparations from rat brain. *Biochem Pharmacol* 1977;26:1435–1439.
30. Garey RE, Heath RG. The effects of phencyclidine on the uptake of [^{3}H]catecholamines by rat striatal and hypothalamus synaptosomes. *Life Sci* 1976;18:1105–1107.
31. Browne RG. Discriminative stimulus properties of PCP mimetics. In: Clouet DH, ed. *Phencycli-*

dine: an update, NIDA Res. Monogr. #64. Rockville, MD: Dept. of Health and Human Services, 1986;pp134–147.
32. Siegel RK. Phencyclidine and ketamine intoxication: a study of four populations of recreational users. In: *Phencyclidine abuse: an appraisal,* NIDA Res Monogr #21. Rockville, MD: Dept. of Health and Human Services, 1978; pp119–147.
33. Vignon J, Pınet V, Cerruti C, Kamenka JM, Chicheportiche R. [^{3}H]N-[1-(2-Benzo9b)thiophencyl)cyclohexyl]piperidine ([^{3}H]BTCP): a new phencyclidine analog selective for the dopamine uptake complex. *Eur J Pharmacol* 1988;148:427–436.
34. Walberg CB, McCarron MM, Schulze BW. Quantitation of phencyclidine in serum by enzyme immunoassay: results in 405 patients. *J Anal Toxicol* 1986;7:106–110.
35. Sircar R, Rappaport M, Nichtenhauser R, Zukin SR. The novel anticonvulsant MK-801: a potent and specific ligand of the brain phencyclidine/σ-receptor. *Brain Res* 1987;435:235–240.
36. Wong EHF, Knight AR, Woodruff GN. [^{3}H]MK-801 labels a site on the *N*-methyl-D-aspartate receptor channel complex in rat brain membranes. *J Neurochem* 1988;50:274–281.

3

Recent Developments in Genetic Linkage Studies of Schizophrenia

James L. Kennedy[1] and Luis A. Giuffra[2]

The search for genetic factors in schizophrenia is an intriguing and mystifying pursuit. Many investigations over the past several decades have generated strong evidence that genes act to predispose some individuals toward developing the disease. Despite these decades of productive research, the final answers to genetic questions in schizophrenia remain elusive. Genetic linkage strategies have recently been successful in locating genes for a number of familial diseases including cystic fibrosis and muscular dystrophy. Locating genes for schizophrenia, however, promises to be a more complex task.

HISTORICAL PERSPECTIVE

In the 1930s and 1940s Kallmann (1) studied the prevalence of schizophrenia in the biological siblings of subjects having schizophrenia and in a control group of step-siblings who were in the same family as the individuals with schizophrenia but not biologically related to them. The biological siblings were seven times more likely to have schizophrenia compared with the step-siblings of the schizophrenic proband. Studies using the adopted-away format (2) revealed the rate of schizophrenia to be higher in the biological siblings of schizophrenic persons reared in other families than in the biologically unrelated social siblings in the adopting family. Kendler and Gruenberg (3) have reanalyzed these data, and the results continue to provide strong support for the hypothesis that genetic factors operate in the etiology of schizophrenia. A different format of adoption study examined the adopted-away offspring of schizophrenic parents; here again, despite a different social environment, the children who were biologically related to schizophrenic parents had a significantly higher rate of schizophrenia than expected (4,5,6).

Investigations of schizophrenia in identical and fraternal twins clearly point to a major role for the involvement of genetic factors. There is a concordance rate of 30% to 70% for schizophrenia in monozygotic twin pairs. Dizygotic twin pairs have 10% to 20% concordance for the disease (reviewed by Kendler, ref 7). Kendler has calculated a heritability of liability statistic (which is based on a multifactorial threshold model) using data from the major twin studies; he concludes that genetic factors play a major, and nongenetic familial factors perhaps a minor, etiologic role in schizophrenia.

Twin and adoption studies thus provide a solid foundation for investigators to search, using restriction fragment length polymorphisms (RFLPs) and genetic linkage studies, for the genes involved in the pathogen-

---

[1]Departments of Human Genetics and Psychiatry, and [2]Section of Neuroanatomy, Yale University School of Medicine, 333 Cedar Street, New Haven, CT 06510.

esis of schizophrenia. As will be discussed later in the chapter, the number of genes involved and their mode of inheritance remain uncertain. Such uncertainties did not exist in the linkage studies of cystic fibrosis or Duchenne's muscular dystrophy; Mendel's laws are unambiguously obeyed by these diseases. In schizophrenia, however, the variable age of onset, incomplete penetrance, and uncertainties in the diagnosis all converge to create a much higher degree of genetic complexity than is the case for simple Mendelian diseases. Nonetheless, even if errors arising from this uncertainty are made in estimates of penetrance (8) or in assumptions regarding the mode of inheritance (9), linkage can still be detected, as shown by simulation studies. In contrast to this relative robustness for the aforementioned errors, linkage analysis may be quite sensitive to errors or changes in the diagnosis, especially if the misdiagnosed person is in the older generation of the family. For related discussion of the broad range of complexities inherent in genetic linkage studies of psychiatric disorders, see Kennedy et al (10,11) and Giuffra and Kidd (12).

TWO STRATEGIES FOR GENETIC LINKAGE

The search for a disease gene can be carried out using two general approaches, each with its advantages and disadvantages. One of these methods is the genome scan. In this approach the investigator collects a relatively large number of DNA markers (perhaps 300 or more) that are distributed throughout the chromosomes. Each of these markers is tested in turn to determine whether the area around the marker includes a gene for the disease in question. The genetic distance that can be investigated on either side of the marker depends primarily on how polymorphic that marker is in the family being investigated. The major advantage of the genome scan is that no a priori hypothesis concerning the pathophysiology of the disease is required. Given the lack of solid hypotheses for the etiology of schizophrenia, this is indeed a significant advantage. An important disadvantage to bear in mind arises statistically as a result of the repeated measures. Testing several hundred markers can lead to false-positive evidence for linkage at a few of these markers due to chance alone. Thus, when testing a large number of markers, a more stringent level of statistical significance (a higher lod score) is required.

The second approach to finding a disease gene is to examine a candidate gene. In contrast to the genome scan, this strategy depends entirely on the ability of the research community to generate a good a priori hypothesis for the etiology of the disorder. Once a good hypothesis for a causative gene is produced, a DNA clone for the candidate must be obtained. A reasonable example of a candidate gene for schizophrenia is the gene for the D_2 dopamine receptor. The D_2 receptor is the major binding site for the neuroleptic medications used to reduce the symptoms of the disease. However, using the HD2G1 clone at the DRD2 locus on the long arm of chromosome 11, Moises et al (13) have shown no evidence for linkage of this dopamine receptor to schizophrenia in a Swedish kindred. An advantage of the candidate-gene strategy is that because the hypothesis is quite specific, it is more amenable to falsification. The major disadvantage to the strategy is the difficult requirement of having a very good a priori hypothesis. In the absence of such a hypothesis, virtually any gene that influences brain development or function could be a candidate. Using these broad criteria there are 50,000 to 70,000 possible candidate genes for schizophrenia.

The next section reviews a series of studies on a segment of chromosome 5 that, as a result of cytogenetic studies of a chromosomal aberration, have become a candidate "region" for linkage to schizophrenia.

CHROMOSOME 5 AND SCHIZOPHRENIA

In the last two years considerable attention has been given to linkage studies of schizophrenia, following a positive report by Sherrington et al (14). Sherrington et al collected, diagnosed, and performed genetic linkage analyses on five Icelandic and two British families, segregating for schizophrenia as well as for a variety of other psychiatric conditions. The focus of their search for a gene underlying schizophrenia in these families was the proximal long arm of chromosome 5 (the region between cytogenetic bands 5q11.2 and 5q13.3). This region was favored after a report by Bassett et al (15) described an uncle-nephew pair in which both were trisomic for this segment and both had schizophrenia. Each patient had subtle facial dysmorphic features, which provided the clue that a chromosomal abnormality might be present. The cytogenetic studies showed that both patients had an extra copy of the 5q11.2–13.3 region translocated and inverted into the long arm of chromosome 1. It was thus thought that this segment of chromosome 5 could contain a gene (or group of genes) underlying susceptibility to schizophrenia. A specific candidate, the glucocorticoid receptor gene, was originally thought to be located within this region (16) and thus raised considerable interest at the time. However, in the course of our mapping studies on chromosome 5, we demonstrated that the glucocorticoid receptor gene is not located in the 5q11.2–13.3 region and that it is not linked to schizophrenia in the Swedish kindred (17,18).

Using linkage analysis with two DNA markers from the candidate region, D5S39 and D5S76, Sherrington et al (14) obtained positive lod scores, leading them to conclude that they had discovered a susceptibility locus for schizophrenia. Intriguingly, when the disease was defined in a much broader way to include cases of major depression, minor depression, phobic disorder, and drug abuse, the evidence for linkage was increased, suggesting a possible common etiologic factor for all of these conditions.

The Sherrington et al report was simultaneously published with a negative result from our group at Yale (18). We studied seven branches of a large multigenerational kindred from Sweden with multiple cases of schizophrenia. We used the same two markers employed by Sherrington et al plus five more, and we obtained strong evidence against linkage of the disease to any site within the entire 5q11.2–13.3 region. More recently we have mapped (10) another marker, D5S6, to a location approximately halfway between the two markers used by Sherrington et al (14), and incorporation of this marker into our multipoint linkage analyses has resulted in even stronger evidence against linkage of schizophrenia in our kindred to the 5q11.2–13.3 region.

A number of additional studies attempting to replicate the positive findings of Sherrington et al have now been completed. In addition to our own study with the Swedish kindred, at least six other investigations have been carried out, none of which has been able to suggest evidence of linkage of markers in the 5q11.2–13.3 region to schizophrenia. A large study was conducted by St Clair and colleagues (19). These authors found no evidence for linkage, regardless of whether the schizophrenia phenotype was defined broadly or narrowly. Fifteen families were studied with DNA being prepared from 166 members for RFLP analysis. The data were analyzed using four separate models for diagnostic classification. The first model defined a set of affected cases consisting of schizophrenia, schizoaffective disorder, bipolar disorder, and unspecified functional psychosis. This model was assigned a penetrance of 66%. In the second model, major depressive disorder was also included and penetrance rose to 77%. The third model included as affected all family members with psychiatric diagnoses, including schizotypal personality disorder (penetrance = 94%). St Clair et al (19) mention analyzing the data in a fourth way restricting affected cases to schizophrenia, schizoaffective disorder, and unspecified functional psychosis, a model wherein the penetrance was set at 44%; however, multipoint analyses for this more conservative definition of the phenotype were not presented.

In five of the 15 families a parent with affective disorder gave birth to children with schizophrenia. This situation did not arise in the families from Iceland and England studied by Sherrington et al (14). St Clair et al (19) argued, however, that in the six families in which there were no cases of bipolar illness the lod score analyzed separately was still below -2, indicating that the presence of bipolar affective disorder in some families could not by itself explain the negative findings.

Another investigation of chromosome 5 and schizophrenia was reported by Detera-Wadleigh et al (20). In this study five American families were examined from which 64 members had provided DNA samples. The authors used a very high penetrance of 95% to demonstrate exclusionary lod scores of less than -2. At a lower penetrance of 60% the multipoint analyses could not rule out linkage in the region between the loci. As was the case with the studies of Sherrington et al (14) and St. Clair et al (19), when a broader range of diagnoses was included, the magnitude of the lod score increased. Fifteen individuals in the study had an affective disorder diagnosis, two of which were bipolar disorder. The authors state that in the multipoint analyses their linkage exclusion does not depend on the inclusion of the families with bipolar disorder, arguing that bipolar disorder did not have a major effect in determining the results. However, only one of the two individuals with bipolar disorder had RFLP typing.

Another study by Kaufmann et al (21) examined two families used in the Detera-Wadleigh et al (20) report plus two additional American families. Because of the overlap in families used, the two studies cannot be considered as two independent failures to replicate the positive linkage result of Sherrington et al. However, Kaufmann et al used a more diagnostically conservative approach and a statistically more stringent one, using an affected-only model which considered as affected only those individuals with either chronic schizophrenia or schizo-affective disorder and considering as phenotype unknown all other individuals. Their lod scores were significantly negative at only one point across the 5q11.2–13.3 region, at the D5S6 locus. In the multipoint analysis linkage was tested across five RFLP markers and at no point in the distribution was the lod score positive, indicating absence of linkage for this region to schizophrenia.

Aschauer et al (22) examined three black and four white families from the Midwest of the USA. Samples of DNA were obtained from 57 individuals, and three diagnostic levels were investigated: (a) schizophrenia only, (b) schizophrenia plus schizoaffective and schizotypal disorders, and (c) all psychiatric diagnoses. Heterozygote penetrances for these levels were 54%, 64%, and 85% respectively. Linkage to the marker D5S76 could be rejected for all three models of affected status. The broadest level of diagnostic inclusion generated the widest area of exclusion. One nuclear family of four individuals with two affected members produced slightly positive lod scores, but there was no statistically significant evidence of linkage heterogeneity among the seven families.

Deihl et al (23) have reported preliminary evidence for exclusion of linkage between 5q 11.2–13.3 markers and schizophrenia in a large number of families collected in western Ireland. Macciardi et al (24) have studied families from northern Italy and also find no evidence for linkage of schizophrenia to markers in the 5q11.2–13.3 region. The final analyses from these two studies are not yet published.

The interpretation of all of these investigations of chromosome 5 in relation to schizophrenia is not straightforward. Presumably, when one examines a disorder as complex as schizophrenia, one should not be surprised by complex results. If the Bassett et al (15) report is included, then two studies suggest that a gene or genes on the proximal long arm of chromosome 5 play a role in susceptibility to schizophrenia and other psychiatric disorders. Seven studies indicate that there is no linkage of markers in this chromosomal region to schizophrenia or other psychiatric disorders. The conclusion most readily imposed on the data is that schizophrenia is etiologically heterogeneous: in some families there is a gene on chromosome 5 causing predisposition to the disease, and in other families there are other genes, or no genes, involved. However, given the large number of families now investigated for linkage to 5q11.2–13.3 across several ethnic groups with no evidence of positive results, the gene for schizophrenia on chromosome 5, if it exists, must play a role only rarely.

Examination of the pairwise data from each individual family across the published studies by Kennedy et al (18), St. Clair et al (19), Detera-Wadleigh et al (20), and Aschauer et al (22) reveals that three out of 21 families who were informative for D5S39 showed positive lod scores with schizophrenia. Six out of 21 informative families produced positive lod scores at D5S76. None of these positive scores was greater than +0.6, whereas many of the negative scores were less than −2.0. Given such a large proportion of families generating negative scores, it is unusual that Sherrington et al. (14) were able to collect seven families from 2 different countries and find positive lod scores in all 7. Some of the families in the Sherrington et al. (14) study produced negative lod scores, but none of the families showed consistently negative lod scores at both loci. If heterogeneity is true, one would expect one or two of the seven families to show uniformly negative lod scores. The arrangement of data as it stands across the studies could be due to chance variation that clustered the families truly positive for chromosome 5 linkage in the hands of Sherrington et al. Alternatively, chance variation may simply have created spurjiously positive results. Theoretically, the lod score of approximately +7 in the Sherrington et al report means that the probability of this result occurring by chance alone is less than 1 in 1,000,000. However, at this point it is useful to recall that errors in diagnosis, especially false positives, and errors in parameter estimates in the mode of inheritance, can change the lod score significantly. Thus, in view of the impact of diagnostic and parameter errors, the chance of a spuriously positive result may increase.

WHAT IS THE MODE OF INHERITANCE?

The presence of a genetic component as suggested from twin and family studies does not necessarily justify the use of genetic linkage analysis to screen the entire genome in search of the component, since this method has thus far been successful only for single-gene conditions. We should first try to characterize this component and analyze the different methods available to look for it. If the mode of inheritance appears to show a single gene being inherited with the disease, then a genome search with evenly spaced markers should be a good strategy. Candidate genes, when reasonable, are also good starting points.

How can we characterize the genetic component and thus choose our best strategy for the search? The twin and family studies provide us with evidence for the involvement of genes; when carefully done, they also provide us with the opportunity to characterize the genetic component. This is so because genes obey laws of segregation, and segregation patterns provide us with insight as to the potential number of genes involved. When only one gene is causing a disease, its segregation is easily predicted: for a fully penetrant dominant disorder, 50% of the offspring should be affected, and the monozygotic to dizygotic twin ratio (MZ/DZ) of concordance should be 2:1. For a recessive disorder, we expect 25% of the offspring to be affected, and an MZ/DZ ratio of 4:1. In autosomal dominant disorders, the expected decay in the incidence of the disease from first- to second- to third-degree relatives should be close to 1/2. This is true even in the presence of nonallelic genetic heterogeneity (for example, a gene in chromosome 4 *or* a gene in chromosome 6 causing the same phenotype). When diseases show incomplete penetrance, then the percentage of affected individuals is reduced, but not the MZ/DZ ratios or the rate of decay by 1/2. Thus, these two estimates are very powerful to test whether a familial condition is a single-gene disorder, since they are not influenced by the penetrance or by the presence of nongenetic forms of the disease. In schizophrenia they almost unanimously reject a single-gene hypothesis.

Risch (25) has tabulated the risk ratios for relatives of schizophrenics according to their genetic "distance" from the schizophrenic: from monozygotic twins, through dizygotic twin, sibling, and grandparent, to first cousin. He suggests that a model of two or three genes is consistent with the observed decline in risk with degree of relationship. This is neither monogenic nor polygenic, but might be called an "oligogenic" theory of schizophrenia. Although some cases of schizophrenia may be caused by a single gene and others by a relatively large number of genes (polygenic) acting together in an individual, available evidence at the present time supports the oligogenic model of schizophrenia—a few genes cause schizophrenia but not one and not many. The degree to which these genes might interact with one another is not known.

Why, then, do we pursue linkage analysis? A common argument is that linkage analysis has been shown to be a very robust analytical method and that linkage to a disease can be found even in the presence of incorrect assumptions about the mode of inheritance. That is, even if there is a genetic component due to the presence of not one but a few genes (for example, both a gene in chromosome 4 and a gene in chromosome 6 have to be present for the disease to be expressed), linkage could detect at least one of those genes. It is these interactions between a few unlinked genes (through a process called epistasis) that produce the type of results commonly observed in the family and twin studies of schizophrenia: an MZ/DZ ratio greater than 2:1 and a rate of decay with each degree of relationship much faster than by 1/2.

How robust is genetic linkage with the lod-score method to detect one or more epistatic genes? This is not known. If the disease is caused by the interaction of only two or three genes, we might hope to find at least one of them, provided a large sample size is available. But if schizophrenia is due to the epistatic effect of, say, six or more genes, then there is little hope of obtaining a significant linkage result. A random search will exclude all of the genome, but this will not mean there is no genetic component. It will only mean that we started our search under erroneous assumptions about the mode of inheritance. How many genes could be interacting to produce the observed MZ/DZ ratio and rate of decay across relatives observed in schizophrenia? There is no unique answer to this question. The predicted values for the MZ/DZ ratio and rate of decay with degree of relationship for three, four, or more interacting genes start to be so similar that current sample sizes (with large confidence intervals) fail to resolve with certainty among them. Thus, schizophrenia is unlikely to be a single-gene condition, but we cannot resolve the exact number of interacting genes present. It is on this last uncertainty that a significant justification for using lod scores relies. If there are a small number of genes acting together to predispose to schizophrenia, the lod score method should be able to detect at least one of them. However, given that the exact power of linkage analysis is not clearly understood in the presence of epistasis, genetic linkage strategies will continue to present a challenging and complex task.

EXPLORING PHENOTYPIC DEFINITIONS

While the bulk of evidence appears to support an oligogenic model for the genetic factors in schizophrenia, different definitions of the phenotype may lead to other conclusions. The main proponents of a single-major-locus model are Holzman and colleagues who have added to the phenotype of schizophrenia the phenotype of eye movement disorders (EMD). In a recent study (26) the authors provide evidence that when EMD is included as part of the spectrum of definition of schizophrenia as a latent trait for the disease, then the inheritance of schizophrenia plus EMD follows that of a single major locus. Studies of eye movement in the families of schizophrenic probands showed that 45% of the nonschizophrenic first-degree relatives of schizophrenic individuals had EMD. EMD is associated with schizophrenia in 51% to 85% of schizophrenic patients, in contrast to a normal population prevalence of about 8% (27). The EMD finding has been noted in many studies to date with no failures to replicate the results. Holzman et al (26) cite evidence that the dysfunction does not reflect inattention, poor motivation, or neuroleptic drug treatment.

Two studies (28,29) of EMD in monozygotic and dizygotic twins discordant for clinical schizophrenia have been carried out. The monozygotic twins showed a concordance rate for EMD of 77%, and the dizygotic twins, showed almost exactly half that concordance with a rate of 39%. Thus the MZ/DZ ratio is consistent with a single major locus transmission for EMD. Matthysse et al (30) have generated what they refer to as the latent trait model. This model proposes that the genetic transmission of a trait, although itself not observable, can cause either schizophrenia or impaired eye movements or both. The latent trait has a best fit to Mendelian segregation rather than schizophrenia or eye movement dysfunction alone. Although there are controversies regarding the interpretation of eye movement data, the weight of evidence supporting involvement of EMD with schizophrenia makes a molecular genetic linkage study with RFLPs, using the latent trait as the phenotype, an intriguing possibility.

Another trait that may cosegregate with schizophrenia has been described by Moldin and colleagues (31). They have developed a psychometric index composed of 13 Minnesota Multiphasic Personality Inventory (MMPI) indicators that have been shown to measure disturbance in thinking, volition, social relatedness, and expression of affect. Deviation of scores on these indicators is associated with schizophrenia. Psychometric deviance occurs at a rate much higher in the offspring of schizophrenic individuals (23%) than in the offspring of normal controls (2%). Moldin et al suggest that this psychometric index tends to be inherited in families, possibly as an autosomal dominant trait with a single major locus.

SUMMARY

It is abundantly clear from twin, adoption, and family studies that genes play an important role in schizophrenia. Neither the number of genes involved nor their mode of inheritance is clear. In the midst of the controversy regarding modes of inheritance, a report of linkage of DNA markers on the proximal long arm of chromosome 5 has emerged. None of a growing number of attempted replications has been able to confirm this linkage result. Thus a new controversy has arisen in addition to (and partly stemming from) the older debate on mode of inheritance. We have attempted here to convey that genetic linkage studies, as applied to complex disorders such as schizophrenia, are both powerful and labyrinthine. Errors in diagnosis and in model parameters can be quite confounding. Perhaps new ways of defining the phenotype will help reduce the uncertainties arising from current diagnostic structures. A genetic linkage approach, with the two strategies of candidate gene and genome scan, can confirm or falsify specific genetic hypotheses; it also has the valuable advantage that an operant etiologic hypothesis is not necessary when searching for causative genes—genes that may invoke the unexpected, illuminate our understanding, and lead to better treatment for this devastating disease.

REFERENCES

1. Kallman FJ. *The Genetics of Schizophrenia.* New York: J.S. Augustin, 1938.
2. Kety SS, Rosenthal D, Wender PM, Schulsinger F, and Jacobsen B. Mental illness in the biological and adoptive families of adopted individuals who have become schizophrenic: A preliminary report based on psychiatric interviews. In: Fieve RR, Rosenthal D, Brill H, eds. *Genetic Research in Psychiatry,* Baltimore: Johns Hopkins University Press, 1975;147–165.
3. Kendler KS, Gruenberg AM. An independent analysis of the Danish adoption study of schizophrenia: VI. The relationship between psychiatric disorders as defined by DSM-III in the relatives and adoptees. *Arch Gen Psychiat* 1984; 41:555–564.
4. Heston LL. Psychiatric disorders in foster home reared children of schizophrenic mothers. *Brit J Psychiat* 1966;112:819–825.
5. Rosenthal D, Wender PH, Kety SS, Welner J, and Schulsinger F. The adopted-away offspring of schizophrenics. *Am J Psychiat* 1971;128: 307–311.
6. Lowing, PA, Mirsky AF, and Pereira R. The inheritance of schizophrenia spectrum disorders: A reanalysis of the Danish adoptee study data. *Am J Psychiat* 1983;140:1167–1171.
7. Kendler KS. The genetics of schizophrenia and related disorders: A review. In: *Relatives at Risk for Mental Disorder,* Eds DL Dunner, ES Gershon, JE Barrett. New York: Raven Press, 1988;247–263.
8. Clerget-Darpoux F, Bonaiti-Pellie C, Hochez J. Effects of misspecifying genetic parameters in lod score analysis. *Biometrics* 1986;42:393–399.
9. Cox NJ, Hodge SE, Marazita ML, Spence MA, Kidd KK. Some effects of selection strategies on linkage analysis. *Genet Epidemiol* 1988;5: 289–297.
10. Kennedy JL, Giuffra LA, Moises HW, Wetterberg L, Sjogren B, Cavalli-Sforza LL, Pakstis AJ, Kidd JR, Kidd KK. Molecular genetic studies in schizophrenia. *Schiz Bull* 1989;15(3): 383–391.
11. Kennedy JL, Giuffra LA, Wetterberg L, Sjogren B, Pakstis AJ, Kidd JR, Kidd KK. Searching for genes predisposing to neuropsychiatric disorders. In: Berg K, ed. *From Phenotype to Gene in Common Disorders,* Copenhagen: Munksgaard A/S Press, 1990; (in press).
12. Giuffra LA, Kidd KK. Linkage studies in psychiatry. *Int Rev Psychiat* 1990;1(4):231–242.
13. Moises HW, Gelernter J, Grandy DK, Giuffra LA, Kidd JR, Pakstis AJ, Bunzow J, Sjogren B, Wetterberg L, Kennedy JL, Litt M, Civelli O, Kidd KK, Cavalli-Sforza LL. Exlusion of the D_2-dopamine receptor gene as candidate gene for schizophrenia in a large pedigree from Sweden. Abstract, First World Congress on Psychiatric Genetics, Cambridge, 1989.
14. Sherrington R, Brynjolfsson J, Petursson H, Potter M, Dudleston K, Barraclough B, Wasmuth J, Dobbs M, Gurling H. Localization of susceptibility locus for schizophrenia on chromosome 5. *Nature* 1988;336:164–167.
15. Bassett AS, Jones BD, McGillivray BC, Pantzar JT. Partial trisomy chromosome 5 cosegregating with schizophrenia. *Lancet* 1988;i8589:799–801.
16. Weinberger C, Evans R, Rosenfeld MG, Hollenberg SM, Skarecky D, Wasmuth JJ. *Cytogenet Cell Genet* 1985;40:776.
17. Giuffra LA, Kennedy JL, Castiglione CM, Evans RM, Wasmuth JJ, Kidd KK. Glucocorticoid receptor maps to the distal long arm of chromosome 5. *Cytogenet Cell Genet* 1988;49: 313–314.
18. Kennedy JL, Giuffra LA, Moises HW, Cavalli-Sforza LL, Castiglione CM, Pakstis AJ, Sjogren B, Wetterberg L, Kidd KK. Evidence against linkage of schizophrenia with markers on chromosome 5 in a northern Swedish pedigree. *Nature* 1988;336:167–170.
19. St Clair D, Blackwood D, Muir W, Baillie D, Hubbard A, Wright A, Evans HJ. No linkage of chromosome 5q11-q13 markers to schizophrenia in Scottish families. *Nature* 1989;339:305–309.
20. Detera-Wadleigh SD, Goldin LR, Sherrington R, Encio I, deMiguel C, Berrettini W, Gurling H, Gershon ES. Exclusion of linkage to 5q11-13 in

families with schizophrenia and other psychiatric disorders. *Nature* 1989;340:391–393.
21. Kaufman CA, DeLisi LE, Lehner T, Gilliam TC. Physical mapping, linkage analysis of a putative schizophrenia locus on chromosome 5q. *Schiz Bull* 1989;15:441–452.
22. Aschauer HN, Aschauer-Treiber G, Isenberg KE, Todd RD, Knesevich MA, Garver DL, Reich T, Cloninger CR. No evidence for linkage between chromosome 5 markers and schizophrenia. *Hum Hered* 1990;(in press).
23. Diehl S, Su Y, Aman M, MacLean C, Walsh D, O'Hare A, McGuire M, Kidd KK, Kendler KS. Linkage studies of schizophrenia in Irish pedigrees. *Cytogenet Cell Genet* 1989;51:989.
24. Macciardi F, Kennedy JL, Ferrari M, Giuffra LA, Roucco L, Marino C, Rinaldi V, Smeraldi E. Linkage study of schizophrenia to chromosome 5 markers in a northern Italian population. (Submitted.)
25. Risch N. Linkage strategies for genetically complex traits. I. Multilocus models. *Am J Hum Genet* 1990;46:222–228.
26. Holzman PS, Kringlen E, Matthysse S, Flanagan SD, Lipton RB, Cramer G, Levin S, Lange K, Levy DL. A single dominant gene can account for eye movement dysfunctions and schizophrenia in offspring of discordant twins. *Arch Gen Psychiat* 1988;45:641–647.
27. Holzman PS, Proctor LR, Levy DL, Yasillo NJ, Meltzer HY, Hurt SW. Eye-tracking dysfunctions and schizophrenic patients and their relatives. *Arch Gen Psychiat* 1974;31:143–151.
28. Holzman PS, Kringlen E, Levy DL, Proctor LR, Haberman S, Yasillo NJ. Abnormal pursuit eye movement in schizophrenia: Evidence for a genetic marker. *Arch Gen Psychiat* 1977;34:802–807.
29. Holzman PS, Kringlen E, Levy DL, Haberman S. Deviant eye tracking in twins discordant for psychosis, a replication. *Arch Gen Psychiat* 1980;37:627–631.
30. Matthysse S, Holzman PS, Lange K. The genetic transmission of schizophrenia: Application of mendelian latent structure analysis to eye tracking dysfunctions in schizophrenia and affective disorder. *J Psychiat Res* 1986;20:57–65.
31. Moldin SO, Rice JP, Gottesman II, Erlenmeyer-Kimling L. Transmission of a psychometric indicator for liability to schizophrenia in normal families. *Genet Epidemiol* 1990;7:163–176.

4

Gene Expression

Implications for the Study of Schizophrenia and Other Neuropsychiatric Disorders

Edward I. Ginns[1]

The recent reports on linkage of chromosomal regions to schizophrenia, although informative and encouraging, remain preliminary (1–6). Although schizophrenia is the result of both environmental and genetic causes a genetic basis for the disorder can be investigated in large pedigrees with multiple generations of affected individuals. However, attempts to identify a common susceptibility locus for schizophrenia have been thus far unsuccessful (7). This search for the gene or genes that can be implicated in the pathogenesis of schizophrenia has been complicated by the difficulties in the clinical classification of affected individuals, and by the lack of definitive biochemical or other markers for this disorder. Under these circumstances, in order to successfully apply molecular genetic and cell biological approaches to the identification of candidate genes, it is crucial that researchers develop reliable and reproducible measures for the clinical description of affected individuals. This chapter will illustrate differences between human and animal nervous system gene expression that may be important when considering the use of animal models for the study of complex neurologic or psychiatric disorders such as schizophrenia, and also present some of the molecular aspects of abnormalities in gene expression that can cause clinical heterogeneity.

The search through the billions of bases of chromosomal DNA for a genetic basis of schizophrenia has focused on a few candidate regions (Fig. 1). This has resulted from the association of certain genotypes or the chance finding of karyotypic or clinical abnormalities with the disorder. However, the linkage data obtained from probes at these loci are preliminary and are encouraging only in a limited number of pedigrees. It is estimated that there are 50,000 to 100,000 different genes in the human genome (8). However, unlike the simple collinearity of the procaryotic gene to its protein product, the chromosomal representations of many eucaryotic genes are longer than their messenger RNA (mRNA) transcripts (Fig. 2). This occurs because the regions in the mRNA transcripts coding for a protein's primary structure are interrupted by generally larger stretches of noncoding chromosomal DNA (introns) that are delineated by consensus splice donor and acceptor sequences (9). Although the intervening sequences are removed from the mRNA transcript before protein synthesis occurs, their role in determining the final transcript

---

[1]Molecular Neurogenetics Section, Clinical Neuroscience Branch, National Institute of Mental Health, ADAMHA, Bethesda, MD 20892.

FIG. 1. Locating genes responsible for psychiatric illnesses is an immense undertaking at the frontiers of science.

structure or level is unclear. The mRNA is transported out of the nucleus to serve as the template for protein synthesis (translation) by ribosomes in the cytoplasm. The correct maturation and targeting of proteins is the result of multiple cotranslational and posttranslational modifications that can include proteolytic cleavage, carbohydrate addition, disulfide linkage formation, and/or phosphorylation. Carbohydrate addition and modification occurs en route to or within the Golgi apparatus. The final compartmentalization and biological activity of a protein is therefore the result of a complex maturation process. Gene mutations can affect any of these steps resulting in abnormal protein structure and function.

Thus, the clinical heterogeneity observed within neuropsychiatric disorders such as schizophrenia can be a consequence of mutations either in one or in several different genes, each affecting the biological activity, and influencing the processing, cellular compartmentalization, and/or stability of a protein.

In discussing the possible genetic mechanisms responsible for the clinical heterogeneity observed in schizophrenia the following definitions will be helpful. Each of the two chromosome strands (*chromatids*) contains alleles that are alternative forms of a gene at a given chromosomal locus. A *genotype* is the complete allelic description of an individual and is responsible for the

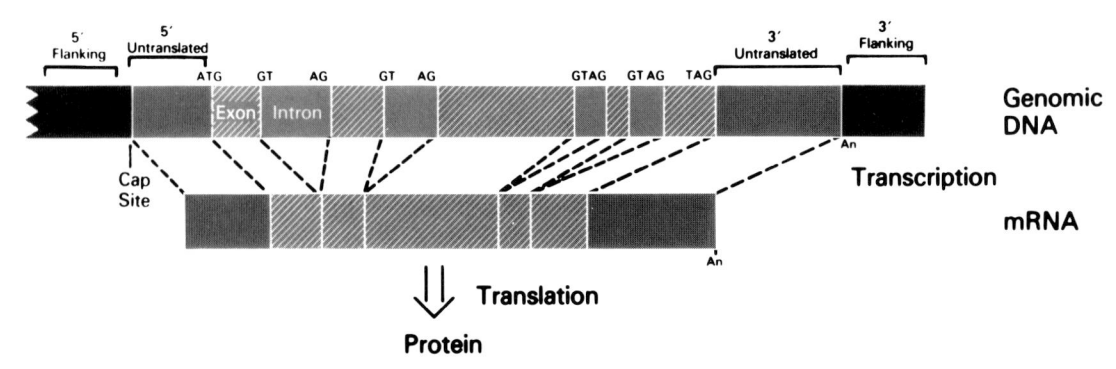

FIG. 2. Schematic representation of eucaryotic transcription and translation.

observable appearance, or *phenotype,* of that individual. A description of an individual's genotypes at several loci is termed the *haplotype.* Genetic heterogeneity results when there are multiple genetic causes of the same or almost identical phenotype. In contrast, a *phenocopy* is an environmentally determined mimic of a genetic disorder. Particularly for disorders as phenotypically heterogeneous as schizophrenia, where both environmental and genetic factors may be important, it is important to use reliable and consistent clinical classification. The uncertainties introduced by lack of a biological marker can be lessened, however, by studying pedigrees with multiple generations of affected individuals, in which case a genetic basis is more likely.

In contrast to autosomal recessive disorders where the heterozygotes are unaffected, autosomal dominant inheritance of a single dose of the mutant gene is sufficient to cause disease. A mutation on one allele can act without influence from other genes, but in many instances the phenotypic expression of a gene is influenced by other modifier genes. In these cases the result is an altered penetrance or expressivity of disease. Additionally, as is the case for retinoblastoma, autosomal dominant disease can result from a somatic cell mutation occurring in the presence of a clinically silent germ-line mutation in the other allele (10).

The age of onset of disease can also be quite heterogeneous, even in large pedigrees where a single gene mutation is suggested. For example, in the majority of cases of Huntington's chorea, disease onset occurs within the wide range of from 26 to 60 years of age (11). Many disorders such as schizophrenia do not manifest until adolescence or adulthood, even though a genetic mutation is presumed. This can be explained as a consequence of the balance between continual cognitive and motor development and the injury caused by the abnormal gene product expressed. Alternatively, developmentally regulated expression of particular proteins, and/or somatic mutations can lead to later-onset symptomatology.

One can now ask: What are the most likely types of mutations occurring? If one considers the observed frequency of mutation types in the human hemoglobin gene to be representative, then single-base substitutions are most frequent (11). These changes in the DNA may or may not result in amino acid substitutions. Even if the primary structure of the protein is changed by an amino acid substitution, this may only result in a silent polymorphism, without any deleterious effect on the biological activity of the protein. In contrast, frameshift mutations, small or large deletions, and other mutation types are much rarer and more likely to affect the activity of the protein. The mechanistic consequences of autosomal dominant mutations include receptor or membrane defects, abnormal subunit assembly or function, and reduced end-product feedback inhibition. Thus, unlike autosomal recessive mutations that generally result in loss of a single protein function, in autosomal dominant disorders the function of several proteins can be disturbed by a mutation in a single protein.

To illustrate the genetic complexity of the human nervous system, I will now compare expression of neurotransmitter synthesizing enzymes in the rat and human. Then I will illustrate the surprising extent of clinical heterogeneity that can result from simple but multiple allelic mutations.

Our laboratory decided to isolate and characterize both complementary DNA (cDNA) and genomic clones for the human enzyme tyrosine hydroxylase. We were stimulated by the suggestion of linkage between bipolar affective disorder and the insulin and Harvey ras-1 genes of chromosome 11p15 (12), in close proximity to the tyrosine hydroxylase gene (13), as well as the clinical and pharmacological data suggesting that alterations in tyrosine hydroxylase might be involved in the pathogenesis of various neuropsychiatric disorders (14). Tyrosine hydroxylase is prominently located within the biosynthetic pathway for catecholamine neurotransmitters, and is the initial and rate-limited enzyme responsible for the conversion of L-tyrosine to 3,4-dihydroxy-L-phenylalanine (L-dopa) in both central and peripheral catecholaminergic neurons.

The isolation of human cDNA clones from both pheochromocytoma and neuroblastoma libraries surprisingly provided evidence for the existence of several isozymes of human tyrosine hydroxylase (15, 16). Although both the rat and human tyrosine hydroxylase genes are similar, spanning 8 kb and containing 13 exons, in contrast to the simple transcriptional unit seen for the rat gene, the human tyrosine hydroxylase gene produces multiple mRNAs with 5' coding-region heterogeneity resulting from alternative splicing (Fig. 3) (17). While the extent of functional significance of multiple mRNAs produced by the human tyrosine hydroxylase gene remains to be determined, these mRNAs do have tissue and regional specific expression.

With the availability of the multiple cDNAs for human tyrosine hydroxylase, baculovirus-derived vectors (16) and retroviral-mediated gene transfer (18) have been used to generate large quantities of active enzyme and stable mammalian cell lines independently expressing the individual isozymes, respectively. The recombinantly produced enzyme and cell lines will facilitate the study of the structural, immunological, kinetic properties, as well as cellular localization of the different isozymes. These studies are important because abnormalities in any one of the isozyme could be responsible for human nervous system disease. Importantly, specific antibody and/or nucleic acid probes may be necessary to identify changes in the expression of a specific isozyme that represents only a small

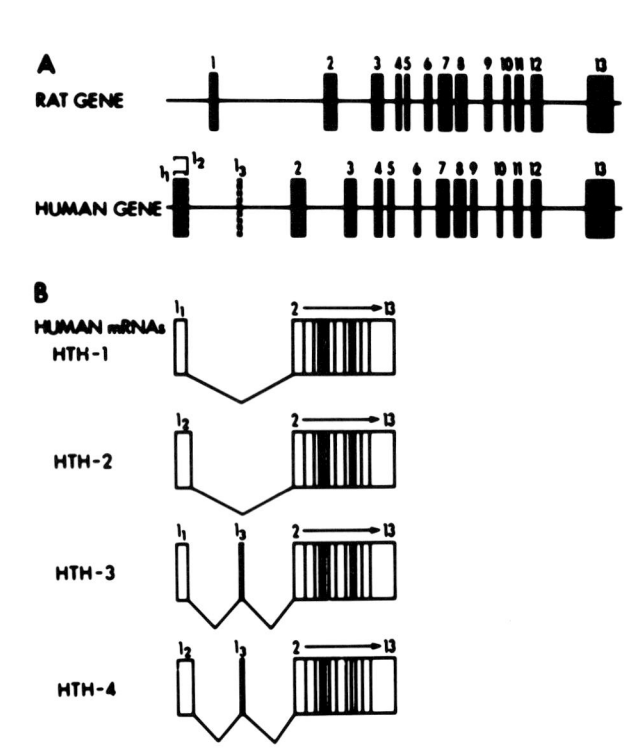

FIG. 3. Comparison of the rat and human tyrosine hydroxylase genes. **A:** Comparison of rat and human exon size and spacing. **B:** Single initiation site but with alternative splicing generating multiple human mRNAs for tyrosine hydroxylase isozymes. Reprinted with permission from ref. 17. Copyright 1987 American Chemical Society.

proportion of total tyrosine hydroxylase activity, but whose deficiency has major pathophysiologic consequences. Because alternative splicing of the tyrosine hydroxylase gene does not occur within all species, the animal models used for the study of the pathogenesis of human neuropsychiatric disorders must be carefully examined (Fig. 4).

In order to illustrate the simplicity of biochemical and genetic mechanisms that can be involved in determining the severity of nervous system abnormalities within a single disease, a discussion of Gaucher's disease, an autosomal recessive disorder, will be informative (19). Most patients with Gaucher's disease are clinically asymptomatic at birth, and the majority of patients have few or no serious problems throughout their lifetime. In type 1 patients, the disease is characterized by enlarged liver and spleen, anemia, low platelets, and skeletal complications, but notably absent is any involvement of the nervous system (Table 1). In contrast, patients with type 2 disease usually have symptom onset by 6 months of

TABLE 1. *Phenotypes of Gaucher's disease*

Type 1   Chronic non-neurologic
Hypersplenism, hepatomegaly, anemia, thrombocytopenia, leukopenia, bone involvement
Type 2   Acute neurologic
Hepatosplenomegaly, trismus, strabismus, head retroflexion, cranial nerve dysfunction, hyperreflexia
Type 3   Chronic neurologic
Variable hepatosplenomegaly, spasticity, ataxia, myoclonus, dementia, oculomotor apraxia, abnormal EEG

age, manifest cranial-nerve and brainstem abnormalities, as well as the other symptoms seen in type 1 disease, and they uniformly succumb to respiratory complications by 3 years of age. In type 3 disease the patients have systemic symptoms similar to those of type 1, but neurologic abnormalities appear during childhood or adolescence and are much milder than those appearing in type 2 disease. In contrast to the stereotypic course seen in type 2 patients, type 1 and type 3 patients have a much broader variation in the time of symptom onset and severity.

The hallmark of this disorder in all three phenotypes of Gaucher's disease is the presence of Gaucher's cells within tissue (19). These macrophage-derived cells accumulate in tissue because of the deficiency of the enzyme glucocerebrosidase, the enzyme in the pathway of glycolipid metabolism that is required for cleaving the glucose moiety from glucosylceramide.

All types of Gaucher's disease are inherited as autosomal recessive, but although it is panethnic, type 1 disease is much more frequent among Ashkenazic Jews, with an estimated range of incidence of 1 in 600 to 1 in 2500. High-resolution in situ hybridization analysis with cDNA probes demonstrated a single locus for glucocerebrosidase at 1q21 (20). The normal human glucocerebrosidase gene has 11 exons and 10 introns contained within approximately 7000 base pairs (21). Also at locus 1q21 is

FIG. 4. "They don't have tails! I wonder if we can still use them as an animal model?"

another region that is highly homologous to the glucocerebrosidase functional gene, but which lacks parts of several exons and splice junctions. These sequence deletions, as well as data from control subjects and Gaucher's patients, suggest that this latter region is a pseudogene (19).

Northern-blot analysis has not been informative for identifying mutations, but the isolation and sequence comparison of genomic clones from normal subjects and Gaucher's patients has led to the characterization of several point mutations (19). A single base mutation (A to G), resulting in a serine rather than asparagine at amino acid position 370, has been found in exon 9 and is seen only in patients with type 1 (nonneuronopathic) Gaucher's disease. In contrast, a single base substitution (C for T) in exon 10, resulting in substitution of proline for leucine at amino acid position 444, is seen predominantly in patients with neurological disease (types 2 and 3). Another mutation found in exon 10 (C to T: arginine to cysteine at 463) is found with high frequency in type 3 patients. Interestingly, no large deletions or chromosomal rearrangements have been found in any patient with Gaucher's disease. The functional consequences and disease spectrum resulting from each of these single base mutations, however, is quite broad.

Active human glucocerebrosidase is a carbohydrate containing protein of 497 amino acids having an apparent molecular weight of 67 kDa (19). The synthesis and

FIG. 5. Cooperation among researchers will help reach the final frontier in determining the genetic bases of psychiatric illnesses.

targeting of human glucocerebrosidase to lysosomes, where it normally functions, involves multiple posttranslational modifications. This protein is initially synthesized with a 2-kDa signal peptide that is removed as the protein enters the cisternae of the endoplasmic reticulum. As the enzyme moves within the endoplasmic reticulum and Golgi apparatus, modification of the four asparagine-linked oligosaccharide chains occurs, and the enzyme is subsequently routed to lysosomes. From Western (22,23), pulse-chase (24), and immunocytochemical (25) analyses, correlations of abnormalities in the biosynthesis of the enzyme clinical phenotype have been made. In type 1 Gaucher's disease the mutant enzyme is unstable, but a mature form of the enzyme is synthesized and active enzyme is present in lysosomes. In types 2 and 3, the neurologic phenotypes of Gaucher's disease, the mature form of the enzyme is virtually absent. The data suggest that the clinical heterogeneity in the disease is a result of differences in enzyme stability and/or compartmentalization of the mutant enzyme as a consequence of single base changes within the glucocerebrosidase gene locus.

It is perhaps startling that such widely different clinical presentations of types 1, 2, and 3 Gaucher's disease can result from just single base allelic mutations. But, given that this occurs, what can we expect for the genetic mutations responsible for catatonic, disorganized, paranoid, undifferentiated, and residual schizophrenia? Could not schizophrenia or, for that matter, other psychiatric disorders be explained by either mutations at a single locus or in multiple gene loci?

For schizophrenia, where no definitive biochemical marker exists and where genetic heterogeneity and phenocopies are common, it is crucial that clinicians develop consistent and reliable diagnostic measures that can form a solid foundation for research into the genetics of schizophrenia. With such an enormous task still ahead, the help of psychiatrists, neurologists, nurses, social workers, cell and molecular biologists, protein chemists, statisticians, physiologists, and pharmacologists working together (Fig. 5) are needed to insure that the goal will be more quickly attained.

REFERENCES

1. Rudduck C, Beckman L, Franzen G, Lindstrom L. C3 and C6 complement types in schizophrenia, *Hum Hered* 1985;35:255–258.
2. McGuffin P, Sturt E. Genetic markers in schizophrenia. *Hum Hered* 1986;36:65–88.
3. Nicol SE, Gottesman II. Clues to the genetics and neurobiology of schizophrenia. *Am Sci* 1983;71:398–404.
4. Byerlet W, Mellon C, O'Connell P, et al. Mapping genes for manic-depression and schizophrenia with DNA markers. *Trends Neurosci* 1989;12:46–48.
5. Sherrington R, Brynjolfsson J, Petursson H, et al. Localization of a susceptibility locus for schizophrenia on chromosome 5. *Nature* 1988;336:164–167.
6. Bassett AS, Jones BD, McGillivray BC, Pantzar JT. Partial trisomy chromosome 5 cosegregating with schizophrenia. *Lancet* 1988;799–801.
7. Kennedy JL, Giuffra LA, Moises HW, et al. Evidence against linkage of schizophrenia to markers on chromosome 5 in a northern Swedish pedigree. *Nature* 1988;336:167–170.
8. Milner RJ, Lai C, Lenoir D, Nave K, Bakhit C, Malfroy B. Brain-specific gene expression. *Biochem Soc Symp* 1987;52:107–117.
9. Beebee T, Burke J. In: Rickwood D, ed. *Gene structure and transcription*. Washington DC: IRL Press, 1988;1–77.
10. Weinberg RA. Finding the anti-oncogene. *Sci Am* 1988;259:44–51.
11. Motulsky V. In: *Human genetics*. New York: Springer-Verlag, 1986; p 114.
12. Egeland JA, Gerhard DS, Pauls DL, et al. Bipolar affective disorders linked to DNA markers on chromosome 11. *Nature* 1987;325:783–787.
13. O'Malley KL, Rotwein P. Human tyrosine hydroxylase and insulin genes are contiguous on chromosome 11. *Nuc Ac Res* 1988.
14. Thoenen H. In: Iversen LL, Iversen SD, Snyder SH, eds. *Handbook of psychopharmacology*, Vol 3. New York: Plenum Press, 1974;443–475.
15. Grima B, Lamouroux A, Boni C, Julien J-F, Javoy-Agid F, Mallet J. A single human gene encoding multiple tyrosine hydroxylases with different predicted functional characteristics. *Nature* 1987;326:707–711.
16. Ginns EI, Rehavi M, Martin BM, et al. Isolation and expression of multiple cDNAs for human tyrosine hydroxylase. *Catecholamine Genes* 1990;23–42.
17. O'Malley KL, Anhalt MJ, Martin BM, Kelsoe

JR, Winfield SL, Ginns EI. Isolation and characterization of the human tyrosine hydroxylase gene: Identification of 5' alternative splice sites responsible for multiple mRNAs. *Biochem* 1987; 26:6910–6914.
18. Ginns EI, Cottingham SL, Schultzberg M, Martin BM, LaMarca ME, Paul SM. Retroviral-mediated gene transfer and expression of active human tyrosine hydroxylase in transplantable cell lines. *Neurosci Abstr* 1989;(in press).
19. Martin BM, Sidransky E, Ginns EI. Gaucher's disease: Advances and challenges. *Adv Pediatr* 1989;(in press).
20. Tsuji S, Choudary PV, Martin BM, et al. Nucleotide sequence of cDNA containing the complete coding sequence for human lysosomal glucocerebrosidase. *J Biol Chem* 1986;261:50.
21. Tsuji S, Choudary PV, Martin BM, et al. A mutation in the human glucocerebrosidase gene in neuronopathic Gaucher disease. *N Engl J Med* 1987;316:570.
22. Ginns EI, Brady RO, Pirruccello S, et al. Mutations of glucocerebrosidase: Discrimination of neurologic and non-neurologic phenotypes of Gaucher disease. *Proc Natl Acad Sci USA* 1982;79:5607.
23. Ginns EI, Tegelaers FPW, Barneveld R, et al. Determination of Gaucher's disease phenotypes with monoclonal antibody. *Clin Chim Acta* 1983;131:283.
24. Erickson AH, Ginns EI, Barranger JA. Biosynthesis of the lysosomal enzyme glucocerebrosidase. *J Biol Chem* 1985;260:14319.
25. Willemsen R, Van Dongen JM, Ginns EI, et al. Ultrastructural localization of glucocerebrosidase in cultured Gaucher's disease fibroblasts by immunocytochemistry. *J Neurol* 1987;234:44.

5

Molecular Approaches to Neuroleptic Action:

Tyrosine Hydroxylase and Cholecystokinin mRNA Levels in the Substantia Nigra and Ventral Tegmental Area

Sandra L. Cottingham, Jacqueline N. Crawley, and David Pickar[1]

The importance of neuroleptic drugs for conceptualizing the pathophysiology of schizophrenia dates from the 1960s when it was first recognized that antipsychotic drugs bind to and block dopamine receptors. The subsequent discovery of the correlation between the affinities of a series of neuroleptics for the D_2 receptor and their potencies as antipsychotics further indicated that neuroleptics produce therapeutic effects by altering CNS dopamine system function (1). The increasing recognition of the limitations of neuroleptic drugs as the primary treatment for a significant number of patients with schizophrenia, however, has renewed attention to the mechanisms by which neuroleptics produce antipsychotic effects. New strategies are being sought to enhance the therapeutic response to neuroleptics while reducing the risk for tardive dyskinesia.

A notable shortcoming in the traditional receptor-blockade model of neuroleptic action is the difference in time course between the receptor-blocking properties of neuroleptics (hours) and the emergence of antipsychotic effects (weeks; ref. 2). Moreover, studies using positron emission tomography (PET) technology have shown that there is substantial occupancy of D_2 receptors in humans following relatively low neuroleptic doses (3) with little relation between drug response and the degree of receptor occupancy (4). In preclinical studies, investigators have explored the time-dependent properties of neuroleptic drugs by comparing the effects of acute and chronic neuroleptic administration on electrophysiological (5) and biochemical measures of dopamine neuronal activity (6). As summarized in Table 1, neuroleptic-induced increases in firing rate and dopamine turnover in subcortical dopamine neurons following short-term administration are reversed during more prolonged administration. The relative "sparing" of nigrostriatal neurons by atypical neuroleptics (e.g., clozapine) may at least partially explain their tendency to produce little or no extrapyramidal side effects. In contrast to nigrostriatal and mesolimbic neurons, mesocortical neurons appear to show diminished responsivity to acute neuroleptic administration without time-dependent characteristics accompanying chronic administration (7).

In clinical experiments, the longitudinal measurement of plasma HVA levels has

[1]Clinical Neuroscience Branch, National Institute of Mental Health, Bethesda, MD 20892.

TABLE 1. *Response of dopamine systems in the central nervous system to neuroleptic administration*[a]

	Acute neuroleptic administration		Chronic neuroleptic administration	
Brain area	Typical[b]	Atypical[b]	Typical[b]	Atypical[b]
Nigrostriatal				
Firing rate[c]	+ + + +	0	Depolarization block	0
Turnover[d]	+ + + +	+	Tolerance[e]	+
Mesolimbic				
Firing rate	+ + +	+ + +	Depolarization block	Depolarization block
Turnover	+ + +	+ + +	Tolerance	Tolerance
Mesocortical				
Firing rate	+	+	+	+
Turnover	+	+	+	+

[a]From Pickar D. Perspectives on a time-dependent model of neuroleptic action. *Schizophr Bull* 1988;14:255–268.
[b]"Typical" refers to neuroleptic drugs that cause extrapyramidal side effects. "Atypical" refers to neuroleptic drugs that tend not to cause extrapyramidal side effects.
[c]Single cell activity.
[d]Dopamine release and metabolism.
[e]Time-dependent reversal of initial increase.

provided an opportunity to examine time-dependent effects of neuroleptic treatment on a peripheral dopamine metabolite that (directly or indirectly) appears to provide a useful reflection of CNS dopaminergic and/or monoaminergic function (see ref. 8). While review of plasma HVA studies is beyond the scope of this chapter, neuroleptic-induced alterations in plasma HVA levels have in aggregate been associated with favorable neuroleptic response (see ref. 2). Given the importance of time-dependent processes to neuroleptic action, delineation of the mechanisms by which neuroleptic drugs produce these changes in neuronal function holds promise for further understanding of antipsychotic mechanisms and for creating models of the CNS substrates of drug response.

Molecular genetics has provided a new set of techniques for studying the mechanism of action of neuroleptics. The effects of drugs on the expression of genes for critical synthetic enzymes, and for peptide transmitters that modulate aminergic function, can be examined in acute and chronic paradigms. In recent experiments we have examined the hypothesis that neuroleptic drugs act at the level of transcription. We have focused our initial efforts on studying tyrosine hydroxylase by using in situ hybridization to quantitate the concentration of tyrosine hydroxylase mRNA in dopaminergic neurons during acute and chronic neuroleptic treatment (9).

Tyrosine hydroxylase, the rate-limiting enzyme in catecholamine synthesis, plays a major role in regulating monoaminergic neuronal function under basal conditions, as well as during stress, and in response to pharmacologic probes. It is known that tyrosine hydroxylase requires a tetrahydrobiopterin cofactor that is present in the brain in subsaturating concentrations (10); thus, fluctuations in affinity of the enzyme for the pterin cofactor could have large effects on its activity. The enzyme also is regulated through phosphorylation by calcium-dependent protein kinase (11,12), cyclic-AMP-dependent kinase (12) and cyclic-GMP-dependent protein kinase (13). In the phosphorylated state the affinity for the pterin cofactor is increased (i.e., the enzyme is more active). Finally, tyrosine hydroxylase is regulated by end-product inhibition, that is, dopamine and norepinephrine feedback inhibits synthesis, although this inhibition occurs only at high catecholamine concentrations and is probably not important in vivo (14).

The effect of neuroleptic (haloperidol) administration on tyrosine hydroxylase activity and pterin cofactor affinity has been studied with fairly consistent results (Table 2). Neuroleptic administration first results in activation of tyrosine hydroxylase by increasing the affinity for its pterin cofactor (15–18). With chronic administration, when firing rates are markedly reduced in many neurons and dopamine turnover returns to baseline, tolerance develops to the activation of tyrosine hydroxylase, although some investigators have reported an increase in amount of tyrosine hydroxylase (V_{max}; ref. 14).

The concentration of tyrosine hydroxylase enzyme is determined in large part by its rate of synthesis. The genes for tyrosine hydroxylase have been cloned and sequenced such that oligonucleotide probes for tyrosine hydroxylase messenger RNA (mRNA) are available (19). Expression of tyrosine hydroxylase mRNA has been studied in several contexts. Regulation of the expression of tyrosine hydroxylase enzyme and mRNA levels has been studied in the adrenal gland, locus ceruleus, substantia nigra, and ventral tegmental area. Administration of reserpine, a catecholamine-depleting drug, has been shown to significantly increase tyrosine hydroxylase enzyme activity (20–26) and tyrosine hydroxylase mRNA levels (27) in the locus ceruleus and adrenal gland. Cold stress has been reported to lead to an increase in tyrosine hydroxylase enzyme in the adrenal and locus ceruleus (28,29) and an increase in tyrosine hydroxylase mRNA in the adrenal gland (30).

In addition to tyrosine hydroxylase, we have used in situ hybridization techniques to study expression of mRNA for cholecystokinin (CCK). Cholecystokinin coexists with dopamine in many neurons in the ventral tegmental area (31) and has been postulated to be related to the pathophysiology of schizophrenia. Preprocholecystokinin mRNA has been reported in the substantia nigra and ventral tegmental area (32–35). Cholecystokinin has been shown to potentiate dopamine-mediated inhibition of neuronal firing rate in the ventral tegmental area (36–38), to modulate release of dopamine from mesolimbic terminals (39–41), and to potentiate dopamine-mediated behaviors (42,43). Chronic administration (2 to 3 weeks) of haloperidol has been reported to increase the concentration of CCK in the substantia nigra and ventral tegmental area (44). Concentrations of CCK in the major projection areas of the substantia nigra and ventral tegmental area, the striatum and nucleus accumbens, have been shown to be unchanged (45) or increased (44,46) by chronic haloperidol administration.

TABLE 2. *Effects of haloperidol treatment on tyrosine hydroxylase enzyme activity*

Reference	Treatment	V_{max}	Affinity for MPH_4	Brain region
Lerner et al (16)	Acute		↑	Striatum
	Chronic	↑	↓	Striatum
Guidotti (18)	Acute		↑	Striatum
	Chronic	0		Striatum, SN, nucleus accumbens
	Chronic	↑		Locus ceruleus
Bacopoulos et al (17)	Acute		↑	Putamen
	Chronic		↓	Cingulate cortex
			↓	Putamen
			↑	Cingulate cortex
Bacopoulos et al (52)	Chronic	0		Caudate, putamen, cingulate cortex, orb. frontal cortex

METHODS

Acute (3 days) and chronic (19 days) regimens of haloperidol administration were chosen to parallel previous neuropsychological, receptor-binding, and clinical studies of changes in dopaminergic function over the time course of haloperidol treatment. The time point of sacrifice (16 hours after the last injection) was chosen as one at which neurophysiological effects on neuronal firing rate are stable (47) and acute effects on enzyme activation are negligible (16). Comparison of changes in tyrosine hydroxylase and CCK mRNA after haloperidol might provide interesting information on whether synthesis of dopamine and CCK are differentially or similarly regulated by such a drug treatment. The methods used for in situ hybridization have been described (9). Briefly, 15 male Sprague-Dawley rats (220 to 225 g) were treated with haloperidol (2 mg/kg IP) or with vehicle twice a day at 8:00 AM and 5:00 PM for 3 days (acute: $n = 5$ for haloperidol treatment, $n = 3$ for vehicle treatment) or 19 days (chronic: $n = 5$ for haloperidol treatment, $n = 2$ for vehicle treatment). Frozen 12 μm sections were taken through the ventral tegmental area and substantia nigra, thaw-mounted onto gelatin-coated slides, and stored at $-70\ °C$. In situ hybridization was performed using ^{35}S-labeled probes as previously described for tyrosine hydroxylase (48) and CCK (35). Labeled sections were exposed to x-ray film, and optical density for the substantia nigra and ventral tegmental area was determined using an image-analysis system (Northern Light lightbox and Sierra Scientific camera; Quick-Capture, Data Translation, Inc, Marlboro, MA; Apple MacIntosh II; and Image 1.06 software, Wayne Rasband, NIMH, Bethesda, MD).

RESULTS

There was no significant difference in tyrosine hydroxylase mRNA levels in the anterior, middle, or posterior ventral tegmental area between control, acute haloperidol, and chronic haloperidol treatments (Fig. 1D–F; Fig. 2A; posterior: $F[2,13] = 0.401$, ns; middle: $F[2,11] = 2.226$, ns; anterior: $t = 1.402$, $df = 7$, ns). There was no significant difference in tyrosine hydroxylase mRNA levels in the substantia nigra between the three groups (Fig. 2B; $F[2,13] = 0.129$, ns).

Similarly, there was no significant difference in CCK mRNA levels in the anterior, middle, or posterior ventral tegmental area between control, acute haloperidol, and chronic haloperidol treatments (Fig. 1A–C; Fig. 2C; posterior: $F[2,15] = 0.461$, ns; middle: $F[2,13] = 0.145$, ns; anterior: $t = 0.578$, $df = 5$, ns). In addition, there was no difference in CCK mRNA in the substantia nigra between the three groups (Fig. 2D; $F[2,12] = 0.124$, ns).

DISCUSSION

This study tested the hypothesis that haloperidol influences dopaminergic function in the substantia nigra and ventral tegmental area by regulating expression of the genes for tyrosine hydroxylase and CCK. Our results suggest that neither acute nor chronic haloperidol administration significantly alters levels of mRNA for tyrosine hydroxylase or CCK. Several technical limitations must be considered that could account for these negative data. First, only two time points were studied, although they were selected to correspond to those previously reported in the literature, in particular in the study of Lerner et al (3 days and 3 weeks; ref. 16). However, a longer time course (e.g., 8 months) might reveal differences that develop more slowly (44). Second, density measurements of film autoradiograms were used to quantify mRNA levels in the substantia nigra and ventral tegmental area. Particularly in the ventral tegmental area, where cells are not as densely packed and homogeneous as in the substantia nigra and locus ceruleus, small

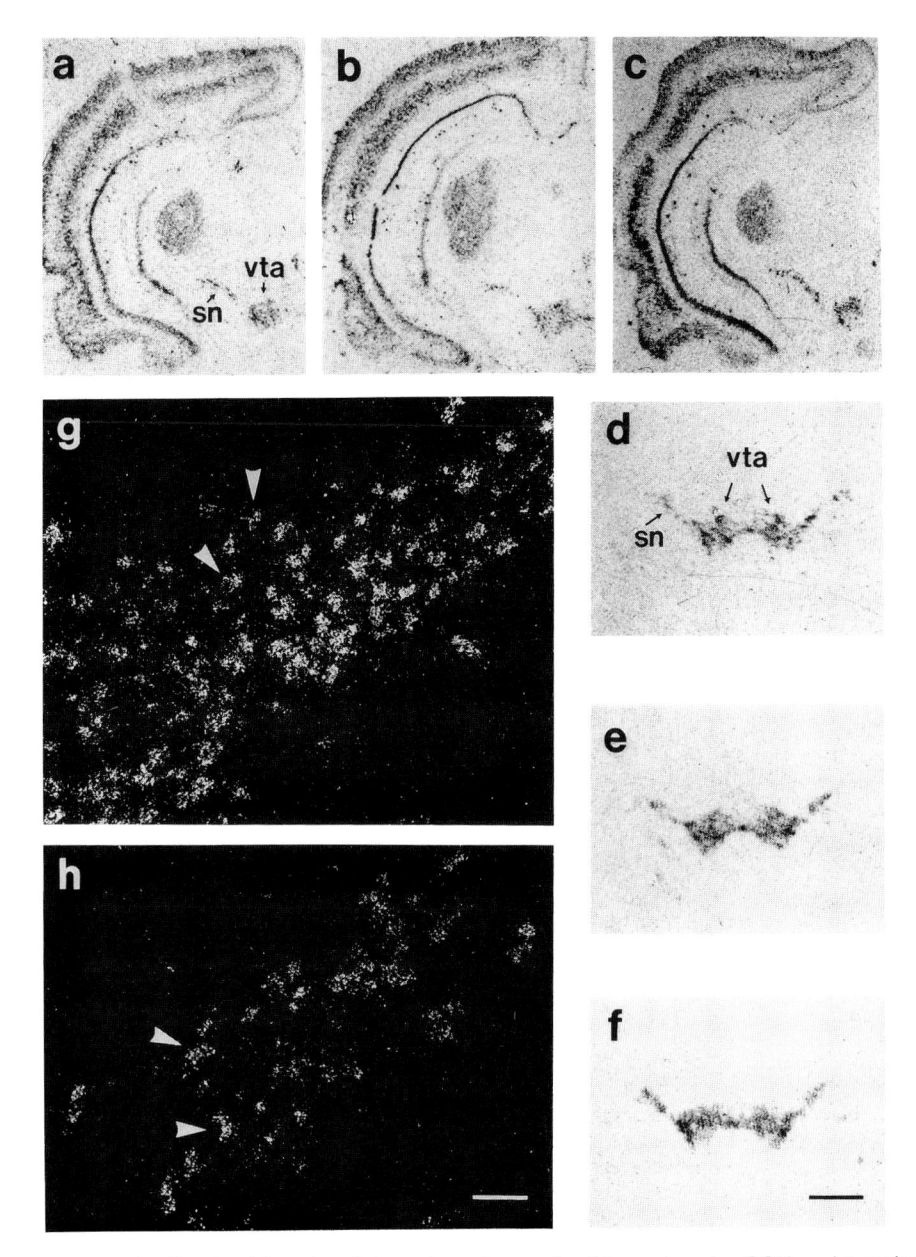

FIG. 1. In situ hybridization histochemistry using oligonucleotide probes for CCK and tyrosine hydroxylase. Film autoradiograms show the distribution of CCK mRNA (**A–C**) and tyrosine hydroxylase mRNA (**D–F**). There was no difference in density in the ventral tegmental area or substantia nigra for either probe among the following haloperidol treatment groups: control (A, CCK; D, tyrosine hydroxylase); acute (B, CCK; E, tyrosine hydroxylase); chronic (C, CCK; F, tyrosine hydroxylase). Darkfield photographs of emulsion-dipped slides demonstrate clusters of silver grains over cells (*arrows*) in the lateral ventral tegmental area and medial substantia nigra for tyrosine hydroxylase (**G**), and in the substantia nigra for CCK (**H**). Calibration bars: A–F, 1.5 mm; G,H: 80 μm.

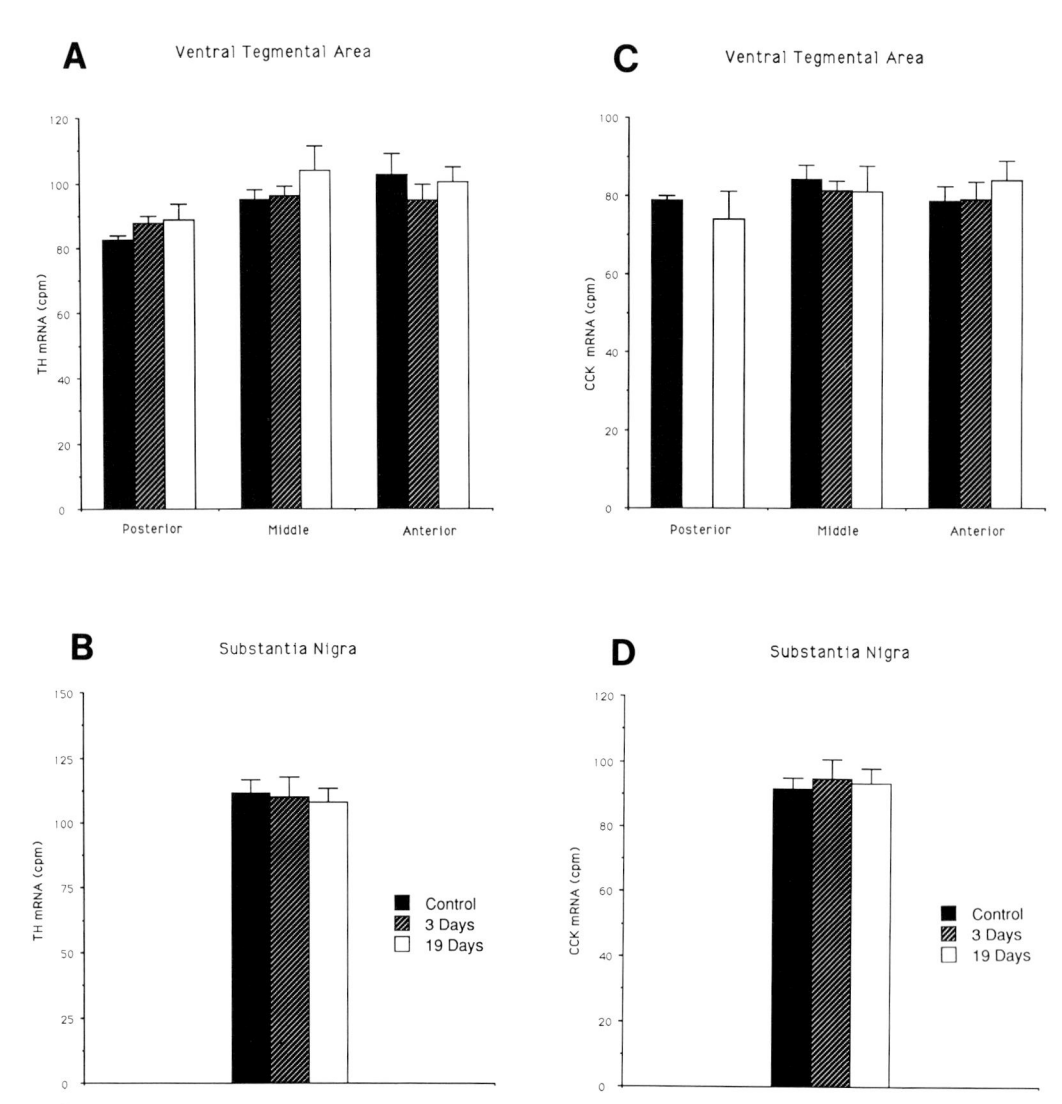

FIG. 2. Effects of acute and chronic haloperidol administration on mRNA levels for tyrosine hydroxylase (**A,B**) and CCK (**C,D**) in the ventral tegmental area (**A,C**) and substantia nigra (**B,D**). Treatment groups are as follows: vehicle (*filled bars*), acute haloperidol administration (2 × 2 mg/kg-d sc × 3 days; *hatched bars*), and chronic haloperidol administration (2 × 2 mg/kg-d sc × 19 days; *open bars*). There were no significant differences between groups in either brain region. Bars represent means ± SEM.

changes could have been undetectable due to dilution by background, or variability in defining the precise area to be quantitated. A more precise cell-by-cell analysis would have been indicated whether any trends in the data from film analysis were detected. A positive result from our laboratory (9) with reserpine treatment in the locus ceruleus, which replicated earlier findings (27), demonstrates that the technique used in the present study would be sufficient to detect large (100%) changes in tyrosine hydroxylase mRNA in a small homogeneous brain nucleus (Fig. 3).

The finding that haloperidol administration does not alter tyrosine hydroxylase

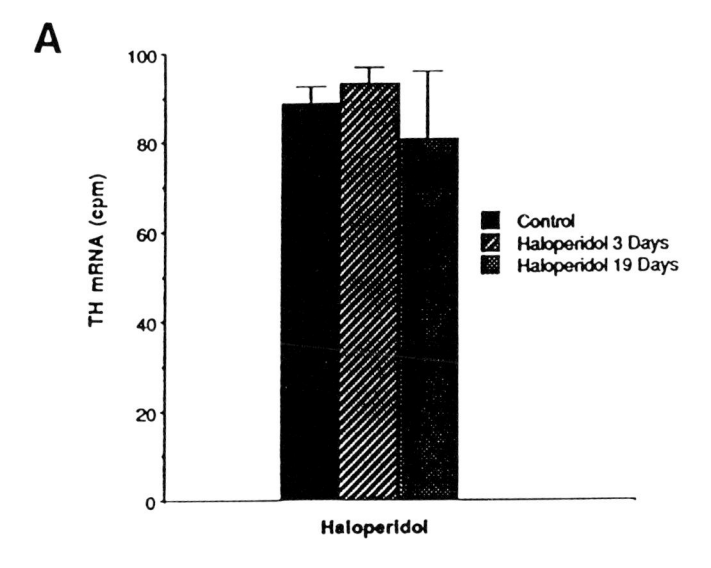

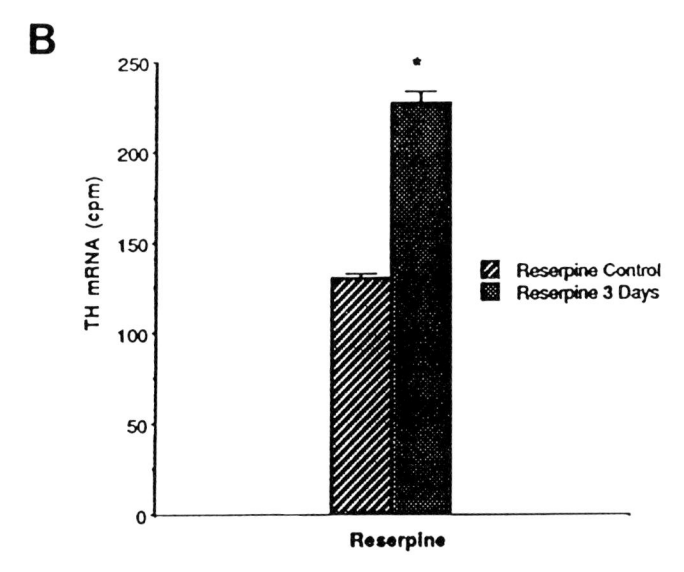

FIG. 3. A: Effect of acute and chronic haloperidol administration on tyrosine hydroxylase mRNA levels in the locus ceruleus. Haloperidol treatment groups are: vehicle (*filled bar*), acute haloperidol administration (2 × 2 mg/kg-d sc × 3 days; *hatched bar*), and chronic haloperidol administration (2 × 2 mg/kg-d sc × 19 days; *shaded bar*). There were no significant differences between groups. Bars represent mean ± SEM. **B:** Effect of reserpine administration (10 mg/kg ip, *shaded bar*) versus vehicle (*closed bar*) on tyrosine hydroxylase mRNA in the locus ceruleus. Bars represent mean ± SEM; *$p < .01$.

mRNA or CCK mRNA concentrations in the substantia nigra or ventral tegmental area suggests that haloperidol may not produce its effects on dopaminergic function at the level of gene transcription. Increases in tyrosine hydroxylase activity following haloperidol administration have been explained by an increase in enzyme affinity for the pterin cofactor (16–18). It has also been reported that tyrosine hydroxylase enzyme activity is regulated by phosphorylation (49–51). These mechanisms would not require increased transcription of tyrosine hydroxylase mRNA. The increase in V_{max} reported by Lerner et al (16) suggests either an increase in mRNA or an accumulation of protein, representing decreased degradation of tyrosine hydroxylase enzyme, or that tyrosine hydroxylase activity is regulated primarily by cofactor affinity and phosphorylation. The present data are consistent with the latter interpretation. The reported increase in CCK concentration in the substantia nigra and ventral tegmental area following chronic haloperidol administration (44) could result from an increased mRNA synthesis or from changes in the regulation of the enzymes that process the CCK precursor, preprocholecystokinin. With CCK, as for tyrosine hydroxylase, the negative data reported herein are more consistent with the latter interpretation.

In conclusion, the negative data on the effects of haloperidol administration on CCK and tyrosine hydroxylase mRNA levels suggest that haloperidol does not exert its effects on dopaminergic function at the level of transcription for tyrosine hydroxylase or CCK in midbrain neurons of the rat. The present data do not, however, categorically rule out a disorder of tyrosine hydroxylase or CCK gene expression in patients with schizophrenia. It is possible that neuroleptics affect dopaminergic systems at the level of gene transcription, not by acting on the tyrosine hydroxylase or CCK genes, but by affecting synthesis of the pterin cofactor, the dopamine receptor, or the enzymes that cleave preprocholecystokinin. As probes for these enzymes and receptors become available, investigations into neuroleptic effects on these mRNA species will become feasible. However, it is interesting to speculate that, rather than providing therapies at the level of genes for transcription, the addition of pterin cofactor early in neuroleptic treatment may be useful for enhancing tyrosine hydroxylase activity and thus improving neuroleptic-induced dopaminergic plasticity in poorly responsive patients.

ACKNOWLEDGMENTS

We wish to express our gratitude to Dr. W. Scott Young for the gift of the CCK and tyrosine hydroxylase oligonucleotide probes and for his kind instruction in the methodology of in situ hybridization histochemistry. SLC is a Pharmacology Research Associate, NIGMS, NIH.

REFERENCES

1. Carlsson A. Antipsychotic drugs, neurotransmitters and schizophrenia. *Am J Psychiat* 1978; 135:164–173.
2. Pickar D. Perspectives on a time-dependent model of neuroleptic action. *Schizophr Bull* 1988;14:255–268.
3. Farde L, Wiesel F-A, Halldin C, Sedvall G. Central D_2-dopamine receptor occupancy in schizophrenic patients treated with antipsychotic drugs. *Arch Gen Psychiat* 1988;45:71–76.
4. Wolkin A, Barouche F, Wolf AP, et al. Dopamine blockade and clinical response: evidence for two biological subgroups of schizophrenia. *Arch Gen Psychiat* 1989;146:905–908.
5. Bunney BS. Antipsychotic drug effects on the electrical activity of dopaminergic neurons. *Trends Neurosci* 1984;1:212–215.
6. Roth RH. Neuroleptics: functional chemistry. In: Coyle JT, Enna SJ, eds. *Neuroleptics: neurochemical, behavioral and clinical perspectives.* New York: Raven Press, 1983;119–156.
7. Bannon MJ, Reinhard JF, Bunney BS, Roth RH. Unique response to antipsychotic drugs is due to the absence of terminal autoreceptors in mesocortical dopamine neurons. *Nature* 1982;296: 444–446.
8. Pickar D, Breier A, Hsiao JK, et al. CSF and plasma monoamine metabolites and their relation to psychosis: implications for regional brain dysfunction in schizophrenia. (Submitted.)
9. Cottingham SL, Pickar D, Shimotake TK, Montpied P, Paul SM, Crawley JN. Tyrosine hydroxylase and cholecystokinin mRNA levels in the substantia nigra, ventral tegmental area and locus ceruleus are unaffected by acute and chronic haloperidol administration. *Cell Mol Neurobiol* 1990; (in press).
10. Levine RA, Miller LP, Lovenberg W. Tetrahydrobiopterin in striatum: localization in dopamine nerve terminals and role in catecholamine synthesis. *Science* 1981;214:919–920.
11. Yamaguchi T, Fujisawa H. Regulation of bovine adrenal tyrosine 3'-mono-oxygenase by phosphorylation-dephosphorylation reaction, catalyzed by adenosine 3'-5'-monophosphate-dependent protein kinase and phosphoprotein phosphatase. *J Biol Chem* 1979;254:503–507.
12. Vulliet PR, Woodgett JR, Ferrari S, Hardie DG. Characterization of the sites phosphorylated on tyrosine hydroxylase by Ca^{2+} and phospholipid-dependent protein kinase, calmodulin-dependent protein kinase and cyclic AMP-dependent protein kinase. *FEBS Lett* 1985;182:335–339.
13. Roskowki R Jr, Vulliet PR, Glass DB. Phosphorylation of tyrosine hydroxylase by cyclic GMP–dependent protein kinase. *J Neurochem* 1987;48:840–845.

14. Cloutier G, Weiner N. Further studies on the increased synthesis of norepinephrine during nerve stimulation of guinea-pig vas deferens preparation: effect of tyrosine and 6,7-dimethyltetrahydropterin. *J Pharmacol Exp Ther* 1973; 186(1):75–85.
15. Zivcovic B, Guidotti A, Costa E. Effects of neuroleptics on striatal tyrosine hydroxylase: changes in affinity for the pteridine cofactor. *Mol Pharmacol* 1974;10:727–735.
16. Lerner P, Nose P, Gordon EK, Lovenberg W. Haloperidol: effect of long-term treatment on rat striatal dopamine synthesis and turnover. *Science* 1977;197:181–183.
17. Bacopoulos NG, Bustos G, Redmond DE, Baulu J, Roth RH. Regional sensitivity of primate brain dopaminergic neurons to haloperidol: alterations following chronic treatment. *Brain Res* 1978;157:396–401.
18. Guidotti A. Regulation of tyrosine hydroxylase after chronic treatment with classic and atypical antischizophrenic drugs. *Adv Biochem Psychopharmacol* 1980;24:1–8.
19. Grima B, Lamouroux A, Blanot F, Faucon Biguet N, Mallet J. Complete coding sequence of rat tyrosine hydroxylase mRNA. *Proc Natl Acad Sci USA* 1985;82:617–621.
20. Mueller R, Thoenen H, Axelrod J. Increase in tyrosine hydroxylase activity after reserpine administration. *J Pharmacol Exp Ther* 1969; 169:74–79.
21. Thoenen H. Introduction of tyrosine hydroxylase in peripheral and central adrenergic neurons by cold-exposure of rats. *Nature* 1970;228:861–862.
22. Reis D, Joh TH, Ross RA, Pickel VM. Reserpine selectivity increases tyrosine hydroxylase and dopamine-β-hydroxylase enzyme protein in central noradrenergic neurons. *Brain Res* 1974; 81:380–386.
23. Zigmond RE. Tyrosine hydroxylase activity in noradrenergic neurons of the locus coeruleus after reserpine administration: sequential increase in cell bodies and nerve terminals. *J Neurochem* 1979;32:23–29.
24. Labatut R, Buda M, Berod A. Long-term changes in rat brain tyrosine hydroxylase following reserpine treatment: a quantitative immunochemical analysis. *J Neurochem* 1988;50: 1375–1380.
25. Schalling M, Dagerlind A, Brene S, et al. Coexistence and gene expression of phenylethanolamine N-methyltransferase, tyrosine hydroxylase, and neuropeptide tyrosine in the rat and bovine adrenal gland: effects of reserpine. *Proc Natl Acad Sci USA* 1988;85:8306–8310.
26. Richard F, Labatut R, Weissmann D, Scarna H, Buda M, Pujol JF. Further characterization of the tyrosine hydroxylase induction elicited by reserpine in the rat locus coeruleus and adrenals. *Neurochem Int* 1989;14:199–205.
27. Faucon Biguet N, Buda M, Lamouroux A, Samolyk D, Mallet J. Time course of the changes of TH mRNA in rat brain and adrenal medulla after a single injection of reserpine. *EMBO J* 1986;5:287–291.
28. Zigmond RE, Schon F, Iversen LL. Increased tyrosine hydroxylase activity in the locus coeruleus of rat brain stem after reserpine treatment and cold stress. *Brain Res* 1974;70:547–552.
29. Fluharty SJ, Snyder GL, Stricker EM, Zigmond MG. Short- and long-term changes in adrenal tyrosine hydroxylase activity during insulin-induced hypoglycemia and cold stress. *Brain Res* 1983;267:384–387.
30. Stachowiak MK, Sebbane R, Stricker EM, Zigmond MH, Kaplan BB. Effect of chronic cold exposure on tyrosine hydroxylase mRNA in rat adrenal gland. *Brain Res* 1985;359:356–359.
31. Hökfelt T, Skirboll L, Rehfeld JF, Goldstein M, Markey K, Dann O. A subpopulation of mesencephalic dopamine neurons projecting to limbic areas contains a cholecystokinin-like peptide: evidence from immunohistochemistry combined with retrograde tracing. *Neuroscience* 1980;5: 2093–2124.
32. Bonnemann C, Giraud P, Eiden LE, Meyer DK. Measurement of mRNA specific for preprocholecystokinin in rat caudatoputamen and areas projecting to it. *Neurochem Int* 1987;10:521–524.
33. Voight MM, Uhl GR. Preprocholecystokinin mRNA in rat brain: regional expression includes thalamus. *Mol Brain Res* 1988;4:247–253.
34. Savastra M, Palacios JM, Mengod G. Regional distribution of the mRNA coding for the neuropeptide cholecystokinin in rat brain studied by in situ hybridization. *Neurosci Lett* 1988;93: 6208–6212.
35. Burgunder J-M, Young WS III. The distribution of thalamic projection neurons containing cholecystokinin messenger RNA, using in situ hybridization histochemistry and retrograde labeling. *Mol Brain Res* 1988;4:179–189.
36. Skirboll LR, Grace AA, Hommer DW, et al. Peptide-monoamine coexistence: studies of the actions of cholecystokinin-like peptide on the electrical activity of midbrain dopamine neurons. *Neuroscience* 1981;6:2111–2124.
37. Hommer DW, Skirboll LR. Cholecystokinin-like peptides potentiate apomorphine-induced inhibition of dopamine neurons. *Eur J Pharmacol* 1983;91:151–152.
38. Freeman AS, Bunney BS. Activity of A9 and A10 dopaminergic neurons in unrestrained rats: further characterization and effects of apomorphine and cholecystokinin. *Brain Res* 1987;405: 46–55.
39. Fuxe K, Andersson K, Locatelli V, et al. Cholecystokinin peptides produce marked reduction of dopamine turnover in discrete areas in the rat brain following intraventricular injection. *Eur J Pharmacol* 1983;67:329–331.
40. Lane RF, Blaha CD, Phillips AG. In vivo electro-chemical analysis of cholecystokinin-induced inhibition of dopamine release in the nucleus accumbens. *Brain Res* 1986;397:200–204.
41. Ruggeri M, Ungerstedt U, Agnati LF, Mutt V, Harfstrand A, Fuxe K. Effects of cholecystokinin peptides and neurotensin on dopamine release and metabolism in the rostral and caudal part of the nucleus accumbens using intracere-

bral dialysis in the anesthetized rat. *Neurochem Int* 1987;10:509–520.
42. Crawley JN, Stivers JA, Blumstein LK, Paul SM. Cholecystokinin potentiates dopamine-mediated behaviors: evidence for modulation specific to a site of coexistence. *J Neurosci* 1985;5:1972–1983.
43. Crawley JN. Microinjection of cholecystokinin into the rat ventral tegmental area potentiates dopamine-induced hypolocomotion. *Synapse* 1989; 3:346–355.
44. Radke JM, MacLennan AJ, Beinfeld MC, et al. Effects of short- and long-term haloperidol administration and withdrawal on regional brain cholecystokinin and neurotensin concentrations in the rat. *Brain Res* 1989;480:178–183.
45. Gysling K, Beinfeld MC. Failure of chronic haloperidol treatment to alter levels of cholecystokinin in the rat brain striatum and olfactory tubercle-nucleus accumbens area. *Neuropeptides* 1984;4:421–423.
46. Frey P. Cholecystokinin octapeptide levels in rat brain are changed after subchronic neuroleptic treatment. *Eur J Pharmacol* 1983;95:87–92.
47. Bunney BS, Walters JR, Roth RH, Aghajanian GK. Dopaminergic neurons: effect of antipsychotic drugs and amphetamine on single-cell activity. *J Pharmacol Exp Ther* 1973;185:560–571.
48. Young WS III, Bonner TI, Brann MR. Mesencephalic neurons regulate the expression of neuropeptide mRNAs in the rat forebrain. *Proc Natl Acad Sci USA* 1986;83:9827–9831.
49. Lovenberg W, Bruckwick EA, Hanbauer I. ATP, cyclic AMP and magnesium increase the affinity of rat striatal tyrosine hydroxylase for its cofactor. *Proc Natl Acad Sci USA* 1975:72:2955–2958.
50. Joh TH, Park DH, Reid DJ. Direct phosphorylation of brain tyrosine hydroxylase by cyclic AMP–dependent protein kinase: a mechanism of enzyme activation. *Proc Natl Acad Sci USA* 1978;75:4744–4748.
51. Vulliet PR, Woodgett JR, Cohen P. Tyrosine hydroxylase: a substrate of cyclic AMP–dependent protein kinase. *Proc Natl Acad Sci USA* 1980; 77:92–96.
52. Bacopoulos NG, Bustos G, Redmond DE Jr, Roth RH. Chronic treatment with haloperidol or fluphenazine decanoate: regional effects on dopamine and serotonin in primate brain. *J Pharmacol Exp Ther* 1982;221:22–28.

PART II
Neurobiology and Physiology of Schizophrenia

6

Neuroplasticity of Mesotelencephalic Dopamine Neurons at the Network and Receptor Level

New Aspects of the Role of Dopamine in Schizophrenia and Possible Pharmacological Treatments

Kjell Fuxe,[1] Luigi F. Agnati,[2] Michele Zoli,[2] Emilio Merlo Pich,[2] Roberta Grimaldi,[2] Börje Bjelke,[1] Sergio Tanganelli,[3] Gabriel von Euler,[1] and Ann-Marie Janson[1]

The neurobiological approach to schizophrenia has focused on the theory of morphofunctional lesions in neural circuits (1,2) as a fundamental pathogenetic cause. The lesion may be of genetic or epigenetic origin. The possibility should be considered that epigenetic influences may trigger the onset of schizophrenia in genetically predisposed subjects. The morphological damage taking place during development may lead to altered information handling, involving especially the prefrontal cortex, the dorsal and ventral striatum, and parts of the limbic system. The role of epigenetic influences in the onset of schizophrenia is illustrated by the role of stress in the development of the disease (3). Thus, it seems as if the ability of the central nervous system (CNS) to adapt to external and internal stimuli by means of morphological and functional plasticity is altered in the schizophrenic brain. An impairment of the highly stress-sensitive mesolimbocortical neurons has in fact been postulated by Weinberger (3). These neurons originate from a subgroup of group A10 in the ventral tegmental area (4–10). It is of substantial interest that the mesocortical dopamine (DA) neurons to the prefrontal cortex appear to contain the highest amounts of glucocorticoid receptor (GR) immunoreactivity among the ventral tegmental and nigral DA neurons (11). These results underline a role of glucocorticoids in the control, especially of the mesocortical DA neurons to the prefrontal cortex and thus possibly in the control of the onset of schizophrenia. The role of glucocorticoids is further underlined by the presence of high amounts of GR immunoreactivity within practically all noradrenaline (NA) and 5-hydroxytryptamine (5HT) neurons, which may also be altered in the schizophrenic brain (11).

---

[1]Department of Histology and Neurobiology, Karolinska Institute, Stockholm, Sweden
[2]Institute of Human Physiology, University of Modena, Modena, Italy
[3]Department of Pharmacology, University of Ferrara, Ferrara, Italy.

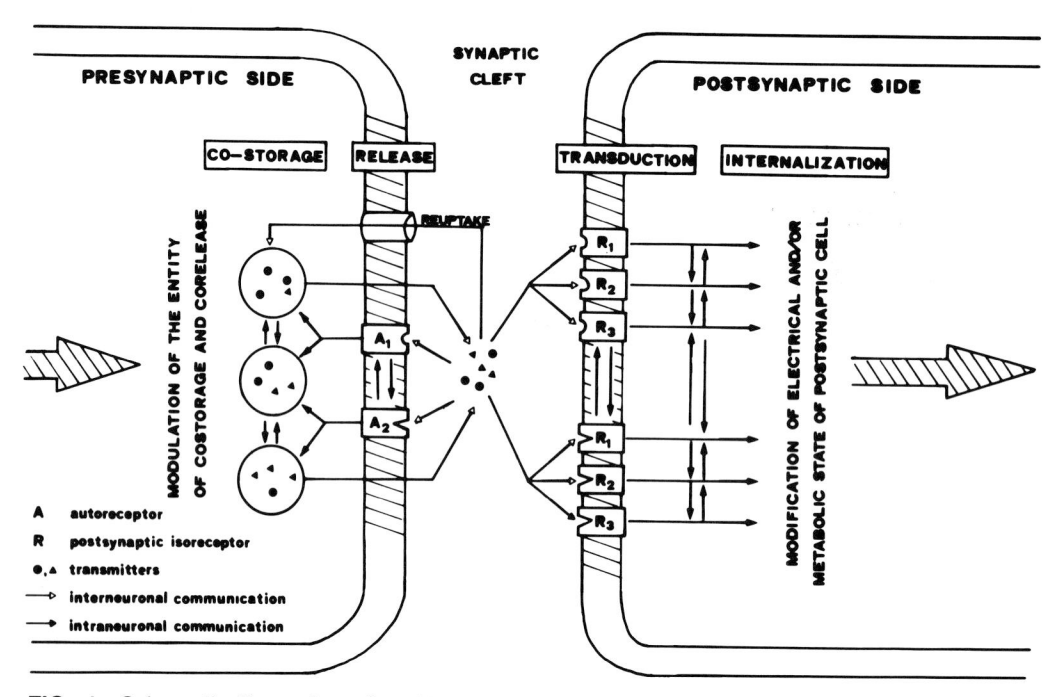

FIG. 1. Schematic illustration of multiple transmission lines in synapses and the existence of receptor-receptor interactions at the pre- and postsynaptic level.

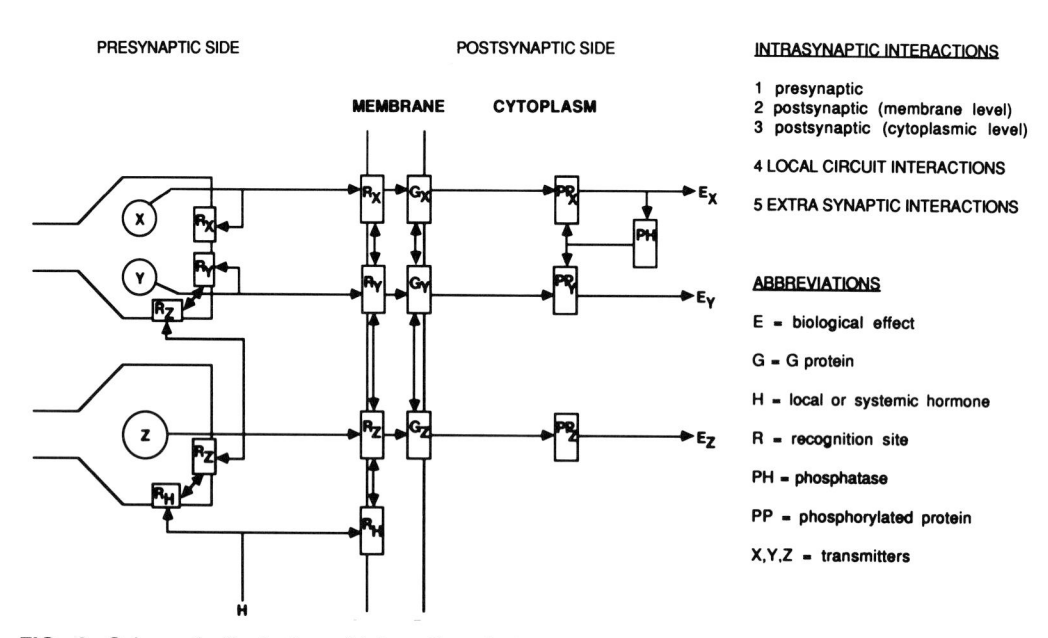

FIG. 2. Schematic illustration of interactions between transmission lines at the intrasynaptic level and at the local circuit level. The hormonal influence on these interactions is also indicated.

Against this background we felt it to be of interest to review our work on morphological and functional plasticity in the ascending meso- and telencephalic DA systems including the complexity of DA neurotransmission and its interactions with other transmission lines (Figs. 1 and 2). Data will be provided to discuss whether an alteration in the wiring (morphological lesion) or in the information handling (functional lesion) of the neural circuits may take place in schizophrenia. In particular, we shall discuss the possibility that pathological changes may selectively affect a transmitter-identified neural system (e.g., dopamine and DA) and, as our data on ischemia indicate (see below), even a single transmission line (i.e., D_1 but not D_2 DA transmission). In this context, it is of particular relevance to consider possible changes in receptor turnover and intramembrane molecular circuits, as exemplified by our findings on the interactions between DA and neurotensin (NT) receptors in limbic and striatal areas. Finally, new aspects on the pharmacological treatment of schizophrenia will be discussed based among other things on the protective effects of gangliosides on mechanical, neurotoxic, and ischemic-induced injuries of the DA neurons (12) and DA receptor-containing nerve cells (13).

EXPERIMENTAL OBSERVATIONS

Prenatal Lesion: Studies in a Model of Microencephalic Rat Based On Prenatal Exposure to Methylazoxymethanol Acetate

It is well known that methylazoxymethanol acetate (MAM) causes a dose-dependent microencephaly together with a relatively maintained body weight when injected into pregnant rats during a particular period of gestation (14). The cytotoxicity of MAM is probably due to its antimitotic action, which results from the methylation of DNA and RNA bases (15). The cerebral cortex and the hippocampal formation are the regions most affected by MAM in the CNS. The effects in the neostriatum, the nucleus accumbens, and the tuberculum olfactorium are substantially less pronounced. In adulthood hypoplasia and cytoarchitectonic abnormality have been demonstrated within the cerebral cortex and the hippocampal formation in MAM-exposed rats (16,17).

Previous studies have demonstrated increased concentrations of NA, DA, 5HT, and acetylcholine within the neocortex and increased concentrations of monoamines in the striatum upon prenatal exposure to MAM. However, the total amount of these neurotransmitters per region were not affected (18,19). Very little is known about the alterations induced by MAM in neuropeptide neurons. Recently we have been involved in an analysis of the vasoactive intestinal polypeptide (VIP), neuropeptide Y (NPY), and cholecystokinin (CCK) immunoreactive (IR) neurons in the neocortex, the hippocampal formation, and the neostriatum including an analysis of tyrosine hydroxylase (TH) IR nerve terminals (20).

We injected MAM into pregnant rats in a dose of 25 mg/kg at gestational day 15, and analyzed the peptide and TH IR neurons in adulthood by means of immunocytochemistry in combination with computer-assisted morphometry and microdensitometry (20). No change was found in the total number of VIP IR neurons of the neocortex and NPY IR neurons of the nucleus caudatus putamen, while CCK and NPY IR neurons in the neocortex and CCK and VIP IR neurons in the hippocampal formation were substantially reduced. The reduction of the latter peptide IR nerve-cell populations is associated with a maintained density due to the overall mass reduction in these areas of MAM-exposed rats. In the basal ganglia TH immunoreactivity was found to be unchanged, but in the neocortex and limbic cortex an increased density of TH IR nerve terminals was demonstrated in MAM-

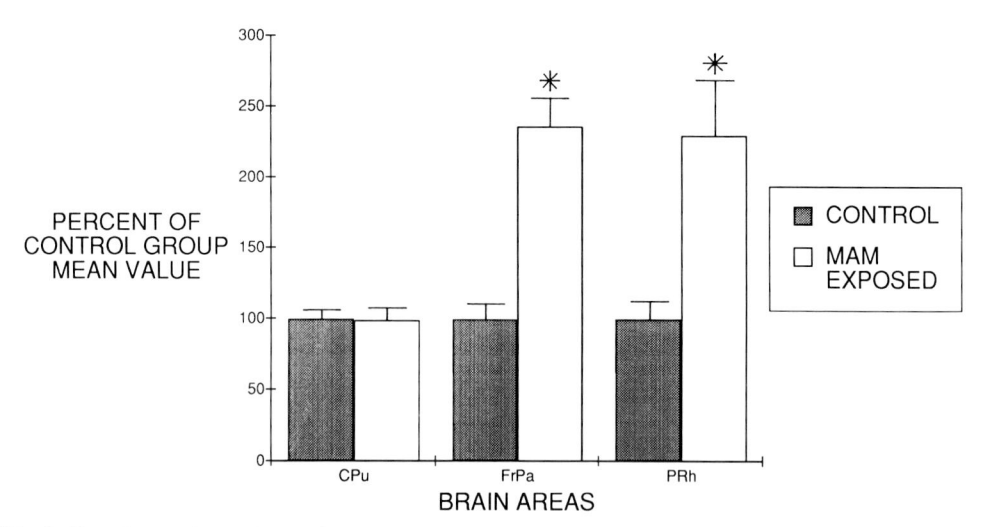

FIG. 3. Densitometric analysis of TH immunoreactivity in three regions of the forebrain of adult rats prenatally exposed to MAM. Means ± SEM are shown for total TH immunoreactivity ($n = 4$). Mann Whitney U-test. Abbreviations: CPu, nucleus caudatus putamen; FrPa, frontoparietal cortex; PRh, perirhinal cortex. *$p < .05$.

exposed rats (Fig. 3 and Table 1); this is consistent with previous studies on cortical NA systems after MAM exposure.

The present results suggest that the VIP and NPY IR neurons of the frontoparietal cortex and the neostriatum, respectively, as well as the ascending DA, NA, and 5HT neurons projecting to the cerebral cortex, develop according to genetically determined programs independent of the interactions with other neuronal populations of the cerebral cortex and the neostriatum.

The VIP IR neurons are uniformly distributed within the cerebral cortex of the rat and appear to represent interneurons always present in the functional unit of the cerebral cortex, the mini column (21,22). Therefore, the fact that the number and uniformity of VIP IR nerve cells is not altered when there is a reduction in the surrounding neuronal populations indicates the possibility that the cortical columnar organization may remain following MAM exposure. In fact, previous data showed that surviving cortical cells can establish normal efferent and afferent connections (20).

The maintained total number of NPY IR nerve cells within the neostriatum again indicates that among the peptide nerve cells certain cell-body populations are differentially affected by MAM exposure, probably related to different developmental periods.

TABLE 1. *Low-magnification densitometric analysis of tyrosine hydroxylase–like immunoreactivity in the forebrain*

Treatment	Optical density (arbitrary units)		
	Nucleus caudatus putamen	Nucleus accumbens	Tuberculum olfactorium
Control	175 ± 8	187 ± 8	238 ± 7
MAM Ac-exposed	172 ± 4	192 ± 4	240 ± 5

The sampled areas are shown in Fig 1. Means ± SEM are shown ($n = 4$ rats per group). The statistical analysis was carried out by the Mann-Whitney U-test.

Of substantial interest was the observation that the NPY IR neuronal population showed an altered distribution within the neostriatum in adulthood with a relative increase in the number of NPY IR nerve cells in fundus striati of MAM-exposed animals (Fig. 4; ref 20).

These observations are of special interest with regard to the neurodevelopmental theory of schizophrenia. Thus, a developmental lesion may not only lead to an overall decrease of the brain region mass (e.g., striatal hypoplasia) but also to substantial alterations in the amount and distribution of selective transmitter-identified nerve-cell populations as shown in this analysis of the NPY IR nerve cells. These events may lead to alterations in the final wiring of the striatal networks during the maturation process. It seems likely that the alterations in the distribution of striatal NPY IR neurons are related to a partial blockade of the developmental spread of these cells from the ventrolateral part into the medial and dorsal part of the neostriatum. Similar events may also take place in other regions such as the prefrontal cortex and may involve the dopaminoceptive cells.

The present observations, however, are of interest not only for the developmental theory of schizophrenia (3) but also for understanding the development of the organization of the brain. As the maintenance of the total number of VIP IR cells in the cerebral cortex (neocortex) and of NPY IR nerve-cell populations within the neostriatum seem to indicate, small transmitter-identified neuronal systems could have a major part in the development of neuronal modules and their interactions. It seems possible that these scattered VIP and NPY neuronal populations could play an essential role in the cytoarchitectonic organization of the neocortex and the nucleus caudatus putamen, respectively, which might be related to certain specific developmental

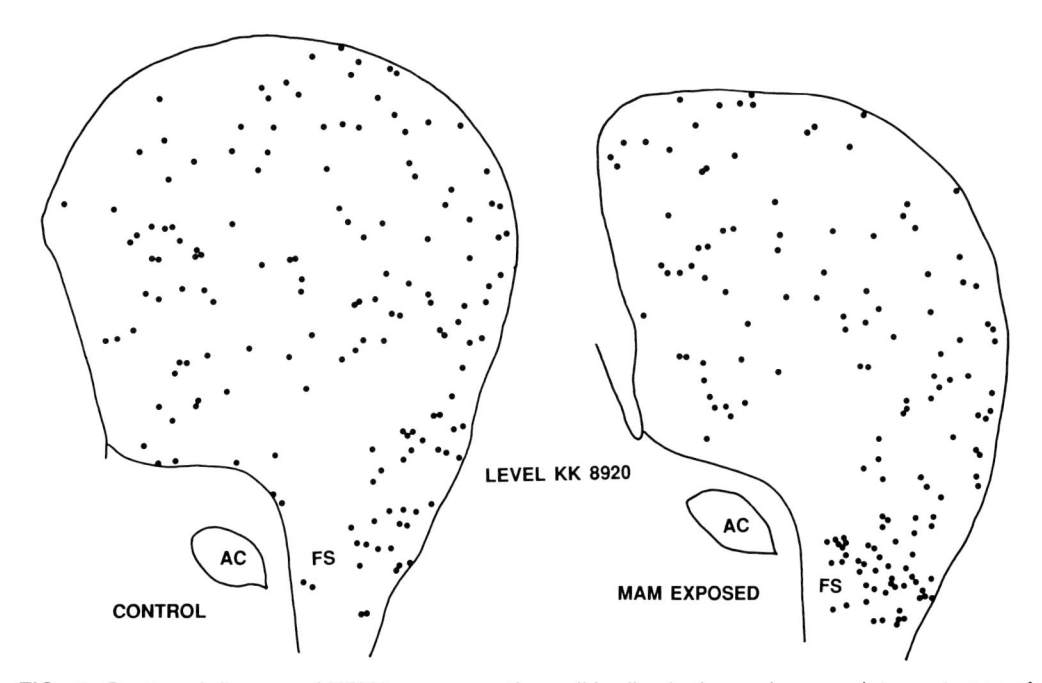

FIG. 4. Scattered diagram of NPY immunoreactive cell bodies in the nucleus caudatus putamen of adult control rats and adult MAM-exposed rats. In the MAM-exposed rat the NPY immunoreactive cell bodies are concentrated in the fundus striati (FS); AC, anterior commissure (20).

characteristics. Based on these observations Zoli et al. (20) postulated that at least some basic features of the modular organization of the nucleus caudatus putamen were preserved in spite of the presence of a mass reduction in these areas. These observations indicate that in a neurodevelopmental model of schizophrenia one may postulate the existence of highly discrete alterations in the wiring of certain brain areas such as the prefrontal cortex, the limbic cortex, and within restricted parts of the basal ganglia in the presence of a cytoarchitectonically maintained organization of the brain.

It is of substantial interest that a NA hyperinnervation appears to exist in the neocortex of MAM-exposed animals (17,20) as well as a dopaminergic hyperinnervation of the limbic cortex (20). However, these hyperinnervations appear to be to some degree age-dependent, since a partial normalization has been observed at 4 months of age (23). These observations may be related to an adaptive reorganization of the catecholamine projections to the cerebral cortex or to a delayed target-dependent neuronal death (see ref 20).

The observations showing hyperinnervation of the DA and NA nerve-terminal networks in the forebrain after MAM treatment are of substantial interest from the standpoint of the neurodevelopmental theory of schizophrenia. Thus, a developmental lesion of the intrinsic circuits in prefrontal and limbic cortical regions and of the basal ganglia may lead to an altered, and possibly increased, influence of ascending monoamine nerve cell due among other things to possible compensatory regrowth phenomena. Based on the results obtained in the MAM model of microencephaly, the impact of DA would be increased in such a network compared with the control animal, if the DA receptors maintain their sensitivity. The possibility should also be considered that an early lesion in the DA innervation of the limbic areas cannot be detected in adult life since a reorganization of the system has taken place. However, the new networks may be more prone to failures under highly demanding situations such as stress conditions.

Adult Lesions

Toxic Lesions: Studies in the MPTP Model of Parkinson's Disease

The chemical 1-methyl-phenyl-5-1,2,3,6-tetrahydropyridine (MPTP) is well known to produce a degeneration of nigrostriatal DA neurons in the black mouse, in monkeys, and in humans (24). MPTP produces neuronal degeneration by being converted into an active metabolite MPP^+ by monoamine oxidase B, after which it is actively taken up by the DA uptake mechanism in the nerve-cell membrane of DA neurons. In this process the neurotoxin becomes accumulated in the DA neurons, where it reaches concentrations sufficient to produce an inhibition of mitochondrial respiration and/or an oxidative stress reaction. In addition, it may also exert detergentlike actions on the nerve-cell membrane of the DA neurons. It should be stressed that the mesolimbic and mesocortical DA neurons are also severely affected by MPTP.

In a recent study it was possible to demonstrate that the ganglioside GM_1 given for 14 days at a dose of 10 mg/kg with onset of treatment 15 minutes after the MPTP injection could partly protect the nigral DA nerve cells against the MPTP-induced degeneration (25). Gangliosides are known to be mainly located in membranes and it seems likely that the exogenous ganglioside GM_1 molecules can be incorporated into the nerve-cell membranes, where they may protect against the detergentlike action of MPTP. The ganglioside GM_1 is located exclusively on the external surface of the plasma membrane and has been implicated in decreased membrane fluidity (26,27). In fact, we have recently been able to show that the toluene-induced increase in mem-

TABLE 2. *Protective effects of ganglioside treatment in various models of brain injury*

Type of lesion	Neural system	Morphological parameters	Improvement of biochemical parameters	Improvement of functional parameters	References
Dimesencephalic hemitransection	Nigrostriatal pathway	Yes	Yes	Yes	12,81,82
MPTP	Nigrostriatal pathway	Yes	NT	NT	25
Forebrain ischemia	Striatum	Yes	NT	Yes	46,83
Severe hypoglycemia	Frontoparietal cortex	NT	Yes	Yes	83
Toluene	Striatum	NT	Yes	NT	84

NT = not tested.

brane fluidity is counteracted by GM_1 in a dose-related manner using the fluorescence polarization of two probes: 1-4-trimethyl-aminophenyl-1,3,5-hexatriene (TMA-DPH) and 1,6 diphenyl-1,3,5-hexatriene (DPH) to measure membrane anisotropy. Thus, GM_1 may stabilize the nerve-cell membrane against a detergentlike activity of MPTP and of MPP+. Actually we have shown that GM_1 can protect against different mechanical, metabolic, and toxic lesions (see Table 2). The ganglioside GM_1 may also bind calcium in vitro (28) and may thus be involved in the control of calcium flow through the nerve-cell membrane (29). In recent work (30) we have been able to demonstrate that the toluene-induced increases in intracellular calcium levels can be partially prevented by pretreatment with the ganglioside GM_1 in a concentration of 50 μM. This action of GM_1 may reflect an interactive interaction, since in this concentration GM_1 by itself reduced the intracellular calcium levels. Thus, it seems likely that this action of GM_1 can also contribute to its protective effect on MPTP-induced degeneration of nigral DA cells, since it is possible that the MPTP treatment may lead to increases in intracellular calcium levels, possibly related to an increase in membrane leakage. Thus, there probably exist multiple targets for the protective actions of gangliosides (Fig. 5).

Based on these observations and on previous work (13) on GM_1 protective activity, gangliosides may protect at least to a certain degree also against other types of neurotoxin-induced lesions (see Table 2). In this respect it should be noted that about 30 years ago the concept of the production of

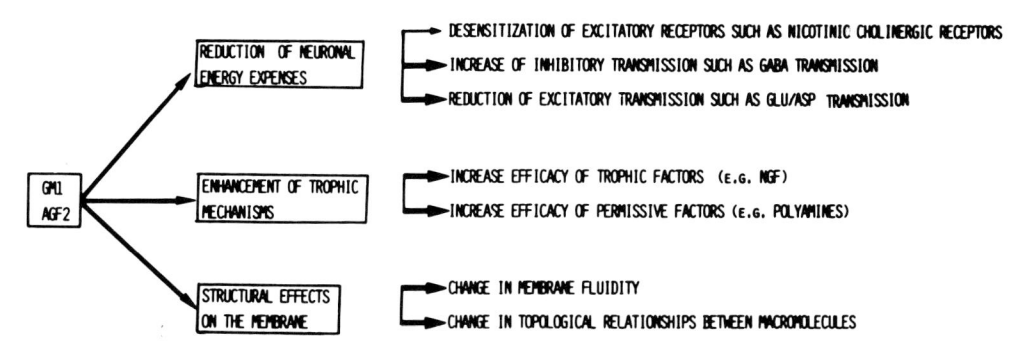

FIG. 5. Possible mechanisms of action of the ganglioside GM_1 and the cyclic GM_1 analogue AGF2.

an endogenous toxin in schizophrenia patients was introduced (for a review see ref 31). Therefore, if neurotoxins were shown to be involved in producing the pathology in the schizophrenic brain, the ganglioside GM_1 should be tested for possible preventive action in subjects at risk (ie, subjects for whom a genetic basis can be assessed); as Slater and Ruth (32) have pointed out, "the evidence is very strong that the genetical constitution of an individual contributes to a large part of his total potentiality of becoming schizophrenic."

In recent work (25,33) we have also studied whether nicotine administered via Azlet minipumps implanted subcutaneously, in amounts producing serum nicotine levels similar to those found in smokers (50 to 60 ng/ml), can exert protective effects against MPTP-induced degeneration of nigrostriatal DA neurons in the black mouse. Studies on TH immunoreactivity within the striatum, using image analysis and biochemical analysis of DA levels in the substantia nigra, provide evidence that chronic nicotine treatment may lead to an increase in the survival of nigrostriatal DA neurons after an MPTP-induced lesion of these cells. It is suggested that the protective action against the MPTP-induced toxicity may be due to a desensitization of excitatory nicotinic cholinoceptors located on the nigral cell bodies and terminals (25). In this way firing rates of the DA nerve cells may be reduced, leading to reduced energy demands, so that energy production may be focused on the maintenance of ion homeostasis in the DA nerve cells, exposed to the MPTP challenge. Also, the ion homeostasis and the survival of the nerve cells may be improved by a reduction of Na^{++} and Ca^{++} ion influx via the ion channel of the nicotine receptor. However, it must be considered that nicotine acutely can counteract MPTP uptake via the DA uptake mechanism by releasing DA. This could be the major mechanism to explain the protective activity of nicotine.

Studies on the effects of chronic nicotine treatment on mechanical lesions of the nigrostriatal DA neurons made via partial hemitransections also show the protective activity of nicotine (25). In this animal model it was found that the lesion-induced disappearance of TH IR cell-body and dendritic profiles in the substantia nigra was significantly counteracted by nicotine treatment, especially with regard to the dendritic profiles. All the morphological and biochemical data obtained can be explained by the hypothesis that the protective effects of nicotine on lesions in the nigrostriatal DA systems are due to a desensitization of excitatory nicotinic cholinoceptors located on the nigral DA nerve cells, leading to a reduction of firing rate and energy demands and improved ion homeostasis (25). Such actions may importantly contribute to a putative antiparkinsonian action of chronic nicotine treatment in humans. Strong support for this hypothesis has been obtained in studies on DA utilization, demonstrating that chronic nicotine treatment markedly and differentially reduces the DA utilization in surviving DA nerve terminal systems of the basal ganglia on the lesioned side, while the DA nerve-terminal networks on the intact side are substantially less affected (Figs. 6 and 7; ref 33). In collaboration with Svensson and Grenhoff we have recently obtained indications that nigral DA nerve cells on the lesioned side of nicotine-treated animals have considerably reduced burst firing rates compared with those found on the lesioned side of saline-treated animals (Grenhoff et al., unpublished observations).

If, in the schizophrenic brain, hyperactivity takes place in discrete ascending DA neuronal populations in response to a putative lesion, chronic nicotine treatment may produce a preferential action on activity in the abnormally active DA neurons, since they may according to our present work be particularly sensitive to desensitization of the excitatory nicotinic cholino-

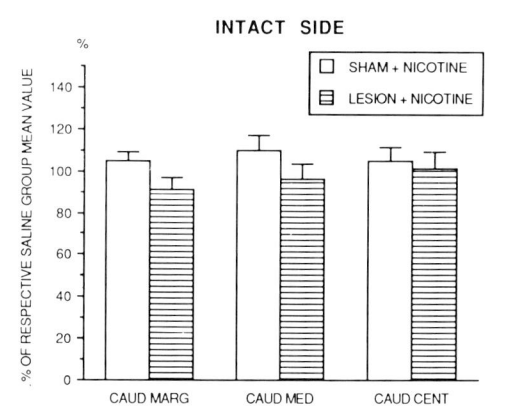

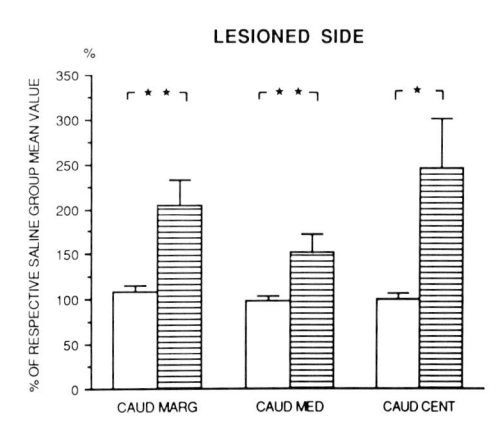

FIG. 6. Effects of chronic nicotine treatment on DA fluorescence in discrete forebrain DA nerve terminal systems of the intact and lesioned sides in the operated male rat. The animals were sham-operated or partially hemitransected at the dimesencephalic junction causing an axotomy of both ascending and descending pathways including the mesostriatal DA system with the exception of its medial component and subsequently treated with (−) nicotine hydrogene (+) tartrate (0.125 mg/kg-h) during 14 days. On the day of the experiment the rats were given saline intraperitoneally 2 hours before decapitation. The sham-operated nicotine-treated group is expressed as a percentage of sham-operated saline-treated group mean values. The hemitransected nicotine-treated group is expressed as a percentage of hemitransected saline-treated group mean values. CAUD MARG, marginal zone of the nucleus caudatus; CAUD MED, medial part of the nucleus caudatus; CAUD CENT, central part of the nucleus caudatus. Means ± SEM, n = 10–12 in all groups except for CAUD MARG, CAUD MED, CAUD CENT on the lesioned side in hemitransected nicotine-treated group (n = 6). The absolute concentrations of catecholamines representing 100% given in nanomoles per gram of tissue wet weight were as follows: in the sham-operated saline-treated group, on the intact side: CAUD MARG = 134 ± 9, CAUD MED = 160 ± 9; CAUD CENT = 153 ± 9; on the lesioned side: CAUD MARG 120 ± 8; CAUD MED = 160 ± 11, CAUD CENT = 145 ± 14. In the hemitransected saline-treated group on the intact side: CAUD MARG = 149 ± 11, CAUD MED = 187 ± 14, CAUD CENT = 153 ± 15; on the lesioned side: CAUD MARG = 38 ± 6, CAUD MED = 51 ± 10, CAUD CENT = 32 ± 6. Two-tailed Mann-Whitney U-test. *$p < .05$, **$p < .01$.

ceptors. Thus, chronic nicotine treatment may have a therapeutic potential in schizophrenia. However, it should be remembered that there exists no evidence of increases in DA release in the schizophrenic brain based on studies of DA metabolite levels in the cerebrospinal fluid. On the other hand, ultrastructural analysis of the substantia nigra (34) has revealed pathological processes in nerve cells as well as dystrophic destruction in afferent systems, which might lead to alterations in the control of DA nerve-cell activity. Also, elevated levels of thalamic DA have been demonstrated in schizophrenia (35). Such a neurochemical change may possibly contribute to sensory dysfunction in schizophrenia.

Metabolic Lesions: Studies on Ischemia-induced Lesions in the Nigrostriatal System

It is well known that the CNS is highly vulnerable to ischemia. The neocortex, the hippocampal formation, and the striatum show a selective vulnerability with severe damage after a brief ischemic episode (36). In the present study the four-vessel occlusion model of transient forebrain ischemia in the rat has been used (37). For details of the model, see Pulsinelli and Brierley (38).

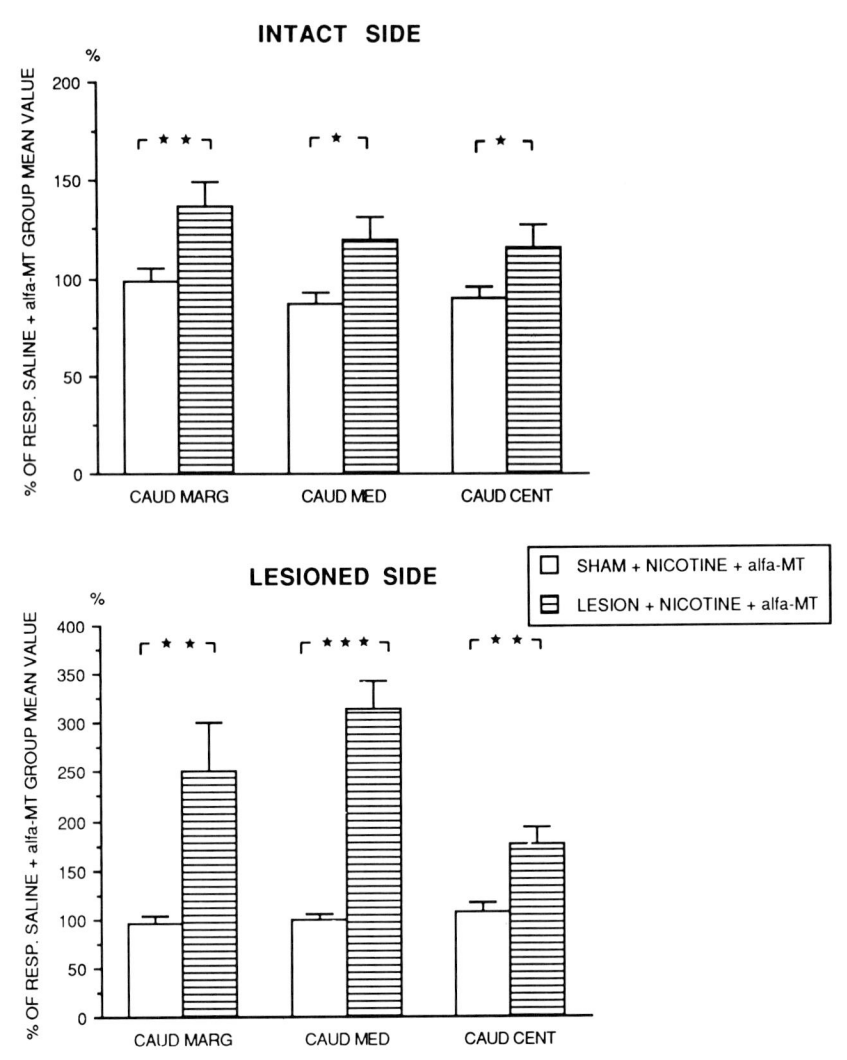

FIG. 7. Effects of chronic nicotine treatment on α-methyltyrosine methylester (α-MT)-induced DA fluorescence disappearance in discrete forebrain DA nerve-terminal systems of the intact and lesioned sides in the operated male rat. The animals were sham-operated or hemitransected and subsequently treated with nicotine (0.125 mg/kg-h) during 14 days (see Fig. 6). On the day of the experiment the rats were given α-MT (250 mg/kg ip) 2 hours before decapitation. The percent amount remaining in the sham-operated nicotine α-MT-treated group is expressed as a percentage of the mean values of the sham-operated saline α-MT-treated group. Similarly, the percent amount remaining in the hemitransected nicotine α-MT-treated group is expressed as a percentage of the mean values of the hemitransected saline α-MT-treated group. Means ± SEM ($n = 12$) in all groups except for CAUD MARG, CAUD MED, and CAUD CENT on the lesioned side in the hemitransected nicotine α-MT-treated group ($n = 9$). The absolute concentrations of catecholamines representing 100% (expressed in nanomoles per gram of tissue wet weight) were as follows: Intact side in the group sham-operated nicotine-treated group: CAUD MARG = 140 ± 5, CAUD med = 176 ± 10, CAUD CENT = 160 ± 12; on the intact side of the hemitransected nicotine-treated group: CAUD MARG = 136 ± 8, CAUD MED = 179 ± 13, CAUD CENT = 153 ± 19; lesioned side in the sham-operated nicotine-treated group: CAUD MARG = 133 ± 10, CAUD MED = 159 ± 11, CAUD CENT = 146 ± 14; lesioned side in the hemitransected nicotine-treated group: CAUD MARG = 50 ± 9, CAUD MED = 74 ± 15, CAUD CENT = 53 ± 11. Statistical analysis according to the two-tailed Mann-Whitney U-test. *$p < .05$, **$p < .01$; ***$p < .002$. For abbreviations see Fig. 6 (33).

Lesions are known to occur in the dorsolateral neostriatum leading to regional deficits in striatal function. Benfenati et al (37) performed the regional analysis of D_1 and D_2 DA transmission 7 days after transient forebrain ischemia, using receptor autoradiography and immunocytochemistry. ^{3}H-SCH-23390, ^{3}H-sulpiride, and ^{3}H-forskolin were used as markers for D_1 receptors, D_2 receptors and adenylate cyclase, respectively (39–41). The intracellular effector mechanisms linked to D_1 receptors were analyzed by means of immunocytochemistry using antibodies against DA-and-cAMP-regulated phosphoprotein (DARPP-32; ref 42). It was found that transient forebrain ischemia produces multiple deficits in DA D_1 transmission in the lateral neostriatum of the rat. In fact, all the markers for D_1 transmission showed a patchy disappearance within the lateral and especially the dorsolateral part of the neostriatum (Fig. 8). Of substantial interest also was the observation that the distribution of D_2 receptors in the neostriatum was unaffected when evaluated 7 days after the ischemic insult (Fig. 9). It should be underlined that the ^{3}H-SCH-23390 and ^{3}H-forskolin binding sites were substantially preserved outside the area of the D_1 receptor and adenylate cyclase disappearance. Furthermore, the patchlike areas of disappearance of D_1 receptors, adenylate cyclase, and DARPP-32-like immunoreactivity in the dorsolateral

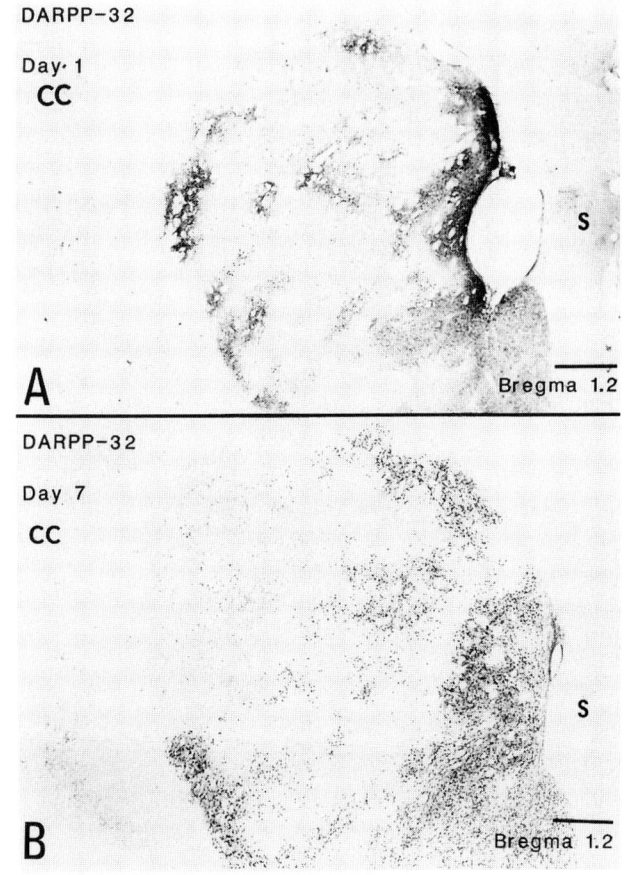

FIG. 8. Coronal section at the Bregma level 1.2 showing DARPP-32 immunoreactivity in the striatum, day 1 (**A**) and day 7 (**B**) after reperfusion. The DARPP-32 immunoreactivity is lost in patches of neostriatum due to the ischemic lesion. The animals were subjected to a four-vessel occlusion (see ref. 38). The bar length is 500 μm.

striatum were associated with a disappearance of nerve cells as evaluated in Nissl stainings.

These results suggest that the observed neurochemical phenomena are related to ischemic injury of dopaminoceptive striatal nerve cells. These observations are in line with the evidence that the D_1 transmission line is exclusively located in intrinsic striatal nerve cells. It should also be stressed that 80% of the D_2 receptors are located on intrinsic striatal neurons (43). Electrophysiological results suggest the coexistence of D_1 and D_2 receptors in a substantial number of striatal nerve cells (44). It seems possible that many of the nerve cells in the lateral part of the neostriatum may survive in the postischemic period but develop multiple severe deficits in D_1 transmission in the presence of intact D_2 receptors. Thus, these cells possess a markedly unbalanced ratio of D_1 to D_2 transmission, altering the metabolism of the striatal nerve cells and their electrical activity. In view of the inhibitory effects of D_1 receptors and the excitatory effects of D_2 receptors, this alteration in the ratio of D_1 and D_2 receptor activity can play an important role in the development of the striatal damage.

Based on the results on a marked reduction in the ratio of striatal D_1 to D_2 receptor density seen after ischemic injury, it is of substantial interest to note the possible existence of a DA receptor subtype imbalance in schizophrenia (45). In postmortem brains from schizophrenic patients a significant 56% increase was observed in D_2 receptor density, while the DA D_1 receptor density was significantly reduced by 43%.

In our analysis of the effects of transient forebrain ischemia on striatal D_1 and D_2 transmission, we have also noticed that after 7 days of reperfusion the reductions of DARPP-32 immunoreactivity are associated with increases of TH immunoreactivity present in the striatal nerve terminals (Fig. 10; ref 13). Thus, a compensatory response appears to have taken place in the DA nerve terminals present in the area with multiple deficits in the D_1 transmission line. It seems possible that such a highly matched response in the presynaptic DA terminals leading to increased TH immunoreactivity can be produced by the secretion of trophic factors from the partly damaged dopaminoceptive striatal nerve cells as well as from nerve terminals innervating this region. The trophic factors may then be

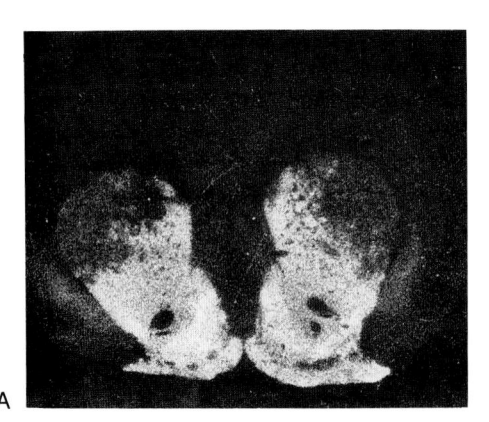

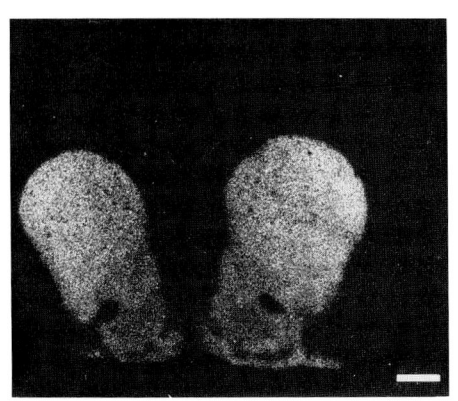

FIG. 9. Autoradiograms of ^{3}H-SCH-23390 (**A:** 1 nM) and ^{3}H-sulpiride (**B:** 15 nM) binding sites in ischemic rat (2 days after reperfusion). Bregma level = 1.2 mm; *bar* = 1 mm.

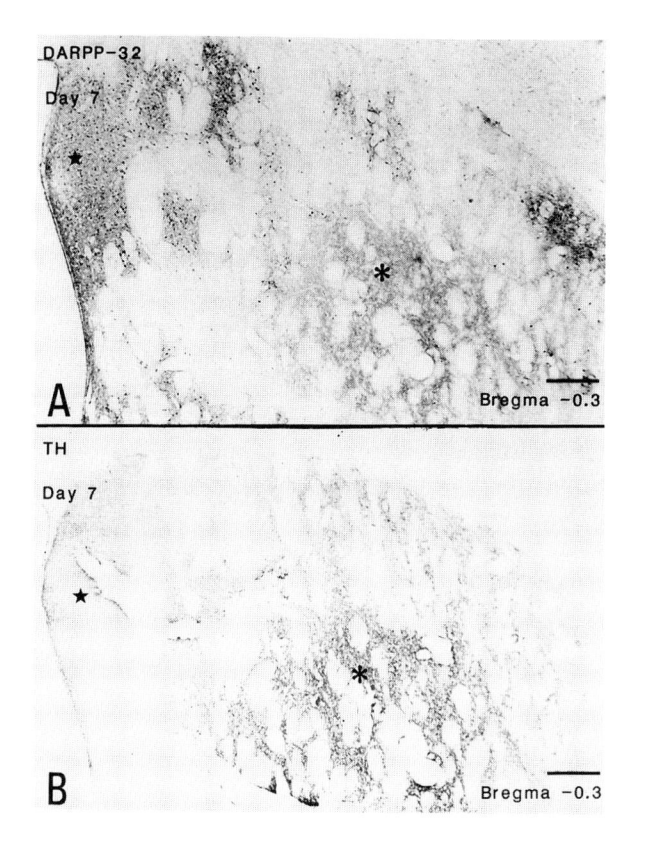

FIG. 10. Coronal section at the Bregma level −0.3 from animals subjected to the four-vessel occlusion. The rats were sacrificed on day 7. **A:** DARPP-32 immunoreactivity shown mainly in the dorsomedial part of the striatum (*star*). The ischemic lesion is primarily found in the central and lateral part of striatum (*asterisk*). **B:** TH immunoreactivity is shown in a consecutive section demonstrating that a loss of DARPP-32 immunoreactivity is often associated with increased TH immunoreactivity (*star*). Bar indicates 100 μm (33).

retrogradely transported to their corresponding DA perikarya in the ventral midbrain, where they may initiate an increased gene expression of proteins essential for the promotion of DA transmission and for a possible sprouting response. It should be considered that such types of discrete compensatory responses may take place also in the schizophrenic brain in those DA nerve-terminal systems innervating the lesioned areas. In conclusion, these data underline the possibility of pathological processes affecting only a subtype specific transmission line at the synaptic level leading to a functional imbalance in the electrometabolic activity of the dopaminoceptive cells. Furthermore, evidence has been provided that such postsynaptic changes can produce profound presynaptic alterations in the DA terminals, which could, however, also represent degenerative phenomena.

In the four-vessel model of transient forebrain ischemia the possible protective effect of the cyclic ganglioside analogue AGF2 was evaluated by means of an immunocytochemical analysis of DARPP-32 immunoreactivity in combination with computer-assisted image analysis at various rostrocaudal levels of the neostriatum (46). It was found that chronic AGF2 treatment in a dose of 5 mg/kg intraperitoneally (IP) for a period of 6 days starting the day after the ischemic insult partly counteracted the disappearance of DARPP-32 immunoreactivity within the dorsolateral neostriatum (Fig. 11). Treatment with AGF2 may accelerate the morphological recovery of striatal nerve cells in the dorsolateral striatum after transient forebrain ischemia. Thus AGF2 appears capable of restoring the biosynthetic pathways, leading to improved DARPP-32 synthesis. It should be considered that the phosphorylated form of this protein produces phosphatase inhibition. In this way, improved phosphorylation processes also take place in other transmission lines colocalized with the D_1 transmission line (47). These morphological and biochemical effects of AGF2 also improved the recovery of striatal function, since ganglioside treatment can increase the step-through latency time and decrease the apomorphine-induced stereotypy score, which are altered in this model of ischemia. It should also be considered that in this way the imbalance in D_1 and D_2 transmission lines is improved, which also may help nerve-cell survival (see above).

The ganglioside GM_1 appears to have multiple sites of action. For example, the ganglioside GM_1 seems capable of switching protein phosphorylation processes from protein kinase C–dependent protein phosphorylation to calcium/calmodulin protein kinase-2–dependent protein phosphorylation (Fig. 12). Inhibition of protein kinase C may be exerted via effects on translocation (48) or through direct effects on protein kinase C in the membrane (49). This switch in the protein phosphorylation processes appears to be important, since protein kinase C–dependent protein phosphorylation mediates many of the effects of the excitatory aminoacid transmitters, which are

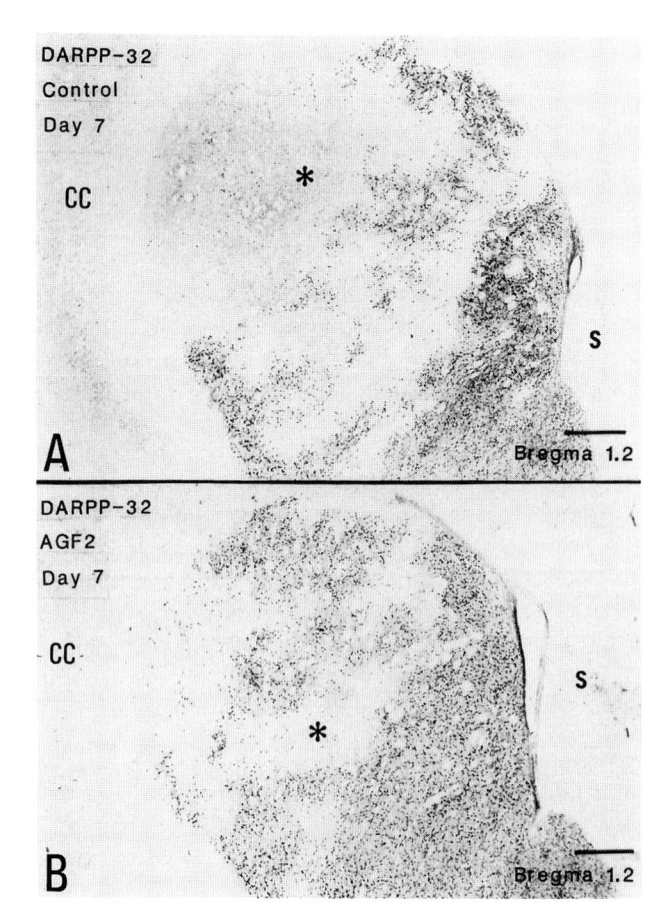

FIG. 11. Coronal section of striatum at day 7 showing DARPP-32 immunoreactivity. The animals were subjected to the four-vessel occlusion. The ischemic lesion is indicated by an *asterisk*. **A:** Animal not subjected to any pharmacological treatment. **B:** 24 hours after the lesion was treated with the GM_1 analogue AGF2. An increase in the DARPP-32 immunoreactivity area is found in the AGF2 group compared with the control group. *Bar* indicates 500 μm (47).

FIG. 12. Schematic representation on possible mechanisms underlying the trophic effects of the ganglioside AGF2 in the Pulsinelli model of transient global cerebral ischemia (13).

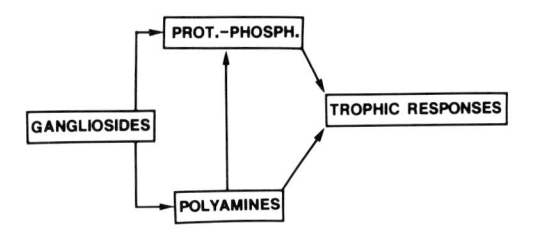

TROPHIC ACTIONS OF GANGLIOSIDES IN STRIATUM MAY INVOLVE

a) MAINTAINED LEVELS OF DARPP-32 AND D1 RECEPTORS

b) POSSIBLE SWITCH FROM PROTEIN KINASE C TO Ca^{++}/CALMODULIN DEPENDENT PROTEIN PHOSPHORYLATION.

c) ACTIVATION BY GANGLIOSIDES OF ORNITHINE DECARBOXYLASE AND SAT ACTIVITY, LEADING TO INCREASED PUTRESCINE FORMATION AND RELEASE, WHICH INTER ALIA INHIBITS PROTEIN KINASE C TRANSLOCATION INTO THE MEMBRANE AND LEADS TO INCREASED RIBOSOMAL RNA SYNTHESIS AND ACCUMULATION.

d) INCREASED ACTIVATION OF ASTROGLIA BY GANGLIOSIDES VIA INCREASED FORMATION AND RELEASE OF PUTRESCINE.

well known to exert neurotoxic actions (50). (For other possible sites of action of GM_1, see ref 13 and also Figs. 5 and 12).

Based on these observations it seems possible that, if the possible reduction of D_1 transmission found in relation to D_2 transmission in the schizophrenic brain is related to injury in dopaminoceptive nerve-cell populations, this may, at least in part, be reversed by ganglioside treatment. We then postulate that gangliosides can also reverse longstanding deficits in nerve cells. This possibility exists, since gangliosides can improve morphological and functional recovery after brain injury (see Table 2; refs 12,51,52).

CONTROL MECHANISMS OF DOPAMINE SYNAPSES

Peptide Modulation of the Dopamine Transmission Lines

Neurotensin/Dopamine D_2 Receptor Interactions. Neurotensin became of interest in the schizophrenic field when Nemeroff and collaborators demonstrated that NT given centrally can exert neurolepticlike activities (53,54). However, NT could not displace DA, DA agonists, or DA antagonists from their respective binding sites in membrane preparations from the brain. Nor could NT antagonize DA-induced activation of adenylate cyclase activity in striatal homogenates (53). Instead, we have in a series of papers (53,55–57) obtained evidence that the neurolepticlike activity of NT is at least in part related to an antagonistic interaction between NT and D_2 receptors in the nerve-cell membrane of dopaminoceptive cells in the forebrain, especially within the nucleus accumbens. This antagonistic interaction between the two receptors probably takes place in the local circuits of the forebrain and may involve also NT/DA co-storing synapses. The possible role of co-transmitters in monoamine neurons is schematically illustrated in Figs 1 and 2.

We could demonstrate that neurotensin in nanomole concentrations produces a concentration-related reduction in the binding affinity of ^{3}H-N-propylnorapomorphine (NPA) in rat striatal and limbic membranes;

the reduction of affinity is on the order of 30% to 40% respectively (Fig. 13). Under the present in vitro conditions NPA only binds to D_2 receptors (57). It has also been found that this marked modulation by NT only takes place at D_2 agonist and not at D_2 antagonist binding sites.

Based on these results it should be investigated whether indeed there exist alterations in the control mechanisms of the DA synapse in schizophrenia, especially in the regulation of the D_1 and D_2 receptor populations. Thus, it should be considered that the wiring of the nerve-cell membrane with regard to its regulation of the D_2 receptor could be altered in schizophrenia, so that the increased number of D_2 receptors found cannot be appropriately regulated with regard to their sensitivity. Obviously the understanding of the mechanisms orienting the decoding of the DA signal towards a certain pattern should be considered of paramount importance for understanding the abnormalities in DA transmission in the schizophrenic brain. From a general standpoint, understanding the wiring of receptor circuits of the nerve-cell membrane will be as important as understanding the wiring by which neurons are organized (58). The hypothesis is introduced that one major error in schizophrenia is the loss of the restraining influence of a number of adjacent receptors on D_2 receptor efficacy exerted on D_2 receptors via intramembrane receptor–receptor interactions (D_2 receptor dysregulation hypothesis).

Presynaptic Modulation by Neurotensin Receptors of D_2 Receptors

This analysis has given an important functional correlate to the binding studies reported above. Thus, in microdialysis experiments in the neostriatum it has been possible to show that NT in concentrations of 10 nM in the perfusate can modulate the D_2 autoreceptor function (59). Thus, this concentration (see Fig. 14) of NT perfused via the microdialysis probe markedly attenuates the inhibitory actions of apomorphine on DA release after systemic administration. Neurotensin alone in this concentration has no effect on DA release. Since only 5% to 10% of the amount perfused will reach the brain tissue outside the probe, NT in concentrations of 1 nM appears to be effective in reducing the D_2 autoreceptor

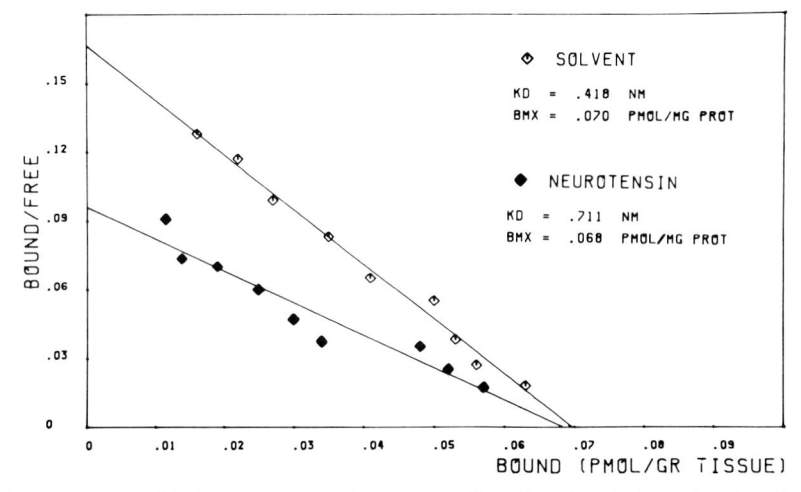

FIG. 13. Representative binding curves and corresponding Scatchard plots showing the effects of 10-nM NT on the binding characteristics of ^{3}H-N-propylnorapomorphine (^{3}NPA)–labeled D_2 dopamine receptors in rat striatal membranes. The experiments were performed under equilibrium conditions.

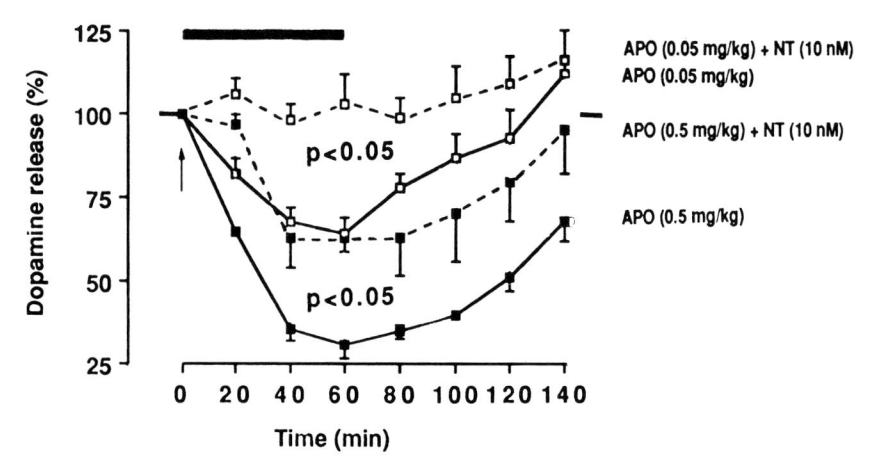

FIG. 14. The effects of local perfusion with neurotensin (NT; 10 n*M*) on the levels of dopamine in neostriatal dialysates were analyzed in a male rat anesthetized with halothane treated with apomorphine (APO; 0.05 and 0.5 mg/kg, SC). The results are expressed as a percentage of the mean of three basal values. Means ± SEM are shown. The *bar* indicates the duration of NT perfusion, and the *arrow* shows when APO was injected. The peak values of reduction of DA release were observed after comparing treatments with apomorphine and apomorphine + NT. The APO effect in both doses is significantly ($p < .01$) counteracted by the NT perfusion (Student's *t*-test); $n = 4-7$ (59).

function. Increasing the dose of apomorphine means that NT can no longer effectively inhibit the apomorphine action on DA release. Results indicate that the reduction in affinity of the D_2 receptors as demonstrated in the experiments on membrane preparations may make an important contribution to the counteraction of the inhibitory action of apomorphine on DA release.

Functional Support for an Antagonistic Postsynaptic Interaction Between Neurotensin and D_2 Receptors

When injected into the nucleus accumbens, NT causes a dose-dependent inhibition of DA-induced locomotor activity, which may indicate postsynaptic interactions (60). Amphetamine-induced locomotion can be counteracted in a similar way (52). The existence of an antagonistic interaction in the nerve-cell membrane between NT and D_2 DA receptors in the nucleus accumbens can explain these findings. Further support for our hypothesis has recently been obtained by Merlo Pich et al. (61; see also ref 62). Thus, it was found that NT antagonism of DA-dependent locomotor hyperactivity is substantially increased after a 6-hydroxy-DA-induced degeneration of the DA nerve-terminal networks of the nucleus accumbens (Fig. 15).

In conclusion, studies on NT/DA D_2 receptor interactions have indicated that NT in the local circuits of the striatum and the nucleus accumbens can inhibit D_2 autoreceptor function and postsynaptic D_2 receptor function. The consequence of this antagonistic interactions at the pre- and postsynaptic level may be a switch from D_2 towards D_1 transmission. Transmission of the D_1 receptor may be absolutely increased in view of the increased release of DA produced by the inhibition of D_2 autoreceptor function and possible reduction of antagonistic D_1/D_2 receptor interactions (see ref 63). Thus, one important role of NT in striatal and limbic circuits may be to switch the synapse from D_2 to D_1 transmission.

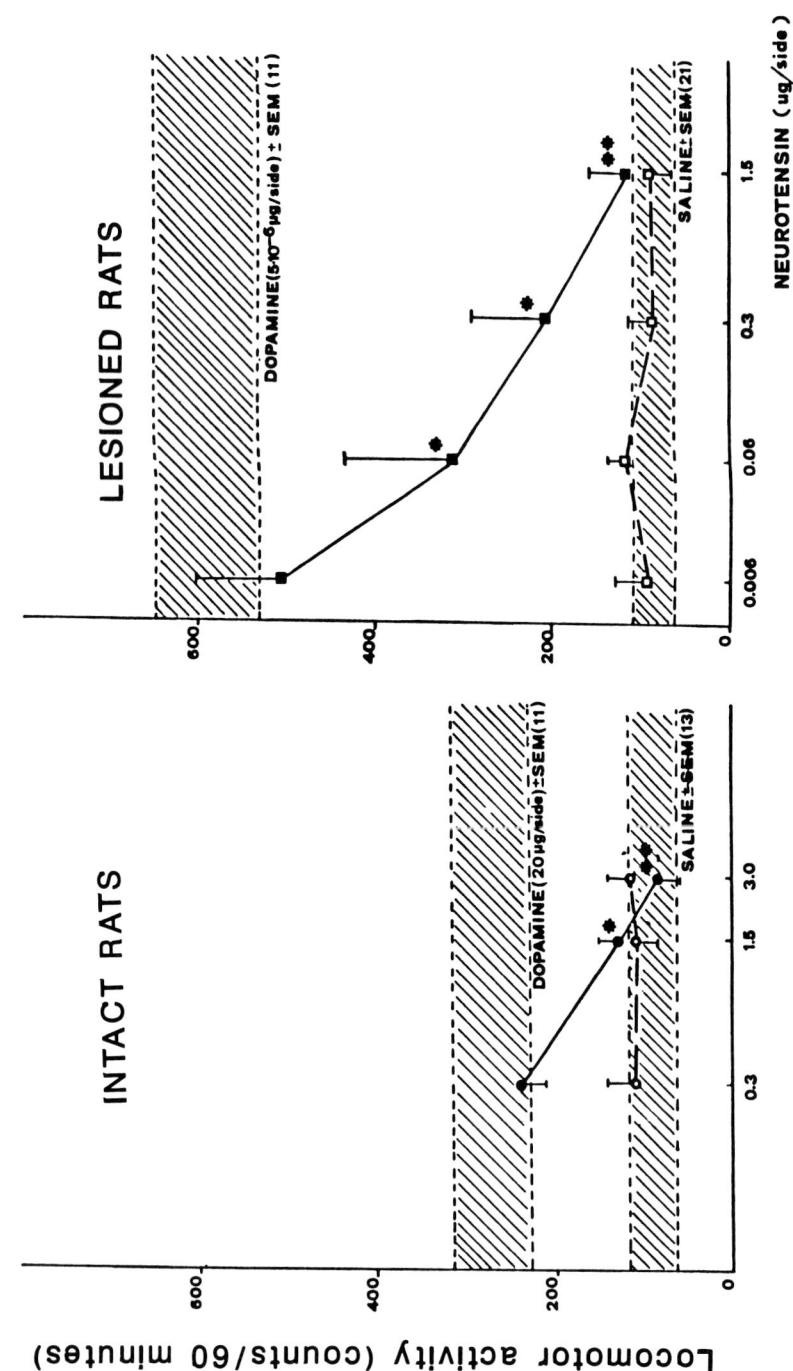

FIG. 15. Effects of bilateral microinjections of various doses of NT and a fixed dose of DA into the nucleus accumbens in vehicle-treated rats (left panel) and 6-OH-DA-lesioned rats (right panel). DA, 5 pg/side and 20 μg/side, was given to 6-OH-DA-lesioned rats and vehicle-treated rats, respectively. The data (means ± SEM) represent the number of photocell interruptions per 60 minutes. Shaded areas represent the mean ± SEM of rats microinjected with a fixed dose of DA alone or saline. Six to eight animals were used for each dose tested. Statistical comparisons were carried out versus the respective control groups (6-OH-DA-lesioned and vehicle-treated rats microinjected with DA alone) by means of Dunnett's test. $*p < .05$; $**p < .01$ (61). $\square$, $\bigcirc$ = saline + NT. $\blacksquare$, $\bullet$ = DA + NT.

Effects of Neuroleptics on Neurotensin Concentrations in Forebrain Regions

The studies with neuroleptic drugs have further emphasized that DA neurotransmission can regulate NT transmission. Thus, acute increases of NT levels have been demonstrated in the neostriatum and nucleus accumbens without any effects on NT levels in amygdaloid and anteromedial frontal cortex upon acute treatment with selective D_2 receptor antagonists or unselective D_1 and D_2 receptor antagonists (64–66). Instead the D_1 receptor antagonist SCH-23390 acutely induces a selective reduction of striatal NT levels. Of substantial interest are the results that chronic treatment with clozapine and fluperlapine, which do not produce extrapyramidallike side effects, does not lead to increases of NT levels in the nucleus accumbens and striatum. In contrast, drugs that do produce extrapyramidallike side effects, such as chlorpromazine and haloperidol, increase NT levels in the neostriatum and nucleus accumbens also upon chronic treatment. The hypothesis is now given that the development of extrapyramidallike side effects such as hyperkinesias is related to a blockade of NT release, leading to an accumulation of NT within interneurons in the forebrain. Based on the above effects, the D_2 receptor appears to facilitate NT release, while the D_1 receptor may inhibit NT release. The lack of extrapyramidallike side effects seen with chronic treatment for clozapine and fluperlapine may then be related to a proper ratio of blockade of D_1 and D_2 receptors, so that NT can again be released. As stated above, the D_2 receptor function may then become counteracted both pre- and postsynaptically leading to maintenance of DA release and inhibition of D_2 but not of D_1 receptor function, reducing the development of D_2 receptor supersensitivity (Fig. 16).

POSSIBLE NEW ASPECTS ON THE PHARMACOLOGICAL APPROACH TO TREATING SCHIZOPHRENIA

Prevention by the Ganglioside GM_1 of the Development of D_2 Receptor Upregulation Following Chronic Haloperidol Treatment

Agnati et al (67) have demonstrated that simultaneous daily treatment with the gan-

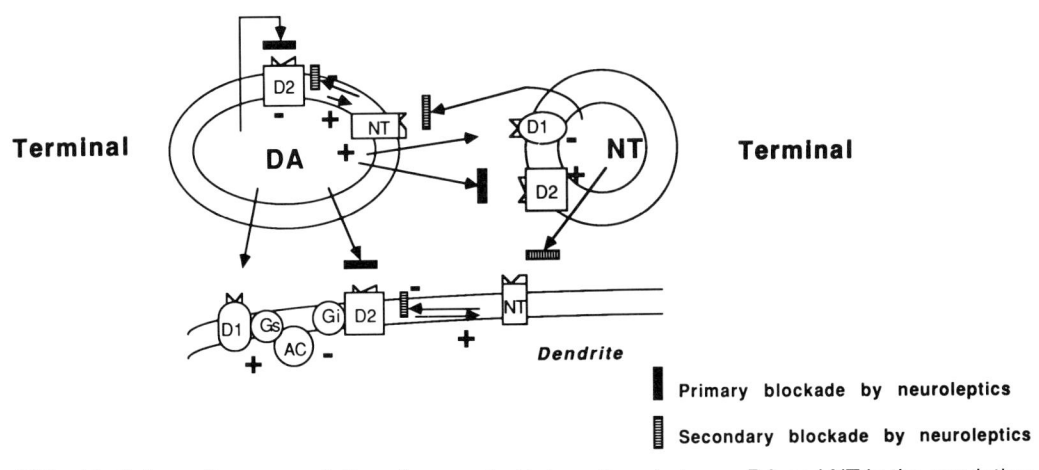

FIG. 16. Schematic representation of suggested interactions between DA and NT in the regulation of dopamine transmission lines by neuroleptics in the basal ganglia. The primary blockade of dopamine D_2 receptors by neuroleptics and the selective stimulation of D_1 receptors may inhibit NT release from adjacent NT nerve terminals, leading to a decreased inhibition of dendritic D_2 receptors and of D_2 autoreceptors by NT receptors.

glioside GM_1 in doses of 10 mg/kg-day significantly counteracted the increase in D_2 receptor density produced by haloperidol (0.7 mg/kg IP) given chronically. The radioligand used was ^3H-spiperone and the ganglioside GM_1 did not influence the affinity of these binding sites either alone or in combination with haloperidol treatment. The mechanism of action for the ability of GM_1 to prevent the upregulation of D_2 receptors upon D_2 receptor blockade is unknown but could involve multiple sites of action including effects on gene expression of D_2 receptors. It may be that the ganglioside GM_1, through effects on membrane fluidity, adenylate cyclase, and protein kinase C (26,30,49,68,69), improves the coupling of the D_2 receptors and its biological effector in the membrane; if so, a low dose of haloperidol will not be able to block the D_2 receptor function sufficiently to alter the turnover of the D_2 receptors so that an increase in D_2 receptor density takes place. Present findings are also supported by behavioral evidence that the ganglioside GM_1 can counteract the development of behavioral supersensitivity seen following the blockade of D_2 receptors (Toffano et al., unpublished observations). Thus, it seems possible that the combined treatment with GM_1 and neuroleptics could be of value in the treatment of schizophrenia, since in the presence of the ganglioside GM_1 the electrical effects and consequences of D_2 receptor blockade, using a low dose of haloperidol, may still be obtained without the development of tolerance to the D_2 receptor blockade.

Prevention by Uridine of Enhancement of Dopamine Release Induced by Acute Haloperidol Treatment as Revealed by Microdialysis

The nucleoside uridine improves brain metabolism after a severe hypoglycemia (70). Furthermore, uridine has anticonvulsant actions (71) and effects on central GABAergic transmission (72). Recent indications have also been obtained that chronic uridine treatment reduces striatal D_2 receptor density and increases the turnover rate of these receptors in young but not adult rats (73). Thus, D_2 transmission as well as GABA transmission (74) appears to be modulated by uridine treatment.

Effects of uridine have been further characterized on DA transmission by measurements of striatal release using intracerebral microdialysis and by studying effects on DA-dependent behaviors. In view of the important role D_2 receptor blockade plays for the antipsychotic activity of neuroleptic drugs, it was tested whether uridine could prevent the homeostatic changes occurring in DA release upon chronic haloperidol treatment as analyzed following an acute challenge with haloperidol, since such a challenge leads to a compensatory enhancement of DA release (74).

Uridine (15 mg/kg-d), haloperidol (1 mg/kg-d) and uridine + haloperidol in the doses indicated above were given to rats for 3 weeks. After 1 week of cessation of treatment, basal striatal DA release was analyzed as well as enhancement of DA release produced by an acute dose of haloperidol (2 mg/kg IP). DA release was evaluated by means of intracerebral microdialysis. Behavioral tests involved haloperidol-induced catalepsy and apomorphine-induced stereotypies and were performed about 1 week after drug withdrawal. As seen in Fig. 17, acute administration of haloperidol produced clearcut and sustained increases of DA release in the group treated with haloperidol alone. This peak increase of DA release was delayed and also less pronounced than in the control group. Of substantial interest was the observation that chronic uridine treatment alone or in association with chronic haloperidol treatment significantly reduced the increases of DA release produced by an acute injection of haloperidol. Acute treatment with uridine was ineffec-

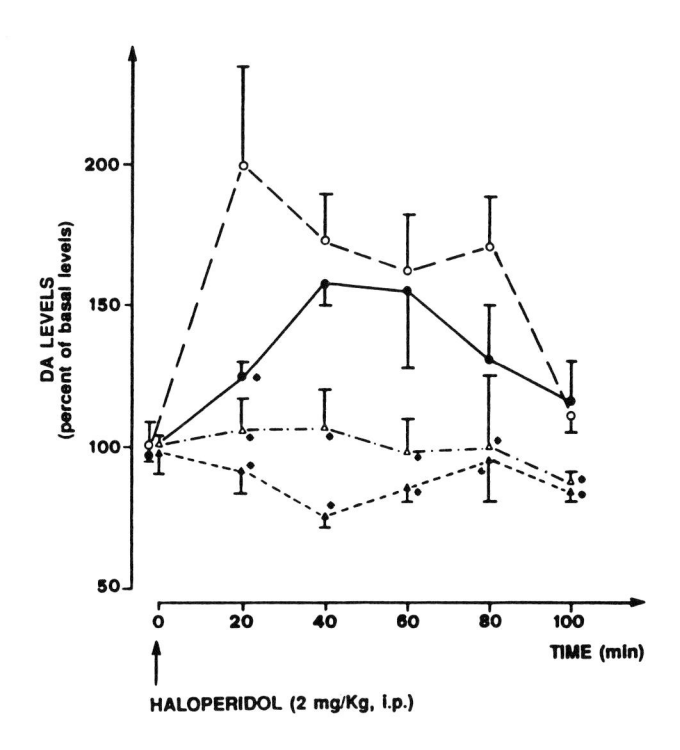

FIG. 17. Time course of DA levels in 20-minute perfusate samples after acute haloperidol administration (2 mg/kg IP) in halothane-anesthetized rats that had been chronically treated with uridiine (*dots and dashes*), uridine + haloperidol (*short dashes*), haloperidol (*solid line*), or saline (*long dashes*) as described in Fig. 1. The results are expressed as percentages of the mean of three basal samples collected before the haloperidol injection. Means ± SEM are shown ($n = 5$). The basal DA levels were not significantly different among the various groups; the mean (± SEM) was 6.87 ± 1.75 fmol/μl. Statistical analysis was performed according to the Dunn test; *$p < .05$ vs control group (saline treatment plus acute haloperidol challenge) (74).

tive in modulating the release induced by an acute haloperidol injection. Behavioral results were in agreement with the neurochemical data. Thus, in the group treated chronically with uridine a significant enhancement in the stereotypy score was demonstrated after injection of apomorphine. Furthermore, the catalepsy induced by an acute haloperidol injection was enhanced in relation to the effects observed in the saline-treated rats.

The important observation in these experiments (74) is the ability of chronic treatment with uridine to counteract the increase in DA overflow caused by an acute treatment with haloperidol. Furthermore, the marked reduction of haloperidol-induced DA release in the neostriatum after chronic treatment with uridine may explain the ability of this treatment to enhance markedly the cataleptic action of acute haloperidol treatment.

The mechanism of action of uridine on DA transmission is presently unknown. However, uridine can competitively inhibit GABA binding to membrane preparations from various brain areas and also counteract bicuculline-induced increases in the cerebellar content of cGMP (72). It seems possible then that uridine can activate GABA receptors. We have previously shown that $GABA_B$ agonists such as baclophen can reduce DA turnover in nigrostriatal and especially mesolimbocortical DA systems (75). Furthermore, the $GABA_B$ agonists were highly effective in counteracting the neuroleptic-induced increases of DA turnover, especially within the subcortical and cortical limbic areas (75–77). Based on these findings we suggested that it may be possible to improve treatment of schizophrenia by combined treatment with neuroleptics and GABAergic drugs, especially $GABA_B$ agonists such as baclophen. It therefore seems reasonable that chronic uridine treatment can enhance the sensitivity of the GABA receptor mechanisms regulating the nigrostriatal as well as the mesolimbic DA neurons. This would explain the ability of chronic uridine treatment to reduce striatal DA overflow. Thus, uridine may potentiate the effects of chronic D_2 DA receptor blockade induced by neuroleptic drugs. Provided that similar events also take place in the mesolimbic DA systems after combined uridine and neuroleptic treatment, there may be a role for uridine in the treatment of schizophrenia. Combined treatment may then allow a reduction of the dose of the neuroleptic compound, which is of value in view of the putative neurotoxic actions of haloperidol (78). In support of our hypothesis are suggestions that the antipsychotic effects of neuroleptics not only involve DA receptor blockade but also the development of reductions in DA release, associated with reductions of plasma HVA levels (79).

Other mechanisms of uridine action should of course also be considered; it seems likely that uridine may act on multiple sites like the gangliosides. Thus, uridine is a precursor for RNA synthesis. Furthermore, in view of, for example, the existence of purine receptors in cellular control systems (70), it cannot be excluded that uridine can act on putative pyrimidine binding sites in brain cells. Another possibility for explaining the cell regulatory function of uridine is that uridine may enhance the formation of cytosine triphosphate (CTP). Uridine can be phosphorylated by a uridine kinase to uridinate monophosphate and subsequently to uridine triphosphate (UTP). The increased levels of CTP would in turn enhance the resynthesis of phosphatidyl inositol, having an important role in signal transduction (80). Such actions may also contribute to the ability of chronic uridine treatment to reduce the level of D_2 receptors and enhance the turnover rate in the striatum of young rats (73).

Taken together, the studies with gangliosides and uridine offer the prospect of new drugs to be used in combination with neuroleptics to improve the treatment of schizophrenia.

CONCLUSIONS

This chapter has reviewed morphological and functional (NT-DA receptor interactions) plasticity phenomena in the ascending mesotelencephalic DA pathways in order to give new insights on the pathogenesis of schizophrenia and give rise to the DA D_2 dysregulation hypothesis of schizophrenia. Even if the final neuropathological outcomes may be similar, "schizophrenia should be considered not as a disease, but, like epilepsy, as a syndrome, recognized by a collection of signs and symptoms, which have diverse pathogenesis" (31). It seems possible that the alterations in the prefrontal and limbic cortex may make important contributions to the appearance of D_2 receptor changes in the basal ganglia of schizophrenic brains. These changes may thus, in part, be the consequence of a diaschisis phenomenon secondary to a primary involvement of the prefrontal cortex. The study on morphological and functional plasticity in the DA systems can give new openings for the pathogenesis and therapy of schizophrenia. Three main issues have been discussed: first is the possibility of protecting the nervous tissue, or of enhancing its morphofunctional reparative responses to metabolic and toxic insults by means of gangliosides and nicotine; second is that NT receptors via an intramembrane receptor-receptor interaction reduces striatal D_2 but not D_1 receptor function pre- and postsynaptically, in turn reducing D_2 receptor supersensitivity development and then the development of schizophrenia and tardive diskinesias; third, is the evidence that a more subtle control of the DA transmission can be obtained by means of the administration of gangliosides (GM_1) and nucleosides (uridine). The results on GM_1 and uridine effects on the response of the DA synapse to chronic neuroleptic treatment demonstrate that it is possible to control the DA-receptor supersensitivity development and to reduce the neuroleptic dosage with maintained inhibition of DA transmission. The relevance of these findings for treatment of schizophrenic patients should be assessed by means of clinical trials.

ACKNOWLEDGMENTS

This work has been supported by a grant (04X-715) from the Swedish Medical Research Council, by the CNR, MRI, and by the Petrus and Augusta Hedlund Stiftelse, and by the American Parkinson's Disease Association. We are grateful to Monia Särd for excellent secretarial help.

REFERENCES

1. Kelsoe JR, Cadet JL, Pickar D, Weinberger DR. Quantitative neuroanatomy in schizophrenia. *Arch Gen Psychiatry* 1988;45:533–541.
2. Stevens CD, Altshuler LL, Bogerts B, Falkai P. Quantitative study of gliosis in schizophrenia and Huntington's chorea. *Biol Psychiatry* 1988;24:697–700.
3. Weinberger DR. Implications of normal brain development for the pathogenesis of schizophrenia. *Arch Gen Psychiat* 1987;44:660–669.
4. Dahlström A, Fuxe K. Evidence for the existence of monoamine-containing neurons in the central nervous system. I. Demonstration of monoamines in the cell bodies of brain stem neurons. *Acta Physiol Scand* 1964;62(Suppl 232):1–55.
5. Fuxe K, Hökfelt T, Johansson O, Jonsson G, Lidbrink P, Ljungdahl ÅA. The origin of the dopamine nerve terminals in limbic and frontal cortex. Evidence for meso-cortico dopamine neurons. *Brain Res* 1974;82:349–355.
6. Hökfelt T, Fuxe K, Johansson O, Ljungdahl Å. Pharmacohistochemical evidence of the existence of dopamine nerve terminals in the limbic cortex. *Eur J Pharmacol* 1974;25:108–112.
7. Hökfelt T, Ljungdahl Å, Fuxe K, Johansson O. Dopamine nerve terminals in the rat limbic cortex: aspects of the dopamine hypothesis of schizophrenia. *Science* 1974;184:177–179.
8. Lindbrink P, Jonsson G, Fuxe K. Selective reserpine-resistant accumulation of catecholamines in central dopamine neurons after DOPA administration. *Brain Res* 1974;67:439–456.
9. Agnati LF, Fuxe K, Andersson K, Benfenati F, Cortelli P, D'Alessandro R. The mesolimbic dopamine system: evidence for a high amine turnover and for a heterogeneity of the dopamine neuron population. *Neurosci Lett* 1980;18:45–51.
10. Thierry AM, Stinus L, Blanc G, Glowinski J. Some evidence for the existence of dopaminergic neurons in the rat cortex. *Brain Res* 1973;50:230–234.
11. Härfstrand A, Fuxe K, Cintra A, et al. Glucocorticoid receptor immunoreactivity in monoaminergic neurons of rat brain. *Proc Nat Acad Sci USA* 1986;83:9779–9783.
12. Agnati LF, Zini I, Zoli M, et al. Regeneration in the central nervous system: Concepts and facts. In: Symon L, ed, *Advances and technical standards in neurosurgery.* Wien: Springer-Verlag, 1988;4–50.
13. Agnati LF, Fuxe K. Nigrostriatal dopamine neurons and protein phosphorylation. Focus on D1 transmission in basal and ischemic states and protective effects of gangliosides. *Lab. Invest.* 1990 (in press).
14. Fisher MH, Welker C, Waisman HA. Generalized growth retardation in rats induced by prenatal exposure to methylazoxymethanol acetate. *Teratology* 1972;5:223–232.
15. Matsumuto H, Higa HM. Studies on methylaxocymethanol, the aglycone of cycasin: methylation of nucleic acid in vitro. *Biochem J* 1966;98:20c.
16. Dambska M, Haddad R, Kozlowski PB, Lee MH, Shek J. Telencephalic architectonics in the brains of rats with graded degree of microencephaly. *Acta Neuropathol, Berlin* 1982;58:203–209.
17. Johnston MV, Coyle JT. Histological and neurochemical effects of fetal treatment with methylazoxymethanol on rat neocortex in adulthood. *Brain Res* 1979;170:135–155.
18. Hallman H, Jonsson G. Monoamine neurotransmitter metabolism in microencephalic rat brain after prenatal methylazoxymethanol treatment. *Brain Res Bull* 1984;13:383–389.
19. Johnston MV, Coyle JT. Cytotoxic lesion and the development of transmitter system. *Trends Neurosci* 1982;5:153–156.
20. Zoli M, Merlo Pich E, Cimino M, et al. Morphometrical and microdensitometrical studies on peptide- and tyrosine hydroxylase–like immunoreactivities in the forebrain of rats prenatally exposed to methylazoxymethanol acetate. *Developmental Brain Res* 1990;51:45–61.
21. Morrison JH, Magistretti PJ, Benoit R, Bloom FE. The distribution and morphological characteristics of the intracortical VIP-positive cell: an immunohistochemical analysis. *Brain Res* 1984;292:269–282.
22. Fuxe K, Hökfelt T, Said SI, Mutt V. Vasoactive intestinal polypeptide and the nervous system: immunohistochemical evidence for localization in central and peripheral neurons, particularly intracortical neurons of the cerebral cortex. *Neurosci Lett* 1977;5:241–246.
23. Abbracchio MP, Cimino M, Di Luca M, Mennuni L, Zaratin P, Cattabeni F. Target-dependency of catecholaminergic afferents in an animal model of microencephaly induced by prenatal methylazoxymethanol administration. *Soc Neurosci Abs* 1988;14:77.7.
24. Markey SP, Johannessen JN, Chiueh CC, Burns RS, Herkenham MA. Intraneuronal generation of a pyridinium metabolite may cause drug-induced parkinsonism. *Nature* 1984;311:464–467.

25. Janson AM, Agnati LF, Fuxe K, et al. GM1 ganglioside protects against the 1-methyl-4-phenyl-1,2,3,6-tetrahydropyridine-induced degeneration of nigrostriatal dopamine neurons in the black mouse. *Acta Physiol Scand,* 1988;132: 587–588.
26. Ando S, Tanaka Y, Kon K. Membrane aging of the brain synaptosomes with special reference to gangliosides. In: Tattemanti RW, Ledeen RW, Sandhoff K, Nagai Y, Toffano G, eds, *Gangliosides and Neuronal Plasticity, Fidia Res Ser,* vol 6. Padova: Liviana Press, 1986;105–112.
27. Toffano G, Savoini G, Aldinio C, et al. Effects of gangliosides on the functional recovery of damaged brain. *Adv Exp Med Biol* 1984;174:475–488.
28. Tettamanti G, Sonnino S, Ghidoni R, Masserini M, Venerando B. Chemical and functional properties of gangliosides. Their possible implication in the membrane-mediated transfer of information. In: *Physics of Amphiphiles: Micelles, Vesicles, and Microemulsions* XC Corso, Soc Italiana di Fisica, Bologna Italy, 1985;607–636.
29. Wieraszko A, Seifert W. Evidence for the functional role of monosialoganglioside GM1 in synaptic transmission in the rat hippocampus. *Brain Research* 1986;371:305–313.
30. Von Euler G, Fuxe K, Bondy S. Ganglioside GM_1 prevents and reverses toluene induced increases in membrane fluidity and calcium levels in rat brain synaptosomes. *Brain Res* 1990; 508:210–214.
31. Trimble MR, ed. *Biological Psychiatry.* New York: Wiley, 1988.
32. Slater E, Roth M, eds. *Clinical Psychiatry.* London: Bailliere, Tindall and Cassel, 1969;246.
33. Fuxe K, Janson AM, Jansson A, Andersson K, Agnati LF. Chronic nicotine treatment reduces dopamine utilization in surviving forebrain dopamine nerve terminal systems after partial dimesencephalic hemitransection. *Arch Pharmacol* 1990;341:171–181.
34. Uranova NA, Levitie OI. Ultrastructure of the substantia nigra in schizophrenia. *Zh Nevropatol Psikhiatr* 1987;87:1017–1024.
35. Oke AF, Adams RN. Elevated thalamic dopamine: possible link to sensory dysfunctions in schizophrenia. *Schizophr Bull* 1987;13:589–604.
36. Kirino T, Tamura A, Sano K. Selective vulnerability of the hippocampus to ischemia—reversible and irreversible types of ischemic cell damage. *Prog Brain Res* 1985;63:39–58.
37. Benfenati F, Merlo Pich E, Grimaldi R, et al. Transient forebrain ischemia produces multiple deficits in dopamine D1 transmission in the lateral neostriatum of the rat. *Brain Res* 1989;498:376–380.
38. Pulsinelli WA, Brierly JB, Plum F. Temporal profile of neuronal damage in a model of transient forebrain ischemia. *Ann Neurol* 1982; 11:491–498.
39. Iorio LC, Barnett A, Leitz FH, Houser VP, Korduba CA. SCH 23390, a potential benzazepine antipsychotic with unique interactions on dopaminergic systems. *J Pharmacol Exp Therap* 1983;226:462–268.
40. Filloux FM, Wamsley JK, Dawson TM. Dopamine D2 auto- and postsynaptic receptors in the nigrostriatal system of the rat brain: localization by quantitative autoradiography with (^{3}H)sulpiride. *Eur J Pharmacol* 1987;138:61–68.
41. Seamon KB, Vaillancourt R, Edwards M, Daly JW. Binding of (^{3}H)forskolin to rat brain membranes. *Proc Natl Acad Sci USA* 1984;81:5081–5085.
42. Hemmings HC Jr, Walaas IS, Ouimet CC, Greengard P. Dopaminergic regulation of protein phosphorylation in the striatum: DARPP-32. *Trends Neurosci* 1987;10:377–383.
43. Joyce JN, Marshall JF. Quantitative autoradiography of dopamine D2 sites in rat caudate-putamen: localization to intrinsic neurons and not to neocortical afferents. *Neuroscience* 1987;20:773–795.
44. Ohno Y, Sasa M, Takaori S. Coexistence of inhibitory dopamine D1 and excitatory D2 receptors on the same caudate nucleus neurons. *Life Sci* 1987;40:1937–1945.
45. Hess EJ, Bracha HS, Kleinman JE, Creese I. Dopamine receptor subtype imbalance in schizophrenia. *Life Sci* 1987;13:1487–1497.
46. Zini I, Grimaldi R, Merlo Pich E, Zoli M, Fuxe K, Agnati LF. Aspects of neural plasticity in the central nervous system. V. Studies on a model of transient forebrain ischemia in male Sprague–Dawley rats. *Neurochem Int* 1990;16:451–469.
47. Zoli M, Grimaldi, Agnati LF, et al. Neurohistochemical studies on striatal lesions induced by transient forebrain ischemia. Evidence for protective effects of the ganglioside analogue AGF2. *Neuroscience Research Communication* 1989;(in press).
48. Vaccarino FM, Guidotti A, Costa E. Ganglioside inhibition of glutamate-mediated protein kinase C translocation in primary cultures of cerebellar neurons. *Proc Natl Acad Sci USA,* 1987; 84:8707–8711.
49. Cimino M, Benfenati F, Farabegoli C, et al. Differential effect of ganglioside GM1 on rat brain phosphoproteins: potentiation and inhibition of protein phosphorylation regulated by calcium/calmodulin and calcium/phospholipid-dependent protein kinases. *Acta Physiol Scand* 1987;130: 317–325.
50. Fuxe K, Roberts P, Schwarcz R. *Excitotoxins.* London: MacMillan Press, 1983.
51. Sabel BA. Anatomic mechanisms whereby ganglioside treatment induces brain repair. What do we really know? In: Stein DG, Sabel BA, eds. *Pharmacological Approaches to the Treatment of Brain and Spinal Cord Injury.* New York: Plenum, 1988;167–194.
52. Feeney DM, Sutton RL. Catecholamines and recovery of function after brain damage. In: Stein DG, Sabel BA, eds. *Pharmacological Approaches to the Treatment of Brain and Spinal Cord Injury.* New York: Plenum, 1988;121–142.
53. Nemeroff CB, Prange AJ Jr, Luttinger D, Her-

nandez DE, King RA, Burgess SK. Similarities and differences in the effects of centrally administered neurotensin and neuroleptics. *Psychopharmacol Bull* 1981;17:145–147.
54. Levant B, Nemeroff CB. The psychobiology of neurotensin. In: Ganten D, Pfaff D, eds. *Current topics of neuroendocrinology: neuroendocrinology of mood*, vol. 8. Berlin: Springer-Verlag, 1988;232–262.
55. Agnati LF, Fuxe K, Benfenati F, Battistini N. Neurotensin in vitro markedly reduces the affinity in subcortical limbic ^{3}H-N-propyl-norapomorphine binding sites. *Acta Physiol Scand* 1983;119:459–461.
56. Von Euler G, Fuxe K. Neurotensin reduces the affinity of D2 dopamine receptors in rat striatal membranes. *Acta Physiol Scand* 1987;131:625–626.
57. Von Euler G, Fuxe K, Benfenati F, Hansson T, Agnati LF, Gustafsson J-ÅA. Neurotensin modulates the binding characteristics of dopamine D2 receptors in rat striatal membranes also following treatment with toluene. *Acta Physiol Scand* 1989;135:443–448.
58. Fuxe K, Agnati LF, Zoli M, Bjelke B, Zini I. Some aspects of the communicational and computational organization of the brain. *Acta Physiol Scand* 1989;135:203–216.
59. Tanganelli S, von Euler G, Fuxe K, Agnati LF, Ungerstedt U. Neurotensin counteracts apomorphine-induced inhibition of dopamine release as studied by microdialysis in rat neostriatum. *T Brain Res* 1989;502:319–324.
60. Kalivas PV, Nemeroff CB, Prange AJ Jr. Neurotensin microinjection into the nucleus accumbens antagonizes dopamine-induced increase in locomotion and rearing. *Neuroscience* 1984;11:919–930.
61. Merlo Pich E, Benfenati F, Farabegoli C, Fuxe K, Agnati LF. Neurotensin antagonism of dopamine dependent locomotor hyperactivity is enhanced after degeneration of accumbens DA nerve terminals. (Submitted.)
62. Agnati LF, Fuxe K, Zoli M, Merlo Pich E, Benfenati F, Zini, Goldstein M. Aspects on the information handling by the central nervous system: Focus on cotransmission in the aged brain. *Prog Brain Res* 1986;68:291–301.
63. White FJ, Wang RY. Electrophysiological evidence for the existence of both D_1 and D_2 dopamine receptors in the rat nucleus accumbens. *J Neurosci* 1986;6:274–280.
64. Govoni S, Hong JS, Yang H-YT, Costa E. Increase of neurotensin content elicited by neuroleptics in nucleus accumbens. *J Pharmacol Exp Ther* 1980;215:413–417.
65. Frey P, Fuxe K, Eneroth P, Agnati LF. Effects of acute and long-term treatment with neuroleptics on regional telencephalic neurotensin levels in the male rat. *Neurochem Int* 1986;8:429–434.
66. Kilts CD, Anderson C, Bissette G, Ely T, Davidson J, Nemeroff C. Differential effects of antipsychotic drugs on the neurotensin content of individual rat brain nuclei. *Proc Am Coll Neuropsychopharmacol*, Abstr 21:102.
67. Agnati LF, Fuxe K, Benfenati F, Battistini N, Zini I, Toffano G. Chronic ganglioside treatment counteracts the biochemical signs of dopamine receptor supersensitivity induced by chronic haloperidol treatment. *Neurosci Lett* 1983;40:293–297.
68. Daly JW. The effects of gangliosides on the activity of adenylate cyclase and phosphodiesterase from rat cerebral cortex. In: Rapport MM, Gorio A, eds. *Gangliosides in neurological and neuromuscular function, development, and repair*, New York: Raven Press, 1981;55–66.
69. Kim JYH, Goldenring JR, DeLorenzo RJ, Yu RK. Gangliosides inhibit phospholipid-sensitive Ca^{2+}-dependent kinase phosphorylation of rat myelin basic proteins. *J Neurosci Res* 1986;15:159–166.
70. Agnati LF, Fuxe K, Eneroth P, Zini I, Härfstrand A, Grimaldi R, Zoli M. Intravenous uridine treatment antagonizes hypoglycemia-induced reduction in brain somatostatin-like immunoreactivity. *Acta Physiol Scand* 1986;126:525–531.
71. Roberts CA. Anticonvulsant effects of uridine: comparative analysis of metrazol and penicillin induced foci. *Brain Res* 1973;55:291–308.
72. Guarnieri P, Guarnieri R, La Bella V, Pindi F. Interaction between uridine and GABA-mediated inhibitory transmission: studies *in vivo* and *in vitro*. *Epilepsy* 1985;26:666–670.
73. Farabegoli C, Merlo Pich E, Cimino M, Agnati LF, Fuxe K. Chronic uridine treatment reduces the level of ^{3}H-spiperone labelled dopamine receptors and enhances their turnover rate in striatum of young rats. Relationship to dopamine dependent behaviours. *Acta Physiol Scand* 1988;132:209–216.
74. Agnati LF, Fuxe K, Ruggeri M, Merlo Pich E, Benfenati F, Volterra V, Ungerstedt, Zini I. Effects of chronic treatment with uridine on striatal dopamine release and dopamine related behaviours in the absence or the presence of chronic treatment with haloperidol. *Neurochem Int* 1989;15:107–113.
75. Fuxe K, Hökfelt T, Ljungdahl ÅA, et al. Evidence for an inhibitory gabergic control of the meso-limbic dopamine neurons: possibility of improving treatment of schizophrenia by combined treatment with neuroleptics and gabergic drugs. *Medical Biol* 1975;53:177–183.
76. Fuxe K, Agnati LF, Everitt BJ, Hökfelt T, Ljungdahl ÅA, Perez de la Mora. Action of β(4-chlorphenyl)GABA, γ-hydroxybutyrolactone, and apomorphine on central dopamine neurons. *Adv Biochem Psychopharmacol* 1977;16:489–494.
77. Fuxe K, Hökfelt T, Agnati LF et al. Regulation of the mesocortical dopamine neurons. *Adv Biochem Psychopharmacol* 1977;16:47–55.
78. Benes F, Paskevich PA, Domesick VB. Haloperidol induced plasticity of axon terminals in rat substantia nigra. *Science* 1983;221:4614–4623.

79. Pickar D, Breier A, Kelsoe J. Plasma homovanillic acid as an index of central dopaminergic activity: studies in schizophrenic patients. *Ann NY Acad Sci* 1988;537:339–346.
80. Hirasawa K, Nishizuka Y. Phosphatidylinositol turnover in receptor mechanism and signal transduction. *Ann Rev Pharmacol Toxicol* 1985;25:147–170.
81. Agnati LF, Fuxe K, Calza L, et al. Gangliosides increase the survival of lesioned nigral dopamine neurons and favour the recovery of dopaminergic synaptic function of rats by collateral sprouting. *Acta Physiol Scand* 1983;119:347–363.
82. Agnati LF, Fuxe K, Calza, et al. Computer assisted morphometry and microdensitometry of transmitter identified neurons with special reference to the mesostriatal dopamine pathway. II. Further studies on the effects of the GM1 ganglioside on the degenerative and regenerative features of mesostriatal dopamine neurons. *Acta Physiol Scand* 1984(Suppl 532):37–42.
83. Zoli M, Ruggeri M, Zini I, et al. Experimental and theoretical aspects on neural plasticity in the central nervous system. VI. Studies on the effects of gangliosides on brain metabolic lesions. *Neurochem Int* 1990;16:469–479.
84. Von Euler G, Fuxe K, Agnati LF, Hansson T, Gustafsson J-ÅA. Ganglioside GM1 treatment prevents the effects of subacute exposure to toluene on N-(^{3}H)propylnorapomorphine binding characteristics in rat striatal membranes. *Neurosci Lett* 1987;82:181–184.

7

Neuropeptides and Schizophrenia

A Critical Review

Charles B. Nemeroff[1]

> We shall learn more about insulin than we will learn about the cause of schizophrenia from the insulin treatment experience.
>
> W. Muncie
> Johns Hopkins University, 1935

Muncie's comment concerning insulin and schizophrenia, now more than 50 years old, is relevant today; in the last two decades an enormous literature has emerged on the neurobiology of the approximately 70 neuropeptides now known to be endogenous in the mammalian brain (1,2). Whether one or another of those neuropeptides is involved in the etiology and pathogenesis of schizophrenia remains unclear. This introduction will briefly describe what is currently known about neuropeptides and their distribution, mode of biosynthesis, inactivation, and so forth. Subsequent sections will summarize the major findings that support or argue against a preeminent role for alterations in neuropeptide systems in schizophrenia. In addition I shall also describe related studies demonstrating that antipsychotic drugs alter neuropeptide systems in the brain and may exert their therapeutic action in part through their action on neuropeptide-containing neurons.

Peptides are comprised of chains of amino acids linked by peptide bonds. They range in size from small peptides such as thyrotropin-releasing hormone (TRH), which is a tripeptide, to large peptides comprised of more than 40 amino acids such as growth hormone-releasing factor (GHRF) or corticotropin-releasing factor (CRF). Table 1 lists the peptides that have been found in the mammalian central nervous system.

For many years the major impetus for research in neuropeptides was a series of discoveries, beginning in 1970, that revealed that the hypothalamic hypophysiotropic hormones, the releasing and release-inhibiting factors, are peptides (3). It is now well established that the peptidergic neurons that contain these releasing hormones project to the median eminence of the hypothalamus, where the peptides are secreted from nerve terminals and transported via the hypothalamopituitary portal system. They bind to membrane receptors in anterior pituitary cells, stimulating or inhibiting adenohypophyseal trophic hormone secretion. By this hierarchical arrangement, hypothalamic neuropeptides control the secretion of all of the endocrine axes. The analytical methodology used to discover the hypothalamic releasing hormones has now been applied to discovering myriad other brain peptides (Table 1), and current estimates suggest that another 200 or so as yet undiscovered peptides exist in brain.

---

[1]Departments of Psychiatry and Pharmacology, Duke University Medical Center, Durham, NC 27710.

TABLE 1. *Neuropeptides identified in mammalian brain*

Adrenocorticotropin (ACTH)	Insulin
Angiotensin	Kallikrein
Atrial natriuretic hormone	Kytorphin
Bombesin (BOM)	Luteinizing hormone (LH)
Bradykinin	α-Melanocyte-stimulating hormone (α-MSH)
Calcitonin	β-Melanocyte-stimulating hormone (β-MSH)
Calcitonin gene-related peptide	Melanocyte-stimulating-hormone–release-inhibiting factor (MIF-I)
Carnosine	
Cholecystokinin (CCK)	Motilin
Corticotropin-releasing factor (CRF)	Neurokinin A
Delta-sleep-inducing peptide (DSIP)	Neuromedin N
Dynorphin	Neuropeptide Y
α-Endorphin	Neurotensin
β-Endorphin	Oxytocin
γ-Endorphin	Pancreatic polypeptide
leu-Enkephalin	Peptide histidine isoleucine
met-Enkephalin	Peptide YY
Galanin	Prolactin (PRL)
Gastrin	Relaxin
Gastric-inhibitory peptide (GIP)	Secretin
Gastrin-releasing peptide	Somatostatin (SRIF, GHIH)
Glicentin	Substance P
Glucagon	Thyroid-stimulating hormone (thyrotropin, TSH)
Gonadotropin-releasing hormone (GnRH, LHRH)	Thyrotropin-releasing hormone (TRH)
Growth hormone (GH)	Vasoactive-intestinal peptide (VIP)
Growth hormone-releasing factor (GHRF, GHRH)	Vasopressin
Inhibin	Vasotocin

There is overwhelming evidence that neuropeptides are important neuroregulators in the CNS, functioning as neurotransmitters or neuromodulators. Each neuropeptide thus far studied exhibits a unique heterogeneous distribution in the brain. For example, cholecystokinin (CCK) is found in high concentrations in the cerebral cortex, whereas neurotensin (NT) is found in high concentrations in limbic areas such as the amygdala and nucleus accumbens. High-affinity neuropeptide binding sites, putative postsynaptic receptors, have been identified by autoradiography and "grind and bind" methods and are found to be heterogeneously distributed in the CNS (4). Peptides are synthesized in neuronal perikarya. The first step is the synthesis of large peptide prohormones frequently comprised of more than 150 amino acids (5). By a poorly understood process the prohormone is cleaved during processing, packaging, and transport to the nerve terminal to liberate the active peptide released when the neuron depolarizes. After peptide release (which, like all neurotransmitters thus far studied, is calcium-dependent), neuropeptides are inactivated by enzymatic inactivation. Little is known about the specificity of peptidases. Recently progress has been made in elucidating the mechanism of signal transduction after neuropeptides bind to their receptors. Second messenger systems that mediate the action of certain neuropeptides include cAMP and cGMP production, and phosphatidyl inositol hydrolysis (6,7). Finally, it is of interest to note the now-well-documented phenomenon of colocalization of neuropeptides and classical neurotransmitters first described by Hokfelt and colleagues (8). Using immunohistochemical methods, the presence of CCK with dopamine (DA), and NT with DA, was demonstrated in certain midbrain neurons in the ventral tegmental area. Similarly, substance P and serotonin are found in brain stem neurons projecting to the spinal cord.

The remainder of this chapter will describe the main strategies for elucidating a role for neuropeptides in the pathogenesis of schizophrenia. These data have been comprehensively reviewed elsewhere (9). In brief these include

1. preclinical studies,
2. cerebrospinal fluid (CSF) and postmortem brain studies,
3. clinical trials of peptides and peptide receptor antagonists,
4. the neuroendocrine window strategy.

RATIONALE FOR STUDYING NEUROPEPTIDES IN SCHIZOPHRENIA

Preclinical Studies

Constraints of space preclude any comprehensive discussion of this vast area. In brief, preclinical studies of neuropeptides comprise essentially the neurobiology of these substances: their distribution and the distribution of their receptors; electrophysiological correlates of their action; and, of particular relevance here, the behavioral effects of neuropeptides. Recent studies using magnetic resonance imaging (MRI) and positron emission tomography (PET), as well as neuropsychological testing and classical neuropathological studies, have implicated the temporal lobe and cortex, as well as the frontal and prefrontal cortex in the pathogenesis of schizophrenia (10). Obviously, any neurotransmitter to be considered a strong candidate as the primary neurochemical abnormality in schizophrenia should be found in brain areas like those mentioned above, which are already implicated in this disorder. Preclinical studies also include ascertaining the activity of neuropeptides in pharmacological screening tests for antipsychotic drugs. These include operant tests such as conditioned avoidance responding (CAR), antagonism of the behavioral effects of psychostimulants such as D-amphetamine and biochemical paradigms such as effects on DA turnover (11). Indeed, such approaches first focused attention on the putative role for β-endorphin and other opioid peptides in schizophrenia (12) and led to more recent work on the putative antipsychotic peptide des-tyr^1-γ-endorphin (13) (see below). Such approaches also led to elucidation of the close relationship between DA neurons and those containing the neuropeptide NT (14,15). Thus NT, as noted above, is colocalized with certain DA neurons; moreover, NT neurons are found in neuroanatomical proximity to DA neurons. Furthermore, NT receptors are found on certain DA nerve terminals. Centrally administered NT, like systemically administered antipsychotic drugs, produces catalepsy, muscle relaxation, hypothermia, inhibition of CAR, blockade of amphetamine-induced hyperactivity, and potentiation of barbiturate-induced sedation. Moreover, NT increases central DA turnover. Clinical studies have supported a role for NT both in mediating the actions of antipsychotic drugs and in the pathogenesis of schizophrenia. Similarly conducted studies with CCK have supported the hypothesis that CCK modulates the activity of DA neurons (16).

Cerebrospinal Fluid and Postmortem Brain Studies

In view of the preclinical data described above demonstrating NT-DA interactions, I and my colleagues have chosen to measure the CSF concentration of NT in schizophrenic patients. In our first study (17) we measured CSF NT concentrations by radioimmunoassay (RIA) in 21 drug-free schizophrenic patients and 12 age- and sex-matched controls. Group mean CSF concentrations of NT-like immunoreactivity (NTLIR) were not significantly different, but the schizophrenic group was shown to consist of two subgroups, one of which had very low CSF concentrations of NTLIR. After neuroleptic treatment, the latter subgroup exhibited normalization of CSF NT concentrations. In subsequent studies

(18,19) we have confirmed and extended our original findings. In our second study, CSF NT concentrations in schizophrenic patients were reduced relative to controls, but no antipsychotic-drug-induced increase was noted. However, we found no difference in CSF NT concentration in drug-free paranoid schizophrenic patients compared with controls. No CSF NT reductions were observed in patients with major depression, anorexia-bulemia, or premenstrual syndrome.

More recently, in collaboration with Garver (20), we measured the CSF concentration of NT in psychotic patients subsequently treated with lithium or haloperidol. Only the delayed antipsychotic drug responders had decreased CSF NT concentrations when compared with controls.

Our group (21) measured CSF concentrations of somatostatin (SRIF) in 10 healthy volunteers, 29 demented patients, 23 patients with major depression, and 10 schizophrenic patients. All three psychiatric diagnostic groups had significantly reduced CSF concentrations of SRIF in comparison with the controls. Thus, decreases in CSF SRIF appear not to be specific to a particular disease state but may reflect cognitive impairment.

Gerner and Yamada (22) assayed CSF concentrations of immunoreactive CCK, SRIF, and bombesin (BOM) in normal healthy volunteers and in drug-free patients with anorexia nervosa, mania, depression, and chronic schizophrenia who were ill for more than 6 months. A small statistically insignificant decrease in BOM-like immunoreactivity (BOMLIR) was observed in the schizophrenic patients in comparison with the controls; no diagnostic group-related differences in CSF concentrations of SRIF- or CCK-like immunoreactivity were found. In a more recent study (23), BOM, SRIF, and CCK were measured by RIA in CSF obtained from normal controls, schizophrenic patients (from California hospitals), and schizophrenic patients (from the National Institute of Mental Health, NIMH). Only the schizophrenic patients from NIMH exhibited significant differences (i.e., elevations in CCK and SRIF concentrations and decreases in BOM) when compared with controls. The finding of increased SRIF concentrations is in contrast to those of Bissette et al (21) in schizophrenia.

Verbanck et al (24) measured CSF concentrations of CCK in controls and in patients with Parkinson's disease, depression, and schizophrenia. Nine patients were drug-free for 6 weeks, and six received haloperidol prior to CSF sampling. The concentration of CCK in CSF was reported to be significantly decreased in the drug-free schizophrenic patients compared with normal controls.

Lindstrom et al (25) measured the CSF concentrations of immunoreactive delta-sleep-inducing peptide (DSIP) in healthy volunteers, schizophrenic patients, and depressed patients. Schizophrenic patients had significantly lower CSF DSIP concentrations than controls, both in the drug-free state and after 4 weeks of neuroleptic treatment.

The potential role of opioid peptides in the pathogenesis of schizophrenia has received considerable attention; consequently there have been many studies in which opioids have been measured in the CSF of schizophrenic patients.

Terenius et al (26) were the first to report alterations in endogenous opioid peptide concentrations in the CSF of schizophrenic patients. Their radioreceptor assay used ^{3}H-dihydromorphine as the ligand and measured total opioid activity without discrimination as to which particular opioid was present. In this original report, the CSF opioid activity of four chronic schizophrenics (ill for at least 10 years but drug-free for 4 weeks) was compared before, and 2 and 4 weeks after, clozapine treatment. Two fractions with opiate receptor activity (fractions I and II) were isolated. Met-enkephalin (ME) coeluted with fraction II, but only the concentration of fraction I was changed after neuroleptic treatment. In a later study, Lindstrom et al (27) reported that when CSF opioid activity, as defined with the same radioreceptor assay, was measured in nine chronic schizophrenic patients after a drug-free period of 1 to 2 months, six of the patients had higher fraction I opioid concentrations than the mean fraction I concentration of 19 normal volunteers. In addition, the schizophrenic patients with high CSF fraction I levels, when retested after treatment with antipsychotic drugs (clozapine, flupenthixol, or chlorpromazine for 12 days to 2 months), exhibited values closer to the mean of the normal controls. In another study (28) using these same methods, CSF fraction I opioid activity was measured in 18 drug-free acute schizophrenics (of which 11 had never received neuroleptics and seven had stopped neuroleptic treatment 4 to 8 weeks before the study) and 24 chronic schizophrenics who had been neuroleptic-free for at least 2 weeks. Two of nine chronic schizophrenic patients, four of six relapsed patients, and six of nine acute schizophrenic patients had elevated mean CSF fraction I opioid concentrations in comparison with the normal controls from the Lindstrom et al (27) study. In another study, Rimon and colleagues (29) found that either fraction I or fraction II CSF opioid activity was elevated above their previously published mean normal control values (27) in 72% of 53 schizophrenic patients who were neuroleptic-free for 1 week.

These elevations did not attain statistical significance when compared with normal controls, but within the schizophrenic group the CSF fraction I opioid activity was significantly higher in the hebephrenic ($N = 23$) than in the undifferentiated subgroup ($N = 21$). No significant correlations were noted between CSF opioid activity of fractions I or II and duration of disease, length of neuroleptic treatment, or psychotic symptoms.

In a preliminary report, Domschke et al (30) measured the CSF concentration of β-endorphin in five acute and seven chronic (over 10 years) schizophrenic patients compared with seven normal controls and ten patients with herniated vertebral discs. All of the psychiatric patients were receiving antipsychotic drug therapy. β-Endorphin was estimated by RIA. Inappropriately analyzing the data, this group claimed that CFS concentrations of β-endorphin had increased in the acute schizophrenic patients and decreased in the chronic schizophrenic patients when compared with the controls.

Burbach et al (31) compared CSF concentrations of β-endorphin and ME in nine neurologically diseased "controls" and nine schizophrenic patients. All patients were currently being treated with neuroleptics. No significant group-related differences in CSF β-endorphin or ME concentrations were observed.

Naber et al (32,33) and Naber and Pickar (34), using a radioreceptor assay for opioid activity and an RIA for β-endorphin, studied the CSF from controls and from drug-free psychiatric patients with a variety of diagnoses, including schizophrenia ($N = 27$), schizoaffective disorder ($N = 17$), depression ($N = 35$), and mania ($N = 13$). The radioreceptor assay used an ME analog, ^{3}H-D-ala-L-leu-enkephalinamide (D-ALA), and the RIA used ^{125}I-β-endorphin as the tracer. Opiate receptor activity was significantly reduced in the schizophrenic males only.

Emrich et al (35,36) and Hollt et al (37) measured the concentration of β-endorphinlike immunoreactivity by RIA in the CSF of eight "normal" controls compared with 15 schizophrenic patients and patients with a variety of other neurological problems. (The CSF in the controls was obtained to diagnose meningitis/encephalitis and found to be negative.) Patients were medication-free for 4 weeks. No significant differences between controls and schizophrenic patients were detected in CSF concentrations.

Van Kammen et al (38) measured both β-endorphin concentration and opioid activity in the CSF from 30 drug-free schizophrenic patients. Concentrations of vasopressin and of angiotensin I and II were also assayed. The results were compared with those obtained in 52 normal controls. Concentrations of β-endorphin, vasopressin, and angiotensin I and II were measured by RIA, and opioid activity was assessed by radioreceptor assay with ^{3}H-D-ALA as the radioligand. The concentration of vasopressin was found to be reduced by approximately 40% ($p < .01$) in the CSF of male schizophrenics; no change in the concentrations of the other peptides was found.

In addition to neuropeptide measurement in the CSF, researchers have examined postmortem brain tissue from schizophrenic patients. As yet, few reports have appeared concerning alterations in neuropeptide concentrations in postmortem brain regions of patients who in life had been diagnosed as schizophrenic.

Crow and his colleagues measured the concentrations of five neuropeptides in brain regions from 12 controls and 14 schizophrenic patients (39,40). The patients were subclassified into type I ($N = 7$) and type II ($N = 7$) based on the presence or absence of "positive" and "negative" symptoms, as described by Crow (41). The neuropeptides NT, substance P, CCK, SRIF, and vasoactive-intestinal peptide (VIP) were assayed by RIA in the temporal, frontal, parietal, and cingulate cortices and in several subcortical regions including the hippocampus, amygdala, globus pallidus, putamen, dorsomedial thalamus, and lateral thalamus. Significant alterations were observed for CCK (reduced in the temporal cortex) and substance P (increased in the hippocampus) in the total group of schizophrenic patients compared with controls. Type II schizophrenic patients had significantly decreased mean concentrations of CCK in the amygdala and significantly decreased SRIF and CCK concentrations in the hippocampus; type I schizophrenic patients had elevated levels of VIP in the amygdala. No significant correlation with age, postmortem delay, or presence of neuroleptic medication was seen for any regional neuropeptide concentration.

My colleagues and I (42) measured the regional postmortem brain concentrations of NT, SRIF, and TRH in controls (free of neurological or psychiatric disease, $N = 50$), patients with Huntington's chorea ($N = 24$), and schizophrenic patients ($N = 46$). Schizophrenic patients were on various neuroleptic regimens before death. No significant differences between controls and schizophrenic patients were seen in NT, SRIF, or TRH concentrations in the caudate nucleus, nucleus accumbens, amygdala, or hypothalamus. A significant decrease in SRIF ($p < .05$) and TRH ($p < .004$) concentrations in Brodmann's area 12 (frontal cortex), and a significant decrease ($p < .05$) in TRH concentration in Brodmann's area 32 (frontal cortex) was observed in the schizophrenic patients when compared with the controls; in contrast, NT content was significantly elevated ($p < .006$) in Brodmann's area 32 (frontal cortex) in the schizophrenic group.

Kleinman et al (43) measured the concentration of four neuropeptides (ME, substance P, NT, and CCK) by RIA postmortem brain regions from normal control subjects ($N = 18$), alcoholic patients ($N = 7$), opiate users ($N = 12$), suicide victims ($N = 19$), and psychotic patients ($N = 40$). The psychotic group was subdivided by RDC criteria into chronic paranoid schizophrenic patients ($N = 11$), chronic undifferentiated schizophrenic patients ($N = 6$), and patients with other psychotic disorders (unspecified functional psychoses and affective psychoses). No significant differences between normals and psychotic patients were found in ME concentrations in the nucleus accumbens, hypothalamus, globus pallidus, or putamen. Similarly, no significant group-related differences in NT concentrations were observed in the nucleus accumbens, globus pallidus, or hypothalamus. Moreover, no significant differences were seen between control and psychotic patients in CCK levels in the amygdala, nucleus accumbens, caudate nucleus, frontal cortex, substantia nigra, hippocampus, or temporal cortex. Met-enkephalin concentrations were reported to be significantly ($p < .05$) decreased in the caudate nucleus of chronic paranoid schizophrenic patients compared with other diagnostic groups or controls; substance P levels were significantly increased in the caudate nucleus of patients with psychoses when compared with patients having diagnoses other than schizophrenia.

Biggins et al (44) measured amygdaloid concentrations of NT and TRH by RIA in normals ($N = 7$) and in patients with senile dementia of the Alzheimer's type ($N = 7$), with depressive illness ($N = 7$), or with schizophrenia ($N = 7$). No significant difference was seen in amygdaloid concentrations of TRH or NT between the four diagnostic groups.

Lightman et al (45) measured the concentration of β-endorphin by RIA in five brain regions (hypothalamus, thalamus, hippocampus, cingulate cortex, and premotor cortex) in schizophrenic patients and controls; no differences in β-endorphin concentrations were found in the samples from the schizophrenic patients.

In view of the work cited above implicating aberrant β-endorphin metabolism in schizophrenia, Weigant et al (46) measured the concentration of α-, β-, and γ-endorphins in postmortem hypothalamic tissue from schizophrenic patients and from controls. The concentrations of α-, and γ-endorphins, but not β-endorphin, were elevated in the hypothalamus of the schizophrenic patients.

Davis et al (47) studied the in vitro metabolism of β-endorphin in the cortex and putamen of schizophrenics and controls. γ-Endorphin formation from β-endorphin in the cortex was found to be reduced in the schizophrenics.

Evidence from Clinical Trials of Peptides and Peptide Receptor Antagonists

Several clinical studies with β-endorphin, enkephalin analogues, and derivatives of the endorphins (eg, des-tyr[1]-γ-endorphin, or DTγE) have been conducted in schizophrenic patients. None of the studies in which β-endorphin or enkephalins were administered to schizophrenic patients revealed any major beneficial effects. These data were previously reviewed in detail (48). In a series of reports, De Wied, van Ree, Verhoeven, and their associates have postulated that schizophrenia is a disorder of endorphin metabolism—an overproduction of α-type endorphins (which purportedly have amphetaminelike properties) and/or an underproduction of γ-type endorphins (which purportedly possess neuroleptic properties). Such theoretical considerations and the preclinical data concordant with these hypotheses have led to clinical trials of DTγE and related peptides in schizophrenic patients.

In the first study (49), six schizophrenic patients, drug-free for one week prior to the clinical trial, received daily intramuscular (IM) treatments with 0.5 to 1.0 mg of DTγE for 10 days. All six patients were reported to show dramatic improvement.

In a second study by the same group (50,51), schizophrenic patients were maintained on neuroleptics during treatment with DTγE. In this double-blind, crossover-designed study, 16 patients received either DTγE (1 mg of IM daily for 16 days) or a placebo. The authors reported significant improvement. The patients became progressively less psychotic, and hallucinations and delusions were reduced.

In contrast to these findings, Emrich and his colleagues (52), in a double-blind trial using daily IM injections of 2 mg of DTγE, found no significant antipsychotic effects of the peptide in 13 patients maintained on neuroleptic medication. Other largely negative studies have been published, including those of Fink and associates (53), Manchandra and Hirsch (54), Meltzer and co-workers (55), and Tamminga and others (56). In these studies and the one by Volavka and colleagues (57), the antipsychotic effects of DTγE, when in evidence at all, were short-lived, barely attained statistical significance, and were not clinically robust.

De Wied and colleagues (58–60) have stated that these negative results from other centers can be attributed to the fact that schizophrenia is a heterogeneous disorder; thus only a subgroup of patients respond to DTγE. In addition, this group of researchers from Utrecht has found that duration of illness, duration of last episode, and patient age correlate negatively with response to DTγE.

Recently Machandra et al (61) have reanalyzed several of the treatment trials (Utrecht, London, Munich, and Chicago) with DTγE by applying a uniform outcome criterion of improvement of a change of 80% or more on rating scale score; these results are more consistent. Marked improvement after DTγE ranged from 15.5% to 30.5% of the patients.

Recently the Utrecht group has studied the clinical effects of des-enkephalin-γ-endorphin (DEγE), the shortest fragment of γ-endorphin with neurolepticlike activity in preclinical studies. Both single-blind and double-blind studies have been conducted (62). In the single-blind study of four patients (one neuroleptic-free), two patients received 1 mg of DEγE IM and two received 10 mg of DEγE IM. All four patients were reported to show a marked amelioration of psychotic symptoms, and two of these were discharged from the hospital. In the double-blind study 19 patients were studied and all received 3 mg of DEγE IM. A significant reduction in BPRS scores was associated with the peptide treatment. Two patients showed no response; four, a slight to moderate response; four, a moderate to marked response; and three, a very marked response.

Three other neuropeptides have been tested clinically for antipsychotic effects: CCK, TRH, and vasopressin. Based on the compelling evidence noted above for colocalization of CCK and DA, researchers have studied the effects of treatment with CCK or the related homologous decapeptide ceruletide on the symptoms of schizophrenia.

Although open studies reported therapeutic effects (63), subsequent double-blind studies revealed no beneficial effects of CCK in schizophrenia (64,65). Similarly disappointing results have been obtained with TRH. Iager et al (66) conducted a 3-month double-blind, placebo-controlled trial with the 1-desamino-8-D-arginine vasopressin (DDAVP), a vasopressin analogue, in ten patients with chronic schizophrenia. Improvement in negative symptoms was observed.

The only neuropeptide antagonists that have been evaluated as antipsychotic agents are the opioid receptor blockers naloxone and naltrexone. Many but not all of the trials have been comprehensively reviewed previously (9). These studies are based on the hypothesis that schizophrenia is associated with excess CNS opioid activity, and therefore the opioid receptor blockade should relieve the symptoms of schizophrenia.

Further impetus for this work was provided by Gunne and associates (67), who in a single-blind pilot study reported that naloxone (0.4 mg IV), temporarily reduced or abolished auditory hallucinations in four cases of chronic schizophrenia. Since this initial report, the effects of naloxone in schizophrenia have been intensively studied, with mixed results.

Lehmann et al (68) conducted single- and double-blind studies of the effects of naloxone (10 mg IV) in seven chronic schizophrenic men. Naloxone was reported to produce statistically significant improvement. In a single case report, Orr and Oppenheimer (69) reported that naloxone (0.4 mg IV), but not a placebo, produced a marked reduction in auditory hallucinations and a mild euphoria on three separate occasions in a 28-year-old chronic schizophrenic patient maintained on antipsychotic drugs.

Watson et al (70) also used a relatively high dose of naloxone (10 mg IV) in a double-blind crossover-designed study. Five patients were maintained on neuroleptics throughout the study, and six were neuroleptic-free for at least two weeks. Two subjects were studied in a single-blind design and nine in a double-blind paradigm. Of the latter nine patients, six reported a clearcut improvement in hallucinations, one showed borderline improvement, and two showed no change. The improvement in clinical state reached statistical significance. In a subsequent study (71), this same group conducted a placebo-controlled, double-blind crossover-designed study to evaluate the effects of naloxone (10 mg IV) in 14 male chronic schizophrenic patients. The results in this study were similar to their first one: A significantly greater reduction in hallucinations was observed following naloxone than with the placebo.

An NIMH study (72) confirmed and extended the findings of the Stanford group. In the double-blind NIMH study, naloxone (15 mg IV) produced significant improvement in abnormal thought content in medicated, but not in unmedicated, chronic schizophrenic patients. A total of 17 patients were studied. A World Health Organization (WHO) Collaborative Study (73,74) confirmed these findings—a naloxone-induced reduction in schizophrenic symptom ratings (eg, auditory hallucinations) in the neuroleptic-treated patients ($N = 19$) but not in the drug-free patients ($N = 13$).

In contrast to these positive findings, several researchers could detect no antipsychotic effects of naloxone. In an early study Janowsky and associates (75) reported that naloxone (1.2 mg IV) produced no change in BPRS items associated with schizophrenic symptomatology in eight male schizophrenic patients. In a study with findings that one could consider both negative and positive, Davis and co-workers (76) found no effect of naloxone (0.4 mg IV) on global assessment or on ratings of hallucinations, psychosis, or conceptual disorganization in 19 (mostly drug-free) schizophrenic patients. However, a single item, unusual thought content, improved significantly after naloxone.

Volavka et al (77), using an almost identical experimental design and dose of naloxone, found no significant effects of the drug in seven chronic, neuroleptic-treated schizophrenic patients. Similarly negative findings were reported by Lipinski and colleagues (78) in seven neuroleptic-treated schizophrenic patients who received naloxone (16 mg IV). Verhoeven and associates (79), who participated in the WHO study on naloxone in schizophrenia, found no effect of naloxone (20 mg subcutaneously [SC]) in a double-blind trial of five chronic schizophrenic patients. In a later study (80), this same group treated ten schizophrenic patients with naloxone (20 mg SC) for four days. No effects of the opioid antagonist were detected in this double-blind study.

Naber and Leibl (81) studied the effects of repeated high-dose naloxone treatment (20 mg SC for 4 days) in seven schizophrenic patients (four treated with neuroleptics). In this double-blind crossover-designed study, no antipsychotic effects were observed at all.

The orally active opiate antagonist naltrexone has also been studied in schizophrenic patients, with largely negative results. Mueser and Dysken (82) have reviewed these studies and summarized the current literature; of 42 schizophrenic patients treated with naltrexone (50 to 800 mg orally for 2 to 6 weeks), only seven improved.

Naloxone appears to exert antipsychotic effects in a *subgroup* of *neuroleptic-treated* chronic schizophrenic patients. The magnitude of the antipsychotic effect is not, however, very robust and appears limited to a reduction in the incidence of auditory hallucinations and/or unusual thought content.

Neuroendocrine Window Strategy

The neuroendocrine window strategy has been utilized for more than 25 years to elucidate the CNS neurotransmitter mechanisms that are awry in major mental disorders such as schizophrenia. Simply stated, the neuroendocrine window strategy is based on the fact that pituitary and peripheral endocrine gland secretion is under the control of the hypothalamic hypophysiotrophic hormones; these in turn are controlled by classical CNS neurotransmitters such as serotonin, dopamine, and acetylcholine. If basal or stimulated pituitary and end-organ endocrine hormone secretion is found to be altered in schizophrenia, then conclusions about alterations in CNS neurotransmitter function could be inferred. This strategy has produced interesting observations, but problems in interpreting such data are readily apparent. Thus, the neurons that innervate neurons containing hypothalamic releasing factor are less likely to be involved in the pathogenesis of schizophrenia as compared, for example, with cerebrocortical neurons. Moreover, there is no reason to believe that the tuberoinfundibular DA neurons that are involved in the control of pituitary hormone secretion would be altered in schizophrenia in the same manner in which forebrain DA systems such as the mesolimbic and mesocortical DA neurons have been postulated to be altered in this disorder. With these caveats in mind, neuroendocrine alterations have been reported in schizophrenia, and these data have been reviewed (83,84). Both basal and stimulated prolactin secretion, largely under inhibitory DA control, is normal in schizophrenic patients. In a small series Asnis and Ryan (85) found that, compared with controls, schizophrenic men had a blunted prolactin response to reserpine.

Basal growth hormone (GH) secretion appears to be normal in schizophrenic patients but apomorphine-induced GH secretion has been reported to be blunted in chronic schizophrenic patients.

The activity of the other endocrine axes—including the pituitary-adrenal, pituitary-thyroid, and pituitary-gonadal systems—are all apparently normal in schizophrenia.

CONCLUSIONS

Neuropeptide studies in schizophrenia have now been conducted in schizophrenia for approximately 20 years. Taken together there is evidence that NT plays a role in the pathogenesis of this disorder, as well as in mediating the action of antipsychotic drugs. In addition, CCK clearly modulates DA neurons and may play a role in schizophrenia. There seems to be a subgroup of schizophrenic patients who show therapeutic responses to naloxone, the opioid receptor antagonist, and another subgroup that responds to the putative endogenous peptide antipsychotic DTγE.

As technical advances in neurobiology occur, it is hoped that postmortem studies will provide novel data on the involvement of neuropeptides in schizophrenia. In addition, development of ligands to measure neuropeptide receptors by PET will yield important data. Clearly, development of lipophilic neuropeptide receptor agonists and antagonists will provide novel putative therapeutic agents in schizophrenia.

ACKNOWLEDGMENTS

This work was supported by NIMH grants MH-39415, MH-42088, MH-40524, and MH-40159. We are grateful to Sheila Walker for preparation of this manuscript.

REFERENCES

1. Palkovits M. Neuropeptides in the brain. In: Martini L, Ganong WF, eds. *Frontiers in neuroendocrinology*, vol 10. New York: Raven Press, 1988;1–44.
2. Martin JB. Neuroendocrinology and brain peptides: an emerging new frontier in neurobiology. In: Shah NS, Donald AG, eds. *Psychoneuroendocrine dysfunction*. New York: Plenum Press, 1984;15–40.
3. Vale W, Rivier C. Hypothalamic hypophysiotropic hormones. In: Iversen LL, Iversen SD, Snyder SH, eds. *Handbook of psychopharmacology*, vol 5. New York: Plenum Press, 1975;195–237.
4. DeSouza EB. Neurotransmitter receptor imaging techniques. In: Nemeroff CB, ed. *Neuropeptides in psychiatry*. Washington, DC: APA Press, 1990; (in press).
5. Eiden LE. The cell biology of the peptidergic neuron: an overview. In: Nemeroff CB, ed. *Neuropeptides in psychiatric and neurological disorders*. Baltimore: Johns Hopkins University Press, 1988;1–17.
6. Chang K-J, Cuatrecasas P. Receptors and second messengers. In: Krieger DT, Brownstein MJ, Martin JB, eds. *Brain peptides*. New York: John Wiley & Sons, 1983;565–593.
7. Muller EE, Nistico G. *Brain messengers and the pituitary*. San Diego: Academic Press, 1989.
8. Hokfelt T, Fried G, Hansen R, et al. Neurons with multiple messengers—distribution and possible functional significance. In: van Ree JM, Matthysse S, eds. *Psychiatric disorders: neurotransmitters and neuropeptides*. Amsterdam: Elsevier, *Prog Brain Res* 1986;65:115–137.
9. Nemeroff CB, Berger PA, Bissette G. Peptides in schizophrenia. In: Meltzer HY, ed. *Psychopharmacology, the third generation of progress*. New York: Raven Press, 1987;727–744.
10. Kleinman JE, Casanova MF, Jaskiw G. Neuropathology of schizophrenia. *Schizophr Bull* 1988;14:209–216.
11. Dunn L, Kilts CD, Nemeroff CB. Animal behavioral models for drug development in psychopharmacology. In: Clark C and Moss WH, ed. *Modern drug discovery technologies* 1990;259–280.
12. Bloom FE, Segal D, Ling N, et al. Endorphins: profound behavioral effects in rats suggest new etiological factors in mental illness. *Science* 1976;194:630–632.
13. Van Ree JM, De Wied D. Endorphins and related peptides in schizophrenia. In: Muller EE, Genazzani R, eds. *Central and peripheral endorphins: basic and clinical aspects*. New York: Raven Press, 1984;325–332.
14. Nemeroff CB. Interactions of neurotensin with dopamine neurons in the mammalian central nervous system: focus on limbic system sites. In: Sandler M, Feuerstein C, Scatton B, eds. *Neurotransmitter interactions in the basal ganglia*. New York: Raven Press, 1987;155–170.
15. Gariano RF, Groves PM. A mechanism for the involvement of colocalized neuropeptides in the actions of antipsychotic drugs. *Biolog Psychiatry* 1989;26:303–314.
16. Altar CA, Boyar WC. Brain CCK-β receptors mediate the suppression of dopamine release by cholecystokinin. *Brain Res* 1989;483:321–326.
17. Widerlov E, Lindstrom LH, Besev G, et al. Subnormal CSF levels of neurotensin in a subgroup of schizophrenic patients: normalization after neuroleptic treatment. *Am J Psychiatry* 1982;139:1122–1126.
18. Lindstrom LH, Widerlov E, Bissette G, et al. Reduced CSF neurotensin concentration in drug-free schizophrenic patients. *Schizophr Res* 1988;1:55–59.
19. Nemeroff CB, Bissette G, Widerlov E, et al. Neurotensin-like immunoreactivity in cerebrospinal fluid of patients with schizophrenia, depression, anorexia nervosa-bulemia and premenstrual syndrome. *J Neuropsychiatr Clin Neurosci* 1989;1:16–20.
20. Bissette G, Garver D, Kelly K, et al. CSF neurotensin concentrations in psychoses. *Soc Neurosci Abstr* 1989;15(in press).
21. Bissette G, Widerlov E, Walleus H, et al. Alterations in cerebrospinal fluid concentrations of somatostatin-like immunoreactivity in neuropsychiatric disorders. *Arch Gen Psychiatry* 1986;43:1148–1154.
22. Gerner RH, Yamada T. Altered neuropeptide concentrations in cerebrospinal fluid of psychiatric patients. *Brain Res* 1982;238:298–302.
23. Gerner RH. Cerebrospinal fluid cholecystokinin and bombesin in psychiatric disorders and normals. In: Post RM, Ballenger JC, eds. *Neurobiology of mood disorders*. Baltimore: Williams & Wilkins, 1984;388–392.
24. Verbanck PMP, Lotstra F, Gilles C, et al. Reduced cholecystokinin immunoreactivity in the cerebrospinal fluid of patients with psychiatric disorders. *Life Sci* 1983;34:67–72.
25. Lindstrom LH, Ekman R, Walleus H, et al. Delta-sleep inducing peptide in cerebrospinal fluid from schizophrenics, depressives, and healthy volunteers. *Prog Neuro-Psychopharm Biol Psychiatr* 1985;9:83–90.
26. Terenius L, Wahlstrom A, Lindstrom LH, et al. Increased CSF levels of endorphins in chronic psychosis. *Neurosci Lett* 1976;3:157–162.
27. Lindstrom LH, Besev G, Gunne L-M, et al. Cerebrospinal content of endorphins in schizophrenia. In: Shah NS, Donald AG, eds. *Endorphins and opiate antagonists in psychiatry*. New York: Plenum Press, 1982;245–256.
28. Rimon R, Terenius L, Kampman R. Cerebrospinal fluid endorphins in schizophrenia. *Acta Psychiatr Scand* 1980;61:395–403.
29. Terenius L, Nyberg F. Opioid peptides in the cerebrospinal fluid of psychiatric patients. In: van Ree JM, Matthysse S, eds. *Psychiatric disorders: neurotransmitters and neuropeptides*. Amsterdam: Elsevier, *Prog Brain Res* 1986;65:207–219.

30. Domschke W, Dickschas A, Mitznegg P. CSF β-endorphin in schizophrenia. *Lancet* 1979;1:1024.
31. Burbach JPH, Loeber JG, Verhoef J, et al. Schizophrenia and degradation of endorphins in cerebrospinal fluid. *Lancet* 1979;2:480–481.
32. Naber D, Pickar D, Post RM, et al. CSF opioid activity in psychiatric patients. In: Perris C, Struwe G, Jansson B, eds. *Biological Psychiatry 1981*. Amsterdam: Elsevier Scientific Publishers, 1981;372–375.
33. Naber D, Pickar D, Post RM, et al. Endogenous opioid activity and β-endorphin immunoreactivity in CSF of psychiatric patients and normal controls. *Am J Psychiatry* 1981;138:1457–1462.
34. Naber D, Pickar D. The measurement of endorphins in body fluids. *Psychiatr Clin North Am* 1983;6:443–456.
35. Emrich HM, Hollt V, Kissing W, et al. A measurement of β-endorphin-like immunoreactivity in CSF and plasma of neuropsychiatric patients. In: Erlich YH, Volavka J, Davis LG, Brunngraber EG, eds. *Modulators, mediators and specifiers in brain function*. New York: Plenum Press, 1979;307–317.
36. Emrich HM, Hollt V, Kissling W, et al. β-endorphin-like immunoreactivity in cerebrospinal fluid and plasma of patients with schizophrenia and neuropsychiatric disorders. *Pharmakopsychiatria* 1979;12:269–276.
37. Hollt V, Emrich HM, Bergmann M, et al. β-endorphin-like immunoreactivity in CSF and plasma of neuropsychiatric patients. In: Shah NS, Donald AG, eds. *Endorphins and opiate antagonists in psychiatry*. New York: Plenum Press, 1982;231–243.
38. Van Kammen DP, Waters RN, Gold PW, et al. Spinal fluid vasopressin, angiotensin I and II, β-endorphin and opioid activity in schizophrenia: a preliminary evaluation. In: Perris C, Struwe G, Jansson B, eds. *Biological Psychiatry 1981*. Amsterdam: Elsevier Scientific Publishers, 1981;339–344.
39. Ferrier IN, Roberts GW, Crow TJ, et al. Reduced cholecystokinin-like and somatostatin-like immunoreactivity in limbic lobe is associated with negative symptoms in schizophrenia. *Life Sci* 1983;33:475–482.
40. Ferrier IN, Crow TJ, Roberts GW, et al. Alterations in neuropeptides in the limbic lobe in schizophrenia. In: Trimble MR, Zaritan E, eds. *Psychopharmacology of the limbic system*. Oxford: Oxford University Press, 1984;244–254.
41. Crow TJ. Schizophrenia. In: Crow TJ, ed. *Disorders of neurohumoural transmissions*. London: Academic Press, 1982;287–340.
42. Nemeroff CB, Youngblood WW, Manberg PJ, et al. Regional brain concentrations of neuropeptides in Huntington's chorea and schizophrenia. *Science* 1983;221:972–975.
43. Kleinman JE, Iadorola M, Govoni S, et al. Postmortem measurements of neuropeptides in human brain. *Psychopharmacol Bull* 1983;19:375–377.
44. Biggins J, Perry EK, McDermott JR, et al. Post-mortem levels of thyrotropin-releasing hormone and neurotensin in the amygdala in Alzheimer's disease, schizophrenia and depression. *J Neurol Sci* 1983;58:117–122.
45. Lightman SL, Spokes EG, Sagnella GA, et al. Distribution of β-endorphin in normal and schizophrenic human brains. *Eur J Clin Invest* 1979;9:377–379.
46. Weigant VM, Verhoef GJ, Burbach PH, et al. Increased concentration of α- and γ-endorphin in postmortem hypothalamic tissue of schizophrenic patients. *Life Sci* 1988;42:1733–1742.
47. Davis TP, Culling-Bergland AJ, Schoemaker H. Specific regional differences of in vitro β-endorphin metabolism in schizophrenics. *Life Sci* 1989;39:2601–2609.
48. Bissette G, Nemeroff CB. The role of neuropeptides in the pathogenesis and treatment of schizophrenia. In: Nemeroff CB, ed. *Neuropeptides in psychiatric and neurological diseases*. Baltimore: Johns Hopkins University Press, 1988;49–75.
49. Verhoeven WMA, van Praag HM, Botter PA, et al. [Des-Tyr¹]-γ-endorphin in schizophrenia. *Lancet* 1978;1:1046–1047.
50. Verhoeven WMA, van Praag HM, van Ree JM, et al. Improvement of schizophrenic patients treated with des-tyr¹-γ-endorphin (DYTE). *Arch Gen Psychiatry* 1979;36:294–298.
51. De Wied D. Endorphins and psychopathology. In: Collu R, et al, eds. *Brain peptides and hormones*. New York: Raven Press, 1982;137–147.
52. Emrich HM, Zaudig M, Kissling W, et al. Des-tyrosyl-γ-endorphin in schizophrenia: a double blind trial in 13 patients. *Pharmakopsychiatria* 1980;13:290–298.
53. Fink M, Papakostas Y, Lee J, et al. Clinical trials with des-tyr-γ-endorphin (GK-78). In: Perris C, Struwe G, Jansson B, eds. *Biological psychiatry*. Amsterdam: Elsevier Scientific Publishers, 1981;393–401.
54. Manchandra R, Hirsch SR. (Des tyr¹)-γ-endorphin in the treatment of schizophrenics. *Psychol Med* 1981;11:401–403.
55. Meltzer HY, Busch DA, Tricon BJ, et al. Effect of (des-tyr)-γ-endorphin in schizophrenia. *Psychiatry Res* 1982;6:313–326.
56. Tamminga CA, Tighe PJ, Chase TN, et al. Des-tyrosine-γ-endorphin administration in chronic schizophrenics. *Arch Gen Psychiatry* 1981;38:167.
57. Volavka J, Hui K-S, Anderson B, et al. Short-lived effect of (des-tyr)-γ-endorphin in schizophrenia. *Psychiatry Res* 1983;10:243–252.
58. Van Ree JM, Verhoeven WMA, Claas FHJ, et al. Antipsychotic action of γ-type endorphins: animal and human studies. In: van Ree JM, Matthysse S, eds. *Psychiatric disorders: neurotransmitters and neuropeptides*. Amsterdam: Elsevier, *Prog Brain Res* 1986;65:221–237.
59. Van Ree JM, De Wied D. Endorphins in schizophrenia. *Neuropharmacology* 1981;20:1271–1277.
60. De Wied D. Psychopathology as a neuropeptide

dysfunction. In: van Ree JM, Terenius L, eds. *Characteristics and function of opioids.* Amsterdam: Elsevier/North Holland Biomedical Press, 1978;113–122.
61. Machandra R, Hirsch SR, Barnes TRE. Criteria for evaluating improvement in schizophrenia in psychopharmacological research (with special reference to gamma endorphin fragments). *Br J Psychiatry* 1988;153:354–358.
62. Verhoeven WMA, van Ree JM, Heezius-van Bentum A, et al. Antipsychotic properties of des-enkephalin-γ-endorphin in treatment of schizophrenic patients. *Arch Gen Psychiatry* 1982;39:648–654.
63. Moroji T, Watanabe N, Aoki N, et al. Antipsychotic effects of ceruletide (caerulein) on chronic schizophrenia. *Arch Gen Psychiatry* 1984;39:485–486.
64. Hommer DW, Pickar D, Roy A, et al. The effects of ceruletide in schizophrenia. *Arch Gen Psychiatry* 1984;41:617–619.
65. Mattes JA, Hom W, Rochford JM. A high-dose double-blind study of ceruletide in the treatment of schizophrenia. *Am J Psychiatry* 1985;142:1482–1484.
66. Iager A-C, Kirch DG, Bigelow LB, et al. Treatment of schizophrenia with a vasopressin analogue. *Am J Psychiat* 1986;143:375.
67. Gunne L-M, Lindstrom L, Terenius L. Naloxone-induced reversal of schizophrenic hallucinations. *J Neural Transm* 1977;40:13–19.
68. Lehmann H, Nair NPV, Kline NS. β-endorphin and naloxone in psychiatric patients: clinical and biological effects. *Am J Psychiatry* 1979;136:762–766.
69. Orr M, Oppenheimer C. Effects of naloxone on auditory hallucinations. *Br Med J* 1978;1:481.
70. Watson SJ, Berger PA, Akil H, et al. Effects of naloxone on schizophrenia: reduction in hallucinations in a subpopulation of subjects. *Science* 1978;201:73–76.
71. Berger PA, Watson SJ, Akil H, et al. The effects of naloxone in chronic schizophrenia. *Am J Psychiatry* 1981;138:913–918.
72. Kleinman JE, Weinberger DR, Rogol A, et al. Naloxone in chronic schizophrenic patients: neuroendocrine and behavior effects. *Psychiatry Res* 1982;7:1–7.
73. Pickar D, Bunney WE, Jr. The endogenous opioid system and psychiatric illness: effects of naloxone administration in schizophrenic and manic patients. In: Perris C, Struwe G, Jansson B, eds. *Biological Psychiatry 1981.* Amsterdam: Elsevier Scientific Publishers, 1981;394–397.
74. Pickar D, Vartanian F, Bunney WE Jr, et al. Short-term naloxone administration in schizophrenic and manic patients. *Arch Gen Psychiatry* 1982;39:313–319.
75. Janowsky DS, Segal DS, Bloom FE, et al. Lack of effect of naloxone on schizophrenic symptoms. *Am J Psychiatry* 1977;134:926–927.
76. Davis GC, Bunney WE, Jr, DeFraitez EG, et al. Intravenous naloxone administration in schizophrenia and affective illness. *Science* 1977;197:74–77.
77. Volavka J, Mallya A, Baig S, et al. Naloxone in chronic schizophrenia. *Science* 1977;196:1227–1228.
78. Lipinski J, Meyer R, Kornetsky C, et al. Naloxone in schizophrenia: negative result. *Lancet* 1979;2:1292–1293.
79. Verhoeven WMA, van Praag HM, de Jong JTVM. Use of naloxone in schizophrenic psychoses and manic syndromes. *Neuropsychobiology* 1981;7:159–168.
80. Verhoeven WMA, van Praag HM, van Ree JM. Repeated naloxone administration in schizophrenia. *Psychiat Res* 1984;12:297–312.
81. Naber D, Leibl K. Repeated high dosage naloxone treatment without therapeutic efficacy in schizophrenic patients. *Pharmakopsychiatria* 1983;16:43–45.
82. Mueser KT, Dysken MW. Narcotic antagonists in schizophrenia: a methodological review. *Schizophr Bull* 1983;9:213–225.
83. Beumont PJV. Endocrinology and schizophrenia. In: Burrows G, Norman H, Rubinstein R, eds. *Handbook of studies on schizophrenia,* part 1. Amsterdam: Elsevier Scientific Publishers, 1986;105–116.
84. Ferrier N. Endocrinology and psychosis. *Br Med Bull* 1987;43:672–688.
85. Asnis GM, Ryan ND. The psychoneuroendocrinology of schizophrenia. In: Rifkin A, ed. *Schizophrenia and affective disorders: biology and drug treatment.* Boston: John Wright, 1983;205–236.

8

Localization and Quantification of μ-Opiate Receptors by ^{11}C-Carfentanil and PET

Application in Schizophrenia

J. James Frost

The primary focus of positron emission tomography (PET) imaging research and schizophrenia has been on dopamine and dopamine receptors. Among the other neurotransmitters and their receptors that have been implicated in the pathogenesis of schizophrenia are the endogenous opioid peptides and opiate receptors. Measurement of opioid peptides in the cerebral spinal fluid (CSF) and therapeutic protocols using naloxone and various opioid peptides (1–13) have suggested a role for the opiate system in schizophrenia, although this is controversial. Further evidence comes from direct measurements of endogenous opioid peptides in post mortem brain tissue as some investigators have reported a decrease in met-enkephalin in the amygdala (14) and caudate nucleus (15). One study reported a decrease in caudate opiate receptors using ^{3}H-naloxone (16), but this was not confirmed in a second study (17). Further rationale for examining opiate receptors in schizophrenia is based on the increasing evidence that the opiate system plays a role in the control of dopamine release and reuptake (18).

There are several regions of the schizophrenic brain of interest for opiate receptor research using PET. These include the basal ganglia, the amygdala, and the limbic system. In several studies, neurochemically and morphologically abnormal amygdalas have been found in schizophrenic patients. Cholecystokinin (CCK) (19) and substance P (14) are decreased in the amygdala and negative-symptom schizophrenia, whereas vasoactive-intestinal peptide (VIP) is increased in the amygdala (19), particularly in positive-symptom schizophrenia. Furthermore, neuroanatomical studies using post mortem methods, x-ray computed tomography (CT) and MRI suggest atrophy and disorder of neuronal architecture in regions including the amygdala, hippocampal and parahippocampal regions, and cingulate cortex (20–25; see additional reports in this volume). Glucose metabolic studies using ^{18}F-fluorodeoxyglucose (^{18}F-FDG) have demonstrated hypometabolism in active schizophrenia in the amygdala, hippocampus, and anterior cingulate cortex (see Chapter 9). It is clear, then, that there are a number of brain regions in addition to the basal ganglia in which opiate receptor quantification is warranted.

Quantitative PET studies of neuroreceptor distribution require the application of tracer kinetic modeling. The following section outlines the approach to modeling ^{11}C-carfentanil binding in human subjects that can be applied to patients with schizophre-

[1]Departments of Radiology and Neuroscience, The Johns Hopkins University School of Medicine, Baltimore, MD 21205.

nia. The third section of this report describes the application of opiate receptor imaging with ^{11}C-carfentanil to patients with temporal-lobe epilepsy. These studies demonstrate the role of receptor studies in understanding the basic pathophysiology of CNS disorders as well as in the surgical management of patients with intractable temporal-lobe epilepsy. Interestingly, several studies have suggested that patients with complex partial epilepsy in mesial temporal EEG abnormalities have more frequent and more severe personality alterations than patients with other focal-seizure disorders or generalized epilepsy. Investigators have demonstrated that the psychosis associated with left-temporal-lobe discharges is characterized by disordered thought, while that associated with right-sided seizure foci is characterized by disordered emotions (26). Sherwin and co-workers reported that more left focused than right-focused patients developed schizophreniform psychoses (27). Neilsen and Kristensen reported increased emotional ability in patients with left- but not right-temporal-lobe foci (28).

LOCALIZATION AND QUANTIFICATION OF MU OPIATE RECEPTORS BY PET

Opiate receptors in rodents have been visualized by light microscopic autoradiography following in vitro (29) or in vivo (30) labeling. Detecting opiate receptors in intact animals following parenteral administration of radioactive ligands requires drugs with very high affinity for receptors (30–33). Opiate receptors have also been localized by autoradiography in the monkey brain following in vivo labeling with ^{3}H-diprenorphine (34).

Carfentanil is an extremely potent analogue of fentanyl that was chosen for PET studies based on its correspondingly high affinity. Several opiate receptor subtypes can be discriminated in binding studies. μ-Receptors tend to be most concentrated in areas such as the thalamus and periaqueductal gray, which are involved in pain perception, whereas δ-receptors are somewhat more concentrated in limbic areas and the pons (35,36). κ-Binding sites are most prominent in the deep layers of the cerebral cortex, the dentate nucleus, the substantia nigra, and the amygdala (36,37). The calculated affinity constants (K_I) of carfentanil for μ-, δ-, and κ-opiate receptors at 37°C are 0.051, 4.7, and 13 nM, respectively. Carfentanil (10 μmolar) fails to affect [^{3}H]3-PPP binding to σ-receptors. Accordingly, carfentanil is quite selective for μ-opiate receptors.

When ^{11}C-carfentanil was administered to a human subject, a strikingly heterogeneous radioactivity distribution was observed as early as 15 minutes after injection (38). The highest radioactivity concentrations were observed in the amygdala, thalamus, and caudate nucleus (Fig 1). Intermediate levels were noted in the frontal and parietal cerebral cortex, cerebellar cortex, cingulate cortex, and hippocampus. Lowest levels were observed in the calcarine cortex, the primary sensory cortex, and white matter. This distribution corresponds closely to the known distribution of opiate receptors in the human CNS determined by in vitro binding.

The opiate antagonist naloxone, when given prior to ^{11}C-carfentanil, produces a dose-dependent inhibition of ^{11}C-carfentanil binding in the human CNS over the dose range of 1.0 to 0.001 mg/kg (39) (ED$_{50}$ = 0.02 mg/kg). In structures such as the amygdala, approximately 90% of the total radioactivity was displaceable by 1 mg/kg naloxone 60 minutes after injection, demonstrating the high percentage specific binding that is achieved with ^{11}C-carfentanil (Fig 1). These studies demonstrate that changes in receptor occupancy can be measured by PET and suggest the use of this method to monitor the local concentration of clinically used opiate agonists and antagonists at receptor sites.

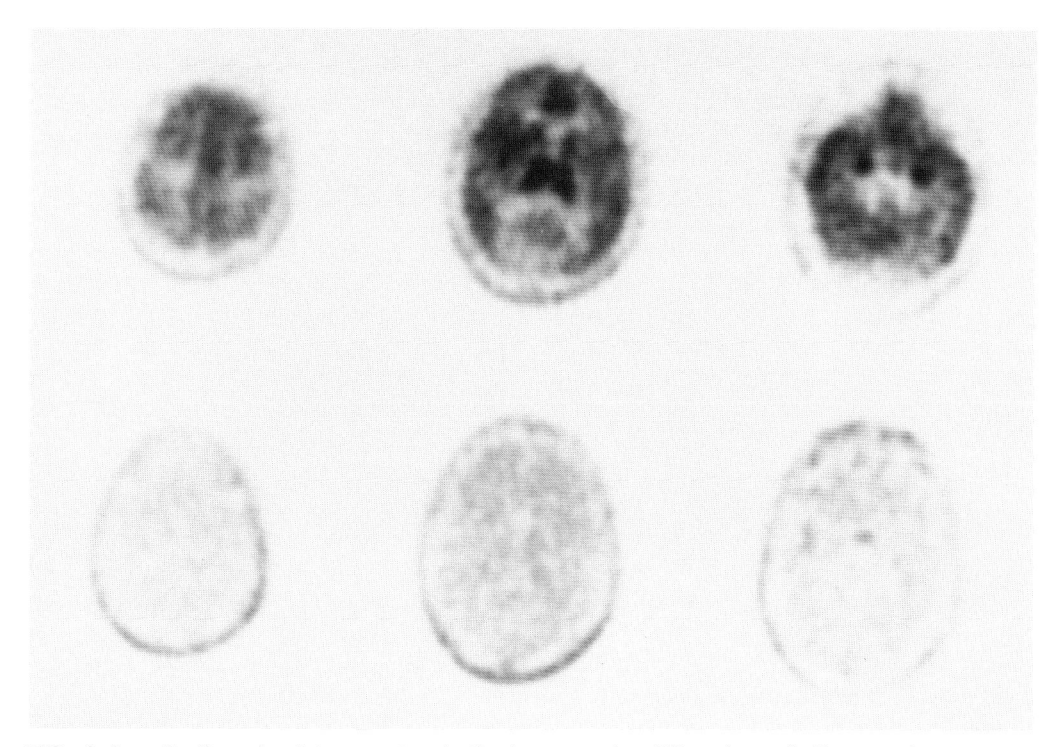

FIG. 1. Localization of opiate receptors in the human using ^{11}C-carfentanil. *Top row:* images were obtained using the NeuroECAT 30 to 60 minutes after intravenous administration of 20 mCi of ^{11}C-carfentanil. *Bottom row:* images were acquired at the same time following intravenous administration of the opiate antagonist naloxone (1 mg/kg) and the same dose of ^{11}C-carfentanil used in the first study. The brightness of each image is normalized for the injected activity, the acquisition time, and radioactive decay. A preferential accumulation of activity is seen in areas known to contain high concentrations of opiate receptors, such as the thalamus, basal ganglia, amygdala, and cortex. Conversely, low activity is seen where opiate receptors exist in low concentrations, such as the occipital cortex, postcentral gyrus, and cerebellum. The images in the bottom row demonstrate the low level of nonreceptor binding in the brain and pituitary gland. Binding is not inhibited in the skull or venous sinuses.

Following the development of ^{11}C-carfentanil, other positron-emitting opiates have been used to image opiate receptors by PET, including ^{11}C-diprenorphine (40,41) and ^{18}F-cyclofoxy (42).

One goal of PET receptor studies is to apply tracer kinetic modeling in order to estimate receptor number and rate constants that are independent of nonspecific processes such as blood flow or blood-brain transport. Tracer kinetic modeling was used to quantify ^{11}C-carfentanil binding to μ-opiate receptors in humans, and in addition, simulation studies were performed to demonstrate the theoretical behavior of the model when receptor and nonreceptor perturbations were introduced (43). Tracer kinetic modeling has been applied previously in other systems to quantify receptor binding in vivo in human and nonhuman studies (31,44–52). Equilibrium and nonequilibrium models have been employed with various levels of simplifying assumptions, and these have not always been validated. It was a primary goal of modeling studies using ^{11}C-carfentanil to use the most complete tracer kinetic approach justified by the data and subsequently utilize simulation experiments to determine when simplified methods of quantification could be employed.

The kinetics of brain ^{11}C-carfentanil in thalamus frontal cortex and occipital cortex was modeled using four compartments. The model consists of a vascular compartment and three tissue compartments that correspond to free tracer, nonspecifically bound tracer, and receptor-bound tracer. Six rate constants were used to model tracer uptake in receptor-rich regions such as the thalamus and frontal cortex. The constants are K_1 and k_2 for transport into and out of the tissue space, k_3 and k_4 for binding to and dissociation from receptors, and k_5 and k_6 for binding to and dissociation from the nonspecific compartment. In a region such as the occipital cortex, which has a negligible concentration of opiate receptors, k_3 and k_4 were set to zero. If plasma and brain concentrations are expressed in units of nanomolar concentration then K_1 will have units of milliliters per minute per milliliter brain tissue and k_2 through k_6 have units of per minute.

The rate constant for transport into the receptor-bound compartment, k_3, is treated as a first-order rate constant. This assumes that the concentration in this compartment, C_3, is always negligible compared with the total concentration of receptors, B_{max}. In this approximation, k_3 equals the product $k_{on} B_{max}$, where k_{on} is the molecular association rate constant and B_{max} is the total number of receptors. The dissociation rate constant k_4 depends on the molecular dissociation rate constant k_{off}, modified by processes such as receptor rebinding (31).

Table 1 shows the individual rate constants and mean values in the thalamus and frontal cortex for five normal volunteers. The values of k_5 and k_6 were determined in the occipital cortex and subsequently used in the analysis of frontal cortex and thalamus kinetics. The mean value of the binding potential ($B_{max}/K_D = k_3/k_4$) is also shown (51).

Simulation studies were conducted to determine whether simple ratios between regions with and without receptors could also be used for quantification. Such a method would be applicable when rigorous tracer kinetic modeling was not feasible. The effect that simulated changes in the value of k_3/k_4 for the thalamus had on the ratio of thalamus to occipital cortex concentrations was evaluated as a function of time. These results were obtained when k_3/k_4 was changed by varying k_3; similar results were obtained by varying k_4. There was only a small change in the thalamus–occipital cortex ratio at early times for different values of k_3/k_4. However, at times later than 20 minutes, when receptor binding predominates, there is a large effect on the value of the thalamus–occipital cortex ratio as k_3/k_4 is varied. As k_3/k_4 approaches zero, the thalamus–occipital cortex ratio remains constant at a value near unity. At large values of k_3/k_4 the increase in the thalamus–occipital cortex ratio becomes progressively smaller for a constant increase in k_3/k_4. When the average thalamus–occipital cortex ratio from 35 to 70 minutes was compared with k_3/k_4, a nearly linear relation was observed (43).

The results of these studies demonstrate that quantitative estimates of in vivo rate

TABLE 1. *Average rate constants for ^{11}C-carfentanil binding in thalamus and frontal cortex*

Region	k_3	k_4	$\dfrac{B_{max}}{K_D}$
Thalamus	0.20 ± 0.07	0.06 ± 0.02	3.4 ± 0.92
Frontal cortex	0.38 ± 0.24	0.22 ± 0.13	1.8 ± 0.33

k_3 = association rate constant (mean ± 1 SD).
k_4 = dissociation rate constant (mean ± 1 SD).
B_{max} = total concentration receptors.
K_D = equilibrium dissociation constant.

constants for μ-opiate receptor binding can be determined using ^{11}C-carfentanil and PET. Rigorous multicompartmental parameter estimation can be used to determine the validity of more simple approaches to quantification (i.e., ratios among different regions).

Simulation studies were helpful in evaluating the behavior of the model when receptor and nonreceptor parameters were perturbed. It is not always feasible or desirable to perform studies suitable for tracer kinetic modeling, for example, in uncooperative or debilitated patients or when extensive sampling of arterial blood or measurement of metabolites is not possible. Therefore, it is helpful to have simplified methods of quantification available. However, it is critical that such methods be validated with respect to their sensitivity to receptor and nonreceptor processes. Methods utilizing ratios among regions can be validated in part through simulations using data from tracer kinetic modeling studies. Without such validation studies, misleading results may be obtained with respect to the presence or absence of receptor changes in patient groups, following inhibition of receptors by drugs, and during physiologic activation of receptor systems.

PET STUDIES IN EPILEPSY

Seizure activity may be regarded as the result of an imbalance between excitatory and inhibitory processes in the brain. Accordingly, several excitatory and inhibitory neurotransmitters and their receptors have been implicated in experimental models of epilepsy and in human epilepsy. During the last decade a large number of studies have been carried out using experimental models of epilepsy to investigate both proconvulsant and anticonvulsant effects of endogenous and exogenous opioid substances (53). Initial studies suggested that opioid peptides were endogenous convulsants based on the production of bursts of epileptiform EEG discharges without true convulsive seizures. Subsequent studies suggested this effect was the result of presynaptic disinhibition of inhibitory pyramidal interneurons in the hippocampus (54). These observations were originally made in rats but subsequently were found not to generalize to other species. Nevertheless, a few isolated studies have shown that in rodents selective μ-opiate ligands can produce generalized convulsions and that these effects are reversed by β-funaltrexamine (an irreversible μ-selective receptor antagonist). Studies using the opiate antagonist naloxone have in general suggested that the endogenous opioids do not play a major role in the initiation or propagation of seizures.

A role for opioid systems in the suppression of seizures in a variety of experimental models of epilepsy is considerably more robust (53). Naloxone-reversible anticonvulsant effects of opioid peptides have been documented in mice, rats, gerbils, rabbits, and baboons through chemical, electrical, and genetic experimental models of human epilepsy. Furthermore, seizures result in the release of an anticonvulsant substance into the CSF, and the anticonvulsant effects of this substance can be reversed by naloxone (55). Immunoreactivity studies indicate the presence of a β-endorphinlike substance and a met-enkephalin precursor (56). Current evidence also suggests that the anticonvulsant effects of both peptide and nonpeptide opioids can be mediated through μ-, δ-, or κ-opiate receptors.

These and other studies taken together suggest that, rather than having a primary role in seizure initiation or propagation, opioid peptides are most involved with the termination or arrest of seizures. Further evidence for a role of opioid systems in seizure mechanisms comes from the observation that opiate receptors are also altered following experimental seizures (57–61).

We have used ^{11}C-carfentanil to investigate the role of opioid systems in human epilepsy using PET. Patients who met the following criteria were identified: (a) they had complex partial seizures; (b) no underlying structural lesion was evident from x-ray CT; and (c) the unilateral temporal-lobe seizure focus had been carefully documented by surface- and depth-electrode EEG recordings. These subjects were studied using ^{11}C-carfentanil as well as ^{18}F-FDG. The latter drug has previously been used to identify reduced utilization of glucose in the vicinity of seizure foci in approximately 70% of patients with temporal-lobe epilepsy (62). Imaging planes were carefully selected using x-ray CT such that the amygdala and temporal neocortex were adequately sampled.

In the initial series of 13 subjects with temporal-lobe epilepsy a significant increase in the binding of ^{11}C-carfentanil in the temporal neocortex ipsilateral to the seizure focus was observed (63). Tracer kinetic modeling indicated that this increase in binding was due to an increase in the number or affinity of opiate receptors rather than to blood flow or blood-brain barrier transport effects. The area of increased ^{11}C-carfentanil binding corresponded to areas with reduced glucose utilization using ^{18}F-FDG, and there was a significant relationship between the elevation in ^{11}C-carfentanil binding and the reduction in glucose utilization. There was no significant increase in the binding in amygdala or hippocampus regions, although two subjects had greatly reduced binding in the amygdala ipsilateral to the seizure focus.

These findings have been confirmed in an additional series of patients with temporal-lobe epilepsy with the primary abnormalities in ^{11}C-carfentanil binding in the temporal neocortex. Isolated patients have continued to show reduced ^{11}C-carfentanil binding in the amygdala ipsilateral to the seizure focus, although the significance of this remains unclear. The observation that the greatest changes in ^{11}C-carfentanil binding is observed in the temporal neocortex as opposed to the amygdala or hippocampus was initially surprising since most partial epilepsy foci are thought to originate in these regions. However, the observations from ^{11}C-carfentanil studies may be consistent with experimental models of epilepsy that suggest that the predominant role of opioid systems is in limiting the propagation and termination of seizures. It is possible that the enhanced activity of the opioid system in the temporal neocortex inhibits the spread of electrical activity originating in the amygdala or hippocampus.

There is considerable variation in the degree to which ^{11}C-carfentanil binding is elevated in the temporal neocortex in clinically homogeneous patients: some subjects show no significant asymmetry while others have been observed with a greater than two-fold asymmetry between the ipsilateral and contralateral temporal neocortices. Additionally, the distribution of increased ^{11}C-carfentanil varies from very focal areas of asymmetry to diffusely increased binding. One subject studied with a frontal-lobe seizure focus also demonstrated elevated ^{11}C-carfentanil binding and reduced glucose utilization in the area of the electrical focus.

Future studies in this area are designed to examine the relationship between elevated ^{11}C-carfentanil binding and EEG data obtained from subdural electrical grid electrodes in patients with intractable epilepsy undergoing evaluation for surgical treatment. To the extent that the distributions of increased ^{11}C-carfentanil binding and abnormal electrical activity are coupled, the noninvasive monitoring of opiate receptors by PET could supplement the more invasive evaluations of patients with intractable seizures. Studies to examine the relationship between clinical seizure parameters such as frequency, duration of individual seizures, duration of illness, etc, are also underway to examine the relationships suggested by studies in experimental epilepsy (i.e., that change in opiate receptors are more related to seizure duration than frequency). It will also be important to investigate the specificity of the observed changes to subjects with idiopathic intractable epilepsy. This will be accomplished by examining alterations in ¹¹C-carfentanil binding in subjects with classical migraine, epilepsy due to a neoplastic process, other types of epilepsy, etc. Since the animal models of epilepsy suggest a role for δ- and κ-opiate receptors in addition to μ-receptors, it will be important to develop labeled PET ligands for δ- and κ-receptors. Preliminary data have suggested that non-μ-opiate receptors are also elevated in temporal lobe epilepsy and that the distribution of altered μ- and non-μ-opiate receptors is different in the same individual; this suggests that there is a differential regulation of μ and non-μ-opiate receptors in epilepsy (64).

In addition to the kappa and delta receptors in epilepsy, there are a number of excitatory and inhibitory neurotransmitter receptors in epilepsy that could be studied using PET. Interestingly, a recent study has suggested a reduced number or affinity of benzodiazepine receptors in temporal-lobe epilepsy (65). The future of these studies lies in improved understanding of the neurochemical mechanisms in epilepsy, the subclassification of epilepsy patients based on neurochemical criteria, rational approaches to drug therapy based on the observation of specific neurochemical abnormalities, and improvements in the noninvasive evaluation of potential subjects for seizure surgery as well as improved definition of the regions to be resected.

CONCLUSION

A variety of lines of evidence continues to suggest that opiate mechanisms may be altered in schizophrenia. To date, the methodologies used to investigate this issue have been largely indirect (ie, CSF analysis or treatment protocols) or have been performed on post mortem tissue. Positron emission tomography now permits in vivo examination of the opiate system through receptor imaging using ¹¹C-carfentanil. Radiolabeled ligands are also being developed for κ-opiate receptors; these ligands are of interest given the psychotomimetic effects of κ-agonists as well as their effects on dopamine kinetics. Also available are advanced tracer kinetic modeling methodologies that permit regional quantification of μ-opiate receptor binding and the ability to account for nonspecific processes such as blood flow or blood-brain barrier transport. These methods already have had application in patients with temporal-lobe epilepsy, where an increase in temporal neocortical opiate receptors has been observed. Studies using PET and ¹¹C-carfentanil in schizophrenic patients have commenced, and the results of these studies should be forthcoming in the near future.

REFERENCES

1. Terenius L, Wahlstrom A, Lindstrom LH, Widerlov E. *Neurosci Lett* 1976;3:157–162.
2. Lindstrom LH, Widerlov E, Gunne LM, et al. *Acta Psychiatr Scand* 1978;57:153–169.
3. Rimon R, Terenius L, Kampman R. *Acta Psychiatr Scand* 1980;61:395–403.
4. Lindstrom LH, Besev G, Gunne LM, et al. In: NS Shah, AG Donald, eds. *Endorphins and opiate antagonists in psychiatry*, Plenum Press, New York, 1982;245–256.
5. DuPont A, Villeneuve A, Bouchard JP, et al. *Lancet* 1978;2:1107.
6. Akil H, Watson SH, Sullivan S, Barchas JD. *Life Sci* 1978;23:121–126.
7. Domschke W, Dickschas A, Mitznegg P. *Lancet* 1979;1:1024.
8. Naber D, Nedopil N, Eben E. *Br J Psychiatry* 1984;144:651–653.
9. Naber D, Pickar D. *Psychiatr Clin North Am* 1983;6:443–456.
10. Naber D, Pickar D, Post RM, et al. In: Perris C, Struwe G, and Jansson B, eds. *Biological psychiatry*, Elsevier, Amsterdam, 1981;372–375.
11. Naber D, Pickar D, Post RM, et al. *Am J Psychiatry* 1981;138:1457–1462.
12. Wen HL, Lo CW, Ho WK. *Clin Chim Acta* 1983;128:367–371.
13. Berger PA, Watson SJ, Akil H, Barchas JD. Martin JB, eds. In: *Neuropeptides in neurologic and psychiatric disease*, New York: Raven Press, 1986;309–333.
14. Bissette G, Nemeroff CV, MacKay AVP. *Prog Brain Res*, Elsevier, Amsterdam 1986;66:161–174.
15. Kleinman JE, Iadarola M, Govoni S, et al. *Psychopharmacol Bull* 1983;19:375–377.
16. Reisine TD, Rossor M, Spokes E, et al. In: Papeu G, Kuhar MJ, Enna SJ eds. *Receptors for*

neurotransmitters and reptile hormones, New York: Raven Press, 1980.
17. Owen F, Bourne RC, Poulter M, et al. *Br J Psychiatry* 1985;146:507–509.
18. Feigenbaum JJ, Fishman RHB, Yanai J. *Substance and Alcohol Actions/Misuse* 1982;3:307–324.
19. Ferrier IN, Robert GW, Crow UJ, et al. *Life Sci* 1983;33:475–482.
20. Nieto D, Escobar A. In: *Pathology of the nervous system,* vol. 3. New York: McGraw-Hill, 1972;2654–2665.
21. Dom R, DeSaedeleer J, Bogerts J, Hopf A. In: *Proceedings of the third world congress of biological psychiatry, Stockholm.* Amsterdam: Elsevier, 1981.
22. Kovelman JA, Scheibel AB. *Biolog Psychiatry* 1984;19:1601–1621.
23. Bogerts B, Meertz E, Schonfelt-Bausch R. *Arch Gen Psychiatry* 1985;42:784–791.
24. Benes FM, Davidson J, Bird ED. *Arch Gen Psychiatry* 1986;43:31–35.
25. Brown R, Colter N, Corsellis JAN, et al. *Arch Gen Psychiatry* 1986;43:36–42.
26. Flor-Henry P. *Epilepsia* 1969;10:363–395.
27. Sherwin, et al. *Arch Neurol* 1982;39:621–625.
28. Nielsen H, Kristenson O. *Acta Neurolog Scand* 1981;64:289–300.
29. Young WS III, Kuhar MJ. *Brain Res* 1979;179:255–270.
30. Pert CB, Kuhar MJ, Snyder SH. *Proc Natl Acad Sci USA* 1976;73:3729–3733.
31. Frost JJ, Wagner HN Jr. *Brain Res* 1984;305:1–11.
32. Perry DC, Mullis KB, Oie S, Sadee W. *Brain Res* 1980;199:49–61.
33. Laduron PM, Janssen PFM, Leysen JE. *Biochem Pharmacol* 1978;27:317–321.
34. Wamsley JK, Azrbin MA, Young WS III, Kuhar MJ. *Neuroscience* 1982;7:595–613.
35. Goodman RR, Snyder SH, Kuhar MJ, Young WS III. *Proc Natl Acad Sci USA* 1980;77:6239–6243.
36. Pfeiffer A, Pasi A, Mehraein P, Herz A. *Brain Res* 1982;248:87–96.
37. Goodman RR, Snyder SH. *Proc Natl Acad Sci USA* 1982;79:5703–5707.
38. Frost JJ, Wagner JH Jr, Dannals RF, et al. *J Comput Assist Tomogr* 1985;9(2):231–236.
39. Frost JJ, Behal R, Mayberg HS, et al. *J Nucl Med* 1986;27:P935.
40. Frost JJ, Mayberg HS, Sadzot B, et al. *J Cereb Blood Flow Metab* 1990;10:484–492.
41. Jones AKP, Luthra SK, Maziere B, et al. *J Neurosci Methods* 1988;23:121–129.
42. Pert CB, Danks JA, Channing MA, et al. *FEBS* 1984;177:281–286.
43. Frost JJ, Douglass KH, Mayberg HS, et al. *J Cereb Blood Flow Metab* 1989;9:398–409.
44. Farde L, Hall H, Ehrin E, Sedvall G. *Science* 1986;231:258–260.
45. Wong DF, Gjedde A, Wagner JH Jr. *J Cereb Blood Flow Metab* 1986A;6:137–146.
46. Wong DF, Gjedde A, Wagner HN Jr, et al. *J Cereb Blood Flow Metab* 1986B;6:147–153.
47. Logan J, Wolf AP, Shieu CY, Fowler JS. *J Neurochem* 1987;48:73–83.
48. Bice AN, Zeeberg BR. *IEEE Trans Med Imag* 1987;6:244–249.
49. Frey KA, Hichwa RD, Ehrenkaufer RLE, Agranoff BW. *Proc Natl Acad Sci USA* 1985;82:6711–6715.
50. Patlak CS, Blasberg RG. *J Cereb Blood Flow Metab* 1985;5:584–590.
51. Mintun MA, Raichle ME, Kilbourn MR, et al. *Ann Neurol* 1984;15:217–227.
52. Perlmutter JS, Larson KB, Raichle ME, et al. *J Cereb Blood Flow Metab* 1986;6:154–169.
53. Tortella FC. *TIPS* 1988;9:366–372.
54. Siggins GR, Henrikson SJ, Chavkin C, Gruol D. *Adv Neurol* 1986;44:501–522.
55. Tortella FC, Long JB. *Science* 1985;228:1106–1108.
56. Tortella FC, Long JB. *Brain Res* 1988;456:139–146.
57. Hitzemann RJ, Hitzemann BA, Blatt S, et al. *Mol Pharmacol* 1987;31:562–566.
58. Holaday JW, Tortella FC, Meyerhoff JL, et al. *Ann NY Acad Sci* 1986;467:249–255.
59. Lee RJ, McCabe RT, Wamsley JK, et al. *Brain Res* 1986;380:76–82.
60. Nakata Y, Chang KJ, Mitchell CL, Hon JS. *Brain Res* 1985;346:160–163.
61. Weiss S, Seeger TF, Ostrowski N, et al. *Soc Neurosci Abstr* 1985;2:1068.
62. Engle J Jr, Babb TL, Phelps ME. In: Engel J Jr, et al, eds. *Fundamental mechanisms of human brain function,* New York: Raven Press, 1987;209–218.
63. Frost JJ, Mayberg HS, Fisher RS, et al. *Ann Neurol* 1988;23:231–237.
64. Frost JJ, Mayberg HS, Meltzer CC, et al. *J Nucl Med* 1989; (abstract in press).
65. Savic I, Roland P, Sedvall G, et al. *Lancet* 1988;863–866.

9

The Limbic System in Schizophrenia

Pharmacologic and Metabolic Evidence

Carol A. Tamminga,[1] Hiro Kaneda,[1] Robert Buchanan,[1] Brian Kirkpatrick,[1] Gunvant K. Thaker,[1] Mary Beth Yablonski,[1] and Henry H. Holcomb[1,2]

Much is known about the presentation, symptoms, and course of schizophrenia (1,2). Observations about its epidemiology have been made and are being gathered (3). Various sets of diagnostic criteria have been developed that, although they may require more "firming," still provide an abundance of diagnostic consistency. Course of illness is being scrutinized for clues to biology and improved treatment (4). The clinical pharmacology of schizophrenia has been studied extensively, although inevitably incompletely, for the same kind of clues (5). Even questions of central nervous system (CNS) structural (6) and functional alteration (7–18; Table 1) have been addressed with imaging technologies to provide interesting leads if not a firm answer.

What remains unknown about schizophrenia are its basic biologic characteristics, its anatomic substrate, its biochemical mediators, and the resultant neural orchestration of its pathophysiology. Similar facts define diseases in other areas of medicine: diabetes, congestive heart failure, ulcers, and the like. Based on the similar spectrum of symptoms in individuals with schizophrenia, the common age of onset, and the rather homogeneous response to dopamine-receptor-blocking drugs, many investigators have tended to assume a single pathophysiologic mechanism (or at least a related set of mechanisms), even when assuming diverse etiologies. Thus the disease may be hypothesized to have a characteristic anatomy and biochemistry. On the other hand, the possibility does exist that schizophrenia is not a single disease but rather a condition like headache, high blood pressure, or anemia for which there exist not only multiple etiologies but multiple pathophysiologies. In this chapter, we will suggest a common neural pathway for schizophrenic manifestations in the brain, perhaps triggered by a variety of agents or etiologies. This anatomy may subserve the psychotic symptoms of the illness and would underlie (perhaps less directly) the social and personality changes characteristic of schizophrenia.

Currently, an anatomic study of the human brain relevant to schizophrenia is timely. This is the case because new technologies, previously unavailable, can now be used to study the functional anatomy of the illness and animal models of psychosis. The regional cerebral metabolic response to a pharmacologic perturbation or to a dis-

[1]Maryland Psychiatric Research Center, University of Maryland Medical School, Baltimore, MD 21228.
[2]Nuclear Medicine Section, Department of Radiology, Johns Hopkins University, Baltimore, MD 21205.

TABLE 1. *PET/FDG studies in schizophrenia*

Reference	N	Conditions	Findings[a]
(7)	17	+N, resting, eyes open	Increased frontal and decreased occipital rCMRglu in S. with neuroleptics ($\times$ 1 yr); striatal rCMRglu increased in S.
(8)	18	+N, resting and task	Negative Sx S fail to increase frontal rCMRglu with task.
(9)	12	−N (> 10 days), resting, eyes open	Whole-brain rCMRglu reduced in S; S have an increased subcortical/cortical gradient.
(10)	16	−N (> 13 d), auditory CPT, eyes closed	CPT performance in S was not related to frontal rCMRglu, but was in normals.
(11)	6	+N, resting, eyes open	Small rCMRglu decreases in S in LIFront and RSTemp cortices
(12)	18	−N, resting, eyes closed	Reduced prefrontal rCMRglu in prefrontal cortex, lentiform n, and thalamus in S.
(13)	10	−N (14 d), +N (5W), resting, eyes open	Reduced frontal and temporal rCMRglu in S. Negative correlation: withdrawal/rCMRglu.
(14)	9	±N	rCMRglu increased by neuroleptic, no differences between S and controls
(15)	6	−N (> 2W), vigilance task	No difference between S and controls
(16)	16	−N (> 2W), right arm electrical shock	Anterior/posterior cortical ratio, rCMRglu: Controls > S.
(17)	13	6 +N, 7 −N, quiet, eyes closed	Decreased frontal rCMRglu in S.
(18)	8	−N, eyes closed, quiet	Reduced rCMRglu in SFront cortex in S.

[a] S = schizophrenics; Sx = symptom; RSTemp = right superior temporal; LIFront = left inferior frontal.

ease-induced change can be assessed by measuring regional glucose changes in the CNS using the ^{14}C-2-deoxyglucose autoradiographic technique in rats (19) or the ^{18}F-2-deoxyglucose (FDG)/positron emission tomography (PET) technique in humans (20). This chapter will examine the cerebral pathways of altered neural activity in a laboratory rat model of psychosis, using phencyclidine (PCP) and one of its agonists, MK801; PCP produces dramatic behavioral effects in animals and psychosis in humans. These areas, along with the circuits they make up, have suggested a novel neural circuit for psychosis in humans. A pharmacologic study of the PCP effect on cerebral neural activity, as measured by glucose utilization, has already suggested a novel circuit involving limbic structures for psychosis that could mediate psychotic symptoms in humans (21). The animal model was then tested in schizophrenic patients with active psychotic symptoms to explore whether limbic structures are associated with psychosis across subtypes of the schizophrenic diagnosis.

PSYCHOTOMIMETIC ACTIONS OF PCP IN NORMAL HUMANS SUGGESTING SCHIZOPHRENIA

Since its original synthesis in the late 1950s, PCP has repeatedly come to the attention of behavioral scientists, first to evaluate its postanesthetic behavioral changes, then to exhaustively study those behavioral effects in normal controls. Now it has become a popular drug of abuse. Originally, PCP was developed as an anesthetic to produce full surgical anesthesia without causing cerebral and respiratory depression (22). The initial attempts to utilize PCP as an anesthetic were plagued by the occurrence of severe postanesthetic behavioral reactions that resembled psychosis, including agitation, bizarre behavior, and hallucinations. Thus, the drug was never pursued for therapeutic application in humans; rather, its sister drug, ketamine, was developed for veterinary and human obstetric use. But these behavioral actions of PCP in humans quickly came to the attention of neurobiologists, because the human reactions to PCP often closely mimicked schizophrenia.

Phencyclidine has been shown to bind selectively and reversibly to its own receptor in the mammalian CNS (see Chapter 2). These receptors are located in highest concentration in the hippocampus, cingulate cortex, and cortical mantle. They are in modestly high concentrations in the striatum and thalamus and only sparsely represented in the midbrain and cerebellum. PCP receptors are located in the calcium ion channel of the cell surface, N-methyl-D-aspartate (NMDA) receptor complex and antagonize NMDA stimulation; the NMDA receptor is positively modulated by a neighboring glycine receptor and negatively modulated by kynurenine and Mg^{2+}. This receptor complex is highly localized to limbic structures (23).

The psychologic responses of normal human subjects to PCP administration include both delirium, with clouded consciousness and altered EEG or vivid psychotic symptoms, and affective responses with no altered consciousness or EEG changes (24). Delirious states can be both acute or chronic, the latter being prolonged well beyond the drug half-life. The drug action may be particularly prolonged because of the formation of active metabolites and the enteric reabsorption of the drug. The psychotomimetic action of PCP, without delirium, causes body-image distortions, perceptions of estrangement, thought disorganization, negativism and hostility, hypnogogic state, and repetitive motor behaviors in normal individuals (25). Investigators have noted close parallels between PCP-induced mentation and schizophrenic thought disorder. It has also been observed that PCP causes disturbances in reaction time, motor learning, and weight discrimination in normal controls that are similar to performance abnormalities found in schizophrenics without PCP. In addition, PCP produces changes in abstraction (proverb interpretation) and sequential thinking (serial sevens) in normal controls which mimic schizophrenic thought characteristics. Neither LSD nor amylbarbital produce these neuropsychologic changes (26) or alter abstract thought or sequential construction in normals (27). Finally, when given to schizophrenic patients, PCP reportedly activates the primary symptoms of their psychotic illness; patients become "profoundly disorganized" and "regressive" (28). Thus, much human behavioral data would suggest that PCP is a unique psychotomimetic compound, different from other psychotomimetics such as LSD or barbiturates in its capacity to induce a mental state similar to schizophrenia itself. As a pharmacologic model, PCP more closely approximates schizophrenia than other psychotomimetic compounds because it produces behaviors strongly reminiscent of schizophrenia in normal humans, induces testable signs in normals like those found in untreated schizophrenics, and worsens the psychopathology in ill schizophrenics.

ACTIONS OF MK801 [(+)-5-METHYL-1-,11-DIHYDRO-5H-DIBENZO[a,d]CYCLOHEPT-5,10-IMINE MALEATE]

MK801 was originally described for its anticonvulsant, anxioloytic, and sympathomimetic properties. Now it is much more widely known as a potent and selective ligand for the PCP receptor in the brain (29,30). Moreover, this compound, like PCP, has been shown to negatively modulate the effects of N-Methyl-D-aspartate (NMDA) at its glutamate receptor subtype without affecting agonist responses at the other glutamate receptors. MK801 binds with high affinity to the PCP receptor and displays biochemical (31), electrophysiologic (32), and behavioral (33) properties of PCP. Through its anti-NMDA action, it is neuron-sparing in animal models of anoxia, neurodegeneration, and stroke. Because the behavioral actions of PCP in humans resemble symptoms in schizophrenia, knowledge of the neural sites and network of MK801 action might be important to the understanding of psychosis.

Because the actions of PCP and presumably MK801 produce a schizophreniclike psychosis in normal humans, the distribution of brain metabolic changes induced by PCP or MK801 in the rat brain could predict a "psychosis circuit" or set of CNS areas that mediate psychosis in humans. These PCP/MK801-induced changes in the rat would be purportedly paralleled to some degree by alterations in metabolism in the human schizophrenic brain.

MK801 Action on Regional Cerebral Glucose Metabolism in Rat Brain

Energy consumption in the mammalian brain derives almost exclusively from glucose catabolism; the activity of neurons in secretion and reuptake of transmitters is thought to be directly proportional to their glucose use (19). Hence, regional glucose utilization can be taken as an index of neuronal synaptic activity in the mammalian CNS. The consumption of glucose by neural tissue can be measured quantitatively and regionally in the rat using the Sokoloff technique and model. The same process can be measured, again quantitatively and regionally albeit with considerably lower resolution, in the human patient using PET with FDG (20). This technique has provided brain biologists with an unprecedented opportunity to study the animal and human CNS for localizing information about behaviors, drug effects, or disease states.

Method. Quantitative glucose metabolism in the rat brain was assessed as previously described (21). In summary, (1.25 mCi/kg) of ^{14}C-2-deoxyglucose (^{14}C-2DG) was administered to laboratory rodents who were pretreated with MK801 or saline. After a 45-minute incorporation period, the animals were sacrificed, their brains were sectioned and autoradiographed, and the optical density of the ^{14}C-2DG in each was read on an IBAS II Image Analysis System. MK801 was administered in doses of 0.1 and 1.0 mg/kg 10 minutes prior to the administration of 2DG. Data were analyzed using multivariate analysis of variance with post hoc *t*-tests for significance.

Results. MK801 increased local cerebral glucose metabolism (LCGM) in predominantly limbic brain structures while reducing metabolism in sensory areas related to audition (Table 2). MK801 had a more restricted effect on regional glucose metabolism than that previously found for PCP in that it increased brain metabolism in limbic circuit structures like the hippocampus, amygdala, and cingulate cortex, but it failed to alter metabolism throughout extrapyramidal structures or in nonsensory cortical areas. In contrast, PCP significantly increased neocortical glucose utilization in entorhinal and visual areas. In the extrapyramidal system, PCP produced consistent increases in glucose utilization, particularly in striatum, globus pallidus, substantia nigra, and red nucleus (Table 3). Metabolism in the lateral habenula, proposed as a marker of antipsychotic drug action, increased with MK801, a change in the same direction as obtained with antipsychotic drugs. The most consistent and profound alterations in brain metabolism following both MK801 and PCP occurred in the limbic system, most particularly in subiculum, anterior cingulate, anteroventral thalamus, and the interpeduncular nucleus.

Interpretation. The hippocampus has a high density of PCP receptors, and certain

TABLE 2. MK801 effect on LCGM in rat (μmol glucose/100 g tissue/min)

Brain area	Saline	0.1 mg/kg	1.0 mg/kg
Neocortical areas:			
Dorsolateral prefrontal	56.2 (3.9)	56.7 (5.6)	55.4 (4.5)
Sensorimotor	67.1 (5.1)	59.8 (7.8)	50.3 (1.8)*
Parietal	61.1 (4.1)	58.7 (6.0)	52.1 (4.2)
Visual	60.3 (3.3)	70.4 (8.8)	69.0 (9.1)
Limbic areas:			
Nucleus accumbens	58.8 (2.3)	75.3 (6.8)*	69.3 (4.6)**
Cingulate cortex	67.0 (3.5)	71.6 (7.0)	77.3 (4.2)**
Lateral septum	36.2 (1.5)	38.0 (4.0)	33.5 (2.1)
Subiculum	53.3 (3.1)	58.3 (5.6)	69.8 (4.1)*
Hippocampus	41.3 (1.4)	49.1 (5.0)	56.1 (1.7)*
Dentate	35.7 (2.1)	40.0 (4.1)	42.6 (1.7)*
Extrapyramidal areas:			
Caudate	66.2 (3.2)	77.2 (9.9)	73.8 (5.7)
Globus pallidus	31.7 (2.5)	39.9 (3.9)	48.1 (4.2)*
Substantia nigra, compacta	46.7 (3.8)	47.6 (4.6)	46.9 (2.4)
Subthalamic nucleus	46.6 (3.0)	58.6 (4.9)**	63.5 (5.2)*
Substantia nigra, reticulata	33.2 (2.3)	38.6 (5.8)	34.6 (3.7)
Brain stem areas:			
Dorsal raphe	47.6 (3.2)	56.0 (3.4)	53.0 (4.6)
Lateral lemniscus	54.1 (3.6)	52.0 (8.3)	66.0 (3.8)*
Inferior colliculus	107.9 (2.9)	79.6 (7.2)*	64.7 (4.0)*
Locus ceruleus	30.9 (0.8)	39.5 (3.5)*	46.3 (3.5)*
Superior olive	73.1 (4.0)	60.9 (4.6)**	80.6 (6.6)
White matter:			
Corpus callosum	20.0 (1.6)	21.8 (2.0)	21.1 (1.8)

*$p < .05$.
**$p < .06$.

TABLE 3. Percent change in LCGM with MK801 compared with PCP

Brain area	MK801/Saline $M \times 100\%$ (1 mg/kg)	PCP/Saline $P \times 100\%$ (4 mg/kg)
Cerebral cortex		
Dorsolateral frontal cortex	98.6	108.6
Sensory motor cortex	75.0*	100.7
Parietal cortex	85.3	128.6
Cingulate cortex, anterior	115.4	164.7*
Extrapyramidal motor		
Caudate	111.5	168.3*
Globus pallidus	151.7*	115.5
Substantia nigra, compacta	100.4	144.0*
Substantia nigra, reticulata	104.2	173.5*
Red nucleus	100.9	130.2
Subthalamic nucleus	136.3*	126.2*
Limbic system and other		
Hippocampus	135.8*	146.5
Subiculum	131.0*	205.2*
Dentate gyrus	119.3	135.8
Nucleus accumbens	117.9	151.9*
Mediodorsal thalamus	134.3*	156.0
Brain stem		
Lateral lemniscus	122.0*	88.9
Inferior colliculus	60.0*	67.1*
Superior olive	110.3	107.6
Dorsal raphe	111.3	104.4
Locus ceruleus	149.8*	130.1*

*$p < .05$.

of its efferent pathways target the subiculum, anterior thalamus, cingulate cortex, and temporal cortex. Indeed, the structures metabolically altered by the selective PCP-receptor agonist MK801 include most of the nuclei in the Circle of Papez, classically proposed to mediate affective, motivational, and cognitive behaviors in animals. As such, these are all areas that may contribute to the psychotomimetic effects of PCP. The hippocampus and its efferent circuits also project to the nucleus accumbens and may interact with the mesolimbic dopamine system, implicated in the antipsychotic action of neuroleptic drugs (12).

Changes in Regional Cerebral Glucose Metabolism in Schizophrenia

Localization of primary areas in human brain with PET/FDG related to psychosis and to schizophrenia are complicated by many methodologic factors; not the least of these are the effects of chronic medication, standardization of mental activity in subjects being scanned, and analysis of the images for the circuitry involved. But, the power of the various technologically new in vivo imaging devices to provide information about human brain function in diseases like schizophrenia enables scientists to begin addressing complex questions of localizing pathophysiology.

The current human studies were carried out to examine the hypothesis generated from the putative animal model of schizophrenia just described, suggesting that psychotic processes utilize limbic pathways for their generation and/or expression, whether in PCP-treated rats or in schizophrenic patients. Subjects were all at rest to provide an initial "basal" comparison between brain metabolism in normal and patient subjects.

Results. We previously reported data from 12 schizophrenic patients and normal controls, demonstrating apparent reductions in cerebral glucose utilization confined to the limbic system (34). Among the schizophrenics, in the hippocampus a 27% decrease in glucose metabolism occurred ($p < .001$), in the anterior cingulate cortex, a 26% decrease ($p < .008$), and in the amygdala area, an 18% decrease ($p < .05$). The relative glucose utilization values (brain area/cerebellum) in these particular areas were all significantly reduced in schizophrenic patients compared with normals; using these relative values, metabolism is seen to have diminished in parts of the temporal lobe as well (Table 4). There were no significant differences between patients and

TABLE 4. *Transposed rCMRglu in schizophrenia at rest, means (SD)*

	Schizophrenia (N = 12)	Normal controls (N = 12)
Limbic system		
Anterior cingulate	1.22 (0.26)**	1.56 (0.36)
Hippocampal cortex	0.91 (0.20)	1.13 (0.29)
Amygdala area	0.78 (0.10)***	0.87 (0.10)
Subcortical gray		
Caudate	1.31 (0.31)	1.36 (0.25)
Putamen	1.31 (0.33)	1.41 (0.30)
Thalamus	1.29 (0.35)	1.30 (0.29)
SN area	0.95 (0.26)	1.10 (0.27)
Neocortex		
Frontal	1.33 (0.26)	1.42 (0.27)
Parietal	1.22 (0.33)	1.32 (0.35)
Temporal	1.04 (0.17)*	1.24 (0.22)
Occipital	1.00 (0.23)	1.15 (0.31)

*$p < .05$.
**$p < .02$.
***$p < .06$.

TABLE 5. *Transposed rCMRglu in deficit vs nondeficit schizophrenia, means (SD)*

	Deficit (N = 4)	Nondeficit (N = 7)	Normal controls (N = 12)
Limbic system			
Anterior cingulate	1.2 (3.9)	1.2 (0.10)	1.56 (0.36)
Hippocampal cortex	0.99 (0.29)	0.82 (0.10)	1.13 (0.29)
Amygdala area	0.76 (0.09)	0.77 (0.12)	0.87 (0.10)
Subcortical grey			
Caudate	1.11 (0.08)	1.34 (0.28)	1.36 (0.25)
Putamen	1.19 (0.17)	1.30 (0.35)	1.41 (0.30)
Thalamus	1.01 (0.10)*	1.38 (0.30)	1.30 (0.29)
SN area	0.91 (0.35)	0.91 (0.11)	1.10 (0.27)
Neocortex			
Frontal	1.08 (0.13)*	1.40 (0.22)	1.42 (0.27)
Parietal	0.96 (0.12)*	1.3 (0.23)	1.32 (0.35)
Temporal	0.93 (0.16)	1.1 (0.12)	1.24 (0.22)
Occipital	0.96 (0.38)	0.89 (0.08)	1.15 (0.31)

*$p < .05$.

controls in frontal or parietal areas in either absolute or relative metabolic values.

Within the group of schizophrenic patients, some subjects evidenced primary and enduring negative symptoms, defined as the deficit syndrome (35), along with their psychotic presentation. These subjects were diagnosed using a standardized diagnostic scheme, the Schedule for Deficit Syndrome. This dichotomization into deficit and nondeficit schizophrenic subjects allowed us to look for metabolic correlates of the deficit symptom complex. The deficit subjects showed reduced glucose metabolism in the thalamus (21%) and in the frontal (15%) and parietal (19%) cortices (Table 5). Nondeficit subjects displayed glucose utilization in these same areas indistinguishable from the normals. These alterations in deficit schizophrenia were apparent and significant using either the absolute glucose metabolism values or relative metabolic data. Both deficit and nondeficit subjects had similar metabolic reductions in the anterior cingulate, hippocampus, and temporal cortex, as suggested by the above data. Another dichotomization into dyskinetic and nondyskinetic schizophrenic subjects (with and without tardive dyskinesia) did not result in a significant effect of this disorder on brain metabolism, even in the caudate or globus pallidus, which are sites generally implicated in the pathophysiology of tardive dyskinesia.

In another preliminary study we quantified the effect of the antipsychotic drug haloperidol on the human schizophrenic limbic system. The data show that haloperidol stimulates glucose utilization in many areas of the limbic cortex, including the hippocampus and the anterior cingulate cortex (Fig. 1). This would suggest that haloperidol is metabolically active in those areas of the limbic system, where we have

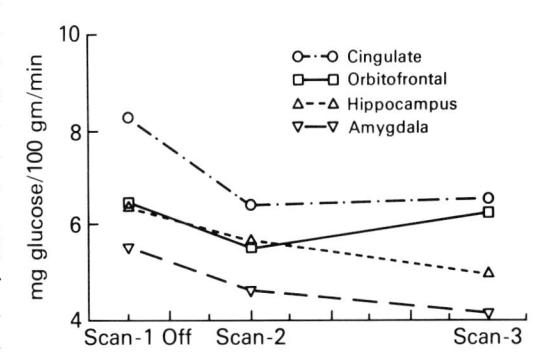

FIG. 1. Regional cerebral glucose metabolism in limbic CNS areas from four schizophrenic patients on haloperidol (scan-1), 5 days off haloperidol (scan-2), and 30 days off haloperidol (scan-3). Glucose metabolism is higher with haloperidol than without haloperidol in all four of these limbic areas.

noted metabolic alteration in schizophrenics. Four schizophrenic subjects underwent repeat PET/FDG scans three times: with haloperidol (fixed therapeutic dose for at least 30 days), 5 days off haloperidol, and drug-free (30 to 35 days off haloperidol). In these preliminary data it is apparent that haloperidol withdrawal alters metabolic activity in the hippocampus, anterior cingulate, and amygdala (Fig. 1). This alteration is in a downward direction, with a progressive drug-free state. Hence, the chronically administered neuroleptic is "corrective" in schizophrenia; that is, it restores the metabolic rate in schizophrenia toward normal levels, as one might predict for neuroleptic treatment.

Interpretation. The hypothesis derived from the MK801/PCP animal model studies proposed that psychosis-associated glucose utilization changes occur in limbic regions. Thus, the metabolic changes found in hippocampus, anterior cingulate, and temporal cortex in this study of schizophrenia were particularly interesting, being in the same brain regions as PCP-induced changes in rats. However, unlike the PCP-induced increases in glucose uptake, the changes found in the group of schizophrenic patients were decreases. Assuming that the animal changes with PCP and human alterations in schizophrenia can be related, various speculations could be raised to address this difference. These would include the greater complexity of circuits in the human brain, or perhaps the contrast between an acute exogenous stimulus compared with a chronic endogenous condition. Thus, the location of this metabolic alteration in a resting state may well be the most salient finding. If these limbic areas are functionally defective in individuals with schizophrenia, they could be tested by drugs or psychologic task performance, a hypothesis that would be testable in subsequent studies.

In this study population those schizophrenics with deficit symptoms (ie, primary and enduring negative symptoms) also showed metabolic reductions in areas of the cortex, particularly the frontal and parietal, and in the thalamus. These kinds of cortical changes have been previously observed in schizophrenia (16,18). Here they are linked to a defined phenomenology, distinct from the psychotic symptomatology of schizophrenia. All the schizophrenics studied demonstrated limbic metabolic alterations, whether deficit or nondeficit. It would be pertinent to note, however, that all subjects were actively psychotic, none in (drug-free) symptom remission.

The brain areas quantified in this glucose utilization experiment in schizophrenic patients have not heretofore been readily apparent in metabolic studies of human brain. The hippocampus is poorly visualized without adequate scanner resolution and slice density. However, these findings are consistent with other reports of post mortem differences between schizophrenic and normal individuals in limbic areas. A reduction in the size of the hippocampus and amygdala in schizophrenic brains as assessed by post mortem morphometric studies has been reported (36). Moreover, there appears to be an increase in lateral ventricular size in post mortem brains and a concurrent reduction in the size of the parahippocampal cortex (37). And there may be an irregularity and reduction in size of neuronal groups in the anterior cingulate cortex (38) and in the entorhinal cortex (39). Recent results cite hippocampal pyramidal cell alterations in schizophrenia (40). The reduction in glucose utilization in limbic areas, as reported in this chapter, is consistent with these published results. Thus, these preliminary PET/FDG data, consistent with the animal studies, suggest that the limbic system, Circle of Papez, may be involved in the manifestations of schizophrenia.

A nidus of dysfunction located in the limbic system (e.g., hippocampus, amygdala, or cingulate cortex) would be consistent not only with these several observations about the schizophrenic brain but also with much of our knowledge about limbic system functions. Indeed, hypotheses implicating the limbic system in schizophrenia have been previously made, based on various kinds of data (42). Moreover, we know that the limbic system, particularly the hippocampus, is highly vulnerable to hypoxia and developmental accident. A limbic system alteration mediating psychotic symptoms in schizophrenia would thus provide a plausible mechanism for perinatal insult resulting eventually in the development of schizophrenia (43).

CONCLUSION

The animal model studies reported here implicate the limbic circuit, specifically the hippocampus, anteroventral thalamus and anterior cingulate cortex, as potentially dysfunctional in the psychosis of schizophrenia. It is therefore of some interest that, in a preliminary analysis of regional brain metabolism in schizophrenic individuals who are without the influence of antipsychotic drugs and at rest, the same areas are affected, albeit in an opposite direction. The localization in schizophrenics of metabolic dysfunction was predicted by PCP- and MK801-induced metabolic alterations in the rat. Metabolic alterations in these limbic areas could, through their cerebral cortical projections, induce various manifestations of cortical dysfunction, as has already been described in schizophrenia. In the deficit state of schizophrenia, metabolism is additionally reduced in several cortical areas, including frontal and parietal areas, and the thalamus. The regional glucose uptake studies presented here provide a preliminary anatomic guide to the illness. Further analysis of these and other similar data are necessary to support this observation. Additional kinds of research, designed to activate the limbic structures functionally, are needed to understand the nature of this putative metabolic change in schizophrenic illness. Analysis of the transmitters and receptors in these areas using post mortem tissue or in vivo imaging are needed to develop the biochemical basis of the metabolic alteration. Certainly, any correlation with state manifestations of psychosis or with trait characteristics of the illness will be important to examine, as will its expression in subgroups of schizophrenic patients. Like findings in the past, these data suggest a focus on limbic structures for further biologic studies in schizophrenia.

REFERENCES

1. Bleuler E. Dementia praecox or the group of schizophrenias. Zinkin J (trans-ed). New York: International University Press, Inc., 1950.
2. Ciompi L. The natural history of schizophrenia in the long term. *British J Psychiatry* 1980; 136:413–420.
3. Tsuang MT, Woolson RF, Fleming JA. Long-term outcome of major psychoses: I. Schizophrenia and affective disorders compared with psychiatrically symptom free surgical conditions. *Arch Gen Psychiatry* 1978;36:1295–1301.
4. Carpenter WT. The phenomenology and course of schizophrenia: treatment implications. In: Meltzer H, ed. *Psychopharmacology*: The third generation of progess. New York: Raven Press, 1987;1121–1128.
5. Tamminga C, Gerlach J. New neuroleptics and experimental antipsychotics in schizophrenia. *Psychopharmacology* 1987;1129–1140.
6. Weinberger DR, Wagner RL, Wyatt RJ. Neuropathological studies of schizophrenia: A selective review. *Schizophrenia Bulletin* 1983;9:193–212.
7. Szechtman H, Nahmias C, Garnett S, Firnau G, Brown G, Kaplan R, Cleghorn J. Effects of neuroleptics on altered cerebral glucose metabolism in schizophrenia. *Arch Gen Psychiatry* 1988; 45:523–532.
8. Volkow ND, Wolf AP, Gelder PV, Brodie JD, Overall JE, Cancro R, Gomez-Mont F. Phenomenological correlates of metabolic activity in 18 patients with chronic schizophrenia. *American J Psychiatry* 1987;144(2):151–158.
9. Gur RE, Resnick SM, Alavi A, Gur RC, Caroff S, Dann R, Silver FL, Saykin AJ, Chawluk JB, Kushner M, Reivich M. Regional brain function in schizophrenia. *Arch Gen Psychiatry* 1987; 44:119–125.
10. Cohen RM, Semple WE, Gross M, Nordahl TE, Holcomb HH, Dowling S, Pickar D. The effect of neuroleptics on dysfunction in prefrontal substrate of sustained attention in schizophrenia. *Life Sciences* 1988;43:1141–1150.
11. Kling AS, Metter EJ, Riege WH, Kuhl DE. Comparison of PET measurement of local brain

glucose metabolism and CAT measurement of brain atrophy in chronic schizophrenia and depression. *Am J Psychiatry* 1986;143:2,175–180.
12. Wiesel FA, Blomqvist G, Greitz T, Nyman H, Schalling D, Stone-Elander S, Widen L, Wik G. Regional brain glucose metabolism in neuroleptic free schizophrenic patients in an acute phase of the disease. *Biological Psychiatry* 392–394.
13. Wolkin A, Jaeger J, Brodie JD, Wolf AP, Fowler J, Rotrosen J, Gomez-Mont F, Cancro R. Persistence of cerebral metabolic abnormalities in chronic schizophrenia as determined by positron emission tomography. *Am J Psychiatry* 1985;142(5):564–571.
14. DeLisi LE, Holcomb HH, Cohen RM, Pickar D, Carpenter W, Morihisa JM, King AC, Kessler R, Buchsbaum MS. Positron emission tomography in schizophrenic patients with and without neuroleptic medication. *Journal of Cerebral Blood Flow and Metabolism* 1985;5:201–206.
15. Jernigan TL, Sargent T, Pfefferbaum A, Kusubov N, Stahl SM. 18Fluorodeoxyglucose PET in schizophrenia. *Psychiatry Research* 1985;16:317–329.
16. Buchsbaum MS, DeLisi LE, Holcomb HH, Cappelletti J, King AC, Johnson J, Hazlett E, Dowling-Zimmerman S, Post RM, Morihisa J, Carpenter W, Cohen R, Pickar D, Weinberger DR, Margolin R, Kessler RM. Anteroposterior gradients in cerebral glucose use in schizophrenia and affective disorders. *Arch Gen Psychiatry* 1984;41:1159–1166.
17. Farkas T, Wolf AP, Jaeger J, Brodie JD, Christman DR, Fowler JS. Regional brain glucose metabolism in chronic schizophrenia. *Arch Gen Psychiatry* 1984;41:293–300.
18. Buchsbaum MS, Ingvar DH, Kessler R, Waters RN, Cappelletti J, van Kammen DP, King AC, Johnson JL, Manning RG, Flynn RW, Mann LS, Bunney WE, Sokoloff L. Cerebral glucography with positron tomography. *Arch Gen Psychiatry* 1982;39:251–259.
19. Sokoloff L, Reivich M, Kennedy C, Des Rosiers MH, Patlak CS, Pettigrew KD, Sakurada O, Shinohara M. The (14C)-deoxyglucose method for measurement of local cerebral glucose utilization: Theory, procedure, and normal values in the concious and anesthetized albino rat. *J Neurochem* 1977;28:897–916.
20. Reivich M, Kuhl D, Wolf A, Greenberg J, Phelps M, Ido T, Casella V, Fowler J, Hoffman E, Alavi A, Som P, Sokoloff L. The (18F) fluorodeoxyglucose method for the measurement of local cerebral glucose utilization in man. *Circulation Research* 1979;44:127–137.
21. Tamminga C, Tanimoto K, Kuo S, Chase TN, Contreras PC, Rice KC, Jackson AE, O'Donohue TL. PCP-induced alterations in cerebral glucose utilization in rat brain: Blockade by metaphit, a PCP-receptor-acylating agent. *Synapse* 1987;1:497–504.
22. Chen G. Sympathomimetic anesthetics. *Can Anesth Soc J* 1973;20:180–185.
23. Maragos WF, Chu DCM, Greenamyre JT, Penney JB, Young AB. Hish correlation between the localization of [3H]TCP binding and NMDA receptors. *Eur J Pharmacol* 1984;123:173–174.
24. Pearlson GD. Psychiatric and medical syndromes with phencyclidine (PCP) abuse. *Johns Hopkins Medical Journal* 1981;148:25–33.
25. Luby ED, Cohen BD, Rosenbaum G, Gottlieb JS, Kelley R. Study of a new schizophrenomimetic drug—serenyl. *Arch Neurol Psychiatry* 1959;71:363–369.
26. Rosenbaum G, Cohen BD, Luby E, Gottlieb JS, Yelen D. Comparison of serenyl with other drugs: Simulation of schizophrenia performance with serenyl, LSD-25, and amylbarbital (amytal) sodium. *Arch Gen Psychiatry* 1959;1:113–118.
27. Cohen BD, Rosenbaum G, Luby ED, Gottlieb JS. Comparison of phencyclidine hydrochloride (serenyl) with other drugs. *Arch Gen Psychiatry* 1962;6:395–401.
28. Luby ED, Gottlieb JS, Cohen BD, Rosenbaum G, Domino EF. *Am J Psychiatry* 1962;119:61–67.
29. Sircar R, Rappaport M, Nichtenhauser R, Zukin SR. The novel anticonvulsant MK-801: a potent and specific ligand of the brain phencyclidine/o-receptor. *Brain Research* 1987;435:235–240.
30. Wong EHF, Kemp JA, Priestly T, Knight AR, Woodruff GN, Iversen LL. The anticonvulsant MK-801 is a potent N-methyl-D-aspartate antagonist. *Proc Natl Acad Sci* 1986;83:7104–7108.
31. Snell LD, Yi SJ, Johnson KM. Comparison of the effects of MK-801 and phencyclidine on catecholamine uptake and NMDA-induced norepinephrine release. *European J of Pharmacol* 1988;145:223–226.
32. French E. Effects of acute and chronic administration of phencyclidine on the A10 dopaminergic mesolimbic system: Electrophysiological and behavioral correlates. *Neuropharmacology* 1988;27:791–798.
33. Willetts J, Balser RL. Phencyclidine-like discriminative stimulus properties of MK-801 in rats, *European J of Pharmacol* 1988;146:167–169.
34. Tamminga CA, Thaker GK, Alphs LD, Chase TN. Limbic system: Localization of PCP drug action in rat and schizophrenic manifestations in humans. In: Schulz SC, Tamminga CA, eds. *Schizophrenic: A scientific perspective*, New York: Oxford Press, 1988.
35. Carpenter WT, Heinrichs DW, Wagman AMI. Deficit and non-deficit forms of schizophrenia: The concept. *Am Journal Psychiatry* 1988;145(5):578–583.
36. Bogerts B, Meertz E, Schonfeldt-Bausch R. Basal ganglia and schizophrenia. *Arch Gen Psychiatry* 1985;42:784–791.
37. Brown R, Colter N, Corsellis JAN, Crow TJ, Frith CD, Jagoe R, Johnstone EC, Marsh L. Postmortem evidence of structural brain changes in schizophrenia. *Arch Gen Psychiatry* 1986;43:36–42.
38. Benes FM, Bird ED. An analysis of the arrange-

ment of neurons in the cingulate cortex of schizophrenic patients. *Arch Gen Psychiat* 1987;44:608–616.
39. Jakob H, Beckmann H. Prenatal developmental disturbances in the limbic allocortex in schizophrenics. *J Neural Transm* 1986;65:303–326.
40. Jeste DV, Lohr JB. Hippocampal pathologic findings in schizophrenia. *Arch Gen Psychiatry* 1989;46:1019–1026.
41. Stevens JR. An anatomy of schizophrenia? *Arch Gen Psychiat* 1973;29:177–189.
42. Stevens JR. Neuropathology of schizophrenia. *Arch Gen Psychiatry* 1982;39:1131–1139.
43. Lewis SW, Owen MJ, Murray RM. Obstetric complications and schizophrenia: methodology and mechanisms. In: Schulz SC, Tamminga CA, eds. *Schizophrenia: Scientific Progress* New York: Oxford Press, 1989;56–68.

10
Autoimmunity and Schizophrenia

Cathy G. McAllister,[1] Mark Hyman Rapaport,[2] David Pickar,[2] and Steven M. Paul[2]

Over the years there have been numerous reports suggesting that immunological factors, such as autoimmunity, may play a role in either the pathogenesis or etiology of schizophrenia (1–5). Observations of aberrant responses in the cellular and humoral immune systems of schizophrenic patients, as compared with healthy controls or patients with other neuropsychiatric disorders, are prevalent in the psychiatric literature. However, these reports have often been conflicting and/or irreproducible by independent laboratories, and the actual role of both immune cells and their products in the development of schizophrenia has been difficult to delineate. Inconsistencies in reports among various laboratories on various immunological parameters in schizophrenia may be due to true clinical and etiological heterogeneity within large groups of schizophrenic patients or the confounding effects of antipsychotic medications on the immune system (6–7). In addition, there have been few if any studies on the complex interactions among immunological, genetic, environmental, and hormonal factors that could potentially contribute to the development of schizophrenia, such as has been shown with several autoimmune disorders, including myasthenia gravis and insulin-dependent diabetes. To this day the question of whether immunologic factors contribute to the pathogenesis of schizophrenia remains unanswered.

With respect to possible autoimmune mechanisms, we have attempted to identify a subgroup of schizophrenic patients who share immunologic stigmata with patients who have known autoimmune disorders. One recently described immunologic feature of several autoimmune disorders is the presence of increased numbers of circulating $CD5^+$ B lymphocytes. $CD5^+$ B lymphocytes are a distinct lineage of B-cells that appear to play a role in autoimmunity in both the mouse and human. These cells, which seldom produce antibodies to conventional antigens, are committed to the production of multispecific antibodies mainly of the IgM class (8), such as rheumatoid factor, and antibodies to single-stranded DNA, as well as the "natural antibodies" (8–10) normally present in healthy individuals. $CD5^+$ B lymphocytes are self-renewing and are located primarily in the peritoneum and are rarely found in the bone marrow, spleen, and lymph nodes (11). $CD5^+$ B lymphocytes are a major B-cell population in spinal cord blood, but in most individuals these cells decrease to a minor subpopulation (less than 5% of peripheral blood lymphocytes, or 20% of peripheral B-cells) by adulthood (11). However in approximately 5% of humans, as well as in autoimmune-prone mice (9,11),

[1]Departments of Psychiatry and Pathology, University of Pittsburgh, Pittsburgh, PA 15213.
[2]The Clinical Neuroscience Branch, National Institute of Mental Health, Bethesda, MD 20892.

the CD5+ B-cells remain elevated in number (greater than 5% of peripheral blood lymphocytes, or 50% of total peripheral B-cells). In addition a subgroup of patients with certain autoimmune disorders, including rheumatoid arthritis, Sjögren's syndrome, progressive systemic sclerosis, and hyperthyroid Graves' disease, have a similar elevation in CD5+ B-cells (9,12–15). However, the role of the CD5+ B-cell and the autoreactive antibodies that it produces, in the development of these autoimmune disorders has not been established.

Another feature of certain autoimmune conditions is the presence of activated T-cells and the corresponding increase in T-cell-associated antigens such as the soluble interleukin-2 (IL-2) receptor (sIL-2R). This 45-kd "receptor," which binds IL-2 with low-affinity kinetics ($k_d = 11.1 \times 10^{-9}M$), is believed to be a released form of the high-affinity membrane-bound IL-2 receptor (16). T lymphocytes, which produce IL-2, express the high-affinity ($k_d = 10^{-12}M$) membrane-bound IL-2 receptor following activation by an exogenous agent (ie, an antigen or mitogen; ref 17). The significance of the soluble (ie, released) form of the IL-2 receptor is unknown. However, sIL-2R may serve an immunoregulatory role either by binding free IL-2 and preventing any further activation of T lymphocytes or by serving as a carrier protein to shuttle IL-2 to cells bearing high-affinity membrane-bound IL-2 receptors. Although the precise role of sIL-2R in autoimmunity has not been established, an elevation in serum levels of sIL-2R has been observed in presumed autoimmune disorders such as systemic lupus erythematosis, Sjögren's syndrome, multiple sclerosis, and rheumatoid arthritis (18–21) as well as animal models of autoimmune disorders such as lupus-prone mice (22). In addition, serum sIL-2R levels have been found to be highly correlated with disease activity in patients with rheumatoid arthritis (19,23).

The purpose of our initial studies was to determine whether schizophrenic patients manifest immunological stigmata similar to those observed in patients with various autoimmune disorders. We have recently examined two characteristics of autoimmune diseases, namely the levels of circulating CD5+ B lymphocytes and serum levels of sIL-2R, in a cohort of schizophrenic pa-

TABLE 1. *Lymphocyte subsets in schizophrenic patients, patients with bipolar affective disorder, and healthy controls[a]*

	N	Age (YR)	Sex (M/F)	Pan T-cell	Suppressor T-cells
Patients:					
Schizophrenic					
All	34	31.3 ± 1.2[b]	21/13	77.0 ± 1.0	22.1 ± 1.1
High[c]	11	30.8 ± 1.7	8/3	75.3 ± 2.1	19.8 ± 1.5
Low[c]	23	31.5 ± 1.5	13/10	77.8 ± 1.0[g]	23.2 ± 1.5
Bipolar	20	41.6 ± 3.1	5/15	75.3 ± 1.3	18.4 ± 1.4
Controls:	33	30.2 ± 0.9	21/12	71.5 ± 1.3	23.3 ± 1.1

[a]Reprinted from *Archives of General Psychiatry* 1989;46:890–894.
[b]Data are presented as the mean value ± the standard error of the mean.
[c]Patients are divided into groups based on a high (> 5.2 %) or low (< 5.2 %) percentage of CD5+ B-cells.
[d]Significantly different from "low"-phenotype schizophrenic patients and controls ($p = .02$).

tients and control subjects. Our goal was to determine whether a subgroup of schizophrenic patients manifests changes in these two parameters, thereby suggesting that certain schizophrenic patients may have an autoimmune component to their disorder.

METHODS

Determination of CD5+ B Lymphocytes

Blood was obtained from schizophrenic patients ($N = 34$),[1] patients with bipolar affective disorder ($N = 20$),[2] and control subjects ($N = 33$). All patients were stabilized on medication, and the schizophrenic patients were age- and sex-matched to the control subjects (Table 1). Blood samples were stained, using a modified lysed whole-blood method (24), with the appropriate monoclonal antibodies (Becton-Dickinson, Montain View, Calif) conjugated with either fluorescein isothiocyanate or phycoerythrin: anti-Leu 1, pan T-cell; anti-Leu 2, suppressor T-cell; anti-Leu 3, helper T-cell; HLA-DR, class II antigens; anti-Leu 12, pan B-cells; anti-Leu 1 and anti-Leu 12, CD5+ B-cell; and analyzed on a FACScan (Becton-Dickinson, San Jose, CA) flow cytometer. Five thousand cells with lymphoid light-scattering characteristics were examined from each sample. The data are expressed as the percentage of lymphocytes that stain with each monoclonal antibody.

Detection of sIL-2R

The serum levels of sIL-2R in 30 schizophrenic patients and 13 age-matched control subjects were determined by a highly sensitive sandwich enzyme-linked immunosorbent assay (25). The data are expressed in units of sIL-2R per milliliter, where 1 unit is equal to 3 pg of soluble IL-2 receptors.

---

[1] Patients were from the NIMH inpatient and outpatient clinics, Bethesda, MD; St. Elizabeth's Hospital Inpatient Research Program, Washington, DC; and the Maryland Psychiatric Research Center, Baltimore, MD.
[2] Patients were either enrolled in the inpatient or outpatient programs, NIMH, Bethesda, MD.

TABLE 1. Continued

Helper T-cells	B-cells	HLA-DR	CD5+ B-cells	
			Lymphocytes (%)	B-cells (%)
44.5 ± 1.1	9.9 ± 0.6	15.3 ± 0.7	3.7 ± 0.4	35.0 ± 2.9
42.6 ± 1.7	12.5 ± 1.3[d]	18.1 ± 1.4[e]	6.8 ± 0.5[f]	52.4 ± 3.5[f]
45.4 ± 1.5	8.8 ± 0.6	14.0 ± 0.6	2.3 ± 0.2	26.7 ± 2.6
43.0 ± 1.5	10.6 ± 1.0	16.3 ± 1.0	2.6 ± 0.4	25.7 ± 2.5
40.4 ± 1.4	9.1 ± 0.7	15.0 ± 0.7	2.8 ± 0.3	31.0 ± 1.8

[e] Significantly different from "low"-phenotype schizophrenic patients ($p = .03$).
[f] Significantly different from all other groups ($p = .0001$).
[g] Significantly different from controls ($p = .006$).

RESULTS

CD5+ B Lymphocytes

Demographic data on all subjects as well as the percentages of total T-cells, suppressor and helper T-cells, total B-cells, cells bearing class II antigens, and CD5+ B lymphocytes are summarized in Table 1. Although the schizophrenic patients and control subjects were matched for age and sex, the group of patients with bipolar affective disorder were older and contained a higher percentage of women. As a group, the schizophrenic patients did not differ in any immunological measurement from the other groups studied. However, when the schizophrenic patients were divided into two groups based on the percentage of peripheral blood lymphocytes that were CD5+ B-cells, the high-phenotype patients had significantly elevated numbers of total B-cells, cells expressing class II antigens, and CD5+ B-cells. (A limit of 2SDs above the mean percentage of CD5+ B lymphocytes for control subjects was chosen to separate high-phenotype from low-phenotype individuals.) The distribution of each patient or control group into high- and low-phenotype groups is shown in Fig. 1(A). There was an increase in high-phenotype frequency in individuals with schizophrenia as compared with bipolar patients and control subjects ($\chi^2 = 10.94$, $p = .004$). To determine whether the elevation in CD5+ B-cells in high-phenotype schizophrenic patients was due to the B-cell hyperplasia observed in this group, we also expressed the data as

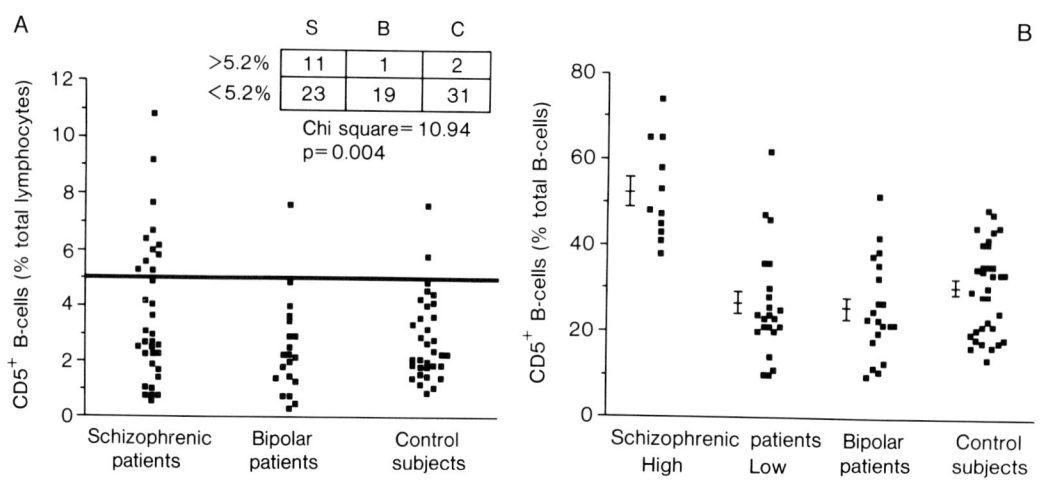

FIG. 1. (A): Distribution of CD5+ B-cells in the peripheral blood of patients with schizophrenia (S), bipolar affective disorder (B), and healthy controls (C). Blood from each subject was analyzed on 1 to 10 separate occasions (see text for details), and each point represents the individual or mean value (percentage of total lymphocytes that are CD5+ B-cells) for each subject. The horizontal line demarcates 2 standard deviations above the mean for control subjects. Points above the line are defined as being in the high range, points below are in the low range. *Inset:* Chi-square analysis of the data indicate a significant ($p = .004$) increase in high-phenotype frequency among the schizophrenic patients. **(B):** Percentage of total peripheral blood B-cells expressing the CD5 surface marker. Total B-cells in each subject were measured by immunoreactivity with anti-Leu 12 monoclonal antibody (see text for details). The schizophrenic patients have been divided into high and low phenotypes as described above. The horizontal bars represent the mean ± SEM for each group. The high-phenotype schizophrenic patients have a significantly elevated percentage of B-cells that express the CD5 marker when compared with all other groups (ANOVA: $F = 15.7$; $p = .001$). (Reprinted from McAllister et al. Increased numbers of CD5+ lymphocytes in schizophrenic patients. *Arch Gen Psychiatry* 1989;46:890–894.)

the percentage of B lymphocytes that are CD5+ B-cells (Table 1 and Fig 1B). The patients with schizophrenia in the high-phenotype group still had elevated numbers of CD5+ B-cells as compared with low-phenotype schizophrenic patients, bipolar patients, and control subjects. (ANOVA: $F = 15.66$, $p = .0001$). Multiple measurements of CD5+ B-cells in the peripheral blood of certain schiozophrenic patients and control subjects revealed no significant fluctuation between high- and low-phenotype ranges (26). In addition, we were able to examine the peripheral blood lymphocytes of a subgroup of schizophrenic patients who were participating in a placebo-controlled medication trial (27). The patients were stabilized on typical neuroleptic medication, then tapered to placebo, and finally stabilized on the atypical neuroleptic clozapine. As shown in Table 2, no significant changes in lymphocytes subsets, including the CD5+ B-cell population, were observed throughout the medication changes.

Soluble IL-2 Receptors

The serum levels of sIL-2R were found to be elevated in the schizophrenic patients ($N = 30$) as compared with age-matched control subjects ($N = 13$). As shown in Fig. 2, the patients had a significantly higher mean serum soluble IL-2 receptor concentration than control subjects (mean U/ml ± SEM: 614 ± 37.2 vs 391 ± 27.4; $t = 3.7$, $p < .001$). Moreover, more than 50% of the patients had sIL-2R levels that were more than 2 SD above the mean value for control subjects. As part of a larger study, we examined the levels of sIL-2R in the sera of 125 schizophrenic patients, 13 bipolar patients, 8 Alzheimer's patients, and 27 control subjects. The schizophrenic patients and the bipolar patients had significantly increased levels of sIL-2R as compared with the control subjects and Alzheimer's patients (28). In addition, we examined the serum sIL-2R levels in a group of schizophrenic patients in both medicated and unmedicated states. Although treatment with neuroleptic medication did increase the level of sIL-2R, the serum of unmedicated schizophrenic patients remained significantly elevated in sIL-2R as compared with control subjects (28).

DISCUSSION

Schizophrenia is a syndrome of completely unknown etiology. Genetic, environmental, as well as immunological factors have been postulated to play a role in schizophrenia. However, an unequivocal casual mechanism has not been established for any of these proposed etiological factors. We have examined schizophrenic patients for immunologic features that are common to patients with known autoimmune disorders. Specifically we quantified both the level of circulating CD5+ B lymphocytes and soluble IL-2 receptors in a population of schizophrenic patients. In each case a proportion of schizophrenic patients shared immunological stigmata with patients having certain autoimmune disorders.

The CD5+ B lymphoctye is morphologically distinct (is larger in size, has larger nuclei, and shows increased cytoplasmic granularity) from the traditional CD5− B-cell (11). CD5+ B lymphocytes have been found to preferentially secrete polyreactive antibodies, mainly of the IgM isotype, that react with a wide range of self-antigens including human IgG Fc fragments, ssDNA, thyroglobulin, and insulin (8). CD5+ B lymphocytes isolated from individuals with certain autoimmune disorders will spontaneously proliferate when maintained in vitro, suggesting that these cells existed in an activated state in vivo. In contrast, CD5− B-cells from these same patients, and CD5+ or CD5− B-cells from control individuals, will not proliferate unless activated by an exogenous stimulus (29).

The level of CD5+ B lymphocytes in pe-

TABLE 2. *Lymphocyte subsets in patients during treatment with neuroleptic medication and placebo (N = 12)[a,b]*

	Pan T-cell	Suppressor T-cell	Helper T-cell
Medication:			
Neuroleptic	72.0 ± 2.5	19.1 ± 1.1	37.3 ± 1.8
Placebo	72.5 ± 1.4	19.8 ± 1.1	38.2 ± 1.5
Clozapine	75.2 ± 2.1	19.1 ± 0.7	40.0 ± 1.7

[a] Lymphocyte subsets were determined by reactivity with monoclonal antibodies as described in the text. Numbers are the mean ± SEM of the percentage of lymphocytes that stain with each marker.
[b] Reprinted from *Archives of General Psychiatry* 1989;46:956–957.

ripheral blood has been found to be under genetic regulation and appears to be a stable phenotypic trait (30). We observed no significant fluctuations in the levels of $CD5^+$ B-cells over a period of months both in several control subjects and in schizophrenic patients who were either stabilized on antipsychotic medication or undergoing medication changes (27). Therefore, the stability of this lymphocyte subset facilitates studies of patients under various clinical conditions.

The presence of increased numbers of $CD5^+$ B lymphocytes is not pathognomonic for autoimmune disorders. For example, an increase in $CD5^+$ B-cells has not been observed in patients with systemic lupus erythematosis (8), although autoimmune mechanisms are strongly suspected to play a role in this disorder. Similarly, only 25% to 50% of patients with rheumatoid arthritis, a disease generally accepted as being autoimmune in nature, have an elevation in $CD5^+$ B-cells (9,31). Therefore, an elevation in $CD5^+$ B lymphocytes could be considered as only a predisposing factor to certain types of autoimmune disorders. The actual development of an autoimmune disease in individuals with the "high" phenotype may therefore also depend on other genetic and environmental factors as well as on medication effects in genetically susceptible patients. We postulate that schizophrenic patients with elevations in the number of $CD5^+$ B lymphocytes may have a disregulation in their immune systems that could contribute to the pathology and perhaps the etiology of their disorder. It is not known at this time whether $CD5^+$ B lymphocytes in the peripheral blood of these individuals are producing autoantibodies that could result in CNS dysfunction. However,

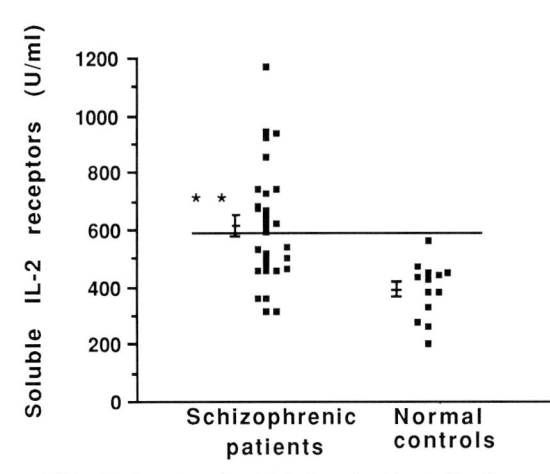

FIG. 2. Levels of soluble interleukin 2 (IL-2) receptors in the serum of schizophrenic patients ($N = 30$) and control subjects ($N = 13$). Soluble IL-2 receptors were measured by a sandwich enzyme-linked immunosorbent assay as described in the text. Each point represents the value for one subject; 1 unit is approximately 3 pg of soluble IL-2 receptor. The horizontal line indicates 2 SD above the mean value for healthy controls. Asterisk, $p < .001$. (Reprinted from Rapaport et al. Elevated levels of soluble interleukin 2 receptors in schizophrenia. *Arch Gen Psychiatry* 1989;46:291–292.)

TABLE 2. Continued

		CD5+ B-cells	
HLA-DR	B-cell	Lymphocytes (%)	B-cells (%)
17.1 ± 1.6	12.7 ± 1.5	4.5 ± 1.1	31.0 ± 3.8
17.5 ± 1.5	14.1 ± 1.3	4.2 ± 0.7	28.4 ± 3.9
15.9 ± 1.3	11.8 ± 1.0	4.2 ± 0.8	32.3 ± 4.4

studies in progress in our laboratories probing the immune repertoire of schizophrenic patients and control subjects should resolve these issues. Specifically, the enumeration of the frequency of cell precursors producing antibodies to self-antigens, including brain proteins, should more accurately reveal a potential bias in the immune response of schizophrenic patients.

We were also able to demonstrate an elevation in the serum levels of soluble IL-2 receptors in certain schizophrenic patients (32), a result confirmed by at least one other group (33). These "receptors" are thought to be shed from activated T lymphocytes, and an increased amount of these proteins in serum indicates a stimulated immune system. An increase in serum sIL-2R has been shown to proceed both the onset of human liver allograft rejection (34) and the signs of active synovitis in patients with rheumatoid arthritis (18). The measurement of sIL-2R may prove to be predictive for clinical relapse in disorders with immunopathogenic mechanisms. We are currently examining the serum levels of sIL-2R in schizophrenic patients during acute episodes and remission states in order to ascertain whether a pattern exists similar to that seen in patients with other autoimmune disorders. We were not able, however, to establish a correlation between schizophrenic patients with a high CD5+ B-cell phenotype and patients with elevated levels of sIL-2R. It remains unclear whether these two groups of patients could potentially have distinct autoimmune disorders that could contribute to their psychoses. However, further attempts by our laboratories to delineate a subgroup of schizophrenic patients with immunologic abnormalities, including "autoimmune" characteristics, should resolve these issues and perhaps serve to select the population of patients that could show clinical improvement by treatment of their immunologic dysfunctions.

ACKNOWLEDGMENTS

We thank Drs A Notkins and P Casali for their careful consideration of our data. We also thank Dr DL Nelson for his assistance with the soluble IL-2 receptor assay.

REFERENCES

1. De Lisi LE, Crow TJ. Is schizophrenia a viral or immunological disorder? *Psychiatr Clin North Am* 1986;9:115–132.
2. Hirata-Hibi M, Higashi S, Tachibana T, Watanabe N. Simulated lymphocytes in schizophrenia. *Arch Gen Psychiatry* 1982;39:88–87.
3. Villemain F, Chatenoud L, Galinowski A, Homo-Delarche F, Ginestet D, Loo H, Zarifian E, Bach J-F. Aberrant T cell–mediated immunity in untreated schizophrenic patients: deficient interleukin-2 production. *Am J Psychiatry* 1989;146:609–616.
4. Ganguli R, Rabin BS, Belle SH. Decreased interleukin-2 production in schizophrenic patients. *Biol Psychiatry* 1989;26:424–427.

5. Knight JG. Dopamine-receptor-stimulating autoantibodies: a possible cause of schizophrenia. *Lancet* 1982;2:1073–1076.
6. Zarrabi MH, Zucker S, Miller F, Derman RM, Romano GS, Hartnett JA, Varma AO. Immunologic and coagulation disorders in chlorpromazine-treated patients. *Ann Int Med* 1979;91:194–199.
7. Johnstone EC, Whaley K. Antinuclear antibodies in psychiatric illness: their relationship to diagnosis and drug treatment. *Br Med J* 1975;2:724–725.
8. Casali P, Notkins AL. CD5+ B lymphocytes, polyreactive antibodies and the human B-cell repertoire. *Immunol Today* 1989;10:364–368.
9. Hardy RR, Hayakawa K, Shimizu M, Yamasaki K, Kishimoto T. Rheumatoid factor secretion from human Leu 1+ B cells. *Science* 1987;236:81–83.
10. Casali P, Burastero SE, Nakamura M, Inghirami G, Notkins AL. Human lymphocytes making rheumatoid factor and antibody to ssDNA belong to Leu 1+ B-cell subset. *Science* 1987;236:77–80.
11. Hayakawa K, Hardy RR. Normal, autoimmune, and malignant CD5+ B cells: the Ly-1 B lineage? *Annu Rev Immunol* 1988;6:197–218.
12. Plater-Zyberk C, Maini RN, Lam K, Kennedy TD, Janossy G. A rheumatoid arthritis B cell subset expressing a phenotype similar to that in chronic lymphocytic leukemia. *Arthritis Rheum* 1985;28:971–976.
13. Taniguchi O, Miyajima H, Hirano T, Noguchi M, Ueda A, Hashimoto H, Hirose S-I, Okumura K. The Leu-1 B-cell subpopulation in patients with rheumatoid arthritis. *J Clin Immunol* 1987;7:441–448.
14. Dauphineé M, Tovar Z, Talal N. B cells expressing CD5 are increased in Sjögren's syndrome. *Arthritis Rheum* 1988;31:642–647.
15. Iwatani Y, Amino N, Kaneda T, Ichihara K, Tamaki H, Tachi J, Matsuzuka F, Fukata S, Kuma K, Miyai K. Marked increase of CD5+ B cells in hyperthyroid Graves' disease. *Clin Exp Immunol* 1989;78:196–200.
16. Rubin LA, Jay G, Nelson DL. The released interleukin-2 receptor binds interleukin-2 efficiently. *J Immunol* 1986;137:3841–3844.
17. Robb RJ, Greene WC, Rusk CM. Low and high affinity cellular receptor for interleukin-2. Implications for the level of Tac antigen. *J Exp Med* 1985;160:1126–1146.
18. Symons JA, Wood NC, DiGiovine FS, Duff GW. Soluble IL-2 receptor in rheumatoid athritis: correlation with disease activity, IL-1 and IL-2 inhibition. *J Immunol* 1988;141:2612–2618.
19. Semenzato G, Bambara LM, Biasi D, Frigo A, Vinante F, Zuppini B, Trentin L, Feruglio C, Chilosi M, Pizzolo G. Increased serum levels of soluble interleukin-2 receptor in patients with systemic lupus erythematosis and rheumatoid arthritis. *J Clin Immunol* 1988;8:447–452.
20. Greenberg SJ, Marcon L, Hurwitz BJ, Waldmann TA, Nelson DL. Elevated levels of soluble interleukin-2 receptors in multiple sclerosis. *N Engl J Med* 1988;319:1019–1020.
21. Manoussakis MN, Papadopoulos GK, Drosos AA, Moutsopoulos HM. Soluble interleukin 2 receptor molecules in the serum of patients with autoimmune diseases. *Clin Immunol Immunopath* 1989;50:321–332.
22. Balderas RS, Josimovic-Alasevic O, Diamantstein T, Dixon FJ, Theofilopoulos AN. Elevated titers of cell-free interleukin 2 receptor in serum of lupus mice. *J Immunol* 1987;139:1496–1500.
23. Campen DH, Horwitz DA, Quismorio FP, Ehresmann GR, Martin WJ. Serum levels of interleukin-2 receptor and activity of rheumatic diseases characterized by immune system activation. *Arthritis Rheum* 1988;31:1358–1364.
24. Direct immunofluorescence staining of cell surface antigens in unseparated blood. In: *Becton Dickinson monoclonal antibody source book*. Mountain View, CA: Becton Dickinson & Co., 1986;2:11.
25. Rubin LA, Kurman CC, Fritz ME, Yarchoan R, Nelson DL. Identification and characterization of a released form of the interleukin-2 receptor. In: Oppenheim JJ, Jacobs DM, eds. *Progress in leukocyte biology: leukocytes and host defense*. New York: Alan R. Liss, 1986;5:95–102.
26. McAllister CG, Rapaport MH, Pickar D, Podruchny TA, Christison G, Alphs LD, Paul SM. Increased numbers of CD5+ B lymphocytes in schizophrenic patients. *Arch Gen Psychiatry* 1989;46:890–894.
27. McAllister CG, Rapaport MH, Pickar D, Paul SM. Effects of short-term administration of antipsychotic drugs on lymphocyte subsets in schizophrenic patients. *Arch Gen Psychiatry* 1989;46:956–957.
28. Rapaport MH, McAllister D, Pickar D, Nelson DL, Paul SM. Unpublished observations, 1989.
29. Burastero SE, Casali P, Wilder RL, Notkins AL. Monoreactive high affinity and polyreactive low affinity rheumatoid factors are produced by CD5+ B cells from patients with rheumatoid arthritis. *J Exp Med* 1988;168:1979–1992.
30. Kipps TJ, Vaughan JH. Genetic influence on the levels of circulating CD5 B lymphocytes. *J Immunol* 1987;139:1060–1064.
31. Plater-Zyberk C, Brennan FM, Feldmann M, Maini RN. 'Fetal-type' B and T lymphocytes in rheumatoid arthritis and primary Sjögren's syndrome. *J Autoimmunity* 1989;2(suppl):233–241.
32. Rapaport MH, McAllister CG, Pickar D, Nelson DL, Paul SM. Elevated levels of soluble interleukin 2 receptors in schizophrenia. *Arch Gen Psychiatry* 1989;46:291–292.
33. Ganguli R, Rabin B. Increased serum interleukin 2 receptor concentration in schizophrenic and brain-damaged subjects. *Arch Gen Psychiatry* 1989;46:292.
34. Adams DH, Hubscher SG, Wang L, Elias E, Neuberger JM. Soluble interleukin-2 receptors in serum and bile of liver transplant recipients. *Lancet* 1989;320:469–471.

11

Neuropharmacologic Techniques in the Molecular Biology of Schizophrenia

George R. Uhl,[1] A. Jayaraman,[1,2] Toshikazu Nishimori,[1] Shoichi Shimada,[1] Marcus Rattray,[1] and Bruce O'Hara[1]

Recent advances in the abilities to manipulate and express genetic information provide an astonishingly broad repertoire of means for studying many important areas of biology, including neurobiology. The power of the techniques already available to study nervous system function, however, has also led to an oppositely directed flow of technology. This chapter documents the use of techniques that are widely employed in neuropharmacology along with molecular biologic approaches to studying molecules of importance for the brain. Pharmacologic, physiologic, and anatomic approaches borrowed directly from neuroscience are thus increasingly finding their way into molecular neurobiology, including the molecular neurobiology of schizophrenia.

RATIONALE: IMPORTANT MOLECULES TO STUDY

Drugs can exert substantial impact on gene expression, and they also function in the brain by interacting with specific gene products. Studies of drug effects on gene expression may have special importance for understanding schizophrenia: Selective impact of neuroleptic drugs on the positive symptoms of the disorder provide one principal biological avenue for insight into disease mechanisms.

Drug Receptors as Gene Products

Genes for the membrane-bound receptors for dopamine and for the major neuroleptic drugs are now being elucidated (1). These members of the so-called type 2 receptor gene family possess seven hydrophobic membrane-spanning domains (2). They display considerable homology to the previously cloned monoaminergic receptor genes. These genes, described in more detail by Caron in Chapter 1, are clearly involved in the initial activities of antischizophrenic neuroleptic drugs. Work that is currently ongoing will demonstrate whether the expression of these receptor genes themselves is significantly altered by neuroleptics.

Drugs can influence receptor molecules through a variety of posttranslational processes, including changes in patterns of phosphorylation and changes in distribution within the cell (membrane versus internalization). Although drug-induced changes in transcriptional rate and/or stability of messenger RNAs (mRNAs) encoding some

[1]Laboratory of Molecular Neurobiology Addiction Research Center, NIDA/NIH, and Departments of Neurology and Neuroscience, Johns Hopkins University School of Medicine, Baltimore, MD 21224.
[2]Department of Neurology, Louisiana State University School of Medicine, New Orleans, LA 70112.

receptors can be observed (eg, refs 3–5), changes at this level may be less common than analogous changes in the expression of neuropeptide genes (see below).

Although the recent expression/homology cloning of several D_1 and D_2 receptor complementary DNAs (cDNAs) has opened the way to studies of its expression at an mRNA level, the genes encoding most neurotransmitter receptors remain to be elucidated. Many other molecules important for synaptic communication also remain to be cloned. Included in this list, as this is written, are the presynaptic transporters that act to terminate the action of released monoamine neurotransmitters.

Transduction Systems

Many different molecules are involved in conveying information from drug occupancy of a cell surface receptor to the nucleus, where these events can influence gene regulation (6). Ligand occupancy of a receptor can enhance its affinity for specific G proteins, as well as change cytoplasmic and transmembrane mono- and divalent ionic fluxes (7). These ionic and G-protein activations can alter specific patterns of phosphorylation and glycosylation of membrane and cytoplasmic constituents. In addition, membrane-derived information-carrying molecules such as phosphatidyl inositol can be modulated. The exact means whereby much of this information is transduced to the specific, appropriate nuclear regions of specific gene regulatory sites is not clear in most circumstances. Although many different G-protein forms have been cloned recently (7), the molecular details of many of the molecules involved in these intracellular communication pathways are poorly understood. Thus, molecular constituents of these intracellular signaling pathways are good candidates for cloning studies.

Glucocorticoid receptors are well-studied molecules that do carry information in this fashion. These cytoplasmic-nuclear shuttle molecules first bind a glucocorticoid molecule in the cytoplasm. The steroid-receptor complex then translocates to the nucleus, where it can recognize a DNA binding site located in the five prime flanking and regulatory regions of steroid-responsive genes (8,9). Direct effects on gene expression are thus major components of the functional activity of steroids. These effects are especially interesting since a psychotomimetic disorder can follow administration of high doses of glucocorticoids in otherwise normal individuals.

Drug Effects on Levels of Gene Expression

Drugs exert substantial effects on the levels of expression of a number of genes. The impact of drugs on peptide neurotransmitter systems can be especially informative (10). In these systems neurotransmission and gene-expression events can be tightly linked (11). In a peptide-containing neuron, every molecule of peptide neurotransmitter that is released must be synthesized *de novo*. Thus, over the long run, if the neuron is not to accumulate or run out of its neurotransmitter, peptide neurotransmitter synthesis must keep pace with physiologically and drug-induced changes in neuronal function.

Several different biochemical mechanisms could conceivably serve to maintain this match. In many neuropeptide systems, however, the rates of many of these steps are little changed by physiologic manipulations. The activities of neuronal enzymes responsible for posttranslational processing of propeptide precursors can be relatively stable in a variety of different circumstances, for example. On the other hand, studies of a variety of different neuropeptide systems have suggested that the rates of transcription of the prepropeptide gene and/or the degree of stabilization of the propeptide mRNA can both combine so that the dynamics in the levels of the mRNA encoding the neuropeptide can often fit well with changes in the functional activity of the neuron in releasing the peptide (12–20). It is often difficult to find changes in levels of peptide neurotransmitters that reflect changes in rates of peptide release (eg, ref 21). If steady-state levels of peptide are maintained relatively unchanged under these circumstances, then the rates of peptide synthesis must more or less match those of peptide release. Changes in neuronal levels of prepropeptide mRNA that correlate well with changes in neuronal function have been shown in practice, in a number of systems. In peptides ranging from atrial natriuretic factor (ANF) to vasopressin, function-related changes in prepropeptide mRNAs have been demonstrated in neuronal and/or endocrine cells (12–20). Study of the levels of particular prepropeptide mRNAs under different circumstances can thus provide one potential marker for changed activity of the mRNA-containing neuron under these different circumstances. Molecular biologic and neurobiologic techniques allowing study of the regulated expression of specific genes are thus of substantial potential significance.

EXPRESSION SYSTEMS

The availability of several different eucaryotic expression systems is key to the successful employment of neuropharmacologic techniques for screening cDNA libraries to verify the presence of clones encoding a certain functional activity. Neuropharmacologic systems are used in conjunction with several different expression systems. These biological systems allow assessment as to whether or not an introduced cDNA or mRNA encodes a given molecule.

Eucaryotic cells can often express genes encoded by DNA segments introduced into the cells' nuclei (22–25). Expression occurs at higher levels if the introduced DNAs are preceded by "promoter" DNA sequences that are recognized by the biochemical machinery of the expressing cell. *Transient expression* can occur after appropriate DNA segments are introduced into the recipient cell's nucleus. DNA within the nucleus, but not incorporated in the host-cell chromosome, will be subject to degradation. Thus, it can cause only brief expression of the introduced genes. Nevertheless, transiently expressing cells can produce appropriately processed mRNA from transcription of introduced DNA. They can produce protein from translation of the mRNA, and even perform posttranslational modifications and membrane insertions with suprising fidelity. Genes encoding several different neurotransmitter receptors, for example, can produce binding sites whose pharmacologic profiles closely reflect their relative functional activities in the brain after transient expression in mammalian cells (1,26–29).

A DNA segment that has penetrated to the nucleus can be incorporated into the host-cell genome in such a fashion that it is passed from generation to generation of cells. This process, *stable expression,* can result in the production of cell lines that express a new phenotypic characteristic encoded by the introduced DNA.

The *Xenopus laevis* oocyte is an excellent system in which to test expression of mRNAs (30–32). The oocyte size (greater than 1 mm in diameter) is an advantage: injection is much easier than into smaller eucaryotic cells. Oocytes are able to translate protein from RNA injected into their cytoplasm and to process and insert membrane-bound translation products in many cases. These oocytes maintain a large transmembrane potential gradient, and thus channel- or receptor-induced depolarizing events related to ligand occupancy of receptors can be electrically monitored. Furthermore, receptors encoded by mRNA obtained from several species can couple with endogenous *Xenopus* G protein and other oocyte mechanisms. This provides a system in which the expression of even some receptors that are dependent on G-protein activation can be assessed. As we will see below, the oocyte's ability to process and insert the translation products of exogenous mRNAs, coupled with its vigorous transmembrane sodium gradient, also provide a suitable system for assessing neurotransmitter uptake.

The other expression system that we will discuss in detail here is the brain. Individual neurons of the brain express significantly different arrays of genes. Indeed, the brain expresses more different genes than virtually any other organ in the body (11). Study of this differential expression and of its regulation is thus a suitable target for application for neurobiologic approaches to molecular biology.

NEUROBIOLOGICAL TECHNIQUES IN MOLECULAR BIOLOGY

Neuropharmacology

Receptor Genes

Neurotransmitter receptors are expressed at low abundance in the nervous system, and their configuration within membranes is key to their biological function. Classical biochemical/molecular biologic approaches to cloning receptor cDNAs involve laborious cross-linking and other labeling strategies, lengthy purification procedures, and painstaking protein microsequencing. These steps are necessary to provide enough protein and/or protein sequence information so that the library screening with antibodies or oligonucleotides can obtain cDNA clones coding for receptor molecules. Recently, however, two applications of a classic neuropharmacologic technique, ligand binding, show promise for direct identification of cDNA clones expressing neurotransmitter receptor molecules.

Civilli and co-workers were able to select a cDNA clone that expressed a D_2 dopamine receptor from a number of potential positive clones by using radioligand binding (1). These workers were able to confirm the identity of this receptor by classic pharmacologic means, displacing radiolabeled spiperone binding with a number of different agents active at dopamine receptors. The relative potencies in displacing binding from cells expressing the appropriate cDNA compared well with the known relative potencies of these same drugs in displacing the same radioligand from brain membrane receptors. This provided strong presumptive evidence that a D_2 receptor had been cloned. This strategy, detailed and contrasted with the classic strategy of biochemical purification in Chapter 1 by Bates et al, provides a promising example of a successful combination of neuropharmacologic and molecular biologic methods.

Further development of this approach with the aid of receptor autoradiographic methods may be possible. The procedure employed by Civilli and co-workers requires individual screening of membranes obtained from cell colonies. We have used a eucaryotic expression system in combination with a filter replica method that has allowed us to sample membrane fragments from many cell colonies distributed over the surface of a culture plate (33,34). The membrane fragments trapped on these filters can thus be screened with classic receptor autoradiographic methods to determine whether any of the cell colonies expresses appropriate DNA-mediated radioligand receptor binding.

We have validated this approach using a known β-adrenergic receptor cDNA. Detection of positive clones expressed at even low levels in initial libraries should be possible. We are currently working to optimize recovery of DNA from positively expressing colonies.

Uptake/Transporter Genes

Neurotransmitter uptake assays, another classic neuropharmacologic tool, can also be used to help identify expression of cDNAs encoding neurotransmitter uptake sites when they are expressed in *Xenopus* oocytes. Our laboratory, along with recent published work from Blakely and associates, finds that injection of messenger RNA from either brain or catecholamine-accumulating PC-12 cells can result in sodium-dependent, temperature-dependent, and time-dependent uptake of catecholamines or neurotransmitter amino acids (35,36). Dopamine uptake into oocytes injected with mRNA extracted from NGF-pretreated PC-12 cells also displays appropriate pharmacologic characteristics. It is blocked by agents including mazindol and cocaine, that block such uptake into brain synaptosomes. These assays can be used to detect the presence of a cDNA encoding an uptake site in a cDNA library, and to help monitor its enrichment and eventual purification through cDNA fractionation procedures. Thus, the ability of these *Xenopus laevis* oocytes to translate and appropriately insert natural or synthetic gene products can be coupled with this neuropharmacologic assay as a potential cloning tool.

Release

Recent applications of classic pharmacological loading-and-release studies in *Xenopus* oocytes have allowed detection of the calcium mobilization events that can also follow receptor occupancy. Oocytes injected with different mRNA preparations were loaded with radiolabeled calcium, washed, and then superfused with unlabeled medium. The release of $^{45}Ca^{2+}$ from some oocytes was dramatically enhanced by application of cholecystokinin (CCK) and other neuropeptides (37). Peptide-dependent release was noted only from oocytes that had been injected with mRNA preparations from receptor-expressing cells. This approach provides a method for monitoring the purification of specific mRNAs and or cDNAs encoding receptors whose coupling to calcium mobilization in the oocyte is superior to their linkage to transmembrane depolarizing events.

Electrophysiology

Classic electrophysiologic techniques, including voltage clamping, can detect the presence of responses to applied drugs and neurotransmitters in *Xenopus* oocytes that are injected with specific mRNAs (30). This approach can be used as a means to approach the cloning of neurotransmitter receptor cDNAs, based on physiologic responsiveness to exogenously applied receptor agonists. Using standard voltage-clamp techniques, electric currents can be recorded across the cell membranes of *Xenopus* oocytes. After injection of mRNAs from appropriate tissue sources, or of RNA synthesized from successively smaller cDNA pools, these eggs can display previously unelicitable responses to drug or neurotransmitter application. These electrical responses can thus be used to monitor purification of particular cDNAs and to aid in receptor cloning. Receptor cDNAs that have been identified in this fashion include those for the serotonin (5-HT$_1$C) and substance K-type tachykinin receptors (38–40).

We have been using *Xenopus* oocytes to identify mRNAs encoding the receptor for the neuropeptide neurotensin. This receptor recognizes one of the principal dopamine cotransmitter peptides and is intensely expressed on dopaminergic cell bodies in the ventral midbrain. In mRNA from rat midbrain, and in mRNA transcribed from cDNA libraries, neurotensin can induce a prolonged depolarization with superimposed transient current fluctuations. This reponse is characteristic of the effect of administering this peptide to mRNA-injected oocytes, which has been described by several other groups (40).

Various ion channels have been cloned in different fashions. Nevertheless, their expression and especially their structure-function relationships have most often been elucidated in a *Xenopus* oocyte test system (eg, ref 41).

Neuroanatomy

In order to appropriately understand gene expression events in the brain, it is necessary to place them in the context of the particular cell types, circuits, and pathways in which they take place. The neuroanatomy of gene neuroscience involves chiefly in situ hybridization (42). Using this anatomic technique, the patterns of expression of many of the genes of neurotransmission have been mapped in the brain. In addition, by applying quantitated autoradiographic and hybridization/wash techniques, one can use these anatomic methods to study gene regulation. Many of the issues regarding quantitation of in situ hybridization signals are directly analogous to those important for quantitated receptor autoradiography (43).

This approach has been used in a number of circumstances. Here we describe our recent use of the technique to document the differential distribution of two of the genes encoding dopamine-cotransmitter neuropeptides within cells of the ventral tegmental area (44). This region assumes major importance in several theories of the pathogenesis of schizophrenia, due to the fascinating pattern of the dopaminergic projections emanating from neurons localized here. Furthermore, many of these cells contain colocalized neuropeptides, neurotensin, and/or CCK (45,46). Using neuroanatomic approaches to mapping expression of the genes, in situ hybridization studies reveal previously unsuspected differences in the disposition of cells expressing neurotensin mRNA in comparison with the localization of those expressing CCK mRNA. Using equivalent-sized oligonucleotide ^{35}S-labeled hybridization probes directed against each of these mRNAs, we have found that CCK mRNA is intensely expressed in neurons of the rostral linear and parabrachialis pigmentosum subunits of the ventral tegmental area. Neurotensin mRNA is also expressed in parabrachialis pigmentosum neurons to a great extent, but it is most intensely expressed in neurons of the caudal linear nucleus. This superimposition of neuroanatomy on studies of gene expression points toward the possibility of dramatically different roles for these two dopamine cotransmitter neuropeptides in projections of the ventral tegmental area.

SUMMARY

Understanding each of these approaches to the study of genes important for brain function requires facility with both molecular biologic and neurobiologic methodologies. Nevertheless, the examples described here indicate that it is likely that neurobiologic methods will continue to exert substantial impact on molecular biologic approaches to the brain. Such continued cross-fertilization can only hasten the day when improved understanding of the structure and regulation of genes important for brain function makes ever increasing inroads into our understanding of normal and pathologic brain function.

ACKNOWLEDGMENTS

We gratefully acknowledge Ms. Debbie Button and Priscilla Heeter for assistance with preparation of the manuscript. We received support from the National Institute of Mental Health, National Institutes of Neurologic Disease and Stroke, McKnight Foundation, Sloan Foundation, American Parkinson's Disease Association, Juvenile Diabetes Association, and, for the personal studies reported here, from the National Institutes of Drug Abuse.

REFERENCES

1. Bunzow JR, Van Tol HHM, Grandy DK, et al. Cloning and expression of a rat D_2 dopamine receptor cDNA. *Nature* 1988;336:783–787.

2. Levitan ES. Cloning of serotonin and substance K receptors by functional expression in frog oocytes. *TINS* 1988;11(2):41–43.
3. Hadcock JR, Malbon CC. Down-regulation of β-adrenergic receptors: Agonist-induced reduction in receptor mRNA levels. *Proc Natl Acad Sci USA* 1988;85:5021–5025.
4. Collins S, Caron MG, Lefkowitz RJ. β_2-adrenergic receptors in hamster smooth muscle cells are transcriptionally regulated by glucocorticoids. *J Biol Chem* 1988;263:9067–9070.
5. Hadcock JR, Malbon CC. Regulation of β-adrenergic receptors by "permissive" hormones: Glucocorticoids increase steady-state levels of receptor mRNA. *Proc Natl Acad Sci USA* 1988;85:8415–8419.
6. Habener JF. Principles of peptide-hormone biosynthesis. In: Martin JB, Reichlin S, Bick KL, eds. *Neurosecretion and brain peptides.* New York: Raven Press, 1981;21–34.
7. Weiss ER, Kelleher DJ, Woon CW, et al. Receptor activation of G proteins. *FASEB* 1988; 2:2841–2848.
8. Hollenberg SM, Weinberger C, Ong ES, et al. Primary structure and expression of a functional human glucocorticoid receptor cDNA. *Nature* 1985;318:635–641.
9. Gehring U. Steroid hormone receptors: biochemistry, genetics, and molecular biology. *TIBS* 1987;12:399–402.
10. Schwart JP, Costa E. Hybridization approaches to the study of neuropeptides. *Annu Rev Neurosci* 1986;9:277–304.
11. Uhl GR, Evans J, Parta M, et al. Vasopressin and somatostatin mRNA in situ hybridization. In: Uhl GR, ed. *In situ hybridization in brain.* New York: Plenum Press, 1986;21–47.
12. Uhl GR, Zingg HH, Habener JF. Vasopressin mRNA in situ hybridization: Localization and regulation studied with oligonucleotide cDNA probes in normal and Brattleboro rat hypothalamus. *Proc Natl Acad Sci USA* 1985;82:5555–5559.
13. Uhl GR, Reppert SM. Suprachiasmatic nucleus vasopressin messenger RNA: Circadian variation in normal and Brattleboro rats. *Science* 1986;232:390–393.
14. Uhl GR, Ryan JP, Schwartz JP. Morphine alters preproenkephalin gene expression. *Brain Res* 1988;459:391–397.
15. Shivers BD, Harlan RE, Romano GJ, et al. Cellular localization and regulation of preproenkephalin mRNA in rat brain. In: Uhl GR, ed. *In situ hybridization in brain.* New York: Plenum Press, 1986;3–20.
16. Eberwine JH, Roberts JL. Glucocorticoid regulation of pro-opiomelanocortin gene transcription in the rat pituitary. *J Biol Chem* 1984; 259:2166–2170.
17. Morris BJ, Hollt V, Herz A. Dopaminergic regulation of striatal proenkephalin mRNA and prodynorphin mRNA: contrasting effects of D_1 and D_2 antagonists. *Neuroscience* 1988;25:525–532.
18. Dobner PR, Tischler AS, Lee YC, et al. Lithium dramatically potentiates neurotensin/neuromedin N gene expression. *J Biol Chem* 1988; 263:13983–13986.
19. Kaplan LM, Gabriel SM, Koenig JI, et al. Galanin is an estrogen-inducible, secretory product of the rat anterior pituitary. *Proc Natl Acad Sci USA* 1988;85:7408–7412.
20. Young WS III, Mezey E, Siegel RE. Quantitative in situ hybridization histochemistry reveals increased levels of corticotropin-releasing factor mRNA after adrenalectomy in rats. *Neurosci Lett* 1986;70:198–203.
21. Barinaga M, Yamonoto G, Rivier C, et al. Transcriptional regulation of growth hormone gene expression by growth hormone-releasing factor. *Nature* 1983;306:84–85.
22. Atchison ML. Enhancers: mechanisms of action and cell specificity. *Annu Rev Cell Biol* 1988; 4:127–153.
23. Ptashne M. How eukaryotic transcriptional activators work. *Nature* 1988;335:683–689.
24. Muller MM, Gerster T, Schaffner W. Enhancer sequences and the regulation of gene transcription. *Eur J Biochem* 1988;176:485–495.
25. Wigler M, Sweet R, Sim GK, et al. Transformation of mammalian cells with genes from procaryotes and eucaryotes. *Cell* 1979;16:777–785.
26. Braun T, Schofield PR, Shivers BD, et al. A novel subtype of muscarinic receptor identified by homology screening. *Biochem Biophys Res Commun* 1987;149:125–132.
27. Strader CD, Sigal IS, Register RB, et al. Identification of residues required for ligand binding to the β-adrenergic receptor. *Proc Natl Acad Sci* 1987;84:4384–4388.
28. Strader CD, Candelore MR, Rands E, et al. β-adrenergic receptor subtype is an intrinsic property of the receptor gene product. *Mol Pharmacol* 1987;32:179–183.
29. Fargin A, Raymond JR, Lohse MJ, et al. The genomic clone G-21 which resembles a β-adrenergic receptor sequence encodes the 5-HT1A receptor. *Nature* 1988;335:358–360.
30. Colman A. Translation of eukaryotic messenger RNA in *Xenopus* oocytes. In: Hames BD, Higgins SJ, eds. *Transcription and Translation.* Washington, DC, IRL Press, 1984;217–302.
31. Masu Y, Nakayama K, Tamaki H, et al. cDNA cloning of bovine substance-K receptor through oocyte expression system. *Nature* 1987;329: 836–838.
32. Bahouth SW, Hadcock JR, Malbon CC. Expression of mRNA of β1-and β2-adrenergic receptors in *Xenopus* oocytes results from structurally distinct receptor mRNAs. *J Biolog Chem* 1988;263:8822–8826.
33. Raetz CRH, Wermuth MM, McIntrye TM, et al. Somatic cell cloning in polyester stacks. *Proc Natl Acad Sci* 1982;79:3223–3227.
34. Rattray M, Lautar S, Uhl GR. Ligand autoradiographic receptor expression I: assessment of transient expression of β-adrenergic receptors in COS cells. *Mol Br Res* 1990;7:249–59.
35. Blakely RD, Robinson MB, Amara SG. Expression of neurotransmitter transport from rat brain mRNA in *Xenopus laevis* oocytes. *Proc Natl Acad Sci* 1988;85:9846–9850.

36. Uhl G, Shimada S, Nishimori T, et al. Dopamine transporter: expression in *Xenopus* oocytes. *Mol Brain Res* (in press).
37. Williams JA, McChesney DJ, Calayag MC, et al. Expression of receptors for cholecystokinin and other Ca^{2+}-mobilizing hormones in *Xenopus* oocytes. *Proc Natl Acad Sci USA* 1988;85:4939–4943.
38. Julius D, MacDermott AB, Axel R, et al. Molecular characterization of a functional cDNA encoding the serotonin 1c receptor. *Science* 1988;241:558–564.
39. Lubbert H, Hoffman BJ, Snutch TP, et al. cDNA cloning of a serotonin $5-HT_{1C}$ receptor by electrophysiological assays of mRNA-injected *Xenopus* oocytes. *Proc Natl Acad Sci USA* 1987;84:4332–4336.
40. Parker I, Sumikawa K, Miledi R, FRS. Neurotensin and substance P receptors expressed in *Xenopus* oocytes by messenger RNA from rat brain. *Proc R Soc Lond* 1986;B229:151–159.
41. Kushner L, Lerma J, Zukin RS, et al. Coexpression of *N*-methyl-D-aspartate and phencyclidine receptors in *Xenopus* oocytes injected with rat brain mRNA. *Proc Natl Acad Sci USA* 1988;85:3250–3254.
42. Uhl GR. *In situ hybridization in brain.* New York: Plenum Press, 1986.
43. Uhl G. In situ hybridization: Quantitation using radiolabeled hybridization probes. In: Conn PM, ed. *Neuroendocrine peptide methodology.* San Diego: Academic Press, 1989.
44. Jayaraman A, Nishimori T, Dobnar P, et al. Cholecystokinin and neurotensin mRNAs are differentially expressed in subnuclei of the ventral tegmental area. (in preparation).
45. Hokfelt T, Everitt BJ, Theodorsson-Norheim E, et al. Occurrence of neurotensinlike immunoreactivity in subpopulations of hypothalamic, mesencephalic, and medullary catecholamine neurons. *J Compar Neuro* 1984;222:543–559.
46. Seroogy K, Schalling M, Brene S, et al. Cholecystokinin and tyrosine hydroxylase messenger RNAs in neurons of rat mesencephalon: peptide/monoamine coexistence studies using in situ hybridization combined with immunocytochemistry. *Exp Brain Res* 1989;74:149–162.

PART III

Behavior and Schizophrenia

12

An Animal Model for Childhood Autism

Memory Loss and Socioemotional Disturbances Following Neonatal Damage to the Limbic System in Monkeys

Jocelyne Bachevalier[1]

Developmental studies of the effects of early brain damage are of great importance for the assessment and understanding of those errors of CNS maturation that cause children to become autistic, dyslexic, learning-disabled, or mentally retarded. This chapter summarizes the initial results of a long-term study of the cognitive and social development of monkeys suffering from an amnesia induced by limbic lesions early in infancy as compared to those rendered amnesic in adulthood, that is, after memories have been formed and possibly consolidated in cerebral tissue outside the limbic system. The accumulating evidence from this ongoing neurobehavioral study provides support for two provocative proposals from the clinical literature. First, early destruction of the limbic memory system is one cause of childhood autism, a syndrome characterized by dramatic social and emotional disturbances not seen in adults with the same neuropathology. Second, the reason a pure case of global anterograde amnesia like the one seen in adults has never been reported in a child is that the clinical picture of an amnesic child, being overlaid with autism, is entirely different from the clinical picture of an amnesic adult.

AN ANIMAL MODEL FOR GLOBAL AMNESIA IN ADULT MONKEYS

Bilateral damage to the medial temporal lobe in humans results in a profound anterograde amnesia. The most striking characteristic of amnesic patients is their inability to remember recent events and to learn many types of new information, even though intelligence, perception, and language are unaffected or minimally impaired. This type of amnesia is also referred to as being "global" in that it extends to many types of information derived from all sensory modalities (19,43). Although the neuropathological evidence has been interpreted as indicating that this temporal-lobe syndrome is due to hippocampal damage (58,59,64), experimental studies in nonhuman primates have suggested the alternative possibility that the syndrome results from combined damage to the hippocampus and the amygdala. The latter proposal is based on a finding in monkeys that, whereas ablation of the hippocampus or amygdala alone resulted in only mild deficits during visual memory tasks, combined

[1] Laboratory of Neuropsychology, National Institute of Mental Health, Bethesda, MD 20892.

ablation of these two structures yielded extremely severe deficits (44).

Indeed, the studies in monkeys have revealed that combined damage to the two limbic structures yields an amnesic syndrome closely resembling the anterograde global amnesia in humans (50). First, in both humans and monkeys, the postoperative memory loss is not all or none but is graded in relation to the amount of conjoint damage to the amygdala and hippocampus, with damage to each of these structures contributing about equally, and with only complete bilateral destruction of both producing a truly profound amnesia (48, 63). Second, the memory defect following combined amygdalohippocampal damage in monkeys, like the clinical syndrome, appears to be global, affecting recognition memory for visual and nonvisual, as well as spatial and nonspatial, stimuli (51,52,57). Third, further investigation has led to the discovery that, in monkeys as in humans, the anterograde amnesia reflected in visual recognition loss results from bilateral damage not only to the medial temporal lobe (44) but also to the medial diencephalon (2,3), the medial prefrontal cortex (9,46) and the basal forebrain (1).

This animal model of human memory disorders has thus provided important new insights into a major neuroanatomic circuit for memory. For vision the neural model proposed by Mishkin and his colleagues (reviewed in ref 45) postulates that visual information is processed sequentially along an occipitotemporal pathway. This ventrally directed chain of cortical visual areas appears to extract stimulus-quality information, such as size, color, shape, and texture, from the retinal input reaching the striate cortex, with the final stations of the inferior temporal cortical area TE synthesizing a complete representation of the object. Storage of the object's representation (and assignment of some meaning or association to it) is realized each time a perception formed in the final station of the visual cortical sensory system activates one or both of two parallel circuits. One circuit is anchored in the amygdala and the other in the hippocampus, and each includes projection target areas in the diencephalon and the ventromedial prefrontal cortex. Each of these structures in turn sends signals to the basal forebrain, which, through its widespread cortical connections, reaches back to the sensory cortical areas. It is postulated that the feedback action of these circuits on sensory areas strengthens synapses among active neurons and perhaps stores the neural representation of the sensory event that had just taken place. Once established, this central representation can be reactivated whenever the same stimulus reappears in the field, yielding visual recognition.

An important similarity between amnesic humans and monkeys is that despite their severe impairment in memory functions, they may still learn new habits and skills in an entirely normal manner. The first piece of evidence for the existence of preserved learning ability in profoundly amnesic subjects came from Milner's dramatic demonstration of a nearly normal rate of improvement in mirror-drawing skill in the severely amnesic patient, H.M., who underwent bilateral surgical removal of the medial temporal lobe to relieve his epilepsy (42). Since the report on H.M., there have been numerous studies showing the ability of amnesic patients to learn despite their inability to remember (16,17,20,65). All these studies demonstrate that gradual learning of skills and habits can proceed independently of the ability to recollect specific events or episodes. A number of studies conducted with nonhuman primates converge on a similar conclusion (48,49,66). For example, despite their rapid forgetting in one-trial recognition, monkeys with combined amygdalohippocampal lesions have no difficulty mastering a multiple-trial concurrent-object discrimination task in which successive trials on a given pair are separated by 24-hour intertrial intervals (35).

One proposal that has been advanced to

explain these paradoxical results is that retaining the effects of experience depends on two fundamentally different neural systems (31,48,49). One is a cognitive or representational system that serves both recognition and recall and utilizes a cortico-limbo-diencephalic circuit; this is the system that is presumed to be impaired in subjects rendered amnesic by limbic or diencephalic lesions. The other is a habit system that mediates the formation of stimulus-response connections; it has been speculated that this habit system depends in large part on a corticostriatal circuit. This is the system that is presumed to be preserved in amnesic subjects.

EARLY- AND LATE-DEVELOPING MEMORY SYSTEMS IN MONKEYS

On the evidence that in adult monkeys there may be two relatively independent systems for retention of information, we sought to compare the functional development of the two systems ontogenetically (7).

First, the development of cognitive memory in infant monkeys was investigated by testing monkeys between 3 months and 4 years of age in a one-trial object-recognition test that was used to demonstrate anterograde amnesia in adult monkeys with limbic lesions (44). In this task, the animal has to remember on the basis of a single trial whether an object had been seen before. Each trial consisted of two parts. First, the animal was confronted with a sample object overlying the baited central well of a test tray, which the animal removed from the well in order to obtain the reward. Ten seconds later the animal was confronted with the sample object and a new object, now overlying the lateral wells of the test tray. In this second part of the trial, the monkey was rewarded for displacing the novel object (delayed nonmatching-to-sample, DNMS). Twenty trials separated by 30-second intervals were given daily, each trial with a new pair of objects chosen from a stock of several hundred (47). First the monkey had to learn the rule of avoiding the familiar item in favor of the new one and thereby show that it could remember each sample for at least a few seconds. Then its recognition memory was taxed further in one of two ways: either through progressive increases of the delay between sample presentation and choice test (from the initial 10-second delay to 30-, 60-, and, finally 120-second delays), or through progressive increases in the number of sample items to be remembered (from the initial single object to three, five, and finally ten objects). The results indicated that 3-month-old monkeys failed to solve the DNMS task until they were approximately 4 months of age. With further maturation there was a gradual improvement in learning ability, yet they did not reach adult levels of proficiency even at 1 year. Only at about 2 years of age did monkeys master the recognition task as efficiently as adult animals (4). Thus, there is an age at which the DNMS task can first be solved and a considerably greater age before it can be solved with full adult proficiency. This slow ontogenetic development of visual recognition memory was shown even more strikingly in the memory performance test. With the longer delays and lists, average scores declined systematically in inverse relation to the group's age.

Like amnesic monkeys, these infant monkeys that could not remember an object they had just seen a few moments ago were nevertheless able to learn in as few trials as normal adults to pick the baited object of two. The relatively early appearance in life of the noncognitive habit system was demonstrated by testing 3-month-old monkeys in a multiple-trial concurrent-object discrimination task that was used to demonstrate the preserved ability in adult monkeys with limbic system lesions (35). In this task a series of 20 pairs of objects were presented as follows. A pair of objects, one baited and one unbaited, was presented simultaneously over the lateral wells of a test tray. After the animal made a choice, there was a 20-second delay, following which the second pair of objects was presented for choice, and so on, until all 20 pairs had been presented once each. The same series of objects was then repeated once every 24 hours until the monkeys reached a criterion of 90 correct choices in 100 trials (24-hour ITI task). Although in this task the intertrial intervals lasted 24 hours, the infant monkeys performed as well as adult monkeys (7).

Together these results strongly suggest that the two learning systems that were found to be separable in the adult monkeys are also developmentally dissociable. Moreover, a similar developmental dissociation was recently demonstrated in human infants (56). In short, the system for noncognitive association (habit system), which is preserved in adult monkeys rendered amnesic by limbic lesions, seems to develop early in infancy. By contrast, the system for cognitive associations (memory system), which is impaired in adult monkeys with limbic lesions, appears to develop late in infancy, presumably because the neural circuit on which it depends has a slow ontogenetic maturation. On the basis of this evidence, we prepared monkeys with neonatal removal of the limbic system (i.e., combined amygdalohippocampal removals) in an attempt to see how cognitive, emotional, and social behavior would develop in animals that might remain amnesic from infancy onward.

MATURATION OF THE HABIT AND MEMORY SYSTEMS

Newborn monkeys received damage either to the limbic system, (ie, amygdalohippocampal complex; Group AH), or to the inferior temporal area TE (Group TE). Four findings in adult monkeys dictated selection of area TE as the site of the comparison lesion:

1. Whereas amygdalohippocampal removals yield a global amnesia, area TE lesions yield a modality-specific memory loss, (i.e., one restricted to vision).
2. Whereas amygdalohippocampal removals impair the ability to form new memories but not the ability to acquire new habits, area-TE lesions yield a severe impairment in both forms of learning (60).
3. Conversely, disturbances in social behavior have been observed after limbic but not after area TE lesions in adulthood.
4. Since both area-TE and amygdalohippocampal lesions produce impairments in visual memory, the use of these two types of ablation permits comparison between the effects of neonatal cortical versus neonatal subcortical lesions on the development of visual memory.

The bilateral lesions shown in Fig. 1 were performed in two unilateral stages at approximately 1 week and 3 weeks of age, respectively. Each animal with a lesion (from Group AH or TE) was age-matched with an unoperated control (Group N).

The formation of visual discrimination habits in the three groups was measured with the 24-hour ITI task when the animals were 3 months old (5,8). Performance of infant monkeys was compared with that of monkeys that had been tested in the same way after receiving identical brain lesions when they were adults. As shown in Fig. 2, damage to the limbic system appeared to leave habit formation intact whether the lesions were early or late. By contrast, lesions of area TE yielded a severe and long-lasting deficit in visual habit formation if the damage occurred late, but they produced only a mild, transitory deficit of this function if the damage occurred early. Indeed, by the second set of visual discriminations (set B), infant monkeys with area-TE damage required no significantly greater number of sessions to learn than did normal adult monkeys (averaging 11 and 10 ses-

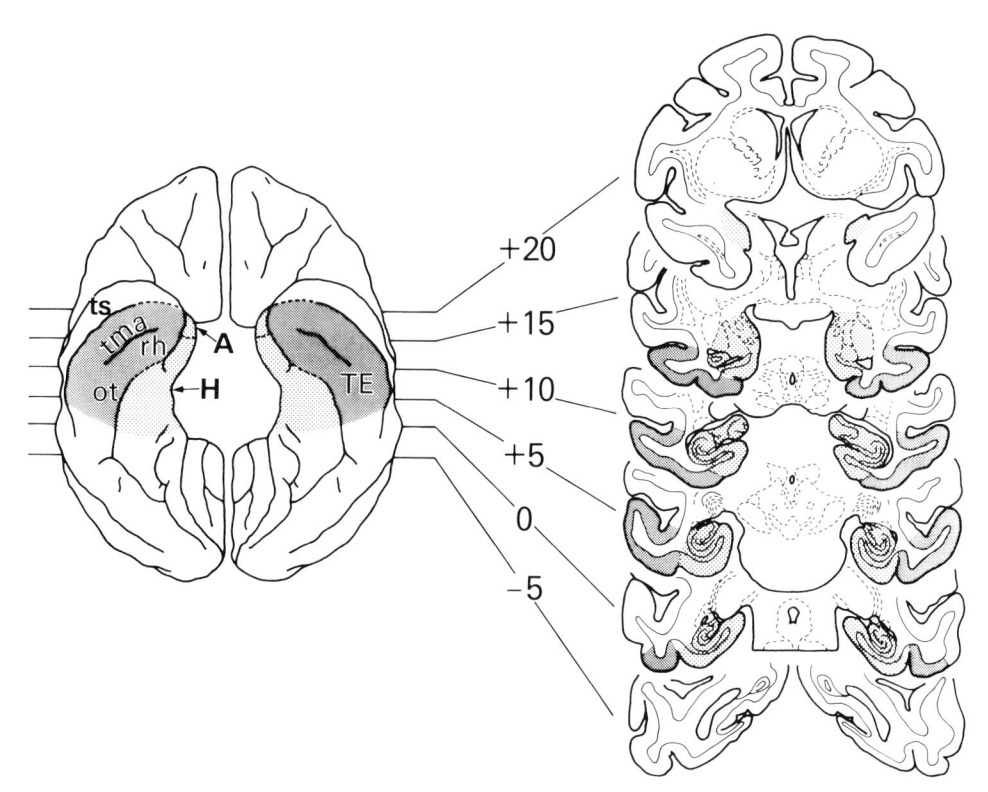

FIG. 1. Ventral surface (*left*) and coronal sections (*right*) illustrating the intended neonatal area-TE lesions (*dark stippling*) and amygdalohippocampal lesions (*light stippling*). A, amygdala; H, hippocampus; ot, occipitotemporal sulcus; rh, rhinal sulcus; tma, anterior middle temporal sulcus; ts, superior temporal sulcus.

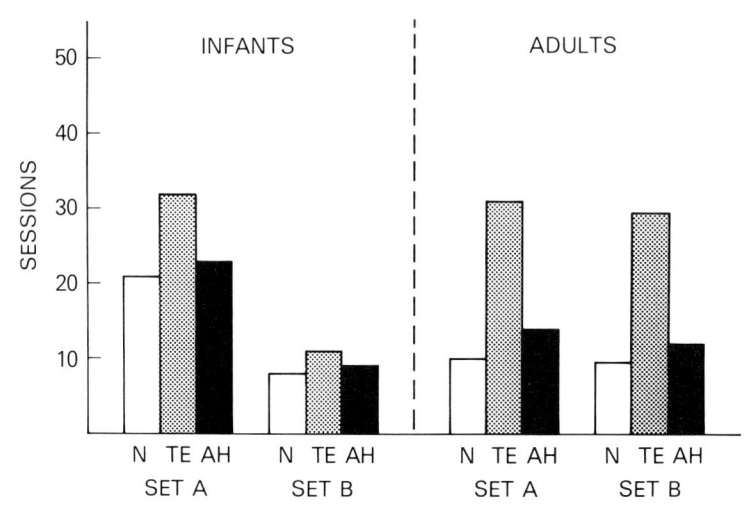

FIG. 2. Average number of sessions to attain criterion on two consecutive sets of discriminations (sets A and B) by 3-month-old monkeys (operated on neonatally) and adult monkeys. N, normal controls; TE, animals with bilateral area TE lesions; AH, animals with bilateral amygdalohippocampal lesions.

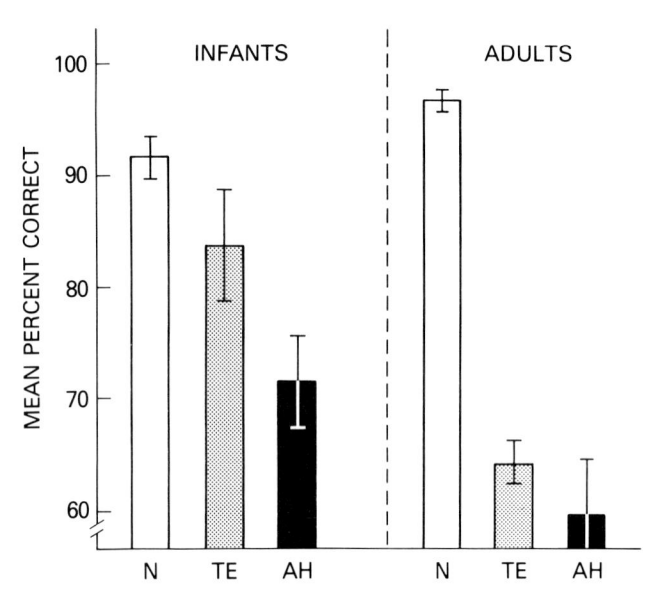

FIG. 3. Average scores on the recognition performance task by 10-month-old monkeys (operated on neonatally) and adult monkeys. Abbreviations same as in Fig. 2.

sions, respectively). These data thus suggest a functional sparing of habit formation following early damage to the inferior temporal cortical area TE. Though not shown in Fig. 2, the results indicated in addition that whereas the impairment in adult monkeys with area-TE lesions was equivalent for the two sexes, the transient impairment in the infant monkeys was apparent in the females only (5). Together with other recent findings showing that female infant monkeys acquire visual discriminations faster than males (6), the data point to an earlier maturation of cortical-area TE in females than in males.

With regard to cognitive memory (as measured by the DNMS task), there is again evidence of a greater compensatory potential after neonatal cortical damage than after neonatal limbic damage (9). Thus, whereas infants with neonatal limbic lesions were severely impaired in visual recognition at 10 months of age, those with neonatal ablation of visual association cortex (area TE) showed significant functional sparing. As shown in Fig. 3, both early and late damage to the limbic structures yielded severe impairment in visual recognition, reflected in drops in performance of 22% for the infants and 32% for the adults (as compared with their normal controls). By contrast, although late damage to area TE resulted in a drop in performance of 29%, early lesions of this cortical area resulted in a drop of only 8%.

Some of the first infants to receive these specific neonatal lesions are now 4-year-old monkeys that have been retested to assess the long-term effects of these early lesions on the formation of noncognitive habits and cognitive memories (10). Their performance on the 24-hour ITI and DNMS tasks was compared to that of 4-year-old monkeys that had received the same lesions in adulthood. At this age the monkeys with neonatal damage to area TE exhibited sparing of both habit and memory formation of the same magnitude as that found earlier when they were 3 and 10 months old. By contrast, the monkeys with neonatal limbic lesions resembled those with late limbic lesions in that they were unimpaired in habit formation but severely impaired in memory.

In summary, these behavioral data are consistent with the notion that association areas of the cortex possess considerable plasticity at birth, implying a degree of functional immaturity. Indeed, compensatory mechanisms appear to operate early to promote permanent recovery from neonatal temporal cortical lesions but not from limbic lesions. In support of this proposal, we have recently obtained direct evidence of neocortical immaturity in the macaque. First, the distribution of both opiate and muscarinic cholinergic receptors appears to be adultlike at birth in subcortical structures and allocortical areas but is not fully developed in any neocortical areas, including area TE (11,54). Second, adult levels of metabolic activity, as measured by the 2-deoxyglucose technique, are not reached in visual association cortex until the animals are about 4 months of age (27,34). These behavioral and neurobiological findings suggest that the relatively poor recognition ability of normal neonates is probably due to slow maturation of the cortical association areas and not to neonatal immaturity of the limbic system. Immaturity of the neocortex could also underlie the absence of a fully functional memory system in human infants and by implication could help explain the phenomenon of infantile amnesia, that is, the lack of memory for the events of infancy and earliest childhood.

DEVELOPMENT OF EMOTIONAL AND SOCIAL BEHAVIORS

The emotional and social development of infant monkeys in the experimental groups was assessed by analyzing their interactions with their age-matched normal controls, with whom they remained throughout their lives, and by comparing these social interactions with those of normal infants raised together (38,39). For this purpose, the infant monkeys were grouped in dyads and triads and placed in a playpen for up to 4 hours every day. These dyads and triads consisted of either one normal animal and one or two animals from the experimental groups AH and TE, or three normal animals. At the ages of 2 and 6 months, animal dyads were placed in a play cage containing toys and towels, and the behavior of each pair was videorecorded for two periods of 5 minutes each, separated by a 5-minute interval, for 6 consecutive days. Frequency and duration of behaviors in the videotapes were scored independently by two observers who assigned the behaviors to one of 14 different behavioral categories. Following are the categories we have analyzed so far:

Approach—social contact initiated by the monkey;

Acceptance of approach—acceptance of social contact initiated by the other monkey;

Dominant approach—immature forms of aggression such as snapping at the other monkey, taking toys away from the other monkey, or pushing the other monkey away;

Active withdrawal—active withdrawal from social approach initiated by the other monkey;

Inactivity—passive behavior;

Locomotor stereotypies—abnormal motor behaviors such as circling or doing somersaults;

Manipulation—manipulations of toys or parts of the cage with the limbs or mouth.

The results indicate that, at both 2 and 6 months of age, pairs of normal animals spent most of their time in social behavior or in object manipulation. There was virtually no behavior considered to be abnormal, such as active withdrawal or locomotor stereotypies, and very little inactivity. Between 2 to 6 months, however, the nature of the social interactions between normal animals did change. Thus, whereas at 2 months social behavior consisted primarily in following the other monkey and clinging to it, this immature behavior was replaced at 6 months by a prevalence of rough-and-tumble play and chasing. By contrast, in the dyads consisting of one normal control and one monkey with a neonatal limbic lesion, several socioemotional disturbances emerged in the latter. At 2 months only, infants with AH lesions had more temper tantrums when first placed in a novel play cage, showed more passive behavior, and manipulated objects less than the controls. Interestingly, at 6 months, these monkeys displayed even more striking pathology in that they now showed a complete lack of social contact, extreme submissiveness including active withdrawal, and gross motor stereotypies. In addition, at 6 months only, monkeys with limbic lesions displayed blank and unexpressive faces, few eye contacts, and poor body expression. Except for increased locomotor stereotypies, no comparable abnormalities were observed in monkeys with lesions of area TE (40). It is becoming clear that the same neonatal damage that leads to a severe cognitive memory disorder can have extremely serious consequences for personality and social development; this is so in part perhaps because of the cognitive memory impairment that is present from infancy onward, but also because of the direct effect of the limbic lesions on mechanisms of emotionality.

SIMILARITIES BETWEEN MONKEYS WITH NEONATAL LIMBIC LESIONS AND AUTISTIC CHILDREN

The developmental time course and the nature of the socioemotional disturbances in animals with neonatal limbic lesions show a marked resemblance to those seen in autism. Early infantile autism is a descriptive term identifying a distinctive disorder of behavioral development in a young child (62). The syndrome, first recognized by Kanner in 1943, was demonstrated to have an early onset, usually before the age of 30 months, and to show a prevalence in male subjects. The principal characteristics are described as follows:

A failure to develop normal social relationships (emotional remoteness, lack of eye contact, indifference to being held, apparent aversion to physical contact, disinterest in playing games with others);
Disturbances of verbal and nonverbal communication;
Development of ritualistic and compulsive behaviors (resistance to change in routine or surroundings, stereotypies, self-stimulatory behavior, abnormal preoccupations, morbid attachments, bizarre collections);
Unusual fears and anxiety.

As described above, the monkeys with neonatal removals of the limbic system develop not only a severe impairment in cognitive memory functions but also abnormal behaviors that bear a striking resemblance to children with the autistic syndrome: failure to develop normal relationships (isolation, withdrawal from other monkeys), blank facial expression and poor body language, lack of eye contact, as well as the presence of locomotor stereotypies such as twirling in circles and doing somersaults.

CLINICAL EVIDENCE FOR INVOLVEMENT OF THE TEMPORAL LOBES IN AUTISM

Despite a considerable number of studies devoted to infantile autism over the last decade or so, the etiology of this syndrome remains unknown. Although the causes may be diverse (55,62), it has become accepted that a primary defect in brain function is present in many if not all autistic children. Furthermore, because there is a common set of behavioral disturbances in autistic individuals, it is likely that a common set of specific brain structures is involved. In fact, there is growing evidence to support the hypothesis that at least one form of infantile autism results from congenital or neonatal neuropathology of the temporal lobes (22,23,26,29,37,53).[1]

First, there are similarities between the disturbed behaviors noted in autism and those found in Klüver-Bucy's syndrome resulting from bilateral removal of the temporal lobes (32). Some of the features of this syndrome are psychic blindness, profound changes in emotional behavior, oral exploration of objects, and dietary changes. The same features, which are similar in many respects to the autistic behaviors listed above, have been reported in a few cases of viral encephalitis in humans (36) as well as in several cases of head trauma, Alzheimer's disease, Pick's disease, and herpes encephalitis (33), all of which are known to have, in common, neuropathology in the medial temporal region.

Second, although autistic children are sometimes described as having excellent memories, the reverse is often closer to the truth. Reports of their excellent memory usually refer to their ability to learn and retain discrimination habits and specific motor skills (61). On tasks requiring long-term memory of information or knowledge, however, they actually perform poorly (61). Indeed, autistic children have been shown to suffer memory defects similar in some respects to those of amnesic adults (14, 15,41). They also perform poorly on imitation tasks (25).

Third, strong implications of medial temporal pathology, and even direct evidence of it, have been found in some cases of autism. Thus, investigators have reported that some autistic children have subtle EEG abnormalities in the temporal lobes (23,28), enlargement of the temporal horn of the lateral ventricles (28), mild abnormalities of the ventricular system and even some major hydrocephalus (30), increased incidence of herpes simplex types 1 and 2, which have a specific affinity for the medial temporal region (24), increased incidence of anoxia, which is also often associated with medial temporal dysfunction (18), and finally and most important, subtle cytoarchitectonic abnormalities found at autopsy in the hippocampus and amygdala (12; 13).

CONCLUSIONS

Cognitive memory and habit formation are two qualitatively different learning processes based on separate neural systems, a corticolimbic and a cortico-nonlimbic system, respectively. Our recent studies of behavioral development in infant monkeys have suggested that these two systems are developmentally dissociable, in that the nonlimbic habit system appears to mature considerably earlier than the limbic memory system. Our long-term investigation of the effects of early lesions on the development of cognitive and socioemotional behavior in primates has indicated that early damage to the limbic system (like damage in adulthood) leaves habit formation intact but severely impairs the formation of new memories. By contrast, neonatal damage to area TE yields relative sparing of both habit and memory formation (as compared with the severe deficit in both functions seen in adults with the same lesions). Thus, association areas of the cortex appear to possess considerable plasticity at birth, implying a degree of functional immaturity. These behavioral data are supported by direct neurobiological evidence of neonatal cortical immaturity, reflected in the homogeneous distribution of opiatergic and cholinergic receptors as well as in the low level of metabolic activity. Together, these behavioral and neurobiological findings sug-

---

[1] Although the discussion in this chapter focuses on the evidence for temporal-lobe involvement in the autistic syndrome, it is important to note that our hypothesis does not exclude the possibility that other structures (such as the cerebellum; see ref 21) may be important in the etiology of autism either as an alternative or an additional locus of neuropathology.

gest that the relatively poor recognition ability of normal neonates, and perhaps by extension the infantile amnesia (i.e., the inability to recollect events of early infancy), is due to slow maturation of the cortical association areas.

Following early damage to the limbic system, the severe memory deficit from birth onward was accompanied by socioemotional abnormalities that are strikingly similar to those seen in autistic children. The results are thus clearly consistent with the clinical evidence implicating medial temporal pathology in autistic behavior. The monkeys with early limbic lesions and autistic children have in common ritualistic and compulsive behaviors, major abnormalities of personality, an absence of social interactions, and memory deficits. It is of interest also that, like autistic children, the experimental monkeys exhibited considerable variability of specific symptoms; this suggests that autism too, rather than resulting from multiple pathologies that each yield a particular subset of autistic symptoms, could result from a common locus of pathology that produces multiple phenotypic displays. Though far from conclusive, the resemblance in the two disorders is sufficiently close to encourage further study of this possible animal model of childhood autism.

REFERENCES

1. Aigner T, Mitchell S, Aggleton JP, DeLong M, Struble R, Wenk G, Price D, Mishkin M. Recognition deficit in monkeys following neurotoxic lesions of the basal forebrain. Soc Neurosci Abstr 1984;10:386.
2. Aggleton JP, Mishkin M. Visual recognition impairment following medial thalamic lesions in monkeys. Neuropsychologia 1983;21:189–197.
3. Aggleton JP, Mishkin M. Memory impairments following restricted medial thalamic lesions in monkeys. Exp Brain Res 1983;52:199–209.
4. Bachevalier J. Ontogenetic development of habit and memory formation in primates. In: Diamond A, ed. Development and neural bases of higher cognitive functions. New York: Academic Press, in press.
5. Bachevalier J, Brickson M, Hagger C, Mishkin M. Age and sex differences in the effects of selective temporal lobe lesion on the formation of visual discrimination habits in rhesus monkeys. Behav Neurosci (in press).
6. Bachevalier J, Hagger C, Bercu BB. Gender differences in visual habit formation in 3-month-old rhesus monkeys. Develop Psychobiol 1989;22:585–599.
7. Bachevalier J, Mishkin M. An early and a late developing system for learning and retention in infant monkeys. Behav Neurosci 1984;98:770–778.
8. Bachevalier J, Mishkin M. Visual recognition impairment follows ventromedial but not dorsolateral prefrontal lesions in monkeys. Behav Brain Res 1986;20:249–261.
9. Bachevalier J, Mishkin M. Cortical vs limbic immaturity: Relationship to infantile global amnesia in monkeys. Soc Neurosci Abstr 1986;12:22.
10. Bachevalier J, Mishkin M. Long-term effects of neonatal temporal cortical and limbic lesions on habit and memory formation in rhesus monkeys. Soc Neurosci Abstr 1988;14:1.
11. Bachevalier J, Ungerleider LG, O'Neill B, Friedman DP. Regional distribution of [^{3}H]naloxone binding in the brain of a newborn rhesus monkey. Develop Brain Res 1986;25:302–308.
12. Bauman ML, Kemper TL. Histoanatomic observations of the brain in early infantile autism. Neurology 1985;35:866–874.
13. Bauman ML, Kemper TL. Limbic and cerebellar abnormalities: Consistent findings in infantile autism. J Neuropathol Exp Neurol 1988;47:369.
14. Boucher J. Immediate free recall in early childhood autism: Another point of behavioral similarity with amnesic syndrome. Br J Psychol 1981;72:211–215.
15. Boucher J, Warrington EK. Memory deficits in early infantile autism: some similarities to the amnesic syndrome. Br J Psychol 1976;67:73–87.
16. Brooks DN, Baddeley AD. What can amnesic patients learn? Neuropsychologia 1976;14:111–122.
17. Cohen NJ, Squire LR. Preserved learning and retention of pattern-analyzing skill in amnesia: Dissociation of "knowing how" and "knowing that." Science 1980;210:207–209.
18. Coleman M. A report on the autistic syndrome. In Rutter M, Schopler E, eds. Autism: a reappraisal of concepts and treatment. New York: Plenum Press, 1978;185–199.
19. Corkin S. Tactually-guided maze learning in man: Effects of unilateral cortical excisions and bilateral hippocampal lesions. Neuropsychologia 1965;3:339–351.
20. Corkin S. Acquisition of motor skill after bilateral medial temporal-lobe excision. Neuropsychologia 1968;6:255–266.
21. Courchesne E, Yeung-Courchesne R, Press GA, Hesselink JR, Jernigan TL. Hypoplasia of cerebellar vermal lobules VI and VII in autism. N Eng J Med 1988;318:1349–1354.
22. Damasio AR, Maurer RG. A neurological model

for childhood autism. *Arch Neurol* 1978;35:777–786.
23. DeLong GR. A neuropsychologic interpretation of infantile autism. In: Rutter M, Schopler E, eds. *Autism: a reappraisal of concepts and treatment*. New York: Plenum Press, 1978;207–218.
24. DeLong GR, Bean SC, Brown FR III. Acquired reversible autistic syndrome in acute encephalopathic illness in children. *Arch Neurol* 1981;38:191–194.
25. DeMyer MK. The nature of the neuropsychological disability in autistic children. *J Autism Child Schiz* 1975;5:109–128.
26. Fein D, Pennington B, Markowitz P, Braverman M, Waterhouse L. Towards a neuropsychological model of infantile autism: Are the social deficits primary? *J Am Acad Child Psychiatry* 1986;25:198–212.
27. Hagger C, Bachevalier J, Macko KA, Kennedy C, Sokoloff L, Mishkin M. Functional maturation of inferior temporal cortex in infant rhesus monkeys. *Soc Neurosci Abstr* 1988;14:2.
28. Hauser SL, DeLong GR, Rosman NP. Pneumographic findings in the infantile syndrome. *Brain* 1975;98:667–688.
29. Hetzler BE, Griffin JL. Infantile autism and the temporal lobe of the brain. *J Autism Develop Dis* 1981;9:153–157.
30. Hier DB, Lemay M, Rosenberg PB. Autism and unfavorable left-right asymmetries of the brain. *J Autism Develop Dis* 1979;9:153–157.
31. Hirsh R. The hippocampus and contextual retrieval of information from memory: A theory. *Behav Biol* 1974;12:421–445.
32. Klüver H, Bucy PC. Preliminary analysis of function of the temporal lobe in monkeys. *Arch Neurol* 1939;42:979–1000.
33. Lilly R, Cummings JL, Benson F, Frankel M. The human Klüver-Bucy syndrome. *Neurology* 1983;33:1141–1145.
34. Macko KA, Bachevalier J, Kennedy C, Suda S, Sokoloff L, Mishkin M. Functional development of the ventral cortical visual pathway measured by the 2-deoxyglucose method. *Soc Neurosci Abstr* 1983;9:375.
35. Malamut BL, Saunders RC, Mishkin M. Monkeys with combined amygdalo-hippocampal lesions succeed in object discrimination learning despite 24-hour intertrial intervals. *Behav Neurosci* 1984;98:759–769.
36. Marlowe WB, Mancall EL, Thomas JJ. Complete Klüver-Bucy syndrome in man. *Cortex* 1975;11:53–59.
37. Maurer RG, Damasio AR. Childhood autism from the point of view of behavioral neurology. *J Autism Develop Dis* 1982;12:195–205.
38. Merjanian PM, Bachevalier J, Crawford H, Mishkin M. Socio-emotional disturbances in the developing rhesus monkey following neonatal limbic lesions. *Soc Neurosci Abstr* 1986;12:23.
39. Merjanian PM, Bachevalier J, Pettigrew KD, Mishkin M. Developmental time course as well as nature of socio-emotional disturbances in rhesus monkey following neonatal limbic lesions resemble those in autism. *Soc Neurosci Abstr* 1988;14:2.
40. Merjanian PM, Bachevalier J, Pettigrew KD, Mishkin M. Behavioral disturbances in the developing rhesus monkey following neonatal lesions of inferior temporal cortex (area TE) resemble those in attention-deficit hyperactivity disorder. *Soc Neurosci Abstr* 1989;15:302.
41. Merjanian PM, Nadel L, Jans DD, Granger DA, Lott IT, Kean ML. Involvement of the hippocampus and amygdala in classical autism: A comparative neuropsychological study. *Soc Neurosci Abstr* 1984;10:524.
42. Milner B. Les troubles de la mémoire accompagnant des lésions hippocampiques bilatérals. In: Passouant P, ed. *Physiologie de l'hippocampe*. Paris: Centre de la Recherche Scientifique, 1962;257–272.
43. Milner B. Disorders of learning and memory after temporal lobe lesions in man. *Clin Neurosurg* 1972;19:421–446.
44. Mishkin M. Memory in monkeys severely impaired by combined but not separate removal of amygdala and hippocampus. *Nature* 1978;273:297–298.
45. Mishkin M, Appenzeller T. The anatomy of memory. *Sci Am* 1987;256:80–89.
46. Mishkin M, Bachevalier J. Differential involvement of orbital and anterior cingulate cortices in object and spatial memory functions in monkeys. *Soc Neurosci Abstr* 1986;12:742.
47. Mishkin M, Delacour J. An analysis of short-term visual memory in the monkey. *J Exp Psychol An Behav Proc* 1975;1:326–334.
48. Mishkin M, Malamut BL, Bachevalier J. Memories and habits: Two neural systems. In: Lynch G, McGaugh L, Weinberger NM, eds. *Neurobiology of learning and memory*. New York: Guilford, 1984;65–77.
49. Mishkin M, Petri HL. Memories and habits: Some implications for the analysis of learning and retention. In: Butters N, Squire L, eds. *Neuropsychology of Memory*. New York: Guilford, 1984;287–296.
50. Mishkin M, Spiegler BJ, Saunders RC, Malamut BL. An animal model of global amnesia. In: Corkin S, Davis KL, Growdon JH, Usdin E, Wurtman RJ, eds. *Alzheimer's Disease: A Report of Progress*. New York: Raven Press, 1982;235–247.
51. Murray EA, Mishkin M. Severe tactual memory deficits in monkeys after combined removal of the amygdala and hippocampus. *Brain Res* 1983;270:340–344.
52. Murray EA, Mishkin M. Severe tactual as well as visual memory deficits follow combined removal of the amygdala and hippocampus in monkeys. *J Neurosci* 1984;4:2565–2580.
53. Novick B, Kurtzberg D, Vaughan HG Jr. An electrophysiologic indication of defective information storage in childhood autism. *Psychiatry Res* 1979;1:101–108.
54. O'Neill JB, Friedman DP, Bachevalier J, Unger-

leider LG. Distribution of muscarinic cholinergic receptors in the brain of a newborn monkey. *Soc Neurosci Abstr* 1986;12:809.
55. Ornitz EM. The functional neuroanatomy of infantile autism. *Int J Neurosci* 1983;19:85–124.
56. Overmann WH. Performance on traditional match-to-sample, nonmatch-to-sample, and object discrimination tasks by 12 to 32 month-old children: A developmental progression. In: Diamond A, ed. *Development and neural bases of higher cognitive functions*. New York: Academic Press, 1990.
57. Parkinson JK, Murray EA, Mishkin M. A selective mnemonic role for the hippocampus in monkeys: Memory for the location of objects. *J Neurosci* 1988;8:4159–4167.
58. Penfield W, Mathieson G. Memory. Autopsy findings and comments on the role of the hippocampus in experiential recall. *Arch Neurol* 1974;31:145–154.
59. Penfield W, Milner B. Memory deficit produced by bilateral lesions in the hippocampal zone. *Am Med Assoc Arch Neurol Psychiatry* 1958;79:475–497.
60. Phillips RR, Malamut BL, Bachevalier J, Mishkin M. Dissociation of the effects of inferior temporal and limbic lesions on object discrimination learning with 24-hr intertrial intervals. *Behav Brain Res* 1988;27:99–107.
61. Prior MR. Cognitive abilities and disabilities in infantile autism: A review. *J Abnorm Child Psychol* 1979;7:357–380.
62. Rutter M. Diagnosis and definition. In: Rutter M, Schopler E, eds. *Autism: Reappraisal of Concepts and Treatment*. New York: Plenum Press, 1978;1–26.
63. Saunders RC, Murray EA, Mishkin M. Further evidence that amygdala and hippocampus contribute equally to recognition memory. *Neuropsychologia* 1984;22:785–796.
64. Scoville WB, Milner B. Loss of recent memory after bilateral hippocampal lesions. *J Neurol Neurosurg Psychiatry* 1957;20:11–21.
65. Warrington E, Weiskrantz L. New method of testing long-term retention with special reference to amnesic patients. *Nature (Lond)* 1968;217:972–974.
66. Zola-Morgan S, Squire LR. Complementary approaches to the study of memory: Human amnesia and animal models. In: Weinberger NW, McGaugh JL, Lynch L, eds. *Memory systems of the brain: animal and human cognitive processes*. New York: Guilford Press, 1985;463–477.

13
Stress and Schizophrenia

Alan Breier,[1] Owen M. Wolkowitz,[2] and David Pickar[3]

The relationship between stress and schizophrenia has been an area of active investigation throughout this century. It is generally accepted that stress is not the sole cause of schizophrenia in otherwise healthy individuals. Rather, stress has been considered to be a potential trigger for schizophrenic episodes in those persons with an underlying predisposition for the illness. However, even the role of stress as a trigger for schizophrenic episodes is still controversial largely because of methodological issues related to examining stress in schizophrenic patients (see below). An improved understanding of the relationship between stress and schizophrenia has important implications for the development of new treatments and the elucidation of the pathophysiology of schizophrenia.

There are several critical questions that need to be addressed in examining the association between stress and schizophrenia:

1. Is environmental stress related to the onset and exacerbation of schizophrenia?
2. Do stress-reduction treatments ameliorate symptoms and signs of schizophrenia?
3. Are there abnormalities in the stress response of schizophrenic patients?
4. What mechanisms might underly a putative altered stress response in schizophrenic patients?

In this chapter, we will examine data relevant to the questions above and synthesize these data into a neurobiological model of how stress may relate to schizophrenia.

ENVIRONMENTAL STRESS AND THE ONSET AND EXACERBATION OF SCHIZOPHRENIA

Several studies have examined the role of environmental stress in the development and course of illness of schizophrenia. Both discrete stressful life events and interpersonal stress have been assessed.

Stressful Life Events

The role of stressful life events in the onset of schizophrenic episodes remains controversial, in part because of the formidable methodologic issues involved in studies of stress in schizophrenia. In assessing the relationship between stressful events and schizophrenic episodes, the following methodologic issues should be considered:

1. A comprehensive assessment instrument designed to define and indentify stressful life events should be used.
2. An appropriate control group is needed.

---
[1]Maryland Psychiatric Research Center, Department of Psychiatry, University of Maryland School of Medicine, Baltimore, MD 21201.
[2]Department of Psychiatry, University of California, San Francisco, CA 94143.
[3]Clinical Neuroscience Branch, National Institute of Mental Health, Bethesda, MD 20892.

3. Events should be determined to be either dependent or independent of the schizophrenic episode; that is, it should be determined whether the event resulted from the psychotic episode or is independent of the episode.
4. Sufficient sample sizes are necessary.
5. Accurate determination of the onset of the schizophrenic episode is important.

Studies that have fulfilled the majority of the methodological criteria above are relatively few. Jacobs and Meyers (1) studied the occurrence of recent life events in 62 first-episode schizophrenic patients and 62 community control subjects. They found that significantly more events occurred in the year prior to the first hospitalization in the schizophrenics than in the year prior to assessing the controls. Brown and Birley (2) examined the rate of recent events in a cohort of 50 first-episode and chronic schizophrenic patients and 325 randomly selected controls. They found significantly more stressful life events occurring during a 3-month period prior to the onset of psychotic episodes in the schizophrenic patients. Moreover, after categorizing events as independent of or dependent on the psychotic episode in a subgroup of the subjects, they found that there were more independent stressful events in the schizophrenic patients compared with the controls. In a study of 132 schizophrenic patients living in the community and 132 matched community controls, Schwartz and Myers (3) found that the schizophrenic patients had significantly more stressful life events and that there was a relationship between life events and psychiatric impairment. Thus, the data from these studies indicate that stressful life events are related to the onset of schizophrenia and exacerbations of the illness.

The types of events commonly found among schizophrenic patients are quite different from those found in other psychiatric populations and controls (3–6). For example, events that have been reported to be at increased rates among schizophrenic patients include death of a pet, scheduled court appearance, eviction from a residence, family discord, and change in therapist or treatment setting. These data suggest that for studies of stressful life events and schizophrenia, assessment instruments should be developed specifically for schizophrenic populations and include an inventory of events that are common to schizophrenic patients. The use of such instruments should lead to a more accurate determination of the role stressful events in precipitating psychotic episodes in these patients.

Family Stress

Several studies have demonstrated that family interactions involving high levels of negatively expressed emotion lead to psychotic relapse and rehospitalization in schizophrenic patients (7–12), although there are studies that have failed to confirm this relationship (11–12). The earlier studies demonstrated that over the 9-month outcome period, relapse was rare in low-expressed-emotion households and appeared to be independent of neuroleptic dose and compliance. Later studies, however, have followed patients over a 2-year period and found relapse in about 50% of neuroleptic-free patients in low-expressed-emotion households (13). It appears that comments critical and pejorative of the patient are most likely to lead to relapse and that male schizophrenics are particularly susceptible to these stressful interactions. It has been argued that the high levels of expressed emotion found in families of some schizophrenic patients may be byproducts of having a severely ill family member in the home (11) and thus may be viewed as an interactional phenomenon.

Thus, the data from stressful life events and ambient interpersonal stress studies support the contention that environmental stress is associated with the onset and exacerbation of schizophrenia.

STRESS REDUCTION TREATMENTS FOR SCHIZOPHRENIA

Behavioral Therapies

Behavioral and psychoeducational therapies designed to decrease family stress have been shown to decrease psychotic relapses and attenuate schizophrenic psychopathology (14–17). Falloon and colleagues (16) examined the efficacy of a family-based approach that was designed to enhance problem-solving capacity and thereby decrease family tension in schizophrenic outpatients. Thirty-six schizophrenic patients who returned to stressful parental households after experiencing a psychotic relapse were randomized to either the family management approach or to individual case management, which served as the control treatment. After 9 months the family management group, in comparison with individual-case-management patients, had significantly fewer psychotic relapses, fewer hospitalizations, lower levels of schizophrenic psychopathology (Fig. 1) and were treated with less neuroleptic medication over the outcome period. Hogarty and colleagues (17) examined the effects of psychoeducational family therapy, social skills training, and maintenance neuroleptic treatment in 103 recently discharged schizophrenic and schizoaffective patients residing in high-expressed-emotion households. First-year relapse rates for the treatment arms were as follows: family treatment plus medication, 19%; social skills training plus medication, 20%; combined family treatment, social skills training, and medication, 0%; and medication alone, 41%. It was found that low relapse rates were found in households in which high-expressed-emotion levels were decreased. Thus, a combination of maintenance medication and behavioral treatments oriented towards decreasing family stress was the most effective treatment for long-term outcome.

Pharmacologic Treatment

The most commonly used stress-reducing pharmacological agents are the anxiolytic benzodiazepines. Benzodiazepines have been used as adjuncts to neuroleptic drugs in treating schizophrenic patients, although the cumulative data are inconclusive with regard to their efficacy (18–21). Of nine double-blind studies in which benzodiazepines were added to neuroleptic treatment, four reported favorable results (22–25) and five reported largely negative results (26–30). Many of these studies, however, particularly those conducted in the 1960s, were

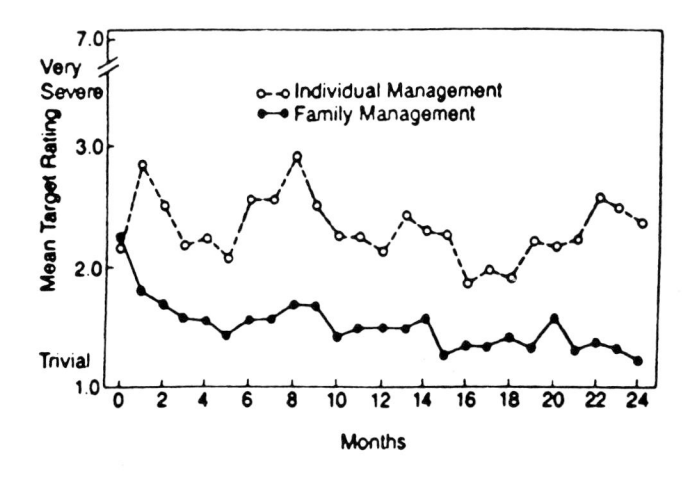

FIG. 1. Mean blind ratings of target symptoms of schizophrenia over 24 months. (Reprinted from *Archives of General Psychiatry* 1985;42:887–896.)

methodologically limited in that they used nonuniform diagnostic groups and nonspecific global rating scales and tended to apply inconsistent statistical analyses. Three of the four completed since 1975 reported benzodiazepines to be synergistic with neuroleptic treatment (22–24). In most studies, regardless of overall group effect, there is evidence for a therapeutic response in some patients; predictors of favorable benzodiazepine response, however, are unclear.

Few studies have directly compared the relative efficacy of different benzodiazepines and newer high-potency benzodiazepines. Csernansky et al (31) compared the efficacy of alprazolam (a triazolobenzodiazepine), diazepam, and placebo added to neuroleptic treatment in schizophrenic outpatients with moderate baseline levels of symptomatology. They found that alprazolam-treated patients had lower symptom scores in the initial weeks of the study but at endpoint analysis there were no significant differences among the three groups. It is possible that significant treatment effects were not demonstrated because the patient group had relatively moderate levels of symptoms at the time of entrance into the study.

We have recently completed a double-blind efficacy study of alprazolam added to neuroleptic medication in schizophrenic inpatients with moderate to high levels of chronic residual positive and negative symptoms (32). In addition, we assessed the effects of alprazolam treatment on plasma homovanillic acid (HVA), a major circulating metabolite of dopamine. Patients were prescribed fluphenazine hydrochloride for a mean of 70.7 days (SD = 54.1 days; range, 41 to 245 days) before alprazolam was added. No adjustments were made in the fluphenazine doses for at least 2 weeks (mean ± SD = 37.8 ± 13.0 days; range, 14 to 58 days) before the addition of alprazolam, and fluphenazine doses were not changed during the study. The mean dose of fluphenazine hydrochloride was 25.4 ± 9.9 mg/d (range, 7 to 40 mg/d). Alprazolam was added at an initial dosage of 0.5 mg/d that was increased in increments of 0.5 mg/d up to a clinically determined dosage (the highest dosage tolerated without undue sedation or other side effects). Treatment at this optimum dosage of alprazolam (mean ± SD = 2.88 ± 1.33 mg/d; range, 1.5 to 5.0 mg/d) was continued for 2 to 4 weeks (mean ± SD = 2.42 ± 0.67 weeks) ("optimum dose treatment period") before alprazolam was tapered by reductions of 0.5 mg every 3 days. Following discontinuation of alprazolam administration, patients were studied for an additional 2 weeks while taking fluphenazine alone. All medications were administered under double-blind conditions, and patients received placebo capsules that appeared identical to the alprazolam capsules. Plasma for HVA and other indices were collected 3 times per week after an overnight fast with the patients at bedrest. HVA levels were determined by high-performance liquid chromatography with electrochemical detection (33).

For the patient group as a whole, the addition of alprazolam to stable doses of fluphenazine resulted in significant reductions in symptom ratings, with return to baseline levels following alprazolam withdrawal (Fig. 2). Significant changes were observed for global ratings of psychosis and anxiety, for the Brief Psychiatric Rating Scale (BPRS) total score, and for BPRS positive and paranoia-suspiciousness symptom subscales (Fig. 2). There was a trend for levels of plasma HVA to change during the course of alprazolam treatment and withdrawal ($p < .1$). Analysis of individual patient responses, however, showed that alprazolam-associated changes in plasma HVA levels were directly correlated with changes in global psychosis ratings ($r = .65$, $p < .05$) and ratings of negative symptoms using the Abrams-Taylor scale for emotional blunting ($r = .59$, $p < .05$). The nature of this relationship can be best appreciated

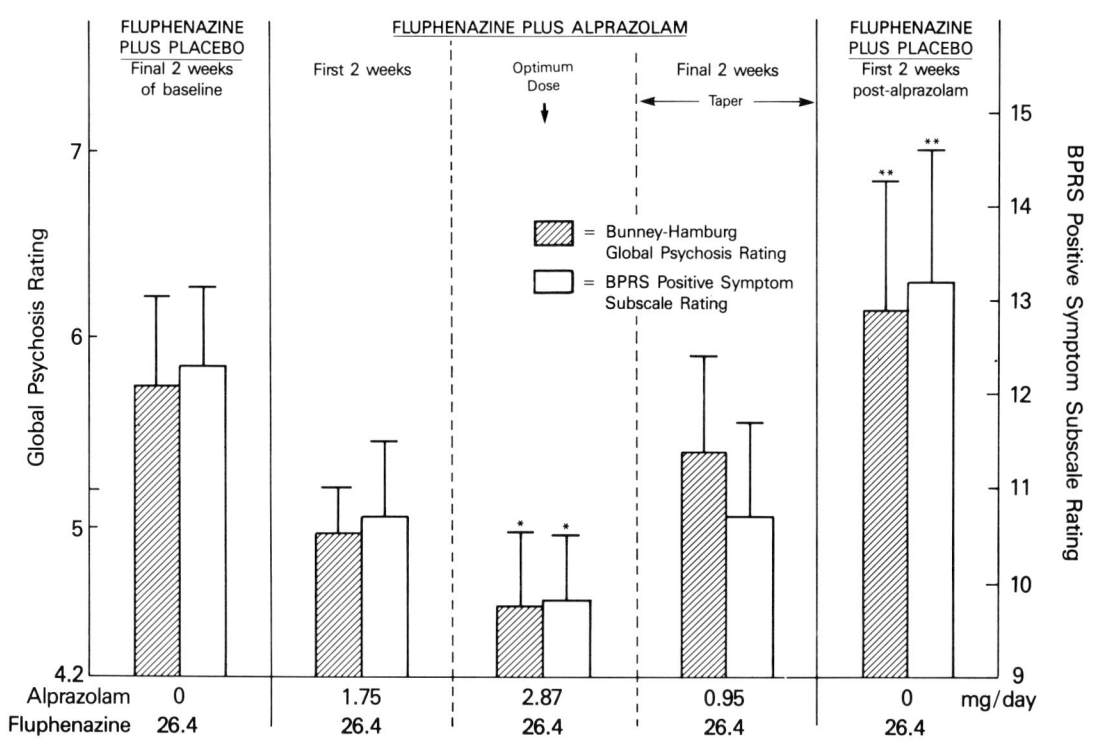

FIG. 2. Changes in mean (±SE) Bunney-Hamburg global psychosis ratings (*shaded bars*) and Brief Psychiatric Rating Scale (BPRS) positive symptom subscale ratings (*open bars*) associated with alprazolam treatment and withdrawal, Mean alprazolam and fluphenazine hydrochloride doses are at bottom. Following are results of analyses of variance. Global psychosis ratings: $F(4,44) = 3.89$, $p<.01$; BPRS positive symptom subscale ratings: $F(4,44) = 3.77$, $p<.01$. *Asterisk* indicates $p<.05$ compared with baseline (post hoc *t*-test); *dagger*, $p<.05$ compared with optimum-dose alprazolam treatment (post hoc *t*-test). (Reprinted from *Archives of General Psychiatry* 1988;45:664–671.)

when responders are compared to nonresponders: Whereas nonresponders showed an increase in plasma HVA levels, responders showed a decrease in plasma HVA levels ($F = 3.28$, $p < .05$; Fig. 3).

These data indicate that the addition of alprazolam to a regimen of the standard neuroleptic fluphenazine in symptomatic schizophrenic inpatients resulted in significant, albeit modest, improvement in psychotic symptoms, notably in "positive" symptoms such as hallucinations, paranoia, and thought disorder. In five of the 12 patients, the improvement during alprazolam treatment was clinically significant, and in two other patients mild improvement was noted. Thus, the significant group improvement was accounted for by the response of one half of the patients.

Although mean ratings of negative symptoms did not significantly decrease during alprazolam treatment, we observed that such symptoms were reduced in patients who showed an overall favorable response to treatment. We have previously reported that both negative and positive schizophrenic symptoms are responsive to neuroleptic treatment (34). Data from the present study further call into question the notion that negative symptoms are pharmacologically unresponsive. With regard to the antipsychotic response itself, changes

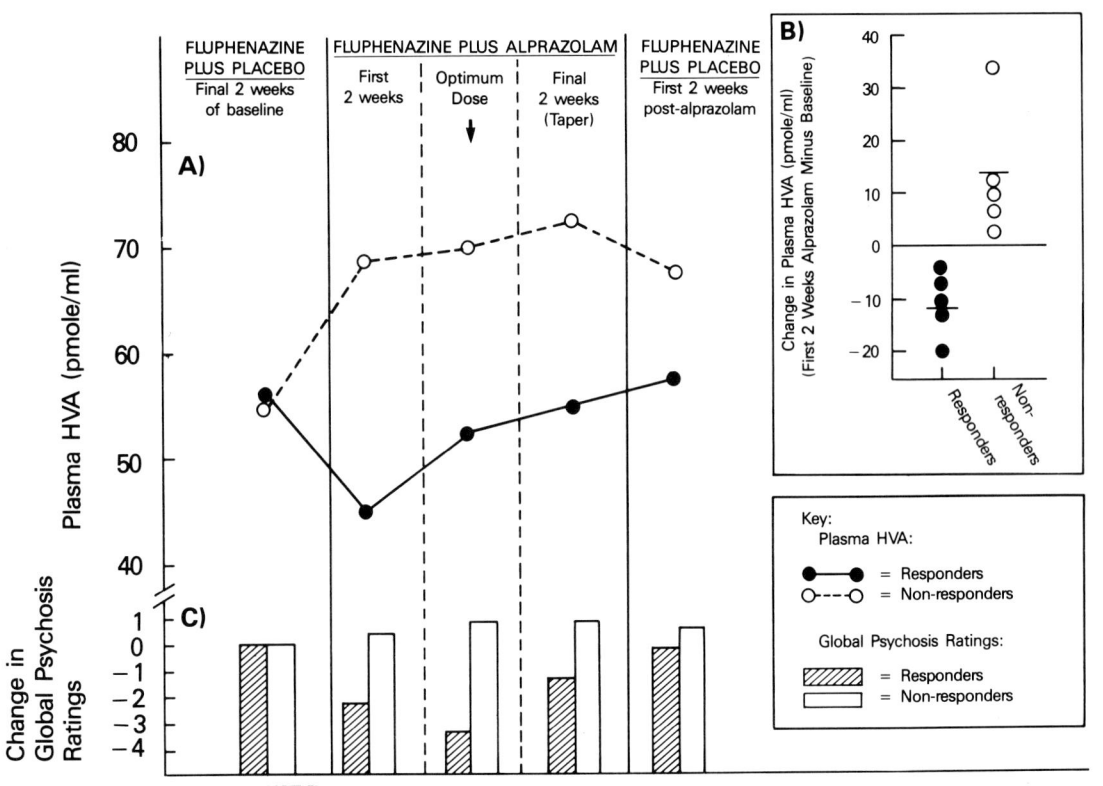

FIG. 3. *Top:* Change in mean plasma homovanillic acid (HVA) levels associated with alprazolam treatment for responders (*shaded bars and circles*) and nonresponders (*open bars and circles*) who showed significantly different plasma HVA responses (analysis of variance: group × time ($F[4,32]$ = 3.28, $p<.05$). This difference was significant during the first 2 weeks of alprazolam treatment ($F[1,8]$ = 17.97, $p<.02$ corrected for multiple comparisons) and tended to be significant during optimum-dose alprazolam treatment ($F[1,8]$ = 7.71, $p<.10$, corrected for multiple comparisons). Considered separately, responders showed significant alprazolam-associated decreases in plasma HVA ($F[4,16]$ = 3.56, $p<.05$) during first 2 weeks of alprazolam treatment ($p<.05$ by post hoc *t*-test), but not during optimum-dose alprazolam treatment. *Inset:* Maximum separation between responders and nonresponders was seen during first 2 weeks of alprazolam treatment. *Bottom:* Change in global psychosis ratings (compared with baseline) for responders and nonresponders. (Reprinted from *Archives of General Psychiatry* 1988;45:664–671.)

in global psychosis ratings were paralleled by changes in global anxiety and depression ratings, although significant main effects of alprazolam administration on anxiety and depression were not observed. It is unknown if the observed antipsychotic effect was etiologically related to improvements in anxiety and/or depression; however, it is clear that core psychotic symptoms, such as hallucinations and delusions, significantly decreased in responding patients.

In our study, patients who were more psychotic or more anxious while taking fluphenazine alone showed the greatest improvement during alprazolam treatment. High levels of baseline anxiety, agitation, or retardation have been reported to predict better responses to neuroleptic-benzodiazepine combinations in other studies. Jimerson et al (35) found that the patients with the best neuroleptic responses also showed the best responses to benzodiazepines when these were administered in high doses as the sole treatment. Our data suggest that neuroleptic-treated patients with greater residual psychotic symptoms show more favorable responses to alprazolam augmentation. These data may explain the discrepant results between this study and the Csernansky study (31) in that alprazolam may be an effective augmenting agent in the more severely ill patients with moderate and high levels of residual symptoms.

The HVA component of our study provides interesting preliminary data suggesting that alprazolam-induced improvement in schizophrenic symptoms is related to decrements in dopamine activity. We and others have shown that standard neuroleptic-induced improvement in schizophrenic symptoms is related to decrements in plasma HVA (36–40). Thus, reduction in plasma HVA may be a correlate of pharmacologically induced symptom amelioration for a range of treatments. Moreover, because benzodiazepines and neuroleptics have direct effects on GABAergic and dopaminergic systems, respectively, the decrement in plasma HVA produced by alprazolam and neuroleptic in this study provides data relevant to hypotheses relating GABA and dopamine in the pathophysiology of altered stress response in schizophrenia (see below).

ASSESSMENT OF THE STRESS RESPONSE IN SCHIZOPHRENIC PATIENTS

In a number of studies researchers have examined neurobiological correlates of the stress response in schizophrenic patients and have reported abnormalities in psychophysiologic function and neuroendocrine responses (41–43), although the effects reported are modest and frequently reflective of a hypofunctional stress response. It has been argued that the decreased response may be secondary to the following: the stressors were not sufficiently robust; cognitive deficits prevent schizophrenic patients from mounting a "normal" stress response; and/or specific neurobiological systems that are hypothesized to be abnormal in schizophrenic patients, such as the dopamine system, have not been directly assessed in previous stress studies (43).

To further examine the mechanisms involved in the stress response of schizophrenic patients, we developed a laboratory stress paradigm that involves intravenous infusion with 2-deoxy-D-glucose (2DG) (44, 45), a glucose analogue that disrupts glycolysis by competitively inhibiting glucose metabolism resulting in intracellular glucopenia. Because neurons are critically dependent on glucose for metabolic activity, the CNS is especially sensitive to the effects of 2DG glucoprivation. In addition, 2DG infusion results in robust activation of central stress systems including the hypothalamic-pituitary-adrenal axis and adrenomedullary system (46–48) and leads to alterations in plasma levels of HVA so that hypotheses related to dopamine activity can be explored (44,45). Moreover, a physical stressor such as 2DG infusion does not require high levels of attention and concentration to elicit a stress response (attributes that are necessary for performance and psychological stress paradigms), so even severely ill and cognitively impaired patients may participate in these studies. Thus, the 2DG metabolic stress paradigm has several advantages for examining the stress response of schizophrenic patients.

Eleven healthy volunteers (seven females and four males) who were free of medications and had no psychiatric or medical illnesses and eight patients (one female and seven males) with diagnoses of schizophrenia from the Diagnostic and Statistical Manual of Mental Disorders III (DSM-III) gave informed consent and participated in the study. The schizophrenic patients were studied while on a minimum of 4 weeks of double-blind placebo-controlled fluphenazine HCl treatment (mean ± SD daily dose: 31 ± 13 mg). The subjects participated in two double-blind randomly assigned test days: A 2DG-infusion (50 mg/kg) test day and a placebo-infusion test day. After an overnight fast the procedure began between 8:00 and 9:00 AM. After 1 hour of bedrest, baseline blood samples were drawn from an indwelling catheter. Either 2DG or placebo (normal saline solution) was then intravenously infused over 30 minutes. Postinfusion blood samples were drawn at the following intervals: +60, +90, +120, and +150 minutes. Levels of HVA were assayed with high-pressure liquid chromatography with electrochemical detection (33), and ACTH and cortisol levels were determined with radioimmunoassay (49,50).

Infusion of 2DG, in comparison with placebo, produced significant elevations in plasma levels of HVA in both the volunteers ($F = 12, p = .0001$) and the neuroleptic-treated schizophrenic patients ($F = 17, p < .0001$). The schizophrenic patients had significantly greater increases in plasma HVA levels ($F = 6.5, p < .005$) in comparison with normal volunteers (Fig. 4). In addition, 2DG administration, in comparison with placebo produced significant elevations in plasma levels of cortisol and ACTH in both healthy volunteers ($F = 65, p < .0001$ and $F = 8.5, p < .001$, respectively)

and schizophrenic patients ($p < .001$ and $p < .01$, respectively). The 2DG-induced increases in cortisol and ACTH levels in volunteers and schizophrenic patients were not significantly different (Fig. 4). There were no significant differences between volunteers and schizophrenic patients for placebo day-plasma indices.

The significant 2DG-related increases in plasma HVA levels in the neuroleptic-treated schizophrenic patients suggest that chronic neuroleptic treatment does not prevent stress-induced increases in dopamine function. These data do not appear to be consistent with preclinical electrophysiologic studies demonstrating that chronic neuroleptic treatment causes dopamine neuron inactivity, a phenomena known as "depolarization blockade" (51,52). Although the effects of stress on dopamine function in chronically treated animals are not well described, neuroleptic-induced depolarization blockade would be expected to block or significantly attenuate the effects of stress on dopamine activity. It is possible, however, that stress-related increases in plasma HVA during chronic neuroleptic treatment are secondary to increased activity of the mesocortical neurons, a subgroup of dopamine neurons. Mesocortical dopamine neurons do not develop neuroleptic-treatment-related depolarization blockade,

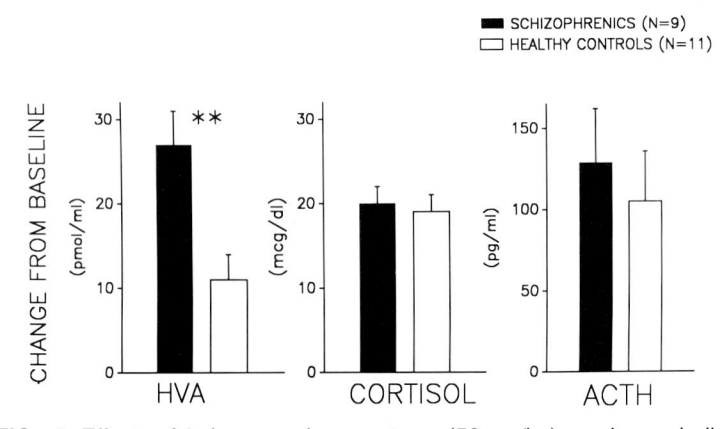

FIG. 4. Effects of 2-deoxy-D-glucose stress (50 mg/kg) on plasma indices.

and they undergo selective increases in activity following stress exposure (53,54). It is also possible that mechanisms in addition to depolarization blockade are required to explain the effects of neuroleptics on dopamine activity.

The significantly greater increases in plasma HVA levels in the schizophrenic patients relative to the volunteers suggest that the schizophrenic patients may have elevated dopamine activity during stress. The failure to demonstrate significant differences in the neuroendocrine parameters between the schizophrenic and volunteer subjects suggests that the altered stress effects in the schizophrenic patients may be relatively specific to dopamine activity. It is unlikely that neuroleptic treatment contributed to the differences in HVA levels between the volunteers and schizophrenic patients unless neuroleptics had the unanticipated effect of increasing plasma HVA levels, an effect not supported by available preclinical and clinical data (37,51,52). Our ongoing studies to determine the effects of stress on dopamine activity in drug-free schizophrenic patients will contribute to assessing the hypothesis that schizophrenia may be associated with heightened stress-related dopamine activity.

MECHANISM FOR ABNORMAL STRESS RESPONSE IN SCHIZOPHRENIA

Several neurotransmitter systems that have been hypothesized to be involved in the pathophysiology of schizophrenia and are activated during stress are candidates for mediating an abnormal stress response in schizophrenia. These include the dopaminergic, norepinephrinergic, GABAergic, peptidergic and glutaminergic systems. Our preliminary data demonstrating that alprazolam responders had decrements in plasma HVA and that schizophrenic patients had significantly greater plasma HVA increases to 2DG-induced metabolic stress provides evidence that there could be alteration in the stress-induced activation of dopamine and/or in dopamine-GABA interaction in schizophrenic patients.

There is a large body of data from preclinical studies demonstrating a relationship between GABA, dopamine, and stress. Pharmacological studies have shown that benzodiazepines and other GABAergic agents decrease nigrostriatal dopamine release (55–57), attenuate neuroleptic-induced increases in HVA in the rat brain (58), and prevent stress-induced increases in dopamine turnover in the frontal cortex and nucleus accumbens (59). Stress-induced increases in prefrontal dopamine activity are selectively influenced by agents whose effects are mediated through the benzodiazepine-GABA receptor complex. Roth and his colleagues (60) have shown that diazepam attenuates stress-induced activation of prefrontal dopamine activity and that this effect is blocked by the specific benzodiazepine receptor antagonist, Ro 15-1788. Moreover, mesoprefrontal dopamine neurons are selectively activated by the anxiogenic benzodiazepine antagonist, FG-7142 (methyl-β-carboline-3-carboxamide) (60). Prefrontal dopamine neurons are of particular interest because they are well documented to selectively activate during a range of stressors including exposure to a novel environment (61), a short-duration foot shock (54), and conditioned fear (62).

A hypothesis in which a functional impairment in GABA-dopamine interaction during stress is invoked to explain schizophrenic episodes is attractive because it serves as a point of convergence of two large bodies of clinical and preclinical literature implicating dopamine and GABA in the pathophysiology of schizophrenia.

SUMMARY AND CONCLUSION

The data presented in this manuscript provide strong evidence that stress plays an important role in at least one subgroup of schizophrenic patients. The environmental stress literature supports the hypothesis that both discrete stressful life events and ambient interpersonal stress precipitate relapse in schizophrenic patients and may trigger the onset of schizophrenia in vulnerable individuals. In addition, both behavioral and pharmacological therapy that is directed at stress reduction improves outcome, decreases relapse, and attenuates symptom levels in schizophrenic patients. Moreover, laboratory-based stress studies suggest that schizophrenic patients have an abnormal stress response, and preliminary data from the metabolic stress studies suggest that schizophrenic patients may have altered dopamine function during stress.

Stress-related alterations in dopamine function, either through direct effects in dopamine activity or through an interaction between dopamine and one of its stress modulators (e.g., GABA), provide a unique interpretation of the dopamine hypothesis of schizophrenia (63,64). It is possible that, in a subgroup of schizophrenic patients, the increased demand resulting from stress amplifies regulatory deficits in dopamine activity that might otherwise not become manifest. This hypothesis would explain the association between the onset of schizophrenia and stressful life periods. In addition, this hypothesis may account for a course of illness common to some schizophrenic patients that is marked by a relapsing pattern with relatively low symptom levels and good functioning in between relapses. It will be important for future studies to attempt to delineate and characterize the putative stress-sensitive subgroup of schizophrenic patients and to determine whether this subgroup has preferential responses to stress-reducing pharmacological (e.g., benzodiazepines) and behavioral treatments and unique pathophysiological processes related to dysfunctional stress mechanisms.

REFERENCES

1. Jacobs S, Myers J. Recent life events and acute schizophrenic psychosis: A controlled study. *J Nerv Ment Dis* 1976;162:75–87.
2. Brown GW, Birley JLT. Crises and life changes and the onset of schizophrenia. *J Health Soc Behav* 1968;9:203–214.
3. Schwartz CC, Myers JK. Life events and schizophrenia: II. Impact of life events on symptom configuration. *Arch Gen Psychiatry* 1977;34:1242–1245.
4. Beck FC, Worthen K. Precipitating stress, crisis theory, and hospitalization in schizophrenia and depression. *Arch Gen Psychiatry* 1972;26:123–129.
5. Jacobs SC, Prusoff BA, Paykel ES. Recent life events in schizophrenia and depression. *Psycholog Med* 1974;4:444.
6. Brown GW, Harris TO, Peto J. Life events and psychiatric disorders. Part 2: Nature of the causal link. *Psycholog Med* 1973;3:159–176.
7. Brown GW, Birley JLT, Wing JK. Influence of family life on the course of schizophrenic disorders: A replication. *Br J Psychiatry* 1972;121:241–258.
8. Vaughn CE, Leff JP. The influence of family and social factors on the course of psychiatric illness: A comparison of schizophrenic and depressed neurotic patients. *Br J Psychiatry* 1976;129:125–137.
9. Vaughn CE, Snyder KS, Jones S, Freeman WB, Falloon IRH. Family factors in schizophrenic relapse: Replication in California of British research on expressed emotion. *Arch Gen Psychiatry* 1984;41:1169–1177.
10. Moline RA, Singh S, Morris A, Melzer HY. Family expressed emotion and relapse in schizophrenia in 24 urban American patients. *Am J Psychiatry* 1985;142:1078–1081.
11. Parker G, Johnston P, Hayward L. Parental 'expressed emotion' as a predictor of schizophrenic relapse. *Arch Gen Psychiatry* 1988;45:806–813.
12. MacMillan JF, Gold A, Crow TJ, Johnson AL, Johnstone EC. IV. Expressed emotion and relapse. *Br J Psychiatry* 1986;148:133–143.
13. Vaughn CE, Leff JP. Patterns of emotional response in relatives of schizophrenic patients. *Schizophr Bull* 1981;7:43.
14. Leff J, Kuipers L, Berkowitz R, Eberlein-Vries R, Sturgeon D. A controlled trial of social intervention in the families of schizophrenic patients. *Br J Psychiatry* 1982;141:121–134.
15. Leff J, Vaughn C. *Expressed emotion in families.* New York: Guilford Press, 1985.
16. Falloon IRH, Boyd JL, McGill CW, Williamson M, Razani J, Moss HB, Gilderman AM, Simpson GM. Family management in the prevention of morbidity of schizophrenia. *Arch Gen Psychiatry* 1985;42:887–896.
17. Hogarty GE, Anderson CM, Reiss DJ, et al. Family psychoeducation, social skills training, and maintenance chemotherapy in the aftercare

treatment of schizophrenia. *Arch Gen Psychiatry* 1986;43:633–642.
18. Arana GW, Ornsteen ML, Kanter F, Friedman HL, Greenblatt DJ, Shader RI. The use of benzodiazepines for psychotic disorders: A literature review and preliminary clinical findings. *Psychopharmacol Bull* 1986;22:77–87.
19. Lingjaerde O. Antipsychotic effect of the benzodiazepines. In: Burrows GD, Norman TR, Davies B, eds. *Antipsychotics*. Amsterdam: Elsevier Science Publishers, 1985;163–172.
20. Donaldson SR, Gelenberg AJ, Baldessarini RJ. The pharmacologic treatment of schizophrenia: A progress report. *Schizophr Bull* 1983;9:504–527.
21. Nestoros JN. Benzodiazepines in schizophrenia: A need for reassessment. *Int Pharmacopsychiatry* 1980;15:171–179.
22. Lingjaerde O. Effect of the benzodiazepine derivative estazolam in patients with auditory hallucinations: A multicentre double-blind, cross-over study. *Acta Psychiatr Scand* 1982;65:339–354.
23. Lingjaerde O, Engstrand E, Ellingsen P, Stylo DA, Robak OH. Antipsychotic effect of diazepam when given in addition to neuroleptics in chronic psychotic patients. A double-blind clinical trial. *Curr Ther Res* 1979;26:505–514.
24. Kellner R, Wilson RM, Muldawer MD, Pathak D. Anxiety in schizophrenia: The responses to chlordiazepoxide in an intensive design study. *Arch Gen Psychiatry* 1975;32:1246–1254.
25. Guz L, Moraea R, Sartoretto JN. The therapeutic effects of lorazepam in psychotic patients treated with haloperidol: A double-blind study. *Curr Ther Res* 1972;14:767–774.
26. Karson CN, Weinberger DR, Bigelow L, Wyatt RJ. Clonazepam treatment of chronic schizophrenia: Negative results in a double-blind, placebo-controlled trial. *Am J Psychiatry* 1982;139:1627–1628.
27. Hanlon TE, Ota KY, Kurland AA. Comparative effects of fluphenazine, fluphenazine-chlordiazepoxide and fluphenazine-imipramine. *Dis Nerv Syst* 1970;31:171–177.
28. Hanlon TE, Ota KY, Agallianos DD, et al. Combined drug treatment of newly hospitalized, acutely ill psychiatric patients. *Dis Nerve Syst* 1969;30:104–116.
29. Holden JMC, Itil TM, Keskiner A, Fink M. Thioridazine and chlordiazepoxide, alone and combined, in the treatment of chronic schizophrenia. *Compr Psychiatry* 1968;9:633–643.
30. Michaux MH, Kurland AA, Agallianos DD. Chlorpromazine-chlordiazepoxide and chlorpromazine-imipramine treatment of newly hospitalized, acutely ill psychiatry patients. *Curr Ther Res* 1966;8:117–152.
31. Csernansky JG, Riney SJ, Lombrozo L, Overall JE, Hollister LE. Double-blind comparison of alprazolam, diazepam, and placebo for the treatment of negative schizophrenic symptoms. *Arch Gen Psychiatry* 1988;45:655–663.
32. Wolkowitz OM, Breier A, Doran A, et al. Alprazolam augmentation of the antipsychotic effects of fluphenazine in schizophrenic patients: Preliminary results. *Arch Gen Psychiatry* 1988;45:664–671.
33. Chang WH, Scheinin M, Burns RS, Linnoila M. Rapid and simple determination of homovanillic acid in plasma using high performance liquid chromatography with electrochemical detection. *Acta Pharmacol Toxicol* 1983;53:275–279.
34. Breier A, Wolkowitz OM, Doran AR, et al. Neuroleptic responsivity of negative and positive symptoms in schizophrenia. *Am J Psychiatry* 1987;144:1549–1555.
35. Jimerson DC, van Kammen DP, Post RM, Docherty JP, Bunney WE. Diazepam in schizophrenia: A preliminary double-blind trial. *Am J Psychiatry* 1982;139:489–491.
36. Pickar D, Labarca R, Linnoila M, et al. Neuroleptic-induced decrease in plasma homovanillic acid and antipsychotic activity in schizophrenic patients. *Science* 1984;225:954–957.
37. Pickar D, Labarca R, Doran AR, et al. Longitudinal measurement of plasma homovanillic acid levels in schizophrenia patients: Correlation with psychosis and response to neuroleptic treatment. *Arch Gen Psychiatry* 1986;43:669–676.
38. Bowers MB, Swigar ME, Jatlow PI, Goicoecha N. Plasma catecholamine metabolites and early response to haloperidol. *J Clin Psychiatry* 1984;6:248–251.
39. Bowers MB, Swigar ME. Acute psychosis and plasma catecholamine metabolites. *Arch Gen Psychiatry* 1987;44:190.
40. Davis KL, Davidson M, Mohs RC, et al. Plasma homovanillic acid concentrations and the severity of schizophrenic illness. *Science* 1985;227:1601–1602.
41. Albus M, Ackenheil M, Engel RR, Muller F. Situational reactivity of autonomic functions in schizophrenic patients. *Psychiatry Res* 1982;6:361.
42. Albus M, Engel RR, Muller K, Zander KJ, Ackenheil M. Experimental stress situations and the state of autonomic arousal in schizophrenic and depressive patients. *Int Pharmacopsychiatry* 1982;17:129.
43. Breier A, Wolkowitz OM, Doran AR, Bellar S, Pickar D. Neurobiological effects of lumbar puncture stress in psychiatric patients and healthy volunteers. *Psychiatry Res* 1988;25:187–194.
44. Breier A, Wolkowitz OM, Rappaport M, Paul SM, Pickar D. Metabolic stress effects in normal volunteers and schizophrenic patients. *Psychopharmacol Bull* 1988;24:431–433.
45. Breier A. Experimental approaches to human stress research: Assessment of neurobiologic mechanisms of stress in volunteers and psychiatric patients. *Biol Psychiatry* 1989;26:438–462.
46. Woolf PD, Lee LA, Leebaw W, et al. Intracellular glucopenia causes prolactin release in man. *J Clin Endocrinol Metab* 1977;45:377–383.
47. Brodows RG, Pi Sunyer FX, Campbell RG.

47. Neural control of counterregulatory events during glucopenia in man. *J Clin Invest* 1973;52:1841–1845.
48. Welle SL, Thompson DA, Campbell RG, Lilavivathana U. Increased hunger and thirst during glucoprivation in humans. *Physiol Behav* 1980;25:397–403.
49. Orth, DN. Adrenocorticotropin hormone. In: Jaffe BM, Behrmen HR, eds. *Methods of Hormone Radioimmunoassay*. New York: Academic Press, 1979.
50. Chrousos GP, Shulte HM, Oldfield EH, et al. The corticotropin-releasing factor stimulation test. *N Eng J Med* 1984;310:622.
51. White FJ, Wang RY. Differential effects of classical and atypical antipsychotic drugs on A9 and A10 dopamine neurons. *Science* 1983;221:1054–1057.
52. Chiodo LA, Bunney BS. Typical and atypical neuroleptics: Differential effects of chronic treatment on A9 and A10 midbrain dopaminergic neurons. *J Neurosci* 1983;3:1607–1619.
53. Bannon MJ, Roth RH. Pharmacology of mesocortical dopamine neurons. *Biol Rev* 1983;35:53–68.
54. Thierry AM, Tassin JP, Blanc G, Glowinski J. Selective activation of the mesocortical DA system by stress. *Nature* 1976;263:242–243.
55. Wood PL. Actions of GABAergic agents on dopamine metabolism in the nigrostriatal pathway of the rat. *J Pharmacol Exp Ther* 1982;222:674–679.
56. Rastogi RB, Lapierre YD, Radhey LS, Nair NPV. Evidence of involvement of dopamine in the action of diazepam: Potentiation of haloperidol and chlorpromazine action in the brain. *Adv Biochem Psychopharmacol* 1980;24:283–289.
57. Singhal RL, Rastogi RB, Lapierre YD. Diazepam potentiates the effect of neuroleptics on behavioral activity as well as dopamine and norepinephrine turnover: Do benzodiazepines have antipsychotic potency? *J Neural Transm* 1983;56:128–138.
58. Keller HH, Shaffner R, Haefely W. Interaction of benzodiazepines with neuroleptics at central dopamine neurons. *Arch Pharmacol* 1976;294:1–7.
59. Fadda F, Argiolas A, Melis MR, Tissari AH, Onali PL, Gessa GL. Stress-induced increase in 3,4-dihydroxyphenylacetic acid (DOPAC) levels in the cerebral cortex and in N accumbens: Reversal by diazepam. *Life Sci* 1978;23:2219–2224.
60. Roth RH, Tam S-Y, Ida Y, Yang J-X, Deutch AY. Stress and the mesocorticolimbic dopamine systems. *Ann N Y Acad Sci* 1988;537:138–147.
61. Tassin JP, Herve D, Blanc G, Glowinski J. Differential effects of a two-minute open field session on dopamine utilization in the frontal cortices of BALB/C and C57 BL/6 mice. *Neurosci Lett* 1980;17:67–71.
62. Deutch QY, Tam S-Y, Roth RH. Footshock and conditioned stress increase 3,4-dihydroxyphenylacetic acid (DOPAC) in the ventral tegmental area but not substantia nigra. *Brain Res* 1985;333:143–146.
63. Carlsson A. Does dopamine play a role in schizophrenia? *Psycholog Med* 1977;7:583–597.
64. Carlsson A. Antipsychotic drugs, neurotransmitters, and schizophrenia. *Am J Psychiatry* 1978;135:164–173.

14
Neuropsychological Study of Schizophrenia

Ruben C. Gur, Andrew J. Saykin, and Raquel E. Gur[1]

In this chapter we will first summarize briefly the current evidence for neuropsychological dysfunction in schizophrenia. Then we will suggest that a range of neuropsychological measures broader than that used in the past is necessary to identify a pattern of deficits characteristic of schizophrenia. In order to understand how this pattern of deficits is related to regional brain dysfunction, it is essential to examine the behavioral measures in light of theoretical advances in understanding brain behavior relations. We will describe an algorithm that one can use to systematically apply theoretical weightings to neuropsychological test scores, indicating the relevance of deficits to hypothesized underlying brain regions. The algorithm yields values for specific regions of interest (ROIs), which reflect the topographic distribution of impairment. The chapter will conclude by presenting some of our data on neuropsychological measures and the results of applying this behavioral-imaging algorithm.

CHARACTERIZATION OF NEUROPSYCHOLOGICAL DEFICITS

Studies of the psychological functioning of patients with schizophrenia have consistently shown cognitive, perceptual and attentional deficits (1–3). The main dimensions examined are abstraction, attention, language and memory.

Impairment in abstraction and "concrete thinking" have long been considered major components of cognitive disorder in schizophrenia (4). Several studies reported poor performance of schizophrenic patients on the Wisconsin Card Sorting Test (5), a measure of abstraction and mental flexibility. Deficits were documented on this and other tests of conceptual skill such as the Halstead Category Test (6–9).

Kraepelin (10) and Shakow (11) viewed attentional dysfunction as a key factor underlying the psychopathology of schizophrenia. Mirsky's studies of vigilance using the Continuous Performance Test (CPT) have pyschometrically documented the impaired attention in patients with schizophrenia (12,13).

There have been differences of opinion as to whether disordered language in schizophrenia is primary, as in aphasia, or whether it reflects underlying thought disorder (14). Andreasen and Grove (15) compared the language behavior of psychotic patients (diagnosed with schizophrenia or mania) with aphasic patients (in which Wernicke's area is affected). They reported that schizophrenic patients had a comparatively mild language disorder. Pronounced speech incoherence was only present in 16%. Language disorder in schizophrenia has been associated with severity in chronic patients (16).

A variety of memory and learning deficits has been described in patients with

---
[1] Brain Behavior Laboratory, and Neuropsychiatry Program, Departments of Psychiatry and Neurology, University of Pennsylvania, Philadelphia, PA 19104.

schizophrenia. In verbal memory studies, relatively normal recognition was found, in contrast to impaired recall of word lists (17–20). Rapid forgetting (18) and more pronounced impairment in new learning than in remote memory (21) have been reported. These features frequently characterize amnesic disorders. It has been suggested that an underlying encoding deficit may account for much of the verbal memory data (18). A selective deficit in retrieval processes has also been described (19), as well as interference effects on verbal learning measures (22). Some findings on memory have been related to clinical severity. Patients with mild illness show a deficit in encoding. This deficit can be diminished by appropriately orienting the patient to the relevant stimuli. More severely ill and chronic patients have an additional postencoding deficit (18).

IMPLICATIONS FOR REGIONAL BRAIN FUNCTION

Impairment on language tests (16), as well as findings of decreased verbal cognitive functions (eg, VIQ* less than PIQ*; refs 7 and 23), implicate left-hemispheric dysfunction in schizophrenia (24–26). Other findings point to frontal-lobe involvement, primarily in higher-level abstraction and mental flexibility on tests such as the Wisconsin Card Sorting Test (WCST) and HCT* (7,27,28). The selective interference effects on verbal learning measures (22) can also be considered a sign of frontal-lobe dysfunction.

The memory and learning deficits implicate mesial limbic and temporal-lobe structures (29,30). The hypothesis of temporal-lobe dysfunction in schizophrenia has also been supported by other evidence (27). Attentional deficits implicate a network of regions in the inferior parietal and frontal lobes as well as of subcortical components (31).

Although the laterality, frontality, and temporal-lobe hypotheses are not mutually exclusive, it would seem essential to examine whether the pattern of deficits in schizophrenic patients reflects specific dysfunction, which is more pronounced than what seems to be a background of global cognitive deficits. This requires consideration of the general problem of establishing "differential deficit" in clinical populations (32). Tests need to have comparable reliability and difficulty, and these must be weighed in identifying the underlying primary deficits of schizophrenia.

Several methodological problems have been identified in neuropsychological studies of schizophrenia. Heaton and Crowley (33) cite the following:

Problems with patient sampling;
Psychiatric diagnosis;
Inadequate neurological evaluation and diagnosis;
Failure to report or control for chronicity of illness;
Lack of comparability between patients and control subjects for age and education;
Inappropriately balancing patients and normals on IQ;
Failure to report or control for past and concurrent somatic therapies.

We would add that substance abuse is another potential confound, with schizophrenics having a high comorbidity.

There is some disagreement on how to select the appropriate control group for the study of schizophrenia. Some studies have employed patients with other psychiatric disorders (eg, affective disorders, nonpsychotic personality disorders). We believe that although there is information to be gained from comparing schizophrenia with these disorders, establishing the sensitivity of the neurobehavioral pattern of deficits and other neuroimaging data logically precedes examination of specificity. This can

---

*VIQ = verbal intelligence quotient; PIQ = performance intelligence quotient; HCT = Halstead Category Test.

best be accomplished by studying patients who have schizophrenia and no other illness and then comparing data from these patients with those of healthy normal controls.

Another issue is the match between patients and controls on IQ and education. Matching on these characteristics, while generally a desirable practice in clinical research, can be a mistake in schizophrenia, which affects the behavioral functions necessary for attaining high IQ scores and high educational levels. The disease itself may also be responsible for the "downward drift" in socioeconomic status (34). Thus, equating patients and controls on these demographic variables will lead to contrasting atypical groups of (overachieving) patients with (underachieving) controls. This issue needs careful scrutiny. In our studies we have attempted to recruit patients and controls from the same general background, and more recently we have used parental education as a measure on which patient and control samples can be balanced (if not technically matched).

In summary, the studies available are limited to a small number of functions examined in any one study. To establish a neuropsychological profile of schizophrenia it is necessary to administer a comprehensive set of measures, tapping major neurobehavioral dimensions, and having adequate reliability. Otherwise, it would be difficult to establish "selective" patterns of deficit against the background level of impairment in schizophrenia. In such a study, the relative importance of deficits could also be established by statistically removing the global impairment factor.

The application of physiologic neuroimaging techniques to psychiatric populations may help advance this research, particularly when physiologic neuroimaging is combined with neuropsychological activation procedures. Since the behavioral abnormalities occur in response to environmental triggers, regional abnormalities in brain activity may be undetected at rest but may become apparent in the pattern of changes in activity produced by task activation. This was seen in a sample of patients with unilateral cerebral infarcts (35). Few studies have examined both resting and activated conditions in psychiatric populations. Gur et al reported that resting (rCBF) was normal in medicated schizophrenics, but abnormalities were pronounced in the asymmetry of activation for the verbal analogies and the spatial line-orientation tasks (36). Schizophrenic patients failed to show the normal left hemispheric activation for the verbal task and showed a "paradoxical" left-hemispheric activation for the spatial task. This supported Gur's (37) hypothesis, based on behavioral studies, that schizophrenia is associated with left-hemispheric dysfunction and with overactivation of the left, dysfunctional hemisphere (37). Further support for the hypothesis was obtained in a sample of unmedicated schizophrenic patients (38). In this group, rCBF showed greater left-hemispheric values, and abnormal activation of the left hemisphere was associated with increased symptom severity. Weinberger et al (28), also using the xenon-133 inhalation technique for measuring rCBF, reported that schizophrenic patients failed to show the normal increase in dorsolateral frontal activity during the performance of the WCST (8). This supports the "frontality" hypothesis.

Obviously, the contribution of neuropsychology to understanding the neural substrates of schizophrenia can best be accomplished by integrating behavioral data with other neuroimaging data in schizophrenia, and comparing them with other neuropsychiatric disorders. This will require improvement in the precision with which the theories and hypotheses of neuropsychology can be stated in reference to regional brain function. Neuropsychology can benefit in turn by putting its hypotheses to test against neuroanatomic and neurophysiologic data. For example, the neuropsychologist can help understand the behavioral effects of frontal-lobe dysfunction by reference to lesion data, neuroanatomic data, performance of schizophrenic patients on tasks requiring the integrity of frontal-lobe regions, and the implementation of "behavioral challenges" in physiologic neuroimaging studies.

METHOD FOR INTEGRATING BEHAVIORAL AND NEUROIMAGING DATA

A key matter for future work is the integration of multifaceted data on regional brain function. In addition to the anatomic information on the integrity of brain regions, such as is now available from x-ray computed tomography (CT) and from magnetic-resonance-imaging (MRI) scans, the positron emission tomography (PET) and xenon-133 techniques provide information on regional brain physiological activity, and topographic EEG techniques complement our armamentarium of data on regional brain function with information on electrical activity. Imaging technologies provide the means for obtaining such multifaceted data in a comprehensible manner, but theory is needed to guide our understanding of how brain activity relates to behavior. The challenge is to integrate behavioral theories on regional brain function with the anatomic and physiologic neuroimaging data.

Theories on brain regulation of human behavior have been tested in clinical populations by correlating behavioral deficits with clinical signs and post mortem findings. Neuropsychological testing in patients with brain disease provides measures of specific behavioral functions (e.g., memory, learning, and praxis). The pattern of scores is used to formulate and test hypotheses on regional brain involvement in the regulation of a specific behavioral function. These are used in clinical practice to interpret the pattern of scores as implicating brain regions affected by a disease process (39–41).

The testing of behavioral hypotheses with neuroimaging technology could be helped by quantification of theoretical statements concerning regional brain involvement in behavior. We have proposed an algorithm that applies such a quantification to standard neuropsychological test scores (42–44). The algorithm transforms neuropsychological test scores into values reflecting regional brain function and permits topographic display of these values. The regional brain values are obtained by the use of expert theoretical ratings of the sensitivity of each neuropsychological test score to lesions in a set of prespecified ROIs. These regional values can be examined statistically to test the behavioral hypothesis against clinical data and other neuroimaging data. Their topographic presentation can facilitate comprehension of the spatial distribution of implicated regions.

Initial implementation of the algorithm was carried out on 32 ROIs using the expert ratings of AJS. The display, and an example of ratings for one of the neuropsychological scores (Block Design), is shown in Fig. 1.

The feasibility of the algorithm was examined by displaying effects of focal and nonfocal lesions in individual cases (43). The topographic displays showed corre-

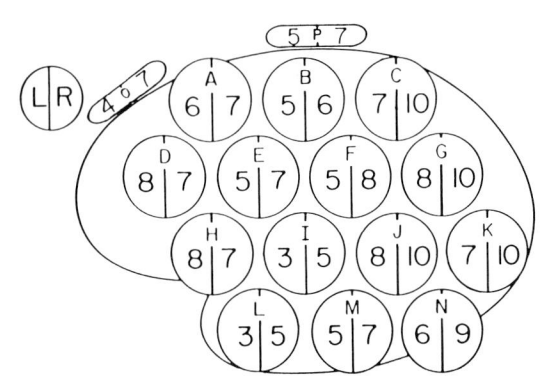

FIG. 1. An example of weights given for the Block Design subtest of the Wechsler Adult Intelligence Scale–Revised (WAIS-R) (Reprinted from *Neuropsychiat Neuropsychol Behav Neurol* 1988;1:53–60.)

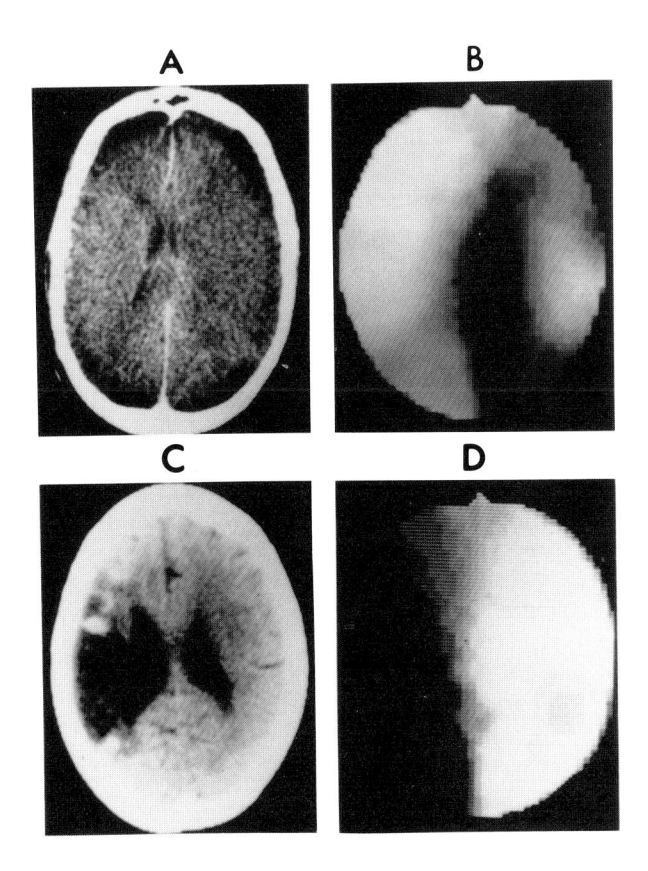

FIG. 2. Computed tomography scans (*left*) and corresponding behavioral images (*right*) of two patients with cerebral infarcts. **A,B:** Right hemisphere. **C,D:** left hemisphere. The CT scans were reversed so that the left hemisphere is to the viewer's left. (Reprinted from *Neuropsychiat Neuropsychol Behav Neurol* 1988;1:53–60.)

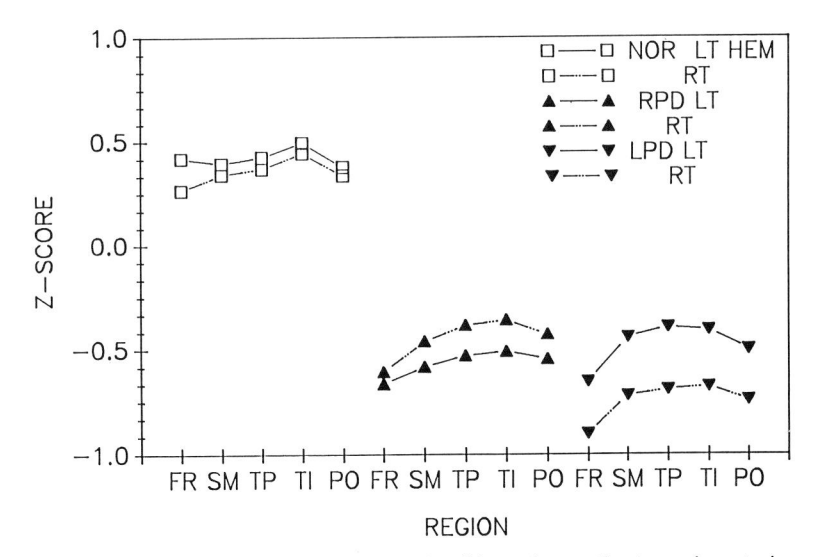

FIG. 3. Lobar neuropsychological values for hemiparkinsonian patients and controls produced by the behavioral-imaging algorithm. Regions: frontal FR, frontal; SM, sensorimotor; TP, temporoparietal; TI, inferior temporal; PO, parieto-occipital. Scores are given for the left hemisphere (*open symbols*) and right hemisphere (*filled symbols*). (Reprinted from Neuropsychiat Neuropsychol Behav Neurol 1988;1:87–96.)

FIG. 4. Interexpert agreement for the initial ratings. The abscissa shows the difference score for each pair of experts (eg, EK–AB stands for EK's ratings minus AB's ratings: for each expert pair, zero corresponds to perfect agreement; negative values indicate that the lefthand expert's ratings are lower than those of the righthand expert (eg, EK>AB); and positive values reflect the opposite. The ordinate shows the frequency of each difference score. (Reprinted from *Neuropsychiat Neuropsychol Behav Neurol* 1990;3:113–124.

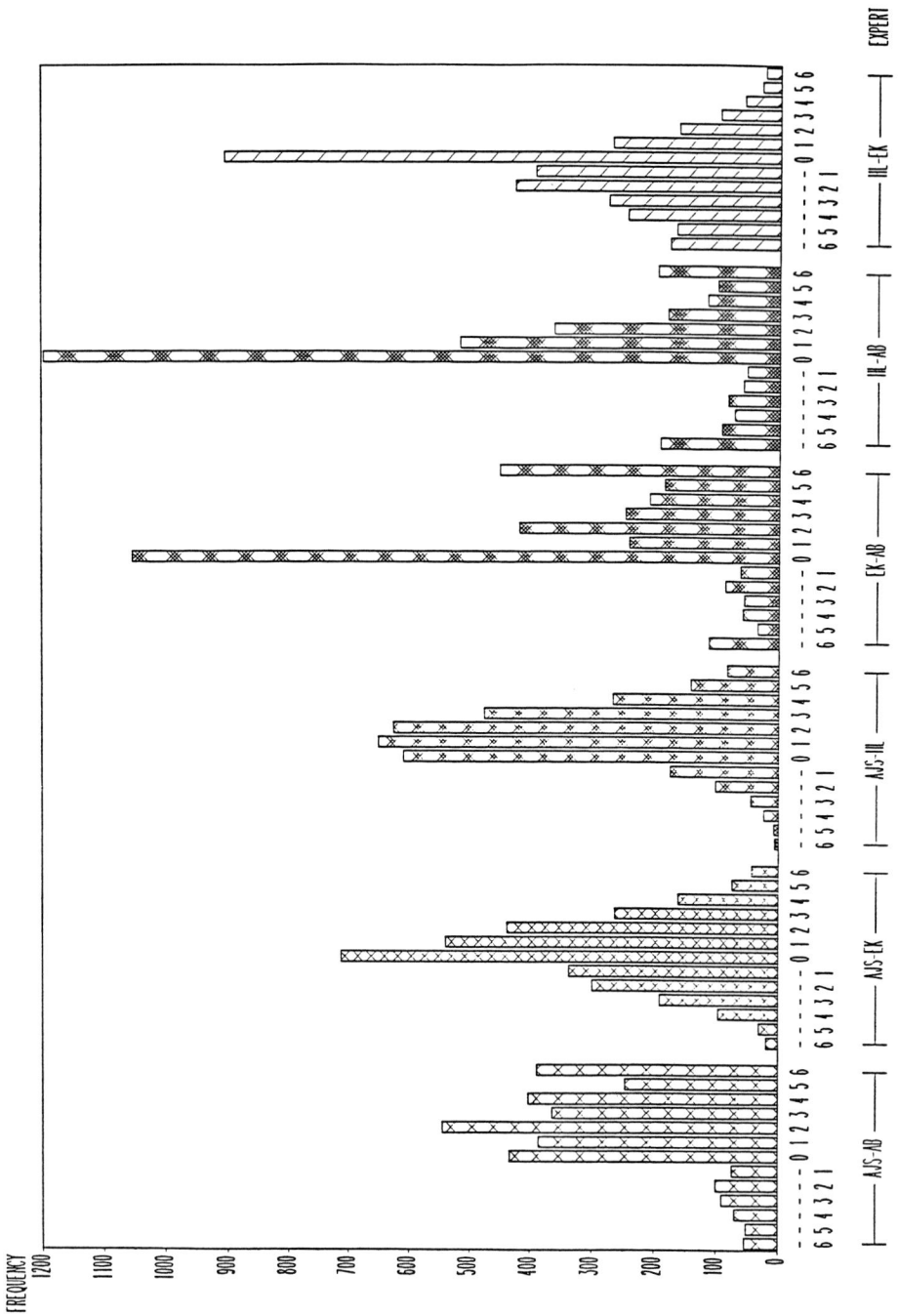

spondence with lesion location in two patients with unilateral stroke (Fig. 2).

The algorithm was then applied to statistical analysis of neuropsychological hypotheses on regional effects of hemiparkinsonism (44). As can be seen in Fig. 3, the presence of unilateral motor symptoms in this population of early-stage parkinsonian patients was associated with cognitive decline in functions associated with the contralateral cerebral hemisphere.

The subjective element in the algorithm consists of the theoretical weightings used in calculating the regional values from the neuropsychological test scores. The ratings of the sensitivity of a given test to brain dysfunction in specified ROIs reflect expert opinion, and a necessary further step in evaluating the heuristic and clinical potential of the algorithm was to establish agreement and reliability indices for this subjective element (45).

To address this we obtained regional weightings from three additional leading experts in clinical neuropsychology, Drs. Arthur Benton, Edith Kaplan, and Harvey Levin. These were obtained for a larger set of 40 ROIs that were located in regions deemed by the experts as most important for behavioral analysis of regional brain functions. The experts also agreed on a core battery of tests that would be likely to produce valid regional values. The expert raters showed satisfactory levels of agreement, with a modal difference of zero for all pairs of raters (Fig. 4).

A STUDY OF SCHIZOPHRENIA

We administered an expanded core battery of neuropsychological tests to schizophrenic patients who received neuroimaging studies as part of our protocols for the Mental Health Clinical Research Center on regional brain function in schizophrenia. Table 1 lists the tests that were administered.

Thus far we have analyzed the data on 16 unmedicated patients with schizophrenia and 18 healthy normal controls. On univariate analysis, controlling for age and education, most tests were performed more poorly by schizophrenics than by controls. The test scores were transformed to their standard equivalents (z-scores) and grouped

TABLE 1. *Neuropsychological battery by function*

1. Abstraction-cognitive (ABS)
   (A) Wisconsin Card Sorting (WCST)
2. Verbal-cognitive (VBL)
   (A) Information (WAIS-R)
   (B) Vocabulary (WAIS-R)
   (C) Comprehension (WAIS-R)
   (D) Similarities (WAIS-R)
3. Spatial-cognitive (SPT)
   (A) Picture Completion (WAIS-R)
   (B) Block Design (WAIS-R)
   (C) Object Assembly (WAIS-R)
4. Semantic/verbal memory (SME)
   (A) Logical Memory (Wechsler Memory Scale)
5. Visual memory (VME)
   (A) Visual Reproduction (Wechsler Memory Scale)[a]
   (B) Memory for Unfamiliar Faces[a]
6. Verbal learning (LRN)
   (A) California Verbal Learning Test
   (B) Paired Associate Learning (WMS)[a]
7. Language (LNG)
   (A) Sentence Comprehension
   (B) Controlled Oral Word Association (MAE)
   (C) Animal Naming (BDAE)
   (D) Boston Naming Test
   (E) Sentence Repetition (MAE)
   (F) Reading (WRAT)
8. Visual perception and attention (VIS)
   (A) Trail Making Test (Parts A and B)
   (B) Digit Symbol (WAIS-R)
   (C) Stroop Test (Word, Color & Interference)
9. Auditory perception and attention (AUD)
   (A) Digit Span (WAIS-R)
   (B) Arithmetic (WAIS-R)
   (C) Rhythm Test (Seashore)
10. Tactile perception & attention (TAC)
    (A) Fingertip Number Writing
11. Motor (MOT)
    (A) Finger Tapping
    (B) Thumb-Finger Sequential Touch

[a]Mean; immediate and delayed.

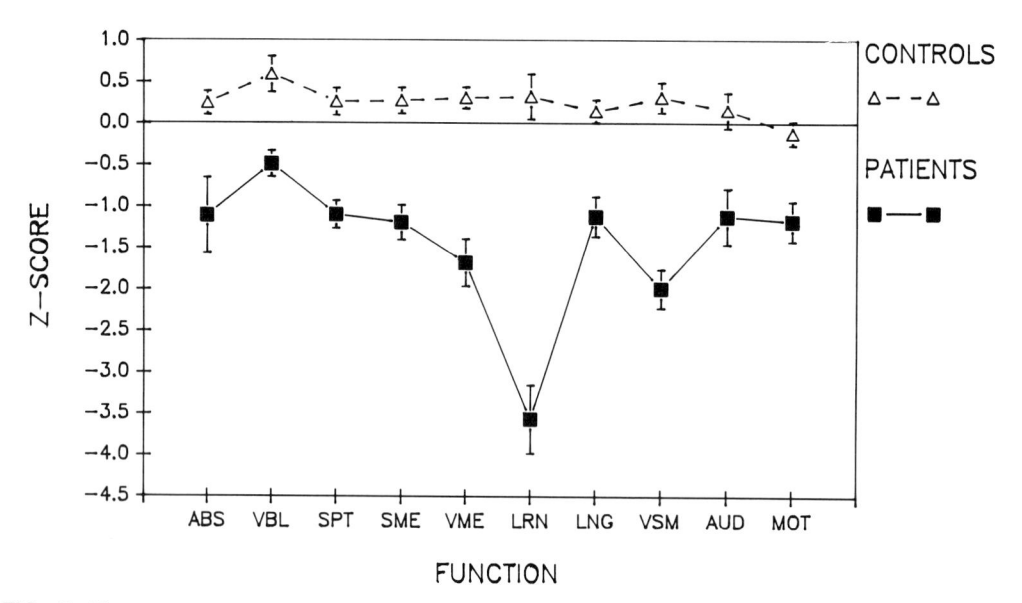

FIG. 5. Mean neuropsychological profile by function (±SEM) for patients with schizophrenia and controls. Functions: ABS, Abstraction; VBL, Verbal Cognitive; SPT, Spatial Cognitive; SME, Semantic Memory; VME, Visual Memory; LRN, Verbal Learning; LNG, Language; VSM, Visual Motor Processing and Attention; AUD, Auditory Processing and Attention; MOT, Motor Speed and Sequencing. MANOVA: Function x Diagnosis interaction, $p<.001$. On contrasts comparing each function to the mean of all other functions, schizophrenics were selectively impaired relative to controls in Verbal Learning and Visual Motor processing.

into the functions listed in Table 1. Figure 5 shows the functional profile of the schizophrenic patients compared with our sample of normal control subjects. MANOVA profile analysis indicated that the greatest deficit was in verbal learning compared with other functions ($p < .001$). Selective impairment in abstraction and mental flexibility (using the WCST) was not supported in this sample.

DIRECTIONS FOR FUTURE RESEARCH AND LONG-TERM POTENTIAL

These initial results illustrate how neuropsychological test scores can be applied to test hypotheses on regional brain dysfunction in schizophrenia. The "behavioral images," however, need to be contrasted with topographic data obtained from anatomic and physiologic neuroimaging modalities to enable a comprehensive understanding of the disturbed brain processes that give rise to the symptoms of schizophrenia. Correlations with clinical status, diagnostic subtypes, and changes in disease severity need to be established. Once this is better explicated, the methods we have described can also be used to evaluate effects of pharmacologic intervention.

New directions can also be pursued. Thus far the cognitive dimension has received the greatest attention in neuropsychological studies of schizophrenia, and particularly the examination of verbal and spatial tasks in relation to hemispheric activation. But emotion and conative or motivational factors could also be studied with the techniques. Studies on regional brain regulation of anxiety, attention, and affect (46–50) can be refined and extended to populations representing a range of normal and abnormal behavior. This could be informative in our understanding of how regional brain areas are involved in the regulation of behavior and could add to the power of neuropsychological understanding of schizophrenia.

The key difficulty, conceptually and practically, is the development of methods for integrating data from both anatomic and physiologic methods. Such integration will be a prerequisite for progress in theory and application. We hope the approach outlined here will provide a step in this direction.

REFERENCES

1. Malec J. Neuropsychological assessment of schizophrenia versus brain damage: a review. *J Nerv Ment Dis* 1978;166:507–516.
2. Heaton RK, Baade LE, Johnson KL. Neuropsychological test results associated with psychiatric disorders in adults. *Psychol Bull* 1978;85:141–162.
3. Goldstein G. The neuropsychology of schizophrenia. In: Grant I, Adams KM, eds. *Neuropsychological assessment of neuropsychiatric disorders*. New York: Oxford University Press, 1986.
4. Goldstein K. The organismic approach. In: Arieti S ed. *American handbook of psychiatry*, vol 2, 1959;1333–1347.
5. Grant DA, Berg EA. A behavioral analysis of degree of reinforcement and ease of shifting to new responses in a Weigl-type card-sorting problem. *J Exp Psychol* 1948;38:404–411.
6. Reitan RM, Wolfson D. *The Halstead-Reitan neuropsychological test battery: theory and clinical interpretation*. Tucson, AZ: Neuropsychology Press, 1985.
7. Flor-Henry P, Yeudall LT. Neuropsychological investigations of schizophrenia and manic-depressive psychoses. In: Gruzelier J, Flor-Henry P (eds), *Hemispheric asymmetries of function in psychopathology*. Amsterdam: Elsevier/North Holland, 1979.
8. Heaton RK. *Wisconsin Card Sorting Test, manual*. Odessa, FL: Psychological Assessment Resources, 1981.
9. Goldberg TE, Weinberger DR, Berman KF, Pliskin NH, Podd MH. Further evidence for dementia of the prefrontal type in schizophrenia? A controlled study of teaching the Wisconsin Card Sorting Test. *Arch Gen Psychiatry* 1987;44:1008–1014.
10. Kraepelin E. *Dementia Praecox*. Barclay E, Barclay S (trans). Edinburgh: Livingstone, 1919.
11. Shakow D. Psychological deficit in schizophrenia. *Behav Sci* 1963;8:275–305.
12. Mirsky AF. Behavioral and electrographic measures of attention in children at risk for schizophrenia. *J Abnorm Psychol* 1977;86:27–33.
13. Mirsky AF. From Worcester to Haifa: fifty years of attention research in neuropsychiatry. Paper presented at the American Psychological Association, Washington, DC, 1986.
14. Schwartz S. Is there a schizophrenic language? *Behav Brain Sci* 1982;5:579–626.
15. Andreasen NC, Grove W. The relationship between schizophrenic language, manic language and aphasia. In: Gruzelier J, Flor-Henry P eds. *Hemispheric asymmetries in function in psychopathology*. Amsterdam: Elsevier/North Holland, 1979.
16. Silverberg-Shalev R, Gordon HW, Bentin S, Aranson A. Selective language deterioration in chronic schizophrenia. *J Neurol Neurosurg Psychiatry* 1981;44:547–551.
17. Koh SD. Remembering of verbal materials by schizophrenic young adults. In Schwartz S, ed. *Language and cognition in schizophrenia*. Hilsdale, NJ: Lawrence Earlbaum, 1978;55–99.
18. Calev A, Venables PH, Monk AF. Evidence for distinct verbal memory pathologies in severely and mildly disturbed schizophrenics. *Schizophr Bull* 1983;9:247.
19. Sengel RA, Lovallo WR. Effects of cueing on immediate and recent memory in schizophrenics. *J Nerv Ment Dis* 1983;171:426–430.
20. Calev A. Recall and recognition in chronic nondemented schizophrenics. *J Abnorm Psychol* 1984;93:172–177.
21. Calev A, Berlin H, Lerer B. Remote and recent memory in long-hospitalized chronic schizophrenics. *Biol Psychiatry* 1987;22:79–85.
22. Stuss DT, Kaplan EF, Benson DF, Weir WS, Chiulli S, Sarazin FF. Evidence for the involvement of orbitofrontal cortex in memory functions: An interference effect. *J Compar Physiol Psychol* 1982;96:913–925.
23. Newlin DB, Carpenter B, Golden CJ. Hemispheric asymmetries in schizophrenia. *Biol Psychiatry* 1981;16:561–582.
24. Flor-Henry P. Lateralized temporal-limbic dysfunction and psychopathology. *Ann NY Acad Sci* 1976;280:777–795.
25. Gur RE. Motoric laterality imbalance in schizophrenia. *Arch Gen Psychiatry* 1977;34:33–37.
26. Gur RE. Left hemisphere dysfunction and left hemisphere overactivation in schizophrenia. *J Abnorm Psychol* 1978;87:226–238.
27. Flor-Henry P, Fromm-Auch D, Schopflocher D. Neuropsychological dimensions in psychopathology. In: *Laterality and Psychopathology*. Amsterdam: Elsevier Bio-Medical Press, 1983.
28. Weinberger DR, Berman KF, Zec RF. Physiologic dysfunction of dorsolateral prefrontal cortex in schizophrenia: I. Regional cerebral blood flow evidence. *Arch Gen Psychiatry* 1986;43:114–125.
29. Mishkin M, Spiegler BJ, Saunders R, Malamut BL. An animal model of global amnesia. In: Corkin S, Davis KL, Growdon JH, Usdin E, Wurtman R, eds. *Toward a treatment of Alzheimer's disease*. New York: Raven Press, 1982;235–247.
30. Zola-Morgan S, Amaral DG, Squire LR. Human amnesia and the medial temporal region: Enduring memory impairment following a bilateral le-

sion limited to field CA1 of the hippocampus. *J Neurosci* 1986;6:2950–2967.
31. Mesulam M-M. A cortical network for directed attention and unilateral neglect. *Ann Neurol* 1981;10:309–325.
32. Chapman LJ, Chapman JP. The measurement of differential deficits. *J Psychiatr Res* 1978;14:303–311.
33. Heaton RK, Crowley TJ. Effects of psychiatric disorders and their somatic treatments on neuropsychological test results. In: Filskov SB, Boll TJ eds. *Handbook of clinical neuropsychology*. New York: Wiley-Interscience, 1981.
34. Dohrenwend BP, Dohrenwend BS. Social status and psychological disorder: a causal inquiry. New York: Wiley, 1969.
35. Gur RC, Gur RE, Silver FL, Obrist WD, Skolnick BE, Kushner M, Hurtig HI, Reivich M. Regional cerebral blood flow in stroke: hemispheric effects of cognitive activity. *Stroke* 1987;18:776–780.
36. Gur RE, Skolnick BE, Gur RC, Caroff S, Rieger W, Obrist WD, Younkin D, Reivich M. Brain function in psychiatric disorders: I. Regional cerebral blood flow in medicated schizophrenics. *Arch Gen Psychiatry* 1983;40:1250–1254.
37. Gur RE. Left hemisphere dysfunction and left hemisphere overactivation in schizophrenia. *J Abnorm Psychol* 1978;87:226–238.
38. Gur RE, Gur RC, Skolnick BE, Caroff S, Obrist WD, Resnick S, Reivich M. Brain function in psychiatric disorders: III. Regional cerebral blood flow in unmedicated schizophrenics. *Arch Gen Psychiatry* 1985;42:329–334.
39. Goodglass H, Kaplan E. *The assessment of aphasia and related disorders,* 2nd ed. Philadelphia: Lea & Febiger, 1983.
40. Reitan RM, Wolfson D. *The Halstead-Reitan neuropsychological test battery: theory and clinical interpretation*. Tucson, Ariz: Neuropsychology Press, 1985.
41. Benton AL, Hamsher K, Varney NR, Spreen O. *Contributions to neuropsychological assessment*. New York: Oxford University Press, 1983.
42. Trivedi SS, Gur RC. Topographic mapping of cerebral blood flow and behavior. *Comput Biol Med* 1989;19:219–229.
43. Gur RC, Trivedi SS, Saykin AJ, Gur RE. "Behavioral imaging"—a procedure for analysis and display of neuropsychological test scores: I. Construction of algorithm and initial clinical application. *Neuropsychiat Neuropsychol Behav Neurol* 1988;1:53–60.
44. Gur RC, Saykin AJ, Blonder LX, Gur RE. "Behavioral Imaging": II. Application of the quantitative algorithm to hypothesis testing in a population of hemiparkinsonian patients. *Neuropsychiat Neuropsychol Behav Neurol* 1988;1:87–96.
45. Gur RC, Saykin AJ, Benton A, Kaplan E, Levin H, Kester DB, Gur RE. "Behavioral imaging": III. Inter expert agreement and reliability of weightings. *Neuropsychiat Neuropsychol Behav Neurol* 1990;3:113–124.
46. Gur RC, Gur RE, Skolnick BE, Resnick SM, Silver FL, Chawluk JB, Muenz L, Obrist WD, Reivich M. Effects of task difficulty on regional cerebral blood flow: relationships with anxiety and performance. *Psychophysiology* 1988;25:392–399.
47. Reivich M, Gur RC, Alavi A. Positron emission tomography studies of sensory stimuli, cognitive processes and anxiety. *Hum Neurobiol* 1983;2:25–33.
48. Reivich M, Alavi A, Gur RC. Positron emission tomographic studies of perceptual tasks. *Ann Neurol* 1984;15:61–65 (supplement).
49. Sackeim HA, Greenberg MS, Weiman AL, Gur RC, Hungerbuhler JP, Geschwind N. Hemispheric asymmetry in the expression of positive and negative emotions: neurological evidence. *Arch Neurol* 1982;39:210–218.
50. Reiman EM, Raichle ME, Robins E, Butler FK, Herscovitch P, Fox P, Perlmutter J. The application of positron emission tomography to the study of panic disorder. *Am J Psychiatry* 1986;143:469–477.

15

Wisconsin Card Sorting Deficits and Diminished Sensorimotor Gating in a Discrete Subgroup of Schizophrenic Patients

Robert W. Butler, Melissa A. Jenkins, Mark A. Geyer, and David L. Braff [1]

It has long been suspected that frontal-lobe dysfunction may play a role in schizophrenia (1,2). Most recently, Weinberger (3) has presented a neurodevelopmental model of schizophrenia that predicts dorsolateral prefrontal dysfunction in schizophrenia through complex feedback mechanisms and interactions between the mesolimbic and mesocortical dopamine systems. The theory suggests that many of the "negative" symptoms of schizophrenia, such as inertia, would be a function of frontal-lobe-mediated deficits while "positive" symptoms, such as hallucinations, are more subcortically mediated. Central to Weinberger's theory is the need for empirical evidence of frontal-lobe deficits in schizophrenia.

A number of studies have documented abnormal frontal-lobe activity in chronic schizophrenia. It has been observed that frontal-lobe metabolism is less active in chronic schizophrenic patients during cognitive tasks when compared with normal subjects using both positron emission tomography (PET) and regional cerebral blood flow (CBF) methodologies (4,5). In addition to metabolic studies of brain function, researchers have investigated the neuropsychology of frontal-lobe function in schizophrenia.

Neuropsychological tests measure cognitive abilities that have been empirically associated with cortical brain functioning. One of the more widely used neuropsychological measures of frontal-brain integrity is the Wisconsin Card Sorting Test (WCST; refs 6,7). The standard WCST consists of 128 cards, each of which contains geometric figures that may vary along several dimensions (eg, color, form, number; see "Methods" below). Patients are instructed to place each card below one of four target or key cards using some principle to guide them. They are not informed of the correct principle but are told whether they are correct or incorrect after their placement of each card. The initial sorting principle is to match according to color. Once a criterion of ten correctly sorted cards is attained, the principle is changed, although the patient is not informed of this change. The test proceeds until the patient has completed six sorting categories of ten cards each or has sorted all 128 cards, whichever occurs first. The type of errors that are elicited may vary, although the most sensitive error type with respect to frontal-lobe dysfunction is the perseverative response, reflecting subjects' difficulty in shifting their strategies or cognitive sets. Although the WCST persev-

[1] Department of Psychiatry, University of California at San Diego, La Jolla, CA 92093.

erative response score is often impaired in brain-damaged patients with varying pathology, it has been shown to be particularly sensitive to frontal-lobe dysfunction (8,9).

A relatively large number of studies have reported that patients with schizophrenia perform in an impaired range on the WCST (10–13). None of these studies, however, definitively addressed the possibility that poor WCST performance might be a function of generalized performance deficits in schizophrenia as opposed to relatively discrete frontal-lobe impairment. Directly investigating this possibility, Goldberg and associates (14) attempted to teach chronic schizophrenic patients how to successfully complete the WCST. They found that considerable instruction did not result in improved WCST performance even though the patients were able to improve their performance on a control task of verbal learning. It should be noted that apparently not all of the subjects completed the Mini-Mental State Examination (MMSE), and the reported group means reflect at least mild to moderate deficits on this test. Also supportive of specific frontal-lobe involvement in schizophrenia are two studies that documented frontal cerebral blood flow (CBF) abnormalities during performance on a modified WCST task (15,16). These studies compared medication-free chronic schizophrenic patients to normal controls and, while failing to demonstrate increased frontal metabolic activity during WCST administration in schizophrenia, reported that posterior resting CBF (rCBF) activity increased in an expected direction during a control task. Nonschizophrenic psychiatric control patients were not tested.

Considerable evidence has been amassed to implicate frontal lobe impairment in schizophrenia, chronic schizophrenia in particular. Much of this evidence, however, has been collected on hospitalized patients who were moderately to severely ill, and in some cases WCST administration methods were modified and altered. Braff and coworkers (17) collected extensive neuropsychological data, including WCST scores, on a group of mild to moderately ill chronic schizophrenic patients who were not hospitalized. Of the 40 schizophrenic patients tested, only five showed significant impairment on the WCST. These authors concluded that, while the specificity of their results remains unclear given that psychiatric controls were not tested and patients were receiving neuroleptic medication, nevertheless, the chronic schizophrenic patients in their study exhibited low-normal performance in conjunction with relatively poorer performance on a variety of other neuropsychological tasks. This pattern of results, when coupled with previously cited studies, supports the possibility that, while deteriorated "Kraepelinian" chronic schizophrenic patients may have frontal-lobe impairment, this may not be true of *all* chronic schizophrenic patients. These conclusions led us to suspect that impaired WCST performance in chronic schizophrenia may be a marker for a relatively discrete subgroup. If so, we would expect this subgroup to show greater evidence of global cognitive dysfunction, a more deteriorated course of illness, and perhaps increased abnormalities on measures of information processing.

Information processing refers to the process by which sensory stimuli are acted on by the central nervous system (CNS) and encoded in ways that are meaningful to humans (18). Abnormalities on information-processing paradigms have been a fairly consistent characteristic of at least some schizophrenic patients (see ref 18). One particularly attractive method of assessing the individual's ability to successfully gate sensory information is the degree of prepulse inhibition of the startle reflex. Weak prestimuli induce a centrally mediated prepulse inhibition of the startle reflex, which is thought to be an important index of central inhibitory processes and effective sensorimotor gating. This paradigm has a number of theoretical and methodological strengths, including relative independence of attentional shifts, automated measurement, and well-known monoaminergic modulation (19). Although impaired prepulse inhibition (PPI) is present in some chronic schizophrenic patients, it is not a ubiquitous phenomenon. The clinical significance of impaired PPI is that it reflects a failure of sensorimotor gating, a process that normally insulates individuals from being overwhelmed by sensory stimuli (18). The possibility that it may be a correlate of poor performance on the WCST has some theoretical support from research that implicates frontal-lobe involvement in perceptual organization (20,21).

We have collected data to investigate the possibility that WCST impairment is present in some but not all chronic schizophrenic patients. Additionally, we have hypothesized that patients who perform in an impaired range on the WCST will also exhibit increased sensorimotor gating abnormalities and a more deteriorated course of symptomatology.

METHODS

Subjects included three groups consisting of 21 RDC-defined chronic and subchronic paranoid schizophrenic patients, 15 psychiatric control patients, and 20 normal control subjects. All psychiatric subjects were inpatients at the time of testing. A number of the psychiatric subjects had histories of substance abuse, but none met criteria for active alcohol dependence at the time of testing. Eleven of the schizophrenic patients were drug-free for at least 3 months prior to testing, and all psychiatric subjects were drug-free for at least 2 weeks. The schizophrenic patient and psychiatric control groups were not significantly different on the MacAndrews Alcoholism Scale. All of the schizophrenic subjects were receiving neuroleptic medication and were in a state of relative clinical stability at the time of testing. The psychiatric control group consisted of six patients with unipolar depression, six patients with bipolar disorder, one patient with borderline personality disorder, and two patients with posttraumatic stress disorder. All subjects reported a negative history for head trauma or other significant neurological involvement.

The three groups were not significantly different in age. The normal control subjects had significantly more years of education (mean = 15.0, SD = 2.1), greater Digit Span Scores for the Wechsler Adult Intelligence Scale–Revised (WAIS-R) (mean = 11.8, SD = 2.2) and WAIS-R Vocabulary Scores (mean = 11.5, SD = 2.1) than the two patient groups. The schizophrenic group was not significantly different from the psychiatric control group in education or the WAIS-R variables. The schizophrenic group had a significantly higher Brief Psychiatric Rating Scale (BPRS) score (mean = 33.6, SD = 9.4) than the psychiatric controls (mean = 20.2, SD = 8.6).

All subjects were administered the WCST in the standard manner (7). On the same day, subjects were tested for PPI of the startle reflex according to our current methods (22). As part of this paradigm, a series of 31 40-msec, 30-psi tactile stimuli (air puffs) were presented at random intervals, with the average interstimulus interval of 15 msec (9 to 23-msec range) through a tube at the subject's neck. Eyeblink startle was measured by electromyogram (EMG) of facial muscles. Half of these stimuli were preceded 120 msec by an 85 dB, 20-msec acoustic prepulse stimulus.

RESULTS

An ANOVA with post hoc testing indicated that the normal control group had significantly fewer perseverative responses on the WCST (mean = 2.8, SD = 6.4) than the two patient groups. The schizophrenic group (mean = 25.0, SD = 15.8), however, was not significantly different from the psy-

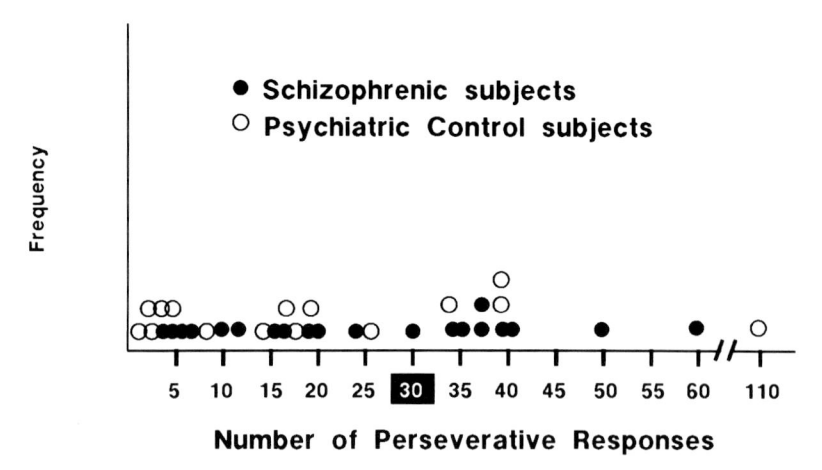

FIG. 1. Frequency distribution of WCST scores Mann-Whitney U-Test ($U' = 22$, $p < .001$).

chiatric control group (mean = 22.6, SD = 27.7) in perseverative responding on the WCST. On closer inspection, however, it appeared that the distributions of perseverative responses were significantly different. These distributions are presented in Fig. 1. A test for homogeneity of variance across these two was significant ($F = 3.06$ $(20,14)$; $p < .05$), confirming the violation of the assumption required for parametric statistical analysis. We then conducted a Mann-Whitney U-Test (see Fig 1) that was highly significant, indicating that the frequency of individuals obtaining greater

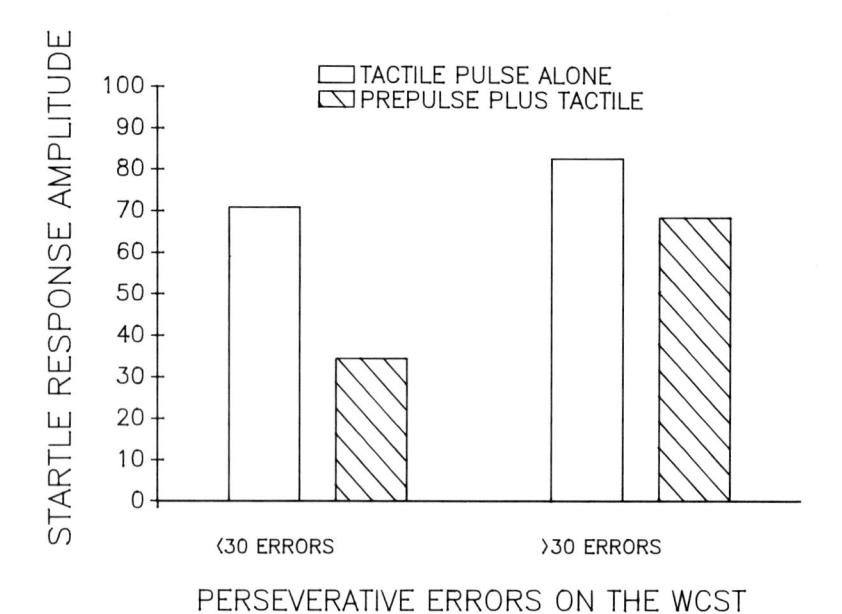

FIG. 2. Tactile prepulse inhibition as a function of perseverative responding on the WCST in schizophrenia. Non-impaired (< 30 errors), $N = 9$; impaired (> 30 errors), $N = 6$.

numbers of perseverative responses on the WCST was higher in the schizophrenic group when compared with the psychiatric control group.

Given that the schizophrenic group appeared to be approximating a bimodal distribution, we then separated this group into two subgroups, impaired ($N = 8$) and nonimpaired ($N = 12$) using 30 perseverative responses on the WCST as the criterion cutoff for impairment (7) and the observation that none of our normal control subjects had obtained a score of greater than 29 perseverative responses. One schizophrenic patient was excluded because of inability to complete the WCST. The two groups were not significantly different in duration of illness, number of previous hospitalizations, age, education, alcohol consumption or on the Scale for the Assessment of Positive Symptoms (SAPS). With regard to PPI of the tactile- (but not auditory) startle reflex, however, the WCST impaired group consistently exhibited less PPI than the nonimpaired group. These data are presented in Fig 2. Statistical analysis was deferred on these measures since individuals who did not exhibit responsivity to the paradigm were removed, which left the sample sizes quite small (WCST impaired, $N = 6$; WCST nonimpaired, $N = 9$).

DISCUSSION

Data are supportive of possible increased sensorimotor gating abnormalities within the subgroup of paranoid schizophrenic patients who demonstrate greater perseverative responding on the WCST. This may reflect a central role of frontal brain dysfunction in some schizophrenic patients that mediates both impaired mental flexibility (eg, WCST) and perceptual disorganization (e.g., decreased sensorimotor gating).

These data are rather intriguing for several reasons. First, researchers have tended to ask whether "schizophrenic patients" show hypofrontality on the WCST or PET. It is more appropriate to ask, which subgroup of schizophrenic patients shows these deficits, and are there markers of this impaired subgroup that can be reliably identified? It is likely that multiple converging methods will give us a fuller picture of these schizophrenia-linked deficits in a subgroup of schizophrenic patients. Certainly, the identification of a schizophrenic subgroup with correlated deficits on the WCST, sensorimotor gating, and PET would be very useful. Would such patients have excess negative symptoms and a Kraepelinian picture? Only future research will answer this question. We will also need to examine the relationship of correlated deficits (of, for example, the WCST and gating) and the issue of possible common underlying mechanisms. Might defective sensorimotor gating in schizophrenic patients result from impaired frontal-lobe inhibitory function, as is hypothesized for perseverative errors on the WCST? This is certainly a possibility and one that will need empirical verification. Future research needs to utilize converging methods regarding this potentially distinct subgroup of schizophrenic patients. Specifically, we will need to administer additional tests of frontal-brain functioning to patients in order to determine the degree of concordance that these independent variables hold. We hypothesize that our WCST and gating-impaired subjects will show frontal brain abnormalities on metabolic measures such as PET, rCBF, and poor performance on other neuropsychological tests sensitive to frontal-lobe integrity (e.g., Auditory Consonant Trigrams, Fluency Measures).

Second, the WCST data are of intrinsic interest. In the current study, nonparametric methods were used due to the violation of parametric assumptions and the small sample sizes. Beyond these issues, on a conceptual basis, nonparametric analyses may be more generally appropriate for these sorts of data. Our study suggests that a central question involves the percentage of schizophrenic patients that perform in an impaired range on the WCST. If schizophrenic patients are indeed characterized by a bimodallike distribution of WCST perseverative responses, then traditional descriptive and parametric statistics may provide misleading pictures, and nonparametric or nonlinear, topographic measures of complexity analysis may prove more useful. These considerations lead us to ask *which specific subgroups* of schizophrenic patients show increased perseverative errors on the WCST. Currently, it seems as if schizophrenic outpatients have relatively normal performance on the WCST (17). Schizophrenic inpatients have more perseverative errors linked to more generalized impairments and also, perhaps, to greater specific frontal-lobe impairment. The next few years should allow researchers to begin providing answers to the question of which schizophrenic patients under which conditions have the greatest impairments on the WCST, gating measures, and other probes of frontal and general brain function.

ACKNOWLEDGMENTS

This research was supported in part by NIMH Grant MH42228 and a State of California Grant DMH 89-7000.

REFERENCES

1. Bleuler E. *Dementia praecox or the group of schizophrenias.* New York: New York International Press, 1950.
2. Greenblatt M, Solomon HC. Concerning a theory of frontal lobe functioning. In: Greenblatt M, Solomon HC, eds. *Frontal lobes and schizophrenia.* New York: Springer-Verlag, 1953; 391–413.
3. Weinberger DR. Implications of normal brain development for the pathogenesis of schizophrenia. *Arch Gen Psychiatry* 1987;44:660–669.
4. Buchsbaum MS, Ingvar DH, Kessler R, et al. Cerebral glucography with positron tomography. *Arch Gen Psychiatry* 1982;39:251–259.
5. Ingvar DH, Franzen G. Distribution of cerebral activity in chronic schizophrenia. *Lancet* 1974; 2:1484–1486.
6. Grant DA, Berg EA. A behavioral analysis of degree of reinforcement and ease of shifting to new responses in a Weigl type card sorting problem. *J Exp Psychol* 1948;38:404–411.
7. Heaton RK. *A manual for the Wisconsin Card Sorting Test.* Odessa, Fla: Psychological Assessment Resources, 1981.
8. Milner B. Effects of different brain lesions on card sorting. *Arch Neurol* 1963;9:90–100.
9. Robinson AL, Heaton RK, Lehman RW, et al. The utility of the Wisconsin Card Sorting Test in detecting and localizing frontal lobe lesions. *J Consult Clin Psychol* 1980;48:605–614.
10. Fey ET. The performance of young schizophrenics and young normals on the Wisconsin Card Sorting Test. *J Consult Psychol* 1951;15: 311–319.
11. Malmo HP. On frontal lobe functions: Psychiatric patient controls. *Cortex* 1974;10:231–237.
12. Kolb B, Whishaw IQ. Performance of schizophrenic patients on tests sensitive to left or right frontal temporal parietal functions in neurologic patients. *J Nerv Ment Dis* 1983;171:435–443.
13. Stuss DT, Benson DF, Kaplan EF, et al. The involvement of orbito frontal cerebrum in cognitive tasks. *Neuropsychologia* 1983;21:235–248.
14. Goldberg TE, Weinberger DR, Berman KR, et al. Further evidence for dementia of the prefrontal type in schizophrenia? A controlled study of teaching the Wisconsin Card Sorting Test. *Arch Gen Psychiatry* 1987;44:1008–1014.
15. Berman KF, Illowsky BP, Weinberger DR. Physiological dysfunction of dorsolateral prefrontal cortex in schizophrenia: IV. Further evidence for regional and behavioral specificity. *Arch Gen Psychiatry* 1988;45:616–622.
16. Weinberger DR, Berman KF, Illowsky BP. Physiological dysfunction of dorsolateral prefrontal cortex in schizophrenia: III. A new cohort and evidence for a monoaminergic mechanism. *Arch Gen Psychiatry* 1988;45:609–615.
17. Braff DL, Heaton RK, Cullum CM, et al. The generalized pattern of neuropsychological deficits in chronic schizophrenic outpatients with relatively normal Wisconsin Card Sorting Results. *Arch Gen Psychiatry* (submitted).
18. Braff DL. Attention, habituation, and information processing in psychiatric disorders. In: Michels R, et al, eds. *Psychiatry,* Vol. 3. Philadelphia: Lippincott Co, 1985;1–12.
19. Braff DL, Geyer MA. Sensorimotor gating and schizophrenia: Human and animal model studies. *Arch Gen Psychiatry* 1990;47:181–188.
20. Luria AR. *Higher cortical functions in man.* New York: Basic Books, 1980.
21. Stuss DT, Benson DF. *The frontal lobes.* New York: Raven Press, 1986.
22. Braff DL, Grillon C, Butler RW, et al. Impaired sensorimotor gating in schizophrenic patients. *Arch Gen Psychiatry* (submitted).

16
Electrophysiological and Behavioral Signs of Attentional Disturbance in Schizophrenics and Their Siblings

Stuart R. Steinhauer,[1,2] Joseph Zubin,[1,2] Ruth Condray, David B. Shaw,[1] Jeffrey L. Peters,[1,2] and Daniel P. van Kammen[1,2]

The identification of individuals at increased risk for the development of schizophrenia requires intensive investigations of potential markers of vulnerability. Consanguinity has been one of the more accurate predictors of the development of schizophrenic disorder. Thus, one of the most important approaches has been the study of twins concordant or discordant for schizophrenia. However, twin findings indicate that there are both genetic and nongenetic components in the etiology of the disorder (1). Complementary strategies involve study of children of schizophrenics (2), including adopted-away offspring (3), and adult first-degree relatives of schizophrenics (4,5). The Pittsburgh project is an ongoing study in which a variety of neurobehavioral measures are being examined in probands and their adult siblings. The program focuses on the information-processing deviations associated with schizophrenia.

The concept of vulnerability to schizophrenia has been employed in order to examine the confluence of different etiological factors, both biological and psychosocial,

[1]Biometrics Research, Department of Veterans Affairs Medical Center, Highland Drive, Pittsburgh, PA 15206.
[2]Western Psychiatric Institute and Clinic, University of Pittsburgh School of Medicine, Pittsburgh, PA 15206.

that contribute to the onset of episodes (6). An examination of patients both during and following episodes can provide information on whether a marker is indicative of current psychopathology (state or episode marker) or of long-term vulnerability (trait) characteristics, present even between episodes (7). Ideally this would include pre-episode status, but such data cannot be collected except in the case of high-risk studies of children or adolescents. However, the presence of the marker among the siblings (or other first-degree relatives) of the patients could indicate either that the marker runs in families or that individuals at high risk who might eventually develop schizophrenia might also exhibit the marker.

More recently it has become clear that members of a proband's family are at greater risk not only for schizophrenia, but for related schizotypal personality disorders, all of which fall into the category of schizophrenia spectrum disorders (4,8,9). This led us to conceptualize the presence of markers among family members in a somewhat more specific manner. If the marker occurred only among those probands and siblings with schizophrenia spectrum disorder, then the marker was likely to be associated with the schizophrenia spectrum. If the marker also appeared at higher rates among those siblings who show nonspectrum disorders (e.g., affective disorder or other personality disorders), then it is a sign of general psychopathology not specific to the schizophrenia spectrum. However, if the marker is also found among siblings with no history of psychiatric problems, then it is most likely to be a true vulnerability marker that is associated with familial status but not specifically predictive of which family members will develop the disorder.

It was necessary to limit the scope of the present studies in several ways. Because many potential markers have been identified (10), it seemed critical to determine which of these to retain for future large-scale family studies. A wide variety of diagnostic, psychophysiological, behavioral, and neuropsychological measures has been included, but pragmatically at a cost of examining only limited numbers of patients and their relatives. The initial research approach has been to test only a single brother of each male proband, although later studies will be extended to female probands and multiple family members. In addition, an attempt is made to recruit randomly selected male siblings, so that the bias for recording only the most conveniently available or willing brother is minimized. In order to obtain a sample of patients who would be maximally functional, recruitment has been targeted at outpatient probands and their families, so that the proband would be capable of participating in most phases of the research. The present overview of attentional factors is based on data from an initial sample of 79 subjects.

OVERVIEW OF SUBJECT SELECTION AND EXPERIMENTAL MEASURES

The 30 schizophrenic probands (mean ± SD = 36.6 ± 6.9 years old), recruited primarily through the Veterans Administration Medical Center, were clinically stable, showing either no current exacerbation of psychotic symptoms, or no change in general clinical state for two monthly interviews prior to laboratory testing. All met RDC and DSM-III criteria for schizophrenia or schizoaffective disorder, mainly schizophrenic type. Of their 30 brothers (37.0 ± 9.2 years old), the participation of the first randomly selected sibling was obtained in 23 cases. Control subjects, recruited through advertising, consisted of 19 males (34.4 ± 7.9 years old) who met criteria for having no history of psychopathology and whose mean socioeconomic and educational levels were matched to the siblings. In addition, exclusion criteria for all subjects included possible brain damage or major medical problems, and siblings were excluded from the present analysis if they met criteria for schizophrenia.

The diagnostic battery for all subjects included the Schedule for Affective Disorders and Schizophrenia (SADS), Lifetime version (11; or SADS—Current version for patient follow-ups), Family History RDC, and drug-use and health questionnaires. Siblings and controls were also administered the Structured Interview for DSM-III Personality Disorders (SIDP; refs 12,13), and the Schedule for Schizotypal Personalities (SSP), which is a section of the Schedule for Interviewing Borderlines (SIB; ref 14). The latter two instruments were employed for evaluation of Axis II personality-related disorders. Psychiatric diagnoses were determined for all subjects following initial clinical evaluations and diagnostic evaluation conferences in which clinical staff and the project psychologist and psychiatrist participated. Diagnoses of schizophrenia spectrum disorder were assigned to four of the siblings (only one of whom had a prior history of alcohol abuse), and diagnoses of non–schizophrenia spectrum disorder (primarily affective disorder or previous alcohol-related problems) were assigned to 15 of the siblings. Siblings with current substance abuse or dependence problems were excluded. Unfortunately, it has been our experience that alcohol-related problems occur at a high rate among the siblings of these patients, making a study of siblings with no history of alcohol-related problems impractical. No psychiatric disorder was diagnosed in the remaining 11 siblings.

The primary psychophysiological evaluation involved the recording of event-related brain potentials (ERPs), pupillary dilation, and heart rate in response to auditory stimulus processing during Counting and Choice Reaction tasks. In addition, smooth-pursuit eye movements, pupillary light reactions, and blink rates were recorded.

Behavioral evaluation included the Continuous Performance Test (CPT) using degraded visual stimuli, the Span of Apprehension task (SOA), and shadowing of dichotically presented material. In collaboration with John Watson and Michael Pogue-Geile, we initiated a neuropsychological test battery that included the Wisconsin Card Sorting Test (WCST), Trails B, the Relational Concepts subscale of the Luria-Nebraska Battery, and subtests of the WAIS-R (Information and Block Design) to assess general intelligence.

EXTRACTING FACTORS OF ATTENTIONAL PERFORMANCE

For an initial examination of data we were faced with the difficult task of trying to discriminate meaningful patterns within this extensive data set. Our attention was therefore drawn to an analysis of neuropsychological data performed by Mirsky (15) in which factor analysis of data from a broad background of neuropsychiatric patients had indicated the following four primary factors attributed to aspects of attentional processing:

Factor 1 (Focus/Execute: perceptual/motor speed) loaded on scores derived from the Trail Making, Talland Letter Cancellation, Digit Symbol Substitution, and Stroop tests.
Factor 2 (Sustain: vigilance) loaded on errors of omission and commission, and reaction time from the CPT.
Factor 3 (Encode: numerical mnemonic) was related to performance on the Digit Span and Arithmetic subtests of the WAIS-R.
Factor 4 (Shift: flexibility) was most heavily loaded on WCST errors.

These results were especially intriguing because of their relation to varieties of attentional disturbance that, as Mirsky noted, had been suggested a decade earlier by Zubin in an analysis of schizophrenic performance (16). Since there was some overlap between the variables included by Mirsky and those in our ongoing research, it seemed feasible to model a similar analysis using a subset of data. The neuropsychological data were limited to the Trails B, Relational Concepts, Block Design scores, and both perseverative and nonperseverative errors on the WCST. Behavioral tests included measures of sensitivity (d') and response criterion (Beta) from the CPT, and performance on the SOA in the nine-distractor condition (in which one of two different target letters is presented tachistoscopically with nine other nontargets).

For psychophysiological evaluation, the amplitude and latency of the P300 component of the ERP (17,18) were measured at multiple scalp sites during basic information-processing tasks. Decreased P300 amplitude among schizophrenics is one of the most reliably documented phenomena (19, 20). Two different auditory stimuli, with different overall frequencies of occurrence, were presented during two separate tasks. In the Counting task, the infrequent tone was counted by the subject. In the Choice Reaction task, separate motor responses were made to infrequent and frequent tones. The infrequent tone gave rise to the largest P300 component. The amplitude and latency of P300 to infrequent tones, measured over the midline parietal cortex, were entered into the analysis.

The loadings of each variable on four fac-

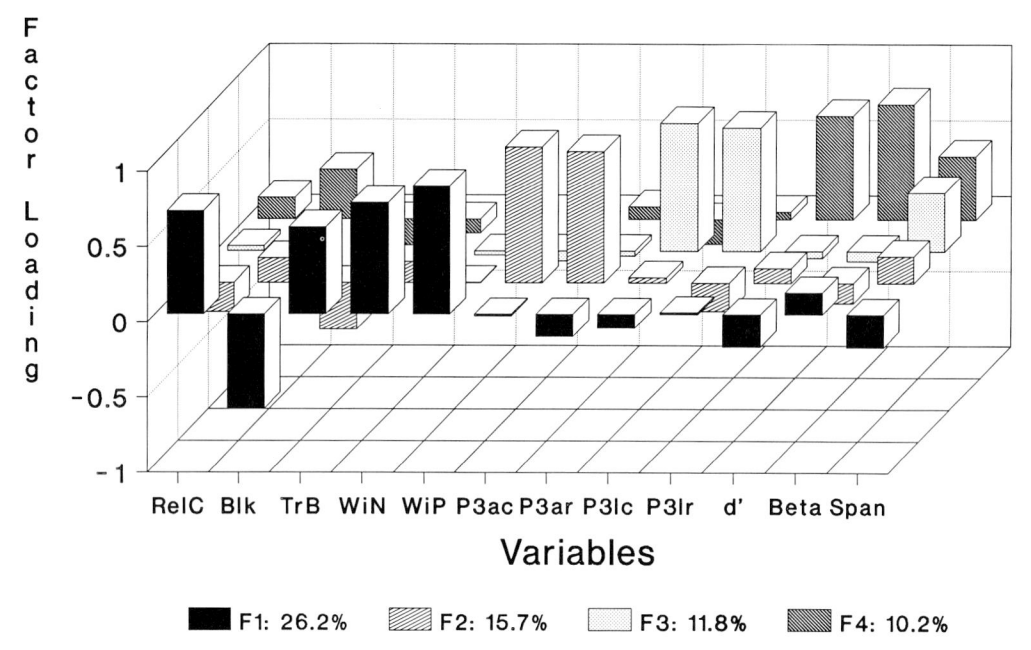

FIG. 1. Elements of attention extracted from the family study. Shown are loadings for individual items on the first four orthogonal factors derived from the factor analysis across all subjects. *Key:* RelC, Relational Concepts; Blk, Block Design; TrB, Trails-B; WiN, Wisconsin Card Sort/Non-Perseverative Errors; WiP, Wisconsin Card Sort/Perseverative Errors; P3ac, P300 amplitude, Counting task; P3ar, P300 amplitude, Choice Reaction task; P3lc, P300 latency, Counting task; P3lr, P300 latency, Choice Reaction task; d', CPT, visual sensitivity; Beta, CPT, response criterion; Span, number correct, Span of Apprehension.

tors resulting from this analysis (totaling 63.9% of the variance) are schematically depicted in Fig. 1. Factor 1, comprised of neuropsychological test measures, appears related to Mirsky's first factor (Focus/Execute) but also includes WCST errors. Factor 4, composed of CPT and SOA scores, is similar to Mirsky's second factor (Sustain). Factor 2 includes the amplitudes of the P300 component on both tasks, while Factor 3 is separately loaded on P300 latency for both tasks. These physiological factors appeared to assess a type of processing independent from that seen with the neuropsychological and behavioral assessments.

Guided by the outcome of the factor analysis, the individual factors were examined. Since the emergence of factors was based on variance of the combined groups and did not necessarily indicate differences among groups of interest, it became important to focus on items composing each of the factors. Differences in neuropsychological performance, most marked for the patients, were also seen for siblings, especially those with spectrum disorders, on the Relational Concepts subtest of the Luria-Nebraska battery, for perseverative errors on the WCST, and on Trails B. (Further description of the neuropsychological data appears elsewhere; see refs. 21,22.)

BEHAVIORAL AND ELECTROPHYSIOLOGICAL COMPARISONS

The remainder of this discussion deals with the vigilance and psychophysiological variables. Comparisons were made among controls, probands, and siblings of the probands meeting criteria for schizotypal personality disorder, other (nonspectrum) psychiatric disorder, and no diagnosis. Because the number of siblings to date who met criteria for schizotypal personality disorder is small, the initial analyses are considered exploratory. Missing data for any subject are indicated by reduced sample size.

The factor associated with sustained attention was related to performance on the CPT and the SOA. Visual sensitivity, as measured by d' level, and response criterion (Beta) are illustrated for all groups in Fig. 2. One-way ANOVAs among all groups yielded a significant effect only for d' ($F[4,73] = 4.29$, $p = .0036$). Probands and the spectrum-disordered siblings showed similar performance levels, and both scored significantly lower than controls. Those siblings with no diagnosis had the highest d' scores. Their performance, like that of the controls, was similar to Nuechterlein's results for controls on a comparable version of the CPT (d' = 2.56; refs. 23 and Nuechterlein, personal communication). The diagnostic groups did not differ significantly on Beta. The d' level findings are especially interesting given a lack of differences in Beta, which measures willingness to respond. This finding held even after the elimination of data for two probands with extremely high Beta values. The differences in visual sensitivity are therefore more likely to reflect basic differences in sensitivity not attributable to the subjects' criteria for responding.

No significant differences were found for the number of correct responses on the SOA. Numerically, probands and siblings with non–schizophrenia spectrum disorders exhibited a lower mean correct score (30.5 and 30.7, respectively, for a maximum of 40 trials) than did siblings with spectrum disorder, siblings with no diagnosis, and controls (with means of 32.5, 32.2, and 32.5, respectively).

Several unusual trends appeared in the analyses of the P300 component of the ERP to the rare stimulus (Fig. 3). None of the ANOVAs of the five groups was significant, though a trend for differences was observed for P300 amplitude in the Counting task ($p < .085$). In both tasks, smaller mean amplitudes can be seen for both probands and for those siblings meeting criteria for schizophrenia spectrum disorder as compared with all other groups. Furthermore, a prolongation of latency is seen in both tasks only for the spectrum-disordered siblings, even when compared with probands.

The lack of a strong P300 amplitude difference between controls and schizophrenic probands is atypical for most studies. (Analyses of all experimental conditions, including both infrequent and frequent stimuli at six electrode sites, did show significant differences between patients and controls for the Counting task, but did not reach significance for the Choice Reaction task.) The relatively stable functional level of our patients, who had remained out of the hospital for a mean of 39.2 months prior to testing, may be related to these effects. These results suggest that P300 amplitude may not reach normal-equivalent levels in remitted patients. This is not necessarily contradictory to previous findings showing that changes in P300 are associated with clinical improvement (24–27). Thus, P300 amplitude findings seem to fit criteria for a "mediating vulnerability factor" (28), a description applied to indicators that may vary with fluctuations in symptomatology but that even during asymptomatic periods never attain normal levels.

The present ERP results for siblings are also difficult to reconcile with the study of Saitoh et al (29), who reported highly reduced P300 amplitudes (based on an amplitude averaged over several time points) recorded from relatives of schizophrenics during a linguistic auditory discrimination task. A possible confound in the Saitoh et

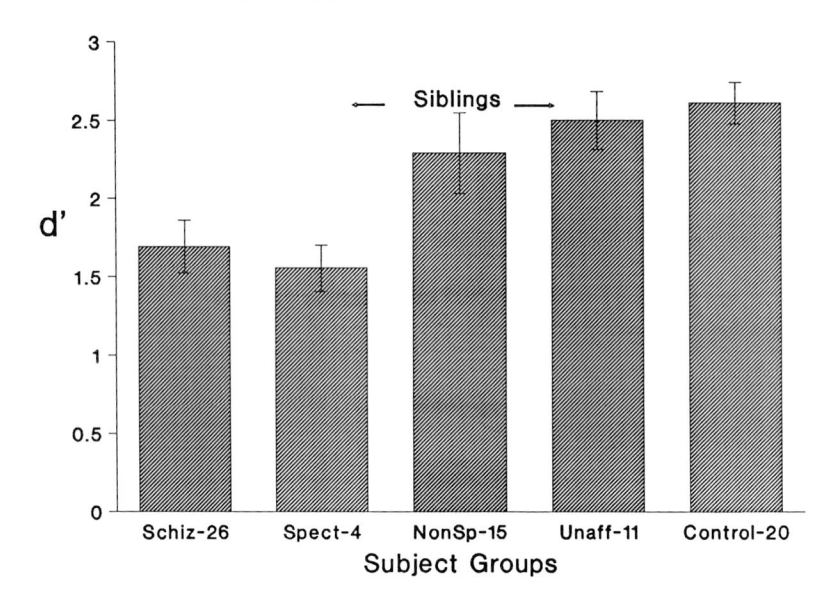

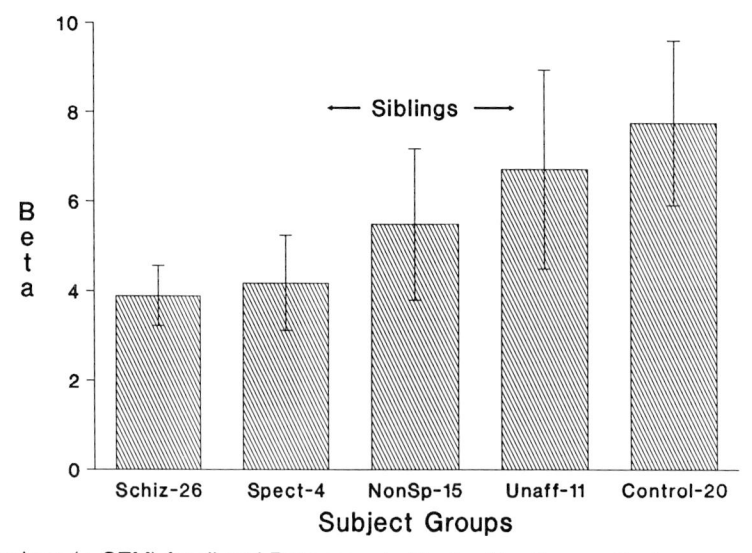

FIG. 2. Mean values (±SEM) for d' and Beta recorded in the Continuous Performance test. From left to right, data are presented for schizophrenic probands (Schiz), siblings with a diagnosis of spectrum disorder (Spect), siblings with other psychiatric disorders (NonSp), siblings with no disorder (Unaff), and controls.

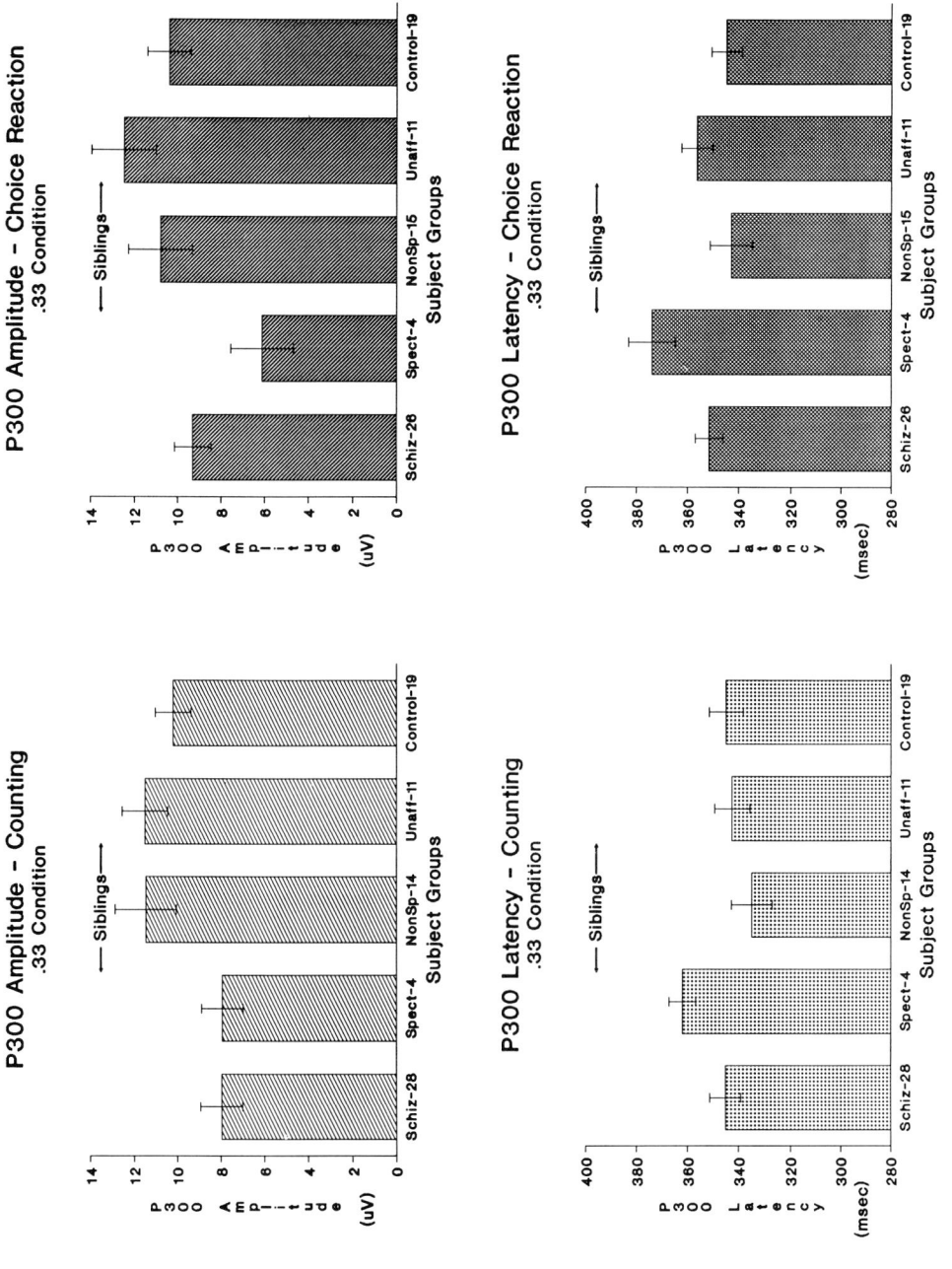

FIG. 3. Mean (±SEM) values for P300 amplitude (*top*) and latency (*bottom*) to the infrequent auditory stimulus in the .33 condition at the midline parietal scalp location for all subject groups, as in Fig. 2. Data are presented for the Counting task (*left*) and for the Choice Reaction task (*right*).

al study is that one half of the relatives of patients who participated were not related to patients also included in their study; however, this alone would probably not account for the discrepancy with the current data.

Among the siblings, only those with schizotypal personality disorder showed trends for both decreased P300 amplitudes and for increased latency. Increased P300 latency in schizophrenics has been reported in other patient samples (20). Both effects are considered deviant characteristics of the ERP response. Whether the lack of statistical significance for spectrum-disordered siblings is due to the small size of this group so far, or is indicative of true measurement error, will require further testing of relatives.

The spectrum-disordered siblings also showed significant decrements in visual sensitivity, similar to those noted in the patients. Across these measures of attention and information processing, a pattern similar to that seen in patients is emerging. It should be noted that among the spectrum-disordered siblings, none had been treated for psychiatric disorder (one had been referred to a social worker for family problems). Thus, the findings are not related to functional impairment identified with psychopathology even among these relatives of patients. Furthermore, it suggests that more refined analyses of symptomatology should be examined. Siever and colleagues (30) have also reported an association between smooth-pursuit eye-movement impairments and schizotypal characteristics, which lends further support to the notion that there is a broad pattern of attentional impairment associated with schizophrenia spectrum disorders, including schizotypal personality disorder. To this end we are studying how the occurrence of symptoms of schizotypal personality disorder among the relatives of patients may relate to laboratory variables, regardless of whether the subject meets clinical criteria for the disorder.

IMPLICATIONS FOR THE CONCEPT OF VULNERABILITY TO SCHIZOPHRENIA

The presence of attentional dysfunctions associated with schizophrenia spectrum disorders provides important information for refining the model of vulnerability to schizophrenia. The schizophrenia spectrum includes both schizophrenic patients and individuals with schizotypal personality disorders of lesser severity. The major components of the vulnerability dimension (6,7) have been thought to reflect primarily genetic factors, enduring biological factors (e.g., viral infection or postnatal brain damage), and/or residual effects of other major life experiences.

It might be expected that those with spectrum disorders lie along a region of greater vulnerability, and that within the same families the schizophrenic patients have the greatest vulnerability. A modification of this notion, suggested by Mirsky and Duncan (31), is that the vulnerability dimension is related to schizophrenogenic brain abnormalities. They suggest that between the threshold for adaptive behavior and the occurrence of schizophrenic episodes is a region in which stress leads to schizotypy or other spectrum disorder.

An alternative possibility is that there is greater similarity in vulnerability among those family members who exhibit schizophrenia spectrum disorders, although they may differ in severity of symptoms. In this case, it is necessary to account for the differential ability of these individuals to cope with stressful life situations. One solution is provided by introducing the moderating effect of tolerance to stress into the vulnerability model (Fig. 4).

According to this depiction of the model, increasing tolerance for individuals with low vulnerability would have little observable effect, since they are least likely to exhibit spectrum disorders at all. For those with greater vulnerability, mechanisms for enhancing tolerance to stress would be more effective in reducing the likelihood of

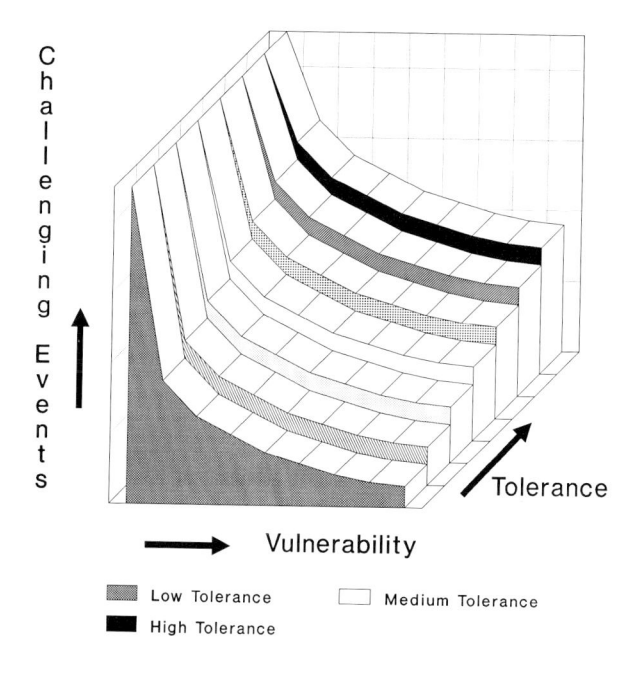

FIG. 4. A modified model of vulnerability to schizophrenia and the effects of tolerance to stress. Changes in the threshold for onset of symptoms are related to variations in individual tolerance to stress. (Adapted from ref. 7.)

expressed symptoms. Several mechanisms for increasing tolerance are well known, including interventions through pharmacotherapeutic and psychotherapeutic treatment. In effect, the model embodies one of the goals in employing such treatments—reducing symptoms by increasing the patient's ability to cope with typical as well as unusual life events.

As depicted, this version of the model also suggests that, in cases involving extremely high degrees of vulnerability, it may be difficult to provide sufficiently powerful interventions for raising the threshold of tolerance. For such individuals, even with the best of the currently known interventions, the likelihood that they will continue to vacillate between stages of minimal and severe symptomatology will remain high.

In pursuing the goal of understanding the factors that contribute to vulnerability to schizophrenia and other schizophrenia spectrum disorders, we are encouraged by the convergent findings from behavioral and psychophysiological studies. Family studies and approaches designed to link laboratory and refined diagnostic tools will provide critical information in efforts to understand the nature of schizophrenia.

ACKNOWLEDGMENTS

This work was supported by the Medical Research Service of the Department of Veterans Affairs, and by NIMH Grant MH43615.

REFERENCES

1. Gottesman II, Bertelsen A. Confirming unexpressed genotypes for schizophrenia. *Arch Gen Psychiatry* 1989;46;867–872.
2. Cornblatt B, Erlenmeyer-Kimling L. Early attentional predictors of adolescent behavioral disturbances in children at risk for schizophrenia. In: Watt NF, Anthony EJ, Wynne LC, Rolf JE, eds. *Children at risk for schizophrenia*. New York: Cambridge University Press, 1984;198–211.
3. Kety S, Rosenthal D, Wender P. Mental illness in the biological and adoptive families of adopted schizophrenics. *Am J Psychiatry* 1971;128:307–311.
4. Kendler K, Gruneberg AM, Strauss JS. An independent analysis of the Danish adoption study of schizophrenia, II: The relationship between

schizotypal personality disorder and schizophrenia. *Arch Gen Psychiatry* 1981;38:982–984.
5. Kendler K, Gruneberg AM. Genetic relationship between paranoid personality and the schizophrenia spectrum disorders. *Am J Psychiatry* 1982;139:1185–1186.
6. Zubin J, Spring B. Vulnerability: A new view of schizophrenia. *J Abnorm Psychol* 1977;86:103–126.
7. Zubin J, Steinhauer S. How to break the logjam in schizophrenia: A look beyond genetics. *J Nerv Ment Dis* 1981;169:477–492.
8. Baron M, Gruen R, Asnis L, Kane J. Familial relatedness of schizophrenia and schizotypal states. *Am J Psychiatry* 1983;140:1437–1442.
9. Baron M, Gruen R, Rainer J, Kane J, Asnis L, Lord S. A family study of schizophrenic and normal control probands: Implications for the spectrum concept of schizophrenia. *Am J Psychiatry* 1985;142:447–455.
10. Zubin J, Steinhauer SR, Day R, van Kammen DP. Schizophrenia at the cross-roads: A blueprint for the 80's. *Compar Psychiatry* 1985;26:217–240.
11. Spitzer RL, Endicott J. The schedule for affective disorders and schizophrenia (SADS). Biometrics Research Unit, New York State Psychiatric Institute, New York, 1975.
12. Pfohl B, Stangl D, Zimmerman M. *Structured Interview for DSM-III Personality Disorders SIDP*, revised edition. Iowa City: Department of Psychiatry, University of Iowa, 1983.
13. Stangl D, Pfohl B, Zimmerman M, Bowers W, Corenthal C. A structured interview for the DSM-III personality disorders. *Arch Gen Psychiatry* 1985;42:591–596.
14. Baron M, Asnis L, Gruen R. The schedule for schizotypal personalities (SSP): A diagnostic interview for schizotypal features. *Psychiatry Res* 1981;4:213–228.
15. Mirsky, AF. The neuropsychology of attention: Elements of a complex behavior. In; Perecman E, ed. *Integrating Theory and Practice in Clinical Neuropsychology.* Hillsdale, NJ: Lawrence Erlbaum Associates (in press).
16. Zubin J. Problem of attention in schizophrenia. In: Kietzman ML, Sutton S, Zubin J, eds. *Experimental Approaches to Psychopathology.* New York: Academic Press, 1975;139–166.
17. Sutton S, Braren M, Zubin J, John ER. Evoked-potential correlates of stimulus uncertainty. *Science* 1965;150:1187–1188.
18. Donchin E, Ritter W, McCallum WC. Cognitive psychophysiology: The endogenous components of the ERP. In: Callaway E, Tueting P, Koslow SH, eds. *Event-related Brain potentials in Man.* New York: Academic Press, 1978;443–496.
19. Zubin J, Sutton S, Steinhauer SR. Event-related potential and behavioral methodology in psychiatric research. In: Shagass C, Josiassen RC, Roemer RA, eds. *Brain Electrical Potentials and Psychopathology.* Amsterdam: Elsevier, 1986;1–26.
20. Pfefferbaum A, Ford JM, White PM, Roth WT. P3 in schizophrenia is affected by stimulus modality, response requirements, medication status, and negative symptoms. *Arch Gen Psychiatry* 1989;46:1035–1044.
21. Watson JR. *Neuropsychological impairment among schizophrenic probands and their siblings.* Doctoral dissertation, University of Pittsburgh, 1988.
22. Pogue-Geile MF, Watson JR, Steinhauer SR, Goldstein G. Neuropsychological impairments among siblings of schizophrenic probands. *Schizophr Res* 1989;2:70.
23. Nuechterlein, KH. Converging evidence for vigilance deficit as a vulnerability indicator for schizophrenic disorders. In: Alpert M, ed. *Controversies in Schizophrenia: Changes and Constancies.* New York: Guilford Press, 1985;175–198.
24. Levit RA, Sutton S, Zubin J. Evoked potential correlates of information processing in psychiatric patients. *Psychol Med* 1973;3:487–494.
25. Steinhauer SR, Zubin J. Vulnerability to schizophrenia: Information processing in the pupil and event-related potential. In: Usdin E, Hanin I, eds. *Biological Markers in Psychiatry and Neurology.* Oxford: Pergamon Press, 1982;371–385.
26. Josiassen RC, Shagass C, Straumanis JJ, Roemer RA. Psychiatric drugs and the somatosensory P400 wave. *Psychiatry Res* 1984;11:151–162.
27. Duncan CC, Morihisa JM, Fawcett RW, Kirch DG. P300 in schizophrenia: State or trait marker? *Psychopharmacol Bull* 1987;23:497–501.
28. Nuechterlein KH, Dawson ME. A heuristic vulnerability/stress model of schizophrenic episodes. *Schizophr Bull* 1984;10:300–312.
29. Saitoh O, Niwa SI, Hiramatsu KI, Kameyama T, Rymar K, Itoh K. Abnormalities in late positive components of event-related potentials may reflect a genetic predisposition to schizophrenia. *Biol Psychiatry* 1984;19:292–303.
30. Siever LJ, Coursey RD, Alterman IS, Zahn T, Brody L, Bernad P, Buchsbaum M, Lake CR, Murphy D. Clinical, psychophysiological, and neurological characteristics of volunteers with impaired smooth pursuit eye movements. *Biol Psychiatry* 1989;26:35–51.
31. Mirsky AF, Duncan CC. Etiology and expression of schizophrenia: Neurobiological and psychosocial factors. *Annu Rev Psychol* 1986;37:291–319.

PART IV

Schizophrenia Spectrum

17

The Biology of the Boundaries of Schizophrenia

Larry J. Siever[1]

Current knowledge regarding schizophrenia and related disorders suggests that these disorders may be represented on a continuum ranging in severity from severe, unremitting "Kraepelinean" schizophrenia to the schizophrenia-related personality disorders with attenuated schizophrenialike traits. The boundaries of these schizophrenia-related disorders are likely to include the schizophrenia-related personality disorders and perhaps the other nonschizophrenic psychotic disorders as well (1). Schizotypal personality disorder is the DSM-III-R prototype of the schizophrenia-related personality disorders. The criteria for schizotypal personality were derived from an examination of case records of the "latent" and uncertain schizophrenic relatives and probands with attenuated schizophrenialike traits in the Danish adoptive studies of Kety and colleagues (2,3) and were later refined in a clinical population (4). Thus, schizotypal personality disorder is the first personality disorder to be empirically defined in part on the basis of a genetic relationship to schizophrenia.

Available evidence from preliminary studies of the phenomenology, genetics, biology, outcome, and treatment response of schizotypal patients supports a close relationship between schizotypal personality disorder and chronic schizophrenia (5–9). In fact, genetic-familial studies of schizophrenic patients suggest that schizotypal personality disorder may be a more common phenotypic expression of a genetic diathesis to the schizophrenia-related disorders (2,10) than is chronic schizophrenia itself. Investigating the biology of schizotypal personality disorder and clarifying its relationship to chronic schizophrenia may therefore have important implications for understanding the pathogenesis of the schizophrenia-related disorders, for formulating the diagnostic boundaries of these disorders, and for defining the affected phenotype in molecular-genetic family studies.

The study of the biology of schizotypal personality disorder has some unique advantages over the investigation of other schizophrenia-related populations. Since chronic and severe illness, long-term hospitalization, and chronic neuroleptic treatment are less prevalent in patients with schizotypal personality disorder than in chronic schizophrenic patients, the systematic study of schizotypal personality disorder and its relationship to chronic schizophrenia affords the opportunity to investigate the schizophrenia-related disorders with less interference from these confounding artifacts. Schizotypal patients are more readily accessible than relatives of schizophrenic patients, and their investigation avoids idiosyncratic factors associated with the study of specific pedigrees of schizophrenic patients.

Family history studies of schizotypal-personality-disorder patients from our lab-

---

[1] Mt. Sinai School of Medicine and Bronx Veterans Administration Medical Center, Bronx, NY 10468.

oratory and other investigative groups suggest that schizotypal personality disorder is transmitted familially as one of several schizophrenia-related disorders, which include chronic schizophrenia, chronic schizoaffective disorder, unspecified psychoses, and schizophrenia-related personality disorders (1,10–16). The more definitive establishment of schizotypal personality disorder in clinical populations as part of a spectrum of schizophrenia-related disorders would necessitate a reexamination of the belief that the schizophrenia spectrum is confined to chronic schizophrenic patients and a subset of their more mildly affected relatives. It would also enable further more sophisticated studies of the schizophrenia-related disorders in this relatively common and clinically accessible population.

Biological similarities between schizotypal personality disorder and chronic schizophrenia would suggest that these disorders are related as part of a spectrum of schizophrenia-related disorders. Biologic abnormalities that occur along this spectrum might serve as genetic markers to identify affected relatives who are not overtly schizophrenic in genetic linkage studies. The character of these biologic abnormalities may provide clues to the underlying pathophysiology of these disorders and perhaps point to likely candidate genes for restriction fragment polymorphism (RFLP) studies. Biologic differences between schizotypal-personality-disorder patients and chronic schizophrenic patients might point to genetic or other biologic factors that protect against or confer an increased vulnerability to the severe, persistent psychosis of schizophrenia.

Biologic measures can be correlated to specific symptom criteria of schizophrenic personality disorders. The criteria for schizotypal personality disorder include deficit symptoms such as social isolation and poor rapport as well as positive psychoticlike symptoms (e.g., ideas of reference and perceptual distortions). As both schizophrenia-related personality disorders and other psychotic disorders are found with increased prevalence in the relatives of schizophrenic patients (1), it is conceivable that some genetic or other biologic factors may be more associated with the core deficit symptoms and others with the psychotic symptoms. The study of schizotypal patients as well as of other nonschizophrenic psychotic patients may help disentangle such factors with greater statistical power than studies of severely ill schizophrenic patients, in whom both deficit and positive symptoms may be prominent.

PSYCHOPHYSIOLOGIC STUDIES

A number of psychophysical tasks or measures that have been identified as abnormal not only in schizophrenic patients but also in schizotypal subjects and individuals at risk for schizophrenia include eye tracking tasks to measure smooth-pursuit eye movements (SPEM), the backward-masking task, and the Continuous Performance Task (CPT). All of these measures reflect potentially related, although not necessarily identical, impairment in attention and information processing that some studies have been reported to be associated with the "core" or deficit symptomatology common to chronic schizophrenia, residual schizophrenia, and the schizophrenia-related personality disorders. These symptoms include affective blunting, social withdrawal, and cognitive slippage. These measures have not been as consistently correlated with the positive psychotic symptoms of hallucinations and delusions, which are restricted to the active psychosis of chronic schizophrenia and occur in attenuated form in only a subset of the schizotypal patients.

Eye-tracking Impairment

Impairment of the SPEM system, required to efficiently track a smoothly moving target, has consistently been reported in 52% to 86% of schizophrenics (17), as compared to 6% to 8% in normal subjects, and in 21% of patients with nonpsychotic disorders. The impairment consists of multiple anticipatory and catch-up saccadic eye movements and lag of the pursuit system itself (18,19). Impairment of SPEM is observed in schizophrenics in remission (20) and is not a function of neuroleptic medication (17). Although SPEM may be abnormal in 30% to 50% of affective disorder patients, particularly bipolar maniacs (17,21), persistence of this impairment in remitted bipolar patients may be attributable to lithium treatment (22,23). Impairment of SPEM in schizophrenic patients may be related to poorer premorbid personality type (24), more recurrent hospitalizations and antipsychotic medication use, which suggests a worsening course (25), severity of illness (26), and severity of thought disorder on the Thought Disorder Inventory (TDI; ref 27), but SPEM impairment is not associated with positive psychotic symptoms in schizophrenic patients (25). Thus, SPEM impairment appears to be a state-independent correlate of schizophrenia that, in the absence of neurologic illness, recent sedative use, or acute decompensation, is relatively specific for the schizophrenia-related continuum of disorders and may be related to severity along this continuum.

Impairment of SPEM may serve as a psychophysiological measure of a broader, underlying disturbance in attentional and information processing, perhaps reflecting frontal cortical dysfunction (28–30). Impaired SPEM of the type observed in chronic schizophrenia seems to be a genetically determined abnormality, since it is observed twice as frequently in monozygotic twins as in dizygotic twins (31). Also, a significantly greater proportion of parents of schizophrenic patients have impaired SPEM than do parents of manic-depressive patients, who do not differ from normal subjects in their prevalence of SPEM impairment (32). However, SPEM impairment and schizophrenia do not invariably segregate together in the relatives of schizophrenic patients. To account for these observations, it has been suggested that the predisposition to schizophrenia is inherited as a latent trait that may be variably expressed as chronic schizophrenia and/or SPEM impairment. A mathematical model, developed from previous family studies of SPEM and schizophrenia, generates specific predictions regarding the prevalence of these disorders in families of schizophrenics (33).

SPEM impairment has been associated with higher scores on the Holzman Thought Disorder Inventory in schizophrenics' relatives even when these relatives were not overtly schizophrenic (34), raising the possibility that SPEM impairment may be associated with schizotypal features in the relatives of schizophrenics. A relationship between schizotypal-like characteristics and SPEM in nonclinical populations has been reported (35,36). Consistently low accuracy tracking in college student volunteers in a "biologic high risk" study was significantly associated with social isolation and incompetence, inadequate rapport, eccentricity, blunted affect, and cognitive and perceptual disturbances, but these tracking scores did not correlate with generalized psychopathologic symptoms, substance abuse, demographic characteristics, or other potentially confounding variables (37). The SPEM impairment was more closely correlated with the deficit symptomatology than the positive symptoms of schizotypal personality disorder and was not associated with other psychopathology. In this study, eye-tracking impairment was also associated with abnormalities on the CPT, longer reaction time, and soft neurological signs (37). Normal volunteers scoring high on the Chapman Physical Anhedonia Scale but not on the Chapman Perceptual Aberration Scale were also found to have significantly more deviant pursuit than control subjects (38). Thus,

SPEM impairment appears to extend beyond the boundaries of chronic schizophrenia to encompass individuals with schizotypal traits as well and seems to be more associated with the core schizotypal disturbances in social relatedness, affective expression, and cognitive and perceptual controls than with the positive psychotic-like symptoms.

Eye-tracking impairment has also been demonstrated in clinically identified schizotypal patients. In studies conducted in four groups at the Bronx VA Hospital, 26 schizotypal patients diagnosed by the Schedule for Interviewing DSM-III personality disorders (SIDP) demonstrated significantly worse eye tracking as measured by qualitative ratings of electro-oculographic records than did 34 normal controls ($p < .05$); 17 patients with other nonschizophrenia-related personality disorders did not differ from the controls. The schizotypal patients evidenced eye-tracking deficits comparable in magnitude to those of a control group of 44 chronic schizophrenic patients, who also differed significantly from the normal controls ($p < .05$). Groups were matched on age and demographic status and history of neuroleptic use; comorbid diagnoses of depression or borderline personality disorder also did not account for the finding. Eye-tracking accuracy was significantly negatively correlated with only one schizotypal criterion: social isolation, as well as with reduced level of desire for social contact.

Continuous Performance Task

The continuous performance task (CPT) is a test in which subjects must monitor a rapidly changing display and respond to the occurrence of a predetermined event. Schizophrenic patients make significantly more errors of omission and commission on this task than normals, and have slower response times than normals when they do it correctly (39). These errors may be conceptualized as a deficit in signal/noise discrimination or attention. High-processing-load versions of the CPT (ie, more demanding tasks using degraded stimuli that are less easy to recognize or sequential target arrays such as the standard A-X method identify attentional deficits in the offspring of schizophrenic patients (40), in individuals with schizotypal features (41), and in relatively stable remitted schizophrenic patients (42,43) as well as in actively symptomatic schizophrenic patients (43,44). These deficits are not seen in affective disorder in patients, their offspring, or other psychiatric disorders outside of the schizophrenia spectrum (44–46). Signal-discrimination deficits on the CPT (47) and a related attentional task, the forced-choice span of apprehension task (48), were found to be associated with fluid thinking but not with the maniclike combinatory cognitive patterns of the Holzman TDI in schizophrenic inpatients and outpatients; impaired CPT performance was also associated with an anergia factor (blunted affect, motor retardation, emotional withdrawal, and disorientation) on the Brief Psychiatric Rating Scale (BPRS), but not with positive psychotic symptomatology. College volunteers selected on the basis of a schizophrenialike profile on the MMPI scales were more likely to show CPT impairment than matched controls (49). Conversely, college volunteers identified on the basis of their high d' test scores reflecting poor signal detection on the CPT showed significant increases in scores on the Chapman Physical Anhedonia Scale compared to controls, but increases did not reach significance on the Chapman Perceptual Aberration Scale. Therefore, the CPT abnormality in signal discrimination observed in individuals with schizophrenia-related disorders, including schizotypal individuals, seems to be related to the core dysfunctions of affect and cognition characteristic of the schizophrenia-related disorders, but not as closely to the positive psychotic symptoms of schizophrenia. Preliminary results of a study at our center of clinically selected schizotypal patients compared to other non-schizophrenia-related personality disorder patients and normal controls suggest that schizotypal patients may also show impairment on the CPT.

Backward Masking

Backward masking is a phenomenon that occurs when a visual stimulus (the target) is presented tachistoscopically and is followed quickly by a second tachistoscopic stimulus (the mask) that commands attention but conveys no additional relevant information. The masking stimulus terminates any visual persistence of the target, which makes the target more difficult to identify. As the time between target and mask is increased, the subject is more easily able to identify the target. The critical or minimum time between the target and mask stimuli necessary to correctly identify the target (i.e., escape the effects of the mask) is a measure of the speed of information processing. Schizophrenic patients require a greater amount of time to escape the mask than do normals or depressed patients (50,51). The information-processing deficit identified by the backward-masking task appears to be a core trait of schizophrenia, but it can also occur as a state-dependent correlate of severe, acute psychotic illness (52). The degree of backward masking impairment has been shown to be associated more specifically with the negative than with the positive symptoms of schizophrenia (53,54).

Evidence in fact suggests that the masking abnormality reflects a fundamental neurophysiological disturbance across the spectrum of schizophrenia disorders. Although free of formal thought disorder, remitted schizophrenics have exhibited the same poor backward-masking performance as actively psychotic schizophrenics (55). Unmedicated schizotypal personality disorder patients are as impaired as chronic schizophrenic patients on the backward-masking task (56,57). The abnormality in masking performance cannot be attributed to artifacts of medication, hospitalization, or positive psychotic symptoms, as poor masking performance has been demonstrated in functioning nonpsychotic college volunteers selected by MMPI profiles associated with schizotypy or schizophrenia (58–64). Masking deficit has been associated with the degree of deviant verbalization as measured by Exner's (65) scoring of Rorschach responses in one of these college populations selected by virtue of its schizophrenia spectrum characteristics (63). Thus, a masking deficit may be observed in schizotypal individuals who are not actively psychotic, suggesting that this measure can robustly identify individuals on the schizophrenia-related continuum.

NEUROCHEMICAL MEASURES

The dopamine system continues to be implicated as important in the pathophysiology of schizophrenia, particularly in relation to psychotic symptoms (66–68), but the interpretation of studies of the dopamine system in schizophrenia is clouded by the fact that chronic neuroleptic treatment, which is nearly universal in schizophrenic patients, may induce alterations in dopamine metabolite concentrations and dopamine receptor sensitivity identical to those observed in schizophrenic patients, potential artifacts that are less prevalent in schizotypal patients. Concentrations of homovanillic acid (HVA) in cerebral spinal fluid (CSF) were significantly higher in a preliminary study of schizotypal personality disorder patients compared with non-schizophrenia-related personality disorder patients, despite a lack of significant difference in demographic or clinical variables or past medication use (Fig. 1). Concentrations of CSF HVA were not correlated with number of days off neuroleptic medication, and four of the five schizotypal patients

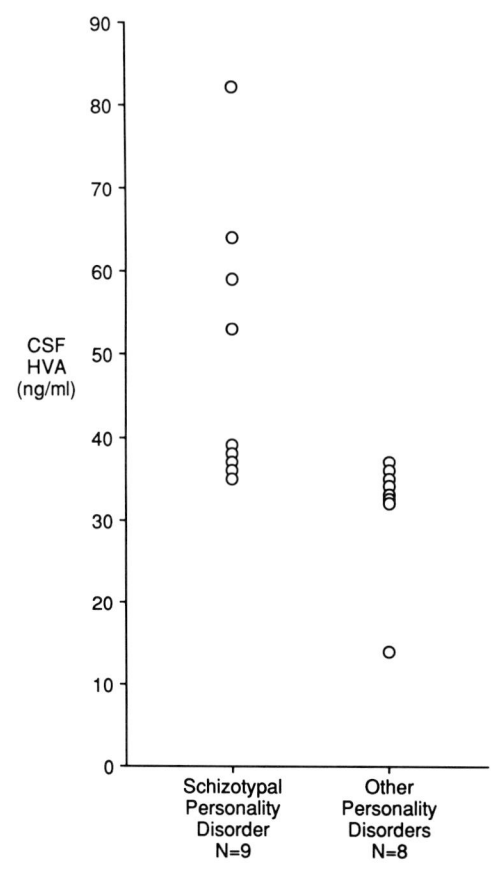

FIG. 1. Cerebrospinal fluid homovanillic acid in schizotypal and other personality disorders.

with CSF HVA concentrations greater than 1 SD above the other personality disorder controls had either never received neuroleptic medication or had not had neuroleptic in the 90 days prior to study. Concentrations of CSF HVA were significantly correlated by the Spearman coefficient with the sum of the positive psychoticlike symptoms (magical thinking, ideas of reference, recurrent illusions, and suspiciousness; $r = .56$, $df = 16$, $p < .05$), but not with the sum of the other deficit-related symptoms ($r = .23$, $df = 16$, $p = $ NS). The individual criteria of suspiciousness or paranoid ideation ($r = .61$, $df = 16$, $p < .01$), recurrent illusions ($r = .55$, $df = 16$, $p < .05$), and inadequate rapport ($r = .50$, $df = 16$, $p < .05$) were significantly correlated with CSF HVA concentrations, while criteria such as social isolation and social anxiety had nonsignificant correlations with CSF HVA. Concentrations of CSF HVA also correlated significantly with the Chapman psychosis-proneness scales in the subsample of patients where this was available (Perceptual Aberration Scale: $r = .83$, $df = 11$, $p < .05$; Physical Anhedonia Scale: $r = .77$, $df = 11$, $p < .05$). These significant preliminary results suggest that CSF HVA may be increased in schizotypal patients compared with individuals with other personality disorder controls and that these increases may be more closely associated with positive psychoticlike symptoms than with deficit symptoms.

In our preliminary studies, plasma HVA concentrations obtained between 9 AM and 10 AM at bed rest with an indwelling intravenous line also proved to be significantly higher in schizotypal patients than in other personality disorder controls. No differences were observed between the two groups in other patient characteristics or prior neuroleptic use (Fig. 2). In another study, conducted at the Schizophrenic Biologic Research Center (SBRC), plasma HVA concentrations in schizotypal patients were also significantly greater than those in 10 AM samples from a group of 14 normal controls (8.8 ± 0.8 ng/ml) (t-test, $p < .01$) tested at the end of an overnight stay (68); aside from the altered time period, in other respects this study was methodologically identical to the present study. Nine of ten of the schizotypal patients were more than 2 SD from the normal mean, while only one of the four other personality disorder controls was increased more than 2 SD from the mean ($p < .05$, Fisher's Exact). There was no significant correlation between time off neuroleptic medication or any of the clinical or demographic variables and plasma HVA concentrations. Four of the seven schizotypal patients with plasma HVA concentrations greater than 14 ng/ml had not received neuroleptic medication within 75 days prior to the plasma HVA

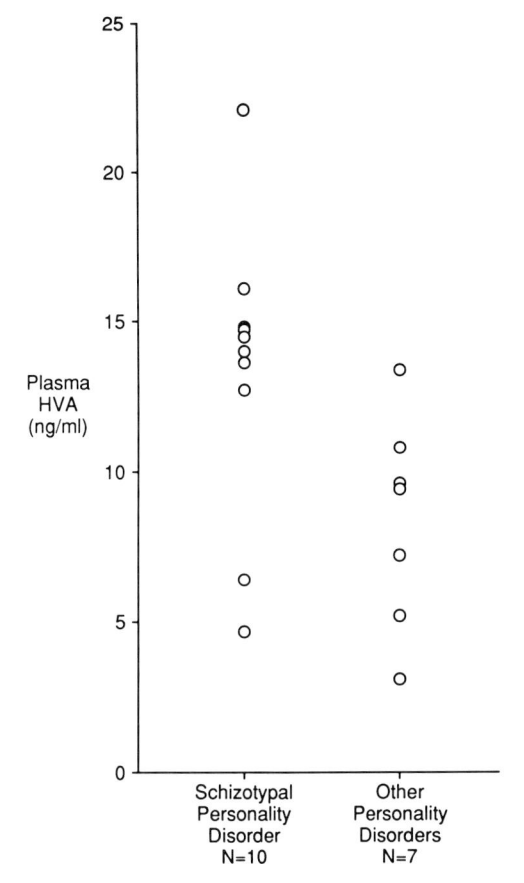

FIG. 2. Plasma homovanillic acid in schizotypal and other personality disorders.

protocol or had never received neuroleptic treatment. Plasma HVA correlated significantly with odd speech ($r = .75$, $df = 12$, $p < .05$), suspiciousness ($r = .54$, $df = 12$, $p < .05$), and inadequate rapport ($r = .57$, $df = 12$, $p < .05$) and nonsignificant correlations greater than .35 were observed for magical thinking ($r = .38$) and ideas of reference ($r = .37$), while correlations with the sum of psychoticlike symptoms and the sum of deficit symptoms did not reach significance. These preliminary results are consonant with the results of the CSF HVA study in suggesting the presence of at least a subgroup of schizotypal patients with altered dopamine function.

Although the measurement of growth hormone (GH) is not a direct test of dopaminergic activity, GH is modulated in part by catecholaminergic activity, and increased GH secretory bursts and increased GH secretion is observed in chronic schizophrenic patients compared with controls and correlated with their psychotic symptom (69). The GH coefficient of variation in our preliminary sample of schizotypal patients was similar to that of chronic schizophrenic patients, who significantly differ from normal controls. There was no difference from a small sample of other personality disorder controls and no correlations with specific schizotypal criteria, so that the specificity of this finding and its relation to psychoticlike symptoms is unclear.

DISCUSSION

A growing body of evidence suggests that the boundaries of schizophrenia encompass schizotypal individuals both among the relatives of schizophrenic patients and among clinically defined personality disorder patients. It appears that schizotypal personality disorder may be a more common schizophrenia-related disorder than chronic schizophrenia itself with implications for the nosology as well as future biological and genetic studies of schizophrenia.

Nosologic Implications

While chronic schizophrenia may be more prevalent in clinical settings and is certainly more costly to treat, individuals with schizophrenia-related personality disorders, who may not seek clinical treatment, may constitute the majority of individuals on the schizophrenia continuum. How far the boundaries of the schizophrenia spectrum extend remains to be determined. Some studies suggest that at least a subgroup of individuals with paranoid personality disorder (70,71) and possibly schizoid personality disorder as defined by DSM-III-R (72) may fall on the schizophrenia spectrum. Genetic studies suggest that even some milder variants of the schizophrenia-related personality disorders that do not fully meet criteria for either schizotypal, paranoid, or schizoid personality disorder should be considered among the schizophrenia-related disorders. It remains to be determined whether such individuals exhibit distinctive traits or symptoms that might distinguish them from other individuals who appear "schizoid" but are unrelated to the schizophrenia spectrum.

For example, social isolation might be attributable to extreme rejection sensitivity (e.g., in avoidant personality disorder), inability to maintain relationships due to chronically unstable behavior (e.g., in borderline personality disorder), or to a genuine lack of desire or capacity to develop interactions with others. The last characteristic might have greater specificity for truly schizophrenia-related personality disorders. Psychoticlike symptoms such as perceptual distortions or paranoid ideation might occur in the context of dissociative episodes, affective episodes, or transient stress-related emotional turmoil as in individuals with borderline or histrionic personality disorder, while it may be that only persistent suspiciousness or perceptual and cognitive distortions characterize truly schizophrenia-related personality disorders. Genetic and biologic studies may be useful in validating an association with the schizophrenia spectrum of more specific and refined traits than those currently defined by DSM-III-R.

It is conceivable that some characteristics of these milder variants of schizophrenia-related personality disorder may even have adaptive advantages. For example, a detached, guarded individual may survive catastrophic events better than more normal individuals. While these considerations are speculative, they might explain the persistence of genes predisposing to schizophrenia despite the documented lower fertility of chronic schizophrenics. The use of genetic and biologic tools (eg, genetic and biologic "high-risk" studies) may help to identify adaptive characteristics of individuals with a relationship to schizophrenia who do not show up in clinical settings.

At our present level of knowledge, it is clear that clinically identified schizotypal-personality-disorder patients should be acknowledged in psychiatric diagnostic classification systems (e.g., DSM-IV) as a schizophrenia-related disorder. However, because it is manifested as a personality disorder and its characteristics may be easily mimicked by non-schizophrenia-related personality disorders, it needs to be included in Axis II as well. Further research needs to be done using genetic and biologic validators to determine the best criteria for this disorder.

Genetic Implications

Genetic studies that identify rigorously diagnosed schizotypal individuals among the relatives of schizophrenic patients may have a greater likelihood of identifying linkage than those that rely only on the identification of chronic schizophrenic individuals. Genetic studies that rely solely on large multiplex pedigrees with numerous chronic schizophrenic individuals may identify atypical populations, while considering schizotypal relatives of chronic schizophrenic patients as "affected" may extend the power of RFLP linkage studies to encompass more typical schizophrenic families. A conservative strategy necessitates stringent criteria; one example is to require the presence of deficit as well as psychoticlike symptoms for the schizotypal-affected relatives to avoid false positives in linkage analyses. The use of biologic correlates such as eye-tracking impairment associated with the schizophrenia spectrum may enhance the confidence in identifying affected relatives over clinical assessment alone.

Since the incidence of both schizophrenia-related personality disorders and psychotic disorders other than chronic schizophrenia are increased in the families of chronic schizophrenic probands, the possibility of more complex genetic transmission models might be considered; for example, one gene might predispose the individual to the deficit symptoms of the schizophrenia-related personality disorders and another gene might predispose to severe psychotic symptoms. While specific models may be premature at this stage, the identification of biologic correlates (which are more specific for the asociality and other deficit symptoms associated with the schizophrenia spectrum) and of other correlates associated more with psychosis generically may augment the power of analyses examining such possibilities in linkage studies.

Pathophysiologic Implications

Studies of the biology of the boundaries may provide clues to the pathophysiology of schizophrenia. Abnormalities in indices of attention and information processing such as eye tracking or backward masking may reflect cortical dysfunction, particularly in association areas crucial to attention such as the dorsolateral prefrontal cortex or the temporal cortex. In fact, SPEM inaccuracy in schizophrenia has also been associated with increased VBR and reversed occipital asymmetry (25,73) and poorer neuropsychological performance on tests of frontoparietal function (25) in schizophrenic patients. It has been argued that the SPEM impairment may derive from impairment in frontal preattentive control of saccadic eye movements (74). Regardless of the precise neuroanatomic substrate for this finding, the SPEM impairment may be associated with other indices of subtle neurologic and attentional dysfunction perhaps as part of an inherited CNS abnormality in the schizophrenia-related disorders.

These variables may be more specifically associated with "negative" or deficit symptoms of the schizophrenia spectrum in both schizophrenic and schizotypal individuals. Abnormalities in dopaminergic metabolism may be more related to active psychotic symptoms in both schizophrenic and schizotypal patients. The mapping of the presence of these abnormalities and their association with specific symptoms in chronic schizophrenia, in other psychotic disorders including psychotic affective disorders, and in the schizophrenia-related personality disorders may increase our understanding of the pathogenesis of schizophrenia and illuminate biologic differences between schizophrenic patients who display chronic, severe psychotic symptoms and schizotypal patients who remain isolated but lead functional lives. Post mortem studies of these populations could additionally help clarify questions of whether psychophysiologic abnormalities and/or deficit symptoms correlate with anatomic abnormalities such as disordered dendritic organization and positive psychoticlike symptoms with altered dopamine concentrations in subcortical areas. In these ways, measurement of biologic correlates along the schizophrenia spectrum may permit the dissection of interacting biological factors in the pathogenesis of schizophrenia.

REFERENCES

1. Kendler KS, Gruenberg AM, Tsuang MT. Psychiatric illness in first-degree relatives of schizophrenic and surgical control patients: A family study using DSM-III criteria. *Arch Gen Psychiatry* 1985;42:770–779.
2. Kety SS, Rosenthal D, Wender PH, et al. Mental illness in the biological and adoptive families of adopted individuals who have become schizophrenic: A preliminary report based on psychiatric interviews. In R Fieve, D Rosenthal, H Brill, eds. *Genetic research in psychiatry*. Baltimore: Johns Hopkins Press, 1975;147–165.
3. Rosenthal D, Wender PH, Kety SS, et al. The adopted-away offspring of schizophrenics. *Am J Psychiatry* 1971;128:307–311.
4. Spitzer RL, Endicott J, Gibbon M. Crossing the border into borderline personality and borderline schizophrenia: The development of criteria. *Arch Gen Psychiatry* 1979;36:17–24.
5. Kendler KS. Diagnostic approaches to schizotypal personality disorder: A historical perspective. *Schizophr Bull* 1985;11:538–553.
6. Torgerson S. Relationship of schizotypal per-

sonality disorder to schizophrenia: genetics. *Schizophr Bull* 1985;11(4):554–563.
7. Siever LJ. Biologic markers in schizotypal personality disorder. *Schizophr Bull* 1985;11:564–575.
8. McGlashan TH. Schizotypal personality disorder. Chestnut Lodge follow-up study. VI. Longterm follow-up perspective. *Arch Gen Psychiatry* 1986;43:329–334.
9. Goldberg SC, Schulz SC, Schulz PM. Borderline and schizotypal personality disorders treated with low-dose thiothixene vs. placebo. *Arch Gen Psychiatry* 1986;43:680–686.
10. Kendler KS, Gruenberg AM, Strauss JS. An independent analysis of the Copenhagen sample of the Danish Abortion Study of Schizophrenia. *Arch Gen Psychiatry* 1981;38:982–984.
11. Kendler KS, Masterson CC, Ungaro R, et al. A family history study of schizophrenia-related personality disorders. *Am J Psychiatry* 1984; 141:424–427.
12. Stone MH. The borderline syndrome: Evolution of the term, genetic aspects and prognosis. *Am J Psychother* 1977;345–365.
13. Soloff PH, Millward JW. Psychiatric disorders in the families of borderline patients. *Arch Gen Psychiatry* 1983;40:37–44.
14. Schulz PM, Schulz SC, Goldberg SC, et al. Diagnoses of the relatives of schizotypal outpatients. *J Nerv Ment Dis* 1986;174:457–463.
15. Baron M, Gruen R, Asnis L, et al. Familial transmission of schizotypal and borderline personality disorders. *Am J Psychiatry* 1985;142: 927–934.
16. Siever LJ, Silverman JM, Horvath TH, et al. Increased morbid risk for schizophrenia-related disorders in relatives of schizotypal personality disordered patients. *Arch Gen Psychiat* 1990;47: 634–640.
17. Lipton RB, Levy DL, Holzman PS, Levin S. Eye movement dysfunctions in psychiatric patients: A review. *Schizophr Bull* 1983;9:13–32.
18. Abel LA, Ziegler AS. Smooth pursuit eye movements in schizophrenics—What constitutes quantitative assessment? *Biol Psychiatry* 1988;24:747–761.
19. Yee RD, Baloh RW, Marder SR, Levy DL, Sakala SM, Honrubia V. Eye movements in schizophrenia. *Invest Ophthalmol Vis Sci* 1987;28:366–374.
20. Iacono WG, Tuason VB, Johnson RA. Dissociation of smooth pursuit and saccadic eye tracking in remitted schizophrenics. *Arch Gen Psychiatry* 1981;38:991–996.
21. Shagass C, Roemer RA, Amadeo M. Eye-tracking performance in psychiatric patients. *Biol Psychiatry* 1974;9:245–260.
22. Iacono WG, Peloquin LJ, Lumry AE, Valentine RH, Tuason VB. Eye tracking in patients with unipolar and bipolar affective disorders in remission. *J Abnorm Psychol* 1982;91:35–44.
23. Levy DL, Dorcas E, Shaughnessy R, Yasillo NJ, Pandey GN, Janicak PG, Gibbons RD, Gavira M, Davis JM. Pharmacologic evidence for specificity of pursuit dysfunction to schizophrenia. *Arch Gen Psychiatry* 1985;42:335–341.
24. Siever LJ, van Kammen DP, Linnoila M, Alterman I, Hare T, Murphy DL. Smooth pursuit eye movement disorder and its psychobiologic correlates in unmedicated schizophrenics. *Biol Psychiatry* 1986;21:1167–1174.
25. Bartfai A, Levander SE, Sedvall G. Smooth pursuit eye movements, clinical symptoms, CSF metabolites and skin conductance habituation in schizophrenic patients. *Biol Psychiatry* 1983; 18:971–986.
26. Keefe RSE, Siever LJ, Mohs RC, Peterson A, Mahon T, Bergman RL, Davis KL. Clinical correlates of eye tracking impairment in individuals with schizophrenia and schizotypal personality disorders. *Int Arch Neurol* 1990;(in press).
27. Solomon CM, Holzman PS, Levin S, Gale HJ. The association between eye tracking dysfunction and thought disorder in psychosis. *Arch Gen Psychiatry* 1987;44:31–35.
28. Holzman PS. Recent studies of psychophysiology in schizophrenia. *Schizophr Bull* 1987;13 (1):49–75.
29. Holzman PS, Levy DL. Smooth-pursuit eye movements and functional psychoses: A review. *Schizophr Bull* 1977;3:15–27.
30. Levin S, Luebke A, Zee DS, Hain TC, Robinson DA, Holzman PS. Smooth pursuit eye movements in schizophrenics: Quantitative measurements with the search-coil technique. *J Psychiatry Res* 1984;18:27–55.
31. Holzman PS, Kringlen E, Levy DL, Haberman S. Deviant eye tracking in twins discordant for psychosis: A replication. *Arch Gen Psychiatry* 1980;37:627–631.
32. Holzman PS, Solomon CM, Levin S, Waternaux CS. Pursuit eye movement dysfunctions in schizophrenia: Family evidence for specificity. *Arch Gen Psychiatry* 1984;41:136–139.
33. Matthysse S, Holzman PS, Lange K. The genetic transmission of schizophrenia: Application of Mendeliam latent structure analysis to eye tracking dysfunctions in schizophrenia and affective disorder. *J Psychiatry Res* 1986;20(1):57–67.
34. Holzman PS, Proctor LR, Levy DL, Yasillo NJ, Meltzer HY, Hurt SW. Eye tracking dysfunctions in schizophrenic patients and their relatives. *Arch Gen Psychiatry* 1974;31:143–151.
35. Siever LJ, Coursey RD, Alterman IS, Buchsbaum MS. Smooth pursuit eye movement impairment: A vulnerability marker for schizotypal personality disorder in a volunteer population. *Am J Psychiatry* 1986;141:1560–1566.
36. Van den Bosch RJ. Eye tracking impairment: Attentional and psychometric correlates in psychiatric patients. *J Psychiatry Res* 1984;18:277–286.
37. Siever LJ, Coursey RD, Alterman IS, Zahn T, Brody L, Bernad P, Buchsbaum M, Lake CR, Murphy DL. Clinical Psychophysiologic and neurologic characteristics of volunteers with impaired smooth pursuit eye movements. *Biol Psychiatry* 1989;26:35–51.
38. Simons RF, Watkins W. Smooth pursuit eye movements in subjects reporting physical anhedonia and perceptual aberrations. *Psychiatry Res* 1985;14:275–289.
39. Nuechterlein KH, Dawson ME. Information

40. Rutschmann J, Cornblatt B, Erlenmeyer-Kimling L. Sustained attention in children at risk for schizophrenia: Report on a continuous performance test. *Arch Gen Psychiatry* 1977;34:571–575.
41. Nuechterlein KH. In: Alpert M, ed. *Controversies in schizophrenia,* New York: Guilford Press, 1987;175–198.
42. Wohlberg GW, Kornetsky C. Sustained attention in remitted schizophrenics. *Arch Gen Psychiatry* 1973;28:533–537.
43. Asarnow RF, MacGrimmon DJ. Residual performance deficit in clinically remitted schizophrenics: A marker of schizophrenia? *J Abnorm Psychol* 1978;87:597–608.
44. Walker E. Attentional and neuromotor functions of schizophrenics, schizoaffectives, and patients with other affective disorders. *Arch Gen Psychiatry* 1981;38:1355–1358.
45. Nuechterlein KH. Signal detection in vigilance tasks and behavioral attributes among offspring of schizophrenic mothers and among hyperactive children. *J Abnorm Psychol* 1983;92:4–28.
46. Erlenmeyer-Kimling L, Cornblatt B. The New York High-Risk Project: A followup report. *Schizophr Bull* 1978;13(3):451–461.
47. Nuechterlein KH, Edell WS, Norris M, Dawson ME. Attentional vulnerability indicators, thought disorder, and negative symptoms. *Schizophr Bull* 1986;12:408–426.
48. Asarnow RF, Steffy RA, MacCrimmon DJ, Cleghorn JM. An attentional assessment of foster children at risk for schizophrenia. *J Abnorm Psychol* 1977;86:267–275.
49. Nuechterlein K. Converging evidence for vigilance deficit as a vulnerability indicator for schizophrenic disorders. In: Albert M ed. *Controversies in schizophrenia: changes and constances.* New York: Guilford Press, 1985;175–198.
50. Braff DL, Saccuzzo DP. The time course of information-processing deficits in schizophrenia. *Am J Psychiatry* 1985;142:170–174.
51. Saccuzzo DP, Hirt M, Spencer TJ. Backward masking as a measure of attention in schizophrenia. *J Abnorm Psychol* 1974;83:512–522.
52. Saccuzzo DP, Braff DL. Information-processing abnormalities: Trait- and state-dependent components. *Schizophr Bull* 1986;12:447–459.
53. Green M, Walker E. Susceptibility to backward masking in schizophrenic patients with positive or negative symptoms. *Am J Psychiatry* 1984;141:1273–1275.
54. Green M, Walker E. Symptom correlates of vulnerability to backward masking in schizophrenia. *Am J Psychiatry* 1986;143:181–186.
55. Miller S, Saccuzzo DP, Braff DL. Information processing deficits in remitted schizophrenics. *J Abnorm Psychol* 1979;88:446–449.
56. Saccuzzo DP, Schubert DL. Backward masking as a measure of slow processing in schizophrenia spectrum disorders. *J Abnorm Psychol* 1981;86:261–266.
57. Braff DL. Impaired speed of information processing in nonmedicated schizotypal patients. *Schizophr Bull* 1981;7:499–506.
58. Sterenko RJ, Woods DJ. Impairment in early stages of visual information processing in nonpsychotic schizotypic individuals. *J Abnorm Psychol* 1978;87:481–490.
59. Merritt RD, Balogh DW. The use of a backward masking paradigm to assess the visual information processing of schizotypics: A re-evaluation of Sterenko and Woods. *J Nerv Ment Dis* 1984;172:216–224.
60. Merritt RD, Balogh DW. Critical stimulus duration: Schizophrenic state or trait? *Schizophr Bull* 1985;11:341–343.
61. Merritt RD, Balogh DW, Leventhal DB. The use of a metacontrast and a paracontrast procedure to assess the visual information processing of schizotypics. *J Abnorm Psychol* 1986;94:74–80.
62. Saccuzzo DP, Braff DL, Sprock J, Sudick N. The schizophrenia spectrum: A study of the relationship among the Rorschach, MMPI, and visual backward masking. *J Clin Psychol* 1984;40:1288–1294.
63. Balogh DW, Merritt RD. Visual masking and the schizophrenia spectrum: Interfacing clinical and experimental methods. *Schizophr Bull* 1987;13(4):679–698.
64. Nakano K, Saccuzzo DP. Schizotaxia, information processing, and the MMPI 2-7-8 code type. *Br J Clin Psychol* 1985;24(3):217–218.
65. Exner JE. *The Rorschach: a comprehensive system,* vol. 1. New York: John Wiley, 1974.
66. Davis KL, Davidson M, Mohs RC, et al. Plasma HVA concentrations correlate with the severity of schizophrenic illness. *Science* 1985;227:1601–1602.
67. Pickar D, Labarca R, Doran A, et al. Longitudinal measurement of plasma homovanillic acid levels in schizophrenic patients. *Arch Gen Psychiatry* 1986;43:669–676.
68. Davidson M, Keefe RS, Mohs RC, et al. Sinemet challenge and relapse in schizophrenia. *Am J Psychiatry* 1987;144:934–938.
69. Davis KL, Fiori M, Davis BM, Mohs RC, Horvath TB, Davidson M. Dopaminergic dysregulation in schizophrenia. *Drug Develop Res* 1986;9:71–83.
70. Kendler KS, Gruenberg AM. Genetic relationship between paranoid personality disorder and the "schizophrenia spectrum" disorders. *Am J Psychiatry* 1982;139:1185–1186.
71. Stevens DA, Atkinson MW, Day DWK, Roth M, Garside RF. Psychiatric morbidity in parents and sibs. of schizophrenics and non-schizophrenics. *Br J Psychiatry* 1975;127:97–108.
72. Gunderson JG, Siever LJ, Spaulding E. The search for a schizotype: Crossing the border again. *Arch Gen Psychiatry* 1983;40:15–22.
73. Weinberger DR. Implications of normal brain development for the pathogenesis of schizophrenia. *Arch Gen Psychiatry* 1987;44:660–670.
74. Levin S. Frontal lobe dysfunctions in schizophrenia—II. Impairments of psychological and brain functions. *J Psychiatr Res* 1984;18:57–72.

18

The Schizophrenia Spectrum Concept

The Chestnut Lodge Follow-up Study

Thomas H. McGlashan[1]

The schizophrenia spectrum concept has followed schizophrenia through the 20th century like a hesperian shadow. No single person can claim responsibility for its articulation; it is itself the creation of a spectrum. Kraepelin (1), for example, first described people with paranoid personalities. These were pervasively mistrustful individuals who frequently developed delusional thinking without functional deterioration. Bleuler (2) defined schizoid or socially isolated personalities, some of whom, according to him, eventually developed schizophrenia, others of whom were found in the families of schizophrenic patients. Zilboorg (3) described cases he termed "ambulatory schizophrenia" (i.e., functioning individuals with mild clinical signs of schizophrenia). He was perhaps the first to distinguish psychopathologic state from trait, and he postulated that while these people did not suffer from the active clinical *state* of schizophrenia, they did possess the same symptomatic *trait* or vulnerability as did patients on the back wards. Around the same time, Helena Deutsch (4) described the "as if" character and regarded it as related somehow to schizophrenia. Striking in her description were deficits in the sense of self: i.e., non-ego-alien depersonalization, inner emptiness, impoverished mutual relationships, and a mirroring or imitative identifications with others.

In the 1950s Sandor Rado (5) hypothesized that schizophrenia begins with an inherited disposition or genotype. The interaction of this genotype with environment produces the schizophrenic phenotype—a type or trait called the *schizotype*. Central to this trait is an inherent incapacity to experience pleasure. "In the schizotype the machinery of psychodynamic integration is strikingly inadequate, because one of its essential components, the organizing action of pleasure—its motivational strength—is innately defective" (ref. 5, p 276). This defect impairs the development of initiative and leads to schizo adaptations such as compensatory overdependence on others (especially parents) and the elaboration of intricate cognitive processes devoid of affect. Anhedonia results in weak emotional bonds and leads to attenuated relationships. The well-compensated schizotype remains a stable schizoid personality. The poorly compensated schizotype develops exaggerated, bizarre behaviors. Schizophrenia proper represents the decompensated schizotype with adaptive incompetence. According to Rado, the nature and severity of the schizo adaptation depends on the genotypic loading, on the one hand, and the degree of familial and environmental stress on the other.

[1] Chestnut Lodge Research Institute, Rockville, MD 20850. *Current affiliation*: Yale Psychiatric Institute, New Haven, CT 06519.

In the 1960s Meehl elaborated on Rado's model (6). He asserted research would establish that, while the content of schizophrenia was learned, it was basically a neurologic disease of genetic origin. To Meehl the inherited schizophrenic genotype consisted of a defect in neural integration.

> Granting its initial vagueness as a construct, requiring to be filled in by neurophysiological research, I believe we should take seriously the old European notion of an integrative neural defect as the only direct phenotypic consequence produced by the genic mutation. . . . This neural integrative defect, which I shall christen schizotaxia is all that can properly be spoken of as inherited. The imposition of a social learning history upon schizotaxic individuals results in a personality organization which I shall call, following Rado, the schizotype (ref. 6, pp 829–830).

His schizotype possessed four central traits: cognitive slippage, anhedonia, ambivalence, and interpersonal aversiveness. Furthermore,

> the four core behavior traits are obviously not innate; but I postulate that they are universally learned by schizotaxic individuals, given any of the actually existing social reinforcement regimens, from the best to the worst. If the interpersonal regimen is favorable . . . he will remain a well compensated, "normal" schizotype, never manifesting symptoms of mental disease. . . . Only a subset of schizotypic personalities decompensate into clinical schizophrenia (ref. 6, p 830).

Kety and colleagues (7) introduced the term *schizophrenic spectrum disorder* in their Danish Adoption Studies of the late 1960s and early 1970s. They used this concept to refer nonpsychotic character pathology frequently present in the biological relatives of schizophrenic probands. These borderline or latent schizophrenic relatives were eccentric, detached, and presented perceptual, cognitive, and interpersonal features resembling schizophrenic symptoms but without the full-blown clinical picture or deteriorating course. They demonstrated a genetic link between these disorders and chronic schizophrenia.

When drafting the Diagnostic and Statistical Manual of Mental Disorders III (DSM-III; ref. 8) in the late 1970s, Spitzer and colleagues (9) reviewed the borderline concept and found it heterogeneous. They postulated that the category *borderline* encompassed at least two constructs: unstable personality, which became borderline personality disorder, and borderline schizophrenia, which became schizotypal personality disorder. They developed criteria for the latter from the spectrum cases of the Danish Adoption Studies.

The 1980s have witnessed an explosion of investigations into the schizophrenia spectrum. Most of the work upholds the distinction made by DSM-III (8) between borderline personality disorder and schizotypal personality disorder and suggests that the latter may be the prototypic spectrum disorder of schizophrenia—the phenotype of the schizophrenic genotype. The other two inhabitants of DSM-III's odd cluster—paranoid personality disorder and schizoid personality disorder—are also candidates. Paranoid personality disorder has been found in the first-degree relatives of patients with schizophrenia and especially in the first-degree relatives of patients with delusional disorders (10). The adoption studies failed to link schizoid personality to schizophrenia, but too little data have been generated about patients meeting current definitions of schizoid personality disorder to draw any conclusions yet.

VALIDATION OF SCHIZOTYPAL PERSONALITY DISORDER IN THE SCHIZOPHRENIA SPECTRUM

Family studies have provided the most consistent validation of schizotypal (SPD) and paranoid personality disorders (PPD) as part of the schizophrenia spectrum. Most studies using DSM-III (8) criteria and personal interviews from this decade confirm a higher prevalence of both disorders in the first-degree relatives of schizophrenic probands versus relatives of normal controls (10–12). The biological and laboratory variables linking schizotypal personality disorder with schizophrenia are striking, especially smooth-pursuit eye movements. They have been reviewed by Siever and colleagues (13–15).

Without generally acceptable diagnostic criteria, studies of the long-term course and outcome of the schizotype were nonexistent prior to this decade. DSM-III (8) and the Chestnut Lodge Follow-up Study (16,17) provided an opportunity to conduct long-term outcome assessments on a group of former inpatients with schizotypal personality disorder and to compare them with a group of patients with schizophrenia and with borderline personality disorder. From the total pool of follow-up subjects, and using ratings achieved mostly on DSM-III, six cohorts were identified for study (18): schizophrenia alone ($N = 53$), mixed schizophrenia and schizotypal personality disorder ($N = 61$), mixed schizophrenia and schizotypal personality disorder plus borderline personality disorder ($N = 30$), schizotypal personality disorder alone ($N = 10$), mixed schizotypal personality disorder and borderline personality disorder ($N = 18$), and borderline personality disorder alone ($N = 81$).

Schizotypal personality disorder was common in this hospitalized sample although rare as a pure syndrome. Only ten (2.2%) of the total sample of 446 study subjects met the DSM-III (8) criteria for SPD without also meeting the criteria for Axis 1 schizophrenia and affective disorder or for Axis 2 borderline personality disorder. At baseline or index admission, the majority of this non-comorbid sample was single (70%). There was a slight predominance of males (60%). All were white and they averaged 1.6 on the Hollingshead-Redlich Scale of Socioeconomic Status (19). Premorbid functioning was poor socially but good instrumentally. Their average IQ was 124 or bright–normal.

Psychopathologically, the average schizotypal patient first developed symptoms at age 19, initially entered their first hospital at age 26, and came to Chestnut Lodge at age 28 after 22 months of outpatient treatment and approximately two hospitalizations totaling 16 months in length. Overall, the schizotypals turned out as expected. They had good intellectual endowment, solid instrumental skills, and had achieved quite satisfactorily in the educational realm. Socially, however, they were withdrawn and seclusive. This was different from (and worse than) the premorbid social functioning of the schizophrenic patients (18).

The sum global functioning scores shown in Fig. 1 summarize many of the long-term trends. This measure covered the entire follow-up period and consists of the sum of the scores on the individual outcome dimensions of hospitalization, time symptomatic, work, and social functioning. There is a consistent augmentation of scores, or better functioning, on moving from the Axis 1 to Axis 2 cohorts. Within Axis 1, global outcome improved slightly (but not significantly) with the addition of schizotypal and borderline traits. Within Axis 2 the borderline and mixed schizotypal-borderline samples scored best and were virtually equivalent. The schizotypal sample emerged intermediate between the Axis 1 schizophrenic and the Axis 2 borderline groups, although the small size of the pure schizotypal cohort prevented any differences from achieving statistical significance. Nevertheless, they scored closer to the Axis 1 groups than they did to their Axis 2 spectrum partners. However, the mixed syndrome functioned much more like borderline personality disorder than like schizotypal personality disorder. Overall, we found the inpatient schizotype to be rare as a singular syndrome but frequent as a co-

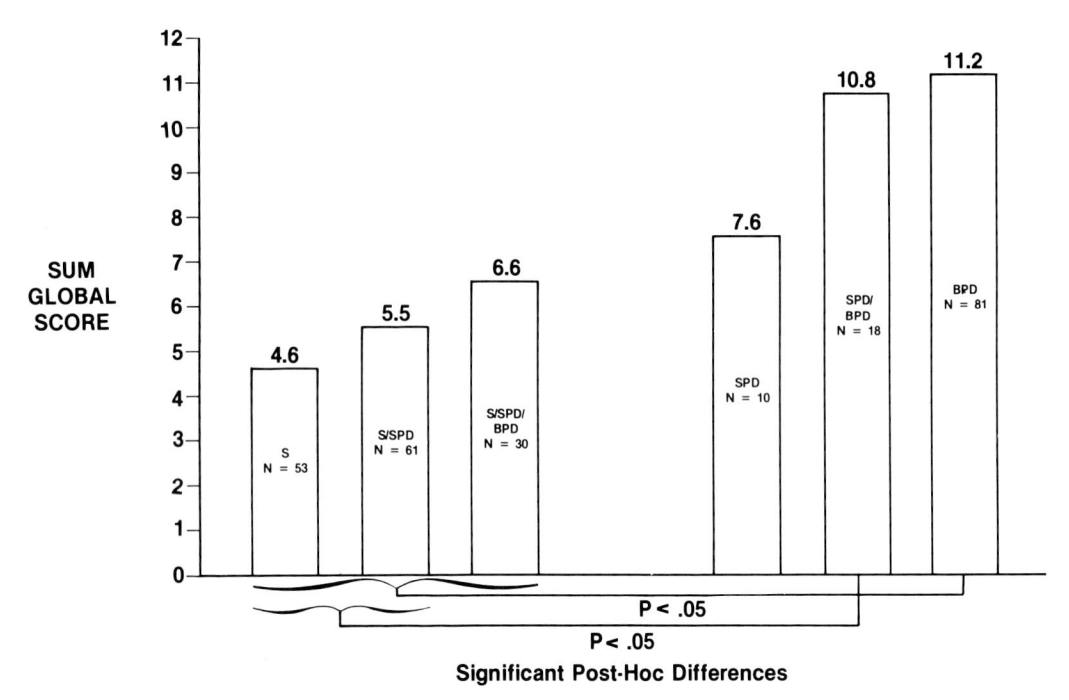

FIG. 1. Schizotypal personality disorder comparison groups, sum global outcome.

morbid entity. From the perspective of long-term outcome, the disorder appeared related to schizophrenia but not to borderline personality disorder.

As noted, there were few pure schizotypes in our study. Combining them with the mixed cohort, however, gave us a respectable baseline sample of 33, 17 males and 16 females. Using this sample, we looked for gender differences in clinical profile and long-term course (20). Such differences are well known and studied in the psychoses like schizophrenia, but not in the personality disorders. As shown in Table 1, our female schizotypal patients were superior to males in premorbid social and sexual functioning, the same trend as in the schizophrenic female patients. They also had a similar gender difference pattern with respect to IQ. Males were socially and sexually isolated up to index admission, and women were superior in symptom severity. At 15-year follow-up, shown in Table 2, schizotypal women were superior in symptom severity and global functioning. Overall, the pattern of gender differences echoed, to a muted degree, the pattern found among our schizophrenic cohort. We suggest these results constitute yet another line of evidence placing schizotypal personality disorder within the schizophrenic spectrum.

Our most compelling evidence of the schizotypes' link with the schizophrenia spectrum came from tracking a subgroup of character-disordered patients from our follow-up study who were independently rediagnosed as schizophrenic at long-term follow-up (21). One hundred five patients came to our hospital meeting criteria for borderline, schizotypal, or both *without* meeting criteria for an Axis 1 schizophrenic or affective disorder. Seventeen percent of these ($N = 18$), however, developed schizophrenia or schizoaffective psychosis an average of 15 years later. Psychosis at follow-up meant the patient demonstrated evidence of positive psychotic symptoms,

TABLE 1. *Schizophrenia and schizotypal personality disorder: baseline sex differences*

			Diagnostic cohort	
Dimension	Variable	Direction	Schizophrenia ($N = 188$)	Schizotypal personality disorder ($N = 33$)
Demography	Married	Yes	♀	
Premorbid	Sexual functioning	Better	♀	♀
	Social functioning	Better	♀	♀
	IQ	Higher	♂	♂
	Prognostic scale	Better	♀	

TABLE 2. *Schizophrenia and schizotypal personality disorder: outcome sex differences*

			Diagnostic cohort	
Dimension	Variable	Direction	Schizophrenia ($N = 163$)	Schizotypal personality disorders ($N = 28$)
Social	Frequency of social contact	Higher	♀	
Psychopathology	Time when symptomatic	Less	♀	
	Symptom severity	Less		♀
Global	Clinical global	Better	♀	
	Health-sickness rating scale	Better		♀

TABLE 3. *Clinical features predicting follow-up diagnosis of schizophrenia among hospitalized patients with character disorders ($N = 105$)*

Diagnostic	Schizophrenia at follow-up	No schizophrenia ($N = 87$)	t (df)	p
DSM-III SPD total	2.8 ± 1.2	1.8 ± 1.4	2.80 (103)	<.006
DSM-III BPD total	3.6 ± 1.5	4.3 ± 1.5	−2.06 (103)	<.04
Gunderson et al total	5.4 ± 1.8	6.4 ± 1.7	−2.30 (103)	<.02

TABLE 4. *Sensitivity of DSM-III schizotypal items among character-disordered patients with ($N = 18$) and without ($N = 87$) follow-up diagnosis of schizophrenia*

DSM-III schizotypal items	Schizophrenia at follow-up ($N = 18$)	No schizophrenia ($N = 87$)	p
Odd communication	22	15	NS[a]
Ideas of reference	11	15	NS
Paranoia/suspiciousness	44	16	.02
Depersonalization/illusions	6	20	NS
Magical thinking	33	3	.0003
Social anxiety	56	44	NS
Social isolation	83	45	.007
Poor rapport	22	22	NS

[a]NS, not significant.

unremitting functional deterioration, and an absence of cyclicity or dominant affective symptoms. The 18 patients so identified were compared with our baseline DSM-III (8) schizophrenic cohort. They were not different from them on any measure of long-term clinical profile—thus upholding the validity of the follow-up diagnosis.

Among the baseline clinical features predicting eventual schizophrenia, as shown in Table 3, were a significantly higher DSM-III SPD score and lower scores for DSM-III borderline personality disorder (BPD) and the Gunderson and Kolb (22) system for borderline. No DSM-III criterion for BPD predicted ultimate schizophrenia. On the other hand, the presence of three DSM-III criteria for schizotypal personality disorder predicted eventual schizophrenia (Table 4): paranoia/suspiciousness, magical thinking, and social isolation. Overall, we found the schizotypal construct very powerful in predicting future schizophrenia.

REFINING THE SPECTRUM CRITERIA

In his seminal paper, Paul Meehl (6) foresaw the need to develop what he called "high validity indicators for compensated schizotypy." He gave as an example subclinical cognitive slippage in the relatives of schizophrenic probands. This effort has indeed grown in the past decade with such biological factors as smooth-pursuit eye movements, platelet monoamine oxidase, and tachistoscopic backward masking (15). These high-validity indicators, along with other classic validating parameters such as treatment response, long-term course and outcome, and genetic linkage, identify samples of core subjects whose phenomenology can inform and upgrade our nosology.

Our follow-up study provided us with an opportunity to test criteria for schizotypal disorder and borderline disorder (23). We asked which of the DSM-III and Gunderson and Kolb (22) symptom criteria were the *most* discriminating among the study cohorts, and which had been partially validated as distinct by their long-term clinical profiles (see Fig. 1). To summarize for the schizotypal cohort in our study, we found (a) a significantly higher frequency of four criteria (odd communication, suspiciousness/paranoia, social isolation, and magical thinking), (b) nonsignificantly higher frequency of two criteria (ideas of reference and social anxiety), and (c) essentially no differences in the frequency of two criteria (inadequate rapport, and illusions/depersonalization/derealization).

We found from the analysis of the Gunderson and Kolb (22) criteria that depression did not discriminate schizotypal disorder and borderline disorder (23). Depression as a symptom was ubiquitous to both disorders and therefore should not be used as a discriminating diagnostic criterion. Finally two of Gunderson and Kolb's (22) criteria may be regarded as non-drug-associated, transient psychotic experiences: brief paranoid experiences and past therapy regressions (23). In our analysis, both were surprisingly more frequent in the schizotypal cohort, the former symptom significantly so. This suggests reconsidering the place of transient psychosis in the borderline spectrum. If the phenomenon is to be included at all, it appears to fit better in the schizotypal mosaic.

Our analysis of the personality disorder characteristics predicting future schizophrenia corroborates these findings (21). Recall that three DSM-III (8) schizotypal-personality-disorder criteria were significantly predictive: magical thinking, social isolation, and suspiciousness/paranoia. The poorest predictor, again, was illusions/depersonalization/derealization. Furthermore, we found brief atypical delusional experience to be highly predictive as well, strongly suggesting that the phenomenology of transient psychosis is part of the schizotypal phenotype, not part of borderline personality disorder.

THE PLACE OF TRANSIENT PSYCHOSES

At the very least, our data raise questions about the place of transient psychoses in this nosology. It may be that brief psychoses are as heterogeneous as prolonged psychoses and that a closer look will identify certain types as associated with borderline personality disorder and the affective disorders while other types will be associated with schizotypal personality disorder and the schizophrenic spectrum. I postulate, for example, that the transient psychotic phenomenologies associated with the schizophrenia spectrum include paranoia; ideas of reference, and bizarre or magical ideation and communication, especially in the context of social isolation. Such symptoms have the "praecox feeling," that is, they seem orthogonal to object relatedness and they betray major gaps in reality testing and interpersonal empathy.

The transient psychotic phenomena associated with borderline personality disorder and the affective disorders, on the other hand, may be highly interpersonal, that is, triggered by conflicted relationships with others and mediated by defenses that are empathically interactive, such as projective identification. Such transient psychotic episodes may also involve symptoms that are either loaded with dyscontrolled affect (rage, anxiety) or heavy with dissociative defenses against overwhelming affect like depersonalization, derealization, dreaminess, and confusion. Such episodes usually preserve reality testing to a greater degree than those associated with the schizophrenia spectrum.

CONCLUSIONS

What questions guide our future investigations? The schizophrenia spectrum concept ultimately goes back to Paul Meehl's (6) schizotaxia or genetic vulnerability to developing schizophrenia and related disorders. One obvious question, therefore, is, What disorders belong to this spectrum and represent the phenotypic expression of this vulnerability? Definite membership goes to schizophrenia, delusional disorder, and schizotypal personality disorder. Probable candidates include schizophreniform disorder (24) and schizoaffective disorder in Axis 1 and paranoid personality disorder and schizoid personality disorder in Axis 2. Finally, possible candidates include a potpourri of disorders, infantile autism and childhood-onset pervasive developmental disorder among the Axis 1 childhood psychoses, affective disorder with mood-incongruent delusions, which may be merged with schizoaffective personality disorder in future nosologies, and certain types of brief reactive psychoses. Possible candidates from Axis 2 are borderline personality disorder, compulsive personality disorder, and avoidant personality disorder.

The second major question to be addressed by future investigators is whether there exist common threads underlying this clinical heterogeneity that link to the schizotaxic vulnerability. Can sign and symptom phenomenology be refined on the basis of validation studies such as the ones outlined here? Finally, are there nonphenomenological phenotypic markers from other disciplines such as biology, electrophysiology, or neuroanatomy that can identify the latent trait or genotype? This domain of inquiry has barely begun and, in conjunction with the recent advances in molecular biology and genetics, holds considerable promise indeed.

ACKNOWLEDGMENTS

This study was supported in part by NIMH grant MH35174-02 and by the Fund for Psychoanalytic Research of the American Psychoanalytic Association. The author wishes to thank Linda Beth Berman for project coordination; Carol Thompson for manuscript preparation; Allison Benesch for chart abstraction and diagnostic evaluation; Renee Marshel and Victoria Solsberry for outcome evaluation; Michael Koontz and John Bartko for statistical consultation; Lawrence Abrams, John Cook, William Flexsenhar, Kathleen Free, Lee Goldman, Anita Gonzalez, Wendy Greenspun, Brian Healy, Tom Martin, Jim Miller, Jack O'Brien, Terry Polonus, Steven Richfield, Susan Voisinet, Robert Welp, and Donald Wright for chart abstraction; and Dexter M. Bullard, Jr, Wells Goodrich, Wayne Fenton, and Robert Heinssen for general consultation and manuscript review.

REFERENCES

1. Kraepelin E. *Dementia praecox and paraphrenia* (1896). Chicago: Chicago Medical Books, 1919.
2. Bleuler E. *Dementia praecox*. New York: International Universities Press, 1950.
3. Zilboorg G. Ambulatory schizophrenia. *Psychiatry* 1941;4:1949.
4. Deutsch H. Some forms of emotional disturbance and their relationship to schizophrenia. *Psychoanal Q* 1942;11:301–321.
5. Rado S. *Psychoanalysis of behavior*. New York: Grune & Stratton, 1956.
6. Meehl P. Schizotaxia, schizotypy, schizophrenia. *Am Psychol* 1962;17:827–838.
7. Kety S, Rosenthal D, Wender P, et al. Mental illness in the biological and adoptive families who have become schizophrenic: a preliminary report based on psychiatric interviews. In: Fieve R, Rosenthal D, Brill H, eds. *Genetic research in psychiatry*. Baltimore: Johns Hopkins University Press, 1975.
8. American Psychiatric Association. *Diagnostic and statistical manual of the mental disorders*, Vol. 3. Washington, DC, 1980.
9. Spitzer RL, Endicott J, Gibbon AM. Crossing the border into borderline personality and borderline schizophrenia: the development of criteria. *Arch Gen Psychiatry* 1979;36:17–24.
10. Kendler KS, Gruenberg AM. Genetic relationship between paranoid personality disorder and the "schizophrenic spectrum" disorders. *Am J Psychiatry* 1982;139:1185–1186.
11. Kendler KS, Gruenberg AM. An independent analysis of the Danish adoption study of schizophrenia: VI. The relationship between psychiatric disorders as defined by DSM-III in the relatives and adoptees. *Arch Gen Psychiatry* 1984;41:555–564.
12. Baron M, Gruen R, Rainer JD, Kane J, Asnis L, Lord S. A family study of schizophrenic and normal control probands: implications for the spectrum concept of schizophrenia. *Am J Psychiatry* 1985;142:447–455.
13. Siever LJ. Biologic correlates of schizotypal personality disorder. *Schizophr Bull* 1985;11:538–553.
14. Siever LJ, Coursey RD, Alterman IS, Buchsbaum MS, Murphy DL. Smooth pursuit eye movement impairment: a vulnerability marker for schizotypal personality disorder in a volunteer population. *Am J Psychiatry* 1984;141:1560–1565.
15. Siever LJ, Klar H. A review of DSM-III criteria for the personality disorders. In: Frances A, Hales R, eds. *American Psychiatric Association Annual Review*, Vol. 5. Washington, DC: American Psychiatric Press, 1986;279–310.
16. McGlashan TH. The Chestnut Lodge follow-up study I. Follow-up methodology and study sample. *Arch Gen Psychiatry* 1984;41:573–585.
17. McGlashan TH. The Chestnut Lodge follow-up study II. Long-term outcome of schizophrenia and the affective disorders. *Arch Gen Psychiatry* 1984;41:586–601.
18. McGlashan TH. Schizotypal Personality Disorder. Chestnut Lodge follow-up study: VI. Long-term follow-up perspectives. *Arch Gen Psychiatry* 1986;43:329–334.
19. Hollingshead AB, Redlich FC. *Social class and mental illness*. New York: John Wiley & Sons, 1957.
20. McGlashan TH, Bardenstein KK. Schizotypal personality disorder: gender differences. *J Personality Disord* 1988;2:221–227.
21. Fenton WS, McGlashan TH. Risk of schizophrenia in character disorders. *Am J Psychiatry* 1989;146:1280–1284.
22. Gunderson JG, Kolb JE. Discriminating features of borderline patients. *Am J Psychiatry* 1978;135:792–796.
23. McGlashan TH. Testing DSM-III symptom criteria for schizotypal and borderline personality disorders. *Arch Gen Psychiatry* 1987;44:143–148.
24. Heinssen RK, McGlashan TH. Schizophreniform psychosis. Paper presented at the annual meeting of the American Psychiatric Association, Montreal, Canada, May 1988.

//
19
Pilot Studies of Schizotypal Subjects

Gunvant Thaker,[1] Marianne Moran,[1] Adrienne Lahti,[1] Helene Adami,[1] Carol A. Tamminga,[1] and S. Charles Schulz[2]

Studies exploring the biological nature of personality disorders, especially the borderline and schizotypal subcategories, only began in earnest in the 1980s. A necessary step in enabling such studies was the establishment of descriptive criteria (6) and then reliable diagnostic criteria (Diagnostic, Interview of Borderlines, or DIB) for borderline personality disorder (7,8). This advance alone predating DSM-III (2) by 5 years attracted investigators who had been trained in the biological approach to schizophrenia and affective disorders. In 1981 there appeared a number of articles focusing on the biology of DIB-identified patients. Using investigational tools developed in their affective-disorder research, Carroll et al (3) and Akiskal (1) used both neuroendocrine (dexamethasone suppression test) and rapid-eye-movement (REM) latency measure obtained from sleep studies to examine objectively identified borderline patients. Their work demonstrated that many borderline patients had findings similar to those of depressed patients. Studies using measurements developed in affective-disorder research extend these original findings. McNamara et al (15) confirmed the REM latency findings, Garbutt et al (4) showed a blunted response to thyroid-stimulating hormone (TSH) similar to depressed subjects, and a number of investigators showed an increased number of affective-disorder patients in the relatives of borderlines (12,20,25,29).

During this early era of research on borderline personality disorder, the major diagnostic criteria employed were those of Gunderson, perhaps because of the extensive work demonstrating the ability of the criteria, when elicited through DIB, to differentiate borderlines from depressed and acute schizophrenic subjects (7). One result of using DIB was that it provided a relatively wide net for a broad category of borderline patients. Patients with a primarily unstable mood would be classified as borderline along with those experiencing brief psychotic episodes or frequent derealization and depersonalization. Development of the DSM-III included dividing the broad range of borderline patients into two groups (28):

1. Borderline personality disorder—these patients closely resembled a group of patients labeled in the early 1970s with an emotionally unstable character disorder (18) except that they were not characterized by brief psychotic episodes.
2. Schizotypal personality disorder—the criteria for this category drew heavily on the "borderline schizophrenia" concept taken from the Danish adoption studies and therefore closely bordered schizophrenia (10).

---
[1]Maryland Psychiatric Research Center, University of Maryland School of Medicine, Baltimore, MD 21228.
[2]Department of Psychiatry, Case Western Reserve University, University Hospitals of Cleveland, Cleveland, OH 44106.

Whereas early studies of DIB-identified borderline patients focused on measures used for investigating affective disorders, a growing body of work in the 1980s began employing measures or medications utilized in schizophrenia research to examine patients with the schizotypal personality disorder (SPD) and those with both borderline and schizotypal disorders (BPD/SPD). Such observations and studies have demonstrated the following:

1. Effectiveness of low doses of neuroleptics for "psychotic" symptoms in schizotypal patients (5,26);
2. Abnormalities in smooth-pursuit eye movements (23);
3. Psychotic episodes (21) or worsening in presenting symptoms with stimulants (14);
4. Correlation of increases in growth hormone (GH, an indirect index of dopaminergic tone) with increases in thought disorder following intake of amphetamines (21);
5. Schizophrenia in the relatives of schizotypes in some but not all studies (13).

Such background indicates that there is ample reason to explore further the biological nature of SPD and SPD/BPD. In addition, there are several good reasons to study SPD. In order to gain further clues about schizophrenia, the study of SPD can be useful since such patients have rarely received medications or been chronically institutionalized. Also, because their "psychosis" is by definition not as severe as in schizophrenia, SPD and SPD/BPD patients can usually participate fully in complicated tests without being distracted by active symptoms such as hallucinations. Also, increased research will lead to improved clinical care. One interesting and unresolved area of discussion in research on SPD is the influence on the results from the sample selected for study. Kendler has reviewed the hypotheses that a "clinical" sample of SPD may differ phenomenologically and in other ways from a "family" sample (9). He asserts that the patients who present for treatment are characterized by positive symptoms of schizotypy (magical thinking) while the relatives of schizophrenic patients are characterized by social withdrawal. Other samples that have proved of interest include the use of high-risk samples, college students for schizotypy, and then testing for measures of attention previously found to be abnormal in schizophrenic patients (23,24).

The sample reported on in this chapter was found in a serendipitous fashion that offers a unique opportunity to study the symptoms and biology of personality. Because the subjects were respondents to an advertisement for normal volunteers and had not received treatment, we were able to study a "psychopathology" unencumbered by "stress." Most inpatient studies are performed shortly after admission to the hospital, which has been necessitated by a decompensation (transient psychotic episode) or suicidal behavior. In the current study this was not a factor.

METHODS

Subject Recruitment

At the inception of this study, normal controls were recruited to establish our laboratory norms for various neuropsychological and neurophysiological measures routinely obtained from our schizophrenic patient samples. An advertisement was placed in a major metropolitan newspaper to recruit subjects. All the interested respondents were screened by a 10-minute telephone interview to rule out obvious psychiatric, medical, and substance abuse history. The remaining subjects, who expressed interest in the studies, were invited for more extensive evaluation.

Clinical Assessments

This consisted of the Structured Interview for Affective Disorders and Schizophrenia, Lifetime version (SADS-L; ref 28), the Structured Interview for DSM-III Personality Diagnoses (SIDP; ref 17), and a semistructured general clinical interview to obtain psychosocial and family history. In the last interview, detailed questions were asked to obtain histories, in first- and second-degree family members of the volunteers, of psychiatric inpatient and outpatient treatments; suicidal behaviors; presence of psychotic, affective, or other psychiatric symptoms; criminal behavior, etc. The information derived from SADS-L and SIDP allowed us to obtain DSM-III Axes 1 and 2 diagnoses and assess comorbidity among these diagnoses, in these research volunteers. Furthermore, estimate of psychiatric morbidity in the family members was made possible from the semistructured clinical interview.

Laboratory Assessments

Oculomotor Paradigms

Eye movements were measured using an infrared technique (Applied Sciences 210 Model). Four eye-movement paradigms were administered to each participant in a random order. The paradigms are described in details elsewhere (30,31). Briefly, subjects were seated comfortably with their head held steady strapped to a chin rest. The stimuli for smooth-pursuit eye movements (SPEM) was provided by projected light moving in sinusoidal wave form (20° amplitude and at 0.5 Hz frequency). The curved screen was placed 48 inches away from the subject. For the remaining paradigms, light-emitting diodes (LEDs) placed 5° apart horizontally provided the target. The LEDs were driven by an electronic switchboard operated manually. In the SPEM task, a global qualitative score from 1 (best) to 5 (worst) was obtained. Also, saccades per cycle (reflecting the average number of saccades per SPEM cycle) and size per saccade (reflecting the average size of the two largest saccades in a SPEM cycle) were measured. In an antisaccade paradigm, instructions were to make a saccade in the direction opposite to the target jump. Saccadic distractibility score (reflecting an inability to inhibit a reflex saccade towards the target) and latencies for reflex saccades and volitional saccades (deliberate saccades away from the target) were measured. Saccadic latency in the traditional saccade task was also measured. Finally, in the fixation tasks, in which the instructions were to fixate in presence or absence of fixation light, scores were obtained reflecting the number of noncorrecting saccades.

Neuropsychological Testing

Neuropsychological testing was performed to characterize the cognitive functioning of the participants. Four subsets of WAIS-R (Arithmetic, Vocabulary, Block Design, and Picture Arrangement) were administered to obtain an estimate of WAIS-R IQ. The IQ testing was completed in one session, which took about an hour. After a small break, the second session of select neuropsychological tests was completed in 1 to 1 1/2 hours. The small battery of tests evaluated perceptuomotor and memory performance of the subjects. The tests included Choice Reaction Time, Trails A and B (32), Verbal Recognition and Recall (33), and Money's Road Map Test of Directional Sense (34).

RESULTS

Sample

In response to the newspaper advertisement, 153 telephone inquiries were made by the interested subjects. After the initial screening and natural attrition, 50 of these subjects were interviewed directly. Out of the 50 subjects who underwent clinical assessments with the SADS-L and SIDP, 16 met DSM-III Axis 1 lifetime diagnoses (schizophrenia/paranoia, 2; major depression, 8; bipolar disorder, 1; current sub-

TABLE 1. *Family history in first- and second-degree relatives*

Subjects	Schizophrenia	Major depression	Suicide	Substance abuse	Criminal behavior
Schizotypal personality disorder ($n=4$)	1	1	0	1	0
Other personality disorders ($n=5$)	0	2	1	5	1
Normals ($n=20$)	1	3	0	8	0

stance abuse, 4; and anxiety disorder, 1). In addition to that, another 10 subjects met DSM-III Axis 2 diagnoses (schizotypal, 4; borderline, 3; antisocial, 6; passive aggressive, 3; and histrionic personality disorders, 1). There was frequent comorbidity among the Axis 2 diagnoses. Compared with those subjects from this sample who were defined as "normal" (those who did not meet the Axes 1 or 2 diagnosis), the personality disorder subjects generally showed more psychopathology in the family members (Table 1).

After screening out all the subjects with Axis 1 diagnosis, laboratory assessments were completed in 12 normal, 4 schizotypal, and 5 other personality diagnoses subjects. Preliminary results are reported here. All subjects with a schizotypal diagnosis, regardless of other Axis 2 traits, were included in the schizotypal group for the purpose of this analysis; the "other" category included all personality disorders with no schizotypal diagnosis. The demographics of subjects in these three groups are presented in Table 2.

Oculomotor Assessments

In this sample, smooth-pursuit eye movements (SPEM) did not differentiate schizotypal subjects from the other groups (Table 3). However, the latency for the volitional saccade was significantly longer in schizotypal subjects compared with the other two groups ($p<.01$; Fig. 1). These differences were evident in spite of equal latencies for the saccades in the traditional saccade shift task (Table 3). In contrast, those subjects with nonschizotypal personality diagnoses performed similar to normals in this measure. These other personality disorder subjects, however, showed significantly higher distractibility scores compared with both normals and schizotypal subjects ($p<.05$). Other eye-movement measures were similar in the three groups.

Neuropsychological Assessments

Subjects in the three groups were very similar in their estimated IQ (Table 2). They

TABLE 2. *Demographic data*

	Normal ($n=13$)	SPD ($n=4$)	Other ($n=5$)
Age in years, mean (SD)	29.8 (5.8)	30.8 (6.0)	28.8 (3.3)
Gender			
Male	6	4	2
Female	7	0	3
Estimated IQ (WAIS-R)	107.0 (15.9)	109.3 (9.3)	100.8 (5.1)

TABLE 3. Oculomotor data, means (SD)

	Normal	SPD	Other
Smooth-pursuit eye movements			
Score	2.29 (0.8)	2.11 (0.6)	2.46 (0.8)
Saccades per cycle	4.11 (1.7)	3.26 (1.7)	3.94 (1.8)
Saccades per size	2.92 (1.0)	2.90 (1.2)	3.86 (1.60)
Saccade paradigm latency	249.5 (40.1)	265.8 (43.8)	224.6 (29.6)
Antisaccade paradigm			
Distractibility (%)*	18.3 (18.3)	23.4 (13.4)	40.1 (26.3)
Volitional latency**	333.4 (47.7)	410.0 (48.8)	259.6 (43.6)

*$p < .05$.
**$p < .01$.

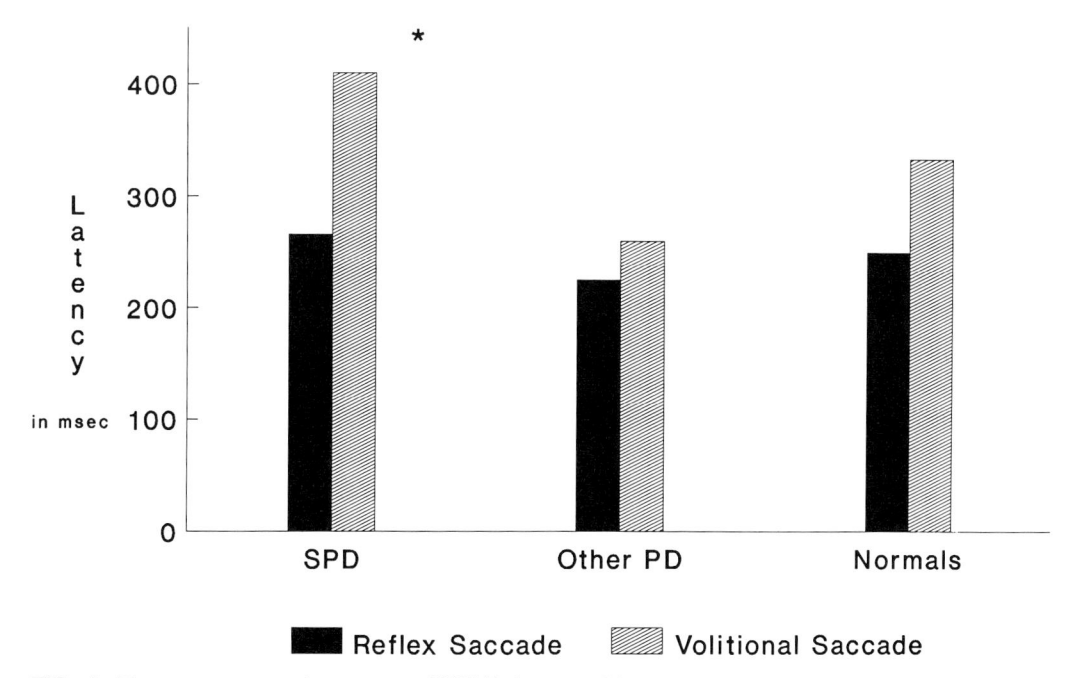

FIG. 1. Two-way repeated measures ANOVA (repeated latency measure X group) showed that in all subjects there was an increase in latency during a volitional saccade compared to a reflex saccade ($F = 92.29$, $df = [1,41]$; $p < .0001$). Also, there was a significant group effect ($F = 7.51$, $df = [2,18]$; $p < .005$) and interaction ($f = 7.83$, $df = [2,41]$; $p < .004$). The post hoc Newman-Lewis test showed that the increase in latency in volitional saccade was significantly greater in the SPD subjects than in the other two groups (*$p < .01$).

TABLE 4. Neuropsychological data, means (SD)			
	Normal	SPD	Other
Money Road Map, # correct	27.9 (4.1)	31.8 (0.5)	29.8 (2.9)
Money Road Map, time in seconds	82.1 (26.8)	77.8 (20.4)	73.6 (5.7)
Trails A, time in seconds	26.8 (5.7)	27.8 (11.6)	28.4 (8.3)
Trails B, time in seconds	66.3 (21.4)	85.0 (13.5)	58.2 (23.7)
Reaction time, time in milliseconds	475.6 (74.1)	489.0 (17.1)	424.8 (20.3)
Verbal recall, # correct	17.5 (4.2)	14.8 (3.1)	16 (4.4)

also performed equally well in most of the other neuropsychological measures (obtained from Trails A, Verbal Recognition, Reaction Time, and Money's Road Map tests; Table 4). However, there were some interesting trends that were observed in the other measures. Schizotypal subjects, who did equally well in Trails A, had relatively more difficulties with Trails B (Table 4). These subjects also made more errors in Verbal Recall. These differences, however, were not statistically significant. In contrast, subjects with other personality disorders performed as well as the normal controls.

DISCUSSION

The findings described above, although derived from a small subject group, are interesting in a number of respects. They demonstrate a high prevalence of Axis 1 and 2 diagnoses in subjects who volunteer for research studies as "normal" controls. This indicates a need for careful clinical assessments of normal controls in order to have normative populations free from psychopathology. The sample of personality disorder subjects, collected in a serendipitous fashion from research volunteers, showed the highest prevalence of antisocial and then schizotypal and borderline personality disorders. The group of schizotypal subjects identified from volunteers was a unique sample of SPD, free from the usual contaminations of patient samples such as institutionalization and pharmacological treatments. The schizotypal subjects in the current study were similar to the two other groups (nonschizotypal personality and normal controls) in their intellectual functioning. In spite of this, they performed poorly in a number of specific neuropsychologic tasks. The pattern of these abnormalities observed in the psychobiological testings was akin to the findings generally reported in schizophrenia (16).

The antisaccade paradigm was the most successful in differentiating schizotypal subjects from the nonschizotypal-personality-disorder subjects and the normals. The volitional saccade latency was significantly increased in these subjects in spite of normal reflex saccade latency. This finding is very similar to observations made in schizophrenic patients, especially those with deficit syndrome (primary and enduring negative symptoms; ref 31). To carry out the antisaccade task correctly, the subject has to shift his or her covert attention towards the target jump to determine it's direction and then shift it back to generate a volitional saccade in the opposite direction. Therefore, either a difficulty in shifting covert attention (e.g., putatively in lesions of the posterior parietal region) or difficulty in generating volitional saccade (e.g., lesions of frontal eye fields) may explain the increased volitional saccade latency.

Smooth-pursuit eye movements, on the other hand, in this population did not separate the schizotypal subjects from the other groups. This is a somewhat surprising finding. Other investigators have noted poor SPEM quality in schizotypal patients compared with normals (23). This non patient, untreated schizotypal subject sample was highly functioning, with normal cognitive abilities (as ascertained by estimated IQ score). It may be possible that the SPEM abnormality is associated with more symptomatic schizotypal subjects with a deteriorating course (22).

The results from the neuropsychological testing also showed a trend toward patterns of deficits generally observed in schizophrenic subjects. Schizophrenic patients, especially remitted individuals, generally do not have as much difficulty with tasks requiring automatic processes. However, tasks that require sustained directed attention, especially in the presence of information loading, differentiate schizophrenic patients from normals. For instance, in contrast to the recognition task, Verbal Recall needs directed attention. Schizophrenic individuals (11), and the schizotypal subjects in the current study, had difficulty with Verbal Recall but not with Verbal Recognition. Similarly, in Trails B, which requires shifting sets, schizotypallike schizophrenic subjects had relatively more difficulty in carrying out the task. These subjects performed as well as normals in Trails A, which is a very similar task as Trails B, but does not require shifting sets.

The uniqueness of this sample lends further meaning to these psychobiological findings. Further exploration is needed to determine whether a sample of schizotypal subjects collected in this fashion are phenomenologically related to the "family" sample of SPD. Like familial SPD and unlike clinical SPD, these subjects were functional and did not seek treatment. They experienced both positive symptoms (mainly magical thinking and recurrent illusions) and negative symptoms (mainly odd speech, inadequate rapport, and social withdrawal). To a lesser extent, they also had nonschizotypal traits (such as impulsivity, affective instability, and unstable relationships) that were equally prevalent in the other personality diagnosis subjects. An SPD sample collected from the general population in this fashion and characterized by a symptom complex akin to familial SPD is a valuable sample to test putative psychobiological markers of schizophrenia. Since phenomenologically they are similar to familial SPD, they are likely to be genetically linked with schizophrenia, but unlike clinical SPD they are not contaminated by treatments. On the other hand, they are free from the environmental risk factors of schizophrenia, which are more likely to be shared by the familial SPD subjects. In that context, it is interesting to note that increased volitional saccade latency was observed to be more frequent in schizophrenic patients with primary and enduring negative symptoms (i.e., deficit syndrome) than in nondeficit-syndrome patients (31). These and other issues are currently being explored.

REFERENCES

1. Akiskal, HS. Subaffective disorders: dysthymic, cyclothymic and bipolar II disorders in the "borderline" realm. *Psychiatr Clin North Am* 1981; 4:25–46.
2. American Psychiatric Association. *Diagnostic and statistical manual of mental disorders III.* Washington, DC, American Psychiatric Association, 1980.
3. Carroll BJ, Greden JF, Feinberg M, et al. Neuroendocrine evaluation of depression in borderline patients. *Psychiatr Clin North Am,* 1981;4: 89–99.
4. Garbutt JC, Loosen PT, Tipermas A, et al. The TRH test in patients with borderline personality disorder. *Psychiatry Res* 1983;9:107–113.
5. Goldberg SC, Schulz SC, Schulz PM, et al. Borderline and schizotypal personality disorders treated with low-dose thiothixene vs placebo. *Arch Gen Psychiatry* 1986;43:680–686.
6. Gunderson JG, Singer MT. Defining borderline patients. *Am J Psychiatry* 1975;132:1–10.
7. Gunderson JG, Kolb J. Discriminating features of borderline patients. *Am J Psychiatry* 1978; 135:792–796.
8. Gunderson JG, Kolb JE, Austin V. The diagnostic inverview for borderline patients. *Am J Psychiatry* 1981;138:896–903.
9. Kendler KS. Diagnostic approaches to schizotypal personality disorder: a historical perspective. *Schizophr Bull* 1985;11:538–553.
10. Kety SS, Rosenthal D, Wender PH, et al. Mental illness in the biological and adoptive families of

adopted individuals who have become schizophrenic: a preliminary report based on psychiatric interviews. In: Fieve RR, Rosenthal D, Brill H, eds. *Genetic research in psychiatry.* Baltimore, Johns Hopkins University Press, 1975.
11. Koh SD, Peterson RD. Encoding orientation and the remembering of schizophrenic young adults. *J Abnorm Psychol* 1978;87:303–313.
12. Loranger AW, Oldham JM, Tulis EH. Familial transmission of DSM-III borderline personality disorder. *Arch Gen Psychiatry* 1982;39:795–799.
13. Lenzenweger MF, Loranger AW. Detection of familial schizophrenia using a psychometric measure of schizotypy. *Arch Gen Psychiatry* 1989;46:902–907.
14. Lucas PB, Gardner DL, Wolkowitz OM, et al. Dysphoria associated with methylphenidate infusion in borderline personality disorder. *Am J Psychiatry* 1987;144:1577–1579.
15. McNamara, E, Reynolds CF III, Soloff PH, et al. EEG sleep evaluation of depression in borderline patients. *Am J Psychiatry* 1984;141:182–186.
16. Nuechterlein KH, Dawson ME. Information processing and attentional functioning in the developmental course of schizophrenic disorders. *Schizophr Bull* 1984;10:160–203.
17. Pfohl B, Stangl D, Zimmerman M. Structured interview for DSM-III personality disorders, SIDP, 2nd ed. Unpublished manual, Iowa City, University of Iowa.
18. Rifkin A, Quitkin F, Carrillo C, Blumberg AG, Klein DF. Lithium carbonate in emotionally unstable character disorder. *Arch Gen Psychiatry* 1972;17:519–523.
19. Schulz SC, van Kammen DP, Rogol AD, Ebert M, Pickar D, Cohen MR, Naber D. Amphetamine increased prolactin but not growth hormone or endorphins in schizophrenic patients. *Psychopharmacol Bull* 1981;17:193–195.
20. Schulz PM, Schulz SC, Goldberg S, et al. Diagnoses of the relatives of schizotypal outpatients. *J Nerv Ment Dis* 1986;174:457–463.
21. Schulz SC, Cornelius J, Schulz PM, Soloff PH. The amphetamine challenge test in patients with borderline disorder. *Am J Psychiatry* 1988;145:809–814.
22. Siever LJ, Coccaro EF, Klar H, Losonczy M, Silverman JM, Davis KL. Biological markers in borderline and related personality disorders. Paper presented at the IVth World Congress of Biological Psychiatry, September, Philadelphia, PA, 1985.
23. Siever LJ, Coursey RD, Alterman IS, Buchsbaum MKS, Murphy DL. Impaired smooth pursuit eye movement: Vulnerability marker for schizotypal personality disorder in a normal volunteer population. *Am J Psychiatry* 1984;141:1560–1566.
24. Siever LJ, Haier RJ, Coursey RD, Sostek AJ, Murphy DL, Holzman PS, Buchsbaum MS. Smooth pursuit eye tracking impairment: relation to other "markers" of schizophrenia and psychologic correlates. *Arch Gen Psychiatry* 1982;39:1001–1005.
25. Soloff PH, Millward JW. Psychiatric disorders in the families of borderline patients. *Arch Gen Psychiatry* 1983;40:37–44.
26. Soloff PH, George A, Nathan RS, et al. Progress in pharmacotherapy of borderline disorders. *Arch Gen Psychiatry* 1986;43:691–697.
27. Spitzer RL, Endicott J. Justification for separating schizotypal and borderline personality disorders. *Schizophr Bull* 1979;5:95–100.
28. Spitzer RL, Endicott J. *Schedule for affective disorders and schizophrenia—lifetime version,* 3rd ed. New York: New York State Psychiatric Institute, Biometrics Research, 1979.
29. Stone MH. Psychiatrically ill relatives of borderline patients: a family study. *Psychiatr O* 1981;58:71–83.
30. Thaker GK, Nguyen JA, Tamminga CA. Increased saccadic distractibility in tardive dyskinesia: functional evidence for subcortical GABA dysfunction. *Biol Psychiatry* 1989;25:49–59.
31. Thaker GK, Kirkpatrick B, Buchanan RW, Ellsberry R, Lahti A, Tamminga CA. Oculomotor abnormalities and their clinical correlates in schizophrenia. *Psychopharmacol Bull* 1989;(in press).
32. Fedio P, Cox CS, Neophytides A, Canal-Frederick G, Chase TN. Neuropsychological profile in Huntington's Disease: Patients and those at risk. In: Chase TN, Wexler NS, Barbeau A, eds. *Advances in neurology* vol. 23. New York, Raven Press, 1979.
33. Calev A, Venables PH, Monk AF. Evidence of distinct verbal memory pathologies in severely and mildly disturbed schizophrenics. *Schizophrenia Bulletin* 1983;9:247–263.
34. Money J. *A standardized road map test of direction sense: manual.* San Rafael, CA, Academic Therapy Publications, 1976.

20

Cerebral Structural Abnormalities in Schizophreniform Disorder and in Schizophrenia Spectrum Personality Disorders

Carlo L. Cazzullo, Antonio Vita, Gian Marco Giobbio, Massimiliano Dieci, and Emilio Sacchetti

Since the introduction of pneumoencephalography (PEG), which was the first technique to allow in vivo visualization of the central nervous system (CNS), many researchers have described cerebral structural anomalies, in particular ventricular enlargement and cortical atrophy, in schizophrenic patients (1–3).

The advent of computed tomography (CT), a safe, noninvasive, and more informative brain-imaging technique, has allowed confirmation and further specification of these first results in larger and better-selected groups of schizophrenics (4–7) as well as in subjects affected by other psychiatric disorders (7–11).

Dilatation of the lateral cerebral ventricles has now been consistently demonstrated in about 25–30% of schizophrenic cases. Patients with ventricular enlargement seem to be characterized by a phenomenological picture in which negative rather than positive symptoms prevail (7, 12), there is greater cognitive and intellectual deterioration (7,13), and they show poorer response to treatment with neuroleptics (6,7,14,15). One problem still unresolved is the timing of the appearance of this anomaly; that is, does it precede the onset of the pathology and is it thus tied to genetic or early environmental factors? Or is it a developmental parameter and thus an effect of the illness, or in any case an epiphenomenon of the events surrounding it?

The studies attempting to answer this question have produced partially discordant results, in part because different parameters and evaluation methods have been used.

The most informative research approaches have been directed towards three areas:

1. Evaluating the ventricular dimension at the onset of schizophrenia or in schizophreniform disorder;
2. Determining the correlation between duration of illness and ventricular size;
3. Analyzing the development of the morphological parameter in tomographic follow-up studies.

In 1982 Weinberger et al (16), in analyzing 35 patients with schizophreniform disorder, observed that the lateral ventricles were significantly larger than those of controls, with pathological enlargement in over 20% of the patients. This value was similar to that found in chronic schizophrenic patients thus indicating the possibility that the anomaly might precede the appearance of

---

[1]Institute of Psychiatry, Milan University School of Medicine, 20122 Milan, Italy.

schizophrenic illness. Substaining this hypothesis, Weinberger and colleagues did not observe any correlation between duration of schizophrenia and ventricular dimensions.

Other studies, however, have shown that ventricular enlargement was most marked in schizophrenic subjects who had been sick for the longest periods of the time. This finding does not necessarily invalidate the hypothesis of the precocity of the abnormality but may be justified by the possibility that the more marked morphological anomalies identify the more serious and temporally long-lasting pathological forms.

Benes et al (17) studied a group of ten schizophrenic patients with a brief disease course and short hospitalization period. They did not find any significant differences in the cerebral ventricular size of their patients and controls. The assessment of the ventricular dimensions was obtained by two linear measures (Evans Index and Cella Media Ratio), which are not totally comparable to the ventricle-to-brain ratio (VBR). Further, when they used VBR, Benes and her co-workers found that the control group (patients suffering from migraine and vertigo) had an abnormally high value that was not consistent with the data in the literature and could have been responsible for the lack of differences between the ventricular dimension of patients and controls.

Neither did Trimble and Kingsley (18) find differences between patients and controls. Their sample, however, was composed of patients who had never been hospitalized; therefore it was a subgroup that was clinically less serious and perhaps also less compromised from a neuromorphological viewpoint.

Nyback et al (19) subjected 13 patients with a diagnosis of schizophrenia or probable schizophrenia (Research Diagnostic Criteria) to CT and found a significant enlargement of the lateral ventricles relative to controls. Dividing patients into subgroups on the basis of age (less than or greater than 45 years), the authors found that only the third ventricle was affected by age; the dimension of the lateral ventricles appeared to correlate with the diagnosis but independent of any chronological parameter.

These findings are consistent with those of Tanaka et al (20), who found a correlation between duration of illness and the dimension of the third ventricle but not with the dimensions of the lateral ventricles.

Schulz et al (21) found significant larger planimetric measures of the lateral ventricles in teenage patients with schizophreniform disorder as compared to age- and sex-matched medical controls. Similar results were obtained by Cazzullo et al (22), who found ventricular enlargement in 46% of their sample of 14 patients with schizophreniform disorder.

Obiols et al (23) analyzed the incidence of ventricular dilatation in 33 young schizophrenic patients (of whom 80%, were less than 30 years) with a brief duration of illness (for 60%, less than 3 years). The study confirmed the presence of enlargement of the lateral ventricles in the schizophrenics and further showed no correlation between VBR and duration of illness or length of hospitalization.

On the contrary, Woods and Wolf (24), analyzing the correlation between ventricular dimensions (with linear indices) and duration of illness, observed that these values were progressively less similar among patients and controls as time passed.

In order to more directly establish whether the structural anomalies observable on CT scans are stable or change over time, three groups (25–27) investigated the temporal development of the tomographic parameter in patients subjected to two CT scans at different periods of time. None of this work revealed any change in the dimension of the lateral ventricles. This observation appears to confirm the early appearance of the cerebral anomaly in schizophrenia.

From this brief review of the available

data, it emerges that there is still a heterogeneity of results relative to CT-scan characteristics of early schizophrenia and related pathologies. This is partially ascribable to the use of nonhomogeneous groups of patients and research protocols that are not fully comparable. This situation suggests the need to carry out further work on the subject.

In order to address the problem of the moment at which the anomaly appears, we considered it interesting to evaluate the dimensions of the cerebral ventricles in patients affected by pathologies correlated with schizophrenia and often preceding its onset, in particular the schizophreniform disorder and personality disorders of the schizophrenia spectrum. Given the lack of data in this regard, we extended the analysis to another morphological parameter, the degree of cortical atrophy.

METHODS

Our study included a group of 29 patients with schizophreniform disorder (19 men and 10 women, with a mean age of 23.3 ± 5.7 years) and a group of 25 patients with personality disorders of the schizophrenia spectrum (19 schizotypal—15 men and 4 women, with a mean age of 20.9 ± 3.3 years; 6 paranoid—5 men and 1 woman, with a mean age of 37 ± 13.2 years). The diagnoses were made according to the Diagnostic and Statistical Manual of Mental Disorders III (DSM-III; ref 28).

The general criteria for inclusion were as follows:

Absence of medical or neurologic illness possibly responsible for neuromorphological anomalies;
No history of alcoholism or of head trauma with loss of consciousness;
No epilepsy, electroshock therapy, or corticosteroid intake in the 3 months prior to the study.

Informed consent was obtained from all of the subjects.

The control group was composed of 74 subjects (43 males and 31 females with a mean age of 26.2 ± 6.1 years) who had undergone cerebral CT as a routine diagnostic examination for minor head trauma without loss of consciousness.

The patients and controls were subjected to CT on an EMI 1010 scanner. The ventricular dimensions were calculated by a manual planimetric method on the CT section in which the lateral ventricles appeared at their largest, as described by Benes et al (17); the ventricular dimensions were expressed as the ratio of the ventricular area to the total cerebral area $\times 100$ (VBR).

Cortical atrophy was measured in a subgroup of patients and controls by using a four-point visual scale, assessing increasing degrees of atrophy (0 = absent, 1 = uncertain or mild, 2 = moderate, and 3 = severe) as indicated by the width of the cortical sulci and the interhemispheric and sylvian fissures (29). The rating was made by using a reference image for each atrophy class.

RESULTS

Schizophreniform Disorder

The comparison of VBR values between the two groups showed that those of the schizophreniform patients were significantly higher than those of the controls (5.96 ± 2.8 and 3.33 ± 2.1, respectively; $t = 5.12$, $p < .001$; see Fig. 1). Of the 29 schizophreniform patients, 9 (31%) had VBR values more than 2 SD above the mean of the controls.

Regarding cortical atrophy, the group of schizophreniform patients had a percentage of pathological values (2 or 3) different from that of the controls (4/18 or 22% vs 1/36 or 2.8%; $\chi^2 = 3.3$, $p = .066$; see Table 1).

These data confirm and extend the results obtained by Weinberger et al (16) and of our previous study (22) in patients with

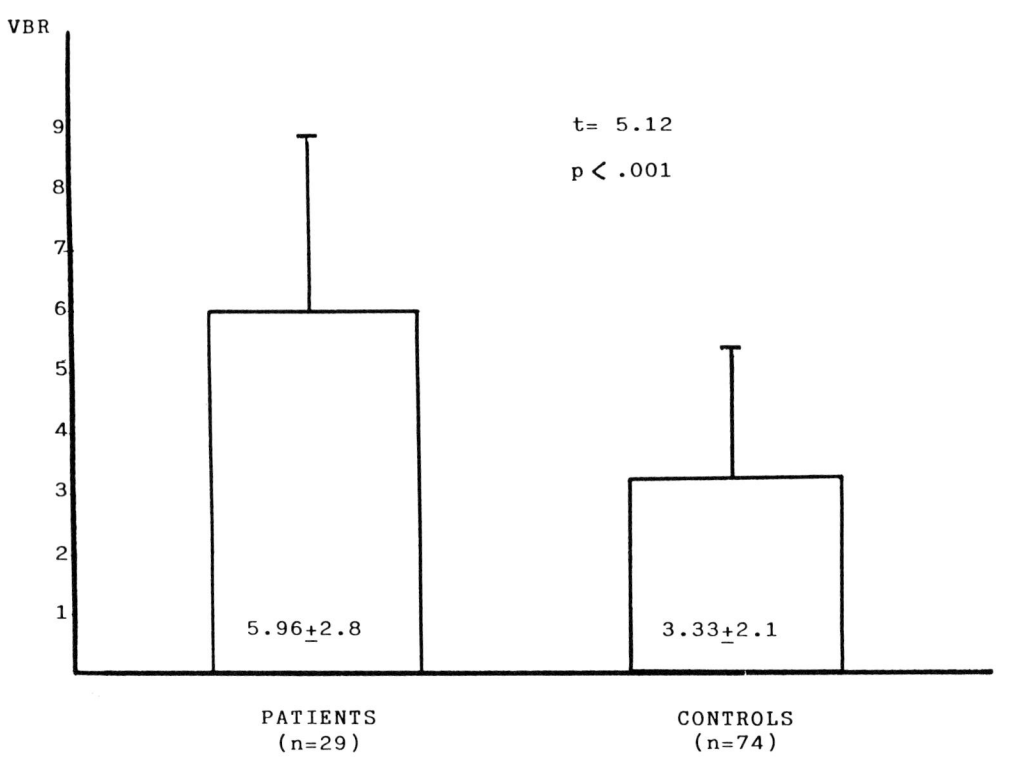

FIG. 1. Cerebral ventricular size in schizophreniform disorder and healthy controls.

VBR: Patients (n=29) 5.96±2.8; Controls (n=74) 3.33±2.1; t = 5.12, p < .001

the same diagnosis of schizophreniform disorder. Such a diagnosis is often provisional, destined to be substituted with that of schizophrenia when a successive and more prolonged psychotic breakdown occurs or when the symptoms persist. Therefore, finding cerebrostructural anomalies in this disorder clearly indicates that they may be present from the very first phases of the psychotic pathology. This factor, together with the scarce or null effect of the duration of illness on the ventricular dimension and the results of the tomographic follow-up studies, suggests that ventricular enlargement is a primary anomaly and is not substantially dependent on factors inherent in the development of the illness.

If the neuromorphological anomalies are already present in the very early months of the illness (since it is extremely improbable that they develop in such a brief period without a serious neurologic symptomatology), we must conclude that these anomalies do precede the clinical onset of the disease.

Finding a high frequency of cases with cortical atrophy confirms the hypothesis that there is an organic cerebral component in initial schizophrenia and indicates the ex-

TABLE 1. Cortical atrophy in patients with schizophreniform disorders, schizotypal and paranoid personality disorders, and in healthy controls

Subjects	Atrophy scores	
	0–1	2–3
Controls	35 (97%)	1 (3%)
Schizophreniform*	14 (78%)	4 (22%)
Schizotypal**	13 (68%)	6 (32%)
Paranoid***	3 (50%)	3 (50%)

*Vs controls: $\chi^2 = 3.3$; $p = .066$.
**Vs controls: $\chi^2 = 6.9$; $p = .009$.
***Vs controls: $\chi^2 = 8.4$; $p = .004$.
All other comparisons are not significant.

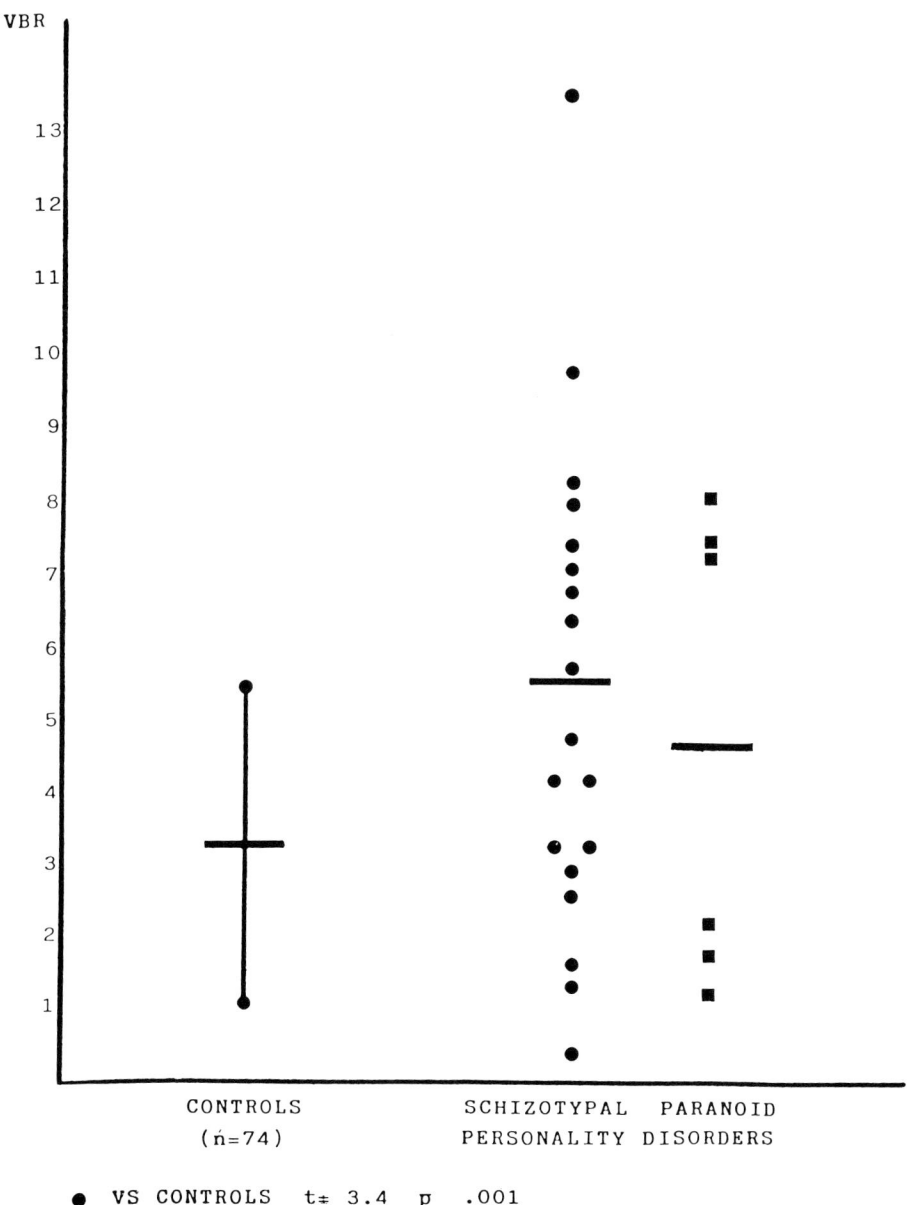

FIG. 2. Cerebral ventricular size in healthy controls and schizophrenic spectrum disorders.

istence of pictures of diffuse atrophy (cortical and subcortical) in a sizable number of schizophreniform patients.

Personality Disorders

The VBR values for personality disorders of the schizophrenic spectrum are presented in Fig. 2. Here too the values of the total group of patients are significantly superior to those of the controls (5.12 ± 3.2 and 3.33 ± 2.1, respectively; $t = 3.22$, $p = .002$).

The analysis of the subdiagnoses demonstrated that the schizotypal but not the paranoid patients had VBR values (5.43 ± 3.2 and 4.75 ± 3) that were significantly different from those of the normal subjects ($t = 3.4, p = .001; t = 1.4, p =$ not significant). Furthermore, the incidence of pathological ventricular dilatation was 24% in the total group and 26% and 17% in schizotypal and paranoid personality disorder subgroups, respectively. Cortical atrophy was present in 36% of the total sample ($\chi^2 = 9.6$, $p = .002$), in 32% of the schizotypal group ($\chi^2 = 6.0, p = .009$), and in 50% of the paranoid group ($\chi^2 = 8.4, p = .004$) (Table 1). This represents one of the first neuromorphological descriptions of personality disorders of the schizophrenic spectrum.

Schulz et al (21) observed essentially normal VBR values in eight young patients with borderline personality disorder as defined by DSM-III criteria. The discrepancy between our results and those of Schulz supports the idea of the specificity of the pathological finding; that is, it is not diffuse among patients with various personality pathologies but may be confined to particular diagnostic groups. This is confirmed by our finding that abnormal VBR values were confined to the schizotypal personality disorder.

In the context of their "High Risk Project" Schulsinger et al. (30) evaluated ventricular dimensions of patients diagnosed as having "borderline disorder" and also found them normal, but these cases were reported to be similar to DSM-III description of schizotypal personality disorder.

Given the discrepancy between the diagnostic criteria employed in Schulsinger et al study and in ours, however, a direct comparison of the results appears to be difficult. Furthermore, the subjects analyzed by Schulsinger et al. (30) were offspring of schizophrenic mothers and thus represented a group at high genetic risk for the development of schizophrenia and probably not representative of the general population of patients with personality disorders. Our finding of ventricular enlargement even in schizotypal subjects clearly indicates that the neuromorphologic anomaly does not necessarily represent a marker of the severity of pathology. Of particular importance is the fact that this disorder may be the early clinical precursor of future severe psychotic pathology and thus may represent an initial stage of the natural history of schizophrenia.

Finally, it is worth mentioning that we found a high percentage of patients in this sample with cortical atrophy. To our knowledge this is the first observation on the subject and warrants further confirmation. This finding, however, should be added to the common biological characteristics shared between schizophrenia and personality disorders of the schizophrenic spectrum and confirms the hypothesis of a close correlation between these disorders beyond familial-genetic considerations. The finding of a specific cortical localization of brain atrophy in patients with the paranoid personality disorder needs further confirmation, given the small number of cases analyzed.

CONCLUSIONS

Considered in the context of the existing literature, our results lend themself to the following considerations. First, the presence of pathological ventricular dilatation and cortical atrophy even in patients with schizophreniform disorders and in those with schizotypal and paranoid personality disorders indicates that the cerebrostructural anomalies are not specific to schizophrenia but represent correlates of a wider spectrum of psychiatric disturbances. In particular, finding the same anomalies in disorders of the Axis 2 of the DSM-III, while revealing a pathological substrate common to these pathologies and schizophrenia, raises a question from a biological point of view about the intrinsic validity of some of the hierarchies proposed by this diagnostic system.

Second, given the genetic link existing between the schizotypal and paranoid personality pathologies and schizophrenia (31), one might suppose that the anomalies observed represent a biological equivalent of the genetic susceptibility to develop schizophrenic illness. However, the results of different studies would indicate a prevalently environmental and not genetic origin of the cerebral structural changes.

Reveley et al (32) noted that the ill member of a pair of monozygotic twins discordant for schizophrenia consistently had larger cerebral ventricles, suggesting that ventricular dilatation might have environmental causes. In a family study of ventricular size, DeLisi et al. (33) demonstrated a genetic component in the definition of VBR, but also a conspicuous effect of the diagnosis, and thus of acquired factors, on ventricular enlargement. Schulsinger et al. (30) further observed that only the schizophrenic member of the schizophrenic mothers' offspring had a pathologically increased VBR.

It seems therefore possible that neuroanatomic anomalies signal the presence of an environmental risk for the development of schizophrenia. In fact, an association has been found between ventricular dilatation and prenatal pathology, in particular obstetrical complications (34) and, as more recently reported, perinatal infective pathology (35). It is possible that these and/or other noxious environmental factors predispose the subject to develop schizophrenia later in life. In some cases this may be preceded by specific personality disturbances and/or brief psychotic episodes that would form an integrative part of the natural history of the disease in some subjects.

Alternatively, it is possible that those factors predispose the individual to the development of a wider pathology spectrum, where determination of the specific clinical expression of each case could be secondary to other factors, whether genetic or not. A definitive response to this problem is entrusted to the results of long-term follow-up studies of subjects in whom various degrees of neuromorphological anomalies are found at an early age.

Third, an open problem is whether the finding of ventricular dilatation and/or widening of the cortical fissures and sulci in a patient with a personality disorder of the schizophrenic spectrum or a schizophreniform disorder does in fact predict the future development of schizophrenia. The only systematic study so far undertaken on schizophreniform patients did find a significant association between ventricular dilatation and a schizophrenic outcome of the disorder (36). Long-term longitudinal studies that evaluate the clinical development in relation to the neuromorphological characteristics of patients with these illnesses are necessary for drawing conclusions on the issue.

The same studies would be entrusted with the task of analyzing whether the presence of cerebrostructural anomalies conditions the clinical presentation, course, and treatment response of acute psychotic disorders as well as the personality disorders in which the anomalies are found. This possibility seems predictable on the basis of the results obtained in schizophrenia, where ventricular dilatation seems to countersign the more severe forms of illness with poor prognosis (4–7). Such a demonstration in pathologies correlated with schizophrenia would confirm the significance of the neuromorphological anomalies as a clinical prognostic marker in psychiatry and would provide an objective, reliable criterion for more rational and individualized planning of treatment.

REFERENCES

1. Jacobi W, Winkler H. Encephalographische Studien an Chronisch Schizophrenen. *Arc Psichiat Nervenkrankenheit* 1927;81:299–332.
2. Asano N. Pneunoencephalographic study of schizophrenia. In: Mitsuda H, ed. *Clinical genetics in psychiatry: problems in nosological classification*. Igaku Ltd, Tokyo, 1967;209–219.
3. Cazzullo CL. Biological and clinical studies on schizophrenia related to pharmacological treatment. *Rec Adv Biol Psychiatry* 1963;5:114–143.
4. Cazzullo CL, Vita A, Sacchetti E. Cerebral ventricular enlargement in schizophrenia: Prevalence and correlates. In: Schulz SC, Tamminga CA, eds. *Schizophrenia: scientific progress*. New York: Oxford University Press, 1989;195–206.
5. Shelton RC, Weinberger DR. X-ray computerized tomography studies in schizophrenia: A review and synthesis. In: Nasrallah HA, Weinberger DR, eds. *Handbook of schizophrenia, vol. 1: The neurology of schizophrenia*. Elsevier Science Publishers, Amsterdam, 1986;207–249.
6. Sacchetti E, Vita A, Calzeroni A, Invernizzi G, Cazzullo CL. Neuromorphological correlates of schizophrenic disorders: Focus on cerebral ventricular enlargement. In: Cazzullo CL, Invernizzi G, Sacchetti E, Vita A, eds. *Etiopathogenetic Hypotheses of Schizophrenia*. MTP Press, Lancaster, 1987;67–91.
7. Andreasen NC. Brain imaging: Application in psychiatry. *Science* 1988;239:1381–1388.
8. Targum DS, Rosen LN, DeLisi LE, et al. Cerebral ventricular size in major depressive disorders. Association with delusional symptoms. *Biolog Psychiatry* 1983;18:329–336.
9. DeLeon M, George AE. Computed tomography in aging and senile dementia of the Alzheimer type. In: Majeux R, Rosen WG, eds. *The dementias*. New York: Raven Press, 1983;103–121.
10. Pearlson GD, Garbacz DJ, Tompkins RH, et al. Clinical correlates of lateral ventricular enlargement in bipolar affective disorder. *Am J Psychiatry* 1984;141:235–256.
11. Rieder RO, Mann LS, Weinberger DR, et al. Computed tomographic scans in patients with schizophrenia, schizoaffective and bipolar affective disorders. *Arch Gen Psychiatry* 1983;40:735–739.
12. Andreasen NC, Olsen SA, Dennert JW, et al. Ventricular enlargement in schizophrenia: Relationship to positive and negative symptoms. *Am J Psychiatry* 1982;139:297–302.
13. Donnelly EF, Weinberger DR, Waldmann IN, et al. Cognitive impairment associated with morphological brain abnormalities on computed tomography in chronic schizophrenic patients. *J Nerv Ment Dis* 1980;168:305–308.
14. Weinberger DR, Bigelow LB, Kleinman JE, et al. Cerebral ventricular enlargement in chronic schizophrenia: An association with poor response to treatment. *Arch Gen Psychiatry* 1980;37:11–18.
15. Vita A, Valvassori G, Boato P, et al. Clinical and prognostic correlates of cerebral ventricular enlargement in schizophrenic disorders. In: Casacchia M, Rossi A, eds. *Schizophrenia: a psychobiological view*. Lancaster: MTP Press, 1989;99–110.
16. Weinberger DR, DeLisi LE, Perman GP, et al. Computed tomography in schizophreniform disorder and other acute psychiatric disorders. *Arch Gen Psychiatry* 1982;39:778–783.
17. Benes F, Sunderland P, Jones BD, et al. Normal ventricles in young schizophrenics. *Br J Psychiatry* 1982;141:90–93.
18. Trimble L, Kingsley D. Cerebral ventricular size in chronic schizophrenia. *Lancet* 1978;i:278–279.
19. Nyback H, Wiesel FA, Berggren BM, et al. Computed tomography of the brain in patients with acute psychosis and in healthy volunteers. *Acta Psychiatr Scand* 1982;65:403–414.
20. Tanaka Y, Hazama H, Kawahara R, et al. Computerized tomography of the brain in schizophrenic patients: A controlled study. *Acta Psychiatr Scand* 1981;63:191–197.
21. Schulz SC, Koller MM, Kishore PR, et al. Ventricular enlargement in teenage patients with schizophrenia spectrum disorder. *Am J Psychiatry* 1983;140:1592–1595.
22. Cazzullo CL, Vita A, Sacchetti E, et al. Cerebral ventricular size in diagnostic subtypes of schizophrenia and in schizophreniform disorder. In: Cazzullo CL, Invernizzi G, eds. *Schizophrenia: an integrative view*. London: John Libbey & Company, 1985;274–292.
23. Obiols, Llandrich JE, Ruscalleda J, Masferrer M. Ventricular enlargement in young chronic schizophrenics. *Acta Psychiatr Scand* 1986;73:42–44.
24. Woods BT, Wolf J. A reconsideration of the relation of ventricular enlargement to duration of illness in schizophrenia. *Am J Psychiatry* 1983;140:1564–1570.
25. Nasrallah HA, Olson SC, McCalley-Whitters M, et al. Cerebral ventricular size in schizophrenia. A preliminary follow-up study. *Arch Gen Psychiatry* 1986;43:157–159.
26. Illowsky BP, Juliano DM, Bigelow LB, et al. Stability of CT scan findings in schizophrenia: Results of an eight year follow-up study. *J Neurol Neurosurg Psychiatry* 1988;51:209–213.
27. Vita A, Sacchetti E, Valvassori G, Cazzullo CL. Brain morphology in schizophrenia: A 2- to 5-year CT scan follow-up study. *Acta Psychiatr Scand* 1988;78:618–621.
28. American Psychiatric Association Committee

on Nomenclature and Statistics. *Diagnostic and statistical manual of mental disorders,* 3rd ed. Washington DC, 1980.
29. Vita A, Sacchetti E, Calzeroni A, Cazzullo CL. Cortical atrophy in schizophrenia. Prevalence and associated features. *Schizophr Res* 1988;1:329–337.
30. Schulsinger F, Parnas J, Petersen ET, et al. Cerebral ventricular size in the offspring of schizophrenic mothers. *Arch Gen Psychiatry* 1984;41:602–606.
31. Baron M, Gruen R, Asnis L, et al. Familial relatedness of schizophrenia and schizotypal states. *Am J Psychiatry* 1983;140:1437–1442.
32. Reveley MA, Reveley AM, Murray RH. Cerebral ventricular enlargement in monogenetic schizophrenia: a controlled study. *Br J Psychiatry* 1984;144:89–93.
33. DeLisi LE, Goldin LR, Hamovit JR, et al. A family study of the association of increased ventricular size with schizophrenia. *Arch Gen Psychiatry* 1986;43:148–153.
34. Owen MJ, Lewis SV, Murray RM. Obstetric complications and cerebral abnormalities in schizophrenia. In: Cazzullo CL, Invernizzi G, Sacchetti E, Vita A, eds. *Etiopathogenetic hypotheses of schizophrenia.* Lancaster: MTP Press, 1987;9–20.
35. Mednick SA, Machon RA, Huttunen MD, et al. Adult schizophrenia following prenatal exposure to an influenza epidemic. *Arch Gen Psychiatry* 1988;45:189–192.
36. DeLisi LE, Schwartz CC, Targum SD, et al. Ventricular brain enlargement and outcome of acute schizophreniform disorder. *Psychiatry Res* 1983;9:169–180.

21

Nonschizophrenic Psychotic Disorders

Peter Berner

In traditional German psychiatry the term *psychosis* refers to mental disorders that have their basis in biological disturbances of brain function. Those disorders for which the somatic origin could be established with certainty were called *organic* psychoses, whereas the remaining group was thought to result from genetic predispositions and labeled as *endogenous* psychoses.

When Kraepelin (1) built up his nosological system, which imposed itself for decades on psychiatric thinking, he envisaged for a while the possibility that the endogenous psychoses could comprise the paraphrenias and paranoia as independent entities in addition to the two main groups, manic-depressive illness and dementia praecox. The catamnestic and family studies of Mayer (2) and Kolle (3), however, persuaded most psychiatrists that these disorders should be regarded as benign forms of schizophrenia (although their data, when critically examined, appear less convincing today). Thus, with the exception of some schools, a simple dichotomy of the endogenous psychoses was widely adopted that distinguished only between affective (named *cyclothymic* by K. Schneider; ref 4) and schizophrenic disorders. In this perspective, nonschizophrenic psychotic disorders, if not of a proven organic nature, are restricted to uni- or bipolar manic-depressive illness.

When Scandinavian psychiatrists such as Wimmer (5) started to use the word *psychotic* to designate the presence of "positive" symptoms, especially hallucinations and delusions, regardless of their supposed origin, another conceptualization of the nonschizophrenic psychotic disorders emerged. This point of view raised the question of which disorders characterized by "psychotic" symptoms have to be categorized as schizophrenic and which do not. German-speaking psychiatrists developed three approaches, frequently applied in combination, to settle this problem:

1. They established an inventory of schizophrenia-characteristic symptoms on theoretical grounds, as did E. Bleuler (6), or on pragmatic grounds, as did Schneider (4).
2. They applied Jasper's "hierarchical principle" (7) stipulating that, in the case of a combination of schizophrenic and cyclothymic symptoms, the former determine the diagnostic attribution.
3. They based the diagnosis on course and outcome, either by postponing its establishment until the end of a long observation or by incorporating prognosis indicators in the cross-sectional diagnostic procedure.

According to Bleuler and Schneider, a nonschizophrenic psychotic disorder is only conceivable in the absence of any "basic" or "first-rank" symptom, respectively. But, because these authors, and in particular some of their disciples, have in-

Psychiatric University Clinic, Allegemeines Krankenhaus der Stadt Wien Währinger Gurtel 18–20, 1090 Vienna, Austria.

sisted that "accessory" or "second-rank" symptoms may also suggest the diagnosis of schizophrenia under certain circumstances (which never have been exactly specified), many schools have incorporated all disorders with "positive" symptoms into schizophrenia. The application of Jasper's hierarchical principle, on the other hand, eliminates the possibility that some psychotic states may belong to the mood disorders or represent an independent schizoaffective entity. Catamnestic studies based on Bleulerian or Schneiderian diagnostic principles (8–10) finally convinced many representatives of these two schools to abandon Kraepelin's assumption that schizophrenia is a chronic, deteriorating process and to ignore course and outcome for diagnostic purposes. The tremendous extension of the boundaries of schizophrenia that emerged from this evolution has been challenged by different diagnostic systems which have proposed, as countermeasures, reversing or abolishing Jasper's hierarchical principle, reintroducing course-related criteria, and defining schizophrenic symptoms more strictly.

Concepts about the nature of endogenous psychoses have, during the last decades, gradually evolved from the assumption of distinct disease entities towards vulnerability models. In this perspective the central question is whether the type of vulnerability underlying schizophrenia is different from the vulnerabilities for cyclothymia or nonschizophrenic psychoses.

Our own research is based on the hypothesis that the particularity of schizophrenic disorders consists of a vulnerability to certain cognitive disturbances and to flatness of affect, whereas mood disorders are characterized by a vulnerability to activation dysregulations. These assumptions are close to the two-factor vulnerability model that Braden (11) proposes for schizoaffective disorders. According to this model, schizoaffective patients on the one hand are vulnerable to episodes of psychosis because of activation dysregulations and on the other are vulnerable to cognitive disturbance. Our model differs, however, from that of Braden insomuch as his notion of cognitive symptoms comprises Schneiderian symptoms and disorganized speech and thinking, whereas in the Vienna model, Schneiderian symptoms may be the direct result of primary cognitive disturbances as well as the consequence of activation dysregulations.

Thus, we agree with the many studies (12) proposing that the characteristic schizophrenic cognitive impairments may be grasped clinically only through the presence of formal thought disorders; in contrast, the Bonn school, characterized by Huber (13) and Klosterkötter (14), assumes that Schneiderian first-rank symptoms also have their roots in the primary cognitive disability considered to lie at the origin of schizophrenia. Klosterkötter has indeed recently demonstrated how first-rank symptoms may gradually emerge from self-experienced basic cognitive disturbances. These observations, however, have not really devaluated Janzarik's (15) studies, which point out how first-rank symptoms may be generated by activation dysregulations. Since these reflections are essential for understanding our concept of nonschizophrenic psychoses, they are briefly outlined below.

Janzarik designates as *dynamic* a fundamental realm embracing affectivity and drive, which contrasts with the *psychic structure* containing behavior patterns and representations (cognitive notions). Parts of this structure become dynamically invested, meaning that they are connected with positive, negative, or ambivalent feelings. Dynamically loaded parts of the structure are called *values* and comprise the *value structure*.

The dynamic, however, is not entirely tied to structural elements. Everybody has at his disposal a certain amount of free-floating dynamics, subject to alterations called *dynamic derailments,* which include manic expansion, depressive restriction, and states of dynamic instability characterized by rapid fluctuations between the aforementioned conditions. (The Vienna school considers irritability and anxiety to be additional, independent derailments.) Derailments effect an actualization of specific values: In states of expansion the positive elements of the structure are actualized, while in states of restriction the negative ones prevail, since positive values find no actualization. In states of dynamic instability, rapid changes in actualization of differently invested parts of the structure occur, whereby ambivalently invested elements of the value structure also become conscious.

All derailments may lead to *delusional impressions* (feeling that one's surroundings are changed in a striking and puzzling way), delusional perceptions, and illusions. In instability states the rapid swings in drive, emotional resonance, and affectivity may become overpowering, making one feel at their mercy; this may explain how hallucinations and feelings of will deprivation, alien influence, depersonalization, derealization, and ambivalence arise.

Thus, dynamic derailments appear to be the main source of Schneiderian symptoms and a part of Bleuler's basic symptoms. Janzarik's assumption that the dynamic derailments may arise in abnormal mental conditions stemming from various origins creates doubts as to the specificity of these phenomena. These suspicions were also strengthened by a series of investigations, for example, those reported by Mellor (16). Thus, the Bonn school, including Huber (13) and Klosterkötter (14), and the Heidelberg school, represented by Janzarik (15,17), propose different models for schizophrenia: Both schools feel that second-rank symptoms may arise from various causes but propose different models for the origin of first-rank symptoms.

The Bonn school assumes that in schizophrenia an inherited or acquired cognitive inadequacy exists that under stress conditions may lead to an impairment of information-processing, to overinclusion, and to response interference. The irritation produced by these phenomena leads, in turn, to disturbances in perception, thought, and behavior patterns as well as to cenesthesias that the patient externalizes and amalgamates with personal experiences into characteristic first-rank symptoms. Dynamic derailments, occurring frequently during the course of schizophrenic psychoses, appear under this perspective as another consequence of the basic irritation.

For the Heidelberg school, the reason for all psychoses is a vulnerability to an acquired or genetically determined dynamic instability, and it is this instability that produces first-rank symptoms. Whether the resulting psychosis is accompanied by formal thought disorders and evolves towards a deficiency state depends, in this view, only on premorbid personality traits. These traits are assumed to be completely independent of the inherited predisposition to psychosis.

The position of the Vienna school is that first-rank symptoms may arise from either impaired information processing or primary dynamic derailments. Thus, in our opinion, they are not suitable for distinguishing between schizophrenia and other psychoses. Taking this point of view into account in the Vienna Research Criteria (VRC; ref 18) we have based the diagnostic attribution to schizophrenia primarily on formal thought disorders (Table 1). The vulnerability for

TABLE 1. *Vienna Research Criteria for schizophrenia: Endogenomorphic–schizophrenic axial syndrome*

Diagnosis:
  Definitive: Criteria A and/or B are present.
  Probable: Only criterion C is present.

Criteria:
  A. Incoherence
    1. Blocking;
    2. Derailment;
    3. Pathologically "muddled speech."
  B. Cryptic neologisms.
  C. Affective blunting.

TABLE 2. *Vienna Research Criteria for endogenomorphic mood disorder: Endogenomorphic–cyclothymic axial syndrome*

A. Appearance of biorhythmic disturbances (Criteria 1 and 2 both necessary):
   1. Diurnal variations in affectivity and drive;
   2. Sleep disturbance (early awakening or prolonged sleep or interrupted sleep).
B. Appearance of a marked change in affectivity following a period of habitual functioning: Euphoric/manic, depressive, dysphoric (= irritable) or anxious.
C. Appearance of a marked change in emotional resonance following a period of habitual functioning.
D. Appearance of a marked change in drive following a period of habitual functioning

Criteria A and (B or C or D) are necessary for a definitive diagnosis.

cyclothymia (ie, endogenous mood disorder), on the other hand, is established in our diagnostic system through the presence of "biological symptoms" such as variations in biorhythms, which we do not consider to be simply an expression of severity (Table 2).

We have developed no operational diagnostic criteria for other psychotic disorders, because our experiences suggest that actual knowledge in this field does not yet allow one to establish distinct delimitations. In regard to delusional disorders we maintain the traditional distinction between paranoid, paranoiac, and paraphrenic states, subdividing the latter into systematic and unsystematic paraphrenias (Table 3).

These denominations are used in a syndromatical perspective for clinical orientation. If the background symptomatology permits no attribution to schizophrenia or cyclothymia (or to both, which leads to the diagnosis of a schizoaffective disorder), then the delusional syndrome is considered to escape nosological classification. Patients characterized by features suggesting an organic brain impairment such as circumstantiality, perseveration, and mnemic and intellectual deficiencies, in spite of negative results obtained by instrumental examination, are designated as "organomorphics." It is important to not forget this group of nonschizophrenic psychoses in view of the experience that psychogenic delusions frequently become chronic when the existence of an organic brain syndrome

TABLE 3. *Vienna Classification of delusion syndromes*

Criteria	Paranoid syndromes	Paranoiac syndrome	Systematic paraphrenia	Unsystematic paraphrenias
Delusional structure				
Paralogically unorganized				X
Logically unorganized	X			X
Paralogically organized	X	X	X	
Constituting elements of delusion:				
Normal, interpretations from:				
Normal perceptions	X	X	X	X
True memories	X	X	X	X
Falsified memories	X	X	X	X
Abnormal, interpretations from:				
Delusional impressions			X	X
Dysesthesias			X	X
Experience of alien influence			X	X
Misidentifications			X	X
Illusions			X	X
Hallucinations			X	X
Spontaneous delusional certitude			X	X
Fabulations			X	X

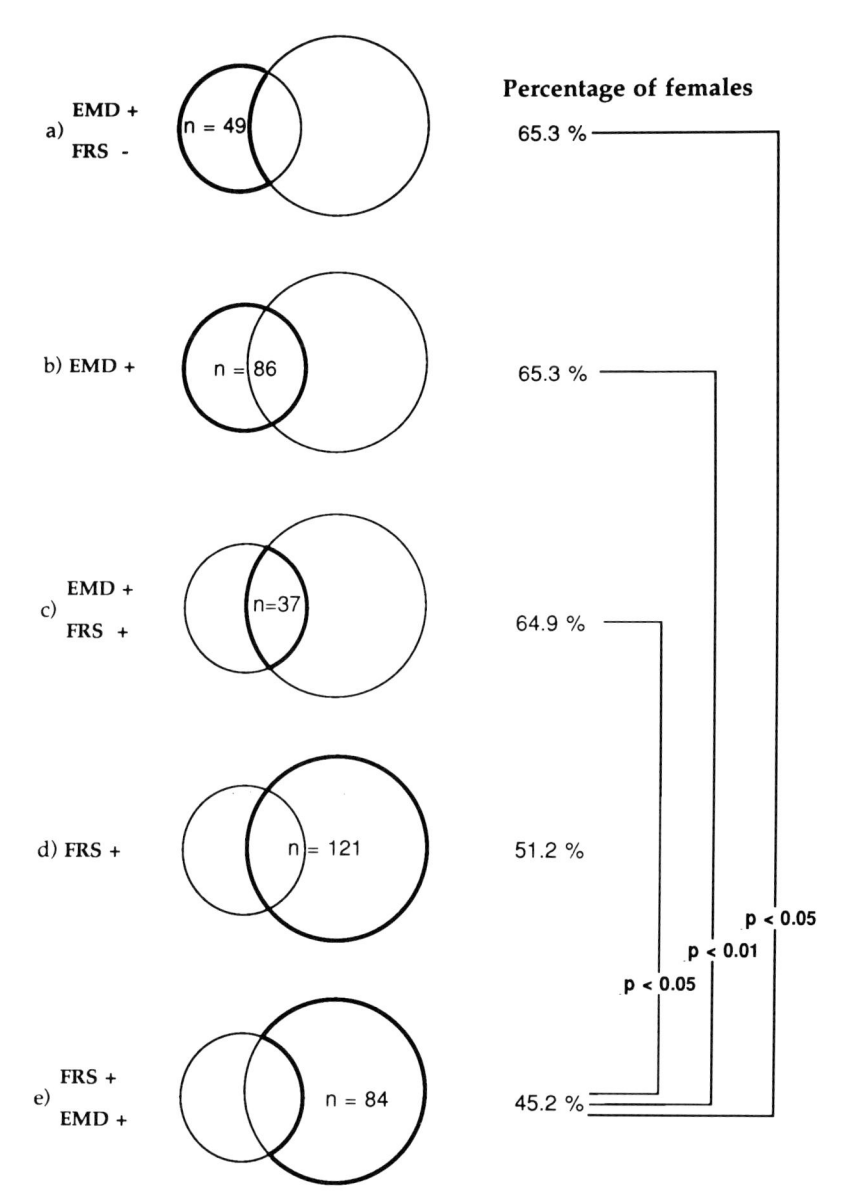

FIG. 1. Overlapping and sexual distribution of patients having at least one Schneiderian first-rank symptom (FRS) with patients meeting the Vienna Research Criteria for an endogenomorphic mood disorder (EMD).

prevents the patient's critical correction of his or her delusion.

Our diagnostic approach is faced with the problem that formal thought disorders are often difficult to grasp cross-sectionally. Similarly, biorhythmic variations may not manifest themselves in all phases throughout the course of endogenous mood disorders. Consequently, the absence of an endogenomorphic schizophrenic or cyclothymic axial syndrome does not preclude the disturbance from belonging to an endogenous schizophrenic or affective disorder; our axial syndromes are intended as research diagnostic criteria, for which specificity is considered of more importance than sensitivity.

The application of our diagnostic system to functional psychoses strongly supports the assumption that a substantial proportion of them belongs to endogenous mood disorders. It also indicates that another group of functional psychoses fits neither into the schizophrenic nor into the cyclothymic group. These statements shall be illustrated by some results of two studies: Fig. 1 shows that out of 200 cases of first-admission functional psychoses (19), 121 had to be considered schizophrenic (group d); however, 37 of them had to be classified as endogenous mood disorders according to VRC (group c). The sex distribution of group c corresponds to the whole group of VRC mood disorders (group b) as well as to the VRC mood disorders without first-rank symptoms (group a). Among the 84 first-rank symptom patients (group e) without a cyclothymic axial syndrome, on the other hand, the male sex prevails. These findings are in keeping with those reported in the literature with regard to the sexual distribution seen in each of these two functional psychoses.

In the second study (20) we have examined 419 first-degree relatives of 77 delusional patients. The results again argue for the assumption of an independent genetic predisposition to schizophrenia and mood disorders (Table 4). Vienna Research Criteria–schizophrenic probands have no first-degree relatives meeting the criteria for an endogenous mood disorder, but they do have a high percentage of VRC-schizophrenic family members. In reverse, VRC-cyclothymic probands have no VRC-schizophrenic relatives but many VRC-cyclothymic-disordered members in their families. Among the relatives of the unclassifiable patients we find a certain percentage of schizophrenic and a somewhat lower proportion of affective disorders, which demonstrates again the heterogeneity of this group. Interestingly, the organomorphic patients have no schizophrenic or

TABLE 4. *Vienna Research Criteria: Diagnosis for 77 delusional patients and mental illnesses among their 419 first-degree relatives*

	Relatives		
Patients	Endogenomorphic–schizophrenic axial syndrome	Endogenomorphic–cyclothymic axial syndrome	Alcoholism
Endogenomorphic–schizophrenic axial syndrome (17 patients, 93 first-degree relatives)	5.38%	0%	1.08%
Endogenomorphic–cyclothymic axial syndrome (13 patients, 76 first-degree relatives)	0%	5.26%	9.21%
Organomorphic axial syndrome (9 patients, 49 first-degree relatives)	0%	0%	14.29%
Unclassifiable (38 patients, 201 first-degree relatives)	2.99%	1%	3.98%

cyclothymic relatives but show the highest percentage of alcoholism in their families; in this context, it is noteworthy to mention that for most of the organomorphic patients chronic alcohol abuse was the obvious cause of their organic brain syndrome.

In conclusion, on the ground of our observations we assume the existence of different vulnerabilities to certain cognitive disturbances and affective flattening, on the one hand, and to endogenous mood disorders on the other. The term *schizophrenic* should, in our opinion, be reserved to the first type. Cases not attributable to one of these two kinds of disturbance are probably of very heterogeneous origin, emerging from multiform combinations of life experiences and personality traits. A portion of these patients may even belong to separate nosological entities. This can especially be assumed for cases corresponding to the syndrome of a "paraphrenia systemica," sustained by a permanently elevated or irritated mood.

REFERENCES

1. Kraepelin E. *Psychiatrie,* 5th ed. Leipzig: Barth, 1896.
2. Mayer W. Über paraphrene Psychosen. *Z ges Neurol Psychiat* 1921;71:187–206.
3. Kolle K. Die primäre Verrücktheit. *Psychopathologische, klinische und genealogische Untersuchungen.* Leipzig: Thieme, 1931.
4. Schneider K. *Klinische Psychopathologie,* 3rd ed. Stuttgart: Thieme, 1950.
5. Wimmer A. *Psykogene sindssygdomsformer.* Copenhagen: St Hans Hospitals Jubilaeumsskrift, 1916.
6. Bleuler E. Dementia praecox oder Gruppe der Schizophrenien. In: Aschaffenburg, ed. *Handbuch der Psychiatrie,* vol. 5. Leipzig–Wien: Deuticke, 1911.
7. Jaspers K. *Allgemeine Psychopathologie.* 4th ed. Berlin–Heidelberg–New York: Springer, 1964.
8. Bleuler M. *Die schizophrenen Geistesstörungen im Lichte langjähriger Kranken- und Familiengeschichten.* Stuttgart: Thieme, 1972.
9. Ciompi L, Müller C. *Lebensweg und Alter der Schizophrenen. Eine katamnestische Langzeitstudie bis ins senium.* Berlin–Heidelberg–New York: Springer, 1976.
10. Huber G, Gross G, Schüttler R. *Schizophrenie. Eine verlaufs- und sozialpsychiatrische Langzeitstudie.* Berlin–Heidelberg–New York: Springer, 1979.
11. Braden W. Vulnerability and schizoaffective psychosis: A two-factor model. *Schizophr Bull* 1984;10(1):71–86.
12. Mundt CH, Lang H. Die Psychopathologie der Schizophrenien. In: Kisker KP et al, eds. *Psychiatrie der Gegenwart.* Berlin–Heidelberg–New York–Tokyo: Springer, 1987.
13. Huber G. Das Konzept substratnaher Basissymptome und seine Bedeutung für Theorie und Therapie schizophrener Erkrankungen. *Nervenarzt* 1983;54:23–32.
14. Klosterkötter J. *Basissymptome und Endphänomene der Schizophrenie.* Berlin–Heidelberg–New York–London–Paris–Tokyo: Springer, 1988.
15. Janzarik W. *Dynamische Grundkonstellationen in endogenen Psychosen.* Berlin–Göttingen–Heidelberg: Springer, 1959.
16. Mellor CS. The present status of first rank symptoms. *Br J Psychiatry* 1982;140:423.
17. Janzarik W. *Schizophrene Verläufe. Eine strukturdynamische Interpretation.* Monographien aus der Gesamtgebiete der Neurologie und Psychiatrie, vol. 126. Berlin–Heidelberg–New York: Springer, 1968.
18. Berner P, Gabriel E, Katschnig H, Kieffer W, Koehler K, Lenz G, Simhandl Ch. *Diagnostic criteria for schizophrenic and affective psychoses.* Washington, DC: American Psychiatric Press, 1983.
19. Berner P, Katschnig H. Approche polydiagnostique en recherche psychiatrique. *Ann Méd-Psycholog* 1984;142(6):825–831.
20. Schanda H. *Paranoide Psychosen.* Stuttgart: Enke, 1987.

22

Ex Multi Uno: A Case for Neurobiological Homogeneity in Schizophrenia

David G. Daniel and Daniel R. Weinberger[1]

In recent years, Bleuler's concept of schizophrenia as a syndrome of etiologically distinct disorders (1) has achieved wide acceptance (2,3). Whereas early attempts to subtype schizophrenia relied almost exclusively on clinical observations, increasingly incisive in vivo brain-imaging techniques have enabled brain structure and metabolism to emerge as the leading tools for subclassifying this disorder. It has been widely believed that these techniques would eventually contribute to a taxonomy of schizophrenia based on biologically distinct subtypes (2,4). Abnormalities in a wide variety of biological parameters have been associated with schizophrenia, including brain morphology (see refs 5 and 6 for reviews), neurophysiology (7–9), neurochemistry (10,11), and performance on tests of neuropsychological function (see ref 12 for review). In most of these studies it has been apparent that only a minority of schizophrenic patients have abnormal values compared to normal controls. That is, the distribution of measurements of the schizophrenic patients usually overlapped with that of the controls but was shifted toward the abnormal end of the spectrum. This pattern of findings has been widely interpreted to signify that a pathological process affects only a minority of schizophrenic patients and that the abnormality in question may be a "marker" for an etiologically distinct subtype of the disorder.

Recent studies of monozygotic twin pairs discordant for schizophrenia suggest that abnormalities in two areas of schizophrenia research that have been frequently discussed with respect to biological heterogeneity—anatomical neuropathological deviations and cerebral metabolic hypoactivity of the frontal lobe—rather than being associated with only a minority of patients, are possibly general characteristics of the disease (51,73). In almost all cases the schizophrenic twin could be discriminated from the normal twin on the basis of these findings, even when both fell well within the range of normal controls (51,73). This suggests that the ubiquitous nature of these findings in schizophrenia may have heretofore been overlooked because of nonspecific variability in brain morphology and physiology. The results suggest that experimental designs that define abnormal measurements by where they fall in relationship to a frequency distribution of normal controls may underestimate the prevalence of neurobiological deviance.

Enlargement in the size of the cerebral ventricles, which has emerged as one of the most frequently replicated findings in the field of schizophrenia research (5), appears to be a case in point. This finding has been demonstrated by a succession of increasingly incisive in vivo structural brain-imag-

---

[1]Clinical Brain Disorders Branch, Intramural Research Program, National Institute of Mental Health, Neuroscience Center at Saint Elizabeth's, Washington, DC 20032.

ing techniques beginning with pneumoencephalography (13–16), then with computed tomography (CT; ref 6), and most recently with magnetic resonance imaging (MRI; refs 17,18). The lateral ventricles have received such extensive study because their size is a sensitive indicator of central nervous system (CNS) pathology that may be diffuse or localized to the structures surrounding them. From the very first quantitative CT study by Johnstone and associates (1976; ref 19), it has been apparent that only a minority of schizophrenic patients have enlarged ventricular size as defined by the normal limits of variability. That is, the distribution of ventricle-to-brain size ratios (VBRs) of the schizophrenic patients usually overlapped that of the controls but was slightly shifted upwards. These findings have been widely interpreted to signify that a pathological process affects the ventricles of only a minority of schizophrenic patients and that ventriculomegaly may be a marker for an etiologically distinct subtype of the disorder. This assumption has held sway in spite of the observation that very small ventricles are as unlikely a finding in patients with schizophrenia as large ventricles are a likely finding (20).

Many classification schemes for schizophrenia assume isomorphism between observed behaviors and biological parameters (3,21). The possibility that lateral ventricular enlargement may define a subpopulation of schizophrenic patients has led a number of investigators to attempt to delineate the clinical, biochemical, and physiological parameters of this subgroup. For instance, on the basis of limited evidence it has been argued that phenomenologically based dichotomous subtypings such as Kraepelinian versus non-Kraepelinian schizophrenia (22–24), disorganized versus paranoid schizophrenia, and Crow's Type 1 versus Type 2 schizophrenia (25) can be differentiated by the presence or absence of structural brain abnormalities (see ref 26 for review). Enlargement of the lateral ventricles has been correlated with the following:

1. Clinical variables, including poor premorbid social adjustment (27,28), impairment on neuropsychological tests (19,29–35), increased frequency of "negative" or "defect" symptoms (19,36, 37), decreased frequency of "positive" symptoms (36–38), persistent unemployment (37), and poor prognosis (39);
2. Measures related to brain dopamine activity including reduced cerebrospinal fluid levels of homovanillic acid (HVA; refs 40–42) and dopamine β-hydroxylase (40), and attenuated response to neuroleptics (27,38,43,44);
3. Deficits in prefrontal blood flow during a prefrontal-specific neuropsychological task (45).

It should be noted, however, that a substantial number of investigations have failed to confirm an association between enlarged ventricles and the following:

Negative symptomatology (38,46–49);
Infrequency of positive symptomatology (46,50);
Cognitive impairment (46,50–53);
Premorbid history (36,50);
Neuroleptic response (46).

These discrepancies probably reflect methodological inconsistencies, sampling differences, and the fact that the relationships are of limited robustness.

The positive findings are compatible with the dichotomous notions that enlarged ventricles in schizophrenia (a) are a marker for a biologically distinct subtype or grouping of subtypes of the disorder, and (b) exist on a continuum in which abnormal ventricular size is associated with perhaps a more severe but qualitatively indistinct form of the same disorder. However, both of these interpretations are posited on the assumption that the underlying pathological process responsible for these observations preferentially or exclusively affects the patients outside the range of normal. This assumption implies that schizophrenic patients whose ventricles are small relative to those of controls lack the pathological process seen in patients with large ventricles.

It may be instructive to test this line of thinking on a better-understood disorder such as acromegaly. In acromegaly enlargement of the extremities of adults occurs because of excessive production of growth hormone by a pituitary adenoma. However, in patients who started out with small hands, this increment might not be sufficient to push their hand size beyond the normal range. Therefore, an investigation based on an examination of the hands of these patients at a single point in time would find some to be enlarged relative to normal hands and some not, possibly leading to the erroneous conclusion that there are subgroups of patients with acromegaly based on hand size. By analogy, it could be argued that all patients with schizophrenia share a common pathophysiological process that augments cerebral ventricular size relative to what would have been, had the patient not had schizophrenia. In patients who started out with small ventricles to begin with, this increment might not be sufficient to push their ventricular size out of the normal range.

Sibling controls provide a means of controlling for normal biological variability and testing the hypothesis that *relative* structural deviation can be detected even when structural parameters fall well within the range of normal controls. Weinberger et al measured lateral ventricular size in 11 sibling groups discordant for schizophrenia and found that the affected sibling group had larger cerebral ventricles in each case, *even when the ventricles of both siblings were small* (54). Reveley and colleagues studied CT scans of 12 twin pairs discordant for schizophrenia and found larger lateral cerebral ventricles in the affected twin in all but one pair (55). DeLisi and co-workers also observed larger ventricular size in schizophrenic patients than in their unaffected siblings (56).

Magnetic resonance imaging provides the best resolution of any currently available in vivo technology for examining brain structure. Suddath et al studied ventricular and temporal-lobe size using MRI in 15 pairs of monozygotic twins who were discordant for schizophrenia (57). Measurements were made on T1-weighted, 5-mm contiguous coronal sections with a semiautomated computerized image-analysis system. Differences between areas measured on MRI scans were examined by matched-pair t-tests. Compared with the normal twin, the right lateral cerebral ventricles were larger in 13 out of 15 affected twins ($p<.001$), the left lateral ventricles were larger in 14 out of 15 affected twins ($p<.003$), and the third ventricle was larger in 13 out of 15 affected twins ($p<.001$). Compared with the normal twin, relative enlargement of the third ventricle and lateral ventricles was visually apparent in 13 out of 15 affected twins even in cases where the ventricles of both twins were small. In addition, 14 out of 15 affected twins had smaller areas of the left anterior hippocampus ($p<.001$), and 13 out of 15 affected twins had smaller areas of the right hippocampus ($p<.02$). These data from studies using sibling controls suggest that subtle anatomic deviations can be observed in most patients with schizophrenia when appropriate controls are available and that these deviations are not unique to a small subgroup of patients.

The finding that monozygotic twins discordant for schizophrenia can be differentiated on the basis of ventricular and hippocampal size suggests an etiologic role for nongenetic factors in the underlying neuropathological process. If a nongenetically induced increment in ventricular size were a marker for a distinct subtype of schizophrenia, then in a large enough sample, the enlarged and unenlarged ventricles might be expected to form two separate distributions with different means, variances, and population proportions. The sample sizes of individual studies have been too small to examine the distribution of ventricular-size values for deviation from unimodality. In order to assess this question, we reviewed all published English-language VBR studies as of December 1987 for which individual data points were available (schizophrenics: $n = 691$; medical controls: $n = 205$; unselected volunteers: $n = 160$); we then culled the individual VBR values from these studies (58). The data were analyzed using a mixture-analysis paradigm developed by Gibbons (59,60) and based in part on earlier work by Day (61). If schizophrenia were composed of two distinct subtypes characterized by the presence or absence of enlarged ventricles, one would have expected the distribution of ventricular size in schizophrenia to be a mixture of at least two normal distributions. Natural log transformation of the data were performed prior to the mixture analysis (60,62) in order to prevent misleading results from small numbers of outliers. Using the mixture-distribution paradigm, the frequency distributions of the log-transformed VBRs of the schizophrenic patients, unselected controls, and medical controls were examined separately in regard to their consistency with a single-component Gaussian distribution (eg, unimodal) versus a mixture of Gaussian distributions (eg, bimodal). In each case the frequency histograms had a unimodal distribution and the improvement in fit of a mixture of distributions over a single distribution was not significant.

We then performed the mixture analysis on the schizophrenic patients combined with all of the controls (both unselected and medical controls). If the model failed to identify the presence of two known populations in this case, then its sensitivity for identifying subpopulations within the schizophrenic patient group could also be questioned. The frequency distribution of log-transformed VBRs of the combined sample of schizophrenic patients and all controls suggested the presence of two-component distributions (ie, bimodality). In this sample the improvement in fit of a mixture of two Gaussian distributions over a single Gaussian distribution was highly significant ($\chi^2 = 114.005$, $df = 2$, $p < .0001$). The lower distribution consisted of 22.5% of the sample, and the higher distribution consisted of 77.5% of the sample. The two-component distributions did not strictly differentiate patients and controls. Of the schizophrenic patients, 12.7% are classified in the lower-component distribution, in contrast to 32.3% of the unselected controls and 36.6% of the medical controls. Because of a controversy in the psychiatric literature over possible differences between the VBRs of medical and unselected controls (63–67), we next performed the mixture analysis on the schizophrenic patients combined separately with the medical controls and with the unselected controls. For each of the two control groups, combination of their VBR values with those of the schizophrenic patients produced a bimodal distribution. The improvement in fit of a mixture distribution over a single normal distribution was highly significant for both the medical controls ($\chi^2 = 144.321$, $df = 2$, $p < .0001$) and the unselected controls ($\chi^2 = 87.104$, $df = 2$, $p < .0001$).

If ventricular size above a certain threshold was a biological marker for a distinct subtype of schizophrenia, VBR values above this threshold would have been expected to cluster apart from the main body of values and the shape of the resulting frequency distribution plot should have been bimodal or at least mixed. Our recent study of data from 691 patients with schizophrenia did not support the notion of a bimodal or multimodal distribution of ventricular size in schizophrenia. Instead, the frequency plot consisted of a relatively smooth continuum that appeared unimodal in shape. When the VBRs of the schizophrenic patients were combined with those of the controls, two visually and statistically distinguishable Gaussian distributions were observed. The distribution indicated that ventricular size in schizophrenia overlaps with that of unselected and medical controls, but is shifted upward. This supports the results of sibling control studies; it also suggests that the assumption that an abnormality in ventricular size can be defined in terms of a single threshold across individuals is probably overly simplistic. A normal genetic endowment for ventricular size might be augmented by a pathological environmental event (eg, prenatal injury) to produce ventricles larger than those of a genetically similarly endowed subject but not necessarily large enough to fall outside the usual range of normal subjects. The observation that the distribution of VBR values far more consistently resembles a unimodal curve shifted upward than a bimodal curve (68,69) is congruous with this hypothesis.

The findings of unimodality in the distribution of ventricular size and relative ventricular enlargement in affected monozygotic twins with normal ventricular size suggests that distinct subpopulations of schizophrenia based on ventricular size do not exist. When viewed with the findings of Suddath et al (57) and Reveley et al (55), this unimodality of VBR values strongly supports the hypothesis that the underlying neuropathological process, which is obvious in patients with extreme VBR values, also exists but to a lesser degree in patients with "normal"-sized cerebral ventricles. Furthermore, the monozygotic twin studies imply that these subtle neuropathological abnormalities are at least partially nongenetic in etiology.

The clinical relevance of structural neuropathological findings is their effect on brain function. Like ventriculomegaly, deficits in prefrontal cortex function as inferred from deficits in prefrontal metabolic activity have frequently, but not invariably, been replicated in the literature. One explanation for the inconsistency is that this is a subgroup phenomenon associated with only a minority of patients. Another possibility is that detection of this finding depends on what the patient is doing during the scanning procedure. It is also possible that subtle differences in metabolic activity may be masked by nonspecific variability among control subjects. Metabolic hypofrontality in schizophrenia has been most consistently demonstrated when the scanning was done while the patient performed the Wisconsin Card Sort Test (WCST), a task that preferentially activates the prefrontal cortex (PFC; refs 70–72). Nevertheless, there remains much overlap in measures of PFC activation between patients and normal controls.

In order to explore this question further we used the XE-133 inhalation technique to measure regional cerebral blood flow (rCBF) in 18 pairs of monozygotic twins, ten of whom were discordant and eight of whom concordant for schizophrenia (73). In each subject rCBF was measured at rest, during a simple numbers matching control task, and during performance of the WCST. In *all* ten twin pairs discordant for schizophrenia, prefrontal rCBF was lower in the schizophrenic twin than in the well twin during performance of the WCST.

It is unproven whether deficits in prefrontal cortex metabolic activity in schizophrenia are a consequence of intrinsic or extrafrontal pathology. What relationship, if any, exists between the prefrontal cortical hypometabolic and anterotemporal structural abnormalities we have reported? A case for a functional relationship between these findings can be made on the basis of animal studies that have identified direct projections from the amygdala and hippocampal complex to the frontal lobe and indirect projections to the frontal lobe via anteromedial limbic structures (74,75). Anatomic data from monkeys demonstrate that direct projections from the PFC and other association cortices converge on the entorhinal and subicular cortices (77–79). Metabolic data from monkeys suggests that the dorsal prefrontal cortex and hippocampus cooperatively mediate performance on *working memory tasks* (76,80). The WCST is a working memory task that requires patients to make decisions based on past experience and to change their behavior based on error feedback (75). As mentioned earlier, in schizophrenia, metabolic hypofrontality has been most consistently demonstrated when imaging is performed during performance of the WCST (70–72). Not surprisingly, patients with schizophrenia tend to perform poorly on the WCST (12).

In view of the animal data, our findings are consistent with the scenario that in schizophrenia, deficits in prefrontal metabolic activity during the WCST arise from disruption in the connectivity of the hippocampal-prefrontal network, possibly due to a primary structural hippocampal lesion. Indirect support for this possibility comes from the results of a study by Berman et al (45) that found an inverse relationship between ventricular size and prefrontal rCBF during the WCST in patients with schizophrenia.

In contrast, patients with schizophrenia perform relatively better on Ravens Progressive Matrices (RPM), another abstract reasoning task, and their pattern of cortical metabolism is relatively normal (71). The RPM requires abstract reasoning and concentration at least as rigorous as does the WCST. However, unlike the WCST, the RPM does not seem to require working memory and does not activate the PFC in normal adults (71,75). If working memory is impaired by dysfunction of prefrontal lobe to anteromedial temporal-lobe connectivity, it could explain why performance and metabolic activation on the WCST is substantially more impaired in schizophrenic patients than on the RPM.

The role these subtle findings play in the pathophysiology of psychotic symptoms of schizophrenia is unclear. Expansion of the lateral and third ventricles may result from reduced tissue volume of structures adjacent to them. Several of these structures, including the hippocampus, fornix, thalamus, and basal ganglia, have at one time or another been implicated in the pathophysiology of schizophrenia. Injuries and epileptic activity in the anteromedial temporal lobe have been associated with psychotic behavior with a relatively high frequency compared with similar lesions in other brain regions (75). Nevertheless, psychotic symptoms are a relatively rare sequel of damage to the anteromedial temporal lobe, and when they occur, the clinical picture usually does not closely resemble schizophrenia (81). In addition, patients with schizophrenia rarely display the profound amnesia seen in patients with bilateral anterior temporal-lobe injuries.

A possibly better clinical-pathological analogy for schizophrenia may be adult-onset metachromatic leukodystrophy (MLD; ref 75), an autosomal recessive disorder of lipid metabolism in which sulfatides accumulate in the brain and other organs (82). A surprisingly high percentage of cases of this disorder present with a schizophrenialike illness before neurological symptoms develop (83–85). The pathological changes of MLD are primarily in the white matter and glia with relative sparing of the cortex and hippocampus. This suggests that, when schizophrenialike symptoms are produced by MLD, they are manifestations of disordered neuroanatomic communication. This is a potential analogy to the scenario described above in which disruptions in the neuroanatomic connectivity of the hippocampal-prefrontal network contribute to the pathophysiology of schizophrenia.

In conclusion, recent data suggest that when nonspecific variation in brain morphology and physiology is properly controlled for, subtle neuropathological features appear to be characteristic findings of the illness, rather than a subgroup phenomenon as previously believed. The finding that monozygotic twins discordant for schizophrenia can be distinguished by these neuropathological features suggest that their etiology is, at least in part, nongenetic. These studies highlight the importance of rigorous matching of controls to patients in order to appreciate subtle quantitative deviations. Our experience suggests that in the absence of ideal controls, physiological activation studies, by permitting the patient to serve as their own controls, are useful in this regard (see refs 70–72 for review).

The motto "ex uno multi," or "many from one" (3), is a reflection of the modern popularity of Bleuler's (1911) syndrome hypothesis of schizophrenia (1,3,11). In this sense, schizophrenia has been considered to be conceptually analogous to syndromes such as mental retardation or epilepsy (3). We believe that recent findings foreshadow a conceptual shift back toward the single-entity disease concept advocated by Emil Kraepelin in 1907 (11,86).

REFERENCES

1. Bleuler E. *Dementia praecox or the group of schizophrenias*. Zinkin J, trans. New York: International University Press, 1950.
2. Kety SS. The syndrome of schizophrenia: unresolved questions for research. *Br J Psychiatry* 1980;136:421–436.
3. Jeste DV, Kleinman JE, Potkin SG, et al. Ex uno multi: subtyping the schizophrenia syndrome. *Biolog Psychiatry* 1982;17:199–222.
4. Baldessarini RJ. Schizophrenia. *N Eng J Med* 1977;297:988–995.
5. Shelton R, Weinberger DR. Brain morphology in schizophrenia. In: Meltzer H, Bunney W, Cowl J, Davis K, eds. *Psychopharmacology: the third generation of progress*. New York: Raven Press, 1987;773–781.
6. Shelton R, Weinberger DR. X-ray computerized tomography studies in schizophrenia: a review and synthesis. In: Nasrallah HA, Weinberger DR, eds. *The neurology of schizophrenia*. Amsterdam: Elsevier N Holland, 1986;207–250.
7. Buchsbaum MS, DeLisi LE, Holcomb H, et al. Anteroposterior gradients in cerebral glucose use in schizophrenia and affective disorders. *Arch Gen Psychiatry* 1984;41:1159–1166.
8. Grebb JA, Weinberger DR, Morihisa JM. EEG and evoked potential findings in schizophrenia. In: Nasarallah HA, Weinberger DR, eds. *The neurology of schizophrenia*. Amsterdam: Elsevier N Holland, 1986;397–406.
9. Berman KF, Weinberger DR. Cerebral blood flow studies in schizophrenia. In: Nasarallah HA, Weinberger DR, eds. *The neurology of schizophrenia*. Amsterdam: Elsevier N Holland, 1986;397–406.
10. Potkin SG, Karoum F, Chuang L-W, et al. Phenylethylamine in paranoid chronic schizophrenia. *Science* 1979;206:470–471.
11. Jeste DV, Doongaji DR, Panjawani D, et al. Paranoid schizophrenia—A cross-cultural confirmation of a biochemical abnormality. *Psychiatry Res* 1981;3:341–352.
12. Goldberg TE, Weinberger DR. Neuropsychological studies of schizophrenia. *Schizophr Bull* 1988;14:179–184.
13. Haug JO. Pneumoencephalographic studies in mental disease. *Acta Psychiatr Scand* 1962;38(suppl)165:1–114.
14. Storey PB. Lumbar air encephalography in chronic schizophrenia: A controlled experiment. *Br J Psychiatry* 1966;112:135–144.
15. Asano N. Pneumoencephalographic study of schizophrenia. In: Mitsuda H, ed. *Clinical genetics in psychiatry: problems in neurological classification*. Tokyo: Igaku-Shoin, 1967.
16. Weinberger DR, Wagner RL, Wyatt RJ. Neuropathological studies of schizophrenia: A selective review. *Schizophr Bull* 1983;9:193–212.
17. Kelsoe J, Cadet J-L, Pickar D, Weinberger DR. Quantitative neuroanatomy in schizophrenia: a controlled MRI study. *Arch Gen Psychiatry* 1988;45:533–541.
18. Suddath RL, Casanova M, Goldberg T, Daniel DG, Kelsoe J, Weinberger DR. Temporal lobe pathology in schizophrenia: a quantitative MRI study. *Am J Psychiatry* 1988;146:464–472.
19. Johnstone EC, Crow TJ, Frith CD, et al. Cerebral ventricular size and cognitive impairment in chronic schizophrenia. *Lancet* 1976;2:924–926.
20. Weinberger DR, DeLisi LE, Perman G, Targum S, Wyatt RJ. Computed tomography scans in schizophreniform disorder and other acute psychiatric patients. *Arch Gen Psychiatry* 1982;39:778–783.
21. Corning WC, Steffy RA. Taximetric strategies applied to psychiatric classification. *Schizophr Bull* 1979;5:294–305.
22. Keefe RSE, Mohs RC, Losonczy MF, et al. Characteristics of very poor outcome schizophrenia. *Am J Psychiatry* 1987;144:889–995.
23. Keefe RSE, Mohs RC, Davidson M, et al. Kraepelinian schizophrenia: a subgroup of schizophrenia? *Psychopharmacol Bull* 1988;24:56–61.
24. Mackay AVP. Positive and negative schizophrenic symptoms and the role of dopamine. *Br J Psychiatry* 1980;137:379–383.
25. Crow TJ. Molecular pathology of schizophrenia: more than one disease process? *Br Med J* 1980;280:66–68.
26. Goetz KL, van Kammen DP. Computerized axial tomography scans and subtypes of schizophrenia: a review of the literature. *J Nerv Ment Dis* 1986;174:31–41.
27. Weinberger DR, Bigelow LB, Kleinman JE, Klein ST, Rosenblatt JE, Wyatt RJ. Cerebral ventricular enlargement in chronic schizophrenia: association with poor response to treatment. *Arch Gen Psychiatry* 1980;37:11–14.
28. DeLisi LE, Schwartz CC, Targum SD, et al. Ventricular brain enlargement and outcome of acute schizophrenic disorder. *J Psychiatry* 1983;9:169–171.
29. Johnstone EC, Crow TJ, Frith CD, et al. The dementia of dementia praecox. *Acta Psychiatr Scand* 1978;57:305–324.
30. Golden CJ, Moses Jr. JA, Zelazowski R, Graber B, Zatz LM, Horvath TB, Berger PA. Cerebral ventricular size and neuropsychological impairment in young chronic schizophrenics. *Arch Gen Psychiatry* 1980;37:619–623.

31. Donnelly EF, Weinberger DR, Waldman IN, Wyatt RJ. Cognitive impairment associated with morphological brain abnormalities on computed tomography in chronic schizophrenic patients. *J Nerv Ment Dis* 1980;168:305–308.
32. Golden CJ, MacInnes WD, Ariel RN, et al. Cross-validation of the ability of the Luria-Nebraska neuropsychological battery to differentiate chronic schizophrenics with and without ventricular enlargement. *J Consult Clin Psychiatry* 1982;50:87–95.
33. Kemali D, Maj M, Galderisi S, et al. Clinical, biological, and neuropsychological features associated with lateral ventricular enlargement in DSM-III schizophrenic disorder. *Psychiatry Res* 1986;21:137–149.
34. Lawson WB, Waldman I, Weinberger DR. Schizophrenic dementia: Clinical and CT correlates. *J Nerv Ment Dis* 1988;176:207–212.
35. Goldberg TE, Kleinman JE, Daniel DG, Myslobodsky MS, Ragland JR, Weinberger DR. Dementia praecox revisited: age disorientation, mental status, and ventricular enlargement. *Br J Psychiatry* 1988;153:187–190.
36. Andreasen NC, Scott AO, Dennert JW, et al. Ventricular enlargement in schizophrenia: relationship to positive and negative symptoms. *Am J Psychiatry* 1982;139:297–302.
37. Pearlson GD, Garbacs DJ, Breakey WR, et al. Lateral ventricular enlargement associated with persistent unemployment and negative symptoms in both schizophrenic and bipolar disorder. *Psychiatry Res* 1984;12:1–9.
38. Luchins DJ, Lewine RRJ, Meltzer HY. Lateral ventricular size, psychopathology, and medication response in the psychoses. *Biolog Psychiatry* 1984;19:29–44.
39. Pandurangi AK, Dewan MJ, Boucher M, et al. A comprehensive study of chronic schizophrenic patients. *Acta Psychiatr Scand* 1986;73:161–171.
40. Van Kammen DP, Mann LS, Sternberg DE, et al. Dopamine β-hydroxylase activity and homovanillic acid in spinal fluid of schizophrenics with brain atrophy. *Science* 1983;220:974–977.
41. Nyback H, Berggren BM, Hindmarsh T. Cerebroventricular size and cerebrospinal fluid monoamine metabolites in schizophrenic patients and healthy volunteers. *Psychiatry Res* 1983;9:301.
42. Jennings WS, Schulz SC, Narasimhachari N, et al. Brain ventricular size and CSF monoamine metabolites in an adolescent inpatient population. *Psychiatry Res* 1985;16:87–94.
43. Luchins DJ, Lewine RJ, Meltzer HY. Lateral ventricular size in the psychoses: relation to psychopathology and therapeutic and adverse response to medication. *Schizophr Bull* 1983;19:518.
44. Schultz SC, Sinicrope P, Kishore P, Friedel RO. Treatment response and ventricular enlargement in young schizophrenic patients. *Psychopharmacol Bull* 1983;19:510–512.
45. Berman KF, Weinberger DR, Shelton RC, Zec RF. A relationship between anatomical and physiological brain pathology in schizophrenia: lateral cerebral ventricular size predicts cortical blood flow. *Am J Psychiatry* 1987;144:1277–1282.
46. Nasrallah HA, Kuperman S, Hamra B, McCalley-Whitters M. Clinical differences between schizophrenic patients with and without large cerebral ventricles. *J Clin Psychiatry* 1983;44:407.
47. Farmer A, Jackson R, Mcguffin P, Storey P. Cerebral ventricular enlargement in chronic schizophrenia: consistencies and contraindications. *Br J Psychiatry* 1987;150:324–330.
48. Ota T, Maeshiro H, Ishido Y, et al. Treatment resistant chronic psychopathology and CT scans in schizophrenia. *Acta Psychiatr Scand* 1987;75:415–427.
49. Takahashi R, Inaba Y, Inanga K, et al. CT scanning and the investigation of schizophrenia. In: Perris C, Struwe C, Jansson B, eds. *Biological psychiatry* 1981. Amsterdam: Elsevier, 1981.
50. Nasrallah HA, Jacoby GC, McCalley-Whitters M, et al. Cerebral ventricular enlargement in subtypes of chronic schizophrenia. *Arch Gen Psychiatry* 1982;319:774–777.
51. Kling AS, Kurtz N, Tachiki K, Orzeck A. CT scans in sub-groups of chronic schizophrenics. *J Psychiatr Res* 1982/83;17:375–384.
52. Owens DGC, Johnstone EC, Crow TJ. Lateral ventricular size in schizophrenia: relationship to the disease process and its clinical manifestations. *Psycholog Med* 1985;15:27–41.
53. Kolakowska T, Williams AO, Jambor K, Ardern M. Schizophrenia with good and poor outcome III: neurological "soft" signs, cognitive impairment and their clinical significance. *Br J Psychiatry* 1985;146:348–357.
54. Weinberger DR, DeLisi LE, Neophytides AN, et al. Familial aspects of CT scan abnormalities in chronic schizophrenic patients. *Psychiatry Res* 1981;4:65–71.
55. Reveley AM, Reveley MA, Clifford CA, et al. Cerebral ventricular size in twins discordant for schizophrenia. *Lancet* 1982;1:540–541.
56. DeLisi LE, Goldin LR, Hamovit JR, et al. A family study of the association of increased ventricular size with schizophrenia. *Arch Gen Psychiatry* 1986;43:148–153.
57. Suddath RL, Christison G, Torrey EF, et al. Quantitative magnetic resonance imaging in twin pairs discordant for schizophrenia. *Schizophr Res* 1989;2:129.
58. Daniel DG, Goldberg TE, Gibbons RD, Weinberger DR. Lack of a bimodal distribution of ventricular size in schizophrenia: a mixture distribution analysis of 1056 cases and controls. (submitted)
59. Gibbons RD. Identifying biological subtypes in psychiatric research. In: Gibbons RD, Dysken M, eds. *Statistical and methodological advances in psychiatric research*. New York: Spectrum Publishers, 1983.
60. Gibbons RD, Dorus E, Ostrow DG, et al. Mixture distributions in psychiatric research. *Biolog Psychiatry* 1984;19:935–961.

61. Day NE. Estimating the components in a mixture of normal distributions. *Biometrika* 1969;56:463–474.
62. Davis JM, Koslow SH, Gibbons RD, et al. Cerebrospinal fluid and urinary biogenic amines in depressed patients and healthy controls. *Arch Gen Psychiatry* 1988;45:705–717.
63. Raz S, Raz N, Bigler ED. Ventriculomegaly in schizophrenia: Is the choice of controls important? *Psychiatry Res* 1988;24:71.
64. Raz S, Raz N, Bigler ED. Ventriculomegaly in schizophrenia: the role of control groups and the perils of dichotomous thinking. *Psychiatry Res* 1988;26:245–248.
65. Smith GN, Iacono WG. Lateral ventricular size in schizophrenia and choice of control group. *Lancet* 1986;i:1450.
66. Smith GN, Iacono WG. Ventricular size in schizophrenia and choice of control subjects. *Psychiatry Res* 1988;26:241–243.
67. Smith GN, Iacono WG, Moreau M, et al. Choice of comparison group and findings of computerized tomography in schizophrenia. *Br J Psychiatry* 1988;153:667–674.
68. Weinberger DR, DeLisi LE, Perman G, Targum S, Wyatt RJ. Computed tomography scans in schizophreniform disorder and other acute psychiatric patients. *Arch Gen Psychiatry* 1982;39:778–783.
69. Weinberger DR. Computed tomography findings in schizophrenia: speculation on the meaning of it all. *J Psychiatr Res* 1984;18:477–490.
70. Weinberger DR, Berman KF, Zec RF. Physiologic dysfunction of dorsolateral prefrontal cortex in schizophrenia. I. Regional cerebral blood flow evidence. *Arch Gen Psychiatry* 1986;43:114–124.
71. Berman KF, Illowsky B, Weinberger DR. Physiologic dysfunction of dorsolateral prefrontal cortex in schizophrenia. IV. Further evidence for regional and behavioral specificity. *Arch Gen Psychiatry* 1988;45:616–622.
72. Weinberger DR, Berman KF, Illowsky B. Physiological dysfunction of dorsolateral prefrontal cortex in schizophrenia. III. A new cohort and evidence for a monoaminergic mechanism. *Arch Gen Psychiatry* 1988;45:609–615.
73. Berman KF, Torrey EF, Daniel DG, et al. Prefrontal cortical blood flow in monozygotic twins concordant and discordant for schizophrenia. *Schizophr Res* 1989;2:129.
74. Nauta WJH, Domesick VB: Neural associations of the limbic system. *Neural Basis Behav* 1982;10:175–206.
75. Weinberger DR. Anteriomedial temporal-prefrontal connectivity: a functional neuroanatomical system implicated in schizophrenia. In: B Caroll, ed. *Psychopathology and the brain.* New York: Raven Press (in press).
76. Friedman HR, Goldman-Rakic PS. Activation of the hippocampus and dentate gyrus by working-memory: a 2-deoxyglucose study of behaving rhesus monkeys, *J Neurosci* 1988;8:4693–4706.
77. Van Hoesen GW, Rosene DL, Mesulam M-M. Subicular input from temporal cortex in the rhesus monkey. *Science* 1979;205:608–610.
78. Goldman-Rakic PS, Selemon LD, Schwartz ML. Dual pathways connecting the dorsolateral prefrontal cortex with the hippocampal formation and the parahippocampal formation in the rhesus monkey. *Neuroscience* 1984;12:719–743.
79. Insausti R, Amaral DG, Cowan WM. The entorhinal cortex of the monkey: II. Cortical afferents. *J Comprehen Neurol* 1987;264:356–395.
80. Goldman-Rakic PS. Circuitry of primate prefrontal cortex and regulation of behavior by representational memory. In: Plumm F, Mountcastle V, eds. *Handbook of physiology.* Washington, DC: American Psychological Society, 1987;373–417.
81. Davison K, Bagley CR. Schizophrenia-like psychoses associated with organic disorders of the central nervous system. *Br J Psychiatry* 1969;113(suppl 1):18–69.
82. Adams RD, Lyons G. *Neurology of hereditary metabolic diseases of children.* New York: Mcgraw-Hill, 1982.
83. Hoes MJ, Lamers KJ, Hommes OR, ter Haar B. Adult metachromatic leukodystrophy: arylsuphatase values in four generations of one family and some reflections about the genetics. *Clin Neurol Neurosurg* 1978;80:174–188.
84. Monowitz P, Kling A, Kohn H. Clinical course of adult metachromatic leukodystrophy presenting as schizophrenia: a report of two living cases in siblings. *J Nerv Ment Dis* 1978;166:500–506.
85. Waltz G, Harik SI, Kaufman B. Adult metachromatic leukodystrophy: value of computed tomographic scanning and magnetic resonance imaging of the brain. *Arch Neurol* 1987;44:225–227.
86. Kraepelin E. *Dementia praecox and paraphrenia* (1907), Barclay RM and Robertson GN, trans. New York: Robert E. Krieger Publishing, 1971.

PART V

Psychosocial Treatments

23

Long-Term Community Care Through an Assertive Continuous Treatment Team

Mary Ann Test,[1] William H. Knoedler,[2] Deborah J. Allness,[3] Suzanne Senn Burke,[4] Roger L. Brown,[5] and Lynn S. Wallisch[6]

While neither the cause nor the cure of schizophrenia is known, substantial evidence is accumulating about the kinds of interventions that may be helpful for preventing relapse, improving the quality of life, and perhaps facilitating gains in social functioning in persons with schizophrenia. Potentially useful interventions, often deriving from the vulnerability–stress model, include biological treatments (1), supportive physical and social environments (2,3), and training and direct assistance with social, work, and daily coping skills (4).

A considerable challenge for service planners and service-system researchers is to develop programs and systems that successfully deliver these empirically supported interventions to patients when they live in community settings, the dominant site of persons with schizophrenia in this postinstitutional era. Toward this end a variety of so-called community support programs have been developed and evaluated. Findings of controlled studies consistently reveal that patients involved in these programs show markedly increased community tenure and often reduced symptomatology when compared with patients not receiving such comprehensive supports (3). Effective program models are widely diverse and include special living arrangements, psychosocial rehabilitation centers, education and support in the family environment, and comprehensive "in community" programs using mobile staff to assist patients.

While findings from studies of programs that provide biological, psychological, and/or social interventions to patients in community settings have yielded positive results, these studies have also uniformly shown that the favorable effects are not sustained after patients are discharged from the special programs (3,5). Our own earlier work provides an example (6). We treated a diagnostically mixed group of patients with serious mental illnesses in a model program called Training in Community Living (TCL) for a period of 14 months. During this time TCL patients exhibited markedly less time in institutions, less symptomatology, more independent living, and somewhat more favorable social and work functioning than patients randomly assigned to a control

---

[1]School of Social Work, University of Wisconsin, Madison, WI 53706.
[2]Program of Assertive Community Treatment, Mendota Mental Health Institute, Madison, WI 53703.
[3]Wisconsin Office of Mental Health, Madison, WI 53707.
[4]Mendota Mental Health Institute, Madison, WI 53704.
[5]Department of Family Medicine, University of Wisconsin, St. Mary's Hospital Medical Center, Madison, WI 53715.
[6]Schizophrenia Research Project, School of Social Work, University of Wisconsin, Madison, WI 53706.

group that received less comprehensive supports. Following discharge from TCL after 14 months, however, most of the gains made by the TCL patients were lost, and by the end of a 14-month follow-up period their community tenure and functioning were quite similar to that of the control group.

It is not clear why, across a range of empirically supported biological and psychosocial interventions, the positive effects of treatment end when the intervention ends, but a likely hypothesis is that the underlying psychobiological vulnerabilities and/or deficits of schizophrenia persist for many patients. This suggests that these patients may need ongoing rather than time-limited special supports in order to survive in the community. Currently, however, many community treatment programs are time-limited. Indeed, little is known either about how to deliver ongoing treatments and supports to patients with schizophrenia in the community or about the impact of such long-term treatment on the course of schizophrenia (7). Most treatment studies are short-term, with the longest ones usually of only two years' duration.

In 1978 we designed a prospective long-term controlled study, which is still in progress, to address this gap in the treatment and service delivery literature (8). We randomly assigned young adults with clearly defined schizophrenia or schizophrenia-related disorders to two different models of progressive community care. Unlike our earlier research, patients in this study are not discharged but remain in their respective treatment conditions for the entire study period. This duration is at least 5 years for all patients and extends to 12 years for those patients who were the first to enter the study. The aims of the study are to contribute to knowledge about how to design and implement effective long-term community care systems and to investigate the course and outcome of persons with schizophrenia when they are treated from early on in active, comprehensive, ongoing, long-term community treatment models. This chapter describes the two treatment systems and the study design and contains findings for the patients' first 2 years on variables assessing community tenure and residential settings.

THE COMMUNITY CARE MODELS

In designing and investigating long-term treatment for persons with schizophrenia, it is neither ethical nor clinically wise to think of delivering a single constant intervention to patients across the years. Rather, the question becomes one of developing and studying a service delivery model or service system that is flexible and that can deliver the entire range of state-of-the-art interventions to patients in the amounts they need, when they need them. Our current research, then, falls into the domains of both treatment research and service-system research. We describe below the two community care models to which patients in the current study are assigned.

Training in Community Living (TCL) Model

The TCL model was developed by Stein and Test in the 1970s specifically to address the characteristics and needs of persons with severe and persistent mental illnesses in community settings (6). The TCL approach was demonstrated in our earlier major controlled study mentioned above to be effective in the short run with diagnostically mixed patients (6,9,10). Additionally, four controlled studies of TCL adaptations in diverse geographic settings found similar positive results (11–13). A comprehensive description of the model as it is being implemented in Madison, Wis, in our current study may be found elsewhere (11) and is briefly summarized below.

The TCL model attempts to provide patients with the following:

- Direct assistance with symptom management (e.g., medications, 24-hour crisis availability, brief hospitalization, and one-to-one clinical relationships);
- An optimally supportive environment (eg, decent residential environments, assistance in meeting basic needs, social supports, education to family and community members);
- Direct assistance with instrumental functioning (e.g., skills teaching; environmental modifications; and assistance in work, social, and daily living activities).

As implemented in our current study, the TCL model differs perhaps most significantly from other community treatment approaches in how it organizes and delivers these services to patients. Three features are critical. First, rather than having an array of providers deliver these diverse biological, psychological, and social services to patients, in TCL the same team of staff deliver almost all of them, thereby optimizing continuity of care across functional areas (14). Second, the same team of staff deliver these services to patients across the years as patients need them, thus facilitating continuity of care across time as well as enabling trusting, supportive long-term relationships between staff and patients to develop. Third, most treatments take place "in vivo," in the natural environment, with staff using assertive outreach and taking services to patients rather than expecting patients to come into an office or facility (15). This prevents dropout and also minimizes the need for having skills learned in one setting generalize to another. Torrey (16) called this approach a "continuous treatment team"; we believe that term captures well the continuity of care and continuity of caregivers that are essential features of TCL.

In the current project, based in Dane County, Wis, the TCL treatment team consists of 14 interdisciplinary staff who assume the above responsibilities for 120 patients (not all of whom are study patients). This community-based team remains responsible for study patients across their entire 5 to 12 years of care. We believe this "assertive continuous team" approach will optimize patients' remaining involved in treatment in an ongoing manner and thus will allow us to evaluate the impact of long-term treatment on persons with schizophrenia.

Comparison System (Dane)

Patients in the control group of the current study are recipients of those services that patients with serious and persistent mental illnesses ordinarily receive in Dane County, Wis (17,18). The Dane system is, like TCL, widely regarded as an extremely good system and serves as a national model for community care. It is grounded in a similar philosophy to TCL and attempts to deliver to patients a similar array of biological, psychological, and social services. It is, however, organized in a different way from TCL. Rather than emphasizing one core team that itself provides to patients most services across functional areas and across time, the Dane system contains many exemplary program components that are invoked at different times depending on the individual patient's needs. These program elements include a crisis team, a day center or psychosocial clubhouse, outpatient psychotherapists, a mobile outreach team, and a variety of special residential options. Case management is usually handled by the program component with which the patient is most centrally involved at any given time.

The Dane system has evolved considerably over the course of the long-term study, and at least one of its important components, the mobile treatment team, was not present until 2 years after the long-term study began. Further, unlike the TCL program, the Dane system has responsibility for all of the publicly funded mentally ill persons in the county. For these reasons and because of the way that it is organized, we hypothesize that study patients in the Dane system will receive very good treatment, but treatment that is less intensive, comprehensive, or continuous than that provided by TCL.

METHOD

Subjects

Patients were admitted to the study as they became available from five in-hospital and two outpatient services. Criteria for study entry were as follows:

1. Ages 18 through 30;
2. Residence in Dane County, Wisconsin;
3. Diagnosis of schizophrenia or schizoaffective disorder according to the Research Diagnostic Criteria (RDC), or schizotypal personality according to DSM-III;
4. Less than 12 months of prior (total accumulated) time in the combination of psychiatric and penal institutions;
5. Informed consent.

Persons with mental retardation, organic brain syndrome, or a primary diagnosis of alcoholism were excluded.

Experimental Design

Patients were randomly assigned to the two different systems of progressive community treatment described above in the ratio of 60% to the TCL program, and 40% to the Dane system. Patients remain in their respective treatment systems for the duration of the study, which ran from 1978 to 1990.

One hundred twenty-two patients meeting our criteria were admitted and randomly assigned (75 to TCL and 47 to Dane) between 1978 and early 1985. They compose the sample for this report as all have now completed 2 years in the study. By the end of the project, these patients were treated and assessed in an ongoing manner for 5 to 12 years.

Assessment and Measuring Instruments

Data regarding patient functioning were collected through face-to-face interviews with patients by independent research staff at time of entry into the study and at 6-month intervals thereafter. Instruments included the Community Adjustment Form (6), the Brief Psychiatric Rating Scale (19), the Brief Symptom Inventory (20), and the Satisfaction with Life Scale (6). Additional data on outcomes and treatments received were collected from several state and county computerized databases.

CHARACTERISTICS OF THE SAMPLE

There were no significant differences by treatment group on any of a wide range of demographic or psychiatric history variables assessed at the patients' time of entry to the study. The sample ($n = 122$) is predominantly white (95.9%), male (67.2%), and never married (86.9%). The mean age at time of study entry was 23.11 years. Seventy-nine percent of the patients were high school graduates.

At the time of study entry the majority of patients (73.8%) received a diagnosis of schizophrenia (via RDC) from independent research diagnosticians. Twenty-three percent of the patients were diagnosed schizoaffective (RDC), and 3.3%, schizotypal personality disorder (DSM-III). The largest proportion (59.8%) were admitted to the study when they were outpatients; 40.2% were inpatients on their day of admission to the study.

The average age of patients' first contact with the mental health system was 19.02 years. Most (81.1%) had been a psychiatric inpatient at some time prior to study admission. These patients with prior hospitalizations revealed a mean of 3.35 previous admissions; they had spent a mean accumulated duration in psychiatric inpatient settings of 64.95 days.

Patients showed varied levels of instrumental functioning during their adult life prior to study admission, but the large majority revealed poor functioning. Additionally, a substantial segment (44.44%) of the sample had been arrested at some time prior to study entry, and many revealed significant use of street substances (21).

The above data and additional variables suggest that most researchers would regard this group as very difficult to treat in the community. The sample shares many of the characteristics of a portion of those patients that Pepper and Ryglewicz (22) have termed "young adult chronics."

RESULTS AFTER TWO YEARS

Findings reported below cover the patients' first 2 years in this in-progress long-term study. We examined all variables for gender as well as for treatment group effects. Only group effects and group-by-gender interactions are discussed below since the gender differences found will be the topic of another paper.

Time in Inpatient Psychiatric Settings and Skilled Nursing Homes

Research staff collected information from patients at the 6-month interviews regarding the number of days they had spent in inpatient psychiatric (IP) or skilled nursing homes (SN) during the previous 6 months. Reports were verified through facility records. We combined time in inpatient psychiatric and skilled nursing homes (IP + SN) in our analyses because in Wisconsin these facilities have much in common. We examined total days in IP + SN during the baseline, initial 6-month, and 7th- through 24th-month periods. The initial 6 months provided information about how the two systems responded to the acute episodes that brought patients into the study, while the subsequent 18-month period covered the poststabilization period during which relapses might be expected. At each of these three time periods we conducted 2×2 ANOVAs (group $\times$ gender) on the rank-transformed scores (days) for those patients with complete living situation data across the first 2 years ($n = 113$; 72 TCL, 41 Dane). Rank transformations were used to address distributional issues in the data (23).

There were no significant group effects on time in IP + SN during the baseline period, again supporting the equivalence of the TCL and Dane groups at study entry. During the six months after study entry, TCL patients spent significantly less time in IP + SN than did Dane (mean = 4.89 vs 22.15 days; $p \leq .001$). This difference was primarily accounted for by the fact that the TCL approach enabled patients who had been in the hospital at the time of study entry to leave far sooner than did hospitalized Dane patients. Specifically, the mean time of return to the community for hospitalized TCL patients was 8.2 days, in contrast with 25.8 days for the Dane group ($p \leq .01$). All patients in both groups had been returned to the community by the end of the first 6 months.

During months 7 through 24 there were large differences between the two treatment systems both in the total time patients spent in IP + SN and in the percentage of patients who spent any time in these facilities during this period. The TCL patients spent a mean of only 5.24 days in IP + SN across this 18-month period, compared to a mean of 44.17 days for Dane patients ($p \leq .001$). Only 19.4% of the TCL patients versus 56.10% of the Dane patients spent any time in IP + SN from months 7 through 24 ($p \leq .001$). Time in IP + SN remained extremely low for TCL patients across the entire 2-year period.

Time Spent in Penal Settings, Homeless Shelters, and in Homelessness

A community program is not successful if patients are avoiding hospitalization but are spending much time in situations clearly indicative of poor quality of life. Therefore, we also studied time spent in jail or other penal settings and in homelessness or homeless shelters. Throughout the first 2 years the time that patients in both groups spent in these settings was small and did not differ significantly between the groups. While a significant number of patients spent some time in penal settings for months 7 through 24 (25.0% of TCL and 29.3% of Dane), their median length of stay was short (2 days for TCL; 2.5 days for Dane). Meanwhile, 6.9% of TCL and 9.8% of Dane patients spent at least one day homeless or in shelters during this period, with median times of 10 and 21 days, respectively.

Community Residential Situations

The goals of both treatment systems in the area of housing were to enable patients to live whenever possible in normative housing (ie, integrated housing available on the open market) and to assist patients in moving out from their parental homes whenever this was the preference of patient and family.

Information about patients' residential settings was obtained during the 6-month interviews. Using time segments, sample size, and analyses identical to those described above for IP + SN, we examined group and gender differences in the number of days that clients had resided with family (older generation), in high-supervision residences (eg, group homes and foster care), in semisupervised settings (eg, sheltered apartments), in rooms, and in scattered apartments or houses.

While there were no differences between the groups in community residential situations prior to study entry, during the initial 6 months TCL patients spent significantly more overnights in independent apartments than did Dane patients ($p \leq .05$) and significantly less time than Dane living with (older generational) family members ($p \leq .05$). These two findings continued for months 7 through 24, with TCL patients spending more time in apartments ($p \leq .001$) and less time with family ($p \leq .05$). The TCL patients also spent less time in semisupervised settings (eg, sheltered apartments) than did Dane patients ($p \leq .05$).

In order to provide a description of where patients were living, we examined how many patients in each group were living in each type of setting for the majority of months 7 through 24. The largest proportion of Dane patients (53.66%) were living in high-supervision settings, primarily with family, while the greatest proportion of TCL patients (73.6%) were living in low-supervision settings, primarily independent apartments. The total data on residential settings indicates that the TCL model was far more successful in obtaining its housing goals than was the Dane system.

Additional Variables

Analyses of data related to additional outcome variables, including symptomatology, subjective distress, and social and work functioning during the first 2 years are currently in progress and will be reported in future papers. Information relating to intervening variables, including biological and psychosocial treatments received, are also being examined.

DISCUSSION

The initial findings reported above from our in-progress long-term study extend our earlier work with the TCL community treatment model in several important ways. First, the highly favorable effects of TCL in reducing hospitalizations, sustaining community tenure, and improving independent living found in our previous research with a diagnostically mixed group of patients are replicated here with a difficult-to-treat group of young adults with clearly defined schizophrenia and schizophrenia-related disorders. Second, the effects of TCL are more favorable than an extremely stringent comparison group, the nationally known Dane county system. Third, unlike our earlier research, the initial early positive effects of TCL on reducing hospitalization and improving community tenure and living were sustained at the 2-year point. This provides initial support for an hypothesis that if supportive interventions are ongoing rather than time-limited, the positive effects of these interventions will be sustained for many persons with schizophrenia.

We were surprised at the size of the differences between the TCL and Dane systems on the variables of time in IP + SN and on the number of patients admitted at all during months 7 through 24. Since the Dane system was not at "full strength" during the very early years of this study (i.e., some important components, such as the Dane system's mobile team, were not yet in place), we reanalyzed the IP + SN data, this time comparing only those TCL and Dane patients who entered the study after the Dane system was fully functional. The differences between the TCL and Dane systems were the same and of similar magnitude, as those found in the analyses reported above. Although we are studying this question further, we speculate at this time that a potentially critical difference between the TCL and Dane systems is in how services are organized. The TCL "assertive continuous treatment team" approach, in which the *same team* provides most services across functional areas and across time, using abundant outreach and "in vivo" techniques, may be essential in keeping patients involved and in making sure that they actually receive those biological and psychosocial interventions that research suggests are helpful.

We look forward to analyses of our incoming data on the longer-term course of these patients, particularly in the area of psychosocial functioning. If reductions in hospitalizations are maintained over time, the resulting foundation of sustained community tenure, when combined with the building blocks of long-term assistance in work and social areas, may facilitate patients making gradual gains in their community functioning.

ACKNOWLEDGMENTS

The study reported here is a collaborative project between the University of Wisconsin–Madison and the Mendota Mental Health Institute of the State of Wisconsin Department of Health and Social Services. This research is supported in part by grant MH40886 from the National Institute of Mental Health.

REFERENCES

1. Kane JM. Treatment of schizophrenia. *Schizophr Bull* 1987;13:133–156.
2. Goldstein MJ. Psychosocial issues. *Schizophr Bull* 1987;13:157–171.
3. Test MA. Community support programs. In: Bellack AS, ed. *Schizophrenia: treatment, management, and rehabilitation*. New York: Grune & Stratton, 1984;347–373.
4. Anthony WA, Liberman RP. The practice of psychiatric rehabilitation: historical, conceptual, and research base. *Schizophr Bull* 1986;12:542–559.
5. Test MA. Effective treatment of the chronically mentally ill: what is necessary? *J Soc Iss* 1981;37:71–86.
6. Stein LI, Test MA. Alternative to mental hospital treatment: I. Conceptual model, treatment program, and clinical evaluation. *Arch Gen Psychiatry* 1980;37:392–397.
7. McGlashan TH. A selective review of recent North American long-term followup studies of schizophrenia. *Schizophr Bull* 1988;14:515–542.
8. Test MA, Knoedler WH, Allness DJ. The long-term treatment of young schizophrenics in a community support program. In: Stein LI, Test MA, eds. *The Training in Community Living model: a decade of experience*. New Directions

for Mental Health Services, no. 26. San Francisco: Jossey-Bass, 1985;17–27.
9. Weisbrod BA, Test MA, Stein LI. Alternative to mental hospital treatment: III. Economic benefit-cost analysis. *Arch Gen Psychiatry* 1980;37:400–405.
10. Test MA, Stein LI. Alternative to mental hospital treatment: III. Social cost. *Arch Gen Psychiatry* 1986;37:1243–1247.
11. Test MA. The Training in Community Living model: delivering treatment and rehabilitation services through a continuous treatment team. In: Liberman RP, ed. *Handbook of psychiatric rehabilitation*. New York: Pergamon Press (in press).
12. Hoult J. Community care of the acutely mentally ill. *Br J Psychiatry* 1986;149:137–144.
13. Bond GR, Miller LD, Krumwied RD, et al. Assertive case management in three CMHC's: a controlled study. *Hosp Community Psychiatry* 1988;39:411–418.
14. Test MA. Continuity of care in community treatment. In: Stein LI ed. *Community support systems for the long-term patient*. New Directions for Mental Health Services, no. 2. San Francisco: Jossey-Bass, 1979;15–23.
15. Brekke JS, Test MA. An empirical analysis of services delivered in a model community support program. *Psychosoc Rehab J* 1987;10(4):51–61.
16. Torrey EF. Continuous treatment teams in the care of the chronically mentally ill. *Hosp Community Psychiatry* 1986;37:1243–1247.
17. Stein LI, Diamond RJ. A program for difficult-to-treat patients. In: Stein LI, Test MA, eds. *The Training in Community Living model: A decade of experience*. New Directions for Mental Health Services, no. 26. San Francisco: Jossey-Bass, 1985;17–27.
18. Stein LI, Diamond RJ, Factor RM. A system approach to the care of persons with schizophrenia. In: Herz MI, Docherty JP, eds. *Handbook of schizophrenia*, vol 5. New York: Elsevier Science Publishers (in press).
19. Overall JE, Klett CJ. *Applied multivariate analysis*. New York: McGraw-Hill, 1972.
20. Derogatis LR, Melisaratos N. The Brief Symptom Inventory: an introductory report. *Psycholog Med* 1983;13:595–605.
21. Test MA, Wallisch L, Allness D, et al. Substance use in young adults with schizophrenic disorders. *Schizophr Bull* (in press).
22. Pepper B, Ryglewicz H, eds. *The young adult chronic patient*. New Directions for Mental Health Service, no. 14. San Francisco: Jossey-Bass, 1982.
23. Conover WJ, Iman RL. Rank transformations as a bridge between parametric and nonparametric statistics. *Am Statistician* 1981;129:124–129.

24

A Review of Psychoeducational Family Approaches

Samuel J. Keith,[1] Susan M. Matthews,[1] and Nina R. Schooler[2]

Research on schizophrenia has been the focus of unprecedented growth in the 1980s. The immense and chronic burden borne by people with this disorder and by their families has emphasized the importance of our commitment to make rapid advances in our state of knowledge about mental illness. Studies of schizophrenia are of course not new. Indeed, the disorder has been the focus of some of the most productive research programs of the National Institute of Mental Health since it was established in the 1940s. Only recently, however, has there emerged a fortuitous blend of challenging hypotheses, scientific technology to test them, and public advocacy of the field.

Indispensable for this growth to occur has been a dramatic change in the perceived role of the family. The era that held the family as causal in schizophrenia has passed, through the intensive efforts in public education to make widely known the results of research that refuted this incorrect and destructive viewpoint. With the termination of the family pathogenesis hypotheses, an explosion of biological and genetic research took place in schizophrenia, strengthening the entire biomedical research process in psychiatry. In their day-to-day lives, however, schizophrenia victims and their families do not grapple with unseen issues of genetics, the biochemistry of nerve cells, or the structure of the brain. They deal instead with profound disturbances in personality and behavior. It is here that new advances in psychosocial factors have become significant, and it is here that we have now come full circle in viewing the family as a valuable asset in the treatment process.

There are currently six controlled studies of family treatment of schizophrenia—one from the 1970s (1) and five from the expressed-emotion (EE) era (2–9). Although the specifics of family management strategies varied, common among them are the following:

1. Enlisting the family in a positive clinical alliance;
2. Providing psychoeducational material about schizophrenia;
3. Providing the family with the principles of management skills in the areas of problem solving and communication;
4. Encouraging families to expand their social networks particularly through mutual interest groups.

The specific components of the psychoeducational treatment packages and results of outcome analyses for the above-mentioned studies as well as their relationship to the family management utilized in the NIMH Treatment Strategies in Schizophrenia Cooperative Agreement Program (10) are reviewed below.

---

[1]National Institute of Mental Health, Rockville, MD 20857.
[2]Western Psychiatric Institute and Clinic, University of Pittsburgh, Pittsburgh, PA 15213.

In the study by Goldstein et al (1), 104 acute schizophrenics, following brief inpatient stays, were randomly assigned to one of four aftercare conditions for a 6-week controlled trial: high dose (1 ml fluphenazine enanthate q 2 weeks) plus family therapy, low dose (0.25 ml fluphenazine enanthate q 2 weeks) plus family therapy, high dose with no family therapy, and low dose with no family therapy.

The family therapy included 6 weekly crisis-oriented family sessions utilizing shared problem solving in an effort to prevent or minimize stresses for the patient and family. The sessions focused on the following areas:

- Exploration of the psychotic experience—discussion of events prior to and during the patient's psychotic break, emphasizing the importance of stress as a trigger of decompensation, and highlighting the value of preventing and coping with stress;
- Identification of stresses—the patient and family reaching consensus on two or three difficulties that present the greatest threat to the patient's current and future stability;
- Joint family and patient planning of stress avoidance and coping strategies—crucial since final plans must be acceptable to all individuals responsible for their enactment;
- Evaluation and refinement of stress-management strategies—based on an examination of attempted plans;
- Anticipatory planning—identifying potentially stressful upcoming events and developing strategies for preventing or managing them.

The results revealed that at the end of the 6-week trial, no patients in the high dose–family therapy group had relapsed. This compares favorably with the other three treatment groups: 9% for low dose, family therapy; 10% for high dose, no family therapy; and 24% for low dose, no family therapy. Overall, only 4.5% of patients receiving family therapy relapsed compared with 17% of those not receiving family therapy, and only 5% of patients receiving the high dose of medication had relapsed versus 16.5% on the low dose. At 6 months following discharge, the pattern of relapse paralleled the pattern at 6 weeks: No relapses were reported for the high dose–family therapy group compared with 17% for the high dose–no family therapy group, 22% for the low dose–family therapy group, and 48% for the low dose–no family therapy group.

Hogarty et al (2) studied 103 patients, residing in high-EE households, with a diagnosis of schizophrenia or schizoaffective disorder, who were assigned to family treatment and medication ($N=22$), social skills training and medication ($N=23$), family treatment and social skills and medication ($N=23$) or to a medication-treated control group ($N=35$). Patients in each treatment condition were seen at least biweekly.

The family treatment condition was designed as an education and management strategy intended to lower the emotional climate of the home while maintaining reasonable expectations for the patient.

> Treatment sought to increase the stability and predictability of family life by decreasing the family's guilt and anxiety, increasing their self confidence, and providing a sense of cognitive mastery through the provision of information concerning the nature and course of schizophrenia as well as specific management strategies thought to be helpful in coping with schizophrenic symptoms on a day-to-day basis [p. 634].

The social skills training focused on assisting the patient to enhance both verbal and nonverbal social behaviors as well as to develop more accurate social perception and judgment. Initial efforts were directed to social skills in dealing with family members. Subsequent training focused on interpersonal relationships beyond the household, in social and vocational rehabilitation settings. Training was structured and included instruction, modeling, role play, feedback, and homework. Therapist support and empathy towards the patient were crucial elements of the program.

Patients assigned to the control condition received maintenance chemotherapy in the context of an individual, supportive, didactic relationship offered by a psychiatric nurse clinical specialist.

The authors reported that for the initial 12 months after discharge, patients considered "treatment takers" relapsed as follows: 19% for family treatment and drug, 20% for social skills training and drug, 0% for combined family treatment and social skills training, and 41% for controls. An examination of drug-compliant patients only reveals similar relapse rates: 11% for family treatment, 17% for social skills training, 0% for combined family treatment and social skills, and 32% for drug controls. An analysis of EE status at 12 months revealed the following:

1. There was no patient relapse in households that changed from high- to low-EE status independent of treatment condition.
2. For households remaining high in EE, only the combination of family treatment and social skills training provided a significant prophylactic effect in relapse (0%), compared with a relapse rate of 33% for family management cases, 29% for social skills training alone, and 42% for controls.

At 2 years after discharge, a clear main effect of family treatment persisted, but the effects of social skills training on relapse were not significant. Approximately one quarter of patients in the family treatment groups relapsed by 2 years, compared with one half of social skills recipients alone and almost two thirds of the controls.

In the Leff study (4, 5), 24 schizophrenic patients, considered to be at high risk for relapse since they were living in frequent contact with high-EE relatives, were randomly assigned to an experimental group, which received social intervention, or to the control group, which received routine outpatient care. All patients were maintained on maintenance-injectable medication.

The social intervention consisted of three elements: an education program, a relatives' group, and family sessions. The aims of the intervention were to reduce face-to-face contact between high-EE relatives and patients and/or to change relatives' EE status from high to low.

The education program consisted of four lectures on etiology, symptoms, course, and treatment and management of schizophrenia, which were provided to each relative in his or her home. The length of sessions was dependent on the family needs. All relatives were provided with written materials.

The relatives' group was jointly attended by both high- and low-EE relatives (patients excluded) and focused on discussion of potential or actual difficulties that relatives experienced. The purpose of the group was to provide a forum for altering the coping styles of high-EE relatives so as to resemble more closely those of low-EE relatives. In addition, the group provided an opportunity for mutual support, for expression of feelings about a problem in a safe atmosphere, and for information exchange. The group met biweekly for 90 minutes and was usually attended by two to seven members. Relatives were encouraged to attend for the entire 9-month study period with optional continued participation thereafter.

Family sessions, lasting 1 hour, were conducted by two professionals (psychiatrist and psychologist) in the home with the patient and available key relatives. Each family was seen in their home on a minimum of one and maximum of 25 occasions. Techniques utilized varied from dynamic interpretations to behavioral intervention.

The control relatives were not offered any treatment.

At 9 months the number of critical comments were significantly reduced in the experimental group. Regarding emotional overinvolvement, a nonsignificant reduction was detected. A reduction in face-to-face contact had fallen below 35 hours per week in six experimental and three control families.

During the 9-month follow-up, 50% of the control patients relapsed compared with 9% of the experimental patients. For experimental families that showed a reduction either in EE or in face-to-face contact below 35 hours per week, no relapses were reported. At 2 years, the relapse rate was less (though not significantly so) for experimental patients (40%) than for control patients maintained on antipsychotic medication (78%; ref 5). Furthermore, among the seven experimental families who achieved one of the therapeutic aims, the relapse rate was 14%. A reanalysis of their data at 2 years lends itself to an interpretation different from the conclusions of the authors of the study. For the 12 control families, nine were included by the authors in the 2-year analysis, and seven relapsed (78%). The other three had medication-noncompliant patients; of these, 2 of 3 relapsed. Adding these back into the analysis yields a relapse rate of 9 out of 12 families, or 75%. For the experimental group, 12 entered, 7 were included by the authors in the 2-year analysis, and 1 relapsed, resulting in a relapse rate of 14%. The remaining five consisted of the following: two were medication-noncompliant patients, both relapsed; in two the patients committed suicide; and one was not included because the EE status was not changed, and the patient relapsed. Adding these five "failures" back into the analysis yields a relapse rate of 6 out of 12 or 50%.

In the Falloon et al study, 36 patients who returned to stressful parental households after florid episodes of schizophrenia were stabilized with optimal neuroleptics and completed a 2-year program of family or individual therapy (6). Patients assigned to family treatment received a mean daily dosage of 245 mg of chlorpromazine, or its equivalent, compared with 338 mg for individually treated cases.

All patients, regardless of treatment assignment, were seen weekly during the initial 3 months, biweekly for the next 6 months, and monthly thereafter. All family therapy sessions (1 hour each) were conducted in the home; initial sessions focused on educational materials, and remaining sessions were devoted to learning problem-solving and the communication skills of expression of positive and negative feelings, reflective listening, requests for behavioral change, and reciprocity of conversation. The strengths and weaknesses of families were determined, and major deficits became the focus of subsequent sessions.

The individual therapy condition was clinic-based and was intended to provide information about the nature, course, and treatment of schizophrenia, rehabilitation counseling, and assistance in coping with everyday problems, primarily from the patient's perspective. The approach was structured and goal-directed in an effort to enhance the community functioning of the patient.

The results indicated that at 9 months, statistically significant advantages were reported for patients assigned to family versus individual treatment as measured by clinical exacerbation (6% vs 44%), target-symptom ratings (2.25% vs 4.10%), symptom remission (56% vs 22%), and community tenure (eg, readmission in 11% vs 50%). At two years, clinicians reported six major episodes of psychopathology for patients assigned to family management compared with 31 major episodes for controls. Also, three individual-therapy cases (17%) had not had a major exacerbation of schizophrenia, compared with 15 family management cases (83%; ref 7). Continued stability and improvement in target symptoms for family management cases was reported.

In the Kottgen study (8), 52 patients were divided into three categories:

1. The treatment group, high-EE status—patients residing in close contact with at least one high-EE relative and receiving

group therapy (separate for patients and relatives; $N = 15$);
2. Control group 1, high-EE status—patients with at least one key high-EE relative and receiving the usual treatment ($N = 14$);
3. Control group 2, low-EE status—patients with no highly emotionally involved key relatives and receiving the usual treatment ($N = 23$).

Group therapy was initiated at a patient's discharge and continued for 2 years. There were two groups for both patients and families—one that met weekly, the other monthly. The authors report many advantages to having separate groups for patients and relatives: it provides the opportunity for participants to continue, even if one partner stops attending; the relatives have an opportunity to exchange views in a safe environment; patients acquire a peer group not otherwise available; etc. The aim of the group meeting was to "disentangle the emotional knots which affect the atmosphere in high EE families." The format included discussions about harmful and insulting situations and strategies to work through them; reducing negative expectations associated with schizophrenia; alleviating the social isolation of families and patients; providing an atmosphere of mutual support; and providing education.

At 9 months after discharge the following were noted: 41% of high-EE patients relapsed compared with 57% of the low-EE patients; for patients receiving group therapy, 33% relapsed, compared with 50% and 55% for the control groups; and medication usage was not significantly different among relapsing patients.

In the Tarrier study, 83 schizophrenic inpatients were divided into high-EE ($N = 64$) and low-EE ($N = 19$) households (9). Patients from high-EE families were randomly assigned to one of four treatment groups: Behavioral Intervention Enactive, Behavioral Intervention Symbolic, Education Only, or Routine Treatment. Patients from low-EE families were randomly assigned to Education Only or Routine Treatment.

The contents of the two 9-month behavioral interventions were identical, but the level of intervention differed. Initially, families received the education program (described below) for two sessions, followed by a stress management program of three sessions, conducted with the relatives. The interventions were designed to teach the relatives to monitor sources of stress and their reactions to it and then to learn more appropriate methods of coping. Finally, there was an eight-session program of goal setting, in which patient and relatives were taught to identify areas of change or need, to set goals to meet these needs, and to establish procedures to achieve the goals. The difference between the two interventions was in how the skills were taught: In Enactive Intervention, skills were taught through enactment or participation, such as rehearsal or role playing, whereas in Symbolic Intervention, skills were taught through verbal instruction, discussion, persuasion, or written material, in which actual behavior changes were represented in a symbolic manner.

Families assigned to the Education Only treatment received a standardized, two-session educational program designed to give the patient and relatives extensive individualized information about schizophrenia and how to manage it in the home environment.

All patients assigned to Routine Treatment were under the care of a multidisciplinary clinical team during their admission and after discharge and were reviewed at outpatient clinics. The research team maintained contact with families for assessment purposes and acted as a link with the clinical team where necessary, but no special intervention was offered.

Results indicated that at 9 months, the high-EE group receiving the behavioral interventions relapsed significantly less (combined 12%, Enactive 17%, Symbolic

8%) than all other treatment groups (including the low-EE sample). No significant differences between the groups were detected in terms of medication compliance, number of months without medication, and oral versus injectable neuroleptics or in contacts with psychiatric services. Significant changes from high-EE to low-EE status were also found in the high-EE groups, with the most profound effect in the groups receiving the behavioral interventions.

In the Treatment Strategies in Schizophrenia (TSS) Program (10), the family treatments are based on a recognition of the role the family plays in supporting gains of schizophrenic patients in the community. Applied and Supportive Family Management share common principles based on this understanding of the family role. These principles include:

Education of the patient and family regarding the nature of schizophrenia as a major mental illness with both biological and psychosocial components;
Importance of stress and the management of stress for such patients;
Understanding that interpersonal relations, particularly those of a sustained close nature, are uniquely stressful for schizophrenic patients;
Need to identify specific stressors and the means for coping with them;
Provision of general case-management support;
Importance of early identification of both general and patient-specific indicators of potential relapse.

During the period of patients' hospitalization or immediately following it, families participate in a one-day psychoeducational workshop based on the survival skills workshop described by Anderson (13): conducted by a psychiatrist and family management clinician (FMC). The goals of the workshop are to provide factual information about schizophrenia; to introduce *principles* of family management based on communication, problem-solving, and stress-reduction skills; to establish a group affiliation designed to reduce isolation, stigma, and anxiety for the family members; and to enlist the family as a therapeutic ally. At the end of the session three booklets are given to each attendee: "What Is Schizophrenia?," "Medication for Schizophrenia," and "The Role of the Family."

In Applied Family Management, emphasis is on improvement in communication and problem-solving skills. Basic behavioral techniques of positive reinforcement, shaping, extinction, modeling, rehearsal, and homework are used. The communication skills training focuses on establishing clear and specific verbal and nonverbal styles of communication. Major goals include developing clear and precise expressions of positive and negative feelings; developing active listening skills through such techniques as clarifying, questioning, and reflection of communication; and developing ways to request positive behavior and set limits for negative behavior. Problem-solving training focuses on improving the coping skills of the family particularly in stress management. Initially, the FMC may assume a directive role, but as the family learns the necessary skills, the clinician becomes less active and serves as a consultant in the sessions. The structured problem solving involves a six-step process:

1. Identification of a specific problem and a full discussion of its definition;
2. Listing of alternative solutions for the problem with the participation of all family members;
3. Discussion of the pros and cons of each proposed solution without acceptance or rejection of any;
4. Selection of a solution with an effort to achieve consensus;
5. Implementation of the planned solution;
6. Subsequent review of efforts after the plan has been attempted or implemented.

The therapy includes a review of the educational materials presented in the workshop, but the patient's participation expands the content substantially since the patient is recognized as the "expert" on the symptoms and direct experience of schizophrenia.

The working assumption of this method is that everyone in the family system is performing at the best level of functioning given the psychological and environmental constraints perceived, and that the coping mechanisms observed are tied to these perceived constraints. In the behavioral assessment the FMC identifies specific assets and deficits of the individual family members. The goals are to establish a therapeutic alliance with each member of the family and to obtain information about individual functioning, as well as the individuals' perceptions about their roles in the family.

Sessions are conducted in the home to capitalize on context-dependent learning to increase generalization of the skills training. Home sessions make it easier to include the patient, the patient's parent(s), or a family member acting *in loco parentis,* and others, whether kin or not, who are actively involved in the family's day-to-day affairs. Providing the family treatment in a familiar environment also serves to reduce tension and encourage additional social-network participation, and treatment compliance is enhanced. Home sessions initiated during the stabilization period are conducted weekly for 3 months (or until 13 sessions have been completed); biweekly for the next 6 months (a second set of 13 sessions); and monthly until the end of the first year. This portion of the program follows closely the Falloon model of Behavioral Family Therapy (11). In addition, however, all patients and families are invited and encouraged to attend monthly family group meetings, conducted by an FMC, for the study duration. Thus, at the end of the first year of treatment, when the home-visits phase is concluded, the monthly group meetings continue as a resource for patients and families.

Supportive Family Management, the second form of family treatment utilized in TSS, is parallel to but distinct from Applied Family Management. Supportive Family Management emphasizes the benefits derived from participation in a group setting with other families: reduction of isolation, mutual support, information sharing, and an expansion of generally considered social networks.

Patients assigned to Supportive Family Management and their families are invited to participate at monthly group meetings for the study duration. The goals of these meetings include sharing information and providing mutual support among families experiencing similar problems of stress, burden, and stigma associated with having a schizophrenic relative. Each session begins with a brief presentation by the FMC on a topic from the Psychoeducation Workshop Manual or a series of curriculum outlines. Following the presentation, families are encouraged to share their experiences and problems and to clarify information about schizophrenia (eg, the often-seen newspaper articles about new "breakthroughs").

Our experience to date has shown that these family treatments can be implemented across a variety of clinical settings, as demonstrated in the preliminary outcome results (12), and that the influence of patient and family participation in such treatments may significantly predict patient outcome. We are witnessing a very important and exciting period of research that we believe may shape future treatment programs designed to integrate the patient, family, and significant others in a balanced and comprehensive treatment approach to schizophrenia.

ACKNOWLEDGMENTS

The authors wish to acknowledge and thank Ian R.H. Falloon, MD, Buckingham Hospital, Buckingham, England, and Christine McGill, PhD, University of California/San Francisco General Hospital for consultation on the design of Applied Family Management, for training of family clinicians, and for continued supervision of clinicians.

The Treatment Strategies in Schizophrenia Cooperative Agreement Program is supported by US Public Health Service (NIMH) grants MH39992 (to John Kane, Hillside Hospital, Glen Oaks, NY), MH39998 (to Alan Bellack, Medical College of Pennsylvania at EPPI, Philadephia), MH40007 (to Ira D. Glick, Payne Whitney Clinic, New York), MH40042 (to William Hargreaves, San Francisco General Hospital), MH40597 (to Philip T. Ninan, Grady Memorial Hospital, Atlanta), and contracts 88MO41599501D and 89MH76823301D (to Nina R. Schooler).

REFERENCES

1. Goldstein MJ, Rodnick EH, Evans JR, et al. Drug and family therapy in the aftercare of acute schizophrenics. *Arch Gen Psychiatry* 1978;35: 1169–1177.
2. Hogarty GE, Anderson CM, Reiss DJ, et al. Family psychoeducation, social skills training, and maintenance chemotherapy in the aftercare of schizophrenia. *Arch Gen Psychiatry* 1986;43: 633–642.
3. Hogarty GE, Anderson CM, Reiss DJ. Family psychoeducation, social skills training, and medication in schizophrenia: the long and short of it. *Psychopharmacol Bull* 1987;23:12–13.
4. Leff J, Kuipers L, Berkowitz R, et al. A controlled trial of social intervention in the families of schizophrenic patients. *Br J Psychiatry* 1982; 141:121–134.
5. Leff J, Kuipers L, Berkowitz R, et al. A controlled trial of social intervention in the families of schizophrenic patients: two year follow up. *Br J Psychiatry* 1985;146:594–600.
6. Falloon IRH, Boyd JL, McGill CW, et al. Family management in the prevention of exacerbation of schizophrenia: a controlled study. *N Eng J Med* 1982;306:1437–1440.
7. Falloon IRH, Boyd JL, McGill CW, et al. Family management in the prevention of morbidity of schizophrenia. *Arch Gen Psychiatry* 1985;42:87–896.
8. Kottgen C, Sonnichsen I, Mollenhauer K, et al. The family relations of young schizophrenic patients: results of the Hamburg Camberwell Family Interview Study I. *Int J Fam Psych* 1984;5: 61–70.
9. Tarrier N, Barrowclough C, Vaughn C, et al. The community management of schizophrenia: a controlled trial of a behavioral intervention with families to reduce relapse. *Br J Psychiatry* 1988;153:532–542.
10. Schooler NR, Keith SJ, Severe JB, et al. Acute treatment response and short term outcome in schizophrenia: first results of the NIMH Treatment Strategies in Schizophrenia study. *Psychopharmacol Bull* 1989;25:331–335.
11. Falloon IRH, Mueser K, Gingerich S, et al. *Behavioural Family Therapy: A Workbook* England: Buckingham Mental Health Science, 1988.
12. Keith SJ, Bellack A, Frances A, et al. The influence of diagnosis and family treatment on acute treatment response and short term outcome in schizophrenia. *Psychopharmacol Bull* 1989;25: 336–339.
13. Anderson CM, Reiss JL, Hogarty GE. *Schizophrenia in the Family.* Guilford Press, New York, 1986.

25

Management of Risk of Relapse Through Skills Training of Chronic Schizophrenics

William C. Wirshing,[1] Thad Eckman,[1,2] Robert P. Liberman,[1,2] and Stephen R. Marder[1]

The well-documented efficacy of neuroleptic medications in controlling the positive symptoms of schizophrenia has enabled many patients to live in the community. However, deinstitutionalization has been accompanied by poor quality of community life (1) and a revolving-door pattern of frequent rehospitalizations (2,3). Further, even when maintained on apparently adequate medications, patients experience unacceptably high readmission rates, up to 40% within 1 year and 75% within 5 years following hospital discharge (4).

The suboptimal effect of current drug and psychosocial treatments, together with the known deficits in social and living skills of chronic schizophrenic patients (5,6), provide a rationale for developing new interventions. Social skills training directed toward problems in the area of instrumental roles, family relationships, vocation, and friendships and peer support has become an innovative avenue for psychosocial intervention with severely disabled schizophrenic patients. To optimize skills training as a protective treatment factor in schizophrenia, intervention technology needs to be designed with an understanding of the cognitive underpinnings of social skills, including the information-processing dysfunctions that mark the enduring vulnerability schizophrenics show to stress-induced relapse.

SOCIAL COPING AND COMPETENCE

Basic psychobiological and social cognitive processes constitute an individual's social schemata, providing the "raw material" for learning social skills. Social skills are the cognitive, verbal, and nonverbal behaviors that must be used interpersonally to achieve one's needs for community survival and a reasonable quality of life. Social skills include accurate perception of incoming social messages, social problem-solving capacity, and "sending" skills. Coping efforts are the individual's attempts to put into practice the social skills that exist in his or her repertoire. The impact of the person's social skills on the relevant interpersonal field or environment, favorable or unfavorable, defines that person's social competence.

A social schema is a modifiable information structure that is a prototype in memory of a frequently experienced situation (7,8). The individual uses this prototype to interpret instances of related knowledge and to

---

[1] Clinical Research Center for Schizophrenia and Psychiatric Rehabilitation, UCLA School of Medicine, and Department of Psychiatry and Biobehavioral Sciences, West Los Angeles Veterans Administration Medical Center (Brentwood Division), Los Angeles, CA 90073.
[2] Camarillo State Hospital, Camarillo, CA 93011.

integrate new information. In essence, a schema is a person's theory or model that "enables him/her to make assumptions about events that generally occur in a particular situation" (8).

When applied to a particular social situation, a schema consists of the individual's assumptions about the qualities that define a competent performance in that general class of situations, the skills required for that performance, and the response that can be expected of the environment. The more extensive the person's experience in that general class of situations, the more finely differentiated his or her schema will be and the more likely the person will perform competently.

To develop social schemata, certain basic psychobiological functions are necessary including perception, attention, memory, affect, and concept formation. A deficiency in one of these will severely limit the range and distinctiveness of the individual's schemata and any subsequent coping efforts. In addition, developing social schemata requires several higher-order cognitive processes, including the ability to take another person's perspective and to regulate one's own behavior. A deficiency in one of these will result in impoverished social schemata, lower skill level, and impaired social coping.

Thus, social schemata that are poorly developed because of inexperience, a deficiency in the psychobiological functions, or a deficiency in higher-order cognitive processes may result in social incompetence. Inexperience may lead to incorrect assumptions about the nature of a competent performance, about the required skills, or about the type and extent of the environmental responses. The individual's social behaviors may be hastily and poorly fashioned; on the other hand, the person may be inactive because of overestimating the required skills or underestimating his or her abilities. Deficiencies in the higher-order cognitive skills may lead to invalid hypotheses about others' behaviors. Misinterpretations may result, and behaviors may be performed that are inappropriate to the individual's and others' actual goals and intentions. Deficiencies in the basic psychobiological functions may lead to either an inattentiveness to the relevant stimuli or an inability to store them for later processing.

Basic psychobiological functions, behavioral competencies, and social cognition together exert reciprocal influences on self-efficacy and interpersonal problem-solving skills. Self-efficacy is governed both by social schemata and by successful social outcomes (9). The social schemata carried by an individual at any time will affect the person's ability to evaluate correctly a social situation that is about to be encountered, to determine whether the requisite skills to be effective in the situation are in one's repertoire, to know whether a means to implement the skills is at hand, and to evaluate the motivation or desire for using the skills in action. These cognitive and motivational factors represent self-efficacy, and they determine the likelihood and persistence of coping efforts in the situation.

Coping efforts then lead to the use of interpersonal problem-solving skills in the situation. These skills, also affected by the person's social schemata, include social perception (receiving skills), generation of alternatives and their evaluation (processing skills), and verbal and nonverbal behavioral responses (sending skills). Thus, social schemata interact with both self-efficacy and interpersonal problem-solving skills to determine the success or failure of the individual's actual efforts in social transactions. The more success the person experiences in meeting his or her needs through social contacts, the greater the person's social competence. Competence is defined by the outcomes of social interactions and the degree to which a person is able to cope and use interpersonal skills to obtain instrumental and affiliative needs.

Social Skills Training

This model of social behavior serves to identify three major focal points for the design and testing of social skills training methods. The first option is to train the basic psychobiological and cognitive functions that form the person's social schemata. For example, attention span and higher-order abstraction have been improved in preliminary studies carried out in experimental psychopathology laboratories (10,11). A second approach is to train the receiving, processing, and sending skills of individuals using behavioral rehearsal, coaching, reinforcement methods, modeling, and homework. The third strategy is to reprogram the individual's natural environment such that skills—however well or poorly developed—can be assured of support and favorable response by others.

While not requiring the intensive, discrete trials method of training needed by severely regressed and inattentive patients, most individuals with chronic schizophrenia do learn social and independent living skills only through involvement in structured and directive instructional sessions (12,13). The teaching procedures in skills training are based on learning principles and include goal setting, focused instructions, modeling, behavior rehearsal, prompting, social reinforcement, shaping successive approximations to desired behaviors, in vivo practice of skills, and homework assignments.

Social skills training generally resembles a classroom teaching environment more than a traditional therapy setting. Sessions require the active participation of the patients and the therapist and may be conducted with individual patients or in groups. They may be as brief as 10 minutes a day or as long as 2 hours, depending on the attentional capacities of the patients. Multiple training sessions every week are preferred to learning less intensively over a longer period. Role playing, or behavior rehearsal, is the main vehicle for both assessing and teaching social skills that are targeted for intervention on the basis of their functional relation to attaining a specific goal important to the patient. Three types of behavior are usually targeted for modification:

1. Response topography behaviors, such as voice volume, fluency, eye contact;
2. Content behaviors, such as making a positive statement or requesting additional information;
3. Cognitive problem-solving skills, such as developing a list of options when one's initial plan is circumstantially thwarted (14).

Additional arguments for adopting a skills-training, rehabilitation model of chronic schizophrenic disorders are the failure of conventional antipsychotic drugs to adequately remediate the negative symptoms (15); the serious neurological side effects of neuroleptics that often evoke noncompliance (16,17); and the fact that medications by themselves cannot teach patients the coping skills they require for survival and maintenance in the community (18,19). While the future holds the promise of providing clinicians and researchers with the pharmacological tools that will both ablate negative symptoms and lack side effects, it is unlikely that such medications will provide any degree of skills acquisition.

Generally, conventional neuroleptic drugs are thought to exert their primary effects on cognitive disorganization and positive symptoms, and are associated only secondarily and with less impact on improvements in psychosocial functioning. The opposite seems to be the case with well-designed social and psychological therapies. In combination, their beneficial impact on the comprehensive needs of the schizophrenic patient is potentially additive and complementary.

SKILLS TRAINING INTERACTIONS WITH NEUROLEPTIC DRUG THERAPY

We have designed a controlled clinical study to more fully explore the interrelationships among skills training, psycho-

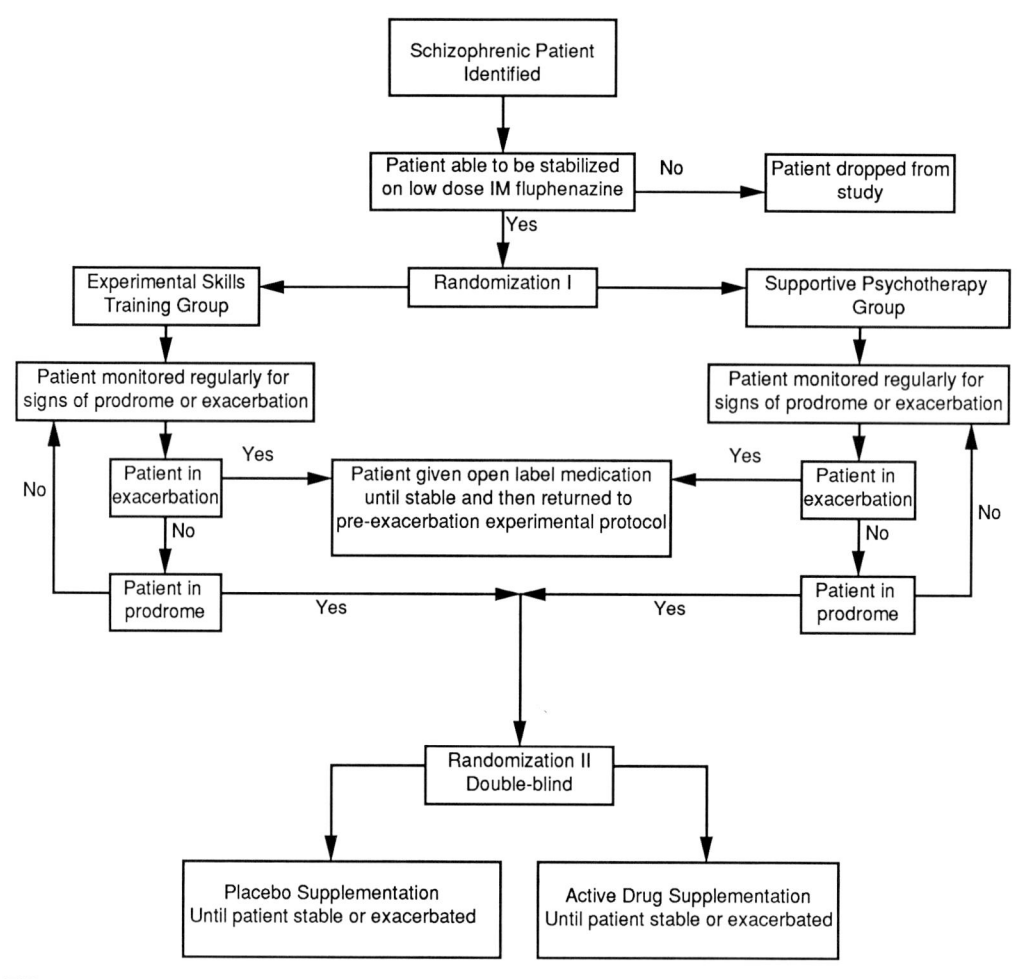

FIG. 1. Flow diagram for the study. There are two randomization points. The first (psychosocial condition) occurs upon entry to the study, and the second (drug condition) occurs when a subject enters his or her first prodromal period.

pharmacology, and psychotic relapse in outpatient schizophrenics. The basic outline of this project is graphically depicted in Fig. 1, and the inclusion and exclusion criteria for choosing subjects are shown in Table 1. Subjects are all diagnosed by DSM-III-R criteria for schizophrenia after having had their psychopathological symptoms elicited in a formal Present State Examination (20). All subjects who reach the first randomization point must have been stabilized as an outpatient for 8 weeks or more on a low dosage of fluphenazine decanoate (5–10 mg IM every 2 weeks). This low dosage was chosen because it is known to be associated with both a lower incidence of extrapyramidal symptoms and a higher rate of relapse than conventional doses (25–50 mg; ref 21). The lower EPS maximized the patient's potential for assimilating skills training material, while the higher rate of relapse mazimized outcome variability.

To offset the higher relapse liability of the low-dosage approach, two potentially mitigating treatment strategies were employed in a 2 × 2 experimental design. The first two

TABLE 1. *Selection criteria for schizophrenic outpatients recruited into Management of Risk of Relapse of Schizophrenia study*

Inclusion criteria:
 1. DSM-III-R diagnosis of schizophrenia;
 2. Stabilized outpatient suitable for maintenance treatment with a low dosage of fluphenazine decanoate (5–10 mg im every 2 weeks);
 3. Age 18–60;
 4. Competent to give informed consent.

Exclusion criteria:
 1. Organic brain disorder;
 2. Mental retardation;
 3. Severe alcohol or other substance abuse;
 4. Severe concomitant medical illness;
 5. History of suicidal or homicidal behavior during exacerbated periods.

TABLE 2. *Skill areas for the two modules used to teach schizophrenic outpatients how to manage their illness*

Skill areas of the Medication Management Module:
 1. General medication information;
 2. Knowing correct self-administration;
 3. Identifying side effects;
 4. Negotiating medication issues with the prescriber;
 5. Understanding long-acting injectable antipsychotic medication.

Skill areas of the Symptom Management Module
 1. Identifying warning signs of relapse (prodrome);
 2. Managing the warning signs of relapse;
 3. Coping with persistent symptoms;
 4. Avoiding alcohol and street drugs.

conditions were a highly prescribed behaviorally oriented skills training program versus a time-matched, "standard" supportive psychotherapy control group; the other two conditions were oral neuroleptic supplementation versus placebo given in double-blind fashion for the duration of each prodromal period.

Skills Training Condition

To produce therapeutic effects synergistic with those of low-dosage neuroleptic therapy, patients were trained in the skills of medication and symptom self-management. Over the course of 6 months in twice-weekly training sessions, patients learned to identify the benefits and side effects of antipsychotic medication, to communicate directly and effectively with their psychiatrist over medication issues, to identify prodromal signs of relapse, and to seek early intervention when these signs developed. Training was carried out in groups of six patients using highly structured and prescribed modules. Each module comprised discrete skill areas, as shown in Table 2.

The specific behaviors comprising the educational objectives of the skill areas were taught through a sequence of eight learning activities as depicted in Fig. 2. The eight learning activities in each skill area are:

Introduction;
Demonstration of skills through video modeling;
skills acquisition through role playing;
Solving resource management problems;
solving outcome problems;
in vivo exercises;
homework exercises;
and booster sessions.

The first five learning activities were taught in the treatment setting and the last three in the natural environment.

In the introduction to each module, the objective was to have the patient identify the goals of the module, the consequences if the goal were achieved, and the steps necessary to achieving the goal. After a module was briefly described, patients were asked the following set of questions:

1. What is the goal of this module?
2. What is the problem?
3. If you get (the goal), what will happen?
4. Do you have time, money, skills, and people to help?
5. What are the steps to get (the goal)?

Following this introduction, which served to give patients insight and motiva-

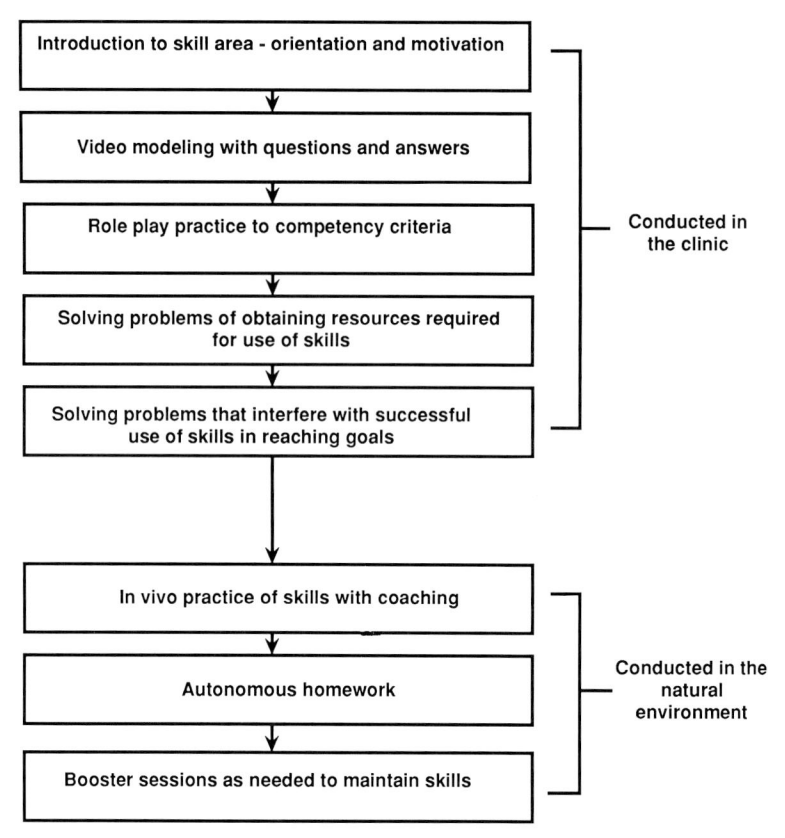

```
┌─────────────────────────────────────────────────────┐
│  Introduction to skill area - orientation and motivation │
└─────────────────────────────────────────────────────┘
                            ▼
┌─────────────────────────────────────────────────────┐
│       Video modeling with questions and answers      │
└─────────────────────────────────────────────────────┘
                            ▼                                  ⎫
┌─────────────────────────────────────────────────────┐        ⎪
│         Role play practice to competency criteria    │        ⎬ Conducted in
└─────────────────────────────────────────────────────┘        ⎪   the clinic
                            ▼                                  ⎪
┌─────────────────────────────────────────────────────┐        ⎪
│    Solving problems of obtaining resources required  │        ⎪
│                   for use of skills                  │        ⎪
└─────────────────────────────────────────────────────┘        ⎪
                            ▼                                  ⎪
┌─────────────────────────────────────────────────────┐        ⎪
│    Solving problems that interfere with successful   │        ⎪
│           use of skills in reaching goals            │        ⎭
└─────────────────────────────────────────────────────┘
                            ▼
┌─────────────────────────────────────────────────────┐        ⎫
│       In vivo practice of skills with coaching       │        ⎪
└─────────────────────────────────────────────────────┘        ⎪
                            ▼                                  ⎬ Conducted in the
┌─────────────────────────────────────────────────────┐        ⎪    natural
│               Autonomous homework                    │        ⎪  environment
└─────────────────────────────────────────────────────┘        ⎪
                            ▼                                  ⎪
┌─────────────────────────────────────────────────────┐        ⎪
│     Booster sessions as needed to maintain skills    │        ⎭
└─────────────────────────────────────────────────────┘
```

FIG. 2. Sequence of structured training components or learning activities of each skill area. The first five learning activities take place in the clinic setting, the next two occur in the patients' natural settings, and the booster sessions can take place in either location.

tion for the training activities, the skills were taught by using a combination of videotaped modeling and role playing. After reviewing the importance and functional utility of the skill and the sequence of steps necessary to achieve the goal, patients viewed a videotaped demonstration that was periodically stopped to assess patients' attentiveness and comprehension. Incorrect answers resulted in replaying the videotape and highlighting the information needed to correctly answer the question when it was repeated.

After all the information had been understood, patients then role played the skill. If a behavior had not been performed or had been performed incorrectly, corrective feedback was given and the patient reenacted the role playing until each skill was correctly role played by all the patients in the group. Patients were next taught to solve a set of "resource management" problems. These were difficulties that they might encounter when they attempted to gather the resources necessary to perform each skill. For example, transportation to the clinic would be a resource necessary for applying the skill of negotiating medication issues with the physician.

Once patients were trained to gather the necessary resources to implement their newly learned skills, they learned to solve problems that might occur when the environment did not respond positively; these were labeled "outcome problems." For example, perhaps a patient decided that he was experiencing medication side effects but discovered that his doctor was out of town. The patient would be guided through a number of problem-solving options for handling such a situation.

The in vivo exercises were designed to have patients perform in the "real world" the skills they had been taught in the training sessions. Patients independently collected resources necessary to perform the skill, and therapists accompanied them during these practice trials to provide corrective feedback and to assess the quality of the performance for additional training.

The homework exercises were much the same as the in vivo exercises except that the staff did not accompany patients. During homework exercises, the patients brought back, whenever possible, some "permanent product" of the exercise that verified its completion. In the Medication Management Module, such a permanent product might be the phone number and address of a local psychiatric emergency room to be used when more familiar medical help, such as the patient's regular psychiatrist, therapist, or case coordinator, was not immediately available.

The intensive treatment phase of the two modules typically lasted for 6 months, followed by less intensive "booster" treatment. The booster exercises were designed to refresh patients' skills after a period of inactivity. These consisted of many of the same role-playing, problem-solving, in vivo, and homework exercises used in the original training. Because of the vicissitudes of community life, the lack of assured material and social reinforcers to sustain learned skills, and the cognitive and memory problems of chronic schizophrenics, these less intensive maintenance sessions were continued throughout the study for up to 2 years. Each of these modules was taught by a team of behavioral therapists ranging in experience from neophyte to 20-year veteran trainer.

The orientation of both of these modules was highly content-specific and depended on the assimilation of a knowledge base involving medications and the symptoms of schizophrenia. Knowledge and skills in these domains were conceptualized as a necessary intermediate step toward improving the social competency of patients in their interactions with family members, significant others, case workers, care givers, and physicians, all in the service of improved coping with stress and self-management of their illness.

Contrast Condition

The patients randomly assigned to the contrast psychotherapy group were exposed to the same amount of therapist contact and peer interaction as their counterparts receiving social skills training. While there was education on the topics of medication and symptomatology, this was not done using the behavioral techniques of the experimental group and there were no systematic problem-solving skills conveyed. The therapist used the techniques of traditional group process and emphasized group cohesion. Such techniques sometimes encouraged the group to "brainstorm" on a particular patient's problem, thereby evoking some implicit group problem solving.

Monitoring Protocol

Once past the initial randomization point, the patients were monitored on a weekly basis for signs of stability, prodrome, or exacerbation. Each of these three clinical states was defined operationally and individually.

The prodromal state was defined as an increase of 30 points or more (out of a possible 100) above baseline on one or more of an individual's prodromal target symptoms. These symptoms were individualized for each subject. They were established at the time of entry to the study through a process of chart review and interviews with subjects, family members, and care givers. Objective prodromal symptoms typically included social withdrawal, hygienic neglect, pacing, hostility, and insomnia; while subjective symptoms included sadness, derealization, confusion, perplexity, or religiosity. The exacerbated state was defined as an increase of three or more points above baseline on either the psychotic or hostile/suspicious cluster scores of the Brief Psychiatric Rating Scale (22).

When a patient first met criteria for a prodrome, the patient was again randomized in double-blind fashion to the drug conditions. He or she then received either the active drug (oral fluphenazine HC1, 5 mg BID) or the placebo (BID) for the duration of this and all subsequent prodromes. Patients who exacerbated were given open-label oral medications until stability was regained.

Thus, the study design is a 2 × 2 factorial experiment: skills training and drug supplementation, skills training and placebo supplementation, supportive psychotherapy and drug supplementation, and supportive psychotherapy and placebo supplementation. Harvested outcome variables included the following:

Number and duration of prodromes and exacerbations;
Latency from prodrome to exacerbation;
Degree of life disruption during an exacerbation;
Amount of open-label medication needed to remediate an exacerbation.

Among the intermediate variables obtained were cognitive mastery and skills acquisition of the material in each of the module's skill areas.

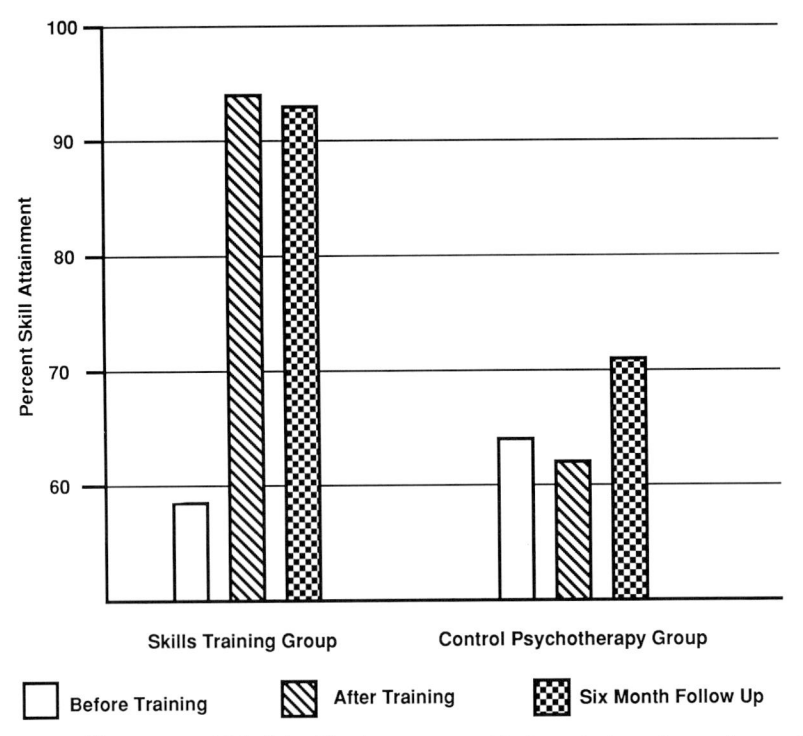

FIG. 3. Symptom Management Module. The improvement in knowledge of symptom self-management, as demonstrated on pre- and posttraining written tests, was significant at the $p = .01$ level for the skills training group. There was no erosion of this knowledge at the 6-month follow-up, and there was no significant change in knowledge for the control group.

INTERIM RESULTS

The study is presently entering year 3 of a planned 5-year span. To date, 53 subjects have reached the first randomization point. Of these, 21 have gone on to develop prodromes and have been randomized to one of the drug conditions.

As shown in Figs. 3 and 4, patients in the experimental skills training group, upon completion of the modules, were able to demonstrate both knowledge assimilation (through written tests) and skills acquisition (through role plays) at higher levels than the contrast group. There were no significant erosions of these skills or knowledge at the 6-month follow-up assessment. The control group showed slight, nonsignificant increases in both knowledge and skills at the 6-month follow-up. There were no significant differences in age, sex, education, length of illness, intelligence, or social functioning between the patients in the skills training or group therapy conditions. Although not depicted, there were similarly significant findings for skills acquisition in the Symptom Management Module and for knowledge mastery in the Medication Management Module.

In examining results from the first randomization point (skills training vs supportive therapy), we found no significant differences (controlling for the drug condition) in the number or length of prodromes; and no significant differences in the number, length, or severity of exacerbations between the skills training group ($N = 27$) and the supportive psychotherapy group ($N = 26$). However, when looking at the time to exacerbation following an initial prodrome

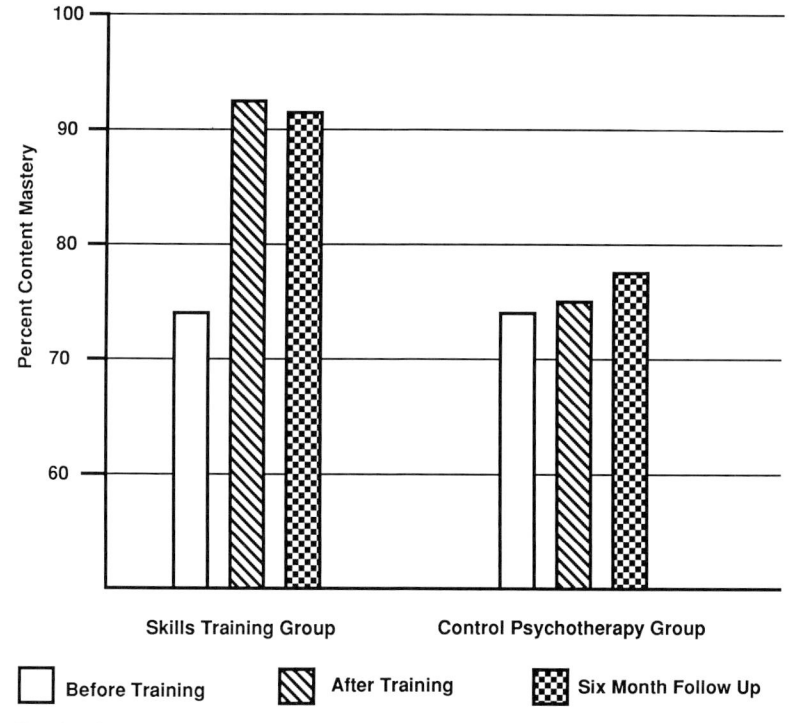

FIG. 4. Medication Management Module. The acquisition of targeted skills, as demonstrated by pre- and posttraining role plays, was significant at the $p = .01$ level for subjects in the skills training condition. There was no erosion of these skills at the 6-month follow-up. The control group's trend toward improvement was nonsignificant at the 6-month follow-up and probably represents "contamination" from implicit training occurring as a result of the study's monitoring protocol.

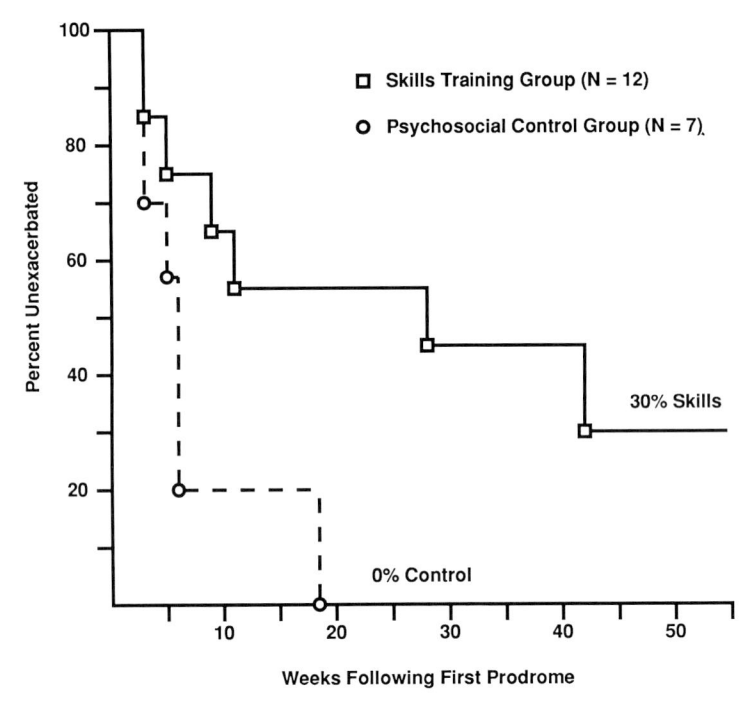

FIG. 5. Survival to exacerbation following the first prodrome for the skills training group and psychosocial control group ($p < .01$ using survival analysis).

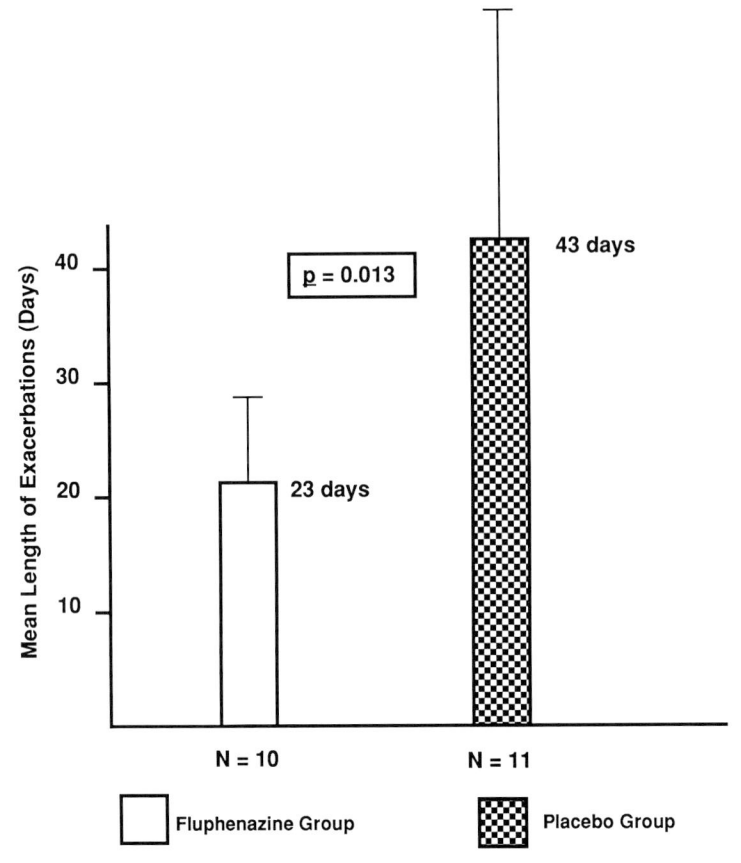

FIG. 6. Mean length of subsequent exacerbations for groups treated with active drug (fluphenazine HCl) and placebo during prodromal periods ($p = 0.013$ using two-tailed t-test).

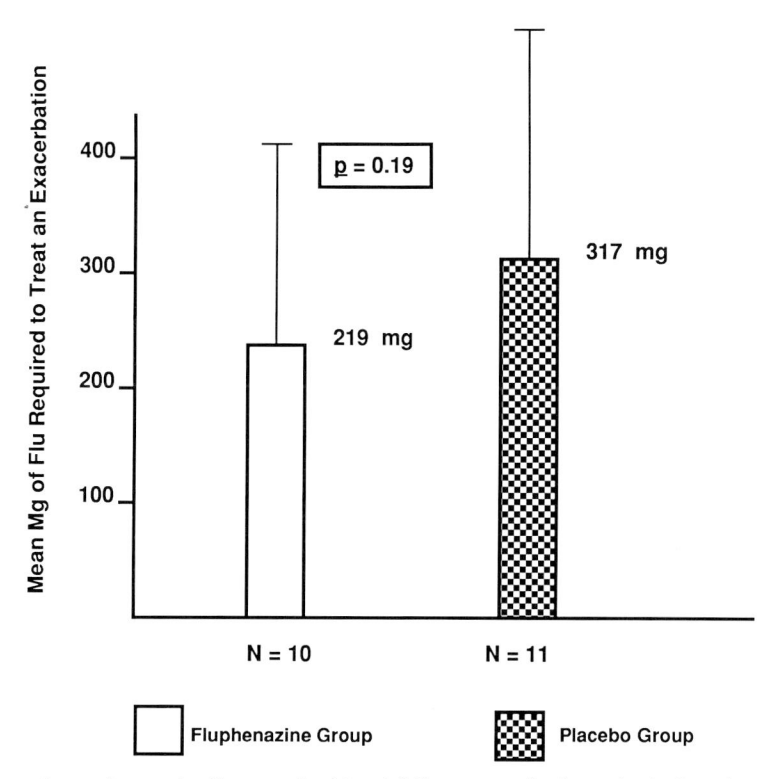

FIG. 7. Mean dose of neuroleptics required to stabilize exacerbations, including dose of fluphenazine supplementations given to the active drug group during prodromal periods.

(second randomization), there was a significant difference (again controlling for the drug condition) with longer survival of patients receiving skills training than those in group therapy (see Fig. 5).

As shown in Fig. 6, patients receiving active fluphenazine supplementation at the time of prodrome ($N = 10$) had a shorter mean length of exacerbation than the placebo group ($N = 11$). As depicted in Fig. 7, there was a nonsignificant difference favoring the active drug supplementation group in the amount of total neuroleptic medication required to treat an exacerbation, including doses given the active group during their prodromal periods.

DISCUSSION

While the findings presented here represent only a partial analysis of the available data at the midpoint of a planned 5-year study, certain trends are suggested.

The results from the assessments of skills acquisition and skills retention indicated that schizophrenic patients were able to assimilate knowledge and skills across a broad range of topics related to medication management and symptom management. These skills appeared durable and, with booster sessions, were retained without substantial erosion over a 6-month period.

These data also suggested that over 6 months the patients in the contrast psychotherapy group may acquire modest amounts of knowledge and skills related to medication and symptom management. This probably resulted from passive teaching, or "contamination," from the monitoring protocol. Since this protocol was heavily weighted with measures of prodromes, psychotic symptomatology, and ication side effects, it seemed reasonable to expect that some of this would be transferred to the subjects in the contrast group.

These early results also suggested that there was generalization of the skills acquired in the training program to the patients' self-management of their illnesses. Patients receiving skills training apparently used the relevant skills they learned to cope better with prodromes, surviving longer without a full-blown relapse. Early intervention with supplemental fluphenazine before the development of overt psychotic symptoms appeared to reduce the severity of ensuing exacerbations. Completion of this study will determine whether skills training and supplemental neuroleptic therapy at times of prodromal symptoms will have an additive influence on preventing, delaying, or reducing the severity of relapses in schizophrenic outpatients.

ACKNOWLEDGMENTS

This project was supported in part by research grants from the Veterans Administration Medical Research Service and the National Institute of Mental Health (MH141573 and MH30911) to Jeffrey Cummings, MD, William C. Wirshing, MD, Stephen R. Marder, MD, and Robert P. Liberman, MD.

The data reported in this chapter were presented at the International Congress on Schizophrenia Research, San Diego, April 1–5, 1989. The authors are grateful for the contributions of the following members of the research team of the "Management of Risk of Relapse" project: Kathleen Johnston-Cronk, Joanne McKenzie, RN, Malca LeBell, PhD, Karen Zimmerman, PhD, Gayla Blackwell, RN, MSW, Edgar Mitchell, Ann Powell, OTR, Bernice Allen, and to Phyllis Lathers, MA, who prepared and edited the manuscript.

REFERENCES

1. Lehman AF, Ward NC, Linn LS. Chronic mental patients: the quality of life issue. *Am J Psychiatry* 1982;134:1271–1276.
2. Talbott JA. *The chronic mental patient: problems, solutions, and recommendations for a public policy.* Washington, DC: American Psychiatric Association, 1978.
3. Goldman HH, Gatozzi J, Taube R. The national plan for the chronically mentally ill. *Hosp Community Psychiatry* 1981;32:16–28.
4. Kohen W, Paul GL. Current trends and recommended changes in extended care placement of mental patients. *Schizophr Bull* 1976;2:575–594.
5. Anthony WA, Liberman RP. The practice of rehabilitation: historical, conceptual, and research base. *Schizophr Bull* 1986;12(4):542–59.
6. Wallace CJ. Functional assessment in rehabilitation. *Schizophr Bull* 1986;12(4):604–624.
7. Rumelhart DE. *Understanding understanding.* La Jolla, Calif: University of California, Center for Human Information Processing, 1981.
8. Glaser R. Education and thinking: the role of knowledge. *Am Psychol* 1984;39:93–104.
9. Bandura A. Self-efficacy: toward a unifying theory of behavioral change. *Psychol Rev* 1977;88:191–215.
10. Brenner HD. Zur bedeutung von basisstorungen für behand lung und rehabilitation. In: Boker W, Brenner HD, eds. *Bewaltigung der Schizophrenie.* Bern: Huber, 1986;142–158.
11. Spaulding W, Storms L, Goodrich V, Sullivan M. Applications of experimental psychopathology to psychiatric rehabilitation. *Schizophr Bull* 1986;12:560–77.
12. Liberman RP, DeRisi WJ, Mueser KT. *Social skills training for psychiatric patients.* New York: Pergamon Press, 1989.
13. Goldstein AP, Sprafkin RP, Gershaw MJ. *Skill training for community living: applying structured learning therapy.* New York: Pergamon Press, 1976.
14. Wallace CJ, Boone SE, Donahoe CP, Foy DW. Psychosocial rehabilitation for the chronic mentally disabled: social and independent living skills training. In: Barlow D, ed. *Behavioral treatment of adult disorders.* New York: Guilford Press, 1985;462–501.
15. Schooler NR. The efficacy of antipsychotic drugs and family therapies in the maintenance treatment of schizophrenia. *J Clin Psychopharmacol* 1986;6:11S–19S.
16. Van Putten T. Why do schizophrenic patients refuse to take their drugs? *Arch Gen Psychiatry* 1974;31:67–72.
17. Kane JM. Compliance issues in outpatient treatment. *J Clin Psychopharmacol* 1985;5:22S–27S.
18. Paul GL. The chronic mental patient: current status, future directions. *Psychol Bull* 1969;71:81–94.
19. Liberman RP, Foy DW. Psychiatric rehabilitation for chronic mental patients. *Psychiat Ann* 1983;13:539–545.

20. Wing JK, Cooper JE, Sartorious N. *Measurement and classification of psychiatric symptoms: an instruction manual in the PSE and CATEGO program.* Cambridge, Engl: Cambridge University Press, 1974.
21. Marder SR, Van Putten T, Mintz J, Lebell M, McKenzie J, May PRA. Low and conventional dose maintenance therapy with fluphenazine decanoate. *Arch Gen Psychiatry* 1987;44:518–521.
22. Overall JE, Hollister LE, Pichot P. Major psychiatric disorders: a four-dimensional approach. *Arch Gen Psychiatry* 1987;16:146–156.

26

A Neuropsychiatric Model of Treatment

Paula T. Trzepacz[1] and Christopher Starratt[2]

We have utilized a multidisciplinary approach to the psychiatric treatment of patients who have both a psychiatric and neurological problem. Such patients may have depression and epilepsy, aggression and head trauma, or amnesias and brain tumors. These dual-diagnosis patients pose some unique and complicated problems for treatment, requiring traditional psychiatric management strategies as well as neurological and cognitive assessments. Our approach combines elements of a rehabilitation model with those of a psychiatric model.

Our treatment team includes psychiatrists, neuropsychologists, nurses, social workers, speech pathologists, neurologists, occupational therapists, and recreational therapists. Intensive assessment by each member of the team precedes the treatment phase. Areas of special concern include the cognitive status of the patient, family system issues, and the interpersonal abilities of the patient. Neuropsychological testing, magnetic resonance imaging (MRI) scans of the brain, single photon emission computed tomography (SPECT) scans of the brain, electroencephalograms (EEGs) and evoked potentials are done routinely. This provides a thorough database on each patient, which allows identification of neuroanatomic areas that are impaired and that may be associated with the psychiatric diagnoses.

ASSESSMENTS AND THERAPIES

Neuropsychological assessment begins with a screening test of various functions, the Mattis Dementia Rating Scale (1). From this test a total score and five subtest scores—attention, initiation and perseveration, construction, conceptualization, and memory—are obtained. If a patient performs adequately on this test, further testing of specific cognitive functions is pursued. A delineation of types of memory or attentional disturbances (e.g., visuospatial vs verbal) is then established. These tests may focus on particular brainstem or cortical areas that are lesioned, and comparisons to deficits on MRI and SPECT scans, and EEGs can then be made. Medications can be chosen to address disturbances of mood or behavior and also to consider their effects on the cognitive and neuroanatomic areas of dysfunction.

Psychopharmacotherapy involves medications to treat depression, mania, psychosis, anxiety, etc, as well as drugs for aggression, seizures, memory deficits, movement disorders, etc. Medications such as propranolol, clonazepam, valproate, carbamazepine, methylphenidate, clonidine, and bromocriptine are used to supplement the more traditional array of psychotropic medications.

Group therapies are an important form of

---

[1]Consultation—Liaison Program, Western Psychiatric Institute and Clinic, University of Pittsburgh School of Medicine, Pittsburgh, PA 15213.
[2]Allegheny Neuropsychiatric Institute, Medical College of Pennsylvania, Oakdale, PA 15071.

treatment for both cognitive and psychosocial dysfunctions. These groups include attentional retraining, memory retraining, and social skills groups. The attentional retraining group involves sustained attention (vigilance) testing and repeated performances by the patient. Feedback is given as the patient performs the tests, and self-monitoring is taught to the patient. Improvements in speed and accuracy are sought. We use attentional tests that are pencil-and-paper tasks, such as the letter cancellation (2), number facility (2), and Trailmaking tests (3). Results are graphed for patients to follow their own performances over time.

The memory retraining group has two levels to accommodate differences in abilities. Level 1 is face-name learning, to associate names with faces of staff members who work with the patients. Level 2 includes verbal paired associate learning, in which a list of unrelated words to remember are embedded into a story as a strategy to enhance memory of the words, and each session involves a retesting of how much the patient remembers. Eventually the patient is able to utilize this story technique to remember his or her own list of words embedded in his or her own story. Level 2 also includes visual imagery training as a strategy to compensate for verbal memory deficits, wherein the patient visually imagines two words interacting (e.g., an elephant wearing a hat).

Patients can be assigned to various social skills groups based on their needs. These groups include perception of emotion, expression of emotion, anger management, and basic social skills. Patients who have some sort of brain injury or pathology commonly have deficits in interpersonal functioning ranging from aggression and impulse dyscontrol to subtler forms of communication problems. These groups address different aspects of such psychosocial problems, and some focus on cognitive-perceptual abilities.

One needs to perceive emotions in others correctly in order to react appropriately. In the perception-of-emotion group, Ekman slides (4) of faces portraying different emotions, such as happiness, sadness, disgust, surprise, and anger, are used. Performances are compared to norms, and patients are given feedback about their performances. They are then trained in ways to notice features of the faces more accurately as a strategy for improving perception of facial emotion in others. Frontal-lobe lesions can produce a decreased *memory* for facial affect, especially for sadness and fearfulness, with happiness and anger somewhat better preserved (5). On the other hand, posterior lesions cause a *misperception* of facial affect, especially fearful faces in patients with right-sided lesions (5).

Expression of emotion is different from perception of emotion, and these two abilities are not necessarily simultaneously impaired. In fact, it appears that different neuroanatomic areas are involved in the perception and expression of emotions (6). Patients observe themselves on a videotape from the group experience and then discuss how they felt in comparison to what they looked like on tape. Feedback from the group is encouraged.

The anger management group is reserved for patients who have difficulty controlling their tempers. Patients identify situations that cause them anger and gain awareness of how they tend to react. They learn de-escalation procedures and relaxation techniques and utilize self-monitoring techniques, including keeping diaries. There is both a behavioral and a psychotherapeutic approach in this group.

The social skills group involves learning and being aware of basic social skills, such as assertiveness, expressing needs appropriately, and giving and receiving compliments. Role playing various scenarios is a prominent modality in this group.

Results from these group therapies, including the cognitive retraining exercises, becomes "grist for the mill" in psychotherapy with the psychiatrist and nurses, or in the milieu activities. Cognitive deficits may be denied and may be part of a patient's retient's resistance and inability to improve psychologically. Retraining groups provide concrete evidence of deficits and any progress the patient has made. In addition, comparisons can be made between problems noted in groups and the patients' psychosocial problems in other situations. A therapeutic alliance can be enhanced by such generalizations.

CASES

Two case examples will illustrate this neuropsychiatric approach, the first case involving epilepsy, aphasia, and depression and the second case a diagnosis of schizoaffective disorder with prior brain injury.

Case 1

Mr C. is a 49-year-old single, righthanded male who had alcohol abuse in remission, seizures since age 20, and global aphasia. Seizures were usually focal, although occasionally generalized, with right-arm motor symptoms and dysarthria. He was taking phenytoin. He was also depressed on admission and had questionable visual and auditory hallucinations. Brief trials on haloperidol and then on nortriptyline did not relieve psychiatric symptoms, and worsened his seizures. An MRI scan showed diffuse brain atrophy, an EEG showed left-hemisphere PLEDS (epileptiform activity), and a MiniMental State Exam (7) score was 11/30 points. A SPECT scan revealed decreased blood flow in the left frontal region. Neuropsychological testing showed a low IQ, reduced executive functions, a fluctuating receptive and expressive aphasia, memory deficits, perseveration on cognitive and motor tasks, decreased visuospatial analytical ability, and an abnormal Mattis score (1) of 92/144. His aphasic symptoms worsened ictally and postictally, such that his speech was more dysarthric with anomia, false starts, and paraphasias.

Carbamazepine was added, and seizure frequency decreased. A trial on bromocriptine was begun at 2.5 mg BID and gradually increased to 7.5 mg TID over a 16-day period. Bromocriptine was chosen for its dopaminergic influences (based on the model of parkinsonism in which dopamine reduces inertia of movements; see ref 8) in hopes of improving his aphasia. This was combined with speech therapy to use only simple syntax and three- to five-word sentences, to increase awareness of comprehensions deficits, and to improve articulation. On bromocriptine a remarkable improvement in speech was noted, including an ability to speak fluently in sentences without perseveration and with fewer false starts.

In attentional retraining group he was initially severely impaired. He improved by 50% in both speed and accuracy of visual scanning on the letter cancellation test over a 4-week period. He was able to self-monitor for reduced errors. Although plagued by frustration and periods of dysphoria, he was very motivated in all groups. His interpersonal communications in the social skills group were enhanced by improvements in speech.

A repeat SPECT scan was normal following the bromocriptine trial. The previous abnormality in the left frontal lobe disappeared and was suggestive of a physiological, not structural problem, perhaps a postictal phenomenon.

Case 2

Mr H. was 29 years old and single. At age 18 he was accidentally electrocuted with entrance of electricity at the right hemisphere. He suffered intermittent psychotic symptoms with multiple psychiatric hospitalizations since that time and was often treated with neuroleptics. He had an aunt with schizophrenia. He was admitted for bizarre and ritualistic behaviors, such as manipulating the television plugs to help his favorite football team to win. He was taking thiothixene, amantadine, and clonazepam. He also had depressive symptoms and passive suicidal ideation. Admission diagnoses included organic delusional disorder and ruled out schizophrenia and depression.

An EEG was normal with a 10-Hz dominant posterior rhythm, and MRI and SPECT scans were both normal. His IQ was low normal, and his Mattis score was normal at 139/144, but there were abstraction, attentional, and visual perceptual deficits. He was overly detailed, overideational, and metaphorical in his thinking, with ideas of reference and magical thinking. He had obsessive-compulsive traits.

He was treated with nortriptyline for depressive symptoms, and clonazepam and amantadine were discontinued. He became frankly manic and nortriptyline was discontinued. Lithium was used to control mania and carbamazepine was added due to the brain-injury component. Milieu therapy provided external structure. He was well motivated.

Despite attentional retraining, his attentional deficits persisted throughout the admission. In the social skills group he utilized role play well and tried to reduce his use of metaphors. One strength was his friendliness. In the emotional expression group he used facial dimensions to help make his expressed affect more appropriate with the help of group feedback. He had very impaired facial emotional perception with a score of only 43% on correctly guessing the Ekman slides on admission. Without specific training he retested 3 weeks later at 74%, and with training he became normal with 92% correct. He practiced making faces in the mirror in his room to identify the information he learned in group.

DISCUSSION

Brain-injured and schizophrenic patients may have some problems in common. Research in schizophrenia has hypothesized abnormalities in the frontal lobes (9,10). The prefrontal cortex (11) is an area involved in executive functions, such as higher-level conceptualizations, social appropriateness, abstraction, initiative, and judgment. Brain-injured and schizophrenic patients have problems in these areas. It is thus reasonable to apply some of the therapeutic techniques used in the rehabilitation of brain-injured patients to populations of schizophrenics (12).

Schizophrenics have deficits in interpersonal skills that may have a cognitive basis. They have deficits in labeling facial emotions, trouble recognizing different expressed emotions, and trouble identifying specific emotions (13). These deficits are not simply due to a verbal labeling problem, however (13).

Schizophrenics also have difficulty with perceptual and cognitive tasks that require *complex* information processing (14). Furthermore, they have attentional deficits especially under distracting conditions, and abstraction problems. However, while brain-injured patients have difficulty with both simple and complex tasks, schizophrenics have deficits only on complex tasks (14). Goldstein believes they bear similarities to patients with frontal-lobe injuries and that schizophrenics with predominantly negative symptoms may have underlying structural brain disease of a dementia pattern (14).

The two cases described illustrate the use of various cognitive and social skills groups that have a cognitive/behavioral orientation. The emphasis on the perception and expression of emotion as neuroanatomic correlates is an important way to think about interpersonal interactions and the deficits that psychiatric patients have that may contribute to what is otherwise felt to be psychosocial in nature. The use of scans such as SPECT (15) may enhance our understanding of cognitive processes. In Case 1 the patient's SPECT deficits in the dominant frontal lobe correlated well with his deficits in speech and executive functions. His aphasia was also due to seizures affecting the entire left hemisphere. By better understanding the cognitive and neuroanatomic aspects of his case, a trial of bromocriptine was attempted based on theoretical knowledge of dopaminergic agents.

The second case illustrated the frontal-lobe deficits that can be due either to a schizophrenic process or to brain injury. Interestingly, only the neuropsychological testing revealed deficits, while the neuro-diagnostic testing was normal. This schizoaffective patient responded with improvements to most of the rehabilitative interventions. There is a practical, concrete nature to these rehabilitative group therapies that even psychotic patients may be able to appreciate and utilize.

We recommend that further work be undertaken in a larger population to determine whether a neuropsychiatric model of treatment that includes cognitive rehabilitation can be effective in schizophrenia. It remains to be seen whether certain subpopulations of schizophrenics respond differently.

REFERENCES

1. Mattis, S. *The Dementia Rating Scale*. Psychological Assessment Resources, 1988.
2. Ekstrom RB, French JW, Harmen HH, Derman D. *Manual for kit of factor referenced cognitive tests*. Princeton, NJ: Educational Testing Service, 1975.
3. Reitan RM. Validity of the Trailmaking test as an indicator of organic brain damage. *Percept Motor Skills* 1985;8:271–276.
4. Ekman P, Friesen W. Pictures of facial affect. Palo Alto, Calif: Consulting psychologists Press, 1976.
5. Prigitano GP, Pribram KH. Perception and memory of facial affect following brain injury. *Percept Motor Skills* 1982;54:859–869.
6. Fried I, Mateer C, Ojeman G, Wohns R, Fedio P. Organization of visuospatial functions in human cortex. *Brain* 1982;105:349–371.
7. Folstein MF, Folstein SE, McHugh PR. Mini-Mental State: a practical method for grading the cognitive state of patients for the clinician. *J Psychiatr Res* 1975;12:189–198.
8. Ross E, Stewart R. Akinetic mutism from hypothalamic damage: successful treatment with dopamine agonists. *Neurology* 1981;31:1435–1439.
9. Weinberger DR, Berman KF, Zec RF. Physiological dysfunction of dorsolateral prefrontal cortex in schizophrenia: I. Regional cerebral blood flow evidence. *Arch Gen Psychiatry* 1986;43:114–124.
10. Morihisi JM, McAnulty GB. Structure and function: brain electrical activity mapping and computed tomography in schizophrenia. *Biol Psychiatry* 1985;20:3–19.
11. Teuber HL. Unity and diversity of frontal lobe functions. *Acta Neurobiol Experimentia* 1972;32:615–656.
12. Erikson RC, Binder LM. Cognitive deficits among functionally psychotic patients: a rehabilitative perspective. *J Clin Exper Neuropsychol* 1986;8:257–274.
13. Feinberg TE, Rifkin A, Schaffer C, Walker E. Facial discrimination and emotional recognition in schizophrenia and affective disorders. *Arch Gen Psychiatry* 1986;43:276–279.
14. Goldstein G. The neuropsychology of schizophrenia. In: Grant I, Adams K, eds. *The neuropsychological assessment of neuropsychiatric disorders*. New York: Oxford University Press, 1986;147–171.
15. Tikofsky RS. SPECT brain studies: potential role of cognitive challenge in language and learning disorders. *Adv Func Neuroimag Spring* 1988:12–15.

PART VI
Pharmacological Treatments

27

Persistence of Antipsychotic Drug Levels and Effects

Bruce M. Cohen,[1,2] Ross J. Baldessarini,[1,2] Alexander Campbell,[1] Tomohiro Tsuneizumi,[1] and Suzann M. Babb[1]

Despite four decades of clinical use and research, many basic pharmacokinetic and pharmacodynamic parameters remain poorly defined for the antipsychotic drugs (1). Among these are the delayed offset of clinical therapeutic effects and side effects often observed following treatment with these agents.

Despite typically quoted half-lives of less than 36 hours (2), residual side effects, such as drug-induced parkinsonism or neuroleptic malignant syndrome, may last for days to weeks after discontinuation of antipsychotic medication (3–5). Similarly, evidence of dopamine blockade may last for weeks in animals after even a *single* moderate dose of haloperidol (6). Therapeutic effects may persist, as well, for extended periods of time after discontinuation of the drug. Many patients, even those with chronic illnesses, may not relapse for months after the termination of treatment (2).

While these persistent effects may be an indirect result of drug exposure, they also may be a consequence of slow elimination of the drug, especially from the brain, with persistence of the drug in the tissue for extended periods of time after administration

[1]Mailman Research Center, McLean Hospital, Belmont, MA 02178.
[2]Departments of Psychiatry and Neuroscience Program, Harvard Medical School, Boston, MA 02115.

(7). In evaluating this possibility, it is important to note that tissue redistribution alone, separate from drug elimination, may continue for days after a single dose of the neuroleptic (8–10). Despite this, few studies have measured neuroleptic concentrations more than 24 hours after administration, and even fewer have measured neuroleptic concentrations for the days to weeks that may be necessary to estimate terminal elimination (7). Thus, accurate estimates of the time necessary for neuroleptics to disappear from the blood and the brain are not available.

In limited experiments in human subjects, metabolites have been observed in the urine for months after single or multiple doses of various phenothiazine and butyrophenone neuroleptic drugs (11–18). Similarly, after a single dose, haloperidol was observed in the plasma by radioimmunoassay (RIA) in three patients 14 days after drug administration (19) and, in a separate study (5), it was observed in the plasma by high-performance liquid chromatography (HPLC) in one patient up to 11 days after drug administration. In each study, the apparent half-life of the drug increased with time after dosing. Thus, at the last measurements taken, half-life was estimated at 4 to 21 *days,* versus the 12 to 36 hours reported from the more numerous studies based on early time points.

In animal studies, tritiated haloperidol

was still observed at substantial concentrations in the tissue 4 days after a single dose was given to rats (20,21). Similarly, haloperidol was observed by gas chromatography (GC) in the serum up to 9 days after a single dose of the drug given to rats, and the half-life of elimination from the serum was estimated to have risen to 4 days at the latest time points evaluated (8).

These results are suggestive of very long retention of neuroleptics in tissue. However, the studies are limited in scope. Most involved only one drug, haloperidol, and in all these studies only four patients and several cohorts of rats were studied. In addition, none of the studies provided an accurate estimate of drug concentration in the brain; most estimated drug concentration in the plasma or serum only. Drug concentrations in the blood may or may not correlate highly with those in the brain and, therefore, may not be adequate to provide evidence on behaviorally relevant drug concentrations at its active site (8,20,22).

This paucity of studies of the persistence and long-term elimination of neuroleptics is partly the result of technological limitations. Until recently, estimates of neuroleptics in tissue at extended times after dosing were impractical due to inadequate sensitivity of the available assay methods (19,23,24). However, with the development of RIA and HPLC techniques sensitive to neuroleptics in the picogram range, such longer-term pharmacokinetic studies became possible. In this chapter, we report on the results of our preliminary studies of the long-term pharmacokinetics of haloperidol and fluphenazine using a sensitive HPLC assay with coulometric electrochemical detection (HPLC-EC).

TIME COURSE OF BEHAVIORAL EFFECTS AND TISSUE LEVELS OF HALOPERIDOL

Haloperidol concentrates markedly in the brain, appearing at levels 20 to 40 times higher than those in the plasma (25,26). In addition, haloperidol and other neuroleptics may be associated preferentially with the cell membrane, in proximity to the receptors through which neuroleptic drugs are presumed to exert their effects (27–29). Therefore, by concentrating at its site of action, even small amounts of haloperidol may produce a significant physiological effect.

Early studies of the long-term effects of acute doses of haloperidol were largely constrained to behavioral observations because, until recently, assays of haloperidol were not adequately sensitive to pursue the possibility that haloperidol remains in the tissue at low concentrations for extended periods of time after dosing. The results of these behavioral studies in rats indicated that haloperidol produced strikingly prolonged, dose-dependent effects following administration of even a single, moderate dose of the drug (6,22,30). Specifically, acute doses of haloperidol around that necessary to produce half-maximal inhibition (ID_{50}, about 0.1 mg/kg) of the stereotypy induced by a single, moderate challenge dose of the direct dopamine agonist R(−)apomorphine continued to reduce the effects of apomorphine given once at various time points over the next several weeks without further administration of haloperidol. Inhibition of apomorphine-induced stereotypy was observed for over a month in animals receiving single higher doses of haloperidol.

While it is possible that these persistent effects of a single dose of haloperidol were independent of the continued presence of the drug in the tissue, a likely factor is the slow disappearance of haloperidol from a critical site in the brain with a half-life paralleling the recovery of responsiveness to apomorphine. The development of more-sensitive assays for haloperidol has allowed us to explore this possibility.

Rats ($N=6$ per group) were injected with single intraperitoneal doses of haloperidol (0.3 mg/kg which is near the ED_{50} value for producing catalepsy; refs 6,22) or of vehicle. At selected times after dosing, separate groups of rats were challenged once only with apomorphine (0.3 mg/kg sc, near its ED_{50} value for producing stereotyped behaviors; ref 31) or sacrificed for determination of haloperidol in the brain. Behavior was rated cumulatively for 60 seconds during each 10 minutes for 1 hour. Drug effect was measured as the reduction in stereotyped behavior in the haloperidol- versus the vehicle-treated rats. Haloperidol concentration in the brain tissue was estimated by HPLC-EC. The technique, modified from Korpi et al (32,33), combined good recovery (75% to 80%) with high sensitivity (approximately 10 pmol/g of wet brain tissue). The results are presented in Fig. 1.

Drug effects and measurable drug in the brain persisted following dosing throughout 3 weeks of study. Inhibition of apomorphine-induced behavior and the log of drug concentration in the brain were highly correlated ($r = .94$, $p < .01$). Drug *effect* disappeared with a half-life of 9.5 days when calculated as the log of the linear regression of values observed for days 1 to 21 after acute administration of haloperidol. Over the same period, haloperidol *in the brain* disappeared with a half-life of 16.7 days.

These results suggest that haloperidol is eliminated from the rat brain with a remarkably slow half-life at times greater than 24

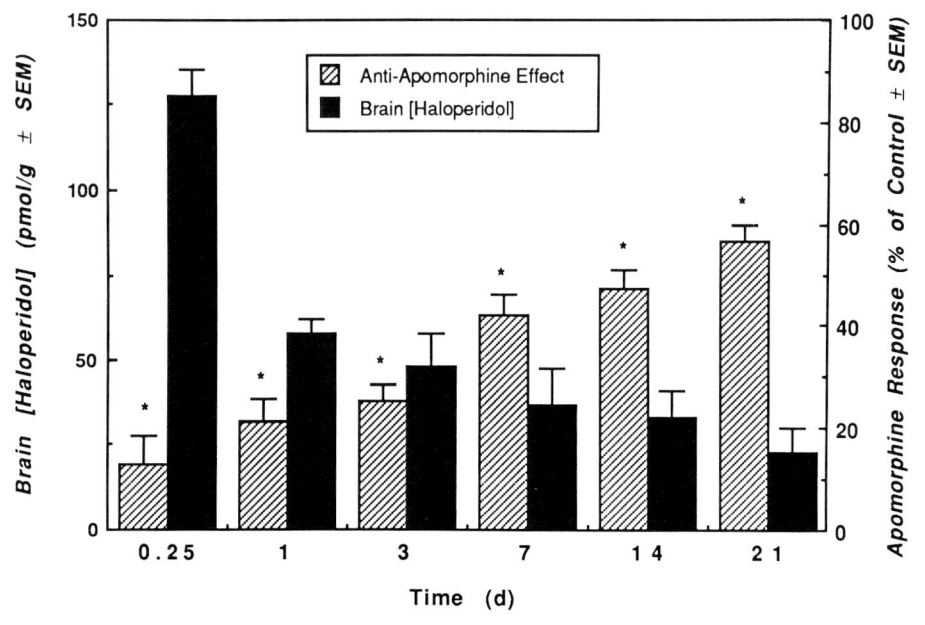

FIG. 1. Time course of inhibition of apomorphine-induced stereotypy and drug concentration in the brain following a single dose of haloperidol. Rats ($N = 6$) received a single intraperitoneal injection of haloperidol (0.3 mg/kg) or of vehicle on day 0. Separate cohorts of rats were sacrificed for determination of haloperidol in the brain by HPLC-EC or received a single injection of apomorphine (0.3 mg/kg sc as the hydrochloride hemihydrate) at the times indicated. No animal received more than one injection of haloperidol or apomorphine. The concentration of haloperidol in the whole brain (minus cerebellum) was estimated in rats not given apomorphine and is expressed as picomoles per gram of wet brain tissue. Stereotyped behavior is scored as the sum of ratings performed for 60-second intervals every 10 minutes for 1 hour after apomorphine injection (maximum score = 18.0) and is expressed as a percentage of that observed in vehicle-treated animals. All injections were given between 11:00 and 13:00 hours on the days indicated. Data are given as means ± SEM; Asterisk indicates stereotypy significantly different from vehicle-treated animals, at $p < .05$ by t-test.

hours after dosing, that substantial amounts of drug remain in the brain for weeks after a single acute dose, and that persistence of the drug in the brain may explain the extended behavioral effects of the drug observed in rats receiving a single dose of haloperidol. In addition, it is interesting that the drug effect appeared to disappear at a faster rate than did the elimination of the drug from the brain. This observation suggests that some functional adaptation—in particular, supersensitivity to the dopamine agonist—may occur during the period following dosing, presumably as a consequence of drug exposure.

TIME COURSE OF BEHAVIORAL EFFECTS AND BRAIN LEVELS OF FLUPHENAZINE

Most past work on the long-term effects of neuroleptic drugs has been performed with haloperidol. Its shorter-acting congener, droperidol, also has been studied, and even this agent inhibited apomorphine-induced behaviors for several days after a single dose in rats. However, the effects of droperidol, even at high doses, are not apparent 1 week after treatment (6).

Haloperidol and droperidol are neuroleptics of the butyrophenone class and are

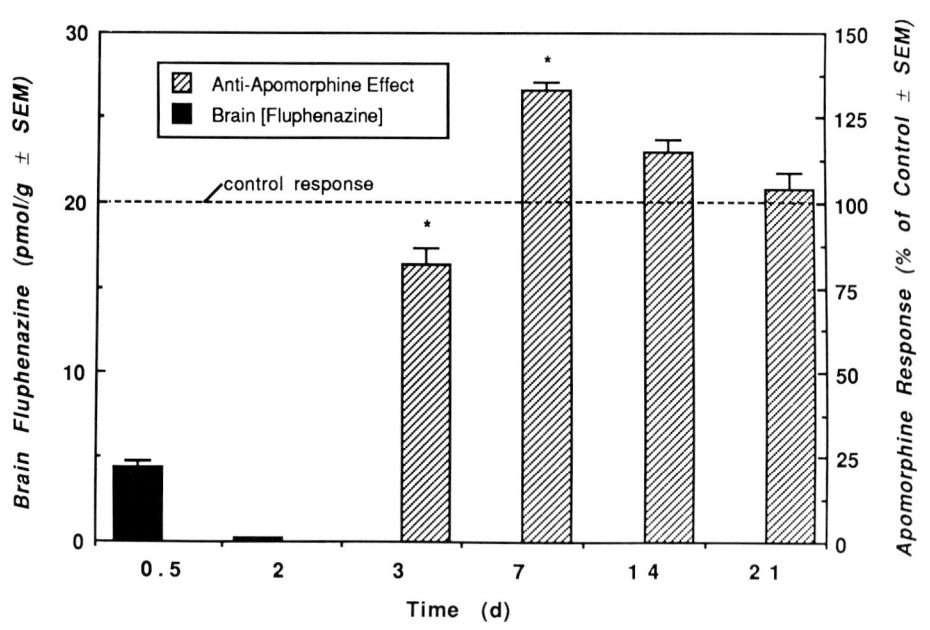

FIG. 2. Time course of inhibition of apomorphine-induced stereotypy and drug concentration in the brain following a single dose of fluphenazine. Rats ($N = 10$) received a single intraperitoneal injection of fluphenazine hydrochloride (1.0 mg/kg) or of vehicle on day 0. Separate cohorts of rats were sacrificed for determination of fluphenazine in the brain by HPLC-EC or received a single injection of apomorphine (0.3 mg/kg sc) at the times indicated. No animal received more than one injection of fluphenazine or apomorphine. Other methods were as described in Fig. 1. Data are given as means ± SEM; asterisk indicates stereotypy significantly different from vehicle-treated animals, at $p < .05$ by t-test; dotted line indicates mean control value of behavioral response to apomorphine. Tissue concentrations of fluphenazine at day 3 were not detectable (i.e., less than 5 pmol/g).

chemically unlike most other antipsychotic drugs. There is little evidence from which to determine if the persistent effects and levels reported with these drugs are properties of neuroleptic agents in general or are limited to butyrophenones and their congeners, or even to haloperidol in particular.

To begin to address this question, we performed studies of the persistence of drug effects and levels of the phenothiazine neuroleptic drug fluphenazine. Like haloperidol, fluphenazine is a high-potency antipsychotic agent and concentrates strikingly (over 40-fold) in brain (26). However, fluphenazine and haloperidol are chemically dissimilar.

Rats ($N = 10$ per group) were treated with a single intraperitoneal dose of fluphenazine (1 mg/kg) or of vehicle. At selected times after dosing, separate cohorts of rats were challenged with apomorphine (0.3 mg/kg, sc) or sacrificed for determinations of fluphenazine in the brain. Assays of behavioral response to apomorphine were as reported for haloperidol. High-performance liquid chromatography with coulometric electrochemical detection for fluphenazine, modified from Svendson and Bird (34) and Stoll et al (35), was sensitive to drug concentrations of 5 pmol/g of wet brain tissue. Results of determinations of drug effect and estimates of the drug in the brain following treatment are presented in Fig. 2.

Despite the sensitivity of the assay, no fluphenazine was observable in the brain by 3 days after drug administration. Also, in contrast to the persistent inhibitory effect observed after treatment with haloperidol, no inhibition of the behavioral effects of apomorphine were observed beyond 2 days after administration of a single dose of fluphenazine. In fact, by 7 days after treatment with fluphenazine, there was evidence of behavioral supersensitivity to apomorphine. This supersensitivity was largely gone by 21 days after drug administration.

DISCUSSION

Documenting the time course of tissue concentrations of the drug and its corresponding effects is critical to defining mechanisms of drug action. This requirement is especially true for neuroleptics, as clinical observation suggests that their ability to produce antipsychotic effects is not immediate but, rather, requires days to weeks of drug exposure and that relapse, too, may not occur quickly but rather is often delayed for weeks to months after the drug is discontinued.

Clinical choices of drug regimens, decisions on the timing and magnitude of dosing, and planning and evaluation of drug withdrawal all depend on accurate estimates of the persistence of drug levels and effects. In addition, it is impossible to design unambiguously informative studies of biochemical and pharmacological parameters in recently treated patients without such information.

Before the present study, several small studies in patients (5,19) and rats (8) had suggested that haloperidol might show a remarkably slow—possibly multiphasic—elimination from blood, but no similar studies had been performed for other neuroleptic drugs. In addition, no previous study had reported on the relationship between drug concentrations in the *brain* and effects of the drug for times greater than 30 hours after dosing (7,8), a time well within the early tissue distribution phases for neuroleptics. The possible dissociation of blood and brain levels of the drug is underscored by recent studies utilizing positron emission tomography (PET) suggesting that elimination of haloperidol from the brain, where it is bound to neurotransmitter receptors, may be slower than elimination from the blood (36). Thus, while determinations of serum or plasma levels of the drug are valuable, they may not be adequate to assess drug levels in the brain, particularly for agents that are strongly tissue-bound.

In the preliminary experiments reported, we estimated drug concentration in the brain and drug effects for weeks after a single dose, given to rats, of either the butyrophenone haloperidol or the phenothiazine fluphenazine. The slow elimination of haloperidol observed in past studies of the drug in the blood of patients and animals was confirmed for brain levels of haloperidol in the present studies. The concentrations of haloperidol in the brain closely correlated with, and so are likely to account for the weeks of behavioral effect observed after even a single, moderate dose of this agent.

A very different time course of drug levels and of direct and secondary drug effects was seen after a single moderate dose of fluphenazine. Fluphenazine disappeared rapidly from brain, and neither drug in the brain nor inhibition of apomorphine were observable within 3 days after treatment. However, the residual effects of drug exposure persisted for as long as 3 weeks, in the form of behavioral supersensitivity to apomorphine.

A similar supersensitivity to apomorphine may have occurred after exposure to haloperidol, obscured by the presence of continued drug in the tissue. This possibility is suggested by the different slopes of disappearance of the drug itself in the brain and of the drug effect (Fig 1).

Thus, it is likely that for both haloperidol and fluphenazine, even single doses of the drug lead to prolonged pharmacologically induced changes in the brain. For haloperidol, slow elimination and persistent dopamine blockade are most prominent, while for fluphenazine, direct drug effects for several days followed by days to weeks of dopamine supersensitivity were evident.

It is not clear whether the differences observed in drug elimination and behavioral supersensitivity in rats would be paralleled by clinically relevant differences in symptoms or side effects after drug discontinuation, especially abrupt discontinuation, in patients receiving haloperidol, fluphenazine, or other neuroleptics. It would be valuable to know if the appearance of withdrawal dyskinesias or symptomatic relapse early after the clinical discontinuation of the drug were more common for fluphenazine than for haloperidol, as the data on relative rates of elimination and development of supersensitivity in the rat outlined above might suggest.

Finally, the persistent pharmacological effects observed with each of the neuroleptics studied suggest that patients recently exposed to antipsychotic drugs are *not* "drug-free" or at least are not free of the *residual effects* of drug exposure *for weeks* after acute treatment. They are certainly not likely to be in an equivalent physiological state to patients who are drug-naive or have not received drugs for months. Moreover, it is not certain whether prolonged treatment leads to even more prolonged effects.

Nor is one patient likely to be in a state equivalent to other patients who have recently received treatment. Rather, our present results suggest that the physiological changes induced by drug exposure may change markedly with time off the drug and may vary widely from drug to drug. Thus, at a time after acute dosing when rats given haloperidol showed continued inhibition of dopamine receptors, rats exposed to fluphenazine showed supersensitivity.

These findings suggest that studies mixing patients who have received different medications or who have been in drug withdrawal for different periods of time risk including subjects in a wide range of drug-induced physiological states from continued monoaminergic inhibition to supersensitivity. Such phenomena may obscure meaningful differences between subject groups. In addition, they may produce apparent differences in individual values or in the group mean or variance for parameters measured that are not disease related but rather are artifacts of recent drug treatment.

Further studies are needed to define the time course of drug levels and effects following treatment with various neuroleptic agents in human as well as animal subjects. In the meantime, great care is needed in interpreting biological findings in patients recently exposed to antipsychotic drugs.

ACKNOWLEDGMENTS

This work was supported in part by USPHS (NIMH) awards and grants MH-31154, MH-36224, MH-42543, MH-43679, and MH-47370, and an award from the Bruce J. Anderson Foundation. Tsuneizumi was partially supported by funds of the Department of Psychiatry, St. Marianna University, Japan. Drug substances were generously donated by McNeil Laboratories (haloperidol; Haldol) and Squibb Corporation (fluphenazine hydrochloride; Prolixin).

REFERENCES

1. Cohen BM. Neuroleptic drugs in the treatment of acute psychosis. In: Casey DE, Christensen AV, eds. *Current trends in psychopharmacology*. Berlin: Springer-Verlag, 1988;47–61.
2. Baldessarini RJ. Drugs and the treatment of psychiatric disorders. In: Gilman AG, et al, eds. *Goodman and Gilman's pharmacologic basis of therapeutics*, 8th ed. New York: Macmillan, 1990 (in press), chap. 19.
3. Curry SH, Marshall JHL, Davis JM, Janowsky DS. Chlorpromazine plasma levels and effects. *Arch Gen Psychiatry* 1970;22:189–196.
4. Itoh H, Ohtsuka N, Ogita K, et al. Malignant neuroleptic syndrome: its present state in Japan in clinical problems. *Folia Psychiatr Neurol Japonica* 1977;31:565–576.
5. Hubbard JW, Ganes D, Midha KK. Prolonged pharmacologic activity of neuroleptic drugs. *Arch Gen Psychiatry* 1987;44:99–100.
6. Campbell A, Baldessarini RJ, Kula NS. Prolonged antidopamine actions of single doses of butyrophenones in the rat. *Psychopharmacology* 1985;87:161–166.
7. Cohen BM, Babb S, Campbell A, Baldessarini RJ. Persistence of haloperidol in brain. *Arch Gen Psychiatry* 1988;45:879–880.
8. Ohman R, Larsson M, Nilsson IM, et al. Neurometabolic and behavioral effects of haloperidol in relation to drug level in serum and brain. *Nauyn-Schmiedebergs Arch Exp Path Pharmakol* 1977;299:105–114.
9. Dahl SG, Strandjord RE. Pharmacokinetics of chlorpromazine after single and chronic dosage. *Clin Pharmacol Ther* 1977;21:437–448.
10. Forsman A, Ohman R. Applied pharmacokinetics of haloperidol in men. *Current Ther Res* 1977;21:396–411.
11. Caffey EM, Forrest IS, Frank TV, Klett CJ. Phenothiazine excretion in chronic schizophrenics. *Am J Psychiatry* 1963;120:578.
12. Forrest IS, Forrest FM. On the metabolism and action mechanism of the phenothiazine drugs. *Exp Med Surg* 1963;21:231–240.
13. Kurland AA, Huang CL, Hallam KJ, Hanlon TE. Further studies of chlorpromazine metabolism and relapse rate. *J Psychiatr Res* 1965;3:27–35.
14. Lutz EG. Dissipation of phenothiazine effect and recurrence of schizophrenic psychosis. *Dis Nerv Syst* 1965;26:355–357.
15. Johnson PC, Charalampous KD, Braun GA. Absorption and excretion and tritiated haloperidol in man (a preliminary report). *Int J Neuropsychiatry* 1967;3(suppl 1):524–525.
16. Cowen MA, Martin WC. Long-term chlorpromazine retention and its modification by steroids. *Am J Psychiatry* 1968;125:139–141.
17. Sved S, Perales A, Palaic D. Chlorpromazine metabolism in chronic schizophrenics. *Br J Psychiatry* 1971;119:589–596.
18. Sakalis G, Curry SH, Mould GP, Lader MH. Physiologic and clinical effects of chlorpromazine and their relationship to plasma level. *Clin Pharmacol Ther* 1972;13:931–946.
19. Ereshefsky L, Jann MW, Saklad SR, Davis CM. Bioavailability of psychotropic drugs: historical perspective and pharmacokinetic overview. *J Clin Psychiatry* 1986;47(9,suppl):6–15.
20. Soudijn W, Van Wijngaarden I, Allewijn F. Distribution, excretion and metabolism of neuroleptics of the butyrophenone type. Part I. Excretion and metabolism of haloperidol and nine related butyrophenone-derivatives in the wistar rat. *Eur J Pharmacol* 1967;1:47–57.
21. Braun, GA, Poos GI, Soudjhn W. Distribution, excretion and metabolism of neuroleptics of the butyrophenone type. Part II. Distribution excretion and metabolism of haloperidol in Sprague-Dawley rats. *Eur J Pharmacol* 1967;1:58–62.
22. Campbell A, Herschel M, Cohen BM, et al. Tissue levels of haloperidol by radioreceptor assay and behavioral effects of haloperidol in the rat. *Life Sci* 1980;27:633–640.
23. Curry SH. Commentary: The strategy and value of neuroleptic drug monitoring. *J Clin Psychopharmacol* 1985;5:263–271.
24. Itoh H, Yagi G, Ohtsuka N, Iwamura K, Ichikawa K. Serum level of haloperidol and its clinical significance. *Prog Neuro-Psychopharmacol* 1980;4:171–183.
25. Cohen BM, Herschel M, Miller EM, et al. Radioreceptor assay of haloperidol tissue levels in the rat. *Neuropharmacology* 1980;19:663–668.
26. Sunderland T, Cohen BM. Blood to brain distribution of neuroleptics. *Psychiatry Res* 1987;20:299–305.
27. Seeman P. Anti-schizophrenic drugs—mem-

brane receptor sites of action. *Biochem Pharmacol* 1977;26:1741–1748.
28. Cohen BM, Zubenko GS. In vivo effects of psychotropic agents on the physical properties of cell membranes in the rat brain. *Psychopharmacology* 1985;86:365–368.
29. Zubenko GS, Cohen BM. Effects of psychotropic agents on the physical properties of platelet membranes in vitro. *Psychopharmacology* 1985;86:369–373.
30. Campbell A, Baldessarini RJ. Prolonged pharmacologic activity of neuroleptics. *Arch Gen Psychiatry* 1985;42:637.
31. Campbell A, Baldessarini RJ, Ram VJ, Neumeyer JL. Behavioral effects of (−)10,11-methylenedioxy - *N* - *n*-propylnorapomorphine, an orally effective long-acting agent active at central dopamine receptors, and analogous aporphines. *Neuropharmacology* 1982;21:953–961.
32. Korpi ER, Phelps BH, Granger H, et al. Simultaneous determination of haloperidol and its reduced metabolite in serum and plasma by isocratic liquid chromatography with electrochemical detection. *Clin Chem* 1983;29:624–628.
33. Korpi ER, Costakos DT, Wyatt RJ. Interconversions of haloperidol and reduced haloperidol in guinea pig and rat liver microsomes. *Biochem Pharmacol* 1985;34:2923–2927.
34. Svendsen CN, Bird ED. HPLC with electrochemical detection to measure chlorpromazine, thioridazine and metabolites in human brain. *Psychopharmacology* 1986;90:316–321.
35. Stoll AL, Baldessarini RJ, Cohen BM, Finklestein SP. Assay of plasma thioridazine and metabolites by high-performance liquid chromatography with amperometric detection. *J Chromatogr Biomed Applic* 1984;307:457–463.
36. Farde L, Wiesel F-A, Halldin C, Sedvall G. Central D_2-dopamine receptor occupancy in schizophrenic patients treated with antipsychotic drugs. *Arch Gen Psychiatry* 1988;45:71–76.

28

Neuroleptic Noncompliance in Schizophrenia

Peter J. Weiden,[1] Lisa Dixon,[2] Allen Frances,[3] Paul Appelbaum,[4] Gretchen Haas,[5] and Bruce Rapkin[6]

Schizophrenia constitutes one of the nation's most costly and devastating public health problems (1). Despite the development of effective drug therapy, this disease has an estimated annual financial cost of 30 billion dollars (2) and causes immeasurable individual suffering and family dysfunction (3). Since a primary goal of researchers in the field is to learn about schizophrenia in order to develop more effective treatments for the future, it seems wise to look at current problems in the delivery of the single most effective treatment of schizophrenia found thus far, the use of neuroleptics. The initial optimism found in early reports on neuroleptics has been tempered partly because of the very high noncompliance rates among patients to these agents (4,5). Noncompliance prolongs psychoses (6), causes unnecessary relapses (7), and increases the potential for violence in the community (8). Therefore, neuroleptic noncompliance is a significant public health problem. Despite this, there has been little systematic study of phenomenology, causes, and management of noncompliance in schizophrenia.

Neuroleptic noncompliance has been separately studied for various routes of delivery (injectable versus oral) and settings (inpatient versus outpatient). Rates of inpatient noncompliance range from a low of 7% to a high of 57% (9–13). The great variability of these reported rates arises from differences in definitions of noncompliance, treatment settings, and patient populations. All of these variables are known to have drastic impacts on drug refusal rates. Using studies in which the inpatient neuroleptic noncompliance was defined as persistent and clinically significant narrows inpatient noncompliance rates to 10% to 30% (14,15). These figures are probably underestimates because they do not take into account patients who refuse hospitalization because of anticipated neuroleptic treatment, nor do they include those apparently compliant inpatients who surreptitiously "cheek" medication (hold it in their mouths and spit it out later when unobserved by staff) and escape detection (16). Also, comparisons between inpatient studies are limited by dramatic setting differences. For example, it probably makes little clinical sense to compare neuroleptic noncompli-

[1]Schizophrenia Service, Hillside Hospital/Long Island Jewish Medical Center, Glen Oaks, NY 11004.
[2]Maryland Psychiatric Research Center, Baltimore, MD 21228.
[3]Department of Psychiatry, New York Hospital-Cornell Medical Center, New York, NY 10021.
[4]Department of Psychiatry, University of Massachusetts Medical Center, Worcester, MA 01655.
[5]Department of Neuropharmacology, Western Psychiatric Institute and Clinic, University of Pittsburgh, Pittsburgh, PA 15213.
[6]Department of Psychology, New York University, New York, NY 10003.

ance rates found in forensic units with those in voluntary private hospitals.

Noncompliance rates for ambulatory schizophrenics are much higher. Naturalistic follow-up studies of adherence to oral neuroleptics have yielded noncompliance rates of 41% to 63% (17–20). Unfortunately, most of these published noncompliance rates reflect dosage deviations in basically compliant chronic patients known to the treatment system in which the study took place. Complete neuroleptic noncompliance often corresponds with treatment dropout, and loss of these patients leads to major ascertainment biases in the remaining sample. In one of the only prospective naturalistic studies starting with an index hospitalization cohort and ending with a 2-year follow-up independent of treatment setting, Serban and Thomas found clinically significant noncompliance rates of 65% in chronic patients and 73% in acute schizophrenics (4). Using a national registry sample, an epidemiologic drug-use survey in Sweden using random cross-sectional sampling techniques revealed a 66% irregular pattern of medication use for schizophrenia (21).

Injectable medication studies provide the most accurate way to assess compliance because compliance is linked with clinic attendance and so can be easily documented. However, longitudinal studies using exclusively the intramuscular (IM) route may yield artificially low noncompliance rates because (a) there is patient selection bias, (b) the IM route does not reflect usual community practices, and (c) the zeal with which the researchers attempt to keep subjects may actually improve noncompliance. Despite these biases towards compliance, naturalistic follow-up studies to depot neuroleptic have obtained noncompliance rates as high as 37% (22), and controlled depot trials have an average 1-year noncompliance rate of 33% (with a maximum of 50%) (23–33). Although at first glance, noncompliance to the IM route found in these studies seems lower than studies involving "oral" neuroleptics, these IM noncompliance rates do not include those patients who refused the outpatient IM maintenance study altogether. Rates of study-entry refusal ranged from 31% to 52%. Therefore, when both initial consent and later compliance rates are considered together, it can be estimated that 56% to 75% of eligible hospitalized patients will not comply with a 1-year depot neuroleptic study. Unfortunately, these studies did not report the reasons for initial study refusal, so the percentage of neuroleptic noncompliers in study-refuser patients remains unknown. Nevertheless, using only the oral studies that control for ascertainment biases and assuming that all early refusers of IM studies are neuroleptic-noncompliant yields consistent noncompliance rates of 60% to 70% within 2 years after discharge, regardless of the route of medication.

METHODOLOGICAL ISSUES

The relative neglect of the study of noncompliance in schizophrenia may be due to assessment problems. Noncompliance is a complex and elusive outcome measure. It is a behavior that is traditionally difficult to operationalize and requires indirect assessment with instruments (eg, self-reports, pill counts, blood-level measurements) that have questionable validity. Given the impact that schizophrenia has on an investigator's ability to obtain psychometric or biological assessments, it is not surprising that the amount of noncompliance research in schizophrenia is not commensurate with the seriousness of the problem.

The ideal assessment of compliance requires simultaneous use of multiple measures to correct for the limitations of any single measure. Measures that have been used include biological assays, pill counts, patient interviews, clinician reports, tracking devices, and clinical outcome. The limitations of these measures are well known

(34,35). While the limitation of measures is ubiquitous to all noncompliance research, it poses a particular problem for the study of neuroleptic noncompliance in schizophrenia. Schizophrenic patients often lead chaotic and disorganized lives and are often poor reporters of their actions. Therefore, the methodology literature will be reviewed with an eye on which measures may be most appropriate for use with schizophrenic patients.

Pill counts are useful in estimating the proportion of prescribed medication that was actually taken, but they may require a level of organization beyond the capacity of many schizophrenic patients. Pill counts in nonpsychotic psychiatric patients found higher rates of minor dosage deviation than simultaneous self-reports (36), but the major episodes of noncompliance were picked up equally well with either interview or pill-count methods. Minor dosage deviations seem beyond the reach of the pill-count methods. Even seemingly compliant, nonpsychiatric patients frequently exaggerate their pill counts. For example, in a well-designed study comparing blood levels of a compliance indicator (phenobarbital added to the active drug tablet), pill counts overestimated compliance at least 32% of the time (37).

Patient interviews, for medical patients, have been found to be an effective (38) and valid (39) measurement of compliance, obviating the need for more complex or costly methods. A major methodological issue is how schizophrenic symptoms interfere with the patient's ability to report compliance (eg, how often symptoms of psychosis or cognitive disorganization will distort the data). Unfortunately, we do not know of any study attempting to validate compliance interview methods in schizophrenia where self-reports may be less (or more) accurate than for other diagnoses. Therefore, a conservative methodological approach seems indicated where patient self-reports are supplemented by family and clinician reports. The use of other data sources will compensate for the limitations inherent in interviewing schizophrenic patients. With that safeguard, noncompliance interview methods in schizophrenia are probably as accurate as noncompliance assessments for other medical and psychiatric diagnoses. If this assumption is correct, using multiple informants for the assessment of neuroleptic noncompliance can find episodes of complete neuroleptic discontinuation but not quantify less extensive dosage deviations.

Biological assays (e.g., serum neuroleptic levels, prolactin levels, and urine phenothiazine screens) have been used as a method for estimating neuroleptic noncompliance. Such measures have the obvious advantage of circumventing the unreliability of patient reports. However, all biological assays to date are limited by large interindividual metabolic variations (40,41) and, more importantly, by the fact that they are basically cross-sectional measures. Therefore, biological assays can be used to reveal whether the patient has had any recent neuroleptic exposure (e.g., within the previous few days for oral neuroleptic) but cannot provide longitudinal data. For example, even if a given patient's pharmacokinetic parameters are established, a plasma haloperidol level that is low compared with the expected compliant value could not distinguish between the patient taking oral haloperidol continuously in less than prescribed doses and the patient taking a single larger oral dose a few days before sampling. Early enthusiasm over biological measures in neuroleptic noncompliance has waned because of these problems. However, the development of a biological assay that provides longitudinal data about the patient's neuroleptic exposure would be an important methodologic advance. An example of this kind of biological measure can be found in the treatment of diabetes. The percentage of glycosylated hemoglobin in red blood cells reveals the glucose control "in-

DETERMINANTS OF NEUROLEPTIC NONCOMPLIANCE

tegrated" over the preceding 6 weeks and thus can estimate compliance over time to a diabetes treatment regimen.

DETERMINANTS OF NEUROLEPTIC NONCOMPLIANCE

Many factors promoting noncompliance have been extensively reviewed in the medical (42) and psychiatric (43) literature. Major determinants of general noncompliance include (a) treatment variables, especially complexity (44–46), cost (47–48), and severity of treatment side effects (49), (b) doctor-patient relationship variables, especially patient dissatisfaction (50–52), (c) psychosocial variables such as poor social support (49), and (d) attitudinal variables, especially elements of the health belief model (42). According to the health belief model, noncompliance is a function of the patient's perception of susceptibility to illness, severity of illness, efficacy of treatment, and costs (practical and emotional) of treatment (53–55). Several of these determinants have been found to be associated with noncompliance in schizophrenia (56–58). Personal characteristics associated with neuroleptic noncompliance include dependency conflicts (59), hostility towards authority (59), and the sense of humiliation about having a chronic mental illness (60). Illness-related characteristics include emotional withdrawal, cognitive disorganization and hostility (61), "psychoticism" (62), and paranoid or grandiose delusions (63). Social characteristics associated with noncompliance include high "expressed emotion" in the family (J. Leff, personal communication) and poor social support, particularly living alone (64). Within the doctor-patient relationship, the strength of the doctor's belief in the prescribed medication has been associated with compliance (64). Consistent with the health belief model, lack of insight (65,66) and denial of illness during hospitalization (67) have been associated with noncompliance.

PSYCHOPHARMACOLOGIC ISSUES IN NEUROLEPTIC NONCOMPLIANCE

Role of Extrapyramidal Syndromes

Extrapyramidal symptoms (EPS) and subjective distress from EPS are understudied determinants of noncompliance. This is particularly unfortunate as EPS are often amenable to psychopharmacological interventions. Van Putten and colleagues, in a series of studies (68–70), found that the presence of akinesia and akathisia after a single test dose of neuroleptic given upon admission predicted future inpatient medication refusal. Recently, this group conducted a fixed-dose acute treatment study in which acutely ill inpatients received daily doses of 5, 10, or 20 mg of haloperidol, and found that those in the 20-mg group were most likely to drop out (71). For outpatients, Hogan and colleagues found that "feeling like a zombie" (presumably subjective akinesia) was the second-strongest predictor of persistently noncompliant patients (as assessed by their clinicians) in a series of self-report items (72). Marder et al (31) reported that 71% of dropouts in an outpatient high dose–low dose fluphenazine study were in the high-dosage group. They postulated that the differential dropout rate was due to akinesia. However, some studies have failed to support the association between EPS and noncompliance or medication refusal (73–76).

One way to explain these disparate results is to postulate that it is the subjective distress attributed to EPS rather than EPS per se that correlates with noncompliance.

Studies vary quite widely in their attempts to measure EPS-related subjective distress. Normal subjects frequently become severely distressed after taking small single doses of neuroleptic (77,78). Neuroleptic dysphoria, as rated by two independent measures, occurs in 48% of schizophrenic admissions (79). Our group (80) found that while neuroleptic-dysphoric inpatients were more likely to refuse treatment, the dysphoric patients who finished their treatment had lower EPS scores and received lower neuroleptic doses than non-dysphorics. We hypothesized that dysphoric patients had a more "normal" distress response and/or a better ability to complain and negotiate lower neuroleptic doses. Research in this area would be facilitated by standardizing the definition(s) of neuroleptic dysphoria and by using subjective EPS distress measures when objective EPS are studied.

Another methodological problem has been the inability to control for the delayed effects of neuroleptic treatment. Since noncompliance is typically studied in cohorts of chronically ill patients for whom good retrospective histories are unavailable, the original reason for noncompliance could be unclear. For example, an acute dystonic reaction in a first-episode schizophrenic patient may cause lasting medication refusal but this relationship could be obscured by the subsequent untreated psychosis. This example may not be that unlikely. Long-term medication refusal from a single bad experience may be analogous to conditioned avoidance paradigms where an acute noxious stimulus produces long-term aversive behavior (e.g., as when someone permanently avoids a restaurant after a bout of food poisoning). There is some evidence that this type of delayed effect occurs after a patient experiences a distressing episode of EPS. Schooler et al (81) reported that noncooperative outpatients in a maintenance treatment study had higher initial EPS scores (usually obtained while the patient was still in the hospital). Similarly, Hogarty (82) reported recruitment difficulties for outpatient studies because of EPS induced during inpatient status, which subsequently diminished when inpatient EPS management improved. In support of the notion that these kinds of adverse effects are remembered for awhile, Seltzer (83) identified fearful anticipation of EPS as the most commonly cited reason for noncompliance in a group of outpatients.

Oral versus Injectable Neuroleptic

A major public health treatment issue is whether the IM route can improve compliance over the oral route. While this hypothesis is intuitively appealing, the literature does not fully support this view. Furthermore, it is not known whether (or for whom) the depot vehicle makes a difference. Possibilities include the following:

1. No differences because only compliant patients agree to the IM route;
2. Apparently higher noncompliance for IM patients as an artifact of the relative ease of documenting IM noncompliance;
3. Higher compliance to IM for those patients who are too apathetic (or lack the social support) to take oral medication;
4. Higher compliance to the IM route because IM refusal is easily detected and allows the clinician to address the problem early on.

To our knowledge, none of these hypotheses has been studied, but similar issues have been considered in studies investigating oral versus IM compliance to medical treatments (e.g., tuberculosis and rheumatic fever). Depot preparations substituted for oral regimens have been shown to be effective for noncompliance to long-term antibiotic treatment in tuberculosis, (84,85) and for initial penicillin prophylaxis for children with rheumatic fever (86). For these infectious diseases (which share with schizophrenia the need for prophylactic treatment and the availability of depot medication), it has been observed that the IM route is particularly effective for indigent or poorly educated patients. Such differences in compliance between the IM and oral routes narrowed after patient education about treatment.

Studies using depot neuroleptics are inconclusive. Several early reports (22,23,87) indicated that crossing over clinic populations from oral to IM neuroleptic reduced relapse rates, presumably because of better compliance. However, other plausible explanations for these findings include time effects of "mirror" studies, the long half-life of IM preparations, and increased clinical attention when the patient stopped coming for injections. Two major prospective studies attempted to answer these problems (30,33). Both of these studies randomly assigned recently discharged outpatients to either route of drug delivery (fluphenazine HCl vs fluphenazine decanoate), and neither study found subsequent differences in relapse rates between oral and IM groups (30). Both studies concluded that surreptitious oral neuroleptic noncompliance did not occur in this sample. Unfortunately, the initial patient selection biases and relatively short 1-year follow-up period prevent this study from being the final word on this issue. A major point proven by these studies is that relapse often occurs for reasons other than noncompliance. Therefore, the evidence that the IM route reduces noncompliance is stronger for maintenance antibiotic treatment of infectious diseases than it is for neuroleptic treatment of schizophrenia.

One might speculate that IM neuroleptic might be most effective in reducing noncompliance for poorly educated or indigent patients. Indeed, the studies that are most favorable for the usefulness of IM neuroleptic (27,87,88) seem to come from clinics with predominantly indigent patient populations. Psychoeducation may have obscured differences between IM and PO in the negative studies.

RETROSPECTIVE NONCOMPLIANCE STUDY

Subjects

All acutely psychotic patients admitted to the Payne Whitney Clinic (PWC) between 1985 and 1987 were screened and recruited by an independent research team. Criteria for admission to this study were that the patient (a) fulfilled SCID DSM-III research criteria for schizophrenic, schizoaffective, or schizophreniform disorder; (b) had voluntarily agreed to hospitalization; (c) demonstrated at least a partial response to acute neuroleptic treatment as measured by a one-point decrease in the Clinical Global Improvement Scale, (d) had at least 4 h/wk of contact with the family of origin; and (e) agreed to the recommendation of outpatient neuroleptic treatment. Many of these patients were recruited to an outpatient maintenance dosage study that offered 2 years of follow-up care including medication, family, and social service support (see below). All patients had signed informed consents for follow-up studies.

Of the 74 patients who fulfilled the above inclusion criteria, 72 (97%) were successfully contacted for this study. The subjects were relatively young (mean age $30.1 \pm 8/5$ years) and were 65% male. They were predominantly schizophrenic (85%) and recently ill (median number of prior hospitalizations = 1.5, median length of prior treatment with neuroleptics = 24 months). Therefore, the typical patient in this sample was younger, had an acute, neuroleptic-responsive schizophrenic disorder, and had a family actively involved in their care. Most of the study subjects (78%) were discharged to the PWC Schizophrenia Clinic in order to participate in the Treatment Strategies in Schizophrenia (TSS) protocol, a multicenter NIMH study investigating in part the risks versus benefits of different dosage strategies of maintenance neuroleptic treatment.

Fluphenazine decanoate was the neuroleptic used for the patients during their participation. Patients leaving this program (by mutual agreement or dropout) received active referral to other treatment programs. Therefore, all patients in this study had adequate access to a neuroleptic treatment program.

Assessments

Patients were retrospectively assessed for up to 2 years after discharge by study raters (AZAM, PJW) who used rating instruments developed by our group. These raters were the patients' primary physician during at least one phase of their inpatient or outpatient treatment. Clinical familiarity with study cases greatly facilitated contact and follow-up for those patients who had dropped out of the PWC treatment setting, and the raters had reasonable working knowledge of pertinent issues for each case. The noncompliance instruments were designed to utilize multiple data sources: chart review, patient interview, family interview, and outside clinician interview. In cases of conflicting reports of compliance (e.g., the patient claimed to always take the neuroleptic while the family stated there was neuroleptic refusal), we used the source that reported the greatest amount of noncompliance. Difficult ratings ($N = 5$) were conferenced with the entire research team in order to reach a consensus noncompliance rating. Assessments were made for each 3-month time block up to the 24-month postdischarge follow-up period.

Instruments

Raters assessed neuroleptic compliance by dichotomous scoring. Each assessment period spanned a 3-month interval. Scoring criteria required that noncompliance had to last for more than 1 week. In order to remain conservative, uncomplicated dosage deviations were categorized as compliance (e.g., occasional forgetting to take a neuroleptic dose, or missing an injection because of inclement weather). Patients who insisted on reducing their maintenance dose but continued with ongoing medication were considered compliant. Behavioral and attitudinal factors thought to be related to neuroleptic compliance and noncompliance were assessed. Assessments included factors hypothesized to promote compliance (e.g., a belief that medications help symptoms, family support for neuroleptic use, etc) as well as those associated with noncompliance. These specific factors were chosen from earlier pilot studies and literature reviews and are listed on Table 1. These factors were rated for *all* patients regardless of their actual compliance. In other words, a noncompliant patient might still score positively for some compliance factors (e.g., fear of relapse, or a good relationship with doctor), but have an overriding reason to be noncompliant (e.g., denial of illness, or distress from side effects).

Data Analysis

Rates of noncompliance over time were determined using survival curve techniques. A maximum total of eight 3-month time intervals were possible for those patients followed for 2 years; shorter follow-up periods used fewer intervals. Demographic and premorbid variables were analyzed for possible association with outcome data. Attitudinal and behavioral factor scores were correlated with the patient's compliance score using the summed score for the entire follow-up period. In order to assess time effects, correlations for each time interval were performed on the group of patients who had been outpatients for at least 1.5 years ($N = 40$). Another way we evaluated noncompliance was to look at the patients' longitudinal compliance pattern. There were four time-course patterns that could be rated reliably: patients who remained compliant (complete compliers), patients who were compliant after discharge but became noncompliant later (early compliers), patients who were noncompliant after discharge but compliant later (early noncompliers), and continually noncompliant patients (complete noncompliers). Only those patients who had completed at least 1.5 years of follow-up ($N = 40$) were analyzed by this method.

TABLE 1. *Attitudinal and behavioral assessments*

Domain	Measure	Definition
1. Environmental	Family structure	Direct supervision of medication and appointments
	Living situation	Alone vs family vs residential
2. Illness	Denial	Only included if considered to be pathologic denial of mental illness
	Disorganization	Could be positive or negative symptoms
	Apathy	Negative symptom only
	Psychosis	Positive symptoms only; includes paranoia and delusions
	Substance abuse	Patient's substance abuse must directly promote neuroleptic noncompliance
3. Family	Belief	A key family member believes in neuroleptic.
	Ambivalence	A key family member is against neuroleptic.
	Family coercion	Threats from family to withdraw involvement or support
4. Distress	Stigma	Patient is stigmatized or humiliated and experiences neuroleptic as a reminder of mental illness
	Akinesia, akathisia, tardive dyskinesia	Ongoing perceived distress from these side effects
5. Treatment	MD/Patient relationship (good/poor)	As perceived by the patient
	Involuntary treatment	Forced neuroleptics, not necessarily involuntary hospitalization
	Access	Includes travel, expense, convenience

Results

Neuroleptic noncompliance was very common. Forty-eight percent of the subjects became noncompliant for at least 1 week within the first postdischarge year. Within 2 years the projected rate (survival analysis) was 73%. It should be noted that, in this cohort, noncompliers frequently reverted back to being compliers. At any given follow-up interval, 30% to 40% of the subjects were noncompliant. Patients displayed different time-course patterns. Forty-five percent of the patients remained completely compliant ($n = 18$), 18% were compliant in the first year but not the second ($n = 7$), 12% were noncompliant in the first year and became compliant in the second year ($n = 5$), and 25% were completely noncompliant throughout ($n = 10$). Of the demographic and illness variables obtained during hospitalization, only age was a predictor of outpatient noncompliance. Younger patients were less likely to comply after discharge ($r = -.31, p < .02$), but the patient's sex, religion, or family background did not predict future noncompliance. No illness or treatment variable (including DSM-III diagnosis, duration of past neuroleptic treatment, or number of past hospitalizations) predicted future outpatient noncompliance. The most prominent predictors of noncompliance were the postdischarge attitudinal and behavioral variables. These include denial of illness ($r = .54, p < .001$), medication coercion ($r = .61, p < .0001$), and the stigma associated with mental illness ($r = .41, p < .001$). Predictors of compliance were a perceived good doctor-patient relationship ($r = .51, p < .001$), the perception that neuroleptics were helpful for ongoing symptom relief ($r = .41, p < .001$), and the perceived fear of future relapse ($r = .28, p < .02$). Strikingly absent in the overall correlations was perceived distress from akathisia, akinesia, or tardive dyskinesia.

Some of the correlations with noncompliance changed as a function of the time since initial discharge. For example, the stigma of being a psychiatric patient was the strongest noncompliance correlate for the first 6 months post-discharge, but the stigma/noncompliance correlations became nonsignificant by the second year. Distress from akinesia at discharge also correlated with first-quarter noncompliance. (Distress from other side effects never correlated with present or predicted future noncompliance.)

In contrast, family attitudes demonstrated a very different time course. Correlations between family ambivalence to medication and patient noncompliance behavior that were initially not significant, became much stronger during the second postdischarge year. Analysis of the compliance pattern groups revealed that the early compliers, after discharge, were much more likely to want to refuse the neuroleptic because of perceived akinesia than were the complete compliers. Distress from akinesia right after discharge was by far the strongest predictive variable between these groups, even though their compliance did not diverge until a year later. The major difference in the second year between early compliers and the complete compliers was the erosion of the families' support of medication treatment by the second year.

CONCLUSIONS AND SPECULATIONS

This study confirms the very high noncompliance rates to neuroleptics in ambulatory schizophrenia. Over the 2 years, approximately three out of four patients refused their neuroleptic treatment for at least 1 week. These findings are consistent with other reviews (89). Even these very high rates are probably underestimates for the outpatient schizophrenic population at large because our subjects were originally voluntary admissions, had contact with their family of origin, and had access to treatment at our clinic after discharge. We were not able to estimate the clinical sequelae of noncompliance in this particular cohort because of methodological problems in determining causality (which came first, relapse or noncompliance?) and because some of the subjects were receiving intermittent neuroleptic treatment in a double-blind protocol (estimated $N = 10$). However, using an estimate of 40% difference in rehospitalization rates between medicated and unmedicated patients, our guess is that noncompliance accounted for at least 20% of the rehospitalizations in this cohort. The data from this study are not amenable to the question of whether the IM route prevents noncompliance since noncompliant patients, after leaving our IM clinic, tended to go back to other treatment settings that used oral neuroleptics. However, it is interesting that this cohort, which began on IM medication, had noncompliance rates comparable to the oral medication studies.

Despite the suggestive nature of the correlational data, the associations with noncompliance are not necessarily causal. For example, the relationship between medication coercion and noncompliance probably comes from the effect noncompliance has on clinician decisions. In order to avoid any assumptions of causality, we decided not to use multivariate analysis but to analyze the data only with pearson correlations. With that cautionary warning, we offer the following speculations about causality. The relative lack of predictive power of demographic variables typically associated with compliance (e.g., sex, number of years ill, and living status) suggests that the traditional predictors of noncompliance do not apply as strongly for schizophrenic patients who still have involved families as they do for other illnesses. Since subjects were selected on the basis of having involved families, this conclusion should not be generalized to all schizophrenics. (This selection criteria for patients with families may also affect the other attitudinal and behavioral correlational findings.) The strongest illness-related predictor was pathological denial of illness, which persisted throughout the follow-up period. As best we could, we attempted to distinguish pathological from nonpathologic denial of illness. (For example, a patient report of "I needed medication because I was hallucinating but now I'm better" would not be rated as denial, but "I never had any emotional problems" would be.) It is unclear to what extent the pathological denial was state-related (e.g., loss of insight occurring with relapse) and how often it was an enduring trait-related aspect of psychopathology. In any case, denial overshadowed obvious psychotic symptoms as the cause of noncompliance in these schizophrenic outpatients.

Distress from side effects was not associated with noncompliance in the overall analysis. Akathisia, which has frequently been associated with inpatient noncompliance, never correlated with present or future noncompliance in this outpatient sample. However, distress from akinesia at discharge was a weak correlate with current noncompliance and a very strong predictor of future noncompliance. It seems, in a post hoc analysis, that the striking delayed effect from akinesia-attributed distress may be mediated through the family. After discharge, many patients comply because of pressure from the family. However, the patient's complaints about akinesia (true or not) may eventually "turn off" the family support of neuroleptic treatment. Since family support of medication promotes compliance, we hypothesize that the loss of such support may be the "final common pathway" for new-onset noncompliance during the patient's second postdischarge year.

In conclusion, it seems that public health planning for the outpatient treatment of schizophrenia should *assume* that most patients become noncompliant to their maintenance neuroleptic regimen. Outpatient services should allow for easy and rapid reentry into a medication treatment program. Psychopharmacological research on schizophrenic outpatients should evaluate whether compliance is feasible even if drug efficacy is found.

ACKNOWLEDGMENTS

This work was supported by NIMH grant MH-43635 First Award to Dr. Peter Weiden.

REFERENCES

1. Frazier S. Statement before the subcommittee on Labor, Health and Human Services, Committee on Appropriations, United States Senate, November 20, 1986.
2. Andrews G, Hall W, Goldstein G, et al. The economic costs of schizophrenia. *Arch Gen Psychiatry* 1985;42:537–543.
3. Sheehan S. *Is there no place on Earth for me?* Boston: Houghton Mifflin Company, 1982.
4. Serban G, Thomas A. Attitudes and behaviors of acute and chronic schizophrenic patients regarding ambulatory treatment. *Am J Psychiatry* 1974;136:991–995.
5. Hare HE, Willcox DRC. Do psychiatric patients take their pills? *Br J Psychiatry* 1967;113:1435–1439.
6. Mason AS, Forrest IS, Forrest FM, Butler H. Adherence to maintenance therapy and rehospitalization. *Dis Nerv Syst* 1963;24:103–104.
7. Johnson DAW, Pasterski G, Ludlow JM, Street K, Taylor RDW. The discontinuation of maintenance neuroleptic therapy in chronic schizophrenic patients: drug and social consequences. *Acta Psychiatr Scand* 1983;67:339–352.
8. Tanay E. Homicidal behavior in schizophrenics. *J Forensic Sci* 1987;32:1382–1388.
9. Van Putten T, May PRA. 'Akinetic depression' in schizophrenia. *Arch Gen Psychiatry* 1977;34:947–950.
10. Gill MJ. Side effects of a right to refuse treatment lawsuit: The Boston State Hospital experience. In: Swazey AE, Swazey JP, eds. *Refusing treatment in mental health institutions: values in conflict*. Ann Arbor: AUPHA Press.
11. Appelbaum PS, Gutheil TG. Drug refusal: a study of psychiatric inpatients. *Am J Psychiatry* 1980;137:340–346.
12. Irwin DS, Weitxell WD, Morgan DW. Phenothiazine intake and staff attitude. *Am J Psychiatry* 1971;127:1631–1636.
13. Callahan LA, Longuire DR. Psychiatric patients' right to refuse psychotropic medication: a national survey. *Ment Disabil Law Reporter* 7:494–499, 1983.
14. Richards AD. Attitudes and drug acceptance. *Br J Psychiatry* 1962;110:46–52.
15. Appelbaum PS, Hoge SK. The right to refuse

treatment: what the research reveals. *Behav Sci Law* 1986;4:279–292.
16. Wilson JD, Enoch MD. Estimation of drug rejection by schizophrenic inpatients, with analysis of clinical factors. *Br J Psychiatry* 1967;113:209–211.
17. Hoffmann RP, Moore WE, O'Dea LF. Medication problems confronted by the schizophrenic outpatient. *J Am Pharm Assoc* 1974;5:252–256.
18. Boczkowski JA, Zeichner A, DeSanto N. Neuroleptic compliance among chronic schizophrenic outpatients: an intervention outcome report. *J Consult Clin Psychol* 1985;53:666–671.
19. Battle EH, Halliburton A, Wallston KA. Self-medication among psychiatric patients and adherence after discharge. *JPNMHS* 1982;20:21–28.
20. Streicker SK, Amdur M, Dincin J. Educating patients about psychiatric medications: failure to enhance compliance. *Psychosoc Rehab J* 1986;4:15–28.
21. Allgulander C. Psychoactive drug use in a general population sample, Sweden: correlates with perceived health, psychiatric diagnoses, and mortality in an automated record-linkage study. *Am J Public Health* 1989;79:1006–1009.
22. Johnson DAW, Freeman HL. Long-acting tranquilizers. *Practitioner* 1972;208:395–400.
23. Chien CP. Drugs and rehabilitation in schizophrenia. In: Greenblatt M, ed. *Drugs in combination therapies*. New York, Grune & Stratton, 1975.
24. Leff JP, Wing JK. Trial of maintenance therapy in schizophrenia. *Br Med J* 1971;3:599–604.
25. Falloon IR, Watt DC, Shepherd M. A comparative control trial of pimozide and fluphenazine decanoate in the continuation therapy of schizophrenia. *Psycholog Med* 1978;8:59–70.
26. McGreadie RG, Dingwall JM, Wiles DH, et al. Intermittent pimozide versus fluphenazine decanoate as a maintenance therapy in chronic schizophrenia. *Br J Psychiatry* 1980;137:510–517.
27. Crawford R, Forrest A. Controlled trial of depot fluphenazine in outpatient schizophrenia. *Br J Psychiatry* 1974;124:385–391.
28. Rifkin A, Quitkin F, Rabiner CJ, Klein DF. Fluphenazine decanoate, fluphenazine hydrochloride given orally, and placebo in remitted schizophrenics. *Arch Gen Psychiatry* 1977;34:43–47.
29. Hogarty GE, Goldberg S. Drug and sociotherapy in the aftercare of schizophrenic patients. *Arch Gen Psychiatry* 1973;28:54–64.
30. Schooler NR, Levine J, Severe JB, et al. Prevention of relapse in schizophrenia. An evaluation of fluphenazine decanoate. *Arch Gen Psychiatry* 1980;37:16–24.
31. Marder SR, Van Putten T, Mintz J, et al. Costs and benefits of two doses of fluphenazine. *Arch Gen Psychiatry* 1985;41:1025–1029.
32. Hogarty GE, Anderson C, Reiss DJ, et al. Family psychoeducation, social skills training, and maintenance chemotherapy in the aftercare treatment of schizophrenia. *Arch Gen Psychiatry* 1986;43:633–642.
33. Hogarty GE, Schooler NR, Ulrich RF, et al. Fluphenazine and social therapy in the aftercare of schizophrenic patients: relapse analysis of a two year controlled study of fluphenazine decanoate and fluphenazine HCL. *Arch Gen Psychiatry* 1979;36:1283–1294.
34. Dunbar J. Adhering to medical advice, a review. *Int J Ment Health* 1981;9:70–87.
35. Rudd P. In search for the gold standard for compliance measurement (editorial). *Arch Intern Med* 1976;139:627–628.
36. Park LC, Lipman RS. A comparison of dosage deviation reports with pill counts. *Psychopharmacologia* 1964;6:299–301.
37. Pullar T, Kumar S, Tindall H, Feely M. Time to stop counting the tablets? *Clin Pharmacol Ther* 1989;46:163–168.
38. Becker MH. Patient adherence to prescribed therapies. *Medical Care* 1985;23:539–555.
39. Morisky D, Green L, Levine DM. Concurrent and predictive validity of a self-reported measure of medication adherence. *Medical Care* 1986;24:67–74.
40. Dahl SG. Plasma level monitoring of antipsychotic drugs: clinical utility. *Clin Pharmacokinetics* 1986;11:36.
41. Jann MW, Ereshefsky L, Saklad SR. Clinical pharmacokinetics of the depot antipsychotics. *Clin Pharmacokinetics* 1985;10:315.
42. Haynes RB, Sackett DL. An annotated bibliography on the compliance of patients with therapeutic regimens. Appendix I. In: *Compliance with therapeutic regimens*. Baltimore: John Hopkins University Press, 1976.
43. Blackwell B. Treatment adherence. *Br J Psychiatry* 1976;129:513–531.
44. Hulka B, Kupper L, Cassel J, et al. Medication use and misuse: physician-patient discrepancies. *J Chron Dis* 1975;28:7–21.
45. Francis V, Korsch BM, Morris MJ. Gaps in doctor-patient communication. *N Eng J Med* 1969;280:535–540.
46. Haynes RB. A critical review of the "determinants" of patient compliance with therapeutic regimens. In: Sackett DL and Haynes RB, eds. *Compliance with therapeutic regimens*. Baltimore: Johns Hopkins University Press, 1975.
47. Alpert JJ. Broken appointments. *Pediatrics* 1964;34:127–132.
48. Donabedian A, Rosenfeld LS. Follow-up study of chronically ill patients discharged from hospital. *J Chron Dis* 1964;17:847–862.
49. Blackwell B. Patient compliance. *N Eng J Med* 1973;289:249–253.
50. Becker MH, Maiman LA. Strategies for enhancing patient compliance. *J Community Health* 1980;6:113–115.
51. Davis MS. Variations in patients' compliance with doctor's advice. *Am J Public Health* 58:274–288.
52. Davis MS, Eichhorn RL. Compliance with medical regimens. *J Health Hum Behav* 1963;4:240–249.
53. Becker MH, Maiman CA. Sociobehavioral de-

terminants of compliance with health and medical care recommendations. *Medical Care* 1975;13:10–24.
54. Kasi SA, Cobb S. Health behavior, illness behavior and sick role behavior. *J Health Illness Behav. Arch Environmental Health* 1966;12:246–266.
55. Rosenstock IM. Why people use health services. *Millbank Mem Fund Q* 44:94–127.
56. Babiker IE. Noncompliance in Schizophrenia. *Psychiatr Devel* 1986;4:329–337.
57. Van Putten T. Noncompliance: problems and solutions. In: Management of schizophrenia. *New York: TransMedica Inc.* 1982;43–50.
58. Van Putten T. Drug refusal in schizophrenia: causes and prescribing hints. *Hosp Community Psychiatry* 1978;29:110–112.
59. Diamond RJ. Quality of life: The patients' subjective response. Presented at the American Psychiatric Association Annual Meeting, Dallas, May 18, 24, 1985.
60. Terkelsen KG. On the humiliation of recovering from psychosis. Presented at the American Psychiatric Association Annual Meeting, May 21, 1985, Dallas.
61. Marder SR, Mebane A, Chien CP, et al. A comparison of patients who refuse and consent to neuroleptic treatment. *Am J Psychiatry* 1983;140:470–472.
62. McEvoy JP, Howe AC, Hogarty GE. Differences in the nature of relapse and subsequent inpatient course between medication compliant and noncompliant schizophrenic patients. *J Nerv Ment Dis* 1984;172:413–416.
63. Van Putten T, Crumpton E, Yale C. Drug refusal in schizophrenia and the wish to be crazy. *Arch Gen Psychiatry* 1976;33:1433–1466.
64. Irwin DS, Weitzell WD, Morgan DW. Phenothiazine intake and staff attitudes. *Am J Psychiatry* 1971;127:1631–1635.
65. Lin IF, Spiga R, Fortsch W. Insight and adherence to medication in chronic schizophrenics. *J Clin Psychiatry* 1979;40:430–432.
66. McEvoy JP, Freter S, Everett G, Geller GL. Insight and the clinical outcome of schizophrenic patients. *J Nerv Ment Dis* 1989;177:48–51.
67. McEvoy JP, Applebaum PS, Apperson LJ, Geller JC, Freter S. Why must some schizophrenic patients be involuntarily committed? The role of insight. *Hosp Comm Psychi* 1989;30:13–171.
68. Van Putten T. Why do schizophrenic patients refuse to take their drugs? *Arch Gen Psychiatry* 1974;31:67–72.
69. Van Putten T, May PRA. Subjective response as a predictor of outcome in pharmacotherapy. *Arch Gen Psychiatry* 1978;35:477–480.
70. Van Putten T, May PRA, Marder SR. Response to antipsychotic medication: the doctors' and consumers' view. *Am J Psychiatry* 1984;141:16–19.
71. Van Putten T, Marder S, Mintz J. A controlled dose comparison of haloperidol in newly admitted schizophrenic patients. *Arch Gen Psychiatry* (in press).
72. Hogan TD, Awad AG, Eastwood R. A self-report scale predictive of drug compliance in schizophrenics: reliability and discriminative validity. *Psycholog Med* 1983;13:177–183.
73. Rodenhauser P. Treatment refusal in the forensic hospital: ill-use of the lasting right. *Bull Am Acad Psychiatry Law* 1984;12:59–63.
74. Rodenhauser P, Schweuker CE, Khanis HJ. Drug treatment in a forensic hospital (unpublished).
75. Marder SR, Swann E, Winslade WJ, et al. A study of medication refusal by involuntary psychiatric patients. *Hosp Community Psychiatry* 1984;35:724–726.
76. Marder SR, Mebane A, Chien CP, et al. A comparison of patients who refuse and consent to neuroleptic treatment. *Am J Psychiatry* 1983; 140:470–472.
77. Henninger G, DiMascio A, Klerman GL. Personality factors in variability of response to phenothiazines. *Am J Psychiatry* 1965;121:1091–1094.
78. Anderson BG, Reber D, Volavka J et al. Prolonged adverse effects from haloperidol in normals. *N Eng J Med* 1981;205:643–644.
79. Hogan TP, Awad AG. Subjective response to neuroleptics and outcome in schizophrenia: A re-examination comparing two measures. *Psycholog Med* (in press).
80. Weiden PJ, Dixon L, Dechillo N, et al. Is neuroleptic dysphoria a healthy response? *Comprehen Psychiatry* 1989;30:546–552.
81. Schooler N. Predictors of stabilization in schizophrenia. Presented at the American Psychiatric Association Annual Meeting, Montreal, Canada, 1988.
82. Hogarty GE. Personal communciation.
83. Seltzer A, Roncari I, Garfinkel P. Effect of patient education on medication compliance. *Am J Psychiatry* 1980;25:638–645.
84. Feinstein R. Spagnuolo M, et al. Prophylaxis of recurrent rheumatic fever. *JAMA* 1968;206:565–568.
85. Ireland HD. Outpatient chemotherapy for tuberculosis. *Am Rev Resp Dis* 1960;82:378–383.
86. Colcher IS, Bass JW. Penicillin treatment of streptococcal pharyngitis: a comparison of schedules and the role of specific counseling. *JAMA* 1972;222:657–659.
87. Denham J, Adamson L. The contribution of fluphenazine enanthate and decanoate in the prevention of readmission of schizophrenic patients. *Acta Psychiatr Scand* 1971;47:420–430.
88. DelGiudice J, Clark WG, Gocha EF. Prevention of recidivism of schizophrenics treated with fluphenazine enanthate. *Psychosomatics* 1977; 34:297–301.
89. Young JL, Zonana HW, Shepler L. Medication noncompliance in schizophrenia: codification and update. *Bull Am Acad Psychiatry Law* 1986;14:105–122.

29

Pharmacological Approaches to the Development of Atypical Antipsychotics

David M. Coward[1]

While antipsychotic agents acting via dopamine D_2 receptor blockade can provide substantial relief of positive schizophrenic symptoms such as delusions and hallucinations, this relief often comes only at the risk of unpleasant subjective and motor side effects. In the acute treatment phase, akathisia, dystonia, and drug-induced parkinsonism are often problematical, and long-term exposure results in a disturbingly high incidence of tardive dyskinesia. Furthermore, approximately one-third of the schizophrenic population is considered to be unresponsive to conventional neuroleptics, and the improvement of negative symptoms seen with most neuroleptics is at best marginal. Nevertheless, the broader understanding of neurotransmitter actions and interactions gained in recent years, coupled with the recognition that clozapine exhibits antipsychotic activity in the virtual absence of extrapyramidal symptoms (EPS) and is effective in many subjects refractory to treatment with classical neuroleptics (1), has raised hopes that the pharmacotherapy of schizophrenia will soon enter a new era.

At the present time the search for more efficacious and better-tolerated antipsychotic agents focuses on three major areas (Table 1). This chapter examines some of these approaches in more detail and, at the same time, illustrates some of the newer selection criteria being employed within the preclinical area.

σ-RECEPTOR BLOCKADE

Clinical observations of the psychotomimetic actions of the benzomorphan SKF 10047 and the subsequent demonstration that these are mediated independently of an interaction with either opiate- or phencyclidine-linked processes, led to the eventual identification of the σ-receptor. Subsequently, it has been shown that σ-receptors are common within limbic structures, can be labeled by haloperidol or (+)-3-PPP, modulate some forms of dopamine function, and by inference could offer a novel means of achieving antischizophrenic activity in the absence of extrapyramidal motor disturbances (2).

While several existing neuroleptics are now known to show appreciable affinity for the σ-receptor, including haloperidol and remoxipride, there is no compelling evidence that the clinical activity of these agents differs from that of neuroleptics lacking an interaction with σ-sites. However, their concomitant interactions with other neurotransmitter systems, particularly dopamine, make it difficult to assess the possible contribution of σ-receptor blockade to their antipsychotic activity. Recently, rimcazole (BW 234U) and BMY 14802 (Fig. 1) have been described as selec-

[1]Sandoz Research Institute Berne Ltd., CH-3001 Berne, Switzerland.

TABLE 1. *Current major approaches in the search for improved antischizophrenic agents*

Mechanistic approach	Specific principle
σ-"opioid"	• σ-receptor blockade
Serotonin	• Selective 5HT$_3$ antagonism • Preferential 5HT$_2$ antagonism (5HT$_2$ > D$_2$)
Dopamine	• Selective D$_2$ antagonism • Partial D$_2$ agonism • Selective D$_1$ antagonism • Preferential D$_1$ antagonism (D$_1$ > D$_2$)

tive σ-receptor antagonists; they exhibit preclinical profiles that only partly overlap with those of other neuroleptics. These agents can inhibit apomorphine-induced climbing behavior in the mouse, fail to induce catalepsy, and indirectly influence the firing rate of mesolimbic (A10) dopamine neurons to a greater extent than nigrostriatal (A9) ones (2). Differences between the effects of the two drugs have been noted in the latter test situation, however, in that chronic administration of rimcazole appears to promote the activity of A10 dopamine neurons (3), whereas BMY 14802 reduces it (4). Clinically, the situation is less clear. While some patients showed improvement on rimcazole in open trials (5), others showed no response or worsened (6). Furthermore, use of this agent appeared to be associated with an increased risk of seizure induction. It now remains to be seen whether BMY 14802, whose actions can be partially differentiated from those of rimcazole (see above), will prove to be safer and perhaps more efficacious in schizophrenic patients.

SEROTONIN-BASED APPROACHES

The possibility of improving the treatment of schizophrenia via the modulation of serotonin activity, while not new, is currently receiving considerable attention. Whereas 5HT$_2$ receptor blockade has long been recognized as a major action of the atypical neuroleptics clozapine and fluperlapine, for example, recent animal data have suggested that both 5HT$_3$ receptor blockade (7) and 5HT$_{1A}$ receptor agonism (8) might offer novel means of alleviating schizophrenia. On the other hand, clarification of the role of serotoninergic modulation in schizophrenia treatment has been compounded by the need to specify which particular issues are being addressed (see below).

Selective 5HT$_3$ Receptor Blockade

The demonstration that selective 5HT$_3$ receptor antagonists such as GR 38032F and ICS 205-930 can profoundly inhibit the behavioral disturbances arising from chronic infusion of dopamine into the rat nucleus accumbens (7) has raised hopes that this type of agent might prove to be antipsychotic without compromising dopamine function within the basal ganglia, thereby avoiding motor side effects. While

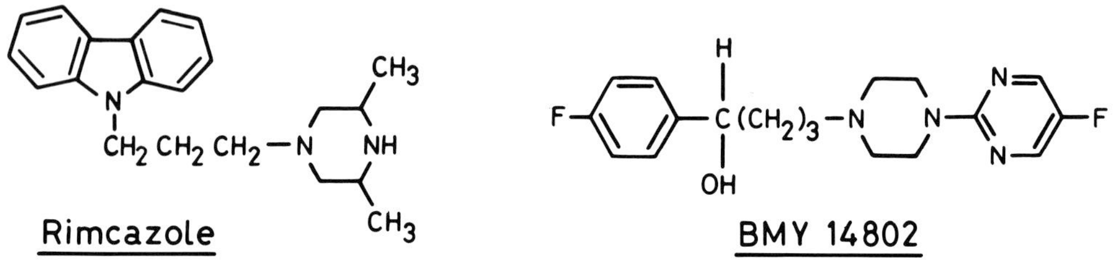

FIG. 1. Chemical structures of the σ-antagonists rimcazole (BW 234U; *left*) and BMY 14802 (*right*).

sufficient clinical feedback is available with this class of agent to confirm a lack of EPS liability, antipsychotic activity, if any, remains to be established. Should they prove to be effective, however, this would go a long way toward establishing hyperactivity within the mesolimbic dopamine system as a cardinal feature of schizophrenia.

5HT$_2$ Receptor Blockade

Interest in 5HT$_2$ receptor blockade arose from the finding that this action could reduce neuroleptic-induced catalepsy in the rat (9–11) and that the atypical neuroleptic clozapine is a strong 5HT$_2$ antagonist. More recently, however, it has been suggested that 5HT$_2$ receptor blockade might confer greater effectiveness against negative symptoms, or could underlie clozapine's activity in formerly treatment-resistant patients. While the clinical confirmation or refutation of these hypotheses has been hampered by the lack of suitable drugs, the availability of risperidone (Fig. 2) should now go a long way towards answering these issues.

This drug combines very strong 5HT$_2$ receptor blockade with strong D$_2$ receptor blockade and, in the rat, is apomorphine-antagonistic and moderately cataleptogenic (12). The available clinical feedback suggests that the drug is an effective antipsychotic agent with possibly more beneficial effects on negative symptoms than are seen with haloperidol (13). On the other hand, the drug does not appear to be devoid of acute EPS (12), and nothing is known about its possible activity in therapy-resistant subjects. Clearly, more feedback is required from controlled studies before the attributes of this type of approach can be ascertained.

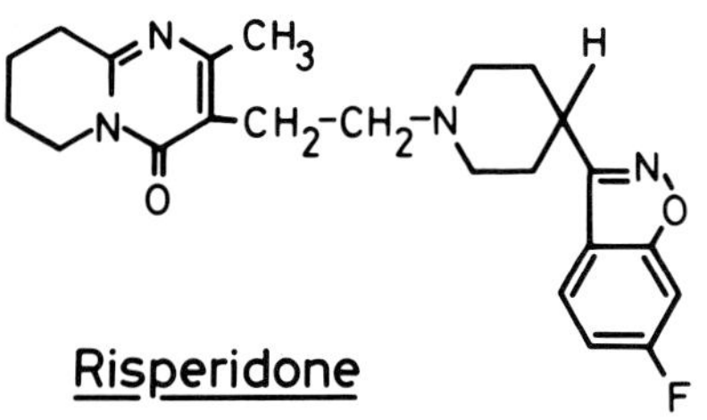

DOPAMINE-BASED APPROACHES

Selective D$_2$ Receptor Blockade

Of the dopamine-based approaches, selective antagonism at one or other of the receptor subtypes has received the most attention in recent years, with several benzamide-based, selective D$_2$ antagonists having been tested clinically. Clinical usage of the prototypic agent sulpiride has been extensive, and it is reasonable to assume that the CNS properties of other benzamides such as raclopride, remoxipride, and amisulpiride will largely reflect those of this agent. The antipsychotic activity of sulpiride is now well established (14,15), and, in addition, there is evidence that this agent exhibits potentially useful "activating" or antiautistic properties (15). On the other hand, the EPS liability of this class of agent is still a matter of discussion. Whereas some investigators have reported little or no drug-induced parkinsonism after sulpiride, acute dystonic reactions to sulpiride have been observed in both monkeys (16,17) and humans (18). Too few patients have been exclusively treated with this class of agent for a sufficient length of time to ascertain whether long-term use of selective D$_2$ receptor antagonists will lead to a reduced liability of developing tardive dyskinesia.

Partial Agonism at D$_2$ Receptors

The notion that partial D$_2$ receptor agonists might offer a means of alleviating both positive and negative symptoms in schizophrenia has gained considerable ground in

FIG. 2. Chemical structure of the preferential 5HT$_2$ antagonist risperidone.

recent years. The compounds of interest combine high affinity with low efficacy at this receptor, and can be regarded as dopaminergic "buffers." This approach assumes that positive symptoms reflect excessive dopaminergic activity within the CNS, and that negative symptoms may partly reflect a dopamine deficit syndrome. Support for the former contention stems from the prevalence of delusions and hallucinations in psychosis resulting from D_2 agonist usage and for the latter derives from the partial amelioration of negative symptoms after L-DOPA (19) or amphetamine treatment (20). In addition to the attributes mentioned above, their intrinsic agonistic properties should avoid the total cessation of postsynaptic activity and thereby result in reduced EPS liability (Fig. 3).

Of the partial D_2 agonists described to date, terguride (21) and SDZ 208-912 (22; Fig. 4) best illustrate the preclinical properties of this type of agent and, in addition, show the different degrees of agonistic and antagonistic weighting that it is possible to achieve. In addition to showing high affinity for the spiperone-labeled D_2 receptor and to inhibiting conditioned avoidance responding in the rat, these partial D_2 agonists prevent apomorphine-induced stereotypies, exhibit little or no cataleptogenic activity, reduce serum prolactin levels, and induce contralateral circling behavior after unilateral, 6-hydroxydopamine lesioning of the substantia nigra (Table 2; Fig. 5). However, SDZ 208-912 is more active than terguride as an inhibitor of apomorphine-in-

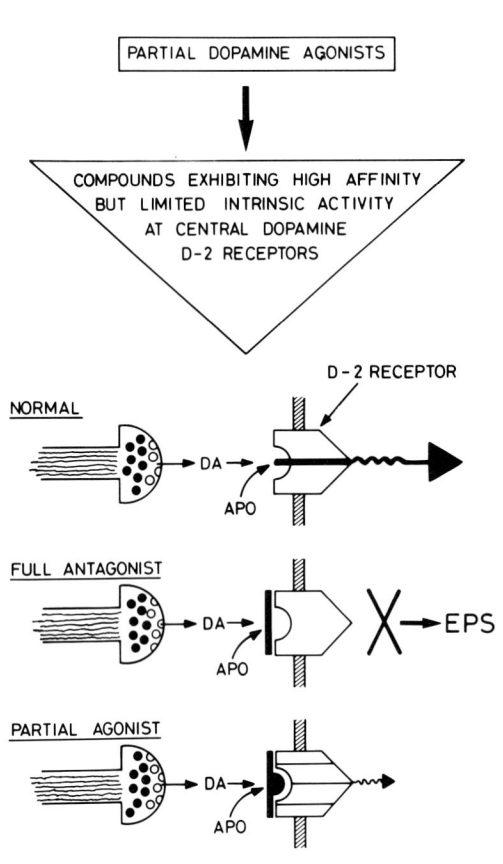

FIG. 3. Illustration of the D_2 partial agonist principle.

FIG. 4. Chemical structures of terguride (*top*) and the aminoergolines SDZ 208-911 and SDZ 208-912 (*bottom*).

TABLE 2. *Comparison of the biochemical and pharmacological properties of various partial D_2 receptor agonists with those of the antagonist haloperidol and the full agonist bromocriptine*

Drug	D_2 affinity (pK_i)	Threshold dose (mg/kg PO)		Prolactin inhibition (ED_{50}, mg/kg SC at 4 h)
		Apomorphine gnawing blockade ($n = 3-6$)	Catalepsy induction ($N = 3-6$)	
Haloperidol	8.2	0.20	0.5	Increased
Terguride	8.4	5.00	>20.0	0.003
SDZ 208-911	8.3	0.20	>20.0	0.002
SDZ 208-912	8.6	0.02	2.0	0.003
Bromocriptine	7.4	—	—	0.007

duced stereotypies, while the reverse is true regarding circling induction. Since they exhibit similar affinities for the D_2 receptor (Table 2), these functional differences must arise from the expression of differing degrees of intrinsic activity at the receptor. Interestingly, the 2-methyl form of SDZ 208-912, SDZ 208-911, shows apomorphine-inhibitory activity similar to that of haloperidol, but is equipotent to terguride as an inducer of circling behavior (see Table 2 and Fig. 5).

The limited clinical feedback available on terguride suggests that its relatively high intrinsic agonistic activity could make it of use in the treatment of negative symptoms (23). However, SDZ 208-911 might be better suited for the treatment of this patient population since it should exhibit a lower risk of positive symptom exacerbation or induction. In the case of SDZ 208-912, low doses have been found to elevate prolactin levels after single administration to healthy volunteers, but to suppress or not affect them after chronic administration to schizophrenic subjects. The prolactin suppression observed in some individuals is unlikely to reflect the emergence of agonistically acting metabolites after chronic application of SDZ 208-912 since no exacerbation of positive schizophrenic symptoms has been observed. Further clinical testing of SDZ 208-912 and SDZ 208-911 should clarify the issue of possible differences in the dopaminergic status of normal and schizophrenic subjects and establish whether partial D_2 agonism is a realistic approach for the improved treatment of schizophrenic psychoses.

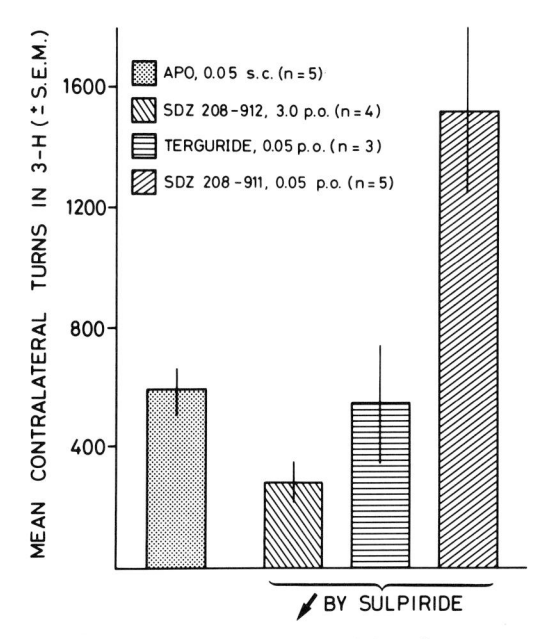

FIG. 5. Relative agonistic activity of apomorphine and various partial D_2 agonists in 6-hydroxydopamine-lesioned rats.

Selective D_1 Receptor Blockade

The clinical viability of selective D_1 receptor antagonism as a means of providing

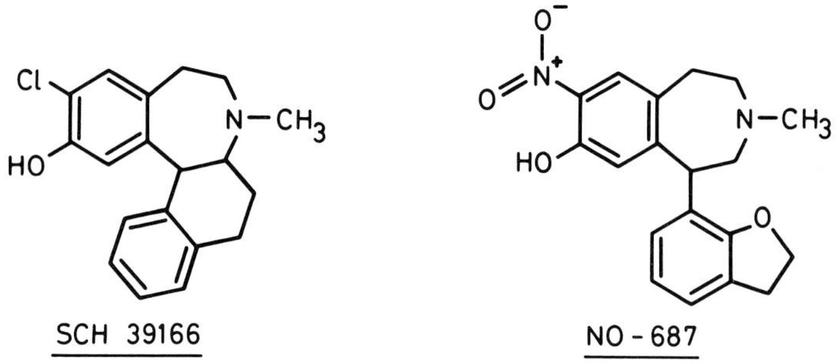

FIG. 6. Chemical structures of the selective D_1 antagonists SCH 39166 (*left*) and NO-687 (*right*).

clinical antipsychotic efficacy remains to be proven, but is strongly supported in particular by SCH 23390's inhibition of dopamine-dependent stereotypies and conditioned avoidance responding in the rodent. Conversely, however, there are indications that this approach will not avoid the problem of acute EPS. Thus, SCH 23390 shows cataleptogenic activity in the rat which, in addition, does not appear to tolerate after repeated administration (24). Cataleptogenic activity also appears to be exhibited by two newer D_1 antagonists, SCH 39166 and NO-687 (Fig. 6), although SCH 39166 is reported to show some degree of separation between its inhibition of conditioned avoidance responding and catalepsy induction in the rat (25). Interestingly, recent electrophysiological studies have shown that repeated administration of SCH 23390 results in chronic depolarization-induced blockade of A10 neuronal activity in the absence of similar impairment within the A9 projection system (26). Such differential effects might confer antipsychotic potential on a compound in the absence of untoward EPS liability, although the true contribution of A9 depolarization blockade to the clinical picture seen with existing neuroleptics is difficult to assess.

Preferential D_1 Receptor Blockade

The proposal that drugs exhibiting proportionally greater blocking activity at D_1 as opposed to D_2 receptors might exhibit nonclassic neuroleptic activity is both new and speculative (27); however, it is supported by a series of empirical findings at both the preclinical and clinical level, and is consistent with the notion that close but not always complementary interactions occur between D_1 and D_2 receptors (28,29). Several key elements have given rise to this hypothesis. Firstly, clozapine, fluperlapine, and similar atypical neuroleptics show higher affinity for D_1 than for D_2 receptors in binding studies (Table 3; ref 30); this relationship is reflected by their functional effects in the whole animal. Thus, transstriatal dialysis studies in the conscious rat show low doses of clozapine to cause a preferential increase of dopamine release, while high doses cause a much greater recovery of dihydroxyphenylacetic acid (DOPAC) relative to dopamine (31). Furthermore, the effects of low but not high doses of clozapine can be prevented by prior treatment with selective D_1 agonists. Haloperidol, in contrast, induces a proportionally greater increase of DOPAC recovery at both low and high doses. Secondly, the classical neuroleptics fluphenazine and *cis*-flupenthixol, which are strong D_1 receptor blockers in vitro, appear to act almost exclusively as D_2 antagonists in the whole animal (24,32). Thirdly, preliminary feedback from PET-scan studies in schizophrenics responding to various neuroleptic therapies suggest that D_2 receptor occupation is least, and D_1 receptor occupation greatest, in subjects receiving clozapine (33,34).

TABLE 3. *Comparison of the affinity of various typical and atypical neuroleptics for dopamine D_1 and D_2 binding sites in vitro*

	IC_{50} (nMol/L)[a]		
Drug	D_1 (SCH 23390)	D_2 (spiperone)	$D_1:D_2$ ratio
Typical:			
Sulpiride	>10,000	233	—
Fluphenazine	17	0.2	77
Haloperidol	365	10	37
Chlorpromazine	110	17	7
Thioridazine	93	31	3
Atypical:			
Tilozepine	94	273	0.34
Clozapine	279	834	0.33
RMI 81582	19	160	0.12
Fluperlapine	96	1,565	0.06

[a]Values represent the means from two or more separate experiments

In spite of the evidence mentioned above, the D_1-bias concept is difficult to accept since both D_1 and D_2 receptor blockades give rise to apomorphine-inhibitory and, more especially, cataleptogenic activity. Nevertheless, we have recently identified a number of novel structures that cause preferential blockade of D_1 receptors, both in vitro and in vivo, but are neverthless devoid of apomorphine-antagonistic, cataleptogenic, or prolactin-elevating properties. Since these compounds do not exhibit clozapine's strong interactions with cholinergic, adrenergic, and serotoninergic systems, these findings appear to support the contention that a D_1 bias might result in atypical neuroleptic properties.

CONCLUSION

Dopamine D_2 receptor blockade provides relief of positive schizophrenic symptoms only at the risk of unpleasant subjective and motor side effects. However, the finding that clozapine exhibits low liability for extrapyramidal side effects (EPS) and is effective in many subjects refractory to treatment with classical neuroleptics has raised hopes that the pharmacotherapy of schizophrenia might soon enter a new era. Several different approaches are being employed preclinically, including selective D_1 or D_2 receptor antagonism, mixtures of these two properties and, more recently, partial agonism. To date, no selective D_1 antagonist has been investigated in the clinic, and selective D_2 antagonism appears to offer marginal rather than major improvement over standard neuroleptic therapy. Partial D_2 agonists act as dopaminergic buffers, and this principle could be useful in treating both positive and negative symptoms. Clarification of whether clozapine's atypical properties are linked to a preferential blockade of D_1 receptors is being addressed by PET-scan investigations in patients, and new compounds are being examined preclinically. Serotonin-based approaches currently focus on $5HT_2$ receptor blockade, either selectively or in combination with D_2 blockade, and the inhibition of $5HT_3$ receptor function. Whereas clinical feedback with $5HT_3$ antagonists is unavailable, there are indications that $5HT_2$ blockade may be relevant for alleviating negative symptoms. However, drugs showing combined $5HT_2/D_2$ receptor blockade are probably not devoid of EPS liability. Drug interactions with σ receptors are also under close scrutiny, although concomitant D_2 and σ-blockade (e.g., haloperidol) would not appear to improve on D_2 blockade alone. Nevertheless, clinical testing of new, selective σ-antagonists is clearly warranted.

REFERENCES

1. Kane J, Honigfeld G, Singer J, Meltzer HY. Clozapine for the treatment-resistant schizophrenic. *Arch Gen Psychiatry* 1988;45:789–796.
2. Deutsch SI, Weizman A, Goldman ME, Morihisa JM. The sigma receptor: a novel site implicated in psychosis and antipsychotic drug efficacy. *Clin Neuropharmacol* 1988;11:105–119.
3. Piontek JA, Wang RY. Acute and subchronic effects of rimcazole (BW 234U), a potential antipsychotic drug, on A9 and A10 neurones in the rat. *Life Sci* 1986;39:651–568.
4. Wachtel SR, White FJ. Electrophysiological effects of BMY 14802, a new potential antipsychotic drug, on midbrain dopamine neurones in the rat: acute and chronic studies. *J Pharmacol Exp Ther* 1988;244:410–416.
5. Davidson J, Miller R, Wingfield M, Zung W, Dren AT. The first clinical study of BW 234U in schizophrenia. *Psychopharmacol Bull* 1982;18:173–176.
6. Chouinard G, Annable L. An early phase II clinical trial of BW 234U in the treatment of acute schizophrenia in newly admitted patients. *Psychopharmacology* 1984;84:282–284.
7. Costall B, Domeney AM, Kelly ME, Naylor RJ, Tyers MB. The antipsychotic potential of GR 38032F, a selective antagonist of 5-HT-3 receptors in the central nervous system. *Br J Pharmac* 1987;90:89P.
8. Wadenberg M-L, Ahlenius S. Suppression of conditioned avoidance by 8-OH-DPAT in the rat. *J Neural Transm* 1988;74:195–198.
9. Carter CJ, Pycock CJ. Possible importance of 5-hydroxytryptamine in neuroleptic-induced catalepsy in rats. *Br J Pharmac* 1977;60:267P.
10. Balsara JJ, Jadhav JH, Chandorkar AG. Effects of drugs influencing central serotoninergic mechanisms on haloperidol-induced catalepsy. *Psychopharmacology* 1979;62:67–69.
11. Balsara JJ, Jadhav JH, Muley MP, Chandorkar AG. Effect of drugs influencing central 5-hydroxytryptaminergic mechanisms on morphine-induced catalepsy in the rat. *J Pharm Pharmacol* 1979;31:255–257.
12. Janssen PAJ, Niemegeers CJE, Awouters F, Schellenkens AHL, Megens AAHP, Meert TF. Pharmacology of risperidone (R 64 766), a new antipsychotic with serotonin-S_2 and dopamine-D_2 antagonistic properties. *J Pharmacol Exp Ther* 1988;244:685–693.
13. Mesotten F, Pietouin M, Wellens I, Heylen S, Gelders Y, Vanden Bussche G. Therapeutic effect and safety of increasing doses of risperidone in psychotic patients. *Psychopharmacology* 1988;96(suppl):238. Abstracts of the XVIth CINP Congress, Munich, 1988.
14. Toru M, Shimazono Y, Kikubo T, Mori Y, Nasu T. A double-blind comparison of sulpiride with chlorpromazine in chronic schizophrenia. *J Clin Pharmacol* 1972;12:221–229.
15. Lewis DM, Bond HR, Curry SH. Sulpiride trial in chronic schizohprenia with comparison of two dosage regimens. *Psychopharmacology* 1983;80:259–262.
16. Liebman J, Neale R, Moen NJ. Differential behavioural effects of sulpiride in the rat and squirrel monkey. *Eur J Pharmacol* 1978;50:377–383.
17. Porsolt RD, Jalfre M. Neuroleptic-induced acute dyskinesias in rhesus monkeys. *Psychopharmacology* 1981;75:16–21.
18. Deniker P, Ginestet D, Loo H. *Maniement des médicaments psychotropes*. Paris: Doin Editeurs, 1980.
19. Gerlach J, Luedorf K. The effect of L-dopa on young patients with simple schizophrenia treated with neuroleptic drugs. *Psychopharmacologia* 1975;44:105–110.
20. Angrist B, Peselow E, Rubinstein M, Corwin J, Rotrosen J. Partial improvement in negative schizophrenic symptoms after amphetamine. *Psychopharmacology* 1982;78:128–130.
21. Wachtel H, Dorow R. Dual action on central dopamine function of transdihydrolisuride, a 9,10-dihydrogenated analogue of the ergot dopamine agonist lisuride. *Life Sci* 1983;32:421–432.
22. Coward DM, Dixon AK, Urwyler S, Vigouret J-M. Pharmacological properties of SDZ 208-912: a potential high potency, non-classical neuroleptic. *Pharmacopsychiat* 1988;21:312–313.
23. Schanz H, Olbrich R, Aufdembrinke B. The partial dopamine agonist transdihydrolisuride and its effects on negative symptoms in schizophrenia. *Psychopharmacology* 1988;96.(suppl):239. Abstracts of the XVIth CINP Congress, Munich, 1988.
24. Hess EJ, Norman AB, Creese I. Chronic treatment with dopamine receptor antagonists: behavioural and pharmacological effects on D_1 and D_2 dopamine receptors. *J Neurosci* 1988;8:2361–2370.
25. Chipkin RE, Iorio LC, Coffin VL, McQuade RD, Berger JG, Barnett A. Pharmacological profile of SCH39166: a dopamine D_1 selective benzonaphthazepine with potential antipsychotic activity. *J Pharmacol Exp Ther* 1988;247:1093–1102.
26. Goldstein JM, Litwin LC. Spontaneous activity of A9 and A10 dopamine neurons after acute and chronic administration of the selective D_1 receptor antagonist SCH 23390. *Eur J Pharmacol* 1988;155:175–180.
27. Coward DM, Imperato A, Urwyler S, White TG. Biochemical and behavioural properties of clozapine. *Psychopharmacology* 1989;99:S6–S12.
28. Murray AM, Waddington JL. The induction of grooming and vacuous chewing by a series of selective D_1 dopamine receptor agonists: two directions of $D_1:D_2$ interaction. *Eur J Pharmacol* 1989;160:377–384.
29. Nomoto M, Jenner P, Marsden CD. The D_1 agonist SKF 38393 inhibits the antiparkinsonian

activity of the D_2 agonist LY 171555 in the MPTP-treated marmoset. *Neurosci Lett* 1988;93:275–280.

30. Andersen PH, Nielsen EB, Gronvald FC, Braestrup C. Some atypical neuroleptics inhibit [^{3}H]SCH 23390 binding in vivo. *Eur J Pharmacol* 1986;120:143–144.

31. Imperato A, Angelucci L. Effects of the atypical neuroleptics clozapine and fluperlapine on the in vivo dopamine release in the dorsal striatum and in the prefrontal cortex. *Psychopharmacology* 1988;96(suppl):79. Abstracts of the XVIth CINP Congress, Munich, 1988.

32. Andersen PH. Comparison of the pharmacological characteristics of [^{3}H]SCH 23390 binding to dopamine receptors in vivo in mouse brain. *Eur J Pharmacol* 1988;146:113–120.

33. Farde L, Wiesel F-A, Halldin C, Sedvall G. Central D_2-dopamine receptor occupancy in schizophrenic patients treated with antipsychotic drugs. *Arch Gen Psychiatry* 1988;45:71–76.

34. Farde L, Wiesel F-A, Nordstrom A-L, Sedvall G. PET examination of human D_1- and D_2-dopamine receptor characteristics. *Psychopharmacology* 1988;96(suppl):79. Abstracts of the XVIth CINP Congress, Munich, 1988.

30

BMY 14802

A Potential Antipsychotic with Selective Affinity for σ-Binding Sites

Duncan P. Taylor, Michael S. Eison, Sandra L. Moon, and Frank D. Yocca

The phenothiazines, thioxanthines, and butyrophenones have undoubtedly been effective in managing the positive symptoms of schizophrenic disorders. From the beginning, however, their propensity to produce acute extrapyramidal symptoms (EPS) was seen as a cautionary sign by physicians, and the later emergence of tardive dyskinesia with the long-term use of these drugs in many patients has become a serious cause for concern. This concern as well as a desire for greater efficacy in the treatment of negative or deficit symptoms of schizophrenia, has led to a continuing search for new agents to use in treating these disorders. One agent resulting from this search is BMY 14802 (Fig. 1); in this chapter we will describe some aspects of its pharmacological and neurochemical profile.

BMY 14802 is active in preclinical behavioral models that predict antipsychotic efficacy. Like conventional antipsychotics, such as chlorpromazine and haloperidol, as well as the atypical agent clozapine, BMY 14802 is active in the inhibition of the conditioned avoidance response (Table 1). This test also detects compounds with general tranquilizing properties. Consistent with the dopamine hypothesis of schizophrenia (2), the in vivo activities induced by the dopamine agonist apomorphine are blocked by antipsychotic drugs. Like clinically effective antipsychotic drugs, BMY 14802 is active in inhibiting apomorphine-induced stereotypy and pole climbing (see Table 1). In the more sophisticated discriminated avoidance task, the typical agent chlorpromazine reduces both avoidance and escape components of the paradigm (Fig. 2). In contrast, BMY 14802 and the atypical agent clozapine selectively reduce only the avoidance component of this test. To the extent that blockade of escape from aversive electroshock may reflect interference with nigrostriatally-mediated motor behavior, these data suggest that these latter agents not only may be effective in the treatment of schizophrenia but also may exhibit a regional selectivity that may obviate the motoric dysfunctions typical of classic antipsychotics. Additional data consistent with this hypothesis have been reported by other laboratories. For instance, amfonelic acid produces hyperlocomotion in rats, presumably by activating the release of dopamine in mesolimbic dopaminergic pathways, and this effect can be blocked by BMY 14802 (5). In addition, BMY 14802

CNS Biology, Pharmaceutical Research and Development Division, Bristol-Myers Squibb Company, Wallingford, CT 06492.

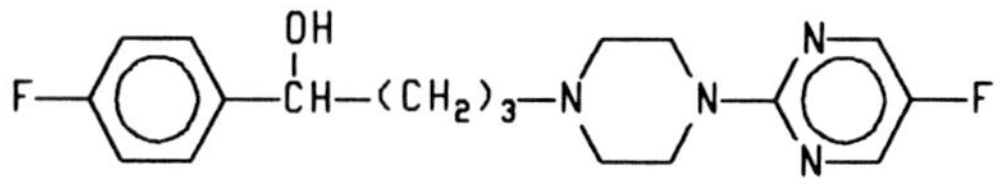

FIG. 1. BMY 14802 was first synthesized by Yevich and Lobeck (1).

abolishes or reduces behaviors associated with correlates of amphetamine-induced psychosis in social primate colonies (6). Finally, chronic administration of BMY 14802 induces depolarization blockade in mesolimbic (A_{10}) dopaminergic cells (those that originate in the ventral tegmental area and project to mesolimbic and mesocortical regions of the brain) but not in nigrostriatal (A_9) dopaminergic cells (7).

BMY 14802 lacks the potential for side effects typical of conventional antipsychotics. Unlike chlorpromazine and haloperidol, BMY 14802 and clozapine do not induce catalepsy, which is a preclinical model of acute EPS and a potential predictor of the propensity to produce tardive dyskinesia (Table 2). BMY 14802 is further distinguished from other antipsychotic agents by its ability to reverse a preexisting cataleptic state induced by the neuroleptic trifluoperazine (see Table 2). Moreover, in contrast to haloperidol, long-term administration of BMY 14802 is not associated with an increase in the number or supersensitivity of striatal D_2 dopamine receptor binding sites (Table 3). These pharmacological effects of BMY 14802 are consistent with the predictions that with long-term pharmacotherapy BMY 14802 may not induce tardive dyskinesia. This suggestion is supported by the observation that repeated administration of BMY 14802 failed to decrease the number of spontaneously active A9 dopaminergic cells (those originating in the substantia nigra and projecting to the extrapyramidal system; see ref 7).

BMY 14802 exhibits an atypical neurochemical profile. The atypical profile of clozapine has been interpreted as reflecting selective effects on dopaminergic neurotransmission in the mesolimbic system without significantly impinging on nigrostriatal processes. BMY 14802 exhibits a clozapinelike profile, not only in its selective inhibition of A10 dopaminergic cell firing relative to A9 cell firing (7), but also in its regional effects on generating the dopamine metabolite dihydroxyphenylacetic acid (DOPAC). The conventional antipsychotic haloperidol consistently produces larger increases in striatal DOPAC levels than in mesolimbic levels (Table 4). In contrast, BMY 14802 at low doses produces selective elevations in DOPAC levels in the nucleus accumbens relative to the striatum. Another distinction between BMY 14802 and haloperidol is that BMY 14802 reduces dopamine levels in both regions while haloperidol has no effect on dopamine levels.

BMY 14802 has an atypical receptor binding profile. How does BMY 14802

TABLE 1. *In vivo testing of selected agents in models that predict antipsychotic efficacy*

Compound	Inhibition of conditioned avoidance response[a] (ED_{50}, mg/kg PO)	Inhibition of apomorphine-induced stereotypy[a] (ED_{50}, mg/kg PO)	Inhibition of apomorphine-induced pole climbing[b] (MED mg/kg PO)[c]
BMY 14802	26	33	60
Clozapine	27	49	10
Haloperidol	2.8	0.5	1
Chlorpromazine	39	10	5

[a]The abilities to inhibit the conditioned avoidance response and apomorphine-induced stereotypy were determined in rats as described in ref 2.
[b]The ability to inhibit apomorphine-induced pole climbing was determined in mice as described in ref 3.
[c]MED reflects minimal effective dose.

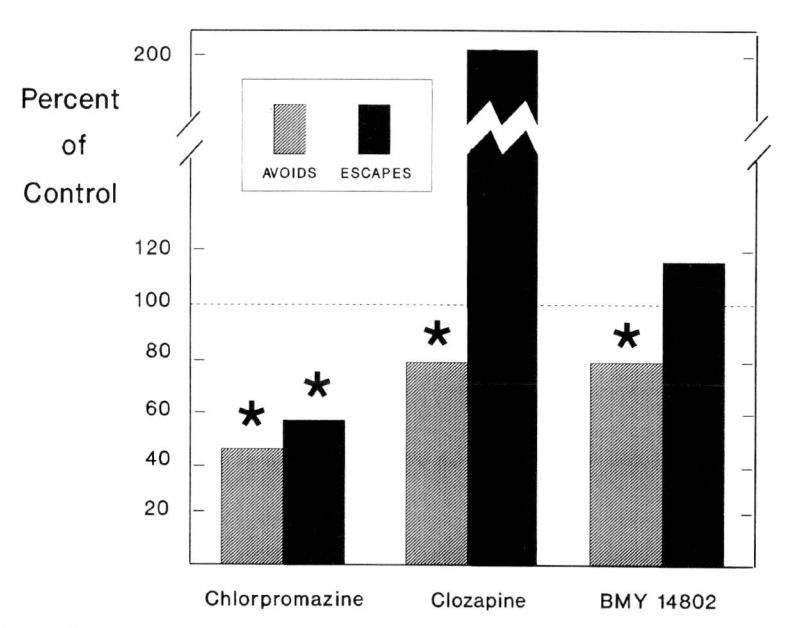

FIG. 2. Actions of selected agents of 100 mg/kg PO on rats in a discriminated avoidance task (adapted from ref 4). Hatched bars indicate avoidance responding as a percentage of vehicle-treated controls. Solid bars represent escape responding as a percentage of vehicle-treated controls. Asterisks denote levels of responding that were significantly different from controls at the $p<.05$ level.

achieve its selective behavioral and neurochemical effects? While conventional antipsychotics exhibit affinity for D_2 dopamine receptor binding sites in vitro, BMY 14802 is distinguished by its low affinity for this receptor site (Table 5). In addition, BMY 14802 does not inhibit D_1 dopamine receptor binding nor does it alter the activity of the D_1 dopamine-stimulated adenylate cyclase. BMY 14802 also exhibits low affinity for a variety of other neurotransmitter receptor binding sites. In particular these include α_1-, α_2-, and β-adrenergic sites, benzodiazepine, glycine (strychnine-sensitive

TABLE 2. In vivo testing of selected agents in models related to motoric dysfunction

Compound	Induction of catalepsy[a] (ED_{50}, mg/kg PO)	Reversal of trifluoperazine-induced catalepsy[b] (ED_{50}, mg/kg PO)
BMY 14802	100[c]	17
Clozapine	200[c]	20[c]
Haloperidol	0.6	—
Chlorpromazine	4.1	—

[a]The ability to induce catalepsy is described in reference 2.
[b]The ability to reverse trifluoperazine-induced catalepsy was determined in rats as described in ref 8.
[c]No activity was seen at this dose.

TABLE 3. Effect of chronic drug administration on D_2 dopamine receptor binding

Treatment[a]	Dose (mg/kg)	B_{max} as percent of vehicle[b]
BMY 14802	15	102
BMY 14802	30	93
Haloperidol	3	127[c]

[a]Drugs were administered orally to rats for 29 days. At least four preparations of striatal membranes pooled from three rats each were assayed by saturation analysis employing [³H]spiperone according to established methods of ref 9.
[b]B_{max} for vehicle-treated animals was 228 fmol of spiperone per milligram of protein.
[c]$p < .05$ vs vehicle

TABLE 4. Effects of drugs on levels of dopamine and DOPAC in brain regions

Drug[a] (mg/kg)	DOPAC[b]		Dopamine[c]	
	Striatum[c]	Nucleus accumbens[c]	Striatum	Nucleus accumbens
BMY 14802				
7.5	125	270	89	61[c]
15	147	196	92	91
30	193	173	85[c]	82[c]
60	203	176	68[c]	75[c]
Haloperidol:				
1.5	355	328	85	86
3	406	347	94	103
6	412	256	101	102
15	365	264	92	89

[a] Drugs were administered orally to rats, and tissues were dissected 1 hour later.
[b] Dopamine and DOPAC levels were determined by high pressure liquid chromatography with electrochemical detection, as described in ref 10.
[c] $p < .05$ vs vehicle control.

and -insensitive subtypes), glutamate (N-methyl-D-aspartate, kainate, and quisqualate subtypes), μ- and κ-opioids, imipramine, nitrendipine, and type 2 serotonergic receptor binding sites (13). Significantly, BMY 14802 does not generate metabolites that might interact with D_2 dopamine binding sites in vivo, as no such activity is present in the serum of animals dosed with BMY 14802 or found in the striatum of rats using ex vivo techniques (13). However, BMY 14802 does exhibit stereoselective and competitive blockade of binding at σ-sites assessed in vitro employing several ligands such as NAN, 3-PPP, and DTG (Table 6; ref 14). Moreover, BMY 14802 has been shown to inhibit the in vivo binding of (+)-[^{3}H]NAN and (+)-[^{3}H]3-PPP to σ-sites in the mouse brain with a potency consistent with in vitro data (Ferris, personal communication; ref 19). In contrast to agents such as NAN and phencyclidine (PCP), which exhibit affinity for both the σ and PCP binding sites, BMY 14802 has virtually no effect on the binding of TCP or MK-801 to PCP sites (Table 6). These data suggest that unlike some agents that bind to σ-receptors, BMY 14802 should lack psychotomimetic properties. Recently we have observed that BMY 14802 has a modest affinity for $5HT_{1A}$ binding sites in rat hippocampal membranes labeled with [^{3}H]8-hydroxy-dipropylaminotetralin (DPAT). This site exhibits stereoselectivity: the dextro-

TABLE 5. Ability of selected agents to act in vitro at dopamine receptors

Compound	Inhibition of D_1 receptor binding[a] (IC_{50}, nM)	Inhibition of (D_1) dopamine-stimulated cAMP accumulation[b] (IC_{50}, nM)	Inhibition of D_2 receptor binding[c] (IC_{50}, nM)
BMY 14802	>100,000	>1,000	6,400
Clozapine	1,100	—	570
Haloperidol	860	250	1.1
Chlorpromazine	550	—	40

[a] D_1 receptor binding was assessed using [^{3}H]SCH 23390 and rat striatal membranes (11).
[b] Dopamine-stimulated cAMP accumulation was assessed in rat striatal homogenates (12).
[c] D_2 receptor binding was assessed using [^{3}H]spiperone and rat striatal membranes (2).

TABLE 6. *Ability of selected agents to inhibit in vitro radioligand binding[a]*

Radioligand: Compound	NAN (15)	3-PPP (16)	DTG (17)	TCP (15)	MK-801 (18)
(+)BMY 14802	43	28	32	>10,000	>100,000
(−)BMY 14802	420	310	140	>10,000	>100,000
Haloperidol	2	1.4	2	>1,000	18,000
(−)Butaclamol	44	41	110	—	7,100
(+)Butaclamol	1,500	1,500	570	—	8,800
Phencyclidine (PCP)	400	640	1,200	34	57

[a]Data are mean K_i values (in nM) from at least three determinations. Abbreviations: NAN, (+)-N-allylnormetazocine; 3-PPP, (+)-3-[3-hydroxyphenyl]-N-(1-propyl)piperidine; DTG, 1,3-di-o-tolyguanidine; TCP, 1-(2-thienyl)cyclohexylpiperidine; MK-801, dizocilipine. Numbers in parentheses are references to methods employed. Binding to σ- and PCP receptors was performed in guinea pig and rat brain, respectively.

rotatory enantiomer has an IC_{50} value of 151 nM, while the levorotatory enantiomer has an IC_{50} value of 189 nM (20). These values represent 1.0% to 1.2% of the potency of DPAT itself. It has been suggested that this activity may play a role in the ability of BMY 14802 to reverse neuroleptic-induced catalepsy (21).

[³H]BMY 14802 selectively labels σ-sites in vitro. How selective is the ability of BMY 14802 to label σ-binding sites? We have investigated the binding of [³H]BMY 14802 in the brain to directly examine the pharmacological specificity of the high-affinity site to which it binds. Our limited studies to date reveal a profile of potency for displacing [³H]BMY 14802 from its binding site by selected agents that is consistent with that observed for the σ-binding site labeled in homogenates by (+)-[³H]3-PPP (Table 7). Moreover, in vitro labeling of brain slices from the rat and guinea pig by [³H]BMY 14802 has revealed high levels of binding in cortical regions, including the hippocampus and cerebellar cortex, the hypothalamus, bed nuclei, periaqueductal gray, and the superficial layers of the superior colliculus, which demonstrate many similarities with previously published data on the localization of (+)-[³H]3-PPP binding (22,23). A representative comparison of the distribution of these two ligands is shown in Fig. 3.

BMY 14802 may be a safer alternative in the treatment of schizophrenia. What is the function of the so-called σ-receptor, this well-defined binding site? Its function is not known, although Bowen and colleagues have recently suggested that the σ receptor is coupled to phosphatidylinositol turnover in peripheral tissues (24). The lack of a known function does not obviate the reality of the receptor but, rather, emphasizes the amount of work yet to be done. Consider that the D_2 dopamine receptor, whose psychiatric and neuroleptic relevance is unquestioned, has no singular, well-defined function. That the σ receptor may be a postsynaptic receptor is suggested by lesion studies (23). When the postsynaptic cells intrinsic to the striatum are destroyed by local injections of the neurotoxin ibotenic acid, σ-binding falls almost 70%. However, when the presynaptic dopaminergic terminals of cells in the substantia ni-

TABLE 7. *Inhibition of in vitro [³H]BMY 14802 binding by selected agents[a]*

Radioligand: Compound	BMY 14802	3-PPP
DTG	8.6	19
Haloperidol	9.4	1.4
BMY 14802	33	110
(−)NAN	8,600	2,000

[a]Data are K_i values (in nM). Abbreviations: see Table 6 footnote. The inhibition of 20 nM of [³H]BMY 14802 (K_D = 73 nM) was assessed using slide-mounted slices of minced guinea pig brain (22). The inhibition of (+)-[³H]3-PPP binding in guinea pig brain homogenates is described in ref 16.

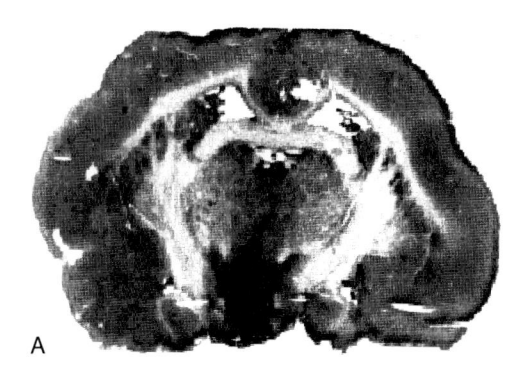

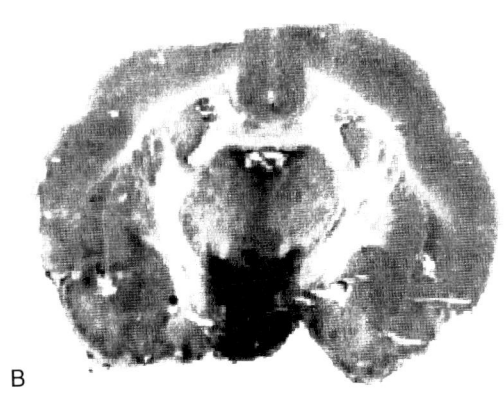

FIG. 3. In vitro labeling of the guinea pig brain through the level of the hypothalamus. **A:** Using [³H]BMY 14802; **B:** using (+)-[³H]3-PPP. Incubation conditions for ³H-14802: 20 nM of ³H-14802 in 50 mM of Hepes buffer for 1 hour at 22°C followed by a 2-minute rinse in buffer alone at 4°C.

gra are destroyed by injection of 6-hydroxydopamine, σ-binding in the striatum falls less than 20%. The relevance of the σ-site to schizophrenia is emphasized by the observation from autoradiographic studies that the nucleus accumbens is enriched in σ-receptors relative to the striatum (23).

We have constructed a heuristic model of how the σ-receptor might influence dopaminergic neurotransmission that attempts to incorporate these observations (Fig. 4). Dopaminergic synapses in the striatum and nucleus accumbens are believed to originate from cell bodies in the substantia nigra (A9) and the ventral tegmental (A10) areas, respectively. Neurochemical or electrical stimulation of these cell bodies results in the propagation of action potentials down axons. At the nerve terminal, stored dopamine is released into the synaptic cleft. Here it acts on the postsynaptic cell to evoke cell firing. Dopamine also acts within the presynaptic terminal at the D_2 dopamine autoreceptor to inhibit the activity of tyrosine hydroxylase, the rate-limiting enzyme for dopamine synthesis. Upon dissociation from postsynaptic dopamine receptors, dopamine is taken up by the presynaptic terminal, where it is inactivated by metabolism to DOPAC. Enhanced cell firing in dopamine projection areas results in decreased firing of cells in the substantia nigra via the nigrostriatal feedback loop.

In our model, acute administration of a D_2 antagonist would block dopamine-induced firing of postsynaptic neurons. This reduced activity would result in increased firing of the presynaptic neuron by virtue of disinhibition by the feedback loop. As a consequence of this increased presynaptic firing, excessive dopamine would be released and metabolized to DOPAC, and DOPAC levels would rise. Because a D_2 antagonist is present, no presynaptic autoreceptor activation would be observed, and there would thus be no reduction of dopamine levels.

In our model, acute administration of a σ-"antagonist" would not block the effect of apomorphine, an agonist at the D_2 receptor, but it would reverse the increase in postsynaptic firing elicited by apomorphine. This would result in an increase in firing of the presynaptic neuron again via disinhibition by the neuronal feedback loop. As before, this increased firing would release excessive dopamine at the synapse, where it is metabolized to DOPAC, and again the levels of this metabolite would rise. Since no D_2 antagonist is present, the D_2 presynaptic autoreceptor would be stimulated by the released dopamine resulting in the inhibition of the enzyme tyrosine hydroxylase. A consequence of this effect would be that neuronal levels of dopamine would fall.

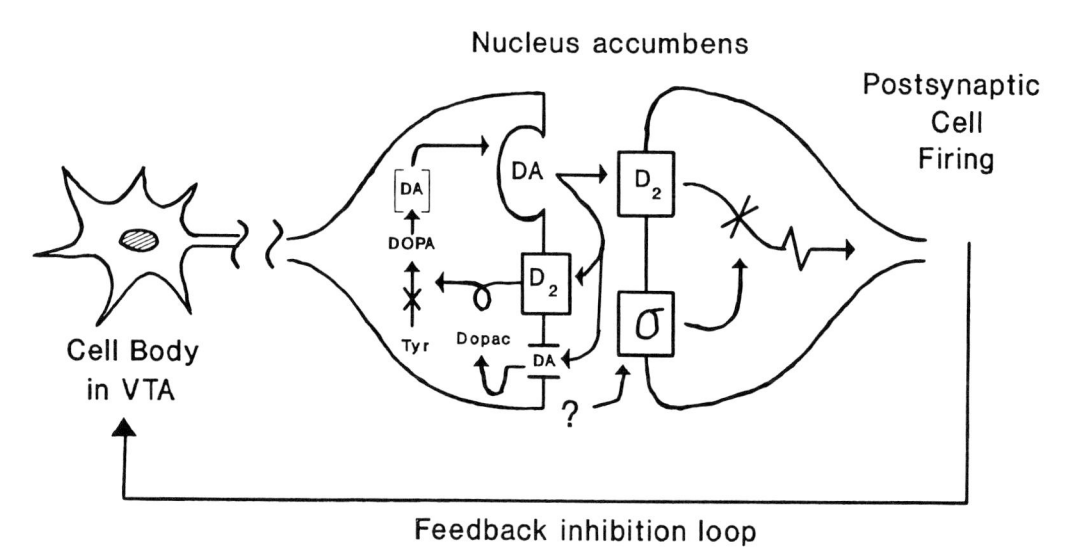

FIG. 4. Schematic diagram of the role of the σ-receptor in dopaminergic neurotransmission. Abbreviations: DA, dopamine; DOPA, dihydroxyphenylalanine; DOPAC, dihydroxyphenylacetic acid; Tyr, tyrosine; VTA, ventral tegmental area. For explanation of the implications, see the text.

We believe that BMY 14802 represents a σ-"antagonist" with actions like those outlined above. BMY 14802 has an appropriate profile in in vitro receptor binding tests (see Tables 5 and 6). Like haloperidol, BMY 14802 has its greatest specificity for σ-sites; however, unlike haloperidol, BMY 14802 shows great selectivity for σ-sites compared with D_2 dopamine receptors. This would suggest that BMY 14802 would have physiological and behavioral effects consistent with a σ-"antagonist" and not with a D_2 dopamine antagonist such as haloperidol.

Furthermore, BMY 14802 stimulates firing of A10 dopaminergic cells at a dose that is about 1/20th that of haloperidol (7). This ratio is consistent with the ratio of affinities of haloperidol and BMY 14802 for σ-receptors. Both agents can reverse the inhibition of A10 cell firing induced by apomorphine, but only haloperidol also blocks the effect of subsequent apomorphine administration. This is consistent with the lack of affinity of BMY 14802 for the D_2 dopamine receptors.

Finally, σ-antagonists would be predicted to have different effects than D_2 antagonists would on the levels of dopamine and its metabolites. The neurochemical profile of BMY 14802 reveals such differences relative to haloperidol (see Table 4). Haloperidol potently and equally elevates levels of the dopamine metabolite DOPAC in both the striatum and nucleus accumbens while leaving dopamine levels in both regions unchanged. In contrast, treatment with BMY 14802 preferentially elevates DOPAC levels to a greater degree in the nucleus accumbens, and a significant decrease in dopamine levels is also observed in this important brain region.

These hypothetical constructs would be of little value unless σ-antagonists had behavioral effects consistent with those predicted for a clinically effective antipsychotic. Like haloperidol, BMY 14802 can attenuate the stereotyped movement elicited by apomorphine in the rat and inhibit the conditioned avoidance response. Both of these tests are classically used to identify potential antipsychotic drug candidates. Moreover, like haloperidol, BMY 14802 has a long duration of action in the inhibition of the conditioned avoidance response. Because BMY 14802 does not bind to D_2 receptors and does not induce catalepsy, a reliable preclinical predictor of movement disorders (see Table 2), it would not be expected to induce the extrapyramidal motor disturbances associated with typical D_2 antagonist antipsychotics.

Therefore, BMY 14802 represents a potential antipsychotic agent with reduced liability for the side effects of currently available drugs. If clinically efficacious, BMY 14802 may treat the symptoms of schizophrenia by a mechanism novel for antipsychotic drugs—selective, stereospecific, and competitive binding to σ-sites.

ACKNOWLEDGMENTS

We are grateful for technical assistance provided by L. Allen, S. Behling, R. Butler, J. Dekleva, D. Hyslop, R. Lamy, E. Ryan, and R. Winneke. We are indebted to M. Haas and J. Loos for artwork and J. Stockla for preparation of the manuscript.

REFERENCES

1. Yevich JP, Lobeck WG Jr. Antipsychotic 1-fluorophenylbutyl-4-(2-pyrimidinyl)piperazine derivatives. US Pat 1986;no. 4,605,655.
2. Yevich JP, New JS, Smith DW, et al. Synthesis and biological evaluation of 1-(1,2-benzisothiazol-3-yl)- and (1,2-benzisoxazol-3-yl)piperazine derivatives as potential antipsychotic agents. J Med Chem 1986;29:359–369.
3. Costall B, Naylor RJ, Nohria V. Climbing behavior induced by apomorphine in mice: a potential model for the detection of neuroleptic activity. Eur J Pharmacol 1978;50:39–50.
4. Sidman M. Avoidance conditioning with brief shock and no exteroceptive warning signal. Science 1953;118:157–158.
5. Matthews RT, McMillen BA, Sallis R, Blair P. Effects of BMY 14802, a potential antipsychotic drug, on rat brain dopaminergic function. J Pharmacol Exp Ther 1986;239:124–131.
6. Schlemmer RF Jr, Davis JM. The effect of BMY 14802 on an amphetamine-induced model of psychosis in primate social colonies. Soc Neurosci Abstr 1986;12:480.
7. Wachtel SR, White FJ. Electrophysiological effects of BMY 14802, a new potential antipsychotic drug, on midbrain dopamine neurons in the rat: acute and chronic studies. J Pharmacol Exp Ther 1987;244:410–416.
8. Riblet LA, Taylor DP, Eison MS, Stanton HC. Pharmacology and neurochemistry of buspirone. J Clin Psychiatry 1982;43 (12, sec 2): 11–16.
9. Taylor DP, Hyslop DK. Chronic administration of buspirone down-regulates 5-HT$_2$ receptor binding sites. Br J Psychiatry 1990; submitted.
10. Mayer GS, Shoup RE. Simultaneous multiple electrode liquid chromatographic-electrochemical assay for catecholamines, indoleamines and metabolites in brain tissue. J Chromatogr 1983; 255:533–544.
11. Billard W, Ruperto V, Crosby G, Iorio LC, Barnett A. Characterization of the binding of ^{3}H-SCH 23390, a selective D$_1$ receptor antagonist ligand, in rat striatum. Life Sci 1984;35:1885–1893.
12. Salomon Y. Adenylate cyclase assay. In: Brooker G, Greengard P, Robison GA, eds. Advances in cyclic nucleotide research, vol. 10. New York: Raven Press, 1979;35–55.
13. Taylor DP, Eison MS, Lobeck WG Jr, Riblet LA, Temple DL, Jr, Yevich JP. BMY 14802: a potential antipsychotic agent that does not bind to D-2 dopamine sites. Soc Neurosci Abstr 1985;11:114.
14. Taylor DP, Dekleva J. Potential antipsychotic BMY 14802 selectively binds to sigma sites. Drug Develop Res 1987;11:65–70.
15. Taylor DP, Dekleva J. BMY 14802: a potential antipsychotic agent that selectively binds to sigma receptors. In: Domino EF, Kamenka J-M, eds. Sigma and phencyclidine compounds as molecular probes in biology. Ann Arbor, Mich: NPP Books, 1988;345–355.
16. Largent BL, Gundlach AL, Snyder SH. Psychotomimetic opiate receptors labeled and visualized with (+)-[^{3}H]3-(3-hydroxyphenyl)-N-(1-propyl)piperidine. Proc Natl Acad Sci USA 1984; 81:4983–4987.
17. Weber E, Sonders M, Quarum M, McLean S, Pou S, Keana JFW. 1,3-Di(2-[5-^{3}H]tolyl)guanidine: a selective ligand that labels σ-type receptors for psychotomimetic opiates and antipsychotic drugs. Proc Natl Acad Sci USA 1986;83:8784–8788.
18. Reynolds IJ, Murphy SN, Miller RJ. ^{3}H-labeled MK-801 binding to the excitatory amino acid receptor complex from rat brain is enhanced by glycine. Proc Natl Acad Sci USA 1987;84:7744–7748.
19. Koe BK, Burkhart CA, Lebel LA. (+)-[^{3}H]3-(3-Hydroxyphenyl)-N-(1-propyl)piperidine binding to sigma receptors in mouse brain in vivo. Eur J Pharmacol 1989;161:263–266.
20. Taylor DP, Behling SH. Unpublished data.
21. McMillen BA, Scott SM, Davanzo EA. Reversal of neuroleptic-induced catalepsy by novel arylpiperazine anxiolytic drugs. J Pharm Pharmacol 1989;40:885–887.

22. Moon SL. The autoradiographic localization of (±)-[³H]BMY 14802, a potential antipsychotic agent. *Soc Neurosci Abstr* 1987;13:457.
23. Gundlach AL, Largent BL, Snyder SH. Autoradiographic localization of sigma receptor binding sites in guinea pig and rat central nervous system with (+)³H-3-(3-hydroxyphenyl)-N-(1-propyl)piperidine. *J Neurosci* 1986;6:1757–1770.
24. Bowen WP, Kirschner BN, Newman AH, Rice KC. σ Receptors negatively modulate agonist-stimulated phosphoinositide metabolism in rat brain. *Eur J Pharmacol* 1988;149:399–400.

31

Presynaptic D_2-Receptor Selectivity of Roxindole (EMD 49 980)

Possible Indirect Effects on Postsynaptic Striatal Cholinergic Neurons

Christoph A. Seyfried,[1] Anton F. Haase,[1] and Henning Böttcher[1]

Based on the dopamine hypothesis of schizophrenia, several dopamine autoreceptor agonists have been developed in recent years as potential neuroleptics. These compounds are hoped to have antipsychotic properties due to a selective action on presynaptic D_2 receptors, thereby reducing dopaminergic impulse flow. Since there is little evidence that pre- and postsynaptic D_2 receptors are qualitatively different, there has been considerable debate as to the mechanism(s) underlying the presynaptic selectivity of these compounds. Recently, striatal presynaptic D_2 receptors have been shown to possess a higher receptor reserve compared with the postsynaptic D_2 receptors (1). It is now widely held that presynaptic selectivity is related to this phenomenon, that dopamine autoreceptor agonists have a lower intrinsic activity than unselective D_2 agonists, for instance apomorphine. However, to substantiate such a mechanism for a particular drug, other possibilities to achieve selectivity or pseudoselectivity have to be excluded: Detection or expression of postsynaptic actions may either be masked by concurrent behavioral effects a drug might have or be functionally counteracted through other transmitter systems that a drug might influence. Thus, postsynaptic D_2-agonist properties of the D_2 and α_2-agonist TL 99 can be revealed by yohimbine cotreatment (2), inhibiting the α_2-mediated sedation. Likewise, in behavioral models, postsynaptic stimulatory effects of B-HT 920 are uncovered by reinstituting the necessary basic D_1 tone with D_1 agonists (3,4). This finding is in accordance with the potent postsynaptic D_2 actions of B-HT 920 in biochemical models (5,6).

Recently we described a novel D_2 agonist (EMD 49 980, roxindole) that is structurally unrelated to either rigid dopamine analogues or to classical ergot derivatives. Roxindole is highly potent and selective for the presynaptic D_2 receptor, in both biochemical and behavioral tests (6,7). However, roxindole also exhibits considerable $5HT_{1A}$-receptor agonist activity and potent 5HT-uptake inhibitory effects. The aim of the present studies was to investigate the possibility that these effects on 5HT systems might functionally antagonize the expression of postsynaptic stimulatory D_2 actions that would result in a pseudoselectivity for presynaptic D_2 receptors.

[1]Department of CNS Research, E. Merck, 6100 Darmstadt, FRG.

MATERIALS AND METHODS

We used male Wistar rats of 190 to 240 g body weight (Iva: WIWU, Ivanovas, Kisslegg, FRG); NSD 1015 (100 mg/kg IP), PCA (p-chloroamphetamine; 5 mg/kg IP), γ-butyrolactone (GBL; 750 mg/kg IP), and apomorphine (SC) were dissolved in saline. For reserpinization (5 mg/kg SC) we used Serpasil® ampoules (Ciba Pharma, Wehr, FRG), containing 1 mg/ml reserpine. All other drugs were dissolved in propanediol-1,2 and administered subcutaneously. Unless otherwise stated, approximate ED_{50} values were graphically derived from dose-response curves with four to eight doses of drug, using three to ten animals per dose.

Other experimental details of the in vivo models have been recently described (6). In vitro efflux of cAMP from striatal prisms was essentially carried out as described by Stoof and Kebabian (8) in a 24-chamber superfusion apparatus at a rate of 0.1 ml/min. The cAMP content of 1-ml fractions was determined in duplicate in 100 μL aliquots by radioimmunoassay (Du Pont/NEN Kit) at a detection limit of 8 fmol/100 μL using the acetylated system. We synthesized EMD 52 500 (7-[4-[4-phenyl-1,2,3,6-tetrahydropyridyl(1)]-butyl]-5H-1,3-dioxolo[4,5f]indole, maleate) in the Department of Medicinal Chemistry, E. Merck.

RESULTS AND DISCUSSION

Roxindole and a close structural analogue of roxindole, the methylenedioxy-derivative EMD 52 500, both potently reversed the GBL-induced rise in striatal DOPA accumulation, indicating presynaptic D_2-agonist activity with potencies below the milligram range and high maximal effects (Fig. 1 and Table 1). In contrast, increases in acetylcholine (AcCh) concentration in the striatum reflecting postsynaptic D_2-agonist activity were rather poor. Similar to roxindole (6), EMD 52 500 induced a maximal increase of 20% to 30% above con-

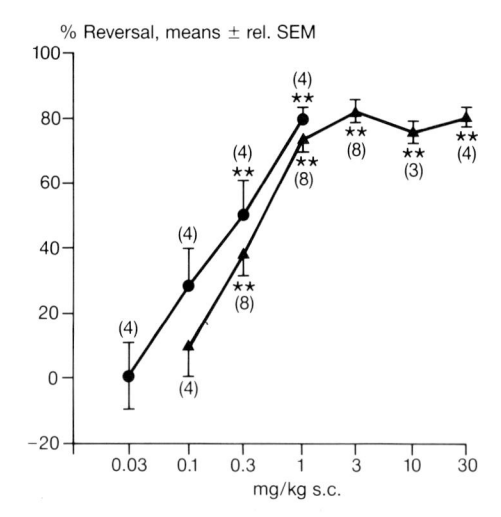

FIG. 1. Reversal of GBL-induced DOPA accumulation in rat striatum by EMD 52 500 70 minutes (*triangles*) and 180 minutes (*circles*) after application. For experimental details, see Table 1. **$p<.01$ vs corresponding controls (t-Dunnett, untransformed data, number of rats in parentheses). Control values in nanograms per gram of fresh weight (means ± SEM of the number of rats in parentheses): for 0% reversal, 5,617 ± 201 ($n=18$) and 5,515 ± 264 ($n=12$) for 70 and 180 minutes, respectively; for 100% reversal, 1,912 ± 93 ($n=8$).

trols at 1 mg/kg SC, and no further increase was noted up to 100 mg/kg SC in contrast to the clearcut, dose-dependent increases seen with B-HT 920 and apomorphine (Fig. 2).

Thus, roxindole and EMD 52 500 proved to have similar selectivity and potency toward presynaptic D_2 receptors, at least in the biochemical models employed. Interestingly, quite different results were obtained with respect to the serotoninergic actions of both drugs. In reserpinized rats (Fig. 3), EMD 52 500 failed to alter the NSD 1015–induced accumulation of 5-hydroxytryptophan (5-HTP) in a dose range of 0.1 to 10 mg/kg SC, indicating lack of $5HT_{1A}$ agonist actions, whereas roxindole reduced 5-HTP accumulation with an ED_{25} value of about 0.6 mg/kg SC (Table 2). Furthermore, with respect to 5HT uptake inhibition (Fig. 4), EMD 52 500 also was inactive at

TABLE 1. Effects of dopamine agonists and antagonists on striatal functions (ED_{50} values, mg/kg SC)[a]

	DOPA accumulation		AcCh concentration	
	Reversal of GBL-induced	Inhibition of reserpine-induced	Elevation	Reduction
Roxindole	0.13	0.071	> 30	—
EMD 52 500	0.46	0.27	>100	—
B-HT 920	0.042	0.03	0.2	—
Apomorphine	0.13	0.051	0.28	—
Chlorpromazine	—	—	—	4.8

[a]Drugs were given 70 minutes before decapitation except apomorphine (45 minutes for DOPA or 15 minutes for AcCh). In the GBL model, GBL was given 40 minutes and NSD 1015, 35 minutes before decapitation. For DOPA accumulation in reserpinized rats, reserpine and NSD 1015 were given 19 hours and 45 minutes, respectively, before decapitation. ED_{50} values are defined as the doses giving 50% reversal of the GBL effect and a 50% change of DOPA or AcCh concentrations in the other models.

relevant doses (0.1 and 1 mg/kg SC), although there was a slight but not dose-dependent increase at 10 and 100 mg/kg SC. Therefore, a clear separation between presynaptic D_2 actions for EMD 52 500, on the one hand, and presynaptic D_2 plus $5HT_{1A}$ agonist activities for roxindole, on the other hand, can be established.

The results of control experiments strengthen this view: As expected from the findings in the GBL model, EMD 52 500 also inhibited DOPA accumulation in reserpinized rats (Fig. 3) similar to roxindole. Under these conditions, dopaminergic potencies of both compounds were about 2 times higher than in the GBL model (Table 1), probably due to development of "supersensitive" D_2 receptors. For measurement of 5HT uptake inhibition in vivo, PCA has to be applied for 3 hours to induce a substantial fall in 5HT levels; consequently, test drugs were given 3.5 hours prior to decapitation.

Therefore, short-acting drugs may not be detected at all or may result in low 5HT uptake inhibition. However, as shown in Fig. 1, EMD 52 500 proved to be a long-acting presynaptic D_2 agonist since ED_{50} values in the GBL model tend to be even lower at 3 hours compared with 1 hour after application (0.3 vs 0.46 mg/kg SC, respectively). Therefore, false-negative results can be excluded for EMD 52 500 under the conditions of the PCA model. In view of the structural similarity of both compounds, the results with EMD 52 500 make it unlikely that the serotoninergic actions of rox-

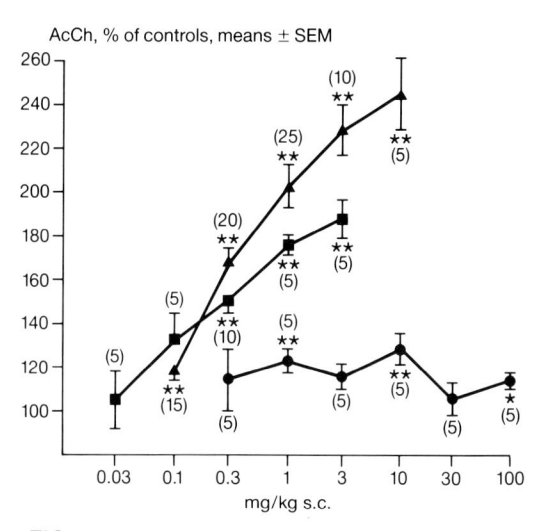

FIG. 2. Increase in rat striatal acetylcholine concentrations by EMD 52 500 (circles), B-HT 920 (triangles), and apomorphine (squares). For experimental details, see Table 1. *$p<.05$; **$p<.01$ vs corresponding controls (t-Dunnett, number of rats in parentheses). Control values in nmol/g of fresh weight (means ± SEM of the number of rats in parentheses): 43.9 ± 1.3 (14) for EMD 52 500; 42.7 ± 1 (21) for B-HT 920; and 39.3 ± 2 (14) for apomorphine.

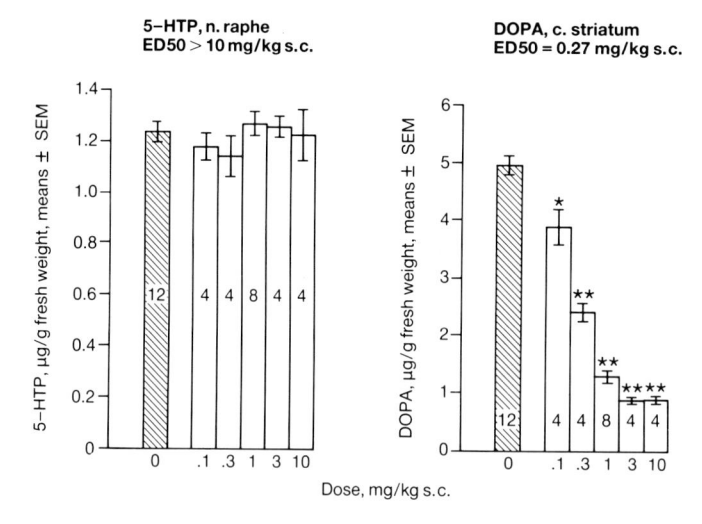

FIG. 3. Inhibition of brain 5-HTP and DOPA accumulation by EMD 52 500 in reserpinized rats. $^*p<.05$, $^{**}p<.01$ vs corresponding controls (number of rats is given in the columns). For details, see Table 2.

indole functionally antagonize increases in striatal AcCh levels by counteracting the expression of any postsynaptic stimulatory D_2 activity that roxindole might have.

The results show that in the novel structural class of indole-butylamines, clear distinctions between dopaminergic and serotoninergic activity can be achieved by only slight structural variations without compromising the remarkable presynaptic D_2 selectivity of this class of compounds. This is especially important in view of possible clinical applications, since EMD 52 500 unfortunately showed unfavorable results in toxicological studies in contrast to roxindole. However, EMD 52 500 proves to be a valuable mechanistic tool for comparative pharmacological studies given the fact that suitable potent and selective $5HT_{1A}$ antagonists for interaction studies with roxindole are still not available.

Recently it has been shown by Harting and Minck (7) that roxindole does not induce stereotypies in rats, even if combined with the D_1-receptor agonist SKF 38 393 to increase D_1-receptor tone. To further study this interesting difference in quality between roxindole and B-HT 920 (see above), the possibility of roxindole having D_1-receptor blocking properties was investigated

TABLE 2. Serotoninergic actions of various drugs in the nucleus raphe (5-HTP accumulation) and hypothalamus (5HT concentration, PCA)

	Inhibition of reserpine-induced 5-HTP accumulation ED_{25} (mg/kg SC)[a]	Antagonism of PCA-induced fall in 5HT concentration ED_{50} (mg/kg SC)[b]
Roxindole	0.58	0.17
EMD 52 500	>10	>100
8-OH-DPAT	0.071	ND[c]

[a]For inhibition of 5-HTP accumulation, drugs were given 70 minutes, reserpine and NSD 1015 19 hours and 45 minutes, respectively, before decapitation. ED_{25} is defined as the dose leading to a 25% decrease in the 5-HTP concentration.

[b]For the PCA antagonism, drugs were given 210 minutes and PCA 180 minutes before decapitation. ED_{50} is defined as the dose resulting in 50% antagonism of the PCA effect.

[c]ND: not determined.

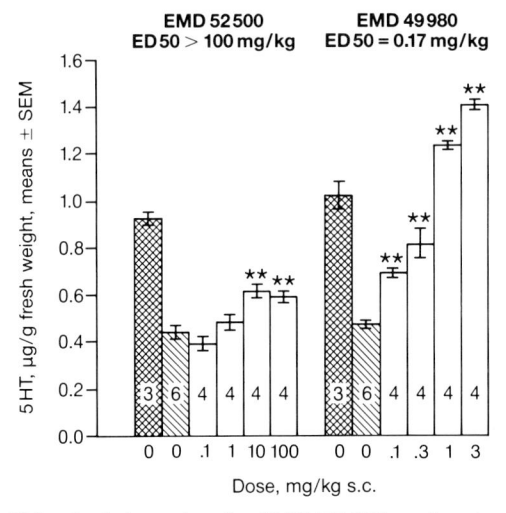

FIG. 4. Antagonism by EMD 52 500 and roxindole (EMD 49 980) of hypothalamic 5HT depletion in PCA-treated rats. $**p<.01$ vs PCA-treated rats (number of rats is given in the columns). For details see Table 2. *Cross-hatched columns*, vehicle treated controls; *hatched columns*, PCA alone; *open columns*, drugs + PCA.

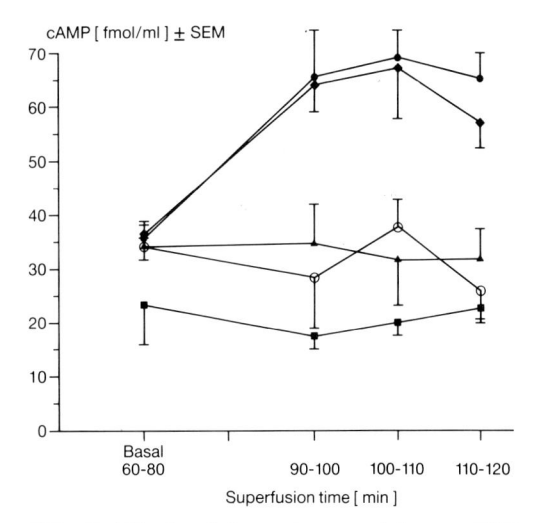

FIG. 5. Effects of dopamine agonists on cAMP release in superfused rat striatal prisms in vitro. $n = 4$ chambers/fraction. *Squares*: controls (basal release); *open circles*: roxindole (0.1 μM); *triangles*: roxindole (30 μM); *closed circles*: SKF 38 393 (10 μM); *diamonds*: SKF 38 393 (10 μM) plus roxindole (30 μM).

in a functional in vitro model, in which cAMP was released from striatal tissue. Figure 5 shows the results of this study. In accordance with the literature, 10 μM of SKF 38 393 significantly increased basal cAMP release by more than 100%, but 30 μM of roxindole completely failed to antagonize this effect of SKF 38 393. Roxindole also failed to significantly stimulate or inhibit basal cAMP release, indicating no activity at D_1 receptors, at least in vitro. These results agree with the low affinity of roxindole in D_1-binding experiments (6), where an IC_{50} in the micromolar range has been measured at the D_1 site as compared to nanomolar affinity to the D_2 site.

In conclusion, our data indicate that neither the serotoninergic actions of roxindole nor any D_1 antagonistic actions—as judged from the in vitro studies—are likely to be responsible as an underlying mechanism for the presynaptic D_2-receptor selectivity of roxindole in the sense that some sort of pseudoselectivity is simulated. Unless other still-unknown properties of this drug can be detected, the most parsimonious explanation is that the intrinsic D_2 activity of roxindole is such that it almost maximally stimulates presynaptic D_2 receptors with only marginal effects at postsynaptic receptors, even at high doses.

REFERENCES

1. Meller E, Helmer-Matyjek R, Bohmaker K, Adler CH, Friedhoff AJ, Goldstein M. Receptor reserve at striatal dopamine autoreceptors: implications for selectivity of dopamine agonists. *Eur J Pharmacol* 1986;123:311–314.
2. Pastor G, Fallon S, Welch JJ, Liebman JM. Postsynaptic dopamine agonist properties of TL-99 are revealed by yohimbine co-treatment. *Eur J Pharmacol* 1983;87:459–464.
3. Hjorth S, Carlsson A. Postsynaptic dopamine (DA) receptor stimulator properties of the putative DA autoreceptor-selective agonist B-HT 920 uncovered by co-treatment with the D-1 agonist SKF 38 393. *Psychopharmacology* 1987;93:534–537.
4. Pifl C, Hornykiewicz O. Postsynaptic dopamine

agonist properties of B-HT 920 as revealed by concomitant D-1 receptor stimulation. *Eur J Pharmacol* 1988;146:189–191.
5. Schmidt CJ, Lobur A, Lovenberg W. Inhibition of K$^+$-stimulated ^{3}H-dopamine and ^{14}C-acetylcholine release by the putative dopamine autoreceptor agonist B-HT 920. *Naunyn-Schmiedeb Arch Pharmacol* 1986;334:377–382.
6. Seyfried CA, Greiner HE, Haase AF. Biochemical and functional studies on EMD 49 980: a potent, selectively presynaptic D-2 dopamine agonist with actions on serotonin systems. *Eur J Pharmacol* 1989;160:31–41.
7. Harting J, Minck KO. Pharmacological characterization of the DA-autoreceptor agonist roxindole. *Naunyn-Schmiedeb Arch Pharmacol* 1989;339:R104.
8. Stoof JC, Kebabian JW. Independent in vitro regulation by the D-2 dopamine receptor of dopamine-stimulated efflux of cyclic AMP and K$^+$-stimulated release of acetylcholine from rat neostriatum. *Brain Res* 1982;250:263–270.

32

Neuroleptic-Induced Anhedonia

Recent Studies

Roy A. Wise[1]

The initial suggestion that acute neuroleptic treatment may cause a state of anhedonia (1–3) was based on animal studies showing that neuroleptics decrease the ability of several normally powerful rewards—amphetamine (4,5), cocaine (6), hypothalamic brain stimulation (7,8), food (3,9), and water (10)—to sustain alley-running or lever-pressing habits in laboratory rats. This hypothesis was initially questioned on two grounds: First, it was argued that the lack of responding in these animals might simply reflect neuroleptic-induced catalepsy or some other form of motoric debilitation (11–14). Second, it was suggested that the dopamine system might be important for mediating some but not all of these rewards (15–20).

After a decade of intense study, it is clear, even to most of those who initially challenged the hypothesis, that neuroleptics *do* block or attenuate the rewarding effects of food (21–23), water (24), amphetamine (25), cocaine (15), and medial forebrain bundle electrical stimulation (26). Moreover, in addition to these early paradigms for discriminating attenuation of reward from impairment of motor function (3–9), several new paradigms have been developed in which neuroleptic-induced re-

ward deficits can be conclusively demonstrated. Where the early paradigms relied on transient periods of normal or elevated responding during neuroleptic treatment, the new paradigms demonstrate the reward-blocking effects of neuroleptics by testing the animals in drug-free conditions the day after neuroleptic administration (22, 24,27,28). For example, rats will show an increased tendency to return to portions of the environment where they have received food (23), amphetamine (29), cocaine (30,31), heroin (27,32), or morphine (33). These conditioned place preferences do not develop if the animals are treated with neuroleptics at the time the rewards are associated with the environmental place, despite the fact that the neuroleptic doses used do not cause any conditioned place aversion in their own right. In addition, rats will show increased responding in extinction (responding after the reward has been discontinued) if a portion of their training occurred under neuroleptic treatment (22,24,28). This increased responding is seen under drug-free conditions and thus could not reflect a motor deficit. Such increased responding parallels the increased extinction responding seen in animals that have been accustomed to the frustration of nonreward by insertion of nonrewarded trials during training. These studies do not challenge the notion that neuroleptics cause motoric impairment, but they do show that

---

[1] Centre for Studies in Behavioral Neurobiology, Department of Psychology, Concordia University, Montreal, PQ, Canada H3G 1M8.

motoric impairment is not a sufficient explanation of the disruption of response habits by neuroleptics. Whatever else they may also do, moderate acute doses of neuroleptics clearly attenuate or block the rewarding impact of food, water, amphetamine, cocaine, and medial-forebrain-bundle brain stimulation (33,34).

The question of whether neuroleptics block the pleasure of all positive rewards (and perhaps the pain of punishment as well; 35,36) is not so easily dealt with. First, we cannot assess pleasure or pain in laboratory animals. Second, while we know that human patients do not like neuroleptics, their subjective reports are varied and may indicate a varied experience with neuroleptic treatment. Third, we can test only a subset of all positive rewards; we can not tap all possibilities. Still, there is a limited number of traditional rewards for the laboratory rat, and while different doses of neuroleptic are required to block the effectiveness of different rewards (in our hands, cocaine and brain stimulation are much more sensitive to pimozide than are food and heroin), we have yet to find a reward that is not blocked or attenuated by acute neuroleptic treatment at moderate doses.

Our recent studies have focused on opiate reward. While opiates have more than one rewarding site of action, they do, at one of their sites of action, activate the same dopaminergic link in reward circuitry implicated in food, water, amphetamine, cocaine, and brain stimulation reward. Moreover, the studies suggest that a putative (37) effect of chronic neuroleptic treatment may produce an even more profound state of anhedonia than that previously reported with acute neuroleptic treatment. At their second site of action, opiates appear to interact with the neurons with which the dopamine link in reward circuitry makes synaptic contact.

This initial interest in opiates was organized by the hypothesis that opiate reward is not affected by neuroleptics. This might have been the case if, as subsequently suggested by others (15), opiate reward were mediated by reward circuitry independent of, but parallel to, the dopaminergic circuitry involved in food, stimulant, and brain stimulation rewards.

Our first study, however, was based on the suggestion of Broekkamp et al (38) that opiates summate with brain stimulation reward because of actions at the dopamine cell bodies of the ventral tegmental area, origin of the dopamine pathways implicated in other rewards (39–41). Morphine injections caudal to the ventral tegmental area inhibit lever pressing for medial-forebrain-bundle brain stimulation reward; injections in more rostral sites (e.g., anterior hypothalamus, nucleus accumbens, and caudate nucleus) are ineffective (38,42). We have subsequently found that opioid injections into the nucleus accumbens do facilitate self-stimulation (43), but the studies of relevance to neuroleptic effects involve the ventral tegmental area.

Beginning with Broekkamp's suggestion that the ventral tegmental area is the site of opiate rewarding actions in the brain, we attempted to train animals to work for rewards of ventral tegmental injections of morphine. Rats readily worked for such injections (44), and these injections caused contraversive circling (45,46), suggesting activation of the mesolimbic dopamine pathway (47). Several additional lines of evidence confirm morphine's activation of the mesolimbic dopamine system: Electrophysiological studies show that morphine disinhibits dopamine neuronal firing (47–49); microdialysis studies show that morphine increases synaptic dopamine levels (50), presumably by increasing dopamine release in proportion to the increased impulse flow.

Since the purpose of central microinjection studies is to localize the sites at which a given drug has a given action, we have been concerned with locating the boundaries of regions where central opiate injections are effective (33,46). The boundaries to the region where ventral tegmental opiate injections are rewarding and produce contraversive circling correspond to the boundaries of the mesencephalic dopamine cell group (33,46). Injections dorsal (51), rostral, caudal, or ventral (33) to the dopamine neurons are ineffective; injections lateral to the ventral tegmental area are less effective and are only effective near the zona compacta (46). Dopamine receptor blockers attenuate or block (15,27,32,52,53) the rewarding effects of opiates, as do ventral tegmental microinjections of opiate antagonists (54,55); these findings confirm that at least a portion of the rewarding effects of intravenous heroin is mediated through this system. Nucleus accumbens injections of opioids are also rewarding (56–58), and nucleus accumbens injections of opiate antagonists also attenuate intravenous heroin reward (54,55). Thus the current view (34,59) is that opiates have two rewarding sites of action: one at the level of the dopamine cell bodies and the other at the level of the dopamine terminals of the nucleus accumbens. Each site has been confirmed in brain stimulation reward studies; opiates have actions at each site that augment brain stimulation reward (43). It is the brain stimulation reward studies that are relevant to the recent hypothesis that chronic neuroleptics can completely shut down the dopamine system by blocking dopaminergic impulse flow (37).

Our currently preferred paradigm for studying the interaction of drugs of abuse with brain stimulation reward is designated the *curve-shift paradigm;* it is a dose-response analysis of the effects of various levels of stimulation (60). In this paradigm we determine the rate of lever pressing under various "doses" of stimulation. Stimulation level can be varied in a number of ways, but variations in stimulation frequency are the most useful; such variations alter the number of action potentials in the population of directly activated reward fibers, but they do not alter the size of the effective field of stimulation (61). A typical "curve" is shown in Fig. 1.

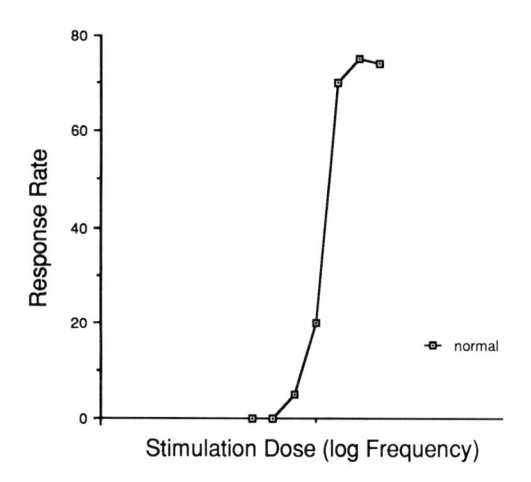

FIG. 1. Rate-frequency function for intracranial self-stimulation involving medial-forebrain-bundle electrodes in an animal given a ventral tegmental injection of physiological saline. A similar "dose-response" function (a rate-*intensity* function) is obtained if stimulation frequency is held constant and stimulation "dose" is varied by manipulating stimulation intensity. However, the rate-frequency function has the advantage of quantitative precision; equal increments on the log frequency scale represent equal increments in reward strength (the relation between intensity changes and reward changes is undetermined; see ref 61).

Treatments that augment the rewarding effects of the stimulation shift this curve to the left, reducing the amount of stimulation needed for a given behavioral output (61). Treatments that attenuate the rewarding effects of the stimulation shift the curve to the right, increasing the amount of stimulation required to motivate a given level of performance. In contrast, treatments that attenuate the performance capacity of the animal decrease the maximal behavioral output of the animal, but do not alter the stimulation frequency required to motivate maximal performance (61,62).

In this paradigm, amphetamine shifts the curve to the left while neuroleptics shift the curve to the right (63,64). If doses of amphetamine and neuroleptic are selected that cause rightward and leftward shifts of equal magnitude (on a log scale), they neutralize one another, leaving performance normal (63,64). Our recent studies involved the effects of ventral tegmental morphine in this paradigm. The working hypothesis was that ventral tegmental morphine should have effects similar to systemic amphetamine, since both treatments ultimately increase dopamine release in the nucleus accumbens (49). As first reported by Broekkamp (38), we have found that ventral tegmental morphine facilitates medial-forebrain-bundle brain stimulation reward (65). It also facilitates the rewarding effects of midline mesencephalic stimulation (66,67). Like systemic amphetamine, ventral tegmental morphine shifts the rate-frequency curve to the left (Fig. 2), reducing the amount of brain stimulation necessary for a designated level of performance.

As previously discussed, systemic neuroleptics shift the curve to the right; when sufficient doses are used, they can also shift the curve down (68). In our experiments, a dose of pimozide was used that shifted the curve both down and to the right (Fig. 3). When ventral tegmental morphine was given after pretreatment with pimozide (the morphine was given 4 hours after the pimozide, at a time approaching peak pimozide effectiveness; see ref 69), morphine reversed the rightward but not the downward shift caused by pimozide—up to a point (Fig. 3). The fact that morphine reversed the rightward but not the downward effect of pimozide confirms the assumption that the rightward and downward shifts are two independent effects of pimozide; the finding fits with the earlier-cited evidence that rightward shifts reflect alterations in the rewarding effects of the stimulation while downward shifts reflect change in the animal's performance capacity. Morphine appears to reverse pimozide's ability to attenuate the rewarding effects of stimulation, but it does not reverse pimozide's high-dose (2,68) effects on performance capacity.

In our first study (66), morphine reversed the effects of pimozide in four animals but caused complete disruption of responding in two others. While the effects seen in the first four animals (subsequently confirmed in additional animals) confirm that dopa-

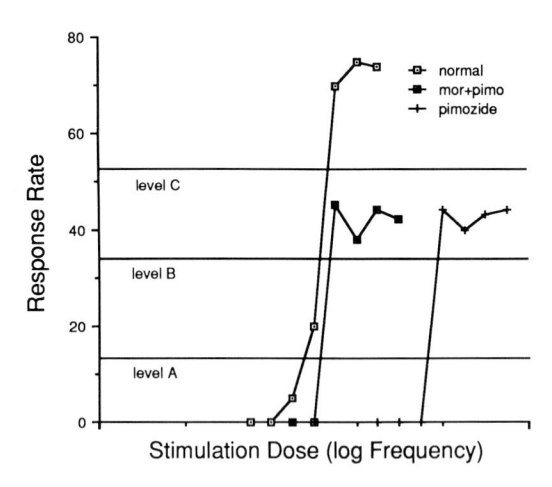

FIG. 3. Rate-frequency functions for an animal given ventral tegmental injections of saline (normal), of morphine (mor) following pretreatment with pimozide (pimo), or of vehicle (normal). Pimozide shifted the rate-frequency function to the right and down; morphine reversed the rightward shift but did not affect the downward shift. Moderate doses are shown; details on the effects of various doses are reported elsewhere (see refs 66,67).

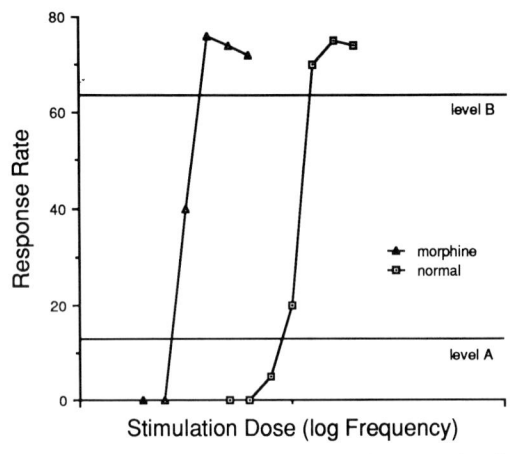

FIG. 2. Rate-frequency functions for an animal given ventral tegmental injections of morphine or saline (normal). Morphine shifted the rate-frequency function to the left, with no change in maximum performance level.

mine plays an important role in the rewarding effects of opiates, it is the effects seen in the remaining two animals that may prove to be of greatest interest to biological psychiatrists. Why should ventral tegmental morphine, which served as an antidote to pimozide in the four animals just mentioned, serve to augment the disruptive effects of pimozide in the two other animals?

One hypothesis is that, while reversing the antireward effects of pimozide, ventral tegmental morphine augments pimozide's cataleptic side effects. We think this unlikely, since, while each drug has sedative side effects, the cataleptic effect of pimozide (70) is quite different from the sedation caused by opiates (71). Moreover, the sites of morphine's sedative actions do not include the ventral tegmental area (72,73), where our morphine was administered. Thus we hypothesize that morphine disrupted responding in the two pimozide-treated animals by overstimulating (or, more precisely, by overdisinhibiting) the dopamine system, driving it into a state of depolarization inactivation. To understand this hypothesis, it is necessary to have some familiarity with the effects of neuroleptics on the firing of dopaminergic neurons.

While neuroleptics serve as competitive antagonists at postsynaptic dopamine receptors, they also block dopamine autoreceptors; thus one effect of acute neuroleptic treatment is to release the dopamine neurons from self-inhibition, increasing their firing rate. When animals are treated chronically with neuroleptics, however, a paradoxical effect is seen; the firing of spontaneously active dopamine neurons is accelerated, but the number of spontaneously active cells is dramatically reduced (37). Bunney and Grace hypothesized that the chronic acceleration of dopaminergic firing caused by 3 weeks of haloperidol treatment might have driven many of the cells into a state of depolarization inactivation (37).

This prescient hypothesis has now been confirmed by extracellular and intracellular recording studies. Grace and Bunney have shown, first, the increasing degrees of stimulation (by electrical stimulation or by local ejections of potassium or glutamate) accelerate these cells from a slow, regular firing pattern to accelerated, bursting patterns (74). Low levels of stimulation cause the cells to fire in couplets; higher levels of stimulation cause triplets and then bursts of four or five firings. When further stimulation is applied, the cells cease firing. If the silent cells are stimulated further with glutamate (a depolarizing agent that normally increases dopamine cell firing), the silent state is not reversed. However, if GABA (a hyperpolarizing agent that normally decreases dopamine cell firing) is given, it reinstates accelerated firing. Intracellular recording (75) confirms that the overstimulated neurons are in a state of depolarization, which is an overexcited state, and not hyperpolarization, which is the state caused by normal inhibitory processes.

Grace and Bunney (37) have suggested that a state of depolarization inactivation of the dopamine system may represent the condition in which psychotic symptoms go into true remission. In this state, the dopamine system is much more effectively antagonized than in the state of acute neuroleptic treatment. With acute treatment, the postsynaptic output of the dopamine system is antagonized, but the synaptic release of dopamine is elevated in partial compensation for the blockade. With chronic treatment the presynaptic release of dopamine is reduced, complementing the postsynaptic receptor blockade. Perhaps it is the presynaptic shutdown of the dopamine neurons that is required for truly effective treatment.

In any case, our hypothesis as to why two of the animals ceased to respond to brain stimulation after the combination of systemic pimozide and ventral tegmental morphine is that the excitatory effects of the two drugs combined to drive a significant portion of the mesolimbic dopamine system into depolarization inactivation. High doses of either neuroleptics (76) or opiates (47) can by themselves cause depolarization inactivation of dopaminergic neurons.

We tested our hypothesis in two additional ways. First, we retested our six animals with a higher dose of morphine. In this condition, morphine disrupted responding in all animals, suggesting that our original dose had been marginal for this effect (67). Second, we attempted to reverse the effects of the new dose by giving ventral tegmental injections of muscimol, a long-acting analogue of the inhibitory transmitter, GABA, that reinstated firing of Grace and Bunney's inactivated single neurons. Muscimol normally inhibits self-stimulation, shifting the rate-frequency function to the right; in these animals, however, it reinstated responding, often bringing the threshold (which muscimol normally elevates) to lower levels than were seen with the neuroleptic alone (77).

These data have two important implications. First, they confirm that opiates interact with dopaminergic reward circuitry. While it is now clear that this interaction is not the only rewarding effect of opiates (54–58), it would appear to account for the rewarding effects of ventral tegmental morphine injections. Moreover, we find that ventral tegmental morphine interacts equally with medial-forebrain-bundle and midline mesencephalic brain stimulation reward, suggesting that both these reward sites depend on dopaminergic systems that morphine can activate (65).

Second, and perhaps more important for biological psychiatry, our data suggest that depolarization inactivation of dopamine neurons can occur with behaviorally relevant doses of neuroleptics and opiates. Depolarization inactivation of the dopamine system is not merely an electrophysiological curiosity; it might be, as Bunney and Grace suggested over a decade ago, a behaviorally relevant phenomenon. It does not play a role in the blockade of psychomotor stimulant reward because psychomotor stimulants increase self-inhibition of dopamine cell firing, acting in the opposite way to morphine on the presynaptic release of dopamine. However, depolarization inactivation of the dopamine system plays a clear role in blockade of opiate reward by neuroleptics, and it offers a viable explanation for the lack of robust compensatory increases in intravenous heroin intake in neuroleptic-treated animals (15,52,53,77). Whereas animals simply take more intravenous amphetamine or cocaine in response to low and moderate doses of neuroleptics (4–6,15), such compensatory responding does not reliably occur with heroin self-administration (15,52,53,77). The likely explanation is that the combination of heroin and neuroleptic causes depolarization inactivation of the dopamine system, resulting in decreased synaptic dopamine rather than the compensatory increases that are seen when increased amphetamine or cocaine are taken. This is clearly a post hoc explanation that requires direct experimental testing (which is underway). One test of the notion would be to use a neuroleptic that does not cause depolarization inactivation of the dopamine system because it does not block the self-regulatory feedback controls of dopamine cell firing. While the self-regulation of dopamine neurons is only partially controlled by autoreceptors, the D_1 dopamine antagonist SCH 23390, which has no effects at dopamine autoreceptors, has less ability than D_2 antagonists to accelerate the firing of dopamine neurons and to cause depolarization inactivation of dopamine cells (78,79). When we challenge intravenous heroin self-administration with SCH 23390, we do find a significant range of doses that cause compensatory increases in heroin self-administration (53); this finding is consistent with the view that depolarization inactivation makes compensatory attempts ineffective when heroin self-administration is challenged by D_2 antagonists.

Thus recent studies add opiates to the list

of rewards that are blocked or attenuated by neuroleptic treatment. Moreover, they suggest that an even more dramatic attenuation of hedonic processes is produced when chronic neuroleptic treatment causes depolarization inactivation of a significant number of dopaminergic neurons, as is hypothesized to occur during effective treatment of schizophrenia. When the phrase "neuroleptic-induced anhedonia" was coined a decade ago, it was intended to attract the interest of biological psychiatrists and call attention to the finding that antipsychotic drugs cause in laboratory animals a state listed as a symptom of the human condition they are used to treat. A part of the paradox may be explained by the distinction between positive and negative symptoms in schizophrenia; perhaps the efficacy of neuroleptics involves alleviation of positive symptoms, while the blunting of reward (if it occurs in psychotic patients) represents a side effect of relevance to negative symptoms. Whatever the explanation, it should be of great interest to biological psychiatrists that both acute and chronic neuroleptic treatments appear to cause affective blunting in laboratory animals.

REFERENCES

1. Wise RA. Neuroleptics and operant behavior: The anhedonia hypothesis. *Behav Brain Sci* 1982;5:39–87.
2. Wise RA. The anhedonia hypothesis: Mark III. *Behav Brain Sci* 1985;8:178–186.
3. Wise RA, Spindler J, de Wit H, Gerber GJ. Neuroleptic-induced "anhedonia" in rats: pimozide blocks the reward quality of food. *Science* 1978;201:262–264.
4. Yokel RA, Wise RA. Increased lever pressing for amphetamine after pimozide in rats: implications for a dopamine theory of reward. *Science* 1975;187:547–549.
5. Yokel RA, Wise RA. Attenuation of intravenous amphetamine reinforcement by central dopamine blockade in rats. *Psychopharmacology* 1976;48:311–318.
6. De Wit H, Wise RA. Blockade of cocaine reinforcement in rats with the dopamine receptor blocker pimozide but not with the noradrenergic blockers phentolamine or phenoxybenzamine. *Can J Psychol* 1977;31:195–203.
7. Fouriezos G, Hansson P, Wise RA. Neuroleptic-induced attenuation of brain stimulation reward in rats. *J Compar Physiol Psychol* 1978;92:661–671.
8. Fouriezos G, Wise RA. Pimozide-induced extinction of intracranial self-stimulation: response patterns rule out motor or performance deficits. *Brain Res* 1976;103;377–380.
9. Wise RA, Spindler J, Legault L. Major attenuation of food reward with performance sparing doses of pimozide in the rat. *Can J Psychol* 1978;32:77–85.
10. Gerber GJ, Sing J, Wise RA. Pimozide attenuates lever pressing for water reinforcement in rats. *Pharmacol Biochem Behav* 1981;14:201–205.
11. Fibiger HC, Carter DA, Phillips AG. Decreased intracranial self-stimulation after neuroleptics or 6-hydroxydopamine: evidence for mediation by motor deficits rather than by reduced reward. *Psychopharmacology* 1976;47:21–27.
12. Koob GF. The dopamine anhedonia hypothesis: a pharmacological phrenology. *Behav Brain Sci* 1982;5:63–64.
13. Tombaugh TN, Anisman H, Tombaugh J. Extinction and dopamine receptor blockade after intermittent reinforcement: failure to observe functional equivalence. *Psychopharmacology* 1980;70:19–28.
14. Gramling SE, Fowler SC, Collins KR. Some effets of pimozide on nondeprived rats licking sucrose solutions in an anhedonia paradigm. *Pharmacol Biochem Behav* 1984;21:617–624.
15. Ettenberg A, Pettit HO, Bloom FE, Koob GF. Heroin and cocaine intravenous self-administration in rats: mediation by separate neural systems. *Psychopharmacology* 1982;78:204–209.
16. Fibiger HC. Drugs and reinforcement mechanisms: a critical review of the catecholamine theory. *Annu Rev Pharmacol Toxicol* 1978;18:37–56.
17. Koob GF, Goeders N. Neuroanatomical substrates of drug self-administration. In: Liebman JM, Cooper SJ, eds. *Neuropharmacological basis of reward*. Oxford: Oxford University Press, 1989;214–263.
18. Mason ST, Beninger RJ, Fibiger HC, Phillips AG. Pimozide-induced suppression of responding: evidence against a block of food reward. *Pharmacol Biochem Behav* 1980;12:917–923.
19. Milgram NW. On the generality of the anhedonia hypothesis. *Behav Brain Sci* 1982;5:69.
20. Phillips AG. Brain reward circuitry: a case for separate systems. *Brain Res Bull* 1984;12:195–201.
21. Beninger RJ, Cheng M, Hahn BL, Hoffman DC, Mazurski EJ, Morency MA, Ramm P, Stewart RJ. Effects of extinction, pimozide, SCH 23390, and metoclopramide on food-rewarded operant responding of rats. *Psychopharmacology* 1987;92:343–349.
22. Ettenberg A, Camp CH. Haloperidol induces a partial reinforcement extinction effect in rats: implications for a dopamine involvement in food reward. *Pharmacol Biochem Behav* 1986;25:813–821.

23. Spyraki C, Fibiger HC, Phillips AG. Attenuation by haloperidol of place preference conditioning using food reinforcement. *Psychopharmacology* 1982;77:379–382.
24. Davis WM, Smith SG. Effect of haloperidol on (+)-amphetamine self-administration. *J Pharm Pharmacol* 1975;27:540–542.
25. Ettenberg A, Camp CH. A partial reinforcement extinction effect in water-reinforced rats intermittently treated with haloperidol. *Pharmacol Biochem Behav* 1986;25:1231–1235.
26. Gallistel CR, Boytim M, Gomita Y, Klebanoff L. Does pimozide block the reinforcing effect of brain stimulation? *Pharmacol Biochem Behav* 1982;17:769–781.
27. Bozarth MA, Wise RA. Heroin reward is dependent on a dopaminergic substrate. *Life Sci* 1981;29:1881–1886.
28. Feldon J, Katz Y, Weiner I. The effects of haloperidol on the partial reinforcement extinction effect (PREE): implications for neuroleptic drug action on reinforcement and nonreinforcement. *Psychopharmacology* 1988;95:528–533.
29. Spyraki C, Fibiger HC, Phillips AG. Dopaminergic substrates of amphetamine-induced place preference conditioning. *Brain Res* 1982;253:185–193.
30. Morency MA, Beninger RJ. Dopaminergic substrates of cocaine-induced place conditioning. *Brain Res* 1986;399:33–41.
31. Nomikos GG, Spyraki C. Cocaine-induced place conditioning: importance of route of administration and other procedural variables. *Psychopharmacology* 1988;94:119–125.
32. Spyraki C, Fibiger HC, Phillips AG. Attenuation of heroin reward in rats by disruption of the mesolimbic dopamine system. *Psychopharmacology* 1983;79:278–283.
33. Bozarth MA. Neuroanatomical boundaries of the reward-relevant opiate-receptor field in the ventral tegmental area as mapped by the conditioned place preference method in rats. *Brain Res* 1987;414:77–84.
34. Wise RA, Bozarth MA. A psychomotor stimulant theory of addiction. *Psychol Rev* 1987;94:469–492.
35. Liebman JM. Understanding neuroleptics: from "anhedonia" to "neuroleptothesia." *Behav Brain Sci* 1982;5:64–65.
36. Rech RH. Neurolepsis: anhedonia or blunting of emotional reactivity? *Behav Brain Res* 1982;5:72–73.
37. Bunney BS, Grace AA. Acute and chronic haloperidol treatment: comparison of effects on nigral dopaminergic cell activity. *Life Sci* 1978;23:1715–1728.
38. Broekkamp CLE, Van den Bogaard JH, Heijnen HJ, Rops RH, Cools AR, Van Rossum JM. Separation of inhibiting and stimulating effects of morphine on self-stimulation behavior by intracerebral microinjections. *Eur J Pharmacol* 1976;36:443–446.
39. Lyness WH, Friedle NM, Moore KE. Destruction of dopaminergic nerve terminals in nucleus accumbens: effect on *d*-amphetamine self-administration. *Pharmacol Biochem Behav* 1979;11:553–556.
40. Roberts DCS, Corcoran ME, Fibiger HC. On the role of ascending catecholaminergic systems in intravenous self-administration of cocaine. *Pharmacol Biochem Behav* 1977;6:615–620.
41. Roberts DCS, Koob GF, Klonoff P, Fibiger HC. Extinction and recovery of cocaine self-administration following 6-OHDA lesions of the nucleus accumbens. *Pharmacol Biochem Behav* 1980;12:781–787.
42. Broekkamp CLE. *The modulation of rewarding systems in the animal brain by amphetamine, morphine, and apomorphine.* Druk: Stichting Studentenpers Nijmegen, 1976.
43. West TEG, Wise RA. Nucleus accumbens opioids facilitate brain stimulation reward. *Soc Neurosci Abstr* 1988;14:1102.
44. Bozarth MA, Wise RA. Intracranial self-administration of morphine into the ventral tegmental area of rats. *Life Sci* 1981;28:551–555.
45. Holmes LJ, Bozarth MA, Wise RA. Circling from intracranial morphine applied to the ventral tegmental area in rats. *Brain Res Bull* 1983;11:295–298.
46. Holmes LJ, Wise RA. Dopamine-dependent contralateral circling induced by neurotensin applied unilaterally to the ventral tegmental area in rats. *Brain Res Bull* 1985;15:537–538.
47. Joyce EM, Iversen SD. The effect of morphine applied locally to mesencephalic dopamine cell bodies on spontaneous motor activity in the rat. *Neurosci Lett* 1979;14:207–212.
48. Matthews RT, German DC. Electrophysiological evidence for excitation of rat ventral tegmental area dopaminergic neurons by morphine. *Neuroscience* 1984;11:617–626.
49. Ostrowski NL, Hatfield CB, Caggiula AR. The effects of low doses of morphine on the activity of dopamine containing cells and on behavior. *Life Sci* 1982;31:2347–2350.
50. Di Chiara G, Imperato A. Drugs of abuse preferentially stimulate dopamine release in the mesolimbic system of freely moving rats. *Proc Natl Acad Sci USA* 1988;85:5274–5278.
51. Phillips AG, LePiane FG. Reinforcing effects of morphine microinjection into the ventral tegmental area. *Pharmacol Biochem Behav* 1980;12:965–968.
52. Gerber GJ, Wise RA. Pharmacological regulation of intravenous cocaine and heroin self-administration in rats: a variable dose paradigm. *Pharmacol Biochem Behav* 1989;32:527–531.
53. Nakajima S, Wise RA. Heroin self-administration in the rat suppressed by SCH 23390. *Soc Neurosci Abstr* 1987;13:1545.
54. Britt MD, Wise RA. Ventral tegmental site of opiate reward: antagonism by a hydrophilic opiate receptor blocker. *Brain Res* 1983;258:105–108.
55. Vaccarino FJ, Bloom FE, Koob GF. Blockade of nucleus accumbens opiate receptors attenuates intravenous heroin reward in the rat. *Psychopharmacology* 1985;86:37–42.
56. Goeders NE, Lane JD, Smith JE. Self-adminis-

tration of methionine enkephalin into the nucleus accumbens. *Pharmacol Biochem Behav* 1984;20:451–455.
57. Olds ME. Reinforcing effects of morphine in the nucleus accumbens. *Brain Res* 1982;237:429–440.
58. Van der Kooy D, Mucha RF, O'Shaughnessy M, Bucenieks P. Reinforcing effects of brain microinjections of morphine revealed by conditioned place preference. *Brain Res* 1982;243:107–117.
59. Wise RA, Rompre P-P. Brain dopamine and reward. *Annu Rev Psychol* 1989;40:191–225.
60. Liebman JM. Discriminating between reward and performance: a critical review of intracranial self-stimulation methodology. *Neurosci Biobehav Rev* 1983;7:45–72.
61. Gallistel CR, Shizgal P, Yeomans J. A portrait of the substrate for self-stimulation. *Psychol Rev* 1981;88:228–273.
62. Stellar JR, Neeley SP. Reward summation function measurements of lateral hypothalamic stimulation reward: effects of anterior and posterior medial forebrain bundle lesions. In: Hoebel BG, Novin DG, eds. *The neural basis of feeding and reward*. Brunswick, Me: Haer Institute, 1982; 431–443.
63. Gallistel CR, Freyd G. Quantitative determination of the effects of catecholaminergic agonists and antagonists on the rewarding efficacy of brain stimulation. *Pharmacol Biochem Behav* 1987;26:731–741.
64. Gallistel CR, Karras D. Pimozide and amphetamine have opposing effects on the reward summation function. *Pharmacol Biochem Behav* 1984;20:73–77.
65. Rompre P-P, Wise R. A study of the interactions of pimozide, morphine and muscimol on brain stimulation reward: behavioral evidence for depolarization inactivation of A10 dopaminergic neurons. *Ann NY Acad Sci* 1988;537:525–528.
66. Rompre PP, Wise RA. Opioid neuroleptic interaction in brainstem self-stimulation. *Brain Res* 1989;477:144–151.
67. Rompre PP, Wise RA. Behavioral evidence for midbrain dopamine depolarization inactivation. *Brain Res* 1989;477:152–156.
68. Stellar JR, Kelley AE, Corbett D. Effects of peripheral and central dopamine blockade on lateral hypothalamic self-stimulation: evidence for both reward and motor deficits. *Pharmacol Biochem Behav* 1983;18:433–442.
69. Atalay J, Wise RA. Time-course of pimozide effects on brain stimulation reward. *Pharmacol Biochem Behav* 1983;18:655–658.
70. Janssen PAJ, Niemegeers CJE, Schellekens KHL, Dreese A, Lenaerts FM, Pinchard A, Schaper WKA, Van Nueten JM. Pimozide, a chemically novel, highly potent and orally long-acting neuroleptic drug. *Arzneim Forsch* 1968; 18:261–279.
71. Segal DS, Browne RG, Bloom FE, Ling N, Guillemin R. β-Endorphine: endogenous opiate or neuroleptic? *Science* 1977;198:411–414.
72. Havemann U, Winkler M, Kuschinsky K. Is morphine-induced akinesia related to inhibition of reflex activation of flexor α-motoneurones? Role of the nucleus accumbens. *Naunyn-Schmiedeb Arch Pharmacol* 1982;320:101–104.
73. Broekkamp CLE, LePichon M, Lloyd KG. Akinesia after locally applied morphine near the nucleus raphe pontis of the rat. *Neurosci Lett* 1984;50:313–318.
74. Grace AA, Bunney BS. Intracellular and extracellular electrophysiology of nigral dopaminergic neurons—2. Action potential generating mechanisms and morphological correlates. *Neuroscience* 1983;10:317–331.
75. Grace AA, Bunney BS. Induction of depolarization block in midbrain dopamine neurons by repeated administration of haloperidol: analysis using in vivo intracellular recording. *J Pharmacol Exp Ther* 1986;238:1092–1100.
76. Hand TH, Hu X-T, Wang RY. Differential effects of acute clozapine and haloperidol on the activity of ventral tegmental (A10) and nigrostriatal (A9) dopamine neurons. *Brain Res* 1987; 415:257–269.
77. Smith SG, Davis WM. Haloperidol effects on morphine self-administration: testing for pharmacological modification of the primary reinforcement mechanism. *Psychol Rec* 1973;23:215–221.
78. Hand TH, Kasser RJ, Wang RY. Effects of acute thioridazine, metoclopramide and SCH 23390 on the basal activity of A9 and A10 dopamine cells. *Eur J Pharmacol* 1987;137:251–255.
79. Skarsfeldt T. Effect of chronic treatment with SCH 23390 and haloperidol on spontaneous activity of dopamine neurones in substantia nigra pars compacta (SNC) and ventral tegmental area (VTA) in rats. *Eur J Pharmacol* 1988;145:239–243.

33

Dopaminergic and Serotoninergic Mechanisms in the Action of Clozapine

Herbert Y. Meltzer[1]

Recent multicenter trials have shown that clozapine may be a more effective antipsychotic agent than chlorpromazine in chronic schizophrenic patients with TD (1) as well as in treatment-resistant schizophrenic patients (2). Some earlier studies also reported clozapine to be equal to or superior to typical antipsychotic drugs in the treatment of schizophrenia (3). We have recently found that clozapine produces gradually increasing improvement in 50% to 60% of treatment-resistant schizophrenic patients for at least the first 12 months of treatment (4). Clozapine was found to be superior to chlorpromazine for both positive and negative symptoms both at 6 weeks and at longer intervals and to produce often dramatic increases in social function. These results agree with retrospective Scandinavian studies (5–7). Clozapine has also been shown not to elevate plasma prolactin levels in humans (8) and to produce fewer extrapyramidal symptoms than typical antipsychotic drugs (9–10). The same is true of other atypical drugs such as melperone (11), fluperlapine (12), and RMI 81582 (13). Furthermore, there is no reliable evidence that either clozapine or melperone produces tardive dyskinesia (TD) or tardive dystonia. Despite this, clozapine can block the symptoms of TD (14).

The four clinical advantages of clozapine might have the same underlying biological basis or have two or more unique etiologies (15). It seems most probable that a common mechanism is involved, but, as discussed below, this is likely to be complex and multifaceted. It seems intuitively likely that low EPS and the apparent absence of TD are based on the same mechanism. As will be discussed later, the lack of effect of clozapine on plasma [prolactin] levels in humans could be due to the ability of clozapine to increase dopamine (DA) release in the median eminence (16), which contains the terminals of the tuberoinfundibular (TIDA) neurons that are critical to control of prolactin secretion. Clozapine also increases DA release in other DA terminal areas (17). The ability of clozapine to increase DA release may be the consequence of a number of aspects of its pharmacology, which could differ from region to region. The intriguing possibility that the enhanced antipsychotic efficacy of clozapine is also based in part on its ability to modulate DA release will be discussed in detail below. Finally, the importance of clozapine as a serotonin (5HT) antagonist and its ability to increase 5HT release will be emphasized and the importance of the relationship between $5HT_2$ and D_2 antagonism considered.

---

[1]Department of Psychiatry, Case Western Reserve University School of Medicine, Cleveland, OH 44106.

SELECTIVE EFFECTS ON MESOLIMBIC VERSUS MESOSTRIATAL DA NEURONS

The basis for neuroleptic-induced EPS has been thought to be blockade of DA D_2 receptors in the striatum (18). Clozapine's affinity for the striatal D_2 receptor is 101 nM, which is low relative to chlorpromazine (3.0 nM) and haloperidol (1.10 nM; ref 19). Nevertheless, the affinity of clozapine for the striatal D_2 receptor is in accord with its clinical potency as an antipsychotic drug (20).

Clozapine has a number of effects on brain dopaminergic activity. It produces a dose-dependent increase in rat striatal homovanillac acid (HVA), the major metabolite of DA, and an increase in DA synthesis (21,22). It also has been shown to antagonize the cataleptogenic effect of the neuroleptic prochlorperazine (21). In vivo dialysis studies have established that clozapine, acutely and chronically, can stimulate DA release from the rat striatum and nucleus accumbens (23). Thus, the blockade of DA receptors in the striatum by clozapine may be reversible, perhaps because of the increased release of DA (21) it provokes (see below). The antiserotoninergic effect of clozapine may also be relevant to this anticataleptogenic effect (see below).

There has been much interest in the possibility that clozapine acts through a selective effect on the mesolimbic system, leaving intact the nigrostriatal system. However, the ability of clozapine to increase DA turnover in the striatum does not appear to differ between the striatum and nucleus accumbens (24–30), but there is some contrary evidence (31). The ability of clozapine to block the symptoms of TD (14) strongly suggests that it does affect the nigrostriatal pathway. However, this might be an indirect effect, through a nondopaminergic mechanism. Clozapine has also been shown to block D_2 receptor binding in the human striatum using ^{11}C-raclopride, but the effect is slightly less than that of other antipsychotic drugs (32). Chronic neuroleptic but not chronic clozapine administration to rodents does not appear to induce striatal D_2 receptor supersensitivity as indicated by behavioral and receptor binding site data (33–39), but two studies have suggested increased stereotypy and D_2 binding sites (40,41). One study reported increased striatal D_1 receptor binding after 9 to 12 months of ^{3}H-piflutixol administration (42), but this needs to be replicated and additional time periods studied, perhaps using a more selective D_1 ligand. The apparent inability of clozapine to produce D_2 receptor supersensitivity could be relevant to the failure of clozapine to produce tardive dyskinesia, but there is no definitive evidence that increased striatal D_2 receptor sensitivity underlies TD.

The effect of acute clozapine administration on DA neuron firing is to increase the rate in the ventral tegmental (A10) but not the nigrostriatal (A9) DA neurons (43–45), although one study reported an increase in the firing rate of both the A9 and A10 neurons. This is more consistent with the results of in vivo dialysis (23). The effect of chronic clozapine administration on the DA neuron firing rate has been reported to be a decrease in the firing rate of the A10 but not of the A9 neurons (43,44). This has been attributed to so-called depolarization inactivation (i.e., an inability of these DA neurons to depolarize due to excessive activity). The selective inactivation of the A10 system was postulated to account for the ability of clozapine to diminish psychotic symptoms, while the maintenance of A9 activity was thought to account for the absence of EPS. This is an interesting hypothesis, but it seems likely that a total inactivation of the A10 neurons would have some major consequences of an adverse nature. Furthermore, the in vivo dialysis suggests that DA release is not selectively decreased in the A10 region by chronic clozapine (23).

Clozapine has been shown to produce an acute increase in the activity of TIDA neurons in the rat (46). This could account for the short-lived increased in prolactin secretion in clozapine-treated rats (47,48). Similar effects have been noted with other atypical antipsychotic drugs (e.g., melperone and amperozide; ref 46). There is some evidence that both neurotensin and 5HT are involved in this effect (47,49). A similar mechanism may account for the lack of effect of clozapine on prolactin secretion in humans.

There is extensive evidence for an effect of clozapine on D_1 DA neurons, which has been reviewed elsewhere (49). Various authors have suggested that this effect can account for the atypical properties of clozapine (50–53). However, clozapine has a modest in vitro affinity for the D_1 DA receptor (146 nM with ^{3}H-SCH 23390 as the ligand; ref 19). This is much less than that of even haloperidol (91 nM), so this is unlikely to be the basis for any unique action mediated through the D_1 mechanism unless there is a marked discrepancy between in vitro affinity and in vivo effects. This will be discussed further after considering the evidence for the importance of the effect of clozapine on 5HT$_2$ mechanisms.

CLOZAPINE AND SEROTONIN

Clozapine has some ability to increase rat brain 5HT turnover (54–56), but it appears rather weak in this regard. Further study on its effect on 5HT turnover in specific areas (e.g., the hippocampus) seem of interest. Clozapine has been found to be a potent 5HT antagonist in vivo (57–64). For example, it blocks the 5-hydroxytryptophan (5-HTP)–induced head twitch in rats (59). This effect of 5-HTP is believed to be mediated by stimulation of 5HT$_2$ receptors. On the other hand, it does not block 5HT$_{1A}$ receptor-mediated effects (63). Clozapine can block the ability of MK-212, a probable 5HT$_2$ agonist, to stimulate corticosteroid secretion in rodents (63) and humans (15). Other antipsychotic drugs, even though they have a high in vitro affinity for 5HT$_2$ receptors (e.g., chlorpromazine), do not have this effect (63,15).

Because of the evidence that 5HT antagonists can inhibit neuroleptic-induced catalepsy (65), as well as for other reasons, there have been numerous suggestions that the atypical properties of clozapine may be related to its 5HT$_2$ antagonism (57,60,63, 64,66). Clozapine, in addition to being a direct acting antagonist of 5HT$_2$ receptors, can downregulate rat cortical 5HT$_2$ receptors (67–69). However, this effect is not unique to atypical antipsychotic drugs since loxapine and chlorpromazine can also do so (69). There is some evidence from studies of brain slices that clozapine can enhance 5HT release (70). This needs to be further studied in intact rats, by in vivo dialysis or other methods. Increased 5HT release, in the face of selective blockade of 5HT$_2$ receptors, can lead to increased stimulation of other 5HT receptor subtypes (e.g., 5HT$_{1A}$, 5HT$_{1D}$, and 5HT$_3$ receptors). We have noted a tendency for chronic clozapine treatment to enhance the ability of buspirone, a 5HT$_{1A}$ agonist, to stimulate cortisol and prolactin secretion in schizophrenic patients (Meltzer et al., in preparation). This could be due to upregulation of 5HT$_{1A}$ receptors as well as to enhanced 5HT release.

CLOZAPINE AND THE 5HT$_2$/D$_2$ RATIO

As just reviewed, there is considerable interest in the possible importance of the D_2, D_1, and 5HT$_2$ antagonist properties of clozapine as the basis for its unique and highly advantageous profile of effects on mesolimbic, mesocortical, nigrostriatal, and TIDA neurons. These same questions have been raised about other atypical antipsychotic drugs.

In a recent study (19), my colleagues and I examined the relative importance of these three attributes by measuring the pK_i values of a large group of typical and atypical antipsychotic drugs for rat striatal D_1 and D_2 and cortical $5HT_2$ receptor binding of antipsychotic drugs. Drugs were classified as atypical if any of the following held:

1. Clinical trials indicated antipsychotic activity with minimal EPS;
2. Clinical experience suggested no causation of TD or elevation of serum prolactin levels;
3. Preclinical studies demonstrated no or weak cataleptic potential.

The compounds studied are listed in Table 1.

We first examined the pK_i values for the three binding sites of a group of 13 typical and 7 atypical antipsychotic drugs for which there is clinical as well as preclinical data, in order to classify them as typical or atypical (the reference compounds). All compounds that produce large increases in serum prolactin levels and/or high EPS were classified as typical. They were used to develop a discriminant function that was then used to classify 17 other drugs less certainly classified as atypical or typical antipsychotic drugs. These 17 compounds comprise the *test* group. The test compounds were a priori classified as typical or atypical on the basis of the clinical criteria cited above, if available, or on the basis of producing weak or no catalepsy in rodents. The classification of the reference and test compounds on the basis of the clinical and preclinical evidence was then compared with that provided by the discriminant function. To confirm our results, a cluster analysis of the compounds based only on the ratio of the pK_i values for the $5HT_2$ and D_2 receptor binding sites was carried out.

The atypical antipsychotic drugs had significantly lower pK_i values for the D_2 but not the $5HT_2$ binding sites. There was a trend for a lower pK_i value for the D_1 binding site for the atypical antipsychotic drugs. The $5HT_2$ and D_1 pK_i values were correlated for the typical antipsychotic drugs, whereas the $5HT_2$ and D_2 pK_i values were correlated for the atypical antipsychotic drugs. The $5HT_2/D_1$ and $5HT_2/D_2$ ratios were significantly lower in the typical compared with the atypical antipsychotic drugs. There was a trend in the same direction for the D_1/D_2 group. There was *no* overlap in the $5HT_2/D_2$ ratio of the atypical group (1.13–1.26) and the typical group (0.81–2.09).

TABLE 1. *Typical and atypical compounds*

Typical		Atypical	
Reference	Test	Reference	Test
Chlorpromazine	Thioridazine	Clozapine	Ritanserin
Trifluoperazine	Mesoridazine	Fluperlapine	Pipamperone
Fluphenazine	Amoxapine	RMI 81582	Rilapine
Perphenazine	Clothiapine	Melperone	Tenilapine
Prochlorperazine	Methiothepin	Amperozide	SCH 23390
Haloperidol	Spiperone	Setoperone	Perlapine
Moperone	Benperidol	Tiospirone	Zotepine
Pimozide			CGS 10746
cis-Flupentixol			HP 370
Thiothixene			FG 5803
Loxapine			
Molindone			
(+)Butaclamol			

A stepwise discriminant function analysis to determine the classification as a typical and atypical antipsychotic drug entered the D_2 pK_i value first, followed by the $5HT_2$ pK_i value. The D_1 pK_i value was not entered. A discriminant function analysis correctly classified 18 out of 20 of these compounds plus 15 of 17 additional test compounds as typical or atypical antipsychotic drugs for an overall correct classification rate of 89.2%. The atypical compounds that were misclassified were zotepine and HP 370. There is, however, controversy about whether zotepine is atypical (19). The typical compounds that were misclassified were loxapine and amoxapine, both of which are closely related to clozapine. The major contributors to the discriminant function factors were the D_2 and $5HT_2$ pK_i values. A cluster analysis based only on the $5HT_2/D_2$ ratio grouped 15 out of 17 atypical plus one typical antipsychotic drug in one cluster and 19 out of 20 typical plus two atypical antipsychotic drugs in a second cluster, for an overall correct classification rate of 91.9%. When the stepwise discriminant function was repeated for all 37 compounds, only the D_2 and $5HT_2$ pK_i values were entered into the discriminant function. These data suggest that determination of D_2 and $5HT_2$ pK_i values may be useful for rapid screening of prospective atypical antipsychotic drugs (ie, compounds that show a behavioral profile characteristic of an antipsychotic drug, with only minimal false positives).

We have discussed the possible importance of serotoninergic-dopaminergic interactions for the mechanism of action of clozapine and the biological basis of schizophrenia in some detail elsewhere (15,19,49). Briefly, the serotoninergic system may modulate the activity of all dopaminergic neurons, either directly or indirectly. In schizophrenia, excessive $5HT_2$ activity may contribute to dysregulation of dopaminergic activity such that there is increased D_2-mediated activity in the mesolimbic system and decreased activity in the mesocortical system, at least in those stages of the illness characterized by positive and negative symptoms. Clozapine, by virtue of its $5HT_2/D_2$ ratio, may decrease dopaminergic activity in the mesolimbic system and enhance it in the mesocortical system.

CONCLUSIONS

The evidence reviewed here suggests that the ability of clozapine to block D_2 and $5HT_2$ receptors and to enhance DA and 5HT release in a coordinated manner are the crucial characteristics that convey its unique clinical effects. If so, all four clinical advantages of clozapine noted in the beginning of the chapter may be related to the influence of this dopaminergic-serotoninergic complex on the nigrostriatal, mesolimbic, mesocortical, and TIDA neurons. Clozapine also has strong anticholinergic effects (71), anti-α-adrenergic effects (22, 72), β-adrenergic blocking properties (73), ability to increase GABA turnover in the striatum and decrease it in the substantia nigra (74), ability to enhance glutamatergic neurotransmission (75), and effects on neurotensin concentrations in discrete brain nuclei (76). It is not possible to be sure if any of those effects independently contributes to the four clinical advantages of clozapine discussed above or whether they are related to the dopaminergic-serotoninergic effects emphasized here and elsewhere (3,19,49). The hypothesis that one mechanism, however complex, is involved in all the unique features of clozapine seems to have the greatest heuristic value at this time.

ACKNOWLEDGMENTS

The work described in this chapter was supported, in part, by USPHS grants MH 41684, MH 41683, USPHS Research Career Scientist Award MH 47808, by NARSAD, and by the Laureate, Cleveland, and Sawyer Foundations. The assistance of Ms Diane Mack in preparing this manuscript is gratefully acknowledged.

REFERENCES

1. Claghorn J, Honigfeld G, Abuzzahab FS, Wang R, Steinbook R, Tuason V, Klerman G. The risks and benefits of clozapine versus chlorpromazine. *J Clin Psychopharmacol* 1987;7:377–384.
2. Kane J, Honigfeld G, Singer J, Meltzer H. Clozapine for the treatment-resistant schizophrenic: a double-blind comparison versus chlorpromazine/benztropine. *Arch Gen Psychiatry* 1988;45:789–796.
3. Honigfeld G, Patin J, Singer J. Clozapine: antipsychotic activity in treatment-resistant schizophrenics. *Adv Ther* 1984;1:77–97.
4. Meltzer HY, Bastani B, Kwon K, Ramirez L, Burnett S, Sharpe J. A prospective study of clozapine in treatment resistant schizophrenic patients. I: Preliminary Report. *Psychopharmacology* 1989;99(suppl):568–573.
5. Juul Polvsen V, Noring V, Fog R, Gerlach J. Tolerability and therapeutic effect of clozapine: a retrospective investigation of 216 patients treated with clozapine for up to 12 years. *Acta Psychiatr Scand* 1985;71:176–185.
6. Kuha S, Miettinen E. Long-term effect of clozapine in schizophrenia: a retrospective study of 108 chronic schizophrenics treated with clozapine for up to 7 years. *Nord Psychiatr Tidskr* 1986;40:225–230.
7. Lindström LH. The effect of long term treatment with clozapine in schizophrenia: a retrospective study in 96 patients treated with clozapine for up to 13 years. *Acta Psychiatr Scand* 1988;77:524–529.
8. Meltzer HY, Goode DJ, Schyve PM, Young M, Fang VS. Effect of clozapine on human serum prolactin levels. *Am J Psychiatry* 1979;136:1550–1555.
9. Angst J, Bente D, Berner P, Heimann H, Helmchen H, Hippius H. Das clinische Wirkungsbild von clozapine (untersuchung mit dem AMP-system). *Pharmakopsychiatrie* 1971;4:200–211.
10. Matz R, Rick W, Oh D, Thompson H, Gershon S. Clozapine, a potential antipsychotic agent without extrapyramidal manifestations. *Curr Ther Res* 1954;16:687–695.
11. Bjerkenstedt L, Härnryd C, Grimm V, Gullberg B, Sedvall B. A double-blind comparison of melperone and thiothixene in psychotic women using a new rating scale, the CPRS. *Arch Psychiatr Nervenkraz* 1978;226:157–172.
12. Woggon B, Angst J, Bartels M, et al. Antipsychotic efficacy of fluperlapine: an open multicenter trial. *Neuropsychobiology* 1984;11:116–120.
13. Young MA, Meltzer HY, Fang VS. RMI-81,582: a novel antipsychotic drug. *Psychopharmacology* 1980;67:101–106.
14. Casey DE. Clozapine: neuroleptic-induced EPS and tardive dyskinesia. *Psychopharmacology* 1989;99:547–548.
15. Meltzer HY. Clozapine: clinical advantages and biological mechanisms. In: Schulz C, Tamminga C, eds. *Schizophrenia: a scientific focus.* New York: Oxford Press, 1988;302–309.
16. Koenig JI, Gudelsky GA, Meltzer HY. Stimulation of corticosterone and β-endorphin secretion by selective 5-HT receptor subtype activation. *Eur J Pharmacol* 1987;137:1–8.
17. Imperato A, Angelucci L. Effects of the atypical neuroleptics clozapine and fluperlapine in the *in vivo* dopamine release in the dorsal striatum and in the prefrontal cortex. *Psychopharmacology* 1988;96(suppl 1):79. Abstracts of the XVI CINP Congress, Munich, 1988.
18. Meltzer HY, Stahl SM. The dopamine hypothesis of schizophrenia: a review. *Schizophr Bull* 1976;2:19–76.
19. Meltzer HY, Matsubara S, Lee J-C. Classification of typical and atypical antipsychotic drugs on the basis of dopamine D-1, D-2 and serotonin$_2$ pK_i values. *J Pharmacol Exp Ther* 1989;251:238–246.
20. Seeman P, Lee T, Chau-wong M, Wong K. Antipsychotic drugs doses and neuroleptic/dopamine receptors. *Nature* 1976;261:717–718.
21. Bartholini G, Haefely W, Jalfre M, Keller HH, Pletscher A. Effect of clozapine on cerebral catecholaminergic neurone systems. *Br J Pharmacol* 1972;46:736–740.
22. Burki HR, Ruch W, Asper H. Effects of clozapine, thioridazine, perlapine and haloperidol on the metabolism of the biogenic amines in the brain of the rat. *Psychopharmacologia (Berl)* 1975;41:27–33.
23. Ichikawa J, and Meltzer HY. The effect of chronic clozapine and haloperidol on basal dopamine release and metabolism in rat striatum and nucleus accumbens studies by *in vivo* microdialysis. *Eur J Pharmacol* 1990;176:371–374.
24. Bartholini G, Keller HH, Pletscher A. Drug-induced changes of dopamine turnover in striatum and limbic system of the rat. *J Pharm Pharmacol* 1975;27:439–442.
25. Westernik BHC and Korf J. Influence of drugs on striatal and limbic homovanillac acid concentration in the rat brain. *Eur J Pharmacol* 1975;33:31–40.
26. Stawarz RJ, Hill H, Robinson SE, Setter P, Dingell JV, Sulser F. On the significance of the increase in homovanillac acid (HVA) caused by antipsychotic drugs in corpus striatum and limbic forebrain. *Psychopharmacologia (Berl)* 1975;43:125–130.
27. Weisel FA, Sedvall G. Effects of antipsychotic drugs on homovanillac acid levels in striatum and olfactory tubercle of the rat. *Eur J Pharmacol* 1975;30:364–367.
28. Walters JR, Roth RH. Dopaminergic neurons: an *in vivo* system of measuring drug interactions

28. with presynaptic receptors. *Naunyn-Schmeideberg's Arch Pharmacol* 1976;296:5–14.
29. Wilk S, Watson E, Stanley ME. Differential sensitivity of two dopaminergic structures in rat brain to haloperidol and to clozapine. *J Pharmacol Exp Ther* 1975;195:265–270.
30. Waldmier PC, Maitre L. On the relevance of preferential increases of mesolimbic versus striatal dopamine turnover for the prediction of antipsychotic activity of psychotropic drugs. *J Neurochem* 1976;27:587–589.
31. Maidment NT, Marsden C. Acute administration of clozapine, thioridazine and metoclopramide increases extracellular DOPAC and decreases extracellular 5-HIAA, measured in the nucleus accumbens and striatum of the rat using *in vivo* voltammetry. *Neuropharmacology* 1987;26:187–193.
32. Fardé L, Wiesel F-A, Halldin C, Sedvall G. Central D2-dopamine receptor occupancy in schizophrenic patients treated with antipsychotic drugs. *Arch Gen Psychiatry* 1988;45:71–76.
33. Sayers AC, Burke AR, Ruch W, Asper H. Neuroleptic-induced hypersensitivity of striatal dopamine receptors in the rat as a model of tardive dyskinesias: effect of clozapine, haloperidol, loxapine and chlorpromazine. *Psychopharmacologis (Berl)* 1975;41:97–104.
34. Gnegy M, Uzunov P, Costa E. Participation of an endogenous Ca^{++}-binding protein activator in the development of drug-induced supersensitivity of striatal dopamine receptors. *J Pharmacol Exp Ther* 1977;202:558–564.
35. Kobayashi RM, Fields JZ, Hrusck RE, Beaumont K, Yamamura HI. Brain neurotransmitter receptors and chronic antipsychotic drug treatment: a model for tardive dyskinesia. In: Usdin E, ed. *Animal models in psychiatry* New York: Pergamon Press, 1978;405–409.
36. Racagni G, Bruno F, Bugatti A, Parenta M, Apud JA, Santini V, Carenzi G, Groppetti A, Cattabeni P. Behavioral and biochemical correlates after haloperidol and clozapine long-term treatment. *Adv Biochem Psychopharmacol* 1980;24:45–52.
37. Seeger TF, Thal L, Gardner EL. Behavioral and biochemical aspects of neuroleptic-induced dopaminergic supersensitivity. Studies with chronic clozapine and haloperidol. *Psychopharmacology* 1982;76;182–187.
38. Rupniak NMJ, Kilpatrick G, Hall MD, Jenner P, Marsden CD. Differential alterations in striatal dopamine receptor sensitivity induced by repeated administration of clinically equivalent doses of haloperidol, sulperide or clozapine in rats. *Psychopharmacology* 1984;84:512–519.
39. Rupniak NMJ, Hall MD, Mann S, Fleminger S, Kilpatrick G, Jenner P, Marsden CD. Chronic treatment with clozapine, unlike haloperidol, does not induce changes in striatal D-2 receptor function in the rat. *Biochem Pharmacol* 1985;34:2755–2763.
40. Smith RC, Davis JM. Behavioral evidence for supersensitivity after chronic administration of haloperidol. *Life Sci* 1976;19:725–732.
41. Allikmets LH, Zarkovsky AM, Nurk AM. Changes in catalepsy and receptor sensitivity following chronic neuroleptic treatment. *Eur J Pharmacol* 1981;75:145–147.
42. Rupniak NMJ, Hall MD, Kelly E, Fleminger S, Kilpatrick G, Jenner P, Marsden CD. Mesolimbic dopamine function is not altered during continuous or chronic treatment of rats with typical or atypical neuroleptic drugs. *J Neural Transm* 1985;62:249–266.
43. Chiodo LA, Bunney BS. Typical and atypical neuroleptics: differential effects of chronic administration on the activity of A9 and A10 midbrain dopaminergic neurons. *J Neurosci* 1983;3:1607–1619.
44. White FJ, Wang RY. Differential effects of classical and atypical antipsychotic drugs on A9 and A10 dopamine cells. *Science* 1983;221:1054–1057.
45. Hand TH, Hu X-T, Wang RY. Differential effects of acute clozapine and haloperidol on the activity of ventral tegmental (A10) and nigrostriatal (A9) dopamine neurons. *Brain Res* 1987;415:257–269.
46. Gudelsky GA, Meltzer HY. Activation of tuberoinfundibular dopamine neurons following the acute administration of atypical antipsychotics. *Neuropsychopharmacology* 1989;2:1:45–51.
47. Gudelsky GA, Berry SA, Meltzer HY. Neurotensin activates tuberoinfundibular dopamine neurons and increases serum corticosterone concentrations. *Neuroendocrinology* 1989;49:604–609.
48. Meltzer HY, Daniels S, Fang VS. Clozapine increases rat serum prolactin levels. *Life Sci* 1975;17:339–342.
49. Meltzer HY. Clozapine: mechanism of action in relation to its clinical advantages. In: Kales A, Stefanis CN, Talbott JA, eds. *Recent advances in schizophrenia*. New York: Springer-Verlag, 1990:237–246.
50. Andersen PH, Nielsen EB, Gronvald FC, Braestrup C. Some atypical neuroleptics inhibit [^{3}H] SCH-23390 binding *in vivo*. *Eur J Pharmacol* 1986;120:143–144.
51. Andersen PH, Braestrup C. Evidence for different states of the dopamine D-1 receptor: clozapine and fluperlapine may preferentially label an adenylate cyclase–coupled state of the D-1 receptor. *J Neurochem* 1986;47:1830–1831.
52. Chipkin RE, Latranyi MB. Similarity of clozapine and SCH 23390 in reserpinized rats suggests a common mechanism of action. *Eur J Pharmacol* 1987;136:371–375.
53. Altar CA, Boyar WC, Wasley A, Gerhardt SG, Liebman JM, Wood WL. Dopamine neurochemical profile of atypical antipsychotics resembles that of D-1 antagonists. *Naunyn-Schmiedeberg's Arch Pharmacol* 1988;338:162–168.
54. Maj J, Sowinska H, Boran L. Palider W. The central action of clozapine. *Pol J Pharmacol Pharm* 1974;26:425–435.
55. Ackenheil M, Beckmann H, Greil W, Hoffmann

G, Markianos E, Raese J. Antipsychotic efficacy of clozapine in correlation to changes in catecholamine metabolism in man. *Adv Biochem Psychopharmacol* 1974;9:647–658.
56. Ruch W, Asper H, Bürki HR. Effect of clozapine on the metabolism of serotonin in rat brain. *Psychopharmacologia (Berl)* 1976;46:103–109.
57. Sulpizio A, Fowler FJ, Macko E. Antagonism of fenfluramine-induced hyperthermia: a measure of central serotonin inhibition. *Life Sci* 1978;22:1439–1446.
58. Fjalland B. Neuroleptic influence on hyperthermia induced by 5-hydroxytryptophan and p-methoxyamphetamine in MAOI-pretreated rabbits. *Psychopharmacology* 1979;63:113–117.
59. Maj J, Baran L, Bigajska BK, Rogoz Z, Skuza G. The influence of neuroleptics on the behavioral effect of 5-hydroxytryptophan. *Pol J Pharmacol Pharm* 1978;30:431–440.
60. Lai H, Carino MA, Horita A. Antiserotonin properties of neuroleptic drugs. In: Yamamura HI, Olsen RW, Usdin E, eds. *Psychopharmacology and biochemistry of neurotransmitter receptor.* Amsterdam: Elsevier, N Holland, 1980; 347–353.
61. Fink H, Morgenstern R, Oelssner W. Clozapine—a serotonin antagonist? *Pharm Biochem Behav* 1984;20:513–517.
62. Friedman RL, Sanders-Bush E, Barrett RL. Clozapine blocks descriptive and discriminative stimulus effects of quipazine. *Eur J Pharmacol* 1985;106:191–193.
63. Nash JF, Meltzer HY, Gudelsky GA. Antagonism of serotonin receptor mediated neuroendocrine and temperature responses by atypical neuroleptics in the rat. *Eur J Pharmacol* 1988; 151:463–469.
64. Rasmussen K, Aghajanian GK. Potency of antipsychotics in reversing the effects of a hallucinogenic drug on locus coeruleus neurons correlates with 5-HT_2 binding affinity. *Neuropsychopharmacology* 1988;1:101–107.
65. Waldmeier PC, Delini-Atula AA. Serotonin-dopamine interactions in the nigrostriatal system. *Eur J Pharmacol* 1979;55:363–373.
66. Altar CA, Wasley AM, Neale RF, Stone GA. Typical and atypical antipsychotic occupancy of D2 and S_2 receptors: an autoradiographic analysis in rat brain. *Brain Res Bull* 1986;16:517–525.
67. Reynolds GP, Garrett NJ, Rupniak N, Jenner P, Marsden CR. Chronic clozapine treatment of rats down-regulates cortical 5-HT_2 receptors. *Eur J Pharmacol* 1983;89:325–326.
68. Lee T, Tang SW. Loxapine and clozapine decrease serotonin (S_2) but do not elevate dopamine (D_2) receptor numbers in the rat brain. *Psychiatry Res* 1984;12:277–285.
69. Matsubara S, Meltzer HY. Acute effects of neuroleptics on 5-HT_2 receptor density in rat cerebral cortex. *Life Science* (in press).
70. Hetey L, Drescher K, Oelssner W. Different influence of antipsychotics and serotonin antagonists on presynaptic receptors modulating the synaptosomal release of dopamine and serotonin. *Wiss Z Humboldt (Univ Berl)* 1982;31:487–489.
71. Racagni G, Cheney DL, Trabucchi M, Costa E. *In vivo* actions of clozapine and haloperidol on the turnover rate of acetylcholine in rat striatum. *J Pharmacol Exp Ther* 1976;196:323–332.
72. Cohen BM, Lipinski JF. *In vivo* potencies of antipsychotic drugs in blocking alpha$_1$ noradrenergic and dopamine D-2 receptors: implications for drug mechanisms of action. *Life Sci* 1986; 39:2571–2580.
73. Gross G, Schümann HJ. Effect of long term treatment with atypical neuroleptic drugs on beta adrenoceptor binding in rat cerebral cortex and myocardium. *Naunyn-Schmiedeberg's Arch Pharmacol* 1982;321:271–275.
74. Maggi A, Cattebeni F, Bruno F, Racagni G. Haloperidol and clozapine: specificity of action on GABA in the nigrostria system. *Brain Res* 1977;133:382–385.
75. Schmidt WJ. Intrastriatal injection of DL-2-amino-5-phosphonovaleric acid (AP-5) induces sniffing stereotypy that is antagonized by haloperidol and clozapine. *Psychopharmacology* 1986;90:123–130.
76. Kilts CD, Anderson CM, Bissette G, Ely T, Nemeroff CB. Differential effects of antipsychotic drugs on the neurotensin concentration of discrete rat brain nuclei. *Biochem Pharmacol* 1988;37:1547–1554.

34

Biochemical Effects of Clozapine in Cerebrospinal Fluid of Patients with Schizophrenia

Jeffrey Lieberman,[1,2] Celeste Johns,[1,2] Simcha Pollack,[1,3] Steven Masiar,[1] Peter Bookstein,[1] Thomas Cooper,[4] Michael Iadorola,[5] and John Kane[1,2]

Clozapine is an atypical neuroleptic with novel pharmacological and clinical properties in comparison to classic neuroleptic drugs (1). Studies have demonstrated that clozapine has superior antipsychotic efficacy in treatment refractory patients (2), may have therapeutic effects on negative symptoms (2) and diminishes impairment in social and vocational functions (3). In addition, clozapine does not cause acute extrapyramidal symptoms (EPS) of parkinsonism and dystonia and appears to lack the capacity (or have a reduced capacity) to produce tardive dyskinesia (TD; ref 4). It may also have therapeutic effects against preexisting TD (4). Despite extensive preclinical and clinical investigation, the pharmacological basis of clozapine's atypical effects is not known. In order to examine clozapine's mechanism of action, we examined cerebrospinal fluid (CSF) and plasma concentrations of biochemical variables in a cohort of patients who were treated with clozapine.

METHODS

Subjects

Patients were referred for clozapine because of treatment-resistant psychosis and/or intolerance to standard pharmacotherapy. Treatment resistance was operationally defined as described previously (2). Treatment intolerance was defined as the presence of severe TD or the occurrence of extreme acute EPS sensitivity to standard neuroleptic drug treatment. In addition, patents had to meet the following criteria:

1. Be between ages 18 and 40 years old;
2. Have a primary psychiatric disorder diagnosed according to (Axis 1 DSM-III) uncomplicated by current substance abuse for which maintenance antipsychotic drug treatment was indicated;
3. Have no current or past history of serious medical illness, particularly idiopathic or drug-induced blood dyscrasia.

In addition, both patients and their families, after being apprised of the potential risks and benefits of clozapine treatment, were required to give informed consent.

---

[1]Hillside Hospital/Long Island Jewish Medical Center, Glen Oaks, NY 11004.

[2]Department of Psychiatry, Albert Einstein College of Medicine, Bronx, NY 10461.

[3]Department of Quantitative Analysis, St. John's University, Jamaica, NY 11439.

[4]Nathan Kline Institute, Orangeburg, NY 10962.

[5]National Institute of Dental Research, NIH, Bethesda, MD 20892.

Procedures

Patients were admitted to the inpatient service and withdrawn from all medication (except occasional doses of amobarbitol and/or chloral hydrate if needed for behavior control) for 14 to 28 days depending on their tolerance of the drug-free period. Prior to the initiation of clozapine, baseline evaluations of patients were performed; these included a behavioral and mental status exam that was scored on the Brief Psychiatric Rating Scale (BPRS), Schedule for Assessment of Negative Symptoms (SANS), Clinical Global Impression Scale (CGI), and a 5- to 10-minute TD exam that was rated on the Hillside Modified version of the Simpson Dyskinesia Scale (SDS; ref 5). Lumbar punctures and venipunctures were simultaneously performed under controlled conditions at baseline and day 21 of clozapine treatment. On the day prior to specimen collection, patients ate their usual breakfast and lunch but had vanilla Sustacal (Meade Johnson) for dinner and then fasted until completion of the procedures. (Vanilla Sustacal has previously been shown to not alter significantly monoamine metabolite levels; see ref 6). The morning of the procedure, patients were kept at bedrest and not permitted to smoke. Lumbar punctures were performed under sterile conditions using a standardized procedure between 8:00 AM and 9:00 AM, with the patient in a recumbent position. Twenty cubic centimeters of CSF were collected. The first 4 cc were sent for routine clinical studies, and the balance were pooled, gently mixed, and then immediately frozen on dry ice. The CSF was then divided into 1- and 2-cc aliquots in eight tubes and immediately frozen at −80°C until laboratory analysis.

Venipunctures were performed under sterile conditions using a standardized technique. Fifteen cubic centimeters of whole blood were withdrawn from an antecubital fossa vein; 5 cc were sent for a complete blood cell count (CBC); 3 cc were placed in a heparinized tube; and 7 cc were put in a tube containing calcium oxalate, then kept on ice until spun in a refrigerated centrifuge for 10 minutes at 800 g. The plasma was decanted and stored in two tubes at −80°C until laboratory analysis.

Identical methods were used for the lumbar puncture (LP) done on day 21 of treatment and for the venipunctures done weekly. The first two 1-cc aliquots of CSF were sent for routine clinical analysis; the third and fourth aliquots were not added to the pooled CSF collection but frozen separately for later analysis of CSF clozapine concentration. Six additional cubic centimeters of blood were drawn, placed in a tube with K^+ ammonium oxylate, centrifuged, decanted, and stored for determination of clozapine level.

Following baseline evaluation, clozapine was started gradually on a twice daily schedule; the dose was titrated as tolerated to 500 mg/d by treatment day 14 and then held fixed for at least 1 week. On treatment day 21, an LP was repeated using the procedure described previously. Subsequently, the daily dose of clozapine was adjusted, as clinically indicated, up to a maximum of 900 mg. Dose adjustments were aimed at achieving optimal treatment response for patients in terms of alleviating psychopathology and minimizing side effects. Patients were evaluated for EPS and behavioral symptoms at weeks 3 and 6 of treatment. Venipunctures were performed weekly for 6 weeks. After the acute treatment period, patients who had shown sufficient improvement to warrant continued treatment with clozapine were discharged and followed as outpatients. Evaluations of psychopathology and TD were performed at 12-week intervals from the start of clozapine treatment. During this follow-up period, the dosage was adjusted on a clinical basis and generally reduced to the lowest effective maintenance dose.

Biochemical Methods

CSF samples were analyzed for levels of homovanillac acid (HVA), 5-hydroxyindoleacetic acid (5-HIAA), phenylethylamine (PEA), norepinephrine (NE), epinephrine (EP), 2-methoxy-4-hydroxyphenylglycol (MHPG), and clozapine, and for 5-met-enkephalin-arg 6-gly 7-leu 8 (Met-Enk) immunoreactivity. Plasma samples were analyzed for clozapine and prolactin concentrations. Methods of the biochemical assays are available on request.

RESULTS

Data from 19 patients were used in the analyses. Their demographic and clinical characteristics are shown in Table 1. The sample was followed for a mean (SD) of 13.1 (6.6) months. The mean daily clozapine) doses received by patients were as follows: at 3 weeks, 404 (121) mg; at 6 weeks, 504 (182) mg; at 12 weeks, 600 (193) mg; and at 1 year, 550 (253) mg. Plasma levels of clozapine and prolactin for the first 6 weeks of treatment are shown in Fig. 1. Clozapine concentrations rose to 466 (360) ng/ml at 6 weeks. Plasma prolactin showed slight transient increases over baseline levels (none of which were statistically significant) and remained within the normal range (5 to 20 ng/mL). Concentrations of

TABLE 1. *Demographic and clinical characteristics of sample (n = 19)*

Age (x yrs ± SD):
  29.5 ± 6.3
Sex:
  68% male
  32% female
Race:
  79% Caucasian
  21% Non-Caucasian
Diagnosis:
  68% Schizophrenia, paranoid
  18% Schizophrenia, undifferentiated
  14% Schizoaffective disorder
Duration of illness (x yrs ± SD):
  9.2 ± 4.6
TD status at entry:
  53% Positive
  47% Negative
Entry criteria:
  68% Treatment refractory
  26% Treatment intolerant
  6% Both

CSF clozapine at week 3 were 5.57 (3.60) ng/ml. Clozapine dose and plasma levels were correlated during the acute treatment phase (combining weeks 1 to 3): $r = .45$, $p = .01$. Clozapine concentrations in plasma for each of the first 3 weeks were positively correlated with CSF-clozapine (measured at week 3): ($r = .58$, $p = .02$; $r = .48$, $p = .05$; $r = 0.46$, $p = .07$).

Baseline and treatment week 3 CSF levels of NE, EP, 5-HIAA, HVA, MHPG, PEA, and Met-Enk are shown in Fig. 2 to 4 and Table 2.

Cerebral spinal fluid variables were examined for correlations within and between measurement time points.

Correlations were found between the following variables:

Between baseline pretreatment levels of NE and 5-HIAA ($r = .41$, $p = .08$), 5-HIAA and MHPG ($r = .31$ $p = .22$), 5-HIAA and HVA ($r = .32$, $p = .18$), 5-HIAA and PEA ($r = -.53$, $p = .09$);

Between baseline and week 3 levels of NE ($r = .53$, $p = .02$), EP ($r = .44$, $p = .08$), 5-HIAA ($r = .88$, $p = .001$), HVA ($r = .82$, $p = .001$), MHPG ($r = .53$, $p = .03$), PEA ($r = .47$, $p = .15$), and Met-Enk ($r = .58$, $p = .04$);

Between week 3 CSF levels of NE and 5-HIAA ($r = .39$, $p = .10$), NE and MHPG ($r = .54$, $p = .03$), EP and Met-Enk ($r = .43$, $p = .19$), HVA and 5-HIAA ($r = .31$, $p = .20$), 5-HIAA and MHPG ($r = .61$, $p = .01$).

In addition, CSF clozapine levels were positively correlated with NE ($r = .46$, $p = .06$) and negatively correlated with HVA ($r = -.32$, $p = .20$) at week 3 of treatment.

The correlation analysis was repeated controlling for height and weight. The pattern of results were generally very similar. The four exceptions are found at week 3: NE and Met-Enk ($r = .73$, $p = .01$); 5-HIAA and HVA ($r = .56$, $p = .02$); MHPG and HVA ($r = .43$, $p = .11$); and finally, the change in Met-Enk with the change in NE ($r = .50$, $p = .12$).

Repeated measures analysis of variance

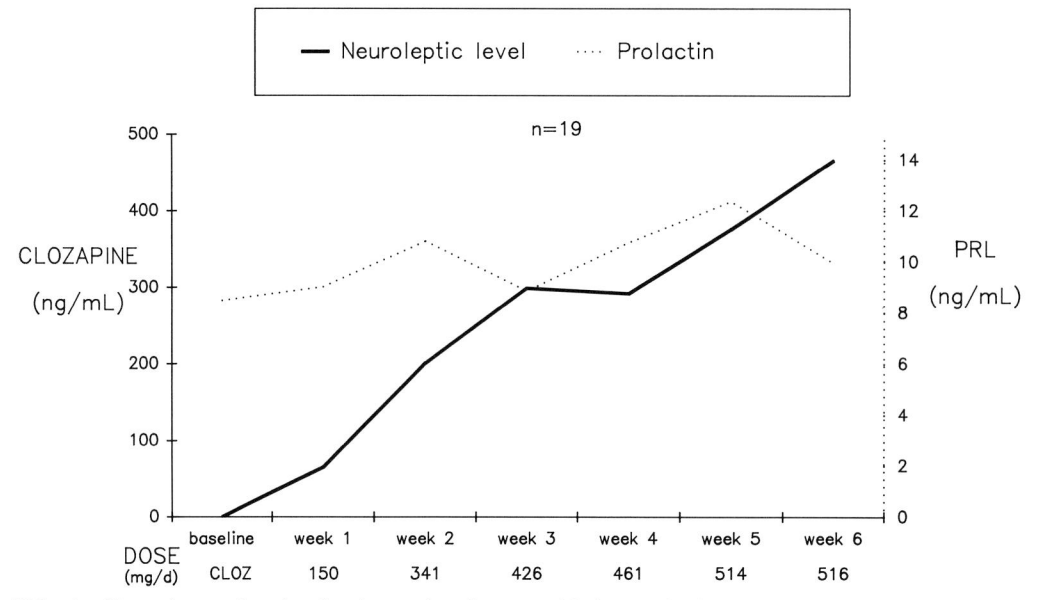

FIG. 1. Clozapine and prolactin plasma levels at weekly intervals during acute treatment.

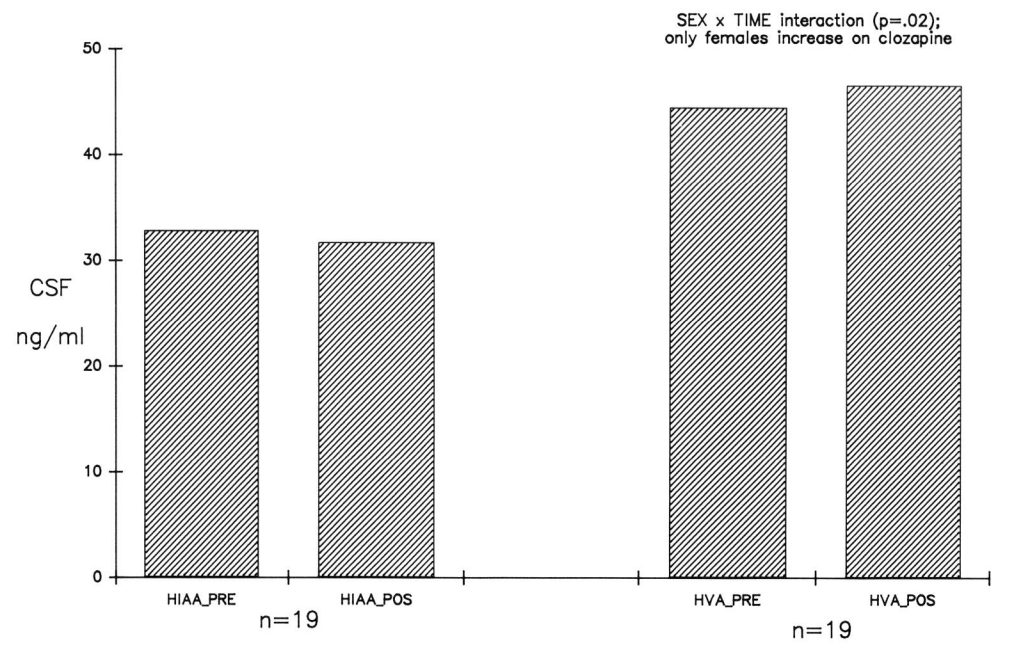

FIG. 2. 5-HIAA and HVA CSF levels prior to (PRE) and following (POS) 21 days of clozapine treatment.

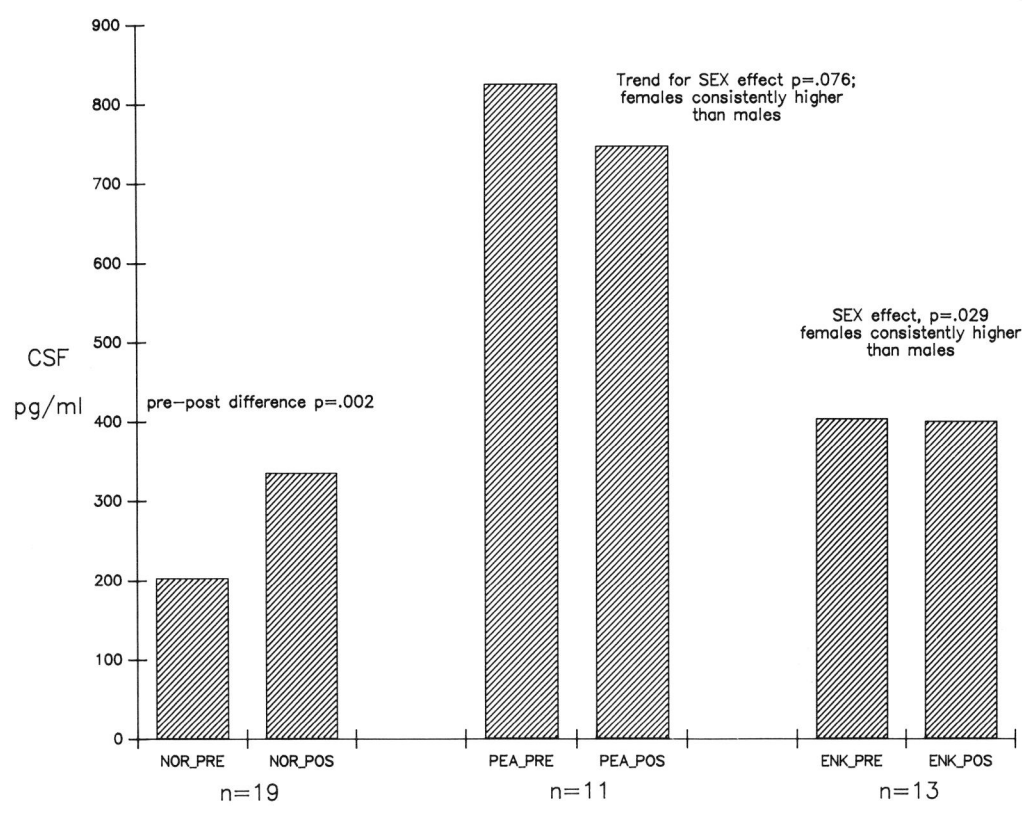

FIG. 3. NE (NOR), PEA, and MET-ENK CSF levels prior to (PRE) and following (POS) 3 weeks of clozapine treatment.

was applied to the seven CSF measures in a univariate fashion using as independent variables treatment (pre/post), sex and TD status at baseline, and covarying for height and weight. The main effects and interactions are discussed below. Due to the small sample size and the exploratory nature of this study, the problem of power was addressed by choosing a p value of .10 for the threshold of significance. In addition, correlational analyses were performed for the change in CSF variables between time points (baseline and week 3; see Table 2).

The most pronounced change was seen in NE, which was significantly increased by clozapine treatment ($F = 20.7$; $df = 1, 8$; $p = .002$). This was more pronounced in TD-positive patients ($n = 8$, TD × treatment, $F = 11.5$; $df = 1,10$; $p = .01$). Levels of CSF clozapine were positively correlated with the change from pretreatment to week 3 in NE ($r = .52$, $p = .03$). Levels of HVA were modestly elevated after clozapine treatment ($F = 5.4$; $df = 1,14$; $p = .036$), but this change was only found in the female group ($n = 6$, sex × treatment, $F = 6.09$; $df = 1,14$; $p = .027$). Changes in CSF HVA and 5-HIAA were positively correlated ($r = .48$, $p = .04$). Further analysis of 5-HIAA using a 5-HIAA/HVA ratio yielded no statistically significant results.

There was a trend for EP levels to be lower after clozapine treatment ($F = 3.58$; $df = 1,6$; $p = .107$), but this result must be interpreted in light of a TD × treatment interaction ($F = 7.75$; $df = 1,6$; $p = .032$).

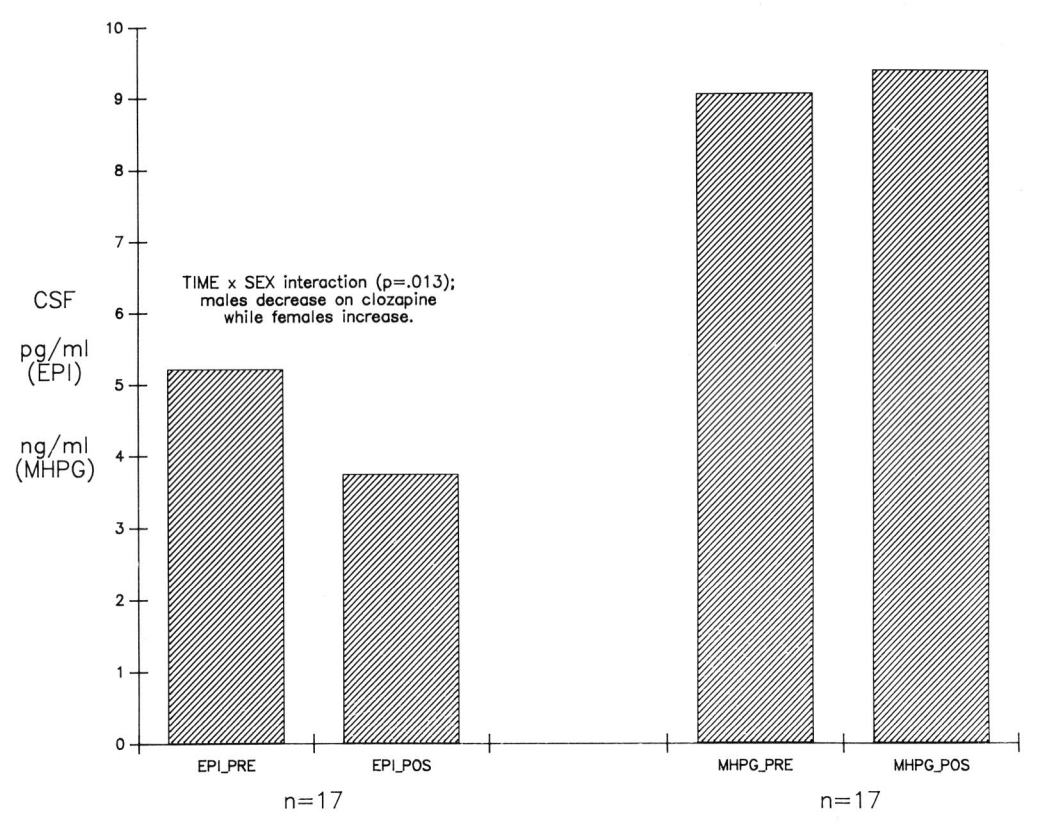

FIG. 4. EP (EPI) and MHPG CSF levels prior to (PRE) and following (POS) 3 weeks of clozapine treatment.

Epinephrine levels in TD-positive patients tended to decrease on clozapine, while TD-negative patients increased. Another interaction between sex and treatment ($F = 11.2$; $df = 1,6$; $p = .015$) further complicated the results. Males showed a decrease in EP on clozapine, while females showed an increase. These two interactions worked independently and additively (i.e., there was no TD × sex × treatment interaction).

There was no change in MHPG after treatment, though TD-positive males had lower average MHPG values (pretreatment and week 3) than TD-positive females. Males who were TD-negative had higher MHPG values than TD-negative females. This TD × sex interaction was marginally significant ($F = 3.61$; $df = 1,12$; $p = .082$). Both PEA and Met-Enk exhibited a sex effect with females ($F = 4.57$; $df = 1,6$; $p = .076$), showing higher values than males ($F = 7.03$; $df = 1,8$; $p = .029$). Correlations that approached the trend level of significance were found between changes from pretreatment to week 3 in MHPG and PEA ($r = .48$, $p = .14$), PEA and Met-Enk ($r = -.47$, $p = .14$), and Met-Enk and HVA ($r = .45$, $p = .12$).

A series of correlational analyses was performed to examine the relationship between biochemical variables and therapeutic response, as measured by the BPRS, SANS, CGI, and SDS. The changes in rating scores from baseline to weeks 3, 6, and 12 of clozapine treatment were used as response variables. No significant correlations between CSF and clinical measures were found.

TABLE 2. Correlations and sample means of CSF measures[a]

	NE	EP	5-HIAA	HVA	MHPG	PEA	Met-Enk	CSF Clozapine	Pretreatment Mean (SD)[b] (ng/ml)	Week 3 Mean (SD)[c] (ng/ml)
NE	**.53** n=19	.06 .00	**.41*** .39*	**.03** −.05	**−.09** .54**	**−.40** .16	**.19** −.03	— .46*	204(120)	336(152)
EP	−.32	**.44*** n=17	**−.42**** −.25	**.02** .00	**−.56**** −.16	**−.29** .19	**−.44** .43	— .23	5.24(4.83)	3.76(2.95)
5-HIAA	−.02	−.13	**.88***** n=19	**.32** .31	**.31** .61***	**−.53*** .01	**.13** .20	— −.08	32.9(11.3)	31.8(9.5)
HVA	.09	−.10	.48**	**.82***** n=19	**−.05** .06	**−.22** .08	**−.35** .35	— −.31	44.6(18.1)	46.6(19.0)
MHPG	.13	−.25	.00	.08	**.53**** n=17	**.16** .16	**−.09** .07	— .16	9.06(1.27)	9.39(1.81)
PGA	−.32	−.01	−.22	.32	.48	**.47** n=11	**−.08** .11	— .03	825(286)	748(309)
Met-Enk	.13	−.35	.08	.45	.15	−.47	**.58**** n=13	— −.13	415(132)	401(151)
CSF Clozapine	.52**	−.16	−.17	−.13	.18	−.09	−.01	— n=18		5.57(3.60)

[a]On diagonal (*underlined*): sample size and correlations between pretreatment and week 3 treatment CSF measures. *Below diagonal:* correlations of baseline–week 3 change scores between CSF measures. *Above diagonal, boldface:* correlations between pretreatment CSF measures. *Above diagonal, lightface:* correlations between week 3 treatment CSF measures.
[b]Means and standard deviations of pretreatment CSF measures.
[c]Means and standard deviations of week 3 treatment CSF measures.
* $p < .10$; ** $p < .05$; *** $p < .01$.

DISCUSSION

The biochemical response to clozapine varies in some respects from published reports of classic neuroleptics (7,8). Clozapine treatment did not alter plasma prolactin levels but increased CSF HVA slightly, mainly in females. This is in contrast to what might be expected with classic neuroleptics that produce robust though transient increases in prolactin and HVA. It is possible that the second lumbar puncture was done after tolerance had begun to develop and therefore missed the initial increase in dopamine (DA) neuronal activity produced by clozapine. This seems unlikely, since prior studies of human CSF HVA indicate that tolerance develops after 28 days or more of treatment. The gradual dose titration schedule might be expected to delay rather than accelerate the tolerance response making it less likely that the repeat LP at 21 days would have missed any treatment induced rise in CSF HVA.

One interpretation is that the lack of change in the plasma prolactin levels and mild increase in CSF HVA mainly of females who are generally more responsive to drug treatment may be due to clozapine's relatively low affinity for D_2 receptors (9) and weak antagonism of nigrostriatal DA neurons. Since this region accounts for a significant proportion of CNS DA metabolism, the reduced turnover produced by clozapine versus standard neuroleptics could result in different HVA response patterns.

The lack of a significant change in CSF 5-HIAA levels with clozapine treatment is consistent with prior studies of standard neuroleptics but surprising in view of clozapine's relatively potent $5HT_2$ antagonism (10). On the other hand, 5-HIAA and HVA are (usually) highly correlated and therefore can be expected to change in concert.

The most robust clozapine effects were seen in the adrenergic system. The dramatic elevation in NE is believed to be due to clozapine's potent α-adrenergic blocking properties (11,12). The role of NE in the pathophysiology of schizophrenia has long been considered important (13). Clozapine's potent actions on NE and its superior antipsychotic efficacy are consistent with this hypothesis, while the lack of any apparent relationship between NE response and therapeutic outcome is not supportive. The fact that the NE response to clozapine was greater in patients with TD suggests adrenergic system involvement in the pathophysiology of TD, as Jeste et al (14) have hypothesized. Somewhat paradoxically, EP levels declined with clozapine treatment. However, this effect is complicated by interactions with both TD status and sex. In addition, the low concentrations of EP (mean of 3 pg/ml) are at the lower limit of the chemical assay's sensitivity and therefore must be interpreted cautiously. In view of the magnitude of the changes in NE and EP levels with clozapine treatment, the apparent lack of change in MHPG is surprising. However, MHPG may not be the most sensitive measure of adrenergic turnover and is not altered by classic neuroleptics (15).

The PEA and Met-Enk results were interesting despite their lack of significant response to clozapine. Levels of PEA were consistently, albeit nonsignificantly ($p = .12$), higher in TD than non-TD patients. Disturbances in phenylalanine metabolism have previously been described as a risk factor for TD development (16). In both rodent and human studies (17) Met-Enk has been found to increase consistently with haloperidol treatment, yet with clozapine no change in mean group concentrations was seen. When individual patient responses were examined, six patients had decreases, five patients had no change, and two patients had increases in Met-Enk levels after clozapine treatment. This peptide, like DA, is most highly concentrated in the corpus striatum and substantia nigra.

In summary, the results of this study demonstrate that clozapine's biochemical properties differ from those of classical neuroleptic drugs as reflected by CSF neurotransmitter concentrations. These results do not establish the biochemical mechanism that mediates clozapine's unique clinical actions but suggest the involvement of NE and the peptidergic neurotransmitter Met-Enk as well as non-D_2-receptor-mediated DA neuronal effects. These properties and their pharmacodynamic mechanisms require further study for their elucidation.

ACKNOWLEDGMENTS

This work was supported by a Research Scientist Development Award (MH-00537) to J. Lieberman, the Mental Health Clinical Research Center of Hillside Hospital, LIJMC (MH-41960), and the Sandoz Research Foundation.

REFERENCES

1. Schmutz J, Eichenberger E. Clozapine. *Chron Drug Discov* 1982;1:39–59.
2. Kane J, Honigfeld G, Singer J, Meltzer H, Clozaril Collaborative Study Group. Clozapine for the treatment-resistant schizophrenic: a double-blind comparison versus chlorpromazine. *Arch Gen Psychiatry* 1988;45:789–796.
3. Lindstrom LH. The effect of long-term treatment with clozapine in schizophrenia: a retrospective study in 96 patients treated with clozapine for up to 13 years. *Acta Psychiatr Scand* 1987;945:1–6.
4. Lieberman JA, Saltz BL, Johns CA, Pollack S, Kane JM. Clozapine effects on tardive dyskinesia. *Psychopharmacol Bull* 1989;25:57–62.
5. Lieberman J, Kane J, Woerner M, Weinhold P. Prevalence of tardive dyskinesia in elderly samples. *Psychopharmacol Bull* 1984;20:22–26.
6. Kendler KS, Mohs RC, Davis KL. The effects of diet and physical activity on plasma homovanillac acid in normal human subjects. *Psychiatry Res* 1983;8:215–223.
7. Van Kammen DP, Peters J, van Kammen WB. Cerebrospinal fluid studies of monoamine metabolism in schizophrenia. *Psychiatr Clin North Am* 1986;9:81–96.
8. Gattaz WF, Walkmeier P, Beckmann H. CSF monoamine metabolites in schizophrenic patients. *Acta Psychiatr Scand* 1982;66:350–360.
9. Arnt J, Hyttel J. Differential inhibition by dopamine D1 and D2 antagonists of circling behavior induced by dopamine agonists in rats with unilateral 6-hydroxy-dopamine lesions. *Eur J Pharmacol* 1984;102:349–359.
10. Friedman RL, Sanders-Bush E, Barrett RL: Clozapine blocks disruptive and discriminative stimulus effects of quipazine. *Eur J Pharmacol* 1985;106:191–193.
11. Burki HR, Ruch W, Asper H, Baggiolini M, Stille G. Effect of single and repeated administration of clozapine on the metabolism of dopamine and noradrenaline in the brain of the rat. *Eur J Pharmacol* 1974;27:180–190.
12. Anden NE, Butcher SG, Corrodi H, Fuxe K, Ungerstedt U. Receptor activity and turnover of dopamine and noradrenaline after neuroleptics. *Eur J Pharmacol* 1970;11:303–314.
13. Van Kammen DP, Antelman S. Minireview: impaired noradrenergic transmission in schizophrenia? *Life Sci* 1984;34:1403–1413.
14. Jeste DV, Lohr JB, Kaufmann CA, Wyatt RJ. Pathophysiology of tardive dyskinesia; evaluation of supersensitivity theory and alternative hypotheses. In: Casey DE, Gardos G, eds. *Tardive dyskinesia and neuroleptics: from dogma to reason.* Washington, D.C.: American Psychiatric Press, 1986;15–32.
15. Wode-Holgodt B, Fryo B, Gullberg B, Sedvall G. Effect of chlorpromazine treatment on monoamine metabolite levels in cerebrospinal fluid of psychotic patients. *Acta Psychiatr Scand* 1977;56:129–142.
16. Richardson M, Suckow R, Whittaker R, Perumal A, Boggiano W, Szirak I, Kushner H. Phenylalanine, phenylethylamine and tardive dyskinesia in psychiatric patients. In: Boulton AA, Jerio AV, Downer R, eds. *Trace Amines: comparative and clinical neurobiology.* Humana Press, 1988;409–422.
17. Iadarola MJ, Berman KF, Karp BP, Suddath R, Mouradian MM, Lieberman J, Kane JM. Cerebrospinal fluid met[5]-enkephalin-arg[6]-gly[7]-leu[8] immunoreactive peptides: differential effect of haloperidol compared to clozapine (in press).

35

Differential Changes in Dopamine and Serotonin Receptors Induced by Clozapine and Haloperidol

Gerald J. LaHoste,[1] Steven J. O'Dell,[1] Clifford B. Widmark,[2] Raymond M. Shapiro,[2] Steven G. Potkin,[2] and John F. Marshall[1]

The widespread use of typical neuroleptics in the treatment of schizophrenia has made it evident that there are limitations to the applications of these drugs. Among the most severe is the high risk of developing extrapyramidal side effects (EPS) and tardive dyskinesia (TD).

Clozapine is representative of a class of agents that, in animal models, lack some of the motoric effects of typical neuroleptics (1–3) but are nonetheless effective in ameliorating the symptoms of schizophrenia. The major advantage of these "atypical" neuroleptics is that they have a very low propensity to induce EPS and possibly TD.

Much effort has been directed toward discovering the mode of action of both typical and atypical neuroleptics in the hope that similarities might reveal the biological basis of antipsychotic activity while differences might elucidate the etiology of EPS and possibly TD. At present, two major classes of hypotheses are offered to account for the differences between typical and atypical neuroleptics. The first suggests that these two groups of neuroleptics may act on the same receptors (primarily D_2 receptors) but at different brain loci. The second suggests that they may act on different receptor systems or that they may affect similar receptor systems to differing degrees.

A variety of evidence suggests that atypical neuroleptics act preferentially on mesocortical and mesolimbic projections of the A10 dopamine (DA) cell group, while typical neuroleptics act on both A10 projections and the mesostriatal projections of A9 DA cells. Electrophysiological evidence shows that either acute or chronic treatment with the typical neuroleptic haloperidol alters the number of spontaneously firing DA neurons in both A9 and A10 areas, while similar treatment with clozapine alters DA neuronal firing only in A10 (4). In neurochemical studies, chronic clozapine treatment decreased DA release in a terminal field of the A10 DA cells, the nucleus accumbens (NAc), while chronic haloperidol treatment resulted in decreased DA release in both the NAc and a terminal field of the A9 DA cells, the caudate putamen (CP; ref 5).

These regional differences in activity between typical and atypical neuroleptics are consistent with the hypothesis that the activity of dopaminergic inputs to limbic and

---

[1]Department of Psychobiology and Center for Neuroscience and Schizophrenia, University of California at Irvine, Irvine, CA 92717.
[2]Department of Psychiatry and Center for Neuroscience and Schizophrenia, University of California at Irvine, Irvine, CA 92717.

cortical regions is of particular importance in generating schizophrenic psychosis. This hypothesis is further supported by electrophysiological studies in which compounds that are effective antipsychotics consistently have an effect on A10 neuronal activity. For example, acute treatment with either haloperidol or clozapine results in increased firing in A10 DA cells (6), whereas acute treatment with the benzamide metoclopramide, a compound nearly devoid of antipsychotic activity, yields increases in A9 neuronal firing without substantially affecting firing rates in the A10 neurons (7).

Irrespective of the loci of action of typical and atypical neuroleptics, these two groups may differ from each other in their receptor binding profiles. It has been shown that the in vitro affinity of a neuroleptic for DA D_2 receptors is correlated with its antipsychotic potential (8,9). However, virtually all known neuroleptics have significant antagonist properties at a variety of other amine receptors, including DA D_1, serotoninergic 5 HT_2, α_1-adrenergic, H_1 histaminergic, and muscarinic cholinergic receptors (5,10–13). Binding to other than D_2 receptors may play a role in either developing or preventing EPS and TD. For example, chronic simultaneous administration of haloperidol and either an anticholinergic (4) or an α_1-adrenergic antagonist (4,5) can mimic the limbic-specific changes in DA cell firing seen after chronic clozapine treatment. However, combining classical neuroleptics with anticholinergic agents neither reduces the risk of TD (14) nor enhances the antipsychotic effect (15). Serotoninergic systems may also play a role in the development of EPS and TD since lesions of the midbrain raphe have been shown to decrease serotoninergic activity and inhibit DA-induced stereotypy. Furthermore, atypical neuroleptics inhibit firing of serotoninergic cells in the dorsal raphe, while typical neuroleptics have no effect (16). Finally, recent studies of DA release and metabolism following acute doses of clozapine suggest that a mechanism related to D_1 antagonism may contribute to the atypical character of this drug (17,18).

To elucidate the neural mechanisms underlying the differing properties of clozapine and the typical neuroleptics, we used quantitative autoradiography to measure changes in DA and serotonin receptors in rats after injection with clozapine or haloperidol for 21 days. The relative doses of these two drugs (30 mg/kg and 1 mg/kg daily, respectively) approximated the relative antipsychotic potencies of these drugs. Levels of D_1, D_2, and $5HT_2$ receptors were determined in the frontal cortex, the caudate putamen, and the nucleus accumbens. Rats that received clozapine chronically showed brain receptor changes markedly different from those in chronic haloperidol-treated animals. Rats treated chronically with haloperidol showed enhanced D_2 binding, while those treated with clozapine did not. In contrast, chronic clozapine treatment resulted in enhanced D_1 binding, whereas these sites were unchanged in haloperidol-treated rats. Finally, clozapine treatment decreased $5HT_2$ receptor binding while haloperidol had no significant effect.

METHODS

Subjects were adult male Sprague-Dawley rats (Charles River) weighing 175 to 200 g at the beginning of chronic drug treatment. They were housed in groups of six to seven with food and water freely available, and a 12:12 light-to-dark cycle. Subjects were injected once daily for 21 days with either clozapine (30 mg/kg IP), haloperidol (1.0 mg/kg IP), or vehicle (1.0 ml/kg IP), as determined by random assignment.

Clozapine (Sandoz Research Institute) and haloperidol (McNeil Pharmaceutical) were dissolved in a minimal volume of acetic acid and then diluted with 0.9% saline. All injected solutions were neutralized with small quantities of 10 N NaOH to as close to pH 7 as possible. Finally, 0.9% saline was added to achieve concentrations of 30 and 1.0 mg/ml, for clozapine and haloperidol respectively. The vehicle consisted of 0.9% saline with acetic acid in proportions equivalent to that for the clozapine and haloperidol solutions, neutralized with NaOH.

Seventy-two hours after the last drug injection, the animals were decapitated; their brains were quickly removed and frozen in isopentane ($-20°C$) for approximately 2 minutes, after which they were stored at $-20°C$. Coronal brain sections were cut on a cryostat at 20 μm thickness and thaw-mounted onto gelatin-coated glass slides. The thawed sections were then vacuum-desiccated for 1 to 2 hours at 4°C and stored at $-20°C$ until used in autoradiographic receptor assays.

To determine D_1 receptor binding, slides were preincubated in 50 mM Tris-buffered saline containing 5 mM KCl, 2 mM CaCl$_2$ and 1 mM MgCl$_2$ (TBSI; pH 7.1) at room temperature for 5 minutes to remove endogenous catecholamines. Slides were then incubated at room temperature for 60 minutes in TBSI plus 0.02% ascorbic acid (TBSIA) and [^{3}H]SCH 23390 at a final concentration of 1.0 nM. Nonspecific [^{3}H]SCH 23390 binding was defined in the presence of 5 μM (+)butaclamol. After incubation, the slides were rinsed at 4°C in TBSIA (2 × 20 seconds) and distilled water (1 × 10 seconds), then rapidly dried by aspiration and moderate heating on a 55°C warming tray.

For D_2 receptor binding, after preincubation in TBSIA for 5 minutes, slides were incubated at room temperature for 60 minutes in TBSIA with [^{3}H]spiroperidol at a final concentration of 0.7 nM and 40 nM ketanserin (to block radioligand binding to 5HT$_2$ receptors). Nonspecific [^{3}H]spiroperidol binding was defined using 1 μM (+)butaclamol. After incubation, slides were rinsed at 4°C in TBSIA (2 × 20 seconds) and distilled water (1 × 10 seconds), then dried by aspiration and mild heating.

For the determination of 5HT$_2$ receptors, preincubation was at room temperature in Tris buffer (pH 7.4) for 5 minutes. Slides were then incubated at room temperature for 60 minutes in a solution of 50 mM Tris containing [^{3}H]ketanserin (final concentration of 2.0 nM with 1 μM prazosin (to block radioligand binding to α_2-adrenergic receptors) and 100 nM tetrabenazine (to block ligand binding to a site associated with monoaminergic nerve terminals). Nonspecific [^{3}H]ketanserin binding was defined with 1 μM methysergide. After incubation, slides were rinsed at 4°C in Tris (2 × 30 minutes) and distilled water (1 × 10 seconds) and then dried under a stream of cool air.

Thoroughly dried slides and tissue standards were apposed to ^{3}H-sensitive Hyperfilm (Amersham) for periods ranging from 2 weeks to 2 months, with the exact exposure time based on the specific activity of the radioligand and the anatomic areas to be analyzed. Tissue standards were prepared by mixing known quantities of [^{3}H]isoleucine into portions of brain homogenate, freezing and sectioning the resultant mixtures, and then vacuum-drying the thaw-mounted radiolabeled tissue "spots," with subsequent storage at $-20°C$.

Autoradiographic images were quantified on a computer-assisted image analyzer. For each sample, analysis began by digitizing an image of the total ligand binding. Image densities were then linearized by calibration against the densities produced by the known radioactivities in our tissue standards. Next, an image of an adjacent tissue section that had been incubated to give only nonspecific binding was digitized and linearized. Applying a pixel-by-pixel subtraction routine, we removed the contribution of the nonspecifically bound radioligand from that of the total binding to yield an image of specific ligand binding. Templates were drawn on these specific binding images to quantify specific receptor densities in discrete anatomic structures.

RESULTS

The binding of D_2 receptors within the CP of vehicle-treated rats displayed the well-described, steep lateral-to-medial decreasing gradient (19). Haloperidol treatment increased the density of D_2 receptors in the CP by 35% to 49% over that of vehicle-treated rats. Although haloperidol also increased D_2 binding in the NAc by 29%, this effect was narrowly nonsignificant (see below). Clozapine treatment did not significantly alter D_2 binding in any region of the CP, although small nonsignificant increases were observed in all subregions (Figs. 1 and 2).

A two-factor analysis of variance (chronic drug × region) yielded significant main effects for chronic drug ($F_{2,15} = 10.16$; $p < .002$) and for region ($F_{4,60} = 188.70$; $p < .001$) on D_2 binding, and a significant interaction term ($F_{8,60} = 2.96$; $p < .01$). The significant interaction term was due to the lack of a significant chronic-drug effect in the NAc ($F_{2,15} = 2.79$; $p = 0.09$), whereas this factor was significant in all CP regions ($p < .01$ in each region). Newman-Keuls tests revealed that the main effect of chronic drug in all CP regions was due to the significant elevation in D_2 binding in the haloperidol group ($n = 7$) relative to either the saline ($p < .01$; $n = 5$) or the clozapine ($p < 0.025$; $n = 6$) groups, which did not differ significantly from each other.

D_1 receptor binding in the CP of rats treated with vehicle displayed slight regional variations in D_1 receptor binding consistent with that previously reported for this region (20). Clozapine treatment increased the density of D_1 receptors by 35% to 50% over that of vehicle-treated rats. The effect of clozapine did not differ significantly across regions, leaving the subtle gradient of D_1 binding intact. Haloperidol treatment, by contrast, did not alter D_1 binding in any subregion of the CP (Figs. 3 and 4), which is in agreement with previous reports (e.g., ref 21).

A two-factor analysis of variance (chronic drug × region) yielded significant main effects for chronic drug ($F_{2,16} = 3.88$; $p < .05$) and for region ($F_{4,64} = 14.33$; $p < .001$) on D_1 binding, while the interaction term was not significant ($F < 1.0$). Newman-Keuls tests revealed that the main effect of chronic drug was due to the significant elevation in D_1 binding in the clozapine group ($n = 6$) relative to either the saline ($p < .05$; $n = 6$) or the haloperidol ($p < .05$; $n = 7$) groups. The saline and haloperidol groups did not differ significantly.

There was a pronounced ventral-to-dorsal gradient in the density of $5HT_2$ receptors in the striata of vehicle-treated animals, with the highest receptor densities being found in the ventral and ventrolateral subregions, including the NAc. Clozapine treatment reduced the density of $5HT_2$ receptors by 40%, but it did so only in areas where appreciable binding is observed in control animals; that is, the reduction was significant in ventral but not dorsal striatal areas, where binding is already quite low (Figs. 5 and 6).

A two-factor analysis of variance (chronic drug × region) yielded a significant main effect for region ($F_{1,14} = 64.15$; $p < .0001$) and a significant drug-by-region interaction ($F_{2,14} = 7.65$; $p < .006$). The interaction effect was due to the fact that clozapine treatment ($n = 6$) significantly decreased $5HT_2$ binding relative to vehicle ($n = 4$) or haloperidol ($n = 7$) treatment in the ventral ($p < .05$) but not the dorsal striatum.

In the cerebral cortex of vehicle-treated animals, $5HT_2$ receptors were found in a distinctive band within the intermediate layers (4 and 5) of the cingulate, frontal, and insular-orbital cortex. Clozapine reduced $5HT_2$ binding by about 33% overall, consistent with its effects in the ventral CP. By contrast, haloperidol did not significantly affect $5HT_2$ binding in any cortical area (Figs. 7 and 8).

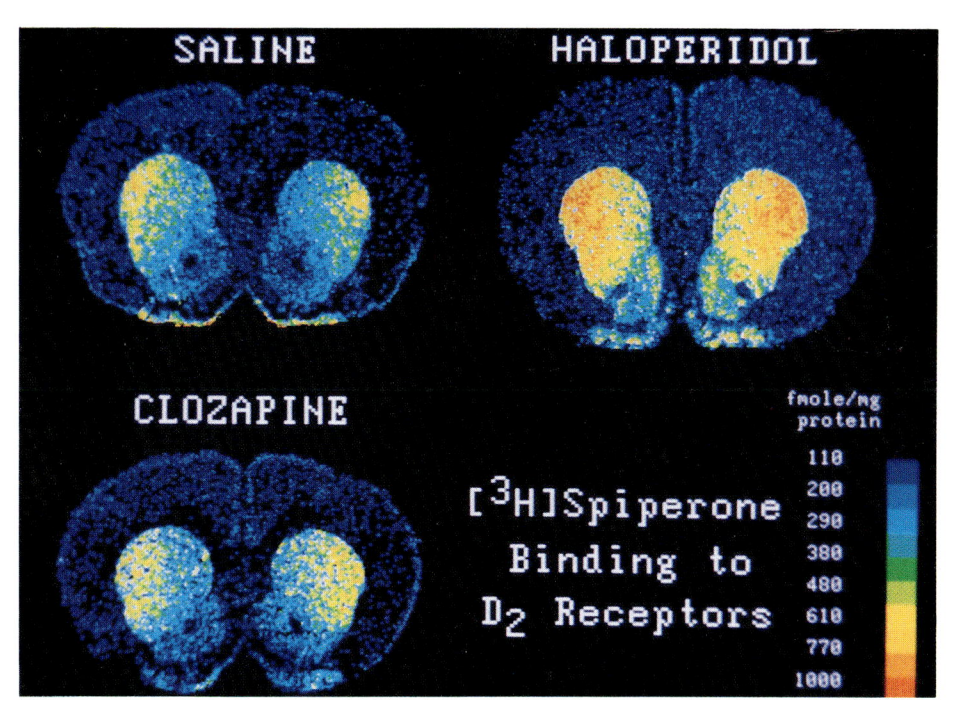

FIG. 1. Autoradiographs showing increased dopamine D_2 receptor binding in all regions of the caudate putamen following chronic administration of haloperidol but not of clozapine.

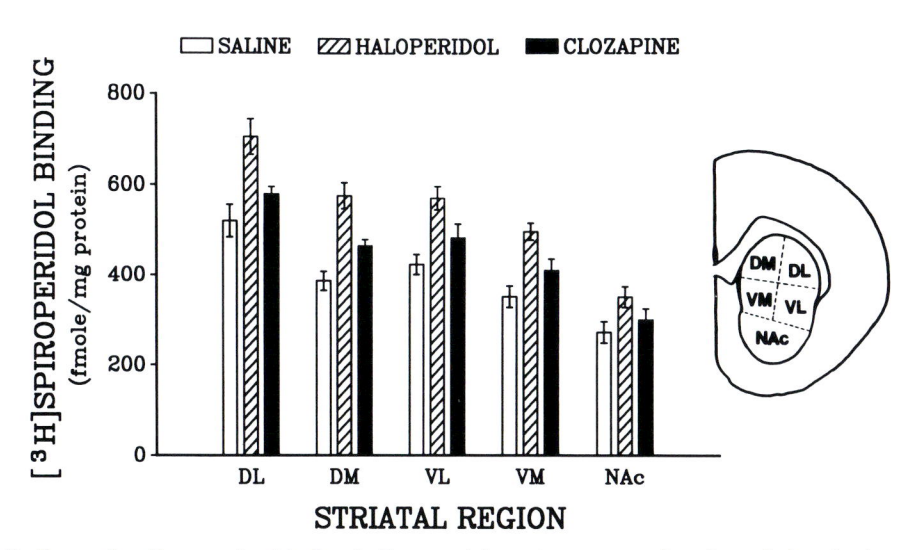

FIG. 2. Dopamine D_2 receptor binding in the caudate putamen as a function of chronic drug treatment and anatomic region. Haloperidol significantly elevated binding in all regions relative to vehicle. Clozapine was without significant effect.

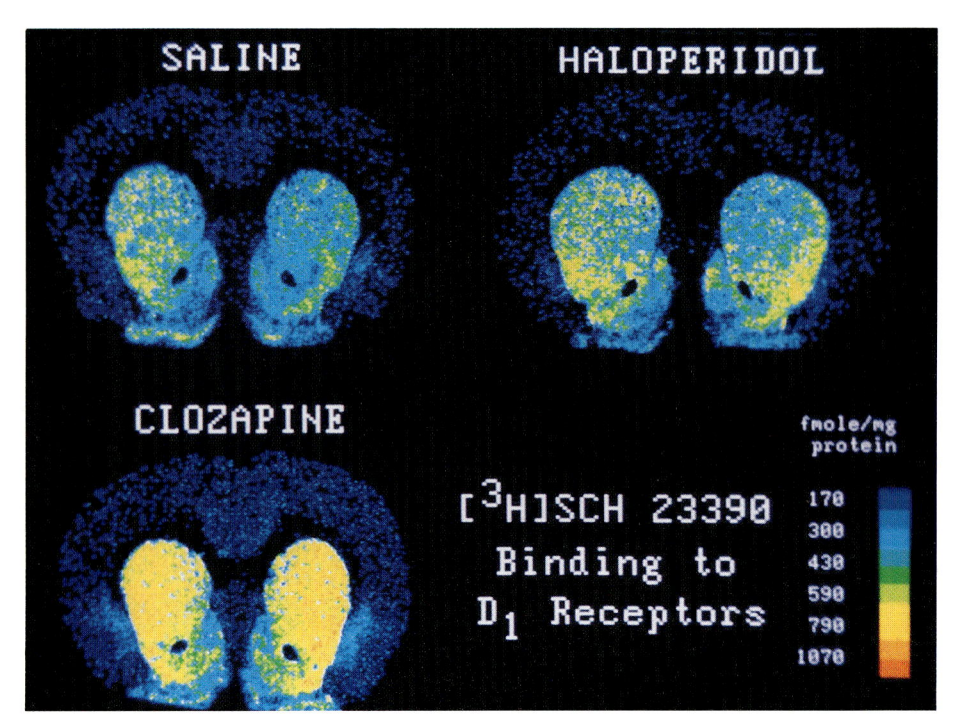

FIG. 3. Autoradiographs showing increased dopamine D_1 receptor binding in all regions of the caudate putamen following chronic treatment with clozapine but not with haloperidol.

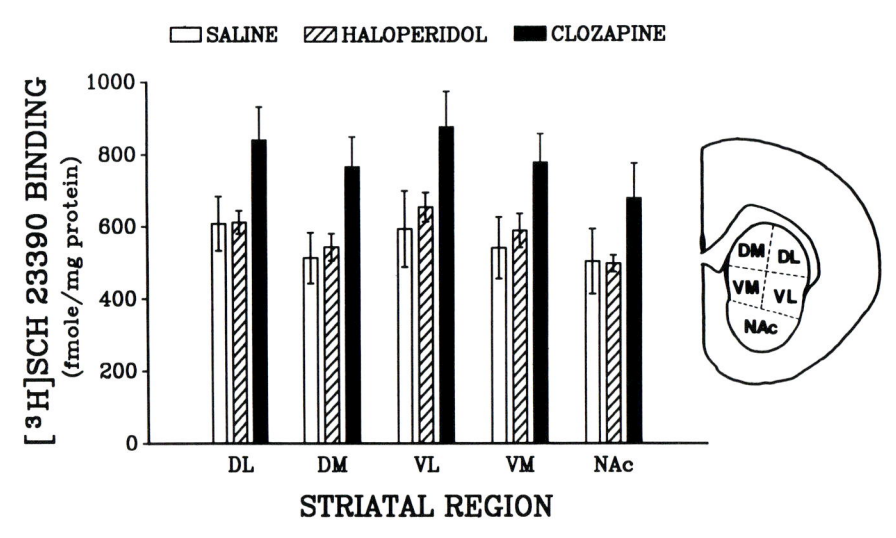

FIG. 4. Dopamine D_1 receptor binding in the caudate putamen as a function of chronic drug treatment and anatomic region. Clozapine significantly elevated binding in all regions relative to vehicle. Haloperidol was without significant effect.

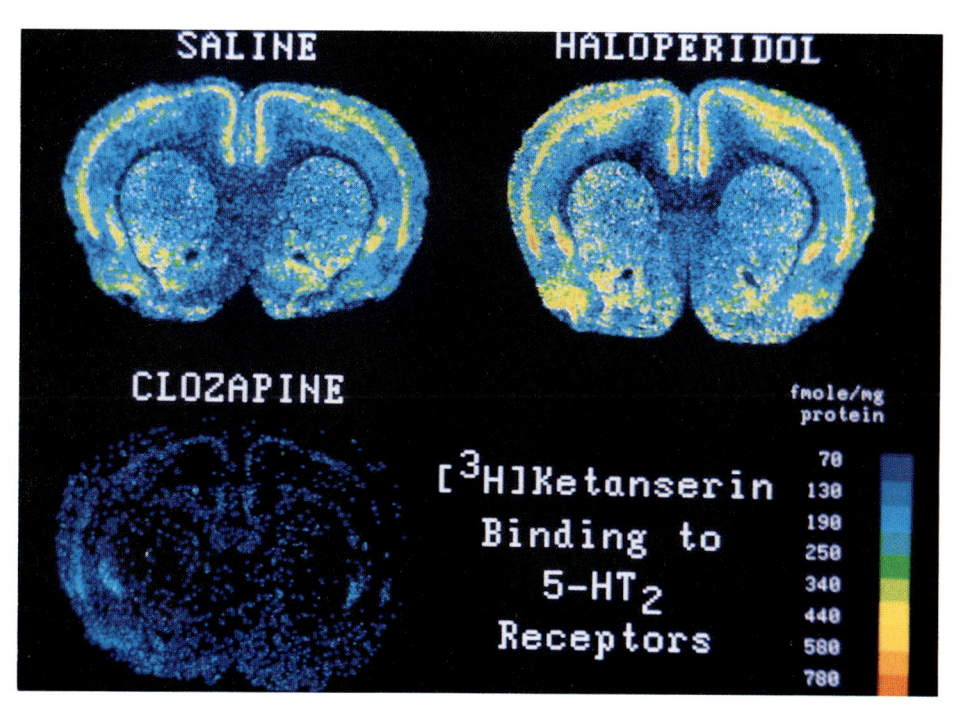

FIG. 5. Autoradiographs showing decreased serotonin 5HT$_2$ binding in the ventral but not the dorsal caudate putamen following chronic administration of clozapine. Haloperidol did not significantly affect 5HT$_2$ receptors.

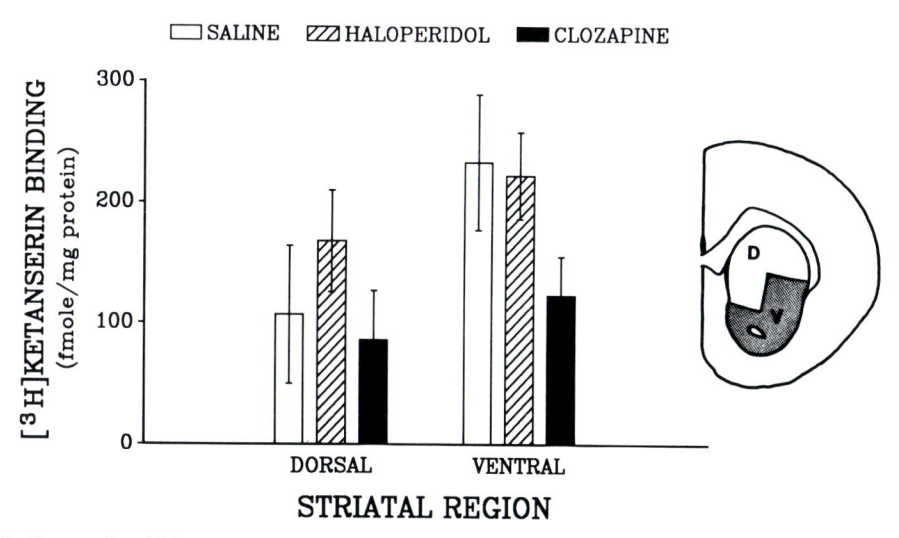

FIG. 6. Serotonin 5HT$_2$ receptor binding in the caudate putamen as a function of chronic drug treatment and anatomic region. Clozapine significantly reduced binding in the ventral but not the dorsal caudate putamen relative to the vehicle. Haloperidol was without significant effect.

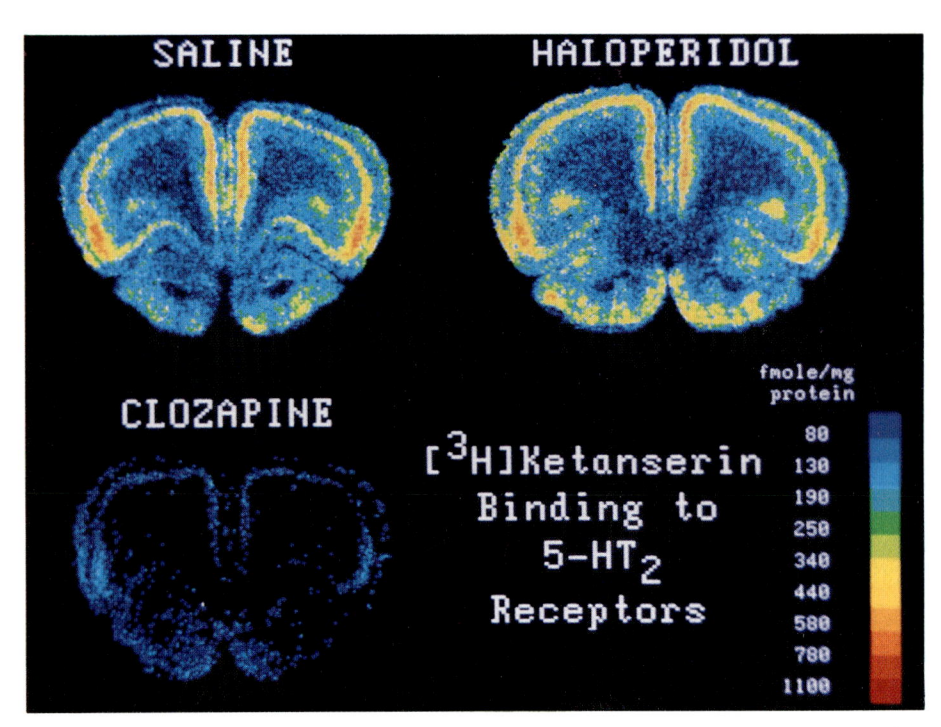

FIG. 7. Autoradiographs depicting decreased serotonin $5HT_2$ binding in the cerebral cortex following chronic use of clozapine. Haloperidol did not significantly affect cortical $5HT_2$ receptors.

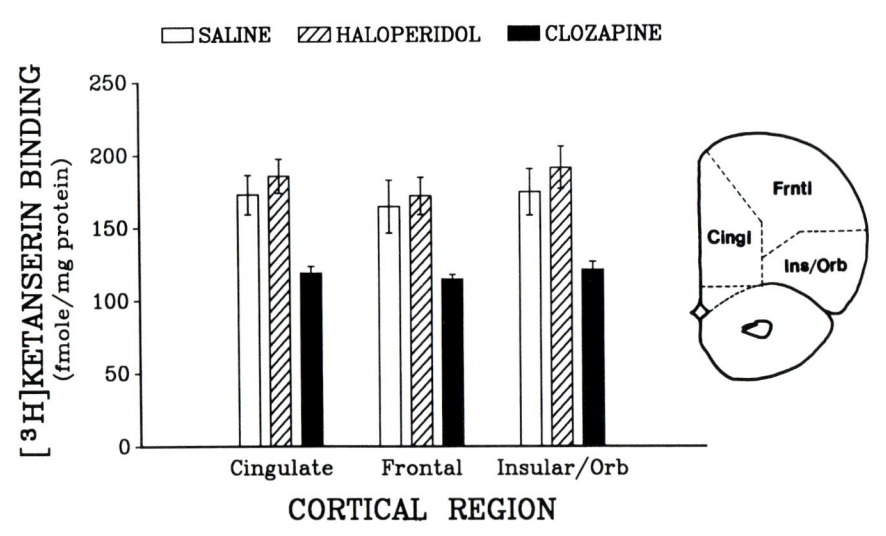

FIG. 8. Serotonin $5HT_2$ receptor binding in the cerebral cortex as a function of chronic drug treatment and anatomic region. Clozapine significantly reduced binding in the cingulate, frontal, and insular-orbital cortex relative to the vehicle. Haloperidol was without significant effect.

A two-factor analysis of variance (chronic drug × region) on the cortical 5HT$_2$ data yielded significant main effects for chronic drug ($F_{2,16} = 8.74$; $p < .003$) and for region ($F_{2,32} = 7.43$; $p < .003$) on 5HT$_2$ binding, while the interaction term was not significant ($F < 1.0$). Newman-Keuls tests revealed that the main effect of chronic drug was due to the significant reduction in 5HT$_2$ binding in the clozapine group ($n = 6$) relative to either the saline ($p < .05$; $n = 6$) or the haloperidol ($p < .05$; $n = 7$) groups, which did not differ significantly from each other.

DISCUSSION

The present findings show that chronic treatment with the atypical antipsychotic clozapine induces DA and serotonin receptor changes that differ from those resulting from chronic treatment with the typical neuroleptic haloperidol. With regard to DA receptors, clozapine produced an apparent upregulation of D$_1$ receptors while leaving D$_2$ receptor density unchanged. By contrast, haloperidol caused an upregulation of D$_2$ receptors while having no effect on D$_1$ binding. These findings are consistent with previously reported binding data in studies involving neuroleptics. For example, data from striatal homogenates has shown that chronic haloperidol treatment upregulates D$_2$ but not D$_1$ sites (22–24). Also, the apparent D$_1$ upregulation produced by chronic clozapine in the present experiment agrees with previous studies of [^{3}H]piflutixol binding in homogenates of clozapine-treated rats (21,24). As in the present experiment, those studies failed to find an effect of chronic clozapine on D$_2$ receptor density.

In addition to their opposing effects on dopamine receptors, clozapine and haloperidol could also be differentiated by their action on 5HT$_2$ receptors. Clozapine induced a substantial decrease in 5HT$_2$ binding sites, whereas haloperidol had no effect on these receptors. This result is confirmed by a report that chronic clozapine administration decreased the density of 5HT$_2$ receptors in the frontal cortex (23,25). However, certain aspects of this clozapine-induced 5HT$_2$ decline call for further investigation. First, acute treatment with clozapine has been shown to result in a decrease of nearly 50% in 5HT$_2$ binding in cortical homogenates within 24 hours (23). This effect is apparently not unique to clozapine, as other 5HT$_2$ antagonists such as mianserin also decrease 5HT$_2$ receptor binding after acute administration (26). Secondly, based on data from other receptor systems, chronic antagonist treatment would have been expected to increase receptor density, rather than producing the decreases in 5HT$_2$ receptors we see after chronic administration of clozapine. Taken together, these findings suggest that the 5HT$_2$ receptor changes observed in the present and other studies may not represent classic receptor regulation.

The D$_1$ and D$_2$ receptor changes induced by clozapine and haloperidol, respectively, did not vary as a function of anatomic region examined. By contrast, the decreases in 5HT$_2$ binding that were seen in the cortex and ventral striatum after chronic clozapine treatment were not seen in the dorsal striatum, where binding in untreated animals is normally very low. Thus, clozapine's effect on 5HT$_2$ receptors in the striatum appears to be selective for the ventral regions, including the NAc. Whether this regional selectivity is due to differences in basal receptor density or to differences in the way that populations of 5HT$_2$-containing neurons in these areas respond to clozapine treatment requires further investigation.

It is widely believed that a drug's antipsychotic efficacy is related to its affinity for D$_2$ receptors (8,9). However, the present findings suggest that chronic clozapine treatment affects D$_1$ receptors to a much greater degree than D$_2$ receptors. Both in vivo and in vitro receptor binding data indicate that clozapine appears to have approximately equal affinities for D$_1$ and D$_2$

receptors (27). However, the absence of D_2 upregulation in the present study suggests either that clozapine's blockade of this receptor is insufficient to stimulate normal regulatory mechanisms or that its long-term effects on the D_2 system are masked by additional nondopaminergic properties of the drug. Regardless of which of these interpretations is correct, these data implicate the D_1 receptor as a component in the mechanism of action of clozapine. Indeed, using transstriatal dialysis in conscious rats, Imperato and Angelucci (18) have recently shown that acute low doses of clozapine preferentially exert D_1-mediated effects on DA release. However, since D_1 receptor regulation is not affected by haloperidol, one might conclude that while D_1 receptor action may be important in suppressing EPS, it may not be necessary for the relief of psychosis. This apparent discrepancy may be resolved by recent studies in rodents showing that D_1 and D_2 receptors interact synergistically, such that antagonists of either receptor type impede dopaminergic transmission (28). If a similar state exists in the brains of schizophrenics, then, like D_2 antagonists, D_1 antagonists could display antipsychotic potential. Although the changes observed in $5HT_2$ receptor binding may be involved in the antipsychotic action of clozapine, the fact that this effect is not common to haloperidol argues against this.

Because clozapine and haloperidol differ greatly in their propensity to induce EPS and TD, the differences in the pattern of receptor binding observed following chronic administration of each of these drugs may be useful in understanding the etiology of these movement disorders. The absence of D_2 receptor upregulation following chronic clozapine treatment may relate to its lesser EPS potential since a D_2 receptor supersensitivity (reflected in increased D_2 radioligand binding) has frequently been invoked as hypothesis for the development of EPS (9). On the other hand, studies in rodents suggest that serotoninergic systems may be involved in the ability of dopaminergic agonists to induce stereotyped behaviors (29,30). Thus, antagonism or chronic downregulation of $5HT_2$ receptors by clozapine may also contribute to its low propensity to induce TD. However, other typical antipsychotics (e.g., chlorpromazine) also have potent $5HT_2$ receptor binding yet still causes EPS and TD (12).

In addition to its action at D_1, D_2, and $5HT_2$ receptors, clozapine is also known to bind to α_1-adrenergic H_1 histamine, and muscarinic cholinergic receptors (5,10–13). The present results do not rule out the possibility that the actions of clozapine may be mediated through either of these additional systems. Nonetheless, the results of the present study suggest a reevaluation of the hypothesis that a drug's antipsychotic potential is strictly related to its affinity for D_2 receptors. The D_1 receptor must now be considered a potential site of action of antipsychotic agents. Furthermore, these results suggest that alterations in D_1 or $5HT_2$ receptors or their interaction may play a role in the low risk of EPS and TD posed by chronic administration of atypical neuroleptics. Thus, our data support the hypothesis that typical and atypical neuroleptics can be differentiated more by their long-term actions at pharmacologically distinct receptors than by differences in regional selectivity for a given receptor type.

ACKNOWLEDGMENTS

The authors gratefully acknowledge the excellent technical assistance of M. Andreini. The clozapine was a generous gift of the Sandoz Research Institute (Berne, Switzerland). This work was supported by PHS research grants NS 22698, NS 20122 and AG 00538 to J.F.M. and Schizophrenia Center grant MH 44188. G.J.L. was supported by National Research Award NS 08563.

REFERENCES

1. Ljungberg T, Ungerstedt U. Classification of neuroleptic drugs according to their ability to inhibit apomorphine-induced locomotion and gnawing: evidence for two different mechanisms of action. *Psychopharmacology* 1978;56:239–247.
2. Niemegeers CJ, Janssen PA. A systematic study of the pharmacological activities of dopaminergic agonists. *Life Sci* 1979;24:2201–2216.
3. Robertson A, MacDonald C. The atypical neuroleptics clozapine and thioridazine enhance amphetamine-induced stereotypy. *Pharmacol Biochem Behav* 1984;21:97–101.
4. Chiodo LA, Bunney BS. Possible mechanisms by which repeated clozapine administration differentially affects the activity of two subpopulations of midbrain dopamine neurons. *J Neurosci* 1985;9:2539–2544.
5. Lane RF, Blaha CD, Rivet JM. Selective inhibition of mesolimbic dopamine release following chronic administration of clozapine: involvement of α_1-noradrenergic receptors demonstrated by *in vivo* voltammetry. *Brain Res* 1988;460:398–401.
6. Hand TH, Hu X-T, Wang RY. Differential effects of clozapine and haloperidol on the activity of ventral tegmental (A10) and nigrostrial (A9) dopamine neurons. *Brain Res* 1987;415:257–269.
7. White FJ, Wang RY. Differential effects of classical and atypical antipsychotic drugs on A9 and A10 dopamine neurons. *Science* 1983;221:1054–1057.
8. Creese I, Burt DR, Snyder SH. Dopamine receptor binding predicts clinical and pharmacological potencies of antipsychotic drugs. *Science* 1976;192:481–483.
9. Seeman P. Brain dopamine receptors. *Pharmacol Rev* 1980;32:229–313.
10. Bradley PB. Psychopharmacology of antipsychotic drugs. In: Bradley PB, Hirsch, eds. *The psychopharmacology and treatment of schizophrenia*. Oxford: Oxford University Press, 1986;27–70.
11. Cohen BM, Lipinski JF. *In vivo* potencies of antipsychotic drugs in blocking α_1-noradrenergic and dopamine D_2 receptors: implications for drug mechanisms of action. *Life Sci* 1986;39:2571–2580.
12. Hyttel J, Larsen J-J, Christensen AV, Arnt J. Receptor-binding profiles of neuroleptics. *Psychopharmacology* 1985;(suppl 2):9–18.
13. Peroutka SJ, Snyder SH. Relationship of neuroleptic drug effects at brain dopamine, serotonin, α-adrenergic and histamine receptors to clinical potency. *Am J Psychiatry* 1980;137:1518–1522.
14. Tarsy D, Baldessarini RJ. The pathophysiologic basis of tardive dyskinesis. *Biol Psychiatry* 1977;12:431–450.
15. Kane J, Honigfeld G, Singer J, Meltzer HY. Clozapine for the treatment-resistant schizophrenic. *Arch Gen Psychiatry* 1988;45:789–796.
16. Gallager DW, Aghajanian GK. Effect of antipsychotic drugs on firing of dorsal raphe cells. *Eur J Pharmacol* 1976;39:341–363.
17. Altar CA, Boyar WC, Wasley A, Gerhardt SC, Liebman JM, Wood PL. Dopamine neurochemical profile of atypical antipsychotics resembles that of D_1 antagonists. *Naunyn-Schmiedeberg's Arch Pharmacol* 1988;338:162–168.
18. Imperato A, Angelucci L. Effects of the atypical neuroleptics clozapine and fluperlapine on the in vivo dopamine release in the dorsal striatum and in the prefrontal cortex. *Psychopharmacology* 1988;(suppl 96):79.
19. Altar CA, O'Neil S, Walter RT Jr, Marshall JF. Brain dopamine and serotonin receptor sites revealed by digital subtraction autoradiography. *Science* 1985;228:597–600.
20. Savasta M, Dubois A, Scatton B. Autoradiographic localization of D1 receptors in the rat brain with [^{3}H]SCH 23390. *Brain Res* 1986;375:291–301.
21. Jenner P, Rupniak NMJ, Marsden CD. Differential alteration of striatal D_1 and D_2 receptors induced by the long-term administration of haloperidol, sulpiride or clozapine. *Psychopharmacology* 1985;(suppl 2):174–181.
22. Jenner P, Marsden CD. Chronic pharmacological manipulation of dopamine receptors in brain. *Neuropharmacology* 1987;26:931–940.
23. Lee T, Tang SW. Loxapine and clozapine decrease serotonin (S_2) but do not elevate dopamine (D_2) receptor numbers in the rat brain. *Psychiatry Res* 1984;12:277–285.
24. Rupniak NMJ, Hall MD, Mann S, et al. Chronic treatment with clozapine, unlike haloperidol, does not induce changes in striatal D_2 receptor function in the rat. *Biochem Pharmacol* 1985;34:2755–2763.
25. Szczepcnik AM, Wilmot CA, Ellis DB. Regional sensitivity of mesolimbic and striatal D_2 receptors to chronic neuroleptic treatment. *Soc Neurosci Abstr* 1987;13:1345.
26. Goodwin GH, Green AR. A behavioral and biochemical study in mice and rats of putative agonists and antagonists for 5-HT_1 and 5-HT_2 receptors. *Br J Pharmacol* 1985;84:743–753.
27. Andersen PH. Comparison of the pharmacological characteristics of [^{3}H]raclopride and [^{3}H]SCH 23390 binding to dopamine receptors *in vivo* in mouse brain. *Eur J Pharmacol* 1988;146:113–120.
28. Walters JR, Bergstrom DA, Carlson JH, Chase TN, Braun AR. D_1 dopamine receptor activation required for postsynaptic expression of D_2 agonist effects. *Science* 1987;236:719–722.
29. Fink H, Oelssner W. LSD, Mescaline and serotonin injected into the medial raphe nucleus potentiates apomorphine hypermotility. *Eur J Pharmacol* 1981;75:289–296.
30. Oberlander C, Demassey Y, Verdu A. Van de Velde D, Bardelay C. Tolerance to the serotonin 5-HT_1 agonist RU 24969 and effects on dopaminergic behavior. *Eur J Pharmacol* 1987;139:205–214.

Subject Index

Subject Index

A

A9 dopamine cell, 351
A10 dopamine cell, 351
Abstraction-cognitive test, 159–160
Acromegaly
  growth hormone, 229
  pituitary adenoma, 229
Adenylyl cyclase, D1 dopamine receptor, 3
Adoption genetic study, 21–22, 25–26
Affective disorder, rapid eye movement, 201
Affinity chromatography
  D1 dopamine receptor, 9–10
  D2 dopamine receptor, 7–8
Akathisia, neuroleptic noncompliance, 290–293
Akinesia, neuroleptic noncompliance, 290–293
Alprazolam
  Brief Psychiatric Rating Scale, 144–145
  homovanillic acid, 144–147
  stress, 144–147
Alzheimer's disease, 137
Ambivalence, schizotype, 194
Ambulatory schizophrenic, neuroleptic noncompliance, 286
Amino acid substitution, autosomal dominant disorder, 33
Amnesia
  global, 129–131
  human, monkey comparison, 130
Amphetamine, neuroleptic anhedonia, 323–324
Amygdala
  cytoarchitectonic abnormality, 137
  met-enkephalin, 91
  neurotensin, 78
  temporal-lobe syndrome, 129–131
Amygdalohippocampal lesion, memory maturation, 132–135
Angel dust. *See* Phencyclidine
Anger management, neuropsychiatry, 270
Anhedonia, 323–329
  schizotype, 193–194
Animal model
  genetic study, 31–37
  global amnesia, 129–131
Apathy, neuroleptic noncompliance, 290–293
Apomorphine, 301
Ashkenazic Jew, Gaucher's disease, 35–36
Assessment instrument, stress, 142

Attentional disturbance
  behavioral sign, 169–177
  electrophysiological sign, 169–177
  sibling, 169–177
Attentional dysfunction, 153–154
Auditory perception, 159–160
Autism, 129–138
  Klüver-Bucy's syndrome, 137
  neonatal limbic lesion, 136
  temporal lobe, 136–137
Autoimmunity, 111–117
Autosomal dominant disorder, amino acid substitution, 33
Autosomal recessive disorder, autosomal dominant disorder, distinguished, 33
Avoidance response, BMY 14802, 307–308

B

B cell, CD5+ B lymphocyte, 111–112
Backward masking, schizotypal personality disorder, 185
Behavior, 127–178
Behavioral data, neuroimaging data, 156–159
Behavioral family therapy, 253
Behavioral therapy, stress, 143
Benzodiazepine, stress, 143–147
Biochemistry, 1–47
Bipolar affective disorder, CD5+ B lymphocyte, 112–115
BMY 14802
  avoidance response, 307–308
  dopamine metabolite hydroxyphenlacetic acid, 308–310, 312–313
Borderline personality disorder, designation, 201
Brain function, regional, 154–156
Brain injury, ganglioside treatment, 57–58
Brief Psychiatric Rating Scale
  alprazolam, 144–145
  fluphenazine, 144–145
  psychosocial treatment, 242
Brief Symptom Inventory, psychosocial treatment, 242
Bromocriptine, 301
  neuropsychiatry, 269
Butyrophenone, 280–281

C

Calcium, cholecystokinin, 123
Carbamazepine, neuropsychiatry, 269

Carfentanil
  epilepsy, 95–97
  mu opiate receptor, 92–95
  naloxone, 92
11C-Carfentanil
  mu opiate receptor, 91–97
  positron emission tomography, 91–92
Caudate nucleus, met-enkephalin, 91
Caudate putamen
  clozapine, 354–358
  haloperidol, 354–358
  5-hydroxytryptamine, 354, 357
CD5+ B lymphocyte, 111–117
  B cell, 111–112
  bipolar affective disorder, 112–115
  immunoglobulin, 111, 115
Cerebral blood flow, 231
Cerebral cortex
  cholecystokinin, 78
  5-hydroxytryptamine, 354, 358
Cerebral metabolic hypoactivity, frontal lobe, 227
Cerebral structural abnormality
  schizophreniform disorder, 209–216
  spectrum personality disorder, 209–216
Cerebral ventricle
  enlargement, 227–233
  size, 209–216
    spectrum disorder, 213–214
Cerebrospinal fluid
  clozapine, 341–349
  postmortem brain study, 79–86
  schizotypal personality disorder, 185–187
Chapman Physical Anhedonia Scale, schizotypal personality disorder, 184
Cheek medication, neuroleptic noncompliance, 285
Chestnut Lodge Follow-up Study, spectrum concept, 193–200
Cholecystokinin, 78
  calcium, 123
  messenger RNA, 41–46
  substantia nigra, 39–46
  ventral tegmental area, 39–46
Chromosome 5, genetic study, 23–25
Circuit level, transmission line, 52–53
Clonazepam, neuropsychiatry, 269
Clonidine, neuropsychiatry, 269
Clozapine, 333–338
  caudate putamen, 354–358
  cerebrospinal fluid, 341–349
  D_1 dopamine receptor, 302–303
  D_2 dopamine affinity, 302–303
  dopamine receptor, 351–360
  epinephrine, 343, 347
  extrapyramidal side effect, 351
  5-hydroxytryptamine, 333, 335–337

  5-hydroxytryptamine acid, 342–344, 347–348
  5-hydroxytryptamine ratio, 335–337
  2-methoxy-4-hydroxyphenylglycol, 343, 347
  prolactin, 343–344
  serotonin, 334
  serotonin receptor, 351–360
  tardive dyskinesia, 351
Cocaine, neuroleptic anhedonia, 323–324
Cognitive impairment, 220
  cerebral ventricle enlargement, 228
Cognitive slippage, schizotype, 194
Communication, family, 247
Community Adjustment Form, psychosocial treatment, 242
Community care, 244
  continuous treatment team, 239–245
Community care model, 240–242
Community living training model, 239–241
Competence, 255–257
Complementary DNA
  messenger RNA, 120
  tyrosine hydroxylase gene, 33–34
Compliance
  neuroleptic
    ambulatory schizophrenic, 286
    patient interview, 287
    prolactin level, 287
    urine phenothiazine screen, 287
  neuroleptic injectable, 289–290
  oral, 289–290
Compulsive behavior, limbic lesion, 136
Continuous performance task, schizotypal personality disorder, 184–185
Continuous Performance Test, 153
Continuous treatment team, community care, 239–245
Control group, selection, 154–155
Coping strategy, family, 248
Cortical atrophy
  personality disorder, 212–214
  schizophreniform disorder, 211–212
Corticotropin-releasing factor, 77
Cytoarchitectonic abnormality
  amygdala, 137
  hippocampus, 137

D

D_1 dopamine receptor, 3–11
  adenylyl cyclase, 3
  affinity chromatography, 9–10
  photoaffinity crosslinking, 5–6
D_2 dopamine affinity, roxindole, 317–321
D_2 dopamine receptor, 3–11
  affinity chromatography, 7–8
  function, 10
  neurotensin, 67–68

neurotensin receptor, 66–67
photoaffinity labeling, 4–5
Dane system, 241–242
Deinstitutionalization, 255
Delusion syndrome, Vienna classification, 222
Delusional impression, 220
Denial, neuroleptic noncompliance, 290–293, 294
^{18}F-2-Deoxyglucose, positron emission tomography, 99–100
Diagnostic, Interview of Borderlines, 201–202
Diagnostic and Statistical Manual of Mental Disorders, borderline category, 194
Dopamine
  atypical antipsychotic, 299–303
  clozapine, 333–338
  homovanillic acid, 144, 334
  peptide modulation, 65–66
  tuberoinfundibular neuron, 333
  uridine, 70–72
Dopamine metabolite hydroxyphenlacetic acid, BMY 14802, 307–310, 312–313
Dopamine nerve terminal, nicotine treatment, 58–59
Dopamine neuron
  mesolimbic vs. mesostriatal, 334–335
  mesotelencephalic, 51–73
  neuroplasticity, 51–73
Dopamine receptor. See also D_1 dopamine receptor; D_2 dopamine receptor
  clozapine, 351–360
  haloperidol, 351–360
  neuroleptic, 39
  purification, 6–10
  specific identification, 4–6
Dopamine synapse, control mechanisms, 65–69
Droperidol, 280–281
Drug. See also Neuroleptic; Pharmacology
  antipsychotic, 277–283, 307–314
    atypical, 297–304
  BMY 14802, 307–314
  gene expression, 120–121
  receptor, gene products, 119–120
Dynamic derailment, 220–221
Dysphoria, neuroleptic noncompliance, 288–289
Dystonia, clozapine, 341

E
Early-developing memory, monkey, 131–132
Education, family, 247–254
Electrophysiologic technique, molecular biology, 123–124
EMD 49 980. See Roxindole
Emotion, negatively expressed, 142
Emotional behavior, development, 135–136

Endogenomorphic-cyclothymic axial syndrome, 221–222
Endogenomorphic-schizophrenic axial syndrome, 221–222
Endogenous psychosis
  cyclothymic disorder, 219
  designation, 219
  schizophrenic disorder, 219
beta-Endorphin, 81–82, 83
des-tyr^1-gamma-Endorphin, 83–84
Met-Enkephalin
  amygdala, 91
  caudate nucleus, 91
Epilepsy, 269, 271
  carfentanil, 95–97
  positron emission tomography, 95–97
Epinephrine, clozapine, 343, 347
Epistatic gene, genetic study, 26–27
Eucaryotic cell, 121
Extrapyramidal symptom, clozapine, 341
Eye contact, limbic lesion, 136
Eye movement disorder
  phenotype, 27
  restrict-fragment-length polymorphism, 27
Eye-tracking impairment, schizotypal personality disorder, 182–184

F
Family
  neuroleptic noncompliance, 290–293
  psychoeducational approach, 247–254
Family stress, relapse, 142
Family treatment, 247–254
  case management support, 252
  interpersonal relation, 252
  potential relapse, 252
  problem solving, 247
  relapse, 249
  relative group, 249
  supportive family management, 253
FDG. See ^{18}F-2-Deoxyglucose
Fluperlapine
  D_1 dopamine receptor, 302–303
  D_2 dopamine affinity, 302–303
Fluphenazine, 262–266
  Brief Psychiatric Rating Scale, 144–145
  time course, 280–282
Food, neuroleptic anhedonia, 323–324
Forebrain
  frontal-lobe activity, cerebral metabolic hypoactivity, 227
  tyrosine hydroxylase, 53–54
Frontal-lobe activity
  cerebral blood flow, 163
  positron emission tomography, 163
Frontal-lobe deficit, 163–168

G

G protein. *See* Guanine nucleotide-binding protein
Ganglioside treatment, brain injury, 57–58
Gaucher's disease, 35–37
Gene expression, drug, 120–121
Genetic implication, schizotypal personality disorder, 188–189
Genetic study, 21–28, 31–37
   adoption, 21–22, 25–26
   chromosome 5, 23–25
   epistatic gene, 26–27
   Sweden, 23
   United States, 24
Genome scan, genetic study, 22
Genotype, 193
   destination, 32–33
Global amnesia, animal model, 129–131
Glucocerebrosidase, Gaucher's disease, 35–37
Glucocorticoid, noradrenaline, 51
Glucocorticoid receptor, 120
   immunoreactivity, 51
Glucose, 99–100
   haloperidol, 105–106
   limbic system, 104–105
   MK801, 102–104
   neocortex, 104–105
   regional cerebral, 104–107
   subcortical grey, 104–105
L-Glutamate
   [^{3}H]MK-801 binding, Hill coefficient, 16
   [^{3}H]MK801 binding, 15–16
GR. *See* Glucocorticoid receptor
Growth hormone, 86
   acromegaly, 229
   schizotypal personality disorder, 187
Growth hormone-releasing factor, 77
Guanine nucleotide-binding protein, 3, 120

H

Habit system, maturation, 132–135
Hallucination, 163
Haloperidol, 69–70
   caudate putamen, 354–358
   dopamine receptor, 351–360
   glucose, 105–106
   limbic system, 105–106
   pterin cofactor, 41
   serotonin receptor, 351–360
   substantia nigra, 41–46
   time course, 278–280, 281–282
   tyrosine hydroxylase, 41
   ventral tegmental area, 41–46
Haplotype, destination, 33
Herpes encephalitis, 137
High-performance liquid chromatography, haloperidol persistence, 277–283

Hippocampus
   cytoarchitectonic abnormality, 137
   temporal-lobe syndrome, 129–131
Homeless shelter, 244
Homelessness, 244
Homework exercise, social skill training, 261
Homovanillic acid
   alprazolam, 144–147
   dopamine, 144, 334
   5-hydroxytryptamine acid, 342–344, 347–348
   schizotypal personality disorder, 185–187
Hostility, neuroleptic noncompliance, 288
Humiliation, neuroleptic noncompliance, 288
5-Hydroxytryptamine, 298–299
   caudate putamen, 354, 357
   cerebral cortex, 354, 358
   clozapine, 333, 335–337
5-Hydroxytryptamine acid
   clozapine, 342–344, 347–348
   homovanillic acid, 342–344, 347–348
5-Hydroxytryptamine ratio, clozapine, 335–337
Hypothalamic brain stimulation, neuroleptic anhedonia, 323–324
Hypothalamic hypophysiotropic hormone, 77–78
Hypothalamus, 77–78

I

IL-2. *See* Interleukin-2
Immunoglobulin, CD5+ B lymphocyte, 111, 115
Inertia, 163
Information-processing deviation, sibling, 169
Inpatient psychiatric setting, 243
Interleukin-2, 113. *See also* Soluble interleukin-2
   T cell, 112–113
Interpersonal aversiveness, schizotype, 194
Intervention, 237–273
Intrasynaptic level, transmission line, 52–53
Ischemia, nigrostriatal system, 61–65
Italy, genetic kin study, 24–25

K

Klüver-Bucy's syndrome, autism, 137
Kraepelinian chronic schizophrenia, 164
Kraepelinian schizophrenia, 181

L

Language, 159–160
Language behavior, Wernicke's area, 153
Late-developing memory, monkey, 131–132
Learning deficit, 153–154
Limbic lesion
   compulsive behavior, 136

SUBJECT INDEX

eye contact, 136
monkey, child comparison, 136
passive behavior, 136
ritualistic behavior, 136
temper tantrum, 136
Limbic system
 damage in, monkey, 129–138
 haloperidol, 105–106
 neonatal damage, 129–138
Living situation, neuroleptic noncompliance, 290–293

M

MacAndrews Alcoholism Scale, 166–167
MAM. See Methylazoxymethanol acetate
Mammalian brain, neuropeptide, 77–78
Mann-Whitney U-Test, 166–167
Marker, sibling, 162
Memory
 early-developing, 131–132
 late-developing, 131–132
 visual, 159–160
Memory loss, 153–154
 amygdalohippocampal complex, 132–135
 limbic damage, 129–138
 modality-specific, 132
 temporal area, 132–135
Memory retraining, neuropsychiatry, 270
Memory system, maturation, 132–135
Mendelian disease, schizophrenia distinguished, 22
Mesolimbocortical neuron, 51
Messenger RNA
 cholecystokinin, 41–46
 complementary DNA, 120
 transcript, 119–120
 tyrosine hydroxylase, 41
Messenger RNA transcript, coding, 31–32
Metachromatic leukodystrophy, 232
2-Methoxy-4-hydroxyphenyglycol, clozapine, 343, 347
(+)-Methyl-1-,11-dihydro-5H-dibenzo[a,d]cyclohept-5,10-imine maleate. See MK801
N-Methyl-D-aspartate, phencyclidine psychosis, 16–17
N-Methyl-D-aspartate-phencyclidine receptor interaction, 14
1-Methyl-phenyl-5–1,2,3,6-tetrahydropyridine, Parkinson's disease, 56–61
Methylazoxymethanol
 neuropeptide Y, 54–56
 tyrosine hydroxylase, 53–54
Methylazoxymethanol acetate, 53–56
Methylphenidate, neuropsychiatry, 269
Microencephalic rat, 53–56

Minnesota Multiphasic Personality Inventory, 27
MK801, 101–102
 glucose, 102–104
 phencyclidine, 100–102
 psychosis, 99–107
MK801[^{3}H] binding
 fast component, 14–15
 L-glutamate, 15–16
  Hill coefficient, 16
 slow component, 14–15
MLD. See Metachromatic leukodystrophy
MMPI. See Minnesota Multiphasic Personality Inventory
Molecular biology, 119–124
Monkey
 global amnesia, 129–131
 limbic system damage, 129–138
 memory development, 131–132
 neonatal damage, 129–138
 neonatal limbic lesion, 136
 social interaction, 135–136
Monozygotic to dizygotic twin ratio, 26–27
Morphine, neuroleptic, 324–328
Morphofunctional lesion, neural circuit, 51
Mu opiate receptor
 carfentanil, 92–95
 ^{11}C-carfentanil, 91–97
 positron emission tomography, 91–97
Multiple transmission line, synapse, 52–53

N

N-(p-azido-m-[^{125}I]-iodophenethyl), dopamine receptor identification, 4–5
NA. See Noradrenaline
Naloxone, carfentanil, 92
[^{125}I]Bromoacetyl-NAPS, dopamine receptor identification, 4–6
Naxolone, 84–86
Neonatal damage
 limbic system, 129–138
 monkey, 129–138
Neonatal limbic lesion
 autism, 136
 monkey, 136
Neural circuit
 metabolic lesion, 61–65
 morphofunctional lesion, 51
 toxic lesion, 56–61
Neural pathway, 99–107
Neuroanatomic technique, molecular biology, 124
Neurobiological homogeneity, 227–233
Neurobiology, 49–126
Neurochemical measure, Rorschach response, 185–187

Neuroendocrine, neurotransmitter function, 86
Neuroimaging data, behavioral data, 156–159
Neuroleptic. *See also* Drug; Pharmacology
  anhedonia, 323–329
  dopamine receptor, 39
  hybridization, 39–46
  injectable, compliance, 289–290
  molecular genetic study, 40–46
  neurotensin, 69
  noncompliance, 285–294
  opiate, 324–328
  oral, compliance, 289–290
  relapse, 281
  skills training, 257–266
  time-dependent property, 39–40
Neuroleptic noncompliance
  ambulatory schizophrenic, 286
  patient interview, 287
  prolactin level, 287
  urine phenothiazine screen, 287
Neuroleptic response, cerebral ventricle enlargement, 228
Neurological psychiatric problem, dual diagnosis, 269–273
Neuropeptide, 77–86. *See also* Peptide
  calcium, 123
  mammalian brain, 77–78
  neurotransmitter, 78
  second messenger system, 78
Neuropeptide neurotensin, *Xenopus laevis*, 123
Neuropeptide Y
  methylazoxymethanol, 54–56
  nucleus caudatus putamen, 54–56
Neuropharmacologic technique, molecular biology, 122–123
Neuroplasticity, dopamine neuron, 51–73
Neuropsychiatry
  anger management, 270
  social skill, 270
Neuropsychological assessment, 269
  schizotypal personality disorder, 204, 206
Neuropsychological battery, 159–160
Neuropsychological deficit, 153–154
Neuropsychological study, 153–161
Neuropsychological testing, schizotypal personality disorder, 203
Neurotensin, 78
  D_2 dopamine receptor, 67–68
  neuroleptic, 69
Neurotensin receptor, D_2 dopamine receptor, 66–67
Neurotransmitter, neuropeptide, 78
Neurotransmitter function, neuroendocrine, 86
Neurotransmitter receptor cDNA, voltage clamping, 123

Neurotransmitter system, stress response, 149
Nicotine treatment, dopamine nerve terminal, 58–59
Nigrostriatal system, ischemia, 61–65
NMDA. *See* N-Methyl-D-aspartate
Noncompliance, neuroleptic, 285–294
Nonschizophrenic psychotic disorder, 219–225
Noradrenaline, glucocorticoid, 51
NPY. *See* Neuropeptide Y
Nucleus accumbens, neurotensin, 78
Nucleus caudatus putamen, neuropeptide Y, 54–56
Nursing home, 243

O

Oculomotor assessment, schizotypal personality disorder, 204–205
Oculomotor paradigm, schizotypal personality disorder, 203
Onset age, 33
Opiate, neuroleptic, 324–328
Opioid peptide, 80–81
  seizure, 95–97
Organic psychosis, designation, 219

P

Paranoid ideation, schizotypal personality disorder, 188
Parkinsonism, clozapine, 341
Parkinson's disease, 1-methyl-phenyl-5-1,2,3,6-tetrahydropyridine, 56–61
Passive behavior, limbic lesion, 136
Pathophysiologic implication, schizotypal personality disorder, 189
Patient interview, neuroleptic noncompliance, 287
PCP. *See* Phencyclidine
Penal setting, 244
Peptide. *See also* Neuropeptide
  modulation, dopamine, 65–66
  peptide receptor antagonist, 83–86
Peptide receptor antagonist, 83–86
Perceptual distortion, schizotypal personality disorder, 188
Personality disorder
  cortical atrophy, 212–214
  schizophrenia-related, 181
PET. *See* Positron emission tomography
Pharmacokinetic, long-term, 278–283
Pharmacology, 69–72, 99–107, 119–124, 275–361. *See also* Drug; Neuroleptic
  atypical antipsychotic, 297–304
  haloperidol, 69–70
  stress, 143–147
  uridine, 70–72
Phencyclidine
  MK801, 100–102

psychosis, 16–17, 99–107
  psychotic episode, 13
  psychotomimetic action, 100–101
Phencyclidine-N-methyl-D-aspartate receptor
    interaction, 13–17
Phenocopy, destination, 32–33
Phenotype, 193
  definition, 27
  destination, 32–33
  eye movement disorder, 27
  Gaucher's disease, 35
Photoaffinity crosslinking, D_1 dopamine
    receptor, 5–6
Photoaffinity labeling, D_2 dopamine receptor,
    4–5
Pick's disease, 137
Pilot study, schizotypal personality disorder,
    201–207
Pituitary adenoma, acromegaly, 229
Pleasure, neuroleptic, 323–329
Positron emission tomography
  ^{11}C-carfentanil, 91–92
  ^{18}F-2-deoxyglucose, 99–100
  epilepsy, 95–97
  mu opiate receptor, 91–97
Postmortem brain study, cerebrospinal fluid,
    79–86
Prenatal lesion, methylazoxymethanol, 53–56
Prepulse inhibition, 164
Prolactin
  clozapine, 343–344
  neuroleptic noncompliance, 287
Propranolol, neuropsychiatry, 269
Psychoeducational therapy, stress, 143
Psychosis
  designation, 219
  MK801, 99–107
  neuroleptic noncompliance, 290–293
  phencyclidine, 99–107
  transient, 199
Psychosocial treatment, 237–273
  community care, 239–245
  community living training model, 239–241
  continuous treatment team, 239–245
  Dane system, 241–242
  neuropsychiatric model, 269–273
  psychoeducational family approach, 247–254
  relapse risk skill training, 255–266
  social skills training, 256–266
Psychotic, designation, 219–220
Psychoticism, neuroleptic noncompliance, 288
Psychotomimetic effect, phencyclidine,
    16–17, 100–101
Pterin cofactor, haloperidol, 41

R

Radioimmunoassay, haloperidol persistence,
    277–283

Rapid eye movement, affective disorder, 201
Ravens Progressive Matrix, 232
Receptor
  drug, gene products, 119–120
  neuropharmacology, 122
Receptor-receptor interaction, synapse, 52–53
Regional cerebral blood flow, XE-133
    inhalation technique, 231
Rehabilitation model, psychiatric model,
    combined, 269–273
Relapse
  family stress, 142
  family treatment, 249
  neuroleptic, 281
  risk management, 255–266
Relative group, family treatment, 249
Restriction fragment polymorphism
  eye movement disorder, 27
  schizotypal personality disorder, 182
RFLP. *See* Restriction fragment
    polymorphism
Rimcazole, 297–298
Risperidone, 299
Ritualistic behavior, limbic lesion, 136
Rodent nervous system, genetic study, 31–37
Rorschach response
  neurochemical measure, 185–187
  schizotypal personality disorder, 185
Roxindole, D_2 dopamine affinity, 317–321

S

Satisfaction with Life Scale, psychosocial
    treatment, 242
Schedule for Affective Disorders and
    Schizophrenia, attentional disturbance,
    170
Schedule for Schizotypal Personalities,
    attentional disturbance, 170
Schizoaffective disorder, two-factor
    vulnerability model, 220
Schizophreniform disorder
  cerebral structural abnormality, 209–216
  cerebral ventricular size, 211–212
  cortical atrophy, 211–212
Schizotypal personality disorder, 181–189,
    195–198, 201–207
  backward masking, 185
  cerebral spinal fluid, 185–187
  Chapman Physical Anhedonia Scale, 184
  continuous performance task, 184–185
  designation, 201
  eye-tracking impairment, 182–184
  genetic implication, 188–189
  growth hormone, 187
  homovanillic acid, 185–187
  neuropsychological assessment, 204, 206
  neuropsychological testing, 203
  oculomotor assessment, 204–205

Schizotypal personality disorder, (contd.)
  oculomotor paradigm, 203
  paranoid ideation, 188
  pathophysiologic implication, 189
  perceptual distortion, 188
  restriction fragment polymorphism, 182
  Rorschach response, 185
  sibling, 169–170
  smooth-pursuit eye movement, 182–184, 189, 203
  social isolation, 188
  Structured Interview for Affective Disorders and Schizophrenia, Lifetime version, 202–204
  Structured Interview for DSM-III Personality Diagnoses, 202–204
  Thought Disorder Inventory, 183
Schizotype
  anhedonia, 193–194
  designation, 193
Second messenger system, neuropeptide, 78
Seizure, opioid peptide, 95–97
Semantic/verbal memory, 159–160
Sensorimotor gating, Wisconsin Card Sorting Test, 163–168
Serotonin
  atypical antipsychotic, 298–299
  clozapine, 333–338
Serotonin receptor
  clozapine, 351–360
  haloperidol, 351–360
Sibling
  attentional disturbance, 169–177
  information-processing deviation, 169
  marker, 162
  schizotypal personality disorder, 169–170
Sigma binding site, antipsychotic, 307–314
Sigma receptor blockade, 297–298
Signal transduction system, 3
sIL-2R. *See* Soluble interleukin-2
Skills training, neuroleptic, 257–266
Smooth-pursuit eye movement, schizotypal personality disorder, 182–184, 189, 203
Social behavior, development, 135–136
Social coping, 255–257
Social isolation, schizotypal personality disorder, 188
Social network, family, 247
Social schema, 255–256
Social skill, 255–257
  neuropsychiatry, 270
  psychosocial treatment, 256–266
Social skills training, 256–266
Socioeconomic status, 155
Socioemotional disturbance, limbic damage, 129–138
Soluble interleukin-2, 112–113, 115–117
Spatial-cognitive test, 159–160

Spectrum concept, 179–235
  clinical state, 193
  symptomatic trait, 193
Spectrum criteria, 198
Spectrum disorder, 193–200
  cerebral ventricular size, 213–214
Spectrum personality disorder, cerebral structural abnormality, 209–216
Spiperone, dopamine receptor identification, 4–6
Stress, 141–150
  alprazolam, 144–147
  assessment instrument, 142
  behavioral therapy, 143
  benzodiazepine, 143–147
  family, 142, 248
  life events, 141–142
  pharmacology, 143–147
  psychoeducational therapy, 143
Stress management, family, 248
Stress reduction, 143–147
Stress response
  assessment, 147–149
  neurotransmitter system, 149
Striatal cholinergic neuron, roxindole, 317–321
Structured Interview for Affective Disorders and Schizophrenia, Lifetime version, schizotypal personality disorder, 202–204
Structured Interview for DSM-III Personality Diagnoses, schizotypal personality disorder, 202–204
Substance abuse, 154
  neuroleptic noncompliance, 290–293
Substantia nigra
  cholecystokinin, 39–46
  haloperidol, 41–46
  tyrosine hydroxylase, 39–46
Synapse
  multiple transmission line, 52–53
  receptor-receptor interaction, 52–53
Syndrome theory, 227

T
T cell, interleukin-2, 112–113
Tactile perception, 159–160
Tardive dyskinesia
  clozapine, 341
  neuroleptic noncompliance, 290–293
Temper tantrum, limbic lesion, 136
Temporal lobe, autism, 136–137
Temporal lobe syndrome, 129–131
Terguride, 300
Tetrahydrobiopterin cofactor, 40–41
TH. *See* Tyrosine hydroxylase
Thought Disorder Inventory, schizotypal personality disorder, 183

Subject Index

Thyroid-stimulating hormone, 201
Thyrotropin-releasing hormone, 77
Tilozepine
   D_1 dopamine receptor, 302–303
   D_2 dopamine affinity, 302–303
Transmission line
   circuit level, 52–53
   intrasynaptic level, 52–53
   multiple, 52–53
Transporter gene, neuropharmacology, uptake gene, 122–123
Trauma, 269, 271–272
Treatment Strategies in Schizophrenia Program, 252
Tuberoinfundibular neuron, dopamine, 333
Tumor, 269
Twin genetic study, 21–22, 25–26
   monozygotic-dizygotic ratio, 26–27
Tyrosine hydroxylase
   forebrain, 53–54
   haloperidol, 41
   messenger RNA, 41
   methylazoxymethanol, 53–54
   neuroleptic treatment, 40–41
   substantia nigra, 39–46
   ventral tegmental area, 39–46
Tyrosine hydroxylase gene, complementary DNA, 33–34

U

Uridine, dopamine, 70–72
Urine phenothiazine screen, neuroleptic noncompliance, 287

V

Valproate, neuropsychiatry, 269
Ventral tegmental area
   cholecystokinin, 39–46
   haloperidol, 41–46
   tyrosine hydroxylase, 39–46
Ventricle-to-brain size ratio, 228
Verbal-cognitive test, 159–160
Verbal learning, 159–160
Vienna Research Criteria, 221–225
Vigilance, 153
Viral encephalitis, 137
Visual memory, 159–160
Visual perception, 159–160
Voltage clamping, neurotransmitter receptor cDNA, 123
Vulnerability, schizophrenia, 177–178

W

Water, neuroleptic anhedonia, 323–324
Wernicke's area, language behavior, 153
Wisconsin Card Sorting Test, 153–154, 160, 231–232
   procedure, 163–164
   sensorimotor gating, 163–168

X

XE-133 inhalation technique, regional cerebral blood flow, 231
Xenopus laevis, 121–124
   neuropeptide neurotensin, 123